In tracing the development of industrial associations in Italy from 1906 to 1934, this study challenges traditional interpretations of the rise of Fascism. Unlike other studies on industrialists and Fascism, which begin with the post–World War I crisis of liberalism, Professor Adler reconstitutes the prior relations between industrialists and Italian liberalism and then situates industrialists within the crisis and the subsequent transition to Fascism. Industrialists are viewed as problematic but loyal members of the old liberal order who at first were skeptical and distant from Fascism and then, with the collapse of any liberal alternative, worked with other traditional elites to preserve as much of the liberal state as possible within the emerging framework of a new and potentially revolutionary Fascist regime.

Applying a hermeneutic approach to public and private texts produced by industrial associations, Adler uncovers the industrialists' self-constitution as a class, especially that subjective dimension of their development which accounts for collective consciousness, a sense of agency, and the will to act politically. Particular attention is paid to the ideological dimension of this development; the formative self-understandings, performative practices, and durable dispositions of this class; as well as their strategic, instrumental, and self-interested interventions in social and political life. Adler's richly textured account, moving between objective structural constraints and subjective political responses, provides a substantive basis for discussions regarding Fascism's continuity with the earlier period of Italian liberalism and where industrialists stood in this transition.

Italian Industrialists
from Liberalism to Fascism

Italian Industrialists from Liberalism to Fascism

The political development of the
industrial bourgeoisie, 1906–1934

Franklin Hugh Adler
Antioch College

CAMBRIDGE
UNIVERSITY PRESS

Published by the Press Syndicate of the University of Cambridge
The Pitt Building, Trumpington Street, Cambridge CB2 1RP
40 West 20th Street, New York, NY 10011-4211, USA
10 Stamford Road, Oakleigh, Melbourne 3166, Australia

First published 1995

Printed in the United States of America

Library of Congress Cataloging-in-Publication Data
Adler, Franklin Hugh, 1944–
Italian industrialists from liberalism to fascism : the political
development of the industrial bourgeoisie, 1906–1934 / Franklin Hugh
Adler.
p.   cm.
ISBN 0-521-43406-8
1. Employers' associations – Italy – Political activity.
2. Industrialists – Italy – Political activity.   3. Liberalism – Italy –
History.   4. Fascism – Italy – History.   5. Italy –
History – 1870–1915.   6. Italy – History – 1914–1945.   I. Title.
HD6948.I8A34   1995
332'.4'094509041 – dc20   95-8060

A catalog record for this book is available from the British Library.

ISBN 0-521-43406-8 hardback

*Dedicated to the memory of my grandfather
Jacob E. Abrams,
a gentle man who loved books*

Contents

vii

Preface

This volume seeks to make two contributions to the study of industrialists and Fascism in Italy. First, in contrast with most of the existing literature, whose terminus a quo is the crisis of Italy's liberal system following World War I, my point of departure is the earlier, Giolittian period, when modern industrial associations first formed, entering into new relations with labor syndicates and the state. Studies that limit themselves to the postwar era tend to take for granted the nature and intensity of longer-term developmental problems regarding social structure, the political system, and the legitimation of power in pre-Fascist Italy. This inattention to prior history consequently obscures the *enracinement* of both the postwar crisis and its unfortunate resolution. Not only are we left with little grasp of the crisis tendencies of Italian liberalism, but we have no sense of the earlier political and sociocultural development of the industrialists, no way of thus ascertaining their prior support for or alienation from the liberal regime.

This study seeks to situate the development of Italian industrialists within the overarching context of Italy's transition from liberalism to Fascism. Rather than accept given interpretations of the relationship between industrialists and Fascism, looking backward into the liberal period for anticipations of proto-Fascist tendencies, my inclination was to study the relationship between industrialists and liberalism without prejudgment and on its own terms and then treat this relationship as an anticipation of the industrialists' later reaction to the crisis of liberalism and confrontation with Fascism.

Second, I have sought to focus significant attention on the ideological development of Italian industrialists. Following Paul Ricoeur's masterful lead,[1] I attempt to probe both the strategic and the constitutive dimensions of ideology. The more conventional strategic, or instrumental, dimension, deriving originally from Marx, concerns the

[1] Paul Ricoeur, *Lectures on Ideology and Utopia* (New York: Columbia University Press, 1986). See also John B. Thompson, *Studies in the Theory of Ideology* (Berkeley and Los Angeles: University of California Press, 1984).

systematic distortion of reality in the furtherance of a particular interest. It is how a group strategically deploys worldviews, concepts, and observations to defend or maximize its position relative to other groups. The lesser-known, constitutive dimension, which Ricoeur derives from Clifford Geertz, addresses what *precedes* this deliberate, self-interested distortion. How is a group subjectively constituted so that it becomes aware of itself and its interest? Here I am concerned with the formative self-understandings and principles from which strategic action is derived, with those durable dispositions, background assumptions, and performative practices that had become almost second nature to Italian industrialists and their world.

This approach to ideology differs significantly from that in Peter Hayes's *Industry and Ideology,* where the author tells the remarkable story of how IG Farben, initially philo-Semitic, ended up with half of its workforce composed of slave labor, including 30,000 inmates of Auschwitz.[2] Hayes chose to focus not on the ideology of industrialists but rather on how an industrial mentality was replaced by an ideological one, on how the "nonideological" bureaucratism and professionalism of industrialists submitted itself and adapted to an increasingly ideological regime. The Italian story is significantly different. In the Giolittian period, Italian industrialists developed a rather sophisticated liberal–technocratic productivist ideology that constituted a core to which they would remain remarkably consistent before, during, and even after Fascism. Unlike the Germans Hayes studied, Italian industrialists were deeply ideological and, in fact, intervened ideologically in the constitution of an evolving Fascist state. When they, too, were forced to accommodate themselves to a Fascist regime, it was from a position of relative autonomy and strength, redefining such basic, if ambiguous, Fascist principles as corporatism in their favor.

The saliency of the German case led advance readers of this manuscript to mistakenly situate it within the context of the Abraham–Turner dispute regarding the role of German industrialists in the rise of National Socialism.[3] In fact, neither the structuralist reductionism of Abraham nor the antitheoretical "nominalism" of Turner (a self-

[2] Peter Hayes, *Industry and Ideology; IG Farben in the Nazi Era* (Cambridge: Cambridge University Press, 1987).

[3] David Abraham, *The Collapse of the Weimar Republic* (Princeton: Princeton University Press, 1981); Henry A. Turner, *German Big Business and the Rise of Hitler* (Oxford: Oxford University Press, 1985). See also the debate between Gerald Feldman and Abraham in *Central European History* 17 (1984): 159–290.

confessed "vulgar factologist") are compatible with the approach taken here, which is to reconstitute the political development of Italian industrialists in the transition from liberalism to Fascism. My interest is in understanding their world of industry and their relation to politics, not in reducing their behavior to structural reflexes or simply demonstrating that they were empirically less complicit in the rise of Fascism than standard interpretations suggest. I am less interested in establishing what industrialists *did not do* in relation to familiar charges made against them than I am in exploring their own sense of agency in the transition from liberalism to Fascism.

My focus is on the formation and development of industrial associations, which, I would argue, represents the best frame of reference. A focus on associations affords a degree of specificity typically absent in analyses that either globally characterize generic attributes and orientations (e.g., industrialists supported this; industrialists felt that) or employ imputed categories (e.g., *grand capital monopoliste,* the industrial–agricultural bloc) that tend to be more derivative of preconceived theoretical predispositions than expressive of the actual self-constitution of the industrial class. Thus, an examination of industrial associations not only militates against vacuous generalizations but leads us directly to those actual organizational vehicles – with determinate structures, functions, compositions, and ideologies – that industrialists deliberately developed to defend and promote their common interests. As real bodies, not imputed constructs, these associations left behind them a rich collection of primary source material (e.g., publications, speeches, internal communications); they themselves were the subjects and objects of well-documented political action.

Not only does a focus on associations afford a high degree of specificity, but associations, by their very nature, are the category most relevant to an examination of the *collective* actions of industrialists. My major concern is not with the idiosyncratic behavior of industrialist X or with the disproportionate influence of industrialist Y, neither of which would tell us much about the industrialists as a class or, for that matter, the distinctive context in which they took common action. Idiosyncratic behavior and disproportionate influence, after all, may be found in all political systems and social situations. Outside an organizational context, they reveal little of collective significance except, of course, via unwarranted imputational leaps of faith. Collective action obviously necessitates collective structures; industrial associations were the collective structures through which industrialists acted in the syndical and political arenas. Obviously, there are limits to this approach, which is less attentive to industrialist activity outside the associational fold and particularly to nonsanctioned activity at the local level. Frank Snowden, for example, has recently indicated that Tuscan industrialists between 1919 and 1922 undertook pro-Fascist action inconsistent with the nuanced policies of Confindustria, the national peak association, in Rome.[4] It is certainly possible that there were other exceptions as well, though exceptions have significance only in relation to the norm, and here the norm, as Snowden himself recognizes, was set by Confindustria.

Current scholarship in European studies has come to recognize the critical role that formally organized interest associations have played in the transition from nineteenth-century, laissez-faire capitalism to twentieth-century, state-administered capitalism.[5] Whereas organized labor associations have long been an object of study, it is only recently that organized business associations have received serious attention. The reason for this imbalance stemmed from the long-held supposition that whereas workers under capitalism had to organize to defend their collective interests, capitalists had their interests protected by the system itself, that the structural economic advantages capitalists enjoyed under capitalism translated directly into political advantages. Thus, capitalists had no reason to organize – this, despite the fact that business associations have existed almost as long as those of labor, but for what ends? In most European nations, Italy included, capitalists organized, first, in response to the development of labor unions, which had been legally prohibited or constrained during the period of laissez-faire capitalism, and, second, in response to state intervention, when capitalists had to confront the political mobilization of organized labor and newly constituted, functional state bureaucracies in some unified, ongoing, and authoritative manner. Under conditions of modern mass democracy, business groups had to act in a formally free political arena where they did not necessarily possess the same competitive advantages they had in the economic

[4] Frank M. Snowden, *The Fascist Revolution in Tuscany, 1919–1922* (Cambridge: Cambridge University Press, 1989).
[5] See, e.g., the essays in Suzanne Berger, ed., *Organizing Interests in Western Europe* (New York: Cambridge University Press, 1981).

sphere. As Philippe Schmitter has pointed out, when business groups adopt a political mode of action, they are in a position fundamentally different from their position in the marketplace. "While in the latter they are distinguished from all other actors by their unique power to control investment, the logic obtaining in a political frame of action puts them at least in principle on the same plane as their opponents." In short, economic advantage has no necessary and direct political translation. "The crucial difference, in other words, from the viewpoint of capital owners between the political and the economic domain is that in the former they have to meet other groups on terms which, unlike the terms regulating economic exchange in the market place, do not grant them an *a priori* advantage."[6]

Beyond the more-immediate issues relating to Italian development and the question of Fascism, it is hoped the present study will contribute as well to this relatively new literature on the organization of business interests, as it deals not only with political problems industrialists confronted under conditions of liberal politics but also with those presented by an authoritarian regime as well. Here, too, economic advantage did not automatically translate into political advantage, and how industrial associations negotiated the transition from liberalism to Fascism, and later operated within a potentially hostile Fascist state, is a case study well worth considering.

Finally, I would like to acknowledge a great intellectual debt to those scholars who carefully read various versions of this manuscript and were generous with their insightful criticism: Philippe Schmitter, Arisitide Zolberg, Lloyd Rudolph, Paul Piccone, Victoria De Grazia, and Roberto Vivarelli. Joseph LaPalombara and Alberto Spreafico helped me contact Italian specialists on Fascism and gave me invaluable hints at the crucial preliminary stage of research. Alberto Aquarone and Renzo De Felice in Rome were of tremendous assistance in helping me understand Fascism and directing me through the intricacies of the Archivio Centrale dello Stato. Valerio Castronovo, Paolo Farneti, and Norberto Bobbio in Turin enriched my understanding of the distinctive nature of Turinese liberalism, as well as the influence industrialization had upon regional and national politics. I owe a very special debt to Mario Abrate, who took a personal interest in my

---

[6] Philippe Schmitter, Wolfgang Streeck, and Alberto Martinelli, "The Organization of Business Interests," Discussion Papers, Wissenschaftszentrum, Berlin, Mar. 1980, p. 13.

project, patiently answering my many questions and making available to me the historical archives of the Lega Industriale di Torino. The staffs of the Archivio Centrale dello Stato, the Biblioteca della Camera dei Deputati, and the Biblioteca di Storia Contemporanea were most helpful and patient in accommodating my inordinate requests. In this regard, I would like to express my personal gratitude to Giovanna Guidi and her staff at the Confindustria library; for more than a year, they graciously responded to all of my research needs, often serving well beyond the call of duty. Without adequate funding, of course, none of this would have been possible; I would like to acknowledge grants from the following sources: the Council for European Studies, the Social Science Research Council, and the National Endowment for the Humanities. Moral encouragement came from a small circle of family and friends on both sides of the Atlantic who gave me indispensable and unconditional support through thick and thin. To my beloved wife, Marie-Hélène, I owe far more than my own words could ever express:

> E sua bieltate è di tanta vertute,
> che nulla invidia a l'altre ne procede,
> anzi le face andar seco vestute
> di gentilezza, d'amore e di fede.
>   Dante Alighieri, *Vita nuova*

Abbreviations

ACS	Archivio Centrale dello Stato
AMMA	Associazione Metallurgici Meccanici e Affini
BLI	*Bollettino della Lega Industriale*
CGL	Confederazione Generale del Lavoro (1906)
CIDI	Confederazione Italiana dell'Industria (1910)
Confindustria	Confederazione Generale dell'Industria Italiana (1919)
ENIOS	Ente Nazionale Italiano per l'Organizzazione Scientifica del Lavoro
FIOM	Federazione Italiana Operai Metallurgici
HAUIT	Historical Archive, Unione Industriale di Torino
LF	*Lavoro Fascista*
LI	*Lavoro d'Italia*
LIT	Lega Industriale di Torino (1906)
OI	*Organizzazione Industriale*

Italian Industrialists
from Liberalism to Fascism

Introduction

Post-Risorgimento liberalism

Liberalism, in Italy and elsewhere in Europe, was essentially a prein-dustrial and predemocratic phenomenon, one that even in the best of cases had to adapt itself painfully to new demands engendered by the process of modernization. Only during the final quarter of the nineteenth century did even the most-advanced European nations begin to assume a distinctively urban–industrial character, as well as extend the franchise to broad strata of the previously excluded population. Industrialization and democratization progressively al-tered the very nature of European politics: elitist and loosely orga-nized bourgeois parties and parliamentary factions found themselves confronted by increasingly large and bureaucratic mass parties; indi-vidual employers found themselves confronted by disciplined trade unions, more often than not affiliated with the new mass parties; the state found itself compelled to permanently intervene in previously autonomous spheres of civil society to ensure social reproduction and maintain civil order. Liberalism, in a word, had to adapt itself to a new epoch of mass politics whose characteristic elements – modern political parties, syndical associations, state intervention – were antic-ipated by neither classical liberal theory nor practice.

That Italian liberalism failed to adapt itself adequately can be readily seen by looking backward over the past century and a half of Italy's history. Liberalism had been the guiding force behind the Risorgimento; from unification to the rise of Fascism, liberalism had been virtually synonymous with national politics. It was the dominant ideology; it was the professed position of the entire *classe dirigente*, it was the juridical foundation of the Constitution. In post-Fascist Italy, liberalism survives as a residual, minor ideology. Liberals are but a marginal party, rarely receiving 5 percent of the vote in a political system dominated by Marxists and Catholics. These two dominant forces of post-Fascist politics, significantly enough, first emerged in pre-Fascist Italy as popular movements largely outside and against liberalism, which excluded mass participation and then, once the larger European trend toward democratization was well under way, failed to integrate the two rapidly growing popular movements within the traditional and essentially unaltered institutional framework. Fascism, within this century-and-a-half period, marks a qualitative divide. With the rise and consolidation of Fascism, liberal dominance comes to an end, never again to reassert itself, but the two popular movements, though suppressed under Fascism, nevertheless ascend thereafter to positions of political dominance. Such a manner of posing the problem, however preliminary and schematic, allows us at least to situate Fascism, anticipating what we shall specify as the internal contradictions of Italian liberalism, as well as delimiting the terrain upon which Fascism, born of liberalism's crisis, took root and flowered.

The primary structural problem of Italian liberalism was an ever deepening contradiction between a developing society and a static institutional framework, a contradiction exacerbated both by factors specific to Italy (e.g., limited capital and natural resources, a traditional culture antagonistic or indifferent to economic development) and by those generic to most belated developers (e.g., peripheral and dependent status in prestructured international markets; little or no time lag between capital accumulation, on the one hand, and "precocious" distributive demands by organized labor, on the other; the tendency to define the domestic situation on the basis of experiences and models peculiar to "advanced" nations, whether appropriate or not). On one side of this contradiction stood a society that rather quickly and abruptly had entered the developmental process, leading to the mobilization of new as well as formerly passive strata that, together, began to advance participatory and distributive claims through the agency of organizational forms (mass parties and labor syndicates) and ideologies (Socialism and revolutionary syndicalism), copied, for the most part, from the advanced nations across the Alps. On the other side stood a nonadaptive, essentially preindustrial and predemocratic institutional framework which could neither respond to the new claims nor integrate the new organizational forms and ideologies.

This institutional framework, which had emerged from the Risorgimento and was linked to a rather unique and transitional social order, was postfeudal yet preindustrial. It had been constituted to mediate among the narrow spectrum of interests specific to the enfranchised 2 percent of the population, mostly large landowners and professionals. Due to the limited degree of political participation and the narrow range of politically articulated interests, this institutional framework was characterized by informal representation, aprincipled trade-offs, and the co-optation of potential opposition through patronage and corruption. This was the social basis of *trasformismo*, the Italian alternative to party and interest-group formation experienced in northern Europe and Great Britain.

The politically enfranchised class, for the most part, subscribed to the cautious, empirical liberalism associated with Cavour. There was little significant opposition from the extreme Right, as few aristocrats entertained a reactionary alternative, a return to the pre-1789 social order; generally speaking, they were already engaged in capitalistic market relations. Similarly, there was little significant opposition from the extreme Left. The peasants were mainly apolitical, though given to spontaneous violence; the bourgeoisie had nothing to gain and everything to lose from social revolution because feudalism already had been abolished; and an industrial proletariat, which might have advanced oppositional claims, had yet to be formed. The church, while dogmatically antiliberal, had ruled itself out of national politics with Pius IX's *Non Expedit*.

Yet by the turn of the century, the process of development had already begun to generate significant social differentiation and political polarization. With the rise of the "social problem" during the 1890s, the apparent adequacy of the Risorgimento institutional framework, linked as it was to a unique and transitional social order, began to show signs of increasing strain. Liberal hegemony, for the first time, was challenged from the outside as Socialism and Catholicism began to articulate the needs of hitherto excluded and passive popular classes, opening up new, oppositional public spheres. At the same time, liberalism began to erode from within. On the one hand, the bourgeois bloc became increasingly fragmented as newer elements, such as industrialists, bankers, and large-scale commercial traders (the so-called productive bourgeoisie), began to articulate and autonomously organize their own sectoral interests, no longer satisfied with their subordinate bourgeois status or confident that the preindustrial bourgeois politicians (sometimes disparaged as the "parasitic bourgeoisie") were willing or able to further their interests or even defend them against the newly emergent mass organizations. On the other hand, liberalism was losing more and more of the younger generation to the two mass movements and to nationalism, a particular expression of bourgeois youth's disaffection from what they viewed as a petty, unadventurous, and corrupt liberal tradition.

Despite eventual democratization and the formal organization of interests, no fundamental alteration or reconstitution of the inherited liberal institutional framework occurred. The increasingly fragmented elements of the bourgeois bloc developed no vehicle to aggregate their separate interests into a common, collective class interest. Most importantly in this regard, they failed to form a national liberal party to compete with the emergent Socialist and Catholic Parties. And when this step was finally taken, twenty days before Mussolini's March on Rome, it was too little, too late. Liberal politicians like Giolitti believed that the new mass movements could be co-opted within the framework of traditional *trasformismo* politics, mistakenly confident that this form of mediation, which had been developed earlier to accommodate the limited upper-class spectrum of interests interior to the agricultural–professional bloc, would prove sufficiently elastic now to embrace the full class spectrum and increasingly organized interests. Liberals found it ever more difficult to bridge the gap between themselves and the newly activated masses, and to do so in such a way that the latter might be preemptively inserted into the traditional institutional framework.

Here Barrington Moore's famous observations regarding the absence of a thoroughgoing bourgeois revolution are highly suggestive. The absence of such a revolution in Italy, and the self-conscious exclusion of the masses at the time of unification, greatly exacerbated the problems of institutional penetration, integration, and legitimacy, generic to all experiences of modernization. At the level of structure, few channels existed within the traditional institutional framework wherein mass parties and syndicates might have functioned. At the level of ideology, it became increasingly difficult for liberals to legitimate themselves, both because liberalism was theoretically bound to the principle of rule by consent and because liberalism lacked any historical linkages in Italy to the non-elites. Given the socially limited nature of the Risorgimento, the Italian bourgeoisie had little prior experience in social mobilization, in providing the nation with an affirmative ideal, universal in scope, with which the bourgeoisie might have learned, in fact, to rule by consensus rather than by coercion. Thus, with further social differentiation, democratization, and the autonomous organization of interests, the liberal political system progressively lost its capacity to mediate, to rule, to even sustain itself. The mass movements were separately unable to impose their programs upon the nation, yet the liberals were no longer capable of ruling in their own right. Fascism, as Renzo De Felice suggests, responded to this fractured, nonhegemonic constellation of class relations as if it were a negative aggregation, imposing a new compulsive system of mediation upon the nation based practically on independent executive authority and ideologically on corporatism as the transcendence of failed liberalism.

Ideologically, liberals never developed a substantive national ideal or legitimating principle to justify their dominance. Italian liberalism, rather than a creed, from the very outset had been a modus operandi, a means by which to strike short-term compromises within a narrowly circumscribed stratum of society. Related to this limited ideological development was retarded party development, and for essentially the same reason: given the exclusive, class-specific electorate, what need was there for alternative political parties, or parties at all, to articulate so restricted a range of interests within such a narrow political arena? Differences within the politically enfranchised stratum could be mediated by personalistic and informal compromise; there was no compelling need, in the absence of organized opposition, to develop superfluous institutional forms such as parties. What would later be called *trasformismo* – or shifting, aprincipled centrist coalitions revolving about dominant personalities – had already been anticipated before unification in Cavour's 1852 *connubio* when the leader of the Center-Right struck a deal with Rattazzi, leader of the Center-Left. As one student of Italian parties comments:

In practice, for the British two-party system an Italian "government party" system was substituted which would dominate national political life for decades to come. This expression defines a ministerial majority which could be based on two political groups but also on an indeterminate number of supporting tendencies, political currents in their complex of single deputies. The incumbent Prime Minister was the epicenter of this convergence which emerged around his person and dissolved the moment he left office, to be reconstituted – in identical or modified form – around another Prime Minister.[1]

Trasformismo, a more corrupt and vulgar version of Cavour's *connubio,* further facilitated the osmosis between Left and Right tendencies within liberalism, inhibiting what some observers maintain might have otherwise led to separate liberal and conservative parties. *Trasformismo* would become the distinctive modality of political life – not a public competition between principled and oppositional parties, but a semipublic and rather autonomous game between *ministriali* and *antiministriali.* The prime minister, who often was also minister of the interior, would use prefects and other discretionary means to "make elections" and "manufacture majorities." Pejorative expressions like "parliamentary incest" and "parliamentary alchemism" characterized this practice, which in the popular consciousness reflected a decline in culture and led to contempt for liberal politics.[2]

The widening gap between a dynamic society and a static institutional framework was apparent in the peculiar insularity of parliamentary life, where the rise and fall of governments had less to do with crisis situations or fundamental differences over public policy than with success or failure in forming and maintaining amorphous *combinazioni* among deputies who, as an almost entirely autonomous group, had themselves elected quite independently of outside forces and interests. In this regard, Paolo Farneti's study of the social composition of Parliament from 1861 to 1914 is most revealing. During the period of the Destra Storica (1861–76), parliamentary leadership was relatively homogeneous and representative of the dominant economic stratum, landowners. According to Farneti, deputies of the Destra Storica had three attributes in common: they came from the nobility, they were landowners, and they had participated in the Risorgimento. This homogeneity of parliamentary leadership and linkage to economic interest declined significantly when the Sinistra Storica came to power. Deputies of the Sinistra Storica, being generally younger and coming from the professional strata, lacked the same shared experiences and direct linkages to the economy. This is particularly important because as Italy industrialized, the number of

---

[1] Francesco Leoni, *Storia dei partiti politici italiani* (Naples: Guida Editore, 1971), pp. 60–1. All translations from foreign-language sources are my own.
[2] John A. Thayer, *Italy and the Great War* (Cambridge: Harvard University Press, 1964), pp. 44–54.

industrialists in Parliament did not significantly increase. The slack, so to speak, was taken up by lawyers and, to a lesser degree, by other professionals (journalists, professors, physicians). Farneti's data indicate that the Italian parliament was composed of proportionately more lawyers and fewer industrialists from 1892 to 1914 than was the case in France and Germany. Furthermore, Farneti concludes that the Italian parliament was composed more of independent political brokers than direct representatives of either industrial or agricultural interests. Because of the limited franchise (1.9 percent of the population under the Destra Storica, extended to 7 percent under the Sinistra Storica through easing property and literacy qualifications), the logic of *trasformismo,* and the capacity to "make elections," these lawyer–politicians rendered themselves far more autonomous than their parliamentary counterparts elsewhere in Europe. For example, Farneti found that the number of Italian deputies who had served in five or more legislatures was three times greater than in France. Italy had proportionally fewer new deputies whose parliamentary careers were interrupted by one or more legislatures out of office.[3] In short, Italian deputies had not only longer parliamentary careers, but longer *uninterrupted* ones. Yet the stability of parliamentary careers, in and of itself, could not ensure the long-term viability of the liberal political system; in fact, it only underscored Parliament's insularity, tending to confirm the view shared by both the extreme Left and the extreme Right that the government was dominated by self-centered "politicians" who in no significant sense represented *le pays réel.*

The contradictions between a dynamically changing society and a static institutional framework dramatically exploded during the 1890s in worker and peasant agitations, declarations of martial law, dissolutions of "subversive organizations," arbitrary arrests, banking crises, political scandals, the assertion of exceptional powers by prime ministers, the dissolution of Parliament and several municipal governments, and the assassination of the king. In 1887, the so-called parliamentary dictatorship of Agostino Depretis passed on to Francesco Crispi, another man of the Left and former lieutenant to Garibaldi during the Sicilian campaign. Crispi, an ardent admirer of Bismarck, combined a policy of domestic repression with imperialism and, in fact, would fall from power with the tragic Italian defeat at Adowa in

---

[3] Paolo Farneti, *Sistema politica e società civile* (Turin: Giappichelli, 1971), pp. 169–71, 194–280.

1896. His tenure in office, plus the repressive governments from 1896 to 1900, constituted a major crisis period for the liberal system that had emerged from the Risorgimento, one that almost brought constitutional rule to an end. Had it not been for Italy's defeat at Adowa, Crispi's combination of imperialism and domestic repression might well have developed into a consolidated dictatorship. His successor, the conservative and unimaginative Marquis di Rudini, initially attempted a policy of social reconciliation: Italy's African claims were scaled down to relative insignificance, an amnesty was granted to most of those condemned during the agitations of 1894, and a government commission was appointed to study the causes of social unrest in Sicily that had radicalized the peasant leagues (*fasci siciliani*).

Conciliation, however, left unaltered the underlying causes of mass unrest; no program of reform was entertained. Sidney Sonnino, a leading conservative who during the 1880s had advocated a program of Tory-like reform, now argued in his famous January 1897 essay *Torniamo allo statuto* for a return to royal prerogatives and the creation of a unified liberal party to do battle against the two new popular movements, Socialism and Catholicism, which now threatened the institutional order. Meanwhile, a bad harvest, compounded by a reduction in American grain imports, caused a precipitous rise in the price of bread and flour products. This would lead to another and far more extensive wave of social unrest in 1898, the so-called *anno terribile*, when rioting broke out in many of the major cities (Rome, Parma, Florence, Naples), as well as throughout the countryside. These agitations culminated in Milan, where in May, responding to a call for a general strike, General Bava Beccaris lost his head and used artillery against unarmed civilians. For having saved the nation from "revolution," the general was decorated by the king. With no evidence of culpability, hundreds were arrested (including Socialist, radical, and Republican deputies), and Socialist and Catholic organizations were dissolved and their journals suppressed. The universities of Rome, Naples, Padua, and Bologna were closed, and civil servants were placed on military footing so that disobedience might be punished under martial law.

Such blatantly anticonstitutional measures threatened di Rudini's ruling coalition when Giuseppe Zanardelli, leader of the Center-Left, resigned from the cabinet at the end of May. In mid-June, di Rudini requested exceptional powers from Parliament that would have further restricted civil liberties, but this was met with opposition from the Left, as well as the Right. With his majority in Parliament now shattered, di Rudini resigned, whereupon the king appointed General Luigi Pelloux prime minister.

With Pelloux, the so-called institutional crisis of the 1890s came to a head, although like his predecessor, he too began his government in a conciliatory manner, appointing some men of the Center-Left to cabinet posts and disregarding the repressive decrees which had been issued under di Rudini. Lacking a program and political skill, Pelloux soon fell under the influence of the conservative *éminence grise* Sonnino. Instead of granting an expected amnesty for those arrested in 1898, in February 1899 Pelloux introduced legislation to control public meetings, limit the press, and send political offenders to penal colonies. When the Center-Left members of his cabinet objected, they were replaced with conservatives. And when debate began on these measures, the extreme Left, fearing that Pelloux might have a majority, resorted to obstructionist tactics. Zanardelli and Giolitti, of the Center-Left, while opposing such tactics, spoke out against the government's demands for limiting debate on so controversial a set of issues. Giolitti, in particular, laid bare the dilemma facing the government: either it could attempt to draw the masses toward the nation's established institutions or it could adopt a futile policy of repression, which would only drive the politicized popular classes to further violence and away from established institutions.

Pelloux finally forbade the Chamber of Deputies (the lower house of Parliament) to meet for six days and on 26 June 1899 withdrew the exceptional bills, presenting in their place a royal decree. At that point, members of the Center-Left, led by Zanardelli and Giolitti, joined the opposition. Obstructionism continued and when the president of the Chamber suddenly declared that debate was closed and the motion would be called, violence broke out: Sonnino and the Socialist Bissolati came to blows, while other Socialist deputies broke the urns in which ballots were cast. Pelloux promptly ordered their arrest and closed the Chamber for three months. Shortly thereafter, he dissolved the Socialist town council of Milan and replaced it with a nominated royal commission.

In February 1900, the Supreme Court (Corte dei Conti) ruled that the royal decree was an unwarranted act of the executive with no more authority than any other bill before Parliament. When in March the decree was again presented to the Chamber of Deputies, obstructionism resumed. The government then attempted to amend the rules of procedure to restrict freedom of debate, whereupon the Extreme Left and the Center-Left abandoned the Chamber. This action would resemble the Aventine secession of 1924, when, in the wake of the Matteotti assassination, opponents of Fascism also left the Chamber. Unlike that instance, which Mussolini unreservedly exploited by having the remaining deputies simply pass repressive legislation, Pelloux chose to dissolve Parliament and call for new elections. He failed to gain the popular mandate he had sought via the elections. Faced with a unified extreme Left and Center-Left and opposed by the prestigious *Corriere della Sera,* the government could obtain only a narrow majority, whereas the declared opposition had doubled their number. Pelloux resigned and the king appointed eighty-year-old Senator Saracco to head a transitional government. Several days later, King Umberto was assassinated, and in February 1901 his son, Vittorio Emanuelle III, appointed a new government headed by the leaders of the Center-Left, Zanardelli and Giolitti, ending the 1898–1900 crisis.

Though the liberal–democrats emerged triumphant from the travail of the 1890s, two observations must be made. First, authoritarian alternatives to the crisis-prone liberal system already had presented themselves. Second, the liberal–democratic victory was more apparent than real. It was based on a short-term, essentially defensive alliance between the extreme Left and Center-Left, destined to fall apart the moment the threat of reaction ended. This alliance was strictly a parliamentary phenomenon, having no basis outside the Chamber among the various social strata and organized groups of the population at large. In no way was the institutional framework itself altered either to integrate the masses or to prepare the liberals for competition, as a modern political party, against the "reds" and "blacks." Instead, Giolitti, who would dominate Italian politics for the next two decades until Mussolini came to power, naively presumed that extending the elastic limits of *trasformismo* from a restricted upper-class spectrum to the popular classes and instituting a limited program of co-optive reform would jointly prove adequate to the task of preserving the nineteenth-century institutional framework within a twentieth-century context of mass politics. The manifold effects of modernization, and in particular the development of modern parties and organized interest groups, were too extensive in scope and too weighty in bearing to be accommodated by any such sleight of hand, even when attempted by the greatest alchemist within the Italian political tradition.

The Giolittian system

In stark contrast with the tumultuous 1890s, the first decade of the new century has been looked back upon as a belle époque. Externally, Europe's long depression gave way to a new period of prosperity and expanded international trade. Not only did Italy passively benefit from this change in the international business cycle, but it experienced its own industrial takeoff, after rather slow and discontinuous progress the preceding decade. That material life had significantly improved for many Italians is indicated by the fact that real wages rose by 21 percent, the highest rate of increase from unification until World War I.[4] For this decade at least, Italy was spared the severe economic distress which had precipitated social unrest earlier. Yet it would be crudely economistic to presume that the coming of good times alone accounted for the relative stability of the new decade, for this would tend to overlook the enlightened political mediations of Giolitti, who had at least temporary success in changing the direction of state policy, though not the institutional framework itself.

Giovanni Giolitti began his career in 1862, working for the Ministry of Justice. The young lawyer rose quickly through the ranks of the state administration, holding important posts in the Ministry of Finance under the governments of the Right and then the Left, until he entered Parliament as a deputy in 1882. It has been said that Giolitti's somewhat atypical bureaucratic background accounted for his predilection to view politics as administration, his preoccupation with economic problems, and his unembellished, pragmatic, commonsense manner, so much at variance with the rhetorical pomposity of many Italian parliamentarians. As Mack Smith notes, "The most common accusation against Giolitti by historians has not been that he was authoritarian or corrupt, but that he was prosaic and pedestrian."[5]

---

[4] Salvatore Salardino, *Italy from Unification to 1919* (New York: Crowell, 1970), p. 115. For time-series data on real wages see Shepard B. Clough, *The Economic History of Modern Italy* (New York: Columbia University Press, 1963), pp. 382–3.
[5] Denis Mack Smith, *Italy* (Ann Arbor: University of Michigan Press, 1959), p. 287.

He made but one attempt to quote Dante in a speech before the Chamber, and got the citation wrong. Yet if he was a cultural philistine, as maintained by the literati of the time, Giolitti nevertheless was unusually adept in parliamentary debate: witty, in full command of the relevant facts, and well prepared with sober arguments.[6] Moreover, he was certainly one of the most enlightened liberals regarding the "social question." Convinced, as he often claimed, that the forward thrust of the masses toward their share of economic and political power was inevitable in fact and fully legitimate in principle, Giolitti maintained that actions taken by the incumbent *classe dirigente* would largely determine whether this mass ascendancy would be violent and subversive of the existing structure or orderly and ultimately conservative.

As early as 1886, Giolitti argued that Italy had a choice between two routes: one imperial, the other democratic. The former would squander the nation's limited resources and necessitate domestic repression; the latter, which he advocated, would favor internal development oriented toward promoting material well-being for the masses, a precondition for their subsequent peaceful entry into national politics.[7] Instead of employing the army as a class militia, repressing every organized attempt by workers to defend their interests, Giolitti recognized both the desirability of syndicates and the right to strike, so long as these remained within the bounds of legality and did not undermine public order. Already in his first ministry (1892–3), cut short by the Banca Romana scandal, Giolitti had advocated a progressive income tax, refused to dissolve workers' syndicates, and took no repressive action against the *fasci siciliani*. When he returned to power in 1901, as minister of the interior under Zanardelli, and in 1903, as prime minister, he set in motion a broad range of reforms (social legislation, public works, lowering taxes on necessities) clearly favoring the lower classes. Responding to conservatives in Parliament, Giolitti declared:

Sonnino is right in saying that the country is sick politically and morally, but the principal cause of its sickness is that the classes in power have been spending enormous sums on themselves and their own interests, and have obtained the money almost entirely from the poorer sections of society. . . . I

[6] Thayer, *Italy and the Great War*, p. 56.
[7] Nino Valeri, *Giolitti* (Turin: UTET, 1971), pp. 206–9.

deplore as much as anyone the struggle between classes, but at least let us be fair and ask who started it.[8]

Social peace was to be ensured by having the state, for the first time, actually promote the welfare of the lower classes and also play an active role in helping institutionalize and regulate class conflict. While prefects continued their traditional political function of "making elections," their social function changed significantly under Giolitti. According to one study of Italian prefects:

They were no longer to side automatically with the industrialists and land-owners in conflicts with labor and to bombard the government with requests for troops, but to mediate such conflicts from a neutral standpoint. Moreover, they were to seek and to remove the causes of social distress and conflict by promoting improvements in the socio-economic conditions of the working classes.[9]

Prefects not only were to help mediate labor conflicts in their municipalities but were to "preoccupy themselves with economic questions, and to interest themselves in salary levels, workers' complaints, and other situations that might lead to industrial strife and peasant disturbances."[10] In this vein, Giolitti established a Labor Office in the Ministry of Agriculture, Industry, and Commerce, charged with the task of collecting and publishing information on labor conditions. He also created an Advisory Council on Labor (Consiglio Superiore del Lavoro) – composed of deputies, functionaries, and representatives of capital and labor – which drafted and presented social legislation to Parliament.

In addition and related to the upturn in the business cycle, the success of Giolitti's program during the first decade of the new century was based on two sets of mediations: (1) Giolitti's sponsorship of a tacit alliance between the new trade-union movement, dominated by reform Socialists, and the new industrial associations (both groups, despite obvious class differences, were jointly committed to further industrialization and developing an institutionalized modus vivendi, based on syndical interaction, to resolve labor conflict without sporadic and violent disruptions to production); and (2) Giolitti's ability

[8] Mack Smith, *Italy*, pp. 214–15.
[9] Robert Fried, *The Italian Prefects* (New Haven: Yale University Press, 1963), p. 148.
[10] Frank Coppa, "Economic and Ethical Liberalism in Conflict: The Extraordinary Liberalism of Giovanni Giolitti," *Journal of Modern History* 42 (June 1970): 200.

to gain the support of Socialists and Catholics, exploiting antagonisms between the two mass movements while seeking, at the same
time, to insert each separately within the ongoing game of *trasformismo.*

The first set of mediations, regarding trade unions and industrial
associations, will be dealt with in detail in Chapter 1. Here we will
only note that this alliance began to break down after 1910, when
economic conditions worsened, closing the margin that had previously allowed for mutually beneficial trade-offs, and when the reformist trade unions proved less able to maintain internal discipline
over their rank and file than was the case with their industrialist counterparts.

We come then to the second set of mediations, regarding Socialists
and Catholics. Until 1912, though with some brief interruptions,
reformists dominated the Socialist Party, as well as the Confederazione Generale del Lavoro (CGL). Because of the progressive role he
had played during the 1898–1900 crisis, Giolitti had gained their
respect. Writing in *Critica Sociale,* Claudio Treves proclaimed:
"There is on the other side a man who has understood us." In
contrast with reactionary bourgeois leaders, he argued, Giolitti would
promote economic development and political liberty, requisite conditions for the further development of the Socialist movement.[11] Seeing
that in France the reformist Alexandre Millerand had entered the
cabinet of Waldeck-Rousseau, and hoping to have the Socialists tied
to his government with a similar assumption of ministerial responsibility, Giolitti offered a cabinet post to Turati in 1903 and to Bissolati
in 1911. Despite their own personal inclinations, both Socialist leaders rejected the offer, fearing acceptance might further split an already
divisive movement. Yet the Socialist Party, in the main, and Socialist
deputies in particular, consistently supported Giolitti until 1912. Giolitti not only expected such support but "punished" reformists when
they let revolutionaries get out of hand. When, for example, revolutionary syndicalists, who tried to take over the Partito Socialísta
Italiano (PSI) in 1904, called for Italy's first general strike, Giolitti
refrained from taking any repressive action but instead dissolved
Parliament and called for national elections. Given the fear engen-

---

[11] *Critica Sociale* 8 (1898–9): 182–4, reprinted in Gastone Manacorda, ed., *Il socialismo nella storia d'Italia,* 2 vols. (Bari: Laterza, 1972), 1:275–83.

dered in the country by the general strike, the PSI lost several seats, while Giolitti's forces gained significantly, such that Giolitti emerged with a large enough majority to allow him to continue independent of Socialist support. Socialist cooperation with Giolitti ended in 1911–12 with two interrelated events: Giolitti's war with Turkey for control of Libya and the assumption of PSI leadership by the revolutionaries.

We turn now to the Catholics. The movement toward Christian Democracy was blocked by two events in 1903–4: the death of Pope Leo XIII and the general strike called by revolutionary syndicalists. Pius X, who succeeded Leo XIII, was a confirmed antimodernist, sharing little of his predecessor's intellectual and social concerns. Fearful that the general strike was a harbinger of revolution, Pius X modified the conditions of the *Non Expedit,* allowing Catholics to vote in those districts where a candidate of the "forces of order" was in danger of being defeated by a "subversive." Though some Catholic candidates also were elected, the Vatican made it clear that they ran as private individuals, not as members of a Catholic party or electoral bloc, for such bodies were not sanctioned. Elected Catholics, as the official phrase went, were *cattolici deputati,* not *deputati cattolici* (deputies who were Catholics, not Catholic deputies). Independent Catholic organizations were either dissolved by the church (e.g., Opera dei Congressi) or condemned (e.g., Muri's Lega Democratica Nazionale) or replaced with associations under strict Vatican control (e.g., Unione Popolare). Catholics participated in the 1913 elections under conditions essentially similar to those of 1904. Before the elections, Giolitti and Count Gentiloni, head of the Unione Elettore Cattolica, entered into a secret pact whereby Catholics would vote for liberal candidates who agreed to certain conditions (including opposition to antireligious and divorce legislation). In 1910–11, when Giolitti's relations with the PSI were still good, he had enacted universal suffrage for men in expectation of Socialist support. However, with the Socialists now against him because of the Libyan War, and likely to make significant gains, Giolitti reached out to the Catholics as an alternative base of mass support. Catholics thus entered political life as a dependent conservative force, not so much out of respect for or trust in Giolitti, but rather because he represented the only available alternative to Socialism. Had Pius X permitted

Christian Democratic development, Catholics might have posed their own political alternative to Socialism and liberalism (as had been the original conception), but this would not occur until Benedict XV became pope, sanctioning in 1918–19 an autonomous Catholic Party and labor confederation.

To the major problem confronting Italy at the turn of the century – the masses' separation from the liberal state – Giolitti had offered bureaucratic and economistic solutions, presuming that were these successful it necessarily would follow that the impetus toward alternative modes of political action would be checked and the satisfied masses, were they ultimately given the vote, would passively affirm the unaltered institutional framework. What remained central to Giolitti's reformist program, its sine qua non, was the capacity to control Parliament, allowing him the independence to rationalize the state apparatus and direct it toward social concerns. However, rather than lay the foundations for a modern political party, which might have afforded him a base in the country, Giolitti merely continued – or rather perfected – the traditional practices of *trasformismo* and "making elections." Hence the paradox of Giolitti: his enlightened social program not only presumed mass passivity but accentuated the worst traits of Italian politics, which had led to such cynicism and lack of legitimacy in the past. The historian Salvemini, in a pamphlet describing Giolitti's corrupt electoral methods, called him *il ministro della malavita* (minister of the underworld), a label which would haunt Giolitti for the duration of his political career. Typical cartoons of the time were no more complimentary. As so often said, Giolitti was the most popular man in Parliament and the most unpopular man in the country.

Between 1910 and 1913, Giolitti's system collapsed. To some degree, this was due to a downward business cycle, which reduced the margin for compromise and class collaboration. Yet the *political* breakdown of the Giolittian system cannot be simply reduced to economics. In large part, the system broke down because of its own internal contradictions, exacerbated, not caused by, the economic downturn. As we have seen, *trasformismo* emerged as a process to mediate among the narrow scope of interests rooted in and specific to the property-holding classes. In an astute observation, Gramsci noted that whereas previously *trasformismo* had involved the "molecular absorption" of individual personalities from the constitutional opposition, Giolitti now attempted to absorb entire oppositional groups from diverse and conflicting social classes.[12] Yet the more inclusive and heterogeneous the interests to be mediated, the less the system could maintain its earlier center of gravity and overall coherence. Concessions made to one group were unacceptable to others, especially under conditions of scarcity. Ideologically, there was no longer a shared consensus among the interested parties. Institutionally, there existed no structure that might have served as an arena for bargaining among formally organized interests, just the preemptive personal mediations of the prime minister.

Universal suffrage was intended to be the culminating keystone of Giolitti's system; instead, it toppled the shaky edifice of the liberal state itself. Giolitti had maintained that this reform ought to be deferred "until the time is mature, when the country is tranquil," arguing that after the masses had experienced material progress, they would be more moderate in orientation and become a conservative force.[13] Italy, indeed, was one of the last western European states to institute universal suffrage for men. By 1911 Giolitti felt that the time was ripe for this culminating step of his ten-year reform program. At the PSI congresses of 1908 and 1910, reformists had consolidated their control. Speaking in Parliament, Giolitti claimed that after eight years of progress, "the Socialist Party had much moderated its program and relegated Karl Marx to the attic."[14]

The prime minister thus sought an opening to the extreme Left by proposing universal suffrage for men, nationalizing life insurance, and offering Bissolati a cabinet post. At the same time, however, he sought to preempt the Nationalist Right by declaring war on Turkey for control of Libya. The war proved catastrophic for Giolitti, who until then had opposed colonial adventures in Africa. He had hoped for the final integration of oppositional forces into the system; instead he saw that system unravel piece by piece. On the other hand, the Nationalists were not won over or mollified by Giolitti. The Libyan campaign only whetted their appetite for further and more aggressive expansionism. On the other hand, Socialists went into strident opposition. Due in no small part to Libya, the reformists who had collaborated with Giolitti were defeated at the 1912 party congress.

Meanwhile, Giolitti, finding himself in a vastly different situation

[12] Antonio Gramsci, *Il Risorgimento* (Turin: Einaudi, 1966), p. 157.
[13] Valeri, *Giolitti*, pp. 206–9.
[14] Mack Smith, *Italy*, p. 257.

on the eve of the 1913 elections from the one he had envisioned when he proposed universal suffrage for men two years earlier, now turned to the Catholics for support and entered into the Gentiloni pact. Yet this, in turn, eroded support for him on the part of laic political forces, primarily the radicals.

Doing all he could to "make" the 1913 election, Giolitti emerged with a majority, but one that was clearly smaller, more heterogeneous and fragile than those of the past when liberals had complete parliamentary control. Liberals now had 318 seats out of 508, 52 fewer than their previous tally of 370 seats; of these 318 seats, 288 had been dependent upon external support from Catholics. Representation of the extreme Left jumped from 112 to 161 seats, and had there been proportional representation, this figure would have been 200 (of the extreme Left's total, the Socialists won 52 seats, which, under proportional representation, would have been 89). Meanwhile, the so-called Catholic deputies increased from 20 to 29, and for the first time, Nationalists found a presence in Parliament with 3 seats.[15] When the radicals withdrew their support upon learning, after the election, of the Gentiloni pact, Giolitti resigned. He was succeeded by the conservative Antonio Salandra, a close associate of Sonnino. Faced with a new wave of social unrest at home and the prospect of territorial conquests abroad, Salandra steered Italy into the First World War against Parliament and popular sentiment. The "executive coup," as we shall see, set an authoritarian precedent for the resolution of the postwar crisis as well.

Industrialization and the rise of an industrial bourgeoisie

As the celebrated economic historian Carlo Cippola notes:

At the beginning of the seventeenth century, Italy, or more exactly Northern and Central Italy, was still one of the most advanced of the industrial areas of Western Europe with an exceptionally high standard of living. By the end of this century, Italy had become an economically backward and depressed area; its industrial structure had almost collapsed, its population was too high for its resources, its economy had become primarily agricultural.[16]

Italy's prosperity had been due mainly to two factors: its large-scale export of manufactured goods (primarily silk and wool) and its pri-

[15] Leoni, *Partiti politici*, pp. 239–42.
[16] Carlo Cippola, "The Decline of Italy: The Case of a Fully Matured Economy," *Economic History Review* 5 (1952): 178.

macy in the commercial fields of banking and maritime service. By the seventeenth century, however, conditions had begun to change. On the one hand, by introducing lower-quality but cheaper textiles, other nations (mainly England, Holland, and France) began to successfully compete in foreign markets that the Italians traditionally had dominated, while Italy fell behind because it adhered to antiquated production techniques and could not otherwise lower costs (labor grew more expensive because of depopulation caused by the great plague; between 1630 and 1657, one-third of the population in Italy's larger cities disappeared). On the other hand, principal trade routes shifted from the Mediterranean to the Atlantic, and England and Holland underwent remarkable development in banking and shipping services at the expense of Italy, undercutting the other pillar of Italian prosperity.[17]

Italy's economic backwardness continued well into the nineteenth century, becoming more severe as England and the northern European countries began to industrialize. Materially, Italy was at a disadvantage because of its topography and lack of mineral resources critical to primary industrialization (coal and iron). Culturally, Italy had been cut off from Europe during the Counter Reformation; its traditional industrial and entrepreneurial classes were narrow in vision and rather unadventurous and were roundly criticized by Risorgimento intellectuals for their lack of interest in science and technology, as well as their conservatism.

At the time of unification, industry accounted for only 20 percent of the gross national product; it was restricted in scope mainly to textiles still at the handicraft and cottage stage and limited geographically to principally the northern regions of Lombardy, Piedmont, and Veneto.[18] No significant changes in scale, technique, or relation to the agricultural sector occurred during the two decades following unification.[19] To some degree, this was due to policies of Cavour and the men of the Right who followed him. As with Italian economists of the time, they were rather dogmatically committed to the tenets of economic liberalism, against tariff protection and state subsidies. Practically, they accepted an economic and political order dominated by the two pow-

[17] Ibid., pp. 178–87.
[18] Rosario Romeo, Breve storia della grande industria in Italia, 1861–1961 (Bologna: Capelli, 1972), pp. 11–26.
[19] Luciano Cafagna, "The Industrial Revolution in Italy, 1830–1914," in Carlo Cippola, ed., The Emergence of Industrial Societies (New York: Harper & Row, 1976), p. 291; Romeo, Breve storia, p. 41.

ers that had been sympathetic to the Italian cause, England and France. Within that order Italy would play a subordinate role, consuming manufactured goods produced abroad while exporting, in return, textiles and food products. Industrial development was confined to these so-called natural industries, and few thought it plausible that Italy might ever become an "industrial nation" as such. Moreover, those who had traveled abroad and had witnessed industrialization firsthand, with its attendant social dislocations and unruly proletariat, questioned the very desirability of Italy pursuing such a path. Even proponents of industry, like Alessandro Rossi and Giuseppe Colombo, maintained that Italy should avoid urban–industrial concentrations ("coketowns" and "mechanicvilles"). Rossi argued that industry should be located in rural areas, where the workforce might conserve its ties to the soil and traditional values; Colombo argued that Milan should preserve its mixed mercantile–light industry character rather than become a center for heavy industry.[20] Nevertheless, as Romeo has pointed out, the first twenty years of a united Italy was a period of significant infrastructure building which prepared the necessary conditions for further industrialization. Most noteworthy was railway construction, with railway lines increasing from 2,175 kilometers in 1860 to 8,713 in 1880. Similar progress was made in road construction (22,500 to 35,500 kilometers), telegraph lines (9,900 to 26,100 kilometers), streetcars (8 to 705 kilometers), and postal service (1,632 to 3,328 offices).[21] Yet this infrastructure building, particularly railroad construction, did little to actually stimulate industrial production itself (contrary to the case elsewhere), because most of the equipment and technical expertise was imported.[22]

Significant industrialization would take place during the last twenty years of the nineteenth century, yet under vastly different interna-

[20] For background on Colombo see Luciano Cafagna, ed., *Il nord nella storia d'Italia* (Bari: Laterza, 1962), pp. 26–51. For background on Rossi see Giuseppe Are, "Alla ricerca di une filosofia dell'industrializzazione nella culture e nei programmi politici in Italia, 1861–1916," *Nuova Rivista Storica* 53 (Jan. 1969): 71–109; Guido Baglioni, *L'ideologia della borghesia industriale* (Turin: Einaudi, 1974), pp. 232–308; Cafagna, *Il nord*, pp. 102–11, 173–96, 223–53; Silvano Lanaro, "Nazionalismo e ideologia del blocco corporativo-protezionista in Italia," *Ideologie* 2 (1967): 36–93.

[21] Romeo, *Breve storia*, p. 38.

[22] Cafagna, "Industrial Revolution in Italy," p. 287; Alexander Gerschenkron, *Economic Backwardness in Historical Perspective* (Cambridge: Harvard University Press, 1962), pp. 84–5; R. A. Webster, *Industrial Imperialism in Italy, 1908–15* (Berkeley and Los Angeles: University of California Press, 1975), p. 6.

tional and domestic conditions. Internationally, the long depression had set in, to which almost all European countries responded by erecting tariff walls in an effort to protect national economies. Domestically, the long depression had two major consequences. First, it led to an accelerated rate of investment in industry, now more attractive than investment in the depressed agricultural sector, and a shift in population from the countryside to the cities and abroad. Second, it led to a change in theory and public policy referred to as "economic Germanism" just as the Left (Sinistra Storica) came to power. Whereas the men of the Right had been doctrinaire economic liberals, basing their economic policy on the export of agricultural goods to unencumbered foreign markets, the men of the Left, by and large, subscribed to the new theory of "national economics" first advanced in Germany. Under this theory, deemed more appropriate to late-developing nations, the state would play an active and direct economic role in fostering growth through subsidies and protection, rather than continue as a so-called "nightwatchman," which left economic growth to the vicissitudes of the international marketplace, monopolized, as was claimed, by the already industrialized nations, which had cynically used "free trade" as an ideological smokescreen to penetrate and then dominate weaker national markets.[23]

This expanded role of the state, when taken in conjunction with the occupational background (lawyers) and moral stature (dubious) of the Left politicians, often led to scandal, corruption, and clientelism. Members of Parliament were not given salaries until 1911, and as Mack Smith quipped, "life in Rome was expensive."[24] It was within this framework that a new state-protected industrial sector was created (steel, armaments, shipbuilding), one that liberal critics from the outset condemned as artificial, parasitic, and incapable of holding its own without massive state support. A prime example of this "political industrialization" was Terni, founded with generous state subsidies to provide steel plate for the merchant marine and for armaments. From the very start, its history was laced with political

---

[23] "Economic Germanism" and "socialism of the chair" emerged in Italy during the mid-1870s. They were promoted by Luigi Luzzatti, Angelo Messedaglia, Fedele Lampertico, and the journal *Giornale degli Economisti,* For background see Are, "Filosofia," pp. 45–133; Cafagna, *Il nord,* pp. 141–261; Clough, *Economic History,* pp. 147, 400; Lucio Villari, "Per la storia del protezionismo in Italia," *Studi Storici* 6 (Oct. 1965): 660–5.

[24] Mack Smith, *Italy,* pp. 163, 201.

jobbery and outright corruption, to say nothing of its overpriced and inferior product.[25] A growing split, though never an outright break, would progressively unfold between this state-supported sector and the later-developing, predominantly export-oriented industrial groups, which in the next century would form industrial associations. Whereas the latter sought tariff reciprocity rather than principled protection, and enlightened syndical practice rather than blind repression, the former were unqualified proponents of economic nationalism, imperialism, corporatism, and, later, Fascism.

Italy's turn toward economic nationalism during the long depression was marked by two increasingly protective tariffs, those of 1878 and 1887, which had been promoted by both industrial and agricultural groups. According to some observers (Gramsci, Procacci, Lanaro, Webster), this marked the origin of a German rye and steel—type power bloc whose antiliberal tendencies eventually led to their support for (or actual imposition of) Fascism. This rather global formulation, however, is subject to several objections. First, no detailed analysis of the mediations between industrial and agricultural groups from 1880 to 1922 has yet been made to either confirm the broad hypothesis or demonstrate precisely how and in what sense Fascism was the culmination of this alliance. Second, of the various industrial groups which advocated protection during the 1880s, little care has been given to differentiating between those who continuously argued for principled protection (i.e., the state-supported sector) and those (e.g., cotton manufacturers) who later opposed protection once the long depression had ended and freer conditions of international trade prevailed. Third, the hypothesis suggests that, at least regarding protection, Italy and Germany were exceptional cases, losing sight of the fact that during this period protection was the rule rather than the exception in Europe, and that Italian rates, if anything, were actually lower than those of France, Germany, Austria, Spain, Greece, and Russia.[26] Fourth, as effective protective devices, the Italian tariffs were clearly counterproductive, since both the volume and the value of imports showed greater increase than during the earlier period of

---

[25] On Terni see Enrico Guaita, "Alle origini del capitalismo industriale italiano: la nascita della Terni," *Studi Storici* 11 (Apr. 1970): 292–312; Webster, *Industrial Imperialism*, pp. 53–60, 175.

[26] Frank J. Coppa, "The Italian Tariff and the Conflict between Agriculture and Industry: The Commercial Policy of Liberal Italy, 1860–1922, *Journal of Economic History* 30 (Dec. 1970): 749, 757–69.

free trade.[27] These objections would seem to indicate that the indus-trial–agricultural bloc hypothesis is rather dubious.

The index of industrial output (1900 = 100) rose steadily from 54 in 1881 to 74 in 1888, only to stagnate from 1888 to 1896, the worst years of the long depression.[28] According to Gerschenkron's data on the rate of industrial growth in Italy, the nation's "big spurt" was experienced during the years 1896–1908, when the annual average rate of growth in industrial output rose to 6.7 percent (compared to 4.6 percent for 1881–8 and 3.8 percent for 1881–1913).[29] Two major factors contributed to this quantitative leap, which led to a rapid transformation of the entire economic structure of the nation. The first was international in nature. In 1896 the long depression ended and Europe began what David Landes has called the "second wind" of the industrial revolution, more technological in nature and based on the large-scale use of new materials and energy sources.[30] Italian participation in this phenomenon is reflected in the develop-ment of hydroelectric power resources, compensating for Italy's lack of coal reserves, and in the ascendancy of new sectors (metalmaking, machines, and chemicals) over the traditional sectors (textiles and food processing). Although the average annual growth rate during the 1896–1908 big spurt was 6.7 percent, the new sectors grew at roughly double this rate (metalmaking, 12.4 percent; machines, 12.2 percent; chemicals, 13.7 percent), while the traditional sectors grew below the 6.7 percent average (textiles, 3.5 percent; food processing, 5.5 percent).[31] Whereas the traditional sectors represented 74.2 per-cent of all manufacturing goods in 1891–5, they fell to 59.2 percent by 1911–15. Conversely, the new sectors rose from 19.8 to 30.6 percent.[32] Still another indication of Italy's participation in the second wind may be seen in data regarding motor power: total motor power

---

[27] Ibid., p. 746.
[28] Gershenkron, *Economic Backwardness*, pp. 75–6.
[29] Ibid., pp. 75–7. Gerschenkron develops the following periodization regarding the annual average rates of growth in Italian industrial output:

1881–8	Moderate growth	4.6%
1888–96	Stagnation	0.3%
1896–1906	Very rapid growth	6.7%

[30] David Landes, "Technological Change and Development in Western Europe, 1750–1914," in *Cambridge Economic History* (Cambridge: Cambridge University Press, 1965), vol. 6, pt. 1, chap. 5; Cafagna, "Industrial Revolution in Italy," p. 304.
[31] Gerschenkron, *Economic Backwardness*, p. 76.
[32] Romeo, *Breve storia*, pp. 68–69.

consumption (coal, electricity, hydrocarbides) rose from an annual average of 25,286 million calories in 1881–90 to an annual average of 48,748 million calories in 1901–5, to 83,116 million calories in 1906–13.[33]

The second contributing factor to Italy's big spurt was the formation of German-style "mixed banks" (Banca Commerciale in 1894; Credito Italiano in 1895), which were founded with German capital after the failure of the French-backed Credito Mobiliare and Banca Generale in 1894 (both modeled after the Credit Mobilier). Whereas the French-backed banks had invested largely in real estate and construction, the mixed banks invested principally in industry and particularly in the new sectors. Moreover, the mixed banks not only made ordinary commercial credit loans in the manner of French-style banks but extended medium- and long-term loans to industry in so bold a manner that liberal critics warned that insufficient reserves were being held to protect depositors' savings.[34] With the formation of these new mixed banks, Italian industry for the first time had access to large and well-administered sources of much needed capital, though, as some maintained, at the cost of entrepreneurial autonomy. The new banks actively intervened in the administration of individual firms and through their investment strategies determined the development of and relations between different industrial sectors. For example, it has been argued that the previously mentioned split between the state-supported sector and the export-oriented groups was mediated and contained by the Banca Commerciale, which invested heavily in both.[35]

One final observation regarding Italian economic development should be made. Unlike in earlier-developing countries, where an initial period of capital formation and industrialization was *followed* by the development of an organized workers' movement, in Italy the two occurred *simultaneously rather than sequentially*. Gerschenkron, noting that the big spurt took place within a context of political

[33] Cafagna, "Industrial Revolution in Italy," p. 299.
[34] Romeo, *Breve storia*, pp. 69–70; Webster, *Industrial Imperialism*, pp. 128–63; Jon S. Cohen, "Italy, 1861–1914," in Rondo Cameron, ed., *Banking and Economic Development* (New York: Oxford University Press, 1972), pp. 58–90; Benedetto Notari, "Banca ed industria in Italia dal 1894 al 1914," *Storia e Politica* 11 (Jan. 1972): 74–92.
[35] Angelo Varni, "Gruppi dirigenti e 'svolta industriale' nel Italia di fine secolo," *Il Politico* 37 (Sept. 1977): 549–61; Procacci, *History of the Italian People*, p. 367.

turmoil and mass militancy, argues that Italy's relatively modest growth rate is at least partially attributable to the fact that the Italian labor movement emerged at the same time that it did in the more-advanced European countries, which had been spared such organized opposition when they themselves began to industrialize.[36]

When we turn from a more or less quantitative treatment of Italian industrialization to a subjective understanding of the sociocultural formation of the industrial bourgeoisie, we must speak with much less precision. Other than Guido Baglioni's pioneering study of the ideological development of this class, there exists no comprehensive analysis of the social origins of industrialists or of their relations with other bourgeois fragments during the nineteenth century. According to Baglioni, who begins his study with an analysis of the attitudes of industrialists as reflected in a parliamentary inquest undertaken between 1870 and 1874, little had changed from the picture presented by Greenfield of the Risorgimento era: that of a largely dependent, unadventurous class that had not as yet developed a consciousness of itself as a distinctive bourgeois fragment or an ideology that would in any way challenge the existent institutional framework or traditional legitimations articulated by the preindustrial *classe dirigente*. As Baglioni put it:

In other words, as opposed to what normally occurs with the affirmation of a capitalist mode of production, they did not question the superiority of the institutional framework with respect to the productive forces and did not exert adequate political pressure to modify it according to the exigencies related to a growing level of development of the industrial apparatus. In practice, they assented to the criteria of legitimation utilized by the old directing groups to maintain domination and to keep the popular classes in their place. They used the same criteria to exercise authority over the new subaltern class, the workers.[37]

In contrast to the enlightened, self-confident, and forward-looking worldview projected twenty-five years later by the first modern industrial association, the Industrial League of Turin (Lega Industriale di Torino; the LIT) Baglioni found no conception on the part of Italian industrialists in 1870–4 regarding either the distinctive nature of the "world of production" (i.e., its particular exigencies, operational logic, authority relations, and primacy over older and less-dynamic sectors)

---

[36] Gerschenkron, *Economic Backwardness*, pp. 85–6.
[37] Baglioni, *Ideologia della borghesia industriale*, pp. 309–65 (quotation from p. 226).

or the "social function," as it would be called later, of the "captain of industry." They seemed quite content passively to "go along with things," accepting their subordinate position within the prevailing bourgeois constellation, having their interests indirectly tutored by a separate political class – different in social origin, cultural formation, and occupation – against whom they advanced no claims.

Given what already has been said about industrialization during the final twenty years of the nineteenth century, it is no wonder that subjective changes began to manifest themselves among the industrialists. On the one hand, the long depression and the consequent European turn toward protection, together with the rise of economic Germanism, led some prominent industrialists not only to publicly question the previously shared consensus regarding the merits of economic liberalism but to become leading advocates of tariff increases in their own right. On the other hand, further quantitative and qualitative articulation of the industrial apparatus, both in itself and in relation to the traditional economic sectors, led to a growing self-consciousness among industrialists and with it a heightened sense of difference from the lawyer–politicians. Rudimentary forms of associations began to appear and an as yet primitive subculture began to develop, furthered, as Baglioni has argued, by the dissemination of "self-help" literature copied from and inspired by the writings of Samuel Smiles[38]

The most outstanding industrialist of the latter nineteenth century with respect to this growing self-consciousness was the wool manufacturer Alessandro Rossi, who owned and managed one of Italy's largest and most modern factories, promoted industrial associations, was a parliamentary deputy and later a senator, and wrote books and essays on such themes as "integral protection" and the "success ethic."[39] Having started as a simple worker in his father's factory and then traveled extensively throughout the industrialized countries, Rossi was the first to stress both the primacy and the distinctiveness of the "world of work," to delineate the specific function and competence of the industrial manager, and to polemicize against the technical illiteracy and traditional prejudice against productive activity on the part of the humanistic bourgeoisie. Though initially an economic liberal, Rossi became an ardent admirer of Germany and especially

[38] Ibid., pp. 309–65.
[39] Ibid., pp. 232–308.

the United States, both strongly protectionist and supportive of industry. "Free trade," he argued, "is the monopoly of the powerful."[40] Protection was the only means by which backward nations could industrialize and "defend national labor" (on the latter point, he was impressed by demonstrations in America, where workers supported high tariffs).[41] While combating social legislation, though not state subsidies to industry, Rossi pioneered such private initiatives as profit sharing and constructing housing, schools, public baths, day-care centers, and a maternity fund for "his" workers. Baglioni refers to this as the "organic paternalism" of Rossi.

Self-help literature, including translations of Smiles's work and tracts by Italians like Strafforello and Lessona, was credited for injecting a "Protestant ethic" into Catholic and status-conscious Italy: suggesting that the individual was the master of his own destiny and rose by virtue of demonstrated merit, not birth; affirming faith in science and progress, while at the same time helping to undercut the traditional prejudice against those who were successful in business activity. Lacking sufficient documentation, it is difficult to gauge precisely what impact this self-help literature had upon the cultural formation of industrialists, other than noting individual instances such as Camillo Olivetti, founder of the office-machine firm, who placed a copy of Smiles's *Self-Help* into the hands of his son and successor Adriano.[42]

However, measured against the contributions that the LIT later would make toward the development of a modern industrial subculture, those of Rossi, self-help literature, and earlier industrial associations were as yet limited in scope and conception. Rossi, as his recent "discoverers" have admitted, was hardly typical or representative of his class in theory or practice. He was rather an exceptional individual with little following in his own time, primarily because his pronounced clericalism ran counter to the laic grain of the predominant liberal culture to which the entire bourgeoisie subscribed. A systematic investigation of twentieth-century industrial literature would reveal that Rossi was largely overlooked, if not completely forgotten,

---

[40] Alessandro Rossi, "Protezionismo integrale," in Cafagna, *Il nord*, pp. 173–86 (quotation from p. 184).
[41] This view was articulated by cotton manufacturers. See the speech delivered in the Chamber of Deputies on 13 April 1878 by Ercole Lualdi, reprinted in Cafagna, *Il nord*, pp. 162–72.
[42] Bruno Caizzi, *Camillo e Adriano Olivetti* (Turin: UTET, 1962), p. 134.

by the next generation of industrialists, who in no sense acknowledged him as either a prophet or a precursor.[43] Despite the modernist
aspects of his thought, Rossi's conception of industrial society was
essentially traditional: he polemicized against urban–industrial development, wanting to preserve intact rural social relations and attitudes; he refused to recognize the legitimacy of workers' associations,
believing that class conflict was an exceptional, rather than an enduring, characteristic of industrial life; and, unlike other advocates of
economic Germanism, he opposed social legislation in principle, believing that his admittedly outstanding private initiatives in this area
would serve as an adequate paternalistic approach for others to emulate. As Baglioni persuasively argues, Rossi's vision was impaired by
a fundamental contradiction: on the one hand, he advocated further
industrialization and expected industrialists to assume leadership of
the bourgeois bloc; on the other, he refused to recognize that further
industrialization would necessarily bring with it a fundamental
change in social structure. He also failed to articulate any alternative
legitimating principles that might have altered the prevailing preindustrial liberal ideology and institutional framework so as to justify
the leadership claims of his ascendant class.[44]

Compared to the later functionalism and Taylorism of the LIT,
self-help literature was but a primitive and limited ideological contribution. It was essentially ahistorical and asocial: isolated and atomized individuals rose and fell by virtue of hard work and demonstrated merit; there was no manifest connection with or analysis of
the "world of work" as such or any sense of collective social life
(i.e., the division of labor, classes, authority relations, associations,
institutions, and politics broadly understood).[45]

The early industrial associations (e.g., Società Promotrice dell'Industria Nazionale, Associazione Fra Gli Industriali Mettallurgici,
Associazione Laniera Italiana) either were narrowly sectoral in membership and interest or were simple vehicles for the dissemination
of trade information. The LIT would be fundamentally different in
structure (an all-inclusive, intersectoral *sindacato padronale*) and

---

[43] As Rossi is rarely even mentioned in industrial association literature, 1906–34, we
question the argument put forth by Lanaro ("Nazionalismo e ideologia"), who
attributes to Rossi a fundamental role in developing a corporatist–protectionist
conception which allegedly informed industrial activity from the 1870s to Fascism.
[44] Baglioni, *Ideologia della borghesia industriale*, pp. 144–5, 301.
[45] Ibid., pp. 355–60.

function (ideological, representational, informational, syndical). The relative maturity of the LIT was not solely a by-product of greater industrialization but, as we shall see, a purposive response to the changed context of industrial relations ushered in by Giolitti. No longer did the state one-sidedly favor capital over labor, employ the army as a class militia to suppress strikes, or promote the interests of industry without counterbalanced reforms for workers. In short, with the coming of Giolitti, industrialists for the first time had to represent and defend themselves in a newly opened arena of syndical and political competition. The new association as such was very much a response to new needs.[46]

[46] Louis Bonnefon-Craponne, *L'Italie au travail* (Paris: Pierre Roger, 1916), p. 24.

1. Associational development during the Giolitti era

We are at the beginning of a new historical period; anyone who is not blind can see it. New mass currents are entering our political life; every day new problems are presenting themselves; new forces are arising with which any government must deal. The very confusion of parliamentary parties demonstrates that the questions which divide us today are no longer those which divided us before. The ascendant movement of the popular classes becomes ever more accelerated. It is an invincible movement because it is common to all civilized nations and because it is supported by the principle of equality among men. No one should delude himself that the popular classes can be impeded from conquering their share of economic and political influence. Those who are the friends of established political institutions have a duty, above all, to persuade these classes – and to persuade them with facts – that from the existing institutions they can expect more than from dreams of the future; that each of their legitimate interests will find efficacious support in the existing sociopolitical order. It depends principally upon us, on the attitude assumed by the constitutional parties in relation to the popular classes, whether the ascendancy of these classes will be a new conservative force, a new element of prosperity and greatness, or whether instead it will be a whirlwind sweeping away the fortune of the Patria![1]

These rather ominous concluding remarks uttered by Giolitti in the Chamber of Deputies on 4 February 1901 foretell what would become his distinctive political project shortly thereafter: conservation of the traditional institutional order through the progressive – though preempted, subordinated, and counterbalanced – insertion of mass demands within a new "liberal–democratic" modus operandi.

The experience of the 1890s had demonstrated that a purely repressive solution to problems posed by mass activation was doubly inadequate. It did not prevent the reoccurrence of bloody civil conflict and it jeopardized the formation of a stable majority in Parliament. Italy found itself presented with two alternatives as the new century began. One was that of the liberal–conservative Sidney Sonnino, advocate of unifying the various liberal factions into a disciplined national party

[1] Giovanni Giolitti, "Lo sciopero di Genova," reprinted in Cafagna, *Il nord,* pp. 355–81 (quotation from pp. 380–1).

to do battle against the "reds" and the "blacks" while realigning the balance of political power away from Parliament in favor of the Crown and executive. The other was that of the liberal–democrat Giolitti, who, rather than form a united political party of the bourgeois bloc against Socialists and Catholics, thereby further polarizing political life and fanning the flames of extremism, preferred using the traditional device of *trasformismo* to absorb these popular movements within the political mainstream. By discouraging the popular movements from persisting as autonomous organizational forces beyond the reach of potential governmental *combinazioni,* and by simultaneously emptying their programs of maximalist demands against the liberal state as such, Giolitti believed that what remained would be minimal *rivendicazioni,* which could be met through the compromise and moderation of parliamentary practice.

Yet the integration of the masses necessitated granting basic participatory privileges: in the first instance, the right to free syndical association and the right to strike; in the second, the extension of the franchise. In Giolitti's eyes, the latter was contingent upon the prior success of the former, for if it could be shown that through legally sanctioned syndical practice workers might extract distributional rewards while leaving the institutional framework and property order intact, then the underlying basis for mass radicalism would be undercut and an extension of suffrage might ultimately serve as stabilizing reform.

Thus, it is not at all surprising that the main subject of the aforesaid parliamentary discourse of 4 February 1901 was the need for syndical freedom and the neutrality of the state in conflicts between labor and capital. The prefect of Genoa, upon authorization from Prime Minister Saracco, had recently dissolved the Camera del Lavoro "for reasons of public order." Such action, wholly consistent with the traditional manner of responding to worker agitation, afforded Giolitti an opportunity to expound what was to become recognized as his principal statement on class conflict and syndical practice.

As with all of Giolitti's views, questions of principle were closely intertwined with a cautious empiricism based on the probable consequence of public policy, which, in turn, was based on observations regarding the direction social relations had taken in the more industrially advanced nations. On the one hand, workers' associations, in principle, had as much right to legal existence as associations which furthered the interests of property; on the other, where workers' associations existed, they pacified, rather than exacerbated, class conflict by tending to prevent economic demands from immediately becoming political ones. Thus, workers' syndicates might well be a necessary instrument in regulating and institutionalizing labor relations, that is, in keeping them within constitutional limits. "I never fear organized forces as I do inorganic forces, because with the former the Government can deal legitimately and effectively, while against inorganic risings there can be only the use of force."

Similarly, although the maintenance of low salaries – the real reason for the suppression of workers' associations, according to Giolitti – might be in the perceived interest of some employers, such was not a legitimate end of the state, which, to the degree it supported one side, would lose its status of absolute impartiality before all citizens. At a more practical level, experience had shown that low salaries were not conducive to industrial expansion: "the malnourished worker is always weaker physically and intellectually; the nations where high salaries are paid are in the forefront of industrial progress." Moreover, "the Government would commit a grave political error, because it would render enemies of the state those classes which constitute in reality the majority of the country." Only by remaining above the struggle between labor and capital could the state "effectively exercise a pacific action, sometimes even a conciliatory one, which is its only legitimate function in this area."

If a strike were to take place, the state should not intervene on behalf of one side or the other, though civil order, the rule of law, and the right to work ("no less sacred than the right to strike") must be guaranteed:

I do not ask privileges either for the workers or the capitalists. The Government ought to remain above these contests. When, I repeat, the law and the right to work are violated, the Government should intervene, and intervene energetically, always maintaining the rule of law. Where the law is not more powerful than all, there can be neither government nor liberty.

Within ten days of this discourse, Giolitti was called upon to assume the post of minister of the interior in the new Center-Left government of Giuseppe Zanardelli, and in November 1903, with the death of Zanardelli, Giolitti became prime minister for the second time. A definitive rupture with the reactionary policy of the 1890s appeared to have taken place. No better indication of this was Giolitti's offer of a cabinet post to the Socialist leader Filippo Turati, who only five years earlier had been unjustly arrested and sentenced to prison following the bloody events of May 1898 in Milan. Although it is true that Giolitti's motives were patently opportunistic (to preempt reformist leadership and divide the Socialist Party in order to ensure the success of his own minimalist program), the unprecedented attempt to stretch the elastic limits of *trasformismo* to the "extraconstitutional Left" indicated the degree to which Giolitti was willing to open political access within his overarching project of conserving the institutional framework by shunting even "extreme" opposition into preestablished channels.

One of the major burdens that all late-developing nations must bear is having to confront simultaneously a number of important problems which "first-comers" could deal with sequentially. For example, in the case of first-comers, an interval of capital accumulation and industrial expansion preceded the formation of workers' syndicates, the legal recognition of strikes, and the passage of social legislation. In Italy, these were of necessity telescoped into one historical period, the Giolitti era. The Italian workers' movement was part of a broader European phenomenon; forms of organization, substantive demands, and modes of agitation became "available" to Italians at virtually the same time they developed in the more-advanced nations. Consequently, they were acted upon immediately and "precociously," before this early stage of capital accumulation and industrial expansion could take place. Despite his failure to modernize the Italian political structure, it was to Giolitti's credit that he recognized the need to simultaneously promote industrial expansion *and* allow for the satisfaction of mass demands through his syndical policy and his proposals for social legislation and public works. There were those who criticized such a balanced policy, arguing that satisfaction of mass demands was a luxury of rich countries and drained capital that might have otherwise been better invested in production.[2] Giolitti, to the contrary, held that these programs were necessary precisely because Italy was poor and backward, that only through the promotion of reform and social peace would industrialization proceed in an orderly fashion, free from the great upheavals that had marked the previous decade.

[2] Giampiero Carocci, *Giolitti e l'eta giolittiana* (Turin: Einaudi, 1971), p. 47.

The first and most immediate outcomes of this change in public policy were a sudden multiplication of workers' syndicates and a notable increase in the rate of strikes. Before 1901, barely more than a few thousand workers had gone on strike, whereas in 1901, there were 1,034 strikes involving 189,271 workers, and in 1902, there were 801 strikes involving 196,699 workers.[3]

In response to this new reality, industrialists reacted by forming their own *sindacati padronali*. Left to fend for themselves, as it were, after having had their interests directly protected by the state, industrialists were now compelled not only to defensively organize themselves against workers' syndicates but, in a more profound sense, to reconsider their relations with other sectors of the bourgeoisie, to redefine their role in civil society, and, accordingly, to restructure their relationship with the state.

The Industrial League of Turin

It was from Turin that a network of modern industrial associations gradually extended to include most of Italy's northern industrial triangle during the pre–World War I period. This associational diffusion began with the Lega Industriale di Torino (1906) and extended to the regional level with the Federazione Industriale Piemontese (1908) and to the entire northern industrial zone with the constitution of the Confederazione Italiana dell'Industria (CIDI; 1910). Less the product of a spontaneous fusion of structurally similar local associations, this development was due rather to the singular effort of a distinctively modern Turinese nucleus whose self-stated mission was the eventual formation of a truly national industrial confederation based on its model of an intersectoral *sindacato padronale*.

The reason for Turin's leadership in this area may be partially explained by its late and intensive entry into the "takeoff" phase of Italian industrialization. The language employed by the LIT was that of a new class, a *borghesia del lavoro* different from the "dependent," earlier industrial associations described in the Introduction. Late entry into industrialization meant that the Turinese industrialists had to confront from the very outset the more modern industrial reality reflected in Giolitti's new reform program, as well as the accumulated

---

[3] Procacci, *History of the Italian People,* p. 374.

syndical experience of the more industrially advanced nations. Intensive industrial development, which abruptly fractured the mercantile–professional character of the city (in contrast with the relatively unbroken continuity experienced in Milan and Genoa), placed special emphasis on the technical imperatives of industrialization, the emergent reciprocal relations which derived from the interdependent needs of all industrial sectors, and the creation of a new ambience supportive of industrial expansion at both the local and the national levels.

Until the turn of the century, the city of Turin and the region of Piedmont were, by quantitative measures, well behind Lombardy and Liguria (e.g., percentage of total population involved in industry, concentration of enterprises, motor power employed). Despite its close proximity to the Alps, electrical energy in Piedmont was less developed than it was even in the Veneto region.[4]

Though Turin would have one of Italy's first Camera del Lavoro, this reflected more the diffusion of French syndicalist influence (the original name of the Camera del Lavoro was the Borsa del Lavoro, after the French Bourse du Travail) than a response to industrial development as such. During the dramatic clashes of 1898, no disturbance of public order was recorded in Turin (though the Camera del Lavoro was dissolved anyway as a precautionary measure). The local section of the Socialist Party was still dominated by "humanistic" middle-class intellectuals (*il socialismo dei professori*) whose commitment to the "moral elevation of the working classes" was far stronger than any desire to stir up the "natural appetites" of the masses by initiating potentially uncontrollable labor agitation.[5] Key factors in the transition of Turin were the availability of capital from the new German-styled mixed banks of Milan (and from abroad) and the abundance of cheap power once electricity replaced coal as the principal source of energy. By 1899, the price of electricity in Turin was the lowest in Italy; as a result of municipal policy, the price was cut by 22 percent in 1907, and by 45 percent between 1907 and 1914.[6]

During the first decade of the new century, Turin experienced

---

[4] On industrial development in Piedmont see Mario Abrate, *Lotta sindacale nella industrializzazione in Italia, 1906–26* (Turin: Franco Angeli, 1967); Pierre Gabert, *Turin, ville industrielle* (Paris: PUF, 1964); Valerio Castronovo, *Economia e società in Piemonte dall'unita al 1914* (Milan: Banca Commerciale Italiano, 1969); Paolo Spriano, *Storia del torino operaia e socialista* (Turin: Einaudi, 1972).

[5] Spriano, *Torino operaia*, pp. 3–60.

[6] Gabert, *Turin*, p. 117.

the highest rate of industrial growth in Italy in terms of both the mechanization of its industries and the increase in its industrial population.[7] Chief beneficiary of this trend was the emerging key sector of Turinese industry, machine manufacturing, of which the automotive industry was the major part. Whereas the total industrial population of the city roughly doubled during the six years between 1905 and 1911 (from 63,247 to 151,672), the increase in this sector was nearly fivefold (from 7,129 to 34,934).[8]

Unlike Milan, where industrialists, as long-standing members of the city's traditional ruling bloc, were largely unsympathetic from the outset to Giolitti's reform program,[9] in Turin industrialists and reform Socialists together formed a new "industrializing bloc" in local politics, jointly interested in replacing the static policies of the traditional merchant–professional ruling bloc with policies oriented toward rapid industrial growth, vocational training, improved social-service facilities, and modernization of the city's infrastructure.[10] Frequently, the pro-Giolitti *La Stampa*, a major force in the city's liberal political life, called upon the industrialists, "new elements with young energy," to participate actively in local politics and replace the older elite. Indeed, in the local elections of 1899, the paper (24 February 1899) called upon "a new bourgeois class endowed with energy and talent, open to all questions, to ascend to municipal responsibility with a new industrial morale."

If, however, such collaboration between reform Socialists and an enlightened bourgeoisie, the social basis of Giolitti's program, enjoyed a propitious beginning at the level of local politics during these early years of Turin's industrial transition, rapid growth and the newly instituted syndical freedom also set the stage for a new era of labor conflict. Among the major agitations which Turin experienced during the beginning years of the new century were a metalworkers strike in January 1901 and a gasworkers strike in February 1902. In the former, the demand for recognition of worker representation within the factory through a *commissione interna* was made for the first time, as was the demand that obligatory membership in the

---

[7] Baglioni, *Ideologia della borghesia industriale,* pp. 495–6; Valerio Castronovo, *Giovanni Agnelli* (Turin: UTET, 1971), p. 47.

[8] Abrate, *Lotta sindacale,* pp. 176–89.

[9] Baglioni, *Ideologia della borghesia industriale,* pp. 366–488.

[10] Castronovo, *Economia e società,* pp. 176–89.

workers' league be a condition for employment. Although salary concessions were made, there was an absolute refusal on the part of employers regarding these two key demands. Particular firmness was displayed toward the *commissione interna,* which, it was argued, "would completely undercut the authority of management and make work impossible."[11] The gasworkers' agitation was distinguished by the support shown by other categories of workers, leading to the city's first general strike.[12]

In 1904, Italy experienced its first national general strike under the leadership of the revolutionary syndicalist Arturo Labriola. In Turin, as elsewhere, there were episodes of unchecked violence, due, in part, to the government's desire to avoid counterproductive repression. Giolitti responded to the 1904 general strike as he would later respond to the factory occupations in the postwar period: by taking no direct action whatsoever. Convinced that the ill-conceived strike would quickly burn itself out, Giolitti saw in the event an opportunity to undercut growing Socialist electoral strength by calling for immediate elections after the strike, a calculated punishment for the reform Socialists, who had allowed revolutionary leadership to upset the new equilibrium.

Finally, 1906 saw an unprecedented number of strikes in all sectors, one barely starting – by chance or design – before the next began. Along with the usual demands concerning hours and wages, once again the issue of the *commissione interna* was raised. Although most industrialists took the position of Ansaldi, refusing the demand "because to concede it would hinder all initiative and all work,"[13] Fiat and other automotive firms, riding the crest of a productive boom and anxious to avoid any interruption of production, gave in. During May 1906, a strike of textile workers quickly gained the sympathy of other workers and, once again, a general strike ensued.

This wave of strikes, as well as the posture assumed by the government, led directly to the formation of the Industrial League of Turin (the LIT) in 1906. On the one hand, workers had displayed an intersectoral solidarity hitherto unknown, compelling one isolated employer after another to generalize concessions granted earlier in the yearlong agitation; on the other, Giolitti's "neutrality" in labor con-

[11] Spriano, *Torino operaia,* pp. 61–72.
[12] Ibid., pp. 72–9.
[13] Ibid., pp. 122–3.

flicts was somewhat less in practice than it had been articulated in theory. The right to work ("no less sacred than the right to strike") was not protected by state authorities. Many were the cases, especially during the general strike of 1904, of seemingly condoned violence and intimidation directed against nonstriking workers. Furthermore, there was resentment toward the government's one-sided application of pressure upon industrialists to make concessions.[14]

Most important, however, was the formation of a national labor confederation on the part of the workers. Since February 1906, the Federation of Italian Metalworkers (Federazione Italiana Operai Metallurgici; the FIOM), the powerful metalworkers syndicate, had been pressing for such a national association modeled on the French Confédération Générale du Travail (CGT). Not without marked contrasts between reformists and revolutionary syndicalists, the General Confederation of Workers (Confederazione Generale del Lavoro; the CGL) was founded in October 1906 with Turin as its official headquarters.[15]

What associational form could the industrialists establish to meet the new challenge? Older industrial associations, formed during the pre-Giolitti period when labor agitation was directly repressed by the state, were either clientelistic in nature, directed at obtaining protective advantages and state contracts, or narrowly technical, concerned with the diffusion of new industrial processes. These older associations tended to be sectoral and, in some cases, like Milan, unwilling to take on an intersectoral form, even after the proven success of the LIT in containing labor conflict.[16] Clearly there was nothing in past Italian experience to serve as a model; however, it is quite likely, given the attention with which the leadership of the LIT followed syndical experience abroad, that the model adopted was based on the various *organizzazioni di difesa padronale* established in England, France, and Germany, which had also been formed, though a decade earlier, in response to the emergence of workers' syndicates.[17]

The LIT was officially founded in July 1906, although preparations had actually begun a year earlier, when a group consisting of some of

---

[14] Abrate, *Lotta sindacale*, pp. 33–9.
[15] On the formation and history of the CGL see Adolfo Pepe, *Storia della CGL*, 2 vols. (Bari: Laterza, 1971).
[16] Abrate, *Lotta sindacale*, pp. 36–8; Baglioni, *Ideologia della borghesia industriale*, pp. 460–502.
[17] Abrate, *Lotta sindacale*, pp. 35–9.

the younger and more dynamic industrialists (Giovanni Agnelli, Luigi Bonnefon Craponne, Cesare Fiorio, the Bocca brothers, and others) took over, in effect, the Società Promotrice dell'Industria, an older Turinese industrial association that had been reduced to little more than ceremonial activity.[18] Under the new direction of Emilio De Benedetti, the Società Promotrice was to become, in theory, a center for political activity, while the newly constructed LIT would concern itself exclusively with syndical activity. In fact, however, it was the LIT that was to be the nucleus for future associational development, both syndical and political, while the Società Promotrice persisted as a political dependency of the LIT until it was finally dissolved by the Fascist government in 1927 as – of all things – a presumed *centro massonico*.

The major functions of the LIT were specified in Article 2 of its constitution: "To guide and defend the collective interests of its members and of Industry; to favor a good understanding with the workers." It was expressly forbidden to hire striking workers from member firms, and should a strike spread, the Administrative Council was empowered to take binding action, including the declaration of partial and general lockouts. Disciplinary measures and fines were enumerated for violations of such provisions.[19]

Though the initial language of the LIT was manifestly combative (but less so than the rhetoric of workers' syndicates), and though its projected strategy entailed retaliation in kind against its adversaries (e.g., a general lockout against a general strike; a blacklist against a boycott), the establishment of the LIT received favorable notices in the press. The celebrated liberal economist Luigi Einaudi, writing in *Corriere della Sera* (31 July 1906), saw in the LIT a necessary counterweight to the workers' associations. Where, as in the more industrially advanced nations, labor conflicts were dealt with by two disciplined and responsible organizations, there was less likelihood of either impulsive action or preoccupation with problems of little importance. The LIT initially had a membership of 200 firms, controlling 27,800 workers; by 1914, membership would grow to 639 firms, controlling 65,319 workers.[20]

The president of the LIT was Luigi Bonnefon Craponne, head of a

[18] On the Società Promotrice see Abrate, *Lotta sindacale;* Castronovo, *Agnelli.*
[19] Abrate, *Lotta sindacale,* p. 406.
[20] Ibid., p. 50.

Turin silk dynasty. Craponne was French by birth but was brought to Turin at the age of two. He received his basic education in Italy and went to Paris to pursue a degree at the Ecole des Hautes Etudes Commerciales. It was the general secretary of the LIT, however, Gino Olivetti, who was to become both "theoretician" and driving force behind not only the LIT but all intermediate associative steps leading up to and including the nationally based Confederazione Generale dell'Industria Italiana (Confindustria), founded in 1919. Gino Olivetti, though also of Jewish origin, was no relation to the noted industrialist Camillo Olivetti, founder of the office-machine firm. A lawyer and never an industrialist in his own right, Gino Olivetti was recognized, by the range of his intelligence and travels, as a prodigious figure in the liberal circles of Turin. At the age of twenty-six, rather than enter politics, Olivetti chose instead to become the LIT's first general secretary. Free to devote himself full-time to the association's activity, he was, in effect, its chief administrator and author of major policy statements appearing in the LIT bulletin, even when these, as in the case of annual addresses delivered by the president, did not bear his name.[21] Forced to resign as general secretary of Confindustria by Mussolini in 1933, Olivetti died in Argentina during the Second World War, having fled Italy in 1938 when the German-inspired racial laws were instituted.

What marked the LIT as Italy's first modern industrial association was its very form, that of a *sindacato padronale.* Implicit in the concept of a *sindacato padronale* was recognition that class conflict was not an epochal phenomenon, destined to ultimately disappear, but had rather become a permanent fact of modern social life. Older, paternalistic concepts of consensual (or at least nonconflictual) labor relations had no place in the LIT's worldview. While Milanese industrialists manifested an aversion toward the adoption of such a tainted term (*sindacato*), as well as the appropriation of this combative form, fearing that these suggested de facto recognition of workers' syndicates,[22] the LIT made recognition of workers' syndicates the necessary point of departure in an attempt to regulate and institutionalize labor relations. Thus, it was hoped, the continuity of production would no

---

[21] Ibid., pp. 40–5; Baglioni, *Ideologia della borghesia industriale,* pp. 502–3; Ernesto Rossi, *Padroni del vapore* (Bari: Laterza, 1955), p. 36. See also *L'Informazione Industriale,* 18 May 1921.
[22] Baglioni, *Ideologia della borghesia industriale,* pp. 462–5.

longer be interrupted by "impulsive" and unmediated agitation on the part of workers or employers. The *sindacato padronale,* although combative when the need arose, was viewed as an equilibrating and pacifying agency and was created (as stated in the first issue of their bulletin), not "to impede or deny the progressive economic and moral betterment of the working class, whose rights it understands and recognizes, but rather to avoid and prevent the damage of disorderly and impulsive movements."[23]

Rather than invoking a reactionary authoritarian solution to challenges posed by the formation of workers' syndicates, the LIT looked to the experience of the more industrially advanced nations, where parallel syndical organizations representing labor and capital appeared as requisite structures for the maintenance of social peace. Olivetti, in a manner strongly suggestive of Einaudi's earlier article, wrote in the first LIT bulletin:

There thus emerged, in the face of workers' associations, industrialists' associations. They emerged, as did the former, first with successive partial modifications of already existing organizations which had been formed for other purposes until more decisive forms developed and took hold. Little by little, in those countries where economic evolution was more advanced and where the spirit of associations was more rooted in the national character (that is, in the Anglo-Saxon countries), a dense network of industrial unions was formed to promote the rights and interests of capital, just as workers' leagues had promoted the rights and interests of labor. The result was this: that the class struggle became more calm, more civil, more orderly, and more useful. Conflicts broke out less frequently, and the economic and moral condition of the nation in general, and of the working class in particular, was elevated.

Though the *sindacato padronale* was seen as a direct consequence of the formation of workers' syndicates ("where the one does not exist, neither does the other"), there was an obvious difference in tactics and objectives: the one was offensive and revolutionary, and the other was defensive and committed to the conservation of the social order.[24] In theory, at least, there was no apparent conflict between the LIT's self-conception and Giolitti's reform project; the LIT invoked no more than the neutrality of the state in labor conflict and had a similar vision of pacification through disciplined contractual practice wherein such conflict would be institutionalized and reduced to mate-

---

[23] *Bollettino della Lega Industriale* (subsequently referred to as *BLI*) 1 (1907): 1.
[24] *BLI* 4 (1910): 4.

rial *rivendicazioni* rather than transformed into political challenges to the social order. In large part, as we shall see, the failure to realize such an outcome was due less to the action of the LIT than to the internal weaknesses of an ideologically divided labor movement torn between reformists and revolutionaries, as well as to the inability of Giolitti to construct a modern institutional framework which might have given his project a structural mooring and a center of gravity. Instead, Giolitti's reform project revolved erratically about ever more contradictory attempts at momentary compromise.

The first and most pressing objective of the LIT was actually overcoming the resistance of industrialists toward joining in this new associative campaign. Here leadership of the LIT had to surmount both the cultural individualism of the Italian bourgeoisie, who allegedly lacked the "spirit of association" found elsewhere, and the passivity of industrialists toward defending their common interests. Industrialists, in particular, had their interests promoted from the outset by the state and, until the turn of the century, had no pressing need to conceive of their interests as being distinct from those of the traditional *classe politica*.

Rather than merely reflect or represent the expressed needs of the industrial class, the LIT was faced with a far more pressing pedagogic task: that, as Craponne put it, of "*creating* a true industrial consciousness"[25] or, so to speak, *teaching the industrialists what their common interests actually were:*

Permit me to say it – and a frank confession cannot hurt us – among us industrialists an exact conception of our function, of our rights, and of our duties is often lacking. The very objections that some raise regarding our organization prove it. Crucial problems have been discussed which concern industry, and if our League had not raised its voice and attracted the attention of industrialists, grave dangers might have befallen our class without anyone having taken notice. Such things happen, not because we lack culture or the ability to deal with questions that directly affect us, but rather because we have become habitually disinterested in such problems.[26]

Their attention ever focused on the multifunctional activities performed by industrial associations in England, France, and Germany (evidenced by countless articles in the LIT bulletin commenting on their potential applicability to Italy), leadership saw its role as one of

[25] Ibid.
[26] Ibid.

pulling the backward Italian industrial class into the modern associational era, serving as a catalyst through which a national industrial consciousness might be organically formed, prodding individual and atomized industrialists to think in terms of a common interest before both the state and other classes, rather than continuing to think in terms of fragmented, particularistic, and disaggregated interests.[27]

This subjective weakness of the Italian industrial class was not viewed by the LIT as being determined solely by the nation's belated industrialization, as if at a certain stage a class in itself automatically becomes a class for itself. Craponne observed: "It is true that our industry is younger, and that our economic struggles are more recent; but this is insufficient reason to explain the actual disorganization of our class."[28] Their own explanation, rightly or wrongly, was based on cultural grounds, on a presumed lack of the "spirit of association" and individualistic shortsightedness which prevented a practical means–ends appraisal of the obvious benefits of organization.

As of now the psychological moment has yet to arrive in which the industrialist begins to abstract momentarily from his particular condition, to forget such things as competition and special interests which divide him from his industrial colleagues, so as to realize and keep in mind that in the present moment the isolated individual or firm tends to become ever less potent in the face of free syndical association, which the new legal order permits. On the one hand, tradition still retains its rule and many prejudices have not disappeared; on the other, the consideration of immediate interests impedes any consideration of ultimate, yet distant, gains.[29]

Nevertheless, there was the perception that eventually an external antagonistic force, pressure from the organized working class, would compel "the industrial class into thinking that among them there exists a commonality of condition in which all particular interests, though divergent in other areas, are interwoven."[30] Thus, it was mainly in the *syndical arena* that the LIT initially put forth its candidacy for class leadership – its program, a national *sindacato padronale*.

Although it was seen as somehow less "natural" and certainly more difficult for industrialists to organize than it was for workers, class

---

[27] Ibid.
[28] *BLI* 3 (1909): 4.
[29] Ibid.; on the lacking "spirit of association" see also *BLI* 1 (1907): 1.
[30] *BLI* 3 (1909): 4.

solidarity was all the more important. Any industrialist who remained outside the associational fold was not merely a "passive element," as, for example, an unorganized worker in the midst of well-organized syndicates was, but a "weakness for the whole class." The LIT believed this to be the case, first, because concessions yielded by one weaker, unorganized industrialist would be quickly generalized, and second, because workers striking the factory of a member firm might find employment with a nonmember firm, thus prolonging the conflict and weakening the market position of the member firm, whose business, in the interim, would gravitate to the nonmember firm. "Strike-breaking is much more dangerous for the industrial class and it is much easier." For that reason, the "totality" of the industrial class would have to be organized:

> It is not enough that one part of the industrialists be organized, it is necessary that all join, or at least enough to represent the near totality of production. Only in this condition can the efficiency be attained that the *organizzazione padronale* must have. Otherwise, organization might be useful, but it will be unable to confront all the battles that lie ahead with a secure anticipation of the outcome.[31]

Ultimately, based on the experience of the more industrially advanced nations, this necessitated a national organization. An uncoordinated series of local associations would not be able to respond effectively to nationally based workers' syndicates in labor conflicts or to represent and defend the common interests of industry at the state level in competition with the CGL.[32]

To define, tutor, and represent the common interests of the industrial class was to recognize that the Giolittian era of syndical freedom and social reform had ushered in a new stage of organized capitalism and that the conception of a self-interested, isolated entrepreneur – mythical hero of the liberal stage of capitalism – was obsolete, if not downright dangerous. As individual interests gave rise to collective interests, the "nightwatchman state" became an interventionist state (or rather, broadened the scope of its intervention to include the promotion of not only agriculture and industry but social needs as well). Hence, the program of an industrial association had to address two sets of problems: labor conflict and interest representation.

---

[31] Ibid.
[32] *BLI* 4 (1910): 5.

The LIT wasted little time over the principled objection of some industrialists that joining a *sindacato padronale* might implicitly recognize the legitimacy of workers' syndicates. "We recognize the workers' syndicates and deal with them." According to the LIT:

We industrialists are people who generally do not engage in abstract discussions or study questions solely from a theoretical perspective. We live in reality and for reality. It is precisely for that reason that we cannot deny those phenomena which the new times have brought. We cannot fail to recognize the workers' movement insofar as it has a real and serious basis. It is rather the presupposition of our organization and, as such, part of its very self-concept that in the realm of economics there are no longer either isolated individuals or isolated interests, but the one and the other so interpenetrate that no modification which affects the conditions of an individual or of an interest is without bearing on the totality of other individuals and interests. Beyond that, the facts of everyday life both here and abroad indicate that it is not by virtue of any a priori negation that we can refuse to see what is happening before our very eyes.[33]

The only issue in dealing with workers' syndicates over which there could be no compromise was that of managerial authority within the factory, the "directing function" of the industrialists. In the words of Craponne:

Above all, however, the LIT is opposed to any intrusion by the workers' organizations into the technical ordering of production; that is a position which I believe is essential for our industry . . . it is not possible to allow a workers' syndicate to enter the factory and to constitute an authority counterposed to that of the industrialist, a competing authority which might impede the efficiency of work and the development of production as planned by him. The function of capital in industry is essentially a directing function.[34]

It should be remembered that worker representation within the factory – in the form of a *commissione interna* – from the outset had been a point of contention in Turin. As we shall see, the preservation of managerial authority within the factory – the "directing function" of the industrialist – was to become the core concern of industrial associations, a presumed "technical imperative" of production that had to be respected both by workers and by the state (regardless of regime type: liberal, Communist, or Fascist). The somewhat murky and unspecified technicopolitical need for complementing a rigidly hierarchical sphere of productive relations with an analogous state

[33] Ibid.
[34] Ibid.

form to ensure such relations certainly contributed to the industrialists' growing estrangement from the Giolittian liberal regime, which was unwilling or unable to ensure civil order outside the factory, much less protect managerial authority within. Yet it also gave rise to increasing tensions later with the Fascist regime, which might have rigorously imposed order inside and outside the factory, but whose totalitarian pretenses raised the danger that productive relations might be controlled and dominated by the state rather than be merely guaranteed by it as an autonomous sphere. This central problem will unfold itself in the course of the present study; the purpose in mentioning it now is simply to alert the reader to the fundamental importance of this uncompromisable programmatic imperative on managerial authority. Recognition of workers' syndicates did not constitute any renunciation of such authority; it was viewed rather as an instrumental step toward regulating those conflicts which revolved around distributive demands and *not* the "technical ordering of production."

As with the LIT's recognition of workers' syndicates, their recognition, as "realists," of the irreversible trend toward greater social legislation presupposed the need for organizational representation of industrial interests before public opinion and the state to ensure that the "exigencies of production" were taken into account and weighed against other interests:

By now the tendency of the modern age is toward an ever greater and ever more direct intervention by the state into social relations. We, as objective observers of social phenomena, must have recognized one fact whose bearing can escape no one: that while we realize it would be vain to oppose this trend, even though at times doubting its benignity, we must seek to influence state action in this arena so that it yields the least possible damage to the industrial class.[35]

For more than a decade, the "social question" had been discussed exclusively from the standpoint of promoting state action to improve the material existence of the working class, frequently by alluding to measures adopted abroad, with little manifest concern for the capacity of Italian industry to support these initiatives. The public forum, in a sense, had been preempted by Socialists and other reformers. In the void left by an absence of industrial associations to defend the "legitimate interests of industry" and the "social function" that the

[35] *BLI* 2 (1908): 3.

industrialists performed, public opinion had been exposed only to caricatures of them as "exploiters," egotistically pursuing their narrow class interest at the expense of the national interest. This was the perception of the industrialists' image not only by the LIT but by other sectors of liberal opinion as well. With a dose of exaggeration, for example, the *Corriere della Sera* of 24 October 1909 noted that industrials had silently submitted to becoming a "corpus vile" for every form of social experimentation because they themselves had failed to publicly defend their interests, as their counterparts had done in England and Germany.

The LIT's substantive position on social reform will be considered shortly; our purpose here is to indicate the perceived ideological need to alter the public perception of industrialists, getting across the message, in the words of Craponne, that "the defense of industry is not reaction."[36] The first step in this direction was for the LIT to establish its superior technical expertise and information-gathering capacity in relation to all other organized interests, including the state bureaucracy itself (this was the actual beginning of a trend highlighted by Joseph LaPalombara in his analysis of Confindustria in the post-Fascist period).[37] The LIT sought to present an image of industrialists as "practical men" who "spoke with facts," not dilettantes who remained at the level of abstract rhetoric. Thus, they hoped to shift the debate on social reform away from pure moralism toward an empirical examination of both the nation's social needs *and* the concrete capacity of Italian industry to support such a burden.

Under Olivetti's direction, the LIT undertook a systematic case study of the various forms of social legislation, both domestic and foreign, and in 1911 published the first manual on the subject to appear in Italy, attempting to codify the often confusing and sometimes contradictory legislative provisions that had been enacted. Similarly, to correct the lack of published industrial-related hard data, the LIT compiled a detailed study of wages, working conditions, regulatory norms, and strikes in Turin that was published in 1907, barely one year after the association's founding. Subsequent statistical studies followed, including an extensive "industrial census" published in 1911.[38]

[36] *BLI* 5 (1911): 2.
[37] Joseph LaPalombara, *Interest Groups in Italian Politics* (Princeton: Princeton University Press, 1964).
[38] Abrate, *Lotta sindacale*, pp. 106–7.

The LIT also sought to represent industry directly before the state by pressing for a reform of the Advisory Council on Labor such that the CIDI, an extension of the LIT, would be recognized as the legitimate voice for all industry and thus have the right to mandate representatives to sit on the council. This attempt, however, was blocked by other industrialists, such as Carlo Tarlarini, who, in the name of the various sectoral Milanese industrial associations, publicly contested the right of the Turin-based *sindacato padronale* to mandate council members, advocating instead election by sectoral category.[39]

The authority to speak in the name of all Italian industry was dependent, to a large degree, upon the territorial extension of the *sindacato pardonale* to the national level; and this, in turn, was dependent upon its proven success over the older associational forms in the most basic of tests: containment of strikes. In the first eighteen months of its existence (from July 1906 to December 1907), 22,176 workers went on strike, with outcomes "completely unfavorable" in thirty-five cases, as opposed to twenty-one cases where the outcome was "totally or partially favorable." In 1908, there were 12,678 striking workers, and only in two cases were outcomes favorable to them.[40] As for resolving conflicts without recourse to strikes, during the period 1906–10, the LIT mediated seventy-one such cases, involving 27,327 workers.[41] Due, in large measure, to the presence of the LIT, Turin's strike rate was consistently half or less than half that of Milan.[42]

More than any other single factor, however, it was the LIT's victory over the first general strike called since its founding that attracted national attention and led directly to a broader diffusion of the *sindacato padronale* form outward from the original Turin nucleus. According to Craponne: "One can say that it was then that our league made its triumphal entry into the social life of the nation, rather than only in the city of Turin."[43] Sectoral associations, lacking any higher form of city, regional, or national intersectoral aggregation, had proven ineffective against strikes that enlisted the solidarity of other categories of workers, the most extreme form of which was the

---

[39] Baglioni, *Ideologia della borghesia industriale*, pp. 464–5.
[40] Castronovo, *Economia e società*, p. 303.
[41] Abrate, *Lotta sindacale*, p. 82.
[42] See appendixes in Pepe, *Storia della CGL*, vol. 2.
[43] *BLI* 2 (1908): 3.

general strike. During the general strike of October 1907, the LIT, through the enactment of a general lockout, received instant national recognition for not only having been the victor but also having forced a bitter division within the ranks of labor between reformists and revolutionaries.[44] From every part of Italy, the LIT received communications "announcing the imminent constitution of industrial leagues modeled on our association," demonstrating that perhaps "the time was ripe to think of establishing a national federation, which might vigorously undertake in Italy those actions which have been taken for some time in other nations by the industrial bourgeoisie."[45]

Though a number of new industrial associations modeled on the *sindacato padronale* enlisted the aid of the LIT for guidance, when the strike wave of 1907 subsided, so too did much of the initial enthusiasm for organizing new associations.[46] A truly national association was some twelve years in the future; however, within three months, the Federazione Industriale Piemontese was formed, followed by the CIDI two and a half years later. Thus, within a brief four years, the LIT extended its associational network from Turin to virtually the entire northern industrial triangle.

Leadership remained in the hands of the Turinese: Craponne was president and Olivetti general secretary of the Federazione Industriale Piemontese and the CIDI, as they had been and continued to be in the LIT. The central headquarters of the new associations, not surprisingly, were in Turin as well. This is not to suggest that Olivetti, itinerant coordinator of the expansion, did not have to overcome considerable localisms and regional rivalries, particularly regarding the composition of the executive councils and location of organizational headquarters. Olivetti ultimately was successful in convincing opponents that Turin was the logical site, since this was where the headquarters of the CGL was also situated. With the formation of the CIDI in 1910, the skeletal structure of the future Confindustria was in place.

With the question of form now largely settled, the next problem that presented itself entailed relations with other sectors of the bourgeois bloc (particularly agricultural and commercial interests), as well as the related issue of political activity. Actually, at the very time the

[44] Abrate, *Lotta sindacale*, pp. 71–3; Spriano, *Torino operaia*, pp. 166–71.
[45] *BLI* 1 (1907): 4–5.
[46] *BLI* 3 (1909): 4.

LIT was extending itself to industrial groups outside Turin, concern
was also raised regarding linkages with other sectors of the *borghesia
produttrice,* which, in some fundamental sense, objectively stood in a
common position before both workers' leagues and the state.[47] The
strike wave of 1907 had affected these sectors as well, and one result
of the LIT's victory in the October general strike was an adoption of
the *sindacato padronale* form by agricultural associations in Piedmont, Lombardy, Emilia, Romagna, and Veneto.[48] However, given
the primacy of organizing industrialists first, it was not until after the
formation of the CIDI that anything more than casual interest was
given to the nonindustrial bourgeois sectors.

As for the political role that the *sindacato padronale* might play,
the LIT initially had no fixed position. It did not, as was often the
case in France, write into its constitution any clause explicitly forbidding the association to indulge in political activity. Cautious empiricists that they were, leaders of the LIT kept a close watch on the
political practice of industrial associations elsewhere in Europe as a
possible guide for their own actions. Because political involvement
was viewed as a potentially divisive factor which might impede the
more pressing task of organizational consolidation, it was not placed
on the immediate agenda. Leadership did, however, follow with great
interest the formation of an industrial party in Germany during the
spring of 1910, but maintained that the time was not ripe to give
"profound consideration to the principal question: whether the industrial class as such ought to take part in political life."[49]

Nevertheless, the reasons that German industrialists gave for forming a political party had significant impact upon the LIT's ideological
formation, especially when the contradictions between their productivist demands and the concessions imposed on them by Giolitti to
maintain his political project of social compromise and mediations
from above could no longer be contained within the traditional politics of *trasformismo.* Among such themes imported from Germany
was that of the "political emancipation of industrialists." Tired of
playing the role of a "laughingstock in the speculation of bourgeois
political parties," which, for reasons of political opportunism, had
sacrificed the interests of industry to the demands of the workers in

[47] *BLI* 2 (1908): 3.
[48] Ibid.
[49] *BLI* 3 (1909): 4.

an age of expanding suffrage, industrialists had to enter the political arena as an autonomous force.[50]

For the moment, however, such a project could not be seriously contemplated. In June 1910, shortly after the constitution of the CIDI, a conference of industrialists and merchants took place in Bologna. One of the major speakers, Cesare Pegna of the Industrialists and Merchants Association of Bologna, proposed the formation of an "industrial party" composed of capitalists and workers. Such a party would be oriented toward "the defense of National Industry"; it would represent a capital–labor industrial bloc based on protection.[51] Against this "corporatist thesis" Olivetti strongly objected, skeptical of such a simplistic concept of class collaboration and fearful that political activity, especially based on principled protection, would undermine the recently achieved organizational unity. Olivetti argued that such a program would divide those industrial sectors interested in free trade from those interested in higher tariffs, as well as alienate agricultural groups. Moreover, Pegna's protectionist program was in fundamental contradiction with Olivetti's liberal vision of industrial development based on private initiative and technical competence. Rather than invoke the aid of the state to secure a privileged position at the expense of the collectivity, Olivetti felt that it would be far better for the state simply to grant industry the freedom to function without excessive fiscal burden and bureaucratic restraint:

According to us, industry ought to ask not so much for excessive tariff protection as to insist that its free development not be impeded by that fiscal injustice under which it moans nor those bureaucratic formalities which entangle it. We dream of an industry strong by virtue of its free and natural expansion, not by means of state privileges; by its own internal strength, not through sacrifices imposed on the nation and on the consumer. And even if to attain this it may be necessary to pass through a period of just protection, we ought never forget that ultimate aim in which our national salvation lies.[52]

In response to the great "southernist" Salvemini, who took the Pegna speech as representative of Italian industry, Olivetti reaffirmed:

Our hopes for the industrial future of Italy are based much more on the assimilative capacity and on the technical and commercial ability of our

---

[50] Ibid., p. 6.
[51] BLI 4 (1910): 6. A complete text of the Pegna speech can be found at the historical archive of the Unione Industriale di Torino (subsequently cited as HAUIT).
[52] BLI 4 (1910): 6.

industrialists than on state intervention. The state ought to take only one action in favor of Italian industry and that would be sufficient: free it from the infinite bureaucratic entanglements in which it struggles and under which it wails.[53]

Under increasing pressure to declare a position on politics, the CIDI formally pronounced its "apolitical" status seven months later:

We are not a party nor do we wish to give rise to one, much less enter into alliances with political parties. Our objective ought to be more vast and more complex: it is not so much in Parliament that we must have notice taken of our ideas, it is in the very consciousness of the nation; in so-called public opinion we must seek to establish a precise idea of the role our industry plays in national life. Just as workers' organizations champion the wishes and desires of labor before the public, we must have heard those issues which affect industry and those necessary exigencies from which it cannot escape.[54]

Although formally "apolitical," the CIDI's position was essentially "prepolitical" in two respects. First, associational consolidation and reciprocal relations with other organized sectors of the *borghesia produttrice* had to progress further before electoral alliances and strategies could be prudently undertaken. Second, the CIDI had to cultivate public opinion, still hostile or indifferent to the industrialists, so that a potential constituency might be established. The CIDI, at too early a stage in its development to involve itself in party politics, chose to bypass the institutional framework of national political life – which made no provisions either for interest groups or for autonomous parties – and, in a sense, to remain "above politics" by playing the role of a public, but nonpartisan, proponent of industry, expounding as the central point of its propaganda a direct identity between the unfettered development of industry, with all its implied objective exigencies, and the "national interest."

This is not to suggest that Parliament manifested no interest in industry. During June 1911, a Gruppo Industriale Parlamentare was formed, consisting of nine senators and forty-eight deputies, to promote the interests of industry and commerce.[55] Yet so far as one can determine from the evidence, this parliamentary group had no direct institutional connection with the CIDI. The fact that the group's existence is mentioned but once in the CIDI's bulletin, and not at all

[53] Ibid., p. 7.
[54] *BLI* 5 (1911): 2.
[55] Ibid., p. 6.

in parliamentary accounts of the period, indicates that its actual life might well have been less significant than its much heralded birth. In a parliamentary realm still dominated by a preindustrial political class and by the personalistic and clientelistic practices of *trasformismo,* such a formalized, functionally specific group, lacking any organizational base outside Parliament, had little chance of playing a significant representational role.

Olivetti, for the moment more concerned with fostering syndical unity than embarking on partisan political action, took great interest in the formation of the Bologna-based Confederazione Nazionale Agraria (July 1910), headed by Oreste Sturani. Not only did this new association assume the form of a *sindacato padronale,* but it also shared a similar analysis of the organizational weakness of the *borghesia produttrice* and the need to "reconstruct the necessary equilibrium in society" now that syndical associations were legally permitted and the working class had demonstrated its own organizational strength. According to Sturani:

We must recognize that the bourgeoisie does not yet have a precise understanding of its rights and duties. We did not recognize our duties when we contemptuously withdrew before the workers' movement, though we knew the fundamental principles upon which modern society is based. We did not recognize our rights when we let escape from our hands direction and primacy in the economic and political life of the country. This double irresponsibility has its roots in only one cause: the lack of any organic energy, a repulsion toward any organizational system. The individualistic presumptions, speculative egoisms, the discord of petty small-town politics, divided us when it was in our highest interest to remain united. And while the workers' movement proceeded with a unitary and vigorous direction, we tried to confront it with single acts of resistance, petty individual tactics, skirmishes, and feigning . . . and we were overcome. Thus, the strong, divided, became weak, and the weak – through organization – became strong and arrogant.[56]

In unison, as Olivetti said, the CIDI and the Confederazione Nazionale Agraria proposed to become the means by which the *borghesia produttrice* might impress public opinion with the

utility and the necessity of the directing function it plays, the social and national importance of the promotion of its interests, and the urgent consideration that social and economic problems be examined from a point of view that takes into account not only humanitarian sentiments or the unilateral

---

[56] A complete text of the Sturani speech can be found at the HAUIT.

interest of the working masses but also a complete and objective vision of the complexity of these various phenomena.[57]

The two associations disagreed, however, on the means by which this *borghesia produttrice* might promote its interest before the public. The CIDI had already declared its apolitical status, but the Confederazione Nazionale Agraria maintained: "To conquer the public consciousness we must also show our strength, and this can only be done through direct intervention in the political life of the nation, especially in electoral politics."[58] Olivetti, recognizing the greater potential for sectoral cleavage within industry than within agriculture, repeated his argument that any source of division, such as politics, ought to be excluded in favor of syndical unity. Although the two associations might eventually assume a common position on economic issues, they ought to refrain from taking any common political action. He noted that for the agrarian associations, emerging in the "red belt" of Emilia–Romagna, every economic battle was at the same time a political one, a situation markedly different from the world of industry, where the two types of conflict could more easily be kept separate and distinct.[59] To do so, to keep "politics outside the factory," presumed the nonpoliticization of the industrialist as well as the worker. Otherwise, politics might become directly linked to their respective "social functions" in the apolitical, technical hierarchy of production.

As if to underscore the syndical, rather than political, imperatives of the *borghesia produttrice*, Olivetti conceived the idea of calling for an international conference, to take place in Turin, which would assemble the various industrial and agricultural associations of Europe to share their syndical experiences, discuss future strategy on the international level, and even entertain the prospect of forming an *internazionale padronale*, which "no less than that of the workers might unite the more potent European industrial organizations and maintain permanent ties to those of agriculture."[60] And so, with the joint sponsorship of the CIDI and the Confederazione Nazionale Agraria, the Primo Congresso Internazionale delle Organizzazioni Padronali dell'Industria e dell'Agricoltura was held between 28 Sep-

[57] *BLI* 5 (1911): 8.
[58] Ibid.
[59] Ibid.
[60] Abrate, *Lotta sindacale*, p. 58.

tember and 1 October 1911. Only the Germans of the Verein Deutscher Arbeitgeberverbande and the Haupstelle Deutscher Arbeit-geberverbande refused the invitation, apparently fearful of being labeled "internationalists" rather than good Wilhelmine "national imperialists." Among those attending were some thirteen associations, including the Comité Central des Forges and the Comité Central des Houilleres de France, three Belgian associations, and the national industrial federations of Austria, Holland, Sweden, Switzerland, and England.[61] Olivetti and Craponne shared the rostrum with such leading international figures as Georges Blondel (of the Fédération des Industriels Français) and Max Kaiser (of the Haupstelle Oesterreichischer Arbeitgeberorganizationen). As if to signal the national importance of such an event, Franceso Nitti, minister of agriculture, industry, and commerce (and future prime minister), was also in attendance.

Little of substance came out of the conference, though its mere occurrence was itself worthy of note. Olivetti's ambitious scheme for an *internazionale padronale* was not seriously considered, although some rather general resolutions concerning the need for continued consultation and cooperation were approved. It appears that the most interested in the project were the Italians and the French, who over the next several years joined in some preparatory efforts for the eventual constitution of an International Office of Industrial Syndicates.[62] Whether such a project died of its own inertia or was stifled by the outbreak of World War I is difficult to ascertain. Only after the war, with the formation of the International Labor Office, would European industrialists enter into a common body, whose heterogeneous structure (composed of representatives of capital, labor, and governments), under the tutelage of the League of Nations, was vastly different from that proposed initially by Olivetti (though Olivetti himself would serve as a representative of Italian industry during the 1920s).

Toward a productivist liberal–technocratic ideology

The LIT's major ideological imperative was to create in the public consciousness an identity between the interests of industry and the

---

[61] Ibid.; see also *BLI* 5 (1911): 10.
[62] Castronovo, *Economia e società*, p. 329.

national interest, a totalizing conception within which the interests of industry would not merely compete with the particularistic interests of other classes and class fragments but purport to reflect the universal aspirations of a modernizing society. The LIT, that is, sought to articulate a national modernization strategy, a concern rarely addressed by other members of the bourgeois bloc, and present the Italian industrialist as its most qualified bearer.

The core of such a conception was the projection of production as the dynamo, or mainspring, of national development, the essential base upon which all other social problems rested. Previous conflictual ideologies, based on scarcity, addressed themselves mainly to the problem of distribution: a zero-sum struggle in which the gain of one party could only be extracted from the equal sacrifice or loss of the other.[63] Productivism not only represented an escape from such zero-sum conflict by increasing the absolute level of wealth but in the context of a relatively poor and developing nation like Italy signaled an escape from an endemic pattern of misery, demographic disequilibrium, spectacular social unrest, and wide-scale emigration. Productivism suggested that it was in the enlightened self-interest of all parties, in the first moment, to stretch the size of the collective pie, so that in the second, more would be available for division. In the words of the spiritual father of this conception, Frederick W. Taylor:

The great revolution that takes place in the mental attitude of the two parties under scientific management is that both sides take their eyes off the division of surplus as the all-important matter, and together turn their attention toward increasing the size of the surplus until the surplus becomes so large that there is ample room for a large increase in wages for the workman and an equally large increase in profits for the manufacturer.[64]

Thus, distribution, hitherto the contentious center of the "social question," now was relegated to a subordinate position, contingent upon and derivative of a new centerpoint, *production*.

The programmatic implications for both the state and the workers' syndicates were clear: no action should be taken to undermine the productive capacity of industry, whether through dysfunctional chal-

---

[63] Charles Maier, "Between Taylorism and Technology: European Ideologies and the Vision of Industrial Productivity in the 1920s," *Journal of Contemporary History* 5 (1970): 27–61.

[64] Reinhard Bendix, *Work and Authority in Industry* (New York: John Wiley, 1956), p. 276.

lenges to managerial authority or through prematurely burdensome social-welfare programs. As Craponne put it:

By now it has been demonstrated that the economic betterment of the working class does not depend solely on the major or minor number of strikes that it has staged. It is the increase in the level of national wealth which has permitted and will continue to permit the rise in salaries. It is the flowering of our industries which also enables the state, in the form of tax revenues, to have the means with which to assist the working class in other ways. If the national level of wealth does not increase, if our industries fall under the load of ever-growing burdens, not even Socialism will be able to repair our economic and social derout.[65]

Similarly, the primacy of class conflict – based as it was on distribution – was replaced by a cooperative, instrumentalist universe of objectively necessary functions within a class-neutral hierarchy of competence and command whose internal logic was based on the attainment of optimal efficiency through means–ends, input–output calculation. Indeed, the most frequently repeated phrase in associational bulletins was "to achieve the maximum effect with the minimum force." This was posed as the standard for all purposive social action, even that of workers' syndicates, and especially, as we shall see, that of the industrialist in the "direction" of his factory.

In textual material already cited, we have frequently encountered the term "function." "Function" and the abovementioned "optimal-efficiency formula" represented basic interrelated elements in the LIT's model of a productive hierarchy. Occasional attempts were even made at raising these to the level of primitive sociological theory:

A modern theory says that each organ has its function and that each function has its organ. This theory, advanced in the field of physiology, has found application even in social relations. Sociologists have wished more than once to demonstrate that the laws which regulate the human body can be adapted to the social body as well. That adaptation cannot go beyond the point of a simple analogy, yet it has served to clarify the concept of a division of labor, the fundamental principle of all social, economic, and political organization in the modern era. Specialization thus has found new and important applications: for every task to be performed, for every function to be exercised, for every objective to be attained, one must create the conditions, ambience, and organs most adaptable in order that the task performed, the function exercised, and the object attained are done so in a more perfect and complete manner and with the minimum expenditure of energy.[66]

[65] *BLI* 3 (1909): 4.
[66] *BLI* 4 (1910): 4.

Within this conception, the industrialist received a new and more modern source of legitimation. No longer was his authority based solely on traditional social standing, moral rectitude, or even financial risk, but rather on his specialized competence and the "social function" he performed:

The function of capital in industry is essentially directive. While, on the one hand, the industrialist assumes the risk of the enterprise and thus sees its dangers and advantages, on the other, he finds himself, through his preparation, in the best position to technically order the factory according to a preestablished plan. Consequently, he is in the best position to realize that cardinal principle of political economy often expressed by the phrase "to achieve the maximum effect with the minimum force."[67]

Such a technocratic conception, as suggested earlier, was intimately related to the particularly intense Turinese industrial experience, one of rapid growth based on technical innovation and dominated by a "new class," captains of industry. By the outbreak of World War I, for example, Giovanni Agnelli, head of Fiat, twice had visited the United States to study Henry Ford's Detroit factories and had been among the first in Europe to construct new factories based on the assembly-line principle. By 1912, a full six to eight years before Taylorism began to have a major impact in Europe,[68] the LIT had already integrated the "scientific management" concept into its prior functionalist–optimality schema.[69] The accentuation of productive rhythm and output, as well as the capacity to regulate the factors of production in accordance with the most efficient use of available technologies, labor, and raw materials, had been an empirical fact as much as the practical basis for a new ideology. No less a figure than Antonio Gramsci would marvel at the modern industrial infrastructure that this *borghesia del lavoro* had constructed in Turin, much as Marx had written earlier in some famous passages in *The Communist Manifesto* praising the technical accomplishments of capitalism's unknowing gravediggers.

This systematic and rather well articulated technocratic component of the LIT's ideology was joined with a more traditional and far less self-reflective liberal component. Liberalism had been the unchallenged civic culture of the Italian bourgeoisie, and the Turinese industrialists emerged from and partook of it as a "natural" part of their

[67] Ibid.
[68] See Maier, "Between Taylorism and Technology."
[69] *BLI* 7 (1913): 11–12.

socialization, so natural that until the rise of Fascism, little consideration was given to whether liberalism indeed constituted the most efficacious political vehicle for the realization of their more immediate technocratic aspirations. In the Introduction, we touched upon the doctrinal weakness and limited penetration of Italian liberalism, relating this to the exclusive, socially circumscribed nature of the Risorgimento. Unlike other cases, where liberalism had been a cause célèbre, emerging from social struggle and mass mobilization, in Italy liberalism was largely an imported and appropriated ideology covering a full spectrum of "democratic" and "conservative" attitudes, identified more with the empirical and essentially formal "art of governing" than a substantive program. In the words of Einaudi, himself one of the greatest liberal *personaggi,* liberalism had "no longer but a tenuous relation with the liberal doctrine. To be 'liberal' was understood as synonymous with 'nonaristocratic,' 'nonrevolutionary,' 'nonanarchist'; in sum, synonymous with people who avoided excess, behaved well, and who did not say bad words." Thanks to the aprincipled alchemy of *trasformismo,* liberalism had become a "mere myth: one of those words which, together with King and Patria, the glorious battles of the national Risorgimento, the Statuto and the Royal March, constituted about all of the spiritual content of political discourses pronounced at the banquets of electoral committees, dedications of bridges, railways, new flags, and similar occasions."[70]

Aside from these sentiments of bonhomie suggested by Einaudi, what the LIT reflected in its liberalism was primarily a commitment to the public–private, state–civil society dichotomies derived from classic political economy. Unlike the state-supported industrial sector, the LIT opposed artificially elevated tariffs and other state-derived advantages, preferring to export and compete in free world markets. The LIT also opposed state intervention in labor conflicts, since this belonged within the realm of civil society; the state should merely guarantee the maintenance of public order, its essential function, and not pretend to have the specialized competence necessary to adjudicate between economic interests:

There was a time when the workers screamed that in every case of labor conflict the state always intervened protecting the capitalists. Now they have discovered that when their agitations are maintained within the limits of legality – and sometimes even when they go a little bit beyond – the state

---

[70] Luigi Einaudi, *La condotta economica e gli effetti sociali della guerra italiana* (Bari: Laterza, 1933), p. 402.

does not take any part in the conflict of interests. They have recognized that the intervention of state authority takes place and is essential only when and because public order has been disturbed. Of course, the industrial class does not ask of the state any more than this. Rather, we believe that it is in its interest to combat state intervention in economic relations between it and the working class in times of peace and in times of war. The state is not capable of evaluating and judging thousands of considerations and thousands of causes which are determinate in such relations.[71]

Besides lacking the competence to act in the economic sphere, the state, according to Olivetti, could never "substitute itself for the spontaneous play of interests."[72] Although the LIT recognized that a new stage of "organized capitalism" had begun, where individual agents were superseded by formally organized interests, these new aggregations were to compete freely within the private sphere of civil society and not enter into clientelistic relations with the state and thereby violate the public–private distinction. Thus, it should be emphasized that although the LIT accepted one element of what eventually became understood as "organized capitalism," the need for disciplined collective action, they *explicitly rejected* what would come to be the other major element of the phenomenon: extensive state intervention. By this they meant the state's domination over civil society, mediating all private relations (that tendency which, in the twentieth century, Pollock, Habermas, and Offe identify as "refeudalization").

The social order, Olivetti claimed, "could not be reduced to a series of syndicates that would set aside all public functions."[73] From their liberal–competitive orientation, the LIT attacked the workers' syndicates for their "corporatism" in attempting to monopolize the labor market by restricting employment exclusively to union members and limiting the number of apprentices. "Now the workers' organizations want to exercise in the field of labor the same function that trusts exercise in the field of industry." The industrialists "can never accept a limitation that might reduce the efficiency of the free play of competition to which they themselves are subject."[74] From the very outset, the LIT identified restrictions on liberal practice, whether by workers' syndicates or the state, as corporatism, and just as "corporatism" was

[71] *BLI* 4 (1910): 7.
[72] *BLI* 3 (1909): 4.
[73] *BLI* 7 (1913): 6.
[74] Abrate, *Lotta sindacale*, p. 75.

a pejorative term in the LIT's lexicon, so, too, would it be later with Confindustria. As we shall see, even when corporatism had become an orthodoxy under Fascism, it was first rejected out of hand by industrial associations, and then, when such a position was no longer formally prudent, corporatism was adeptly redefined in substantively liberal terms to check the integralist and etatist aspirations of Fascist proponents.

Reduced to its essentials, the LIT's liberal–technocratic ideology can be specified by four propositions: (1) production is the basis for national development, and problems of distribution are derivative and contingent upon its unimpeded growth; (2) production is an autonomous sphere, bounded by its own contingencies and action-orienting norms; (3) labor conflict should remain within the realm of civil society and regulate itself through an evolving practice of free competition between opposing syndicates; and (4) the role of the state in economic relations is minimal, and with regard to labor conflict it should remain neutral and limit itself to maintaining order.

Industrial relations and the state

Whereas Taylorism in the United States initially had been identified with the "open-shop movement" and with the view that workers' syndicates could serve no useful function in fully rationalized production,[75] within the Italian context the syndical phenomenon had been so pervasive that no such a priori challenge to syndical legitimacy or futile American-styled attempts at forming yellow unions were objectively possible. As we have seen, the very form of the *sindacato padronale* was a response to that reality. By the end of the first decade of the twentieth century, workers' syndicates had been accepted fully in Italy, while in many of the more-industrialized nations – France, Belgium, Austria, and the United States – the issue was still being debated among employers.[76]

This meant that the LIT had to embrace the syndical phenomenon within its larger functionalist schema, as well as recognize a divergence of interest between workers' and industrialists' syndicates over the question of distribution. The former entailed rendering the workers' syndicate a nonantagonistic partner in preserving the continuity

[75] Bendix, *Work and Authority*, pp. 269–75.
[76] Abrate, *Lotta sindacale*, p. 60.

of production; the latter necessitated a clear demarcation of the scope of issues that could be negotiated (i.e., distributive demands, as opposed to those regarding the "technical ordering of production").

With the emergence of the CGL, and especially after its Modena Congress of 1908 (where the dominant "trade-unionist" faction had declared greater autonomy from the Socialist Party), the LIT noted a general transition from an earlier stage of "blind, impulsive, and anarchistic" anticapitalist struggle to a stage of disciplined, resourceful, and more selective action (based on new techniques copied from abroad: the boycott, passive resistance, and slowdowns) directed at obtaining maximal concessions with minimal losses.[77] In the words of Craponne, they had "abandoned to revolutionaries the tactics of the general strike, often vain as much as an enormous expenditure of energy, and had assumed as their motto the principle of the maximum effect with the minimum force."[78]

The change of orientation was greeted with mixed feelings. On the one hand, the LIT was content that production might no longer be subject to spectacular and "irrational" disruptions and that a reformist bureaucratic organization had emerged with which negotiations and an institutionalization of labor conflict could take place. On the other, it feared the "corporatist," monopolizing tendency of the CGL over the workforce, seeing this as the first step toward an eventual challenge to managerial authority within the factory. "In place of the Marxist system, there has been substituted a corporatist one."[79] Workers' syndicates were becoming "*corporazione di mestiere*"[80] which sought to

guarantee themselves a monopoly over the workforce by compelling the industrialist to employ only its members, diminish the creation of new positions by limiting the number of apprentices, hence reducing the supply, as opposed to the demand, of labor and thus anticipating an ever greater increase in salaries. Workers' syndicates thus sought to guarantee their control over the workforce through the institution of organs like the *commissione interna*, which, in some cases, have already succeeded in imposing salary increases which must be implemented according to their direction.[81]

---

[77] *BLI* 2 (1908): 10–11; 3 (1909): 4.
[78] *BLI* 3 (1909): 4.
[79] *BLI* 2 (1908): 10–11.
[80] *BLI* 3 (1909): 4.
[81] Ibid.

The LIT thus saw its task as one of encouraging the mediating institutional role of workers' syndicates while, at the same time, restricting their competence to questions of distribution and material *rivendicazioni*. "We ought not to be a priori negators of the modern workers' movement; we must rather confront it, redirect it to its real function."[82] According to the logic of productivism, higher salaries could only be obtained with increased output, and this, in turn, was dependent upon the maintenance of a disciplined hierarchy within the factory and allowing the industrialist freely to order the factors of production in accordance with the principle of optimality:

The syndicate is free to help with all the means permitted by law and also with strikes the class that it represents when it is a question of attaining an economic advantage for the workers or contributing to their material elevation. But, at the same time, the benefits obtained for the masses through this action ought to be real and not ephemeral. And ephemeral is precisely what each concession that the workers' syndicate might obtain will be if the industrialist's freedom of action is limited, diminishing in him that thrust of initiative which is necessary for industry's development. Each industry in which he who commands loses the possibility of ordering his machinery and utilizing the workforce in such a manner as to attain with the minimum force the maximum effect goes inescapably to ruin.[83]

Hence, the LIT's position was conciliation on economic questions and the most absolute intransigence on issues concerning productive hierarchy and discipline. "Industry can grant every economic concession whenever the potentiality of the firm can support it, but it cannot accept compromises on the directive function, which is the duty of the industrialist."[84]

Nothing better illustrates this attempt at the institutionalization of labor conflict and the willingness to yield material concessions in exchange for the recognition of managerial prerogatives than the contract negotiated between FIOM and the Consorzio delle Fabbriche di Automobili in Turin during December 1911. The former, as mentioned earlier, was the most prestigious and best-organized workers' syndicate in Italy. For more than seven years, it had led and negotiated every major worker initiative in the machine-manufacturing sector. The latter was formed a month before negotiations for this

[82] *BLI* 4 (1910): 4.
[83] *BLI* 3 (1909): 4.
[84] *BLI* 6 (1912): 1.

contract took place, through the initiative of Olivetti and Agnelli of Fiat. Tempered by a rigid discipline among its members (including the deposit of a blank check which could be put into circulation for violations of discipline), the *consorzio* was directed toward confronting the so-called German tactic of FIOM (striking one firm at a time, serially generalizing concessions won) by negotiating a unitary labor contract that would apply to all of Turin's automotive sector.[85]

In 1910–11, the automotive industry had entered a period of great expansion during which production could not keep pace with demand. Above all, it was necessary to avoid any interruption of work and proceed with a radical technological transformation of existing facilities. Such imperatives were reflected in the newly negotiated contract. On the one hand, FIOM obtained higher wages and shorter hours than in any previous Italian contract, as well as "recognition" in that new workers were to be recruited from its employment office and dues were to be directly deducted from paychecks. On the other, the *consorzio* obtained abolition of the *commissione interna*, the right to fire without notice, the end to any "tolerance" with regard to established work schedules, the deposit of a "caution" by each worker of a week's salary, and, most important, a compulsory process of conciliation that had to be exhausted before any strike could be declared.[86]

Formally, the *consorzio* adhered to the LIT's principle of never conceding a monopoly over the workforce to any labor syndicate; the contract made clear that obligatory membership in FIOM was not a condition of employment. In substance, however, the *consorzio* all but conceded such status to FIOM in the hope of gaining thereby an institutional counterpart which could guarantee that the contract's provisions would be respected. Thus, the continuity of production would be ensured, as well as the formal recognition – by contract – of the industrialists' undisputed authority to unilaterally order the factors of production.

The workers, however, overwhelmingly rejected the contract. A strike was declared, instigated by an autonomous group of revolutionary syndicalists, violating what would have been one of the contact's major provisions, if not the very raison d'être of the regulatory

---

[85] Abrate, *Lotta sindacale*, p. 61; Castronovo, *Economia e società*, pp. 305–6.
[86] Abrate, *Lotta sindacale*, p. 91.

initiative. The conflict ended with the *consorzio*'s complete victory. Retracting all its previous concessions and literally imposing a new *regolamento*, the *consorzio* unilaterally laid down those provisions it deemed necessary to guarantee managerial authority by virtue of its superior syndical force. Once again, there were recriminations between reformists and revolutionaries within the ranks of labor, but the important point to note was the abysmal failure of this important attempt at institutionalizing labor relations through disciplined bilateral negotiations, a failure due less to intransigence on the part of the industrialists than to the organic weakness of the workers' movement.

Other attempts followed at integrating workers' syndicates within a larger institutional and regulatory framework. In February 1912, Olivetti called for the "juridical recognition" of all syndical associations.[87] This request had little in common with the corporatist legislation later to be introduced under Fascism, as the state was to abstain from "any intervention, any interference, any control in the internal structure and functioning of the syndical organization." Rather, Olivetti wanted to ensure basically one thing: that any syndical entity capable of entering into contracts be civilly responsible for its conduct. Since the actual formation of syndicates, no modification of the civil code had been introduced conferring upon them a legal personality and specifing their contractual accountability. Beneath the legal formalism, however, lay an obvious concern that such "licensing" of syndical bodies might lead to more predictable and disciplined labor relations. Without direct state intervention, such a measure might encourage the development of further formalization in this sphere of civil society.

Still another attempt at integration followed in June 1912, when the CIDI and the CGL agreed to establish joint employment offices to help stem the alarming rise in unemployment which gripped the nation during 1912–13. Both organizations recognized a convergence of interest in "normalizing" the labor market.

The CIDI and the CGL, though holding different points of view, cannot help but find accord in this field. It is in the interest of the industrialists that their demand for labor find a copious supply and in a manner that would lead to selection of the most adept worker at a normal level of salary. It is in the interest of the workers that their demands for work find the quickest reception,

[87] *BLI* 6 (1912): 2.

without being constrained to traverse the *via crucis* of a pilgrimage from factory to factory, or to wait in the anxiety of unemployment until an appropriate
offer presents itself. Given this communion of interests, the two organizations
cannot fail to benevolently welcome the appeal made to them to study whether
or not in Italy it may be possible, and upon what basis, to institute joint employment offices. These appear to be a form through which this communion of
interests may give rise to mutual cooperation between the two parties.[88]

Special emphasis was given in the document to the primacy of the
two syndical bodies in two respects: their "natural competence" to
deal with such issues, and how organizational discipline might ensure
the efficacy of such voluntary projects.

The new bodies ought to emerge by mutual consent through the voluntary cooperation of the two interested parties: industrialists and workers. By industrialists and workers we mean not the amorphous and vague mass of the one and
the other but rather the organizations that know the problems that concern
each class and that are in the best position, from the reality of their experience,
to have a general and objective vision; organizations that, above all, are able
to devote serious attention to the initiative, as well as its regular functioning
through the disciplinary bonds that constitute their essence.[89]

Once again, however, the results were somewhat less than the
promise. Since these joint employment offices were not to function in
the case of strikes and lockouts and were oriented more toward
rationalizing an already depressed labor market than creating new
jobs, they could neither function effectively during a period of increased labor agitation nor constitute an effective agency in decreas-
ing unemployment.[90]

Nevertheless, the idea of voluntary and direct relations between the
syndical bodies persisted, and by 1914 bilateral arbitration commissions had been established which were deemed by both parties to be
preferable to state intervention in this area. In the words of Dante
Ferraris, president of the LIT after Craponne resigned:

These organs of conciliation and arbitration, born and maintained through
the free will of the parties, functioning by reciprocal trust, respond better to
their real objectives than official institutions, which are regulated by laws in
a manner not always in conformance with practical necessity, are driven by
the need to function according to cumbersome regulations, and are not

---

[88] Ibid., p. 5. See also Pepe, *Storia della CGL*, 2: 140–4.
[89] *BLI* 6 (1912): 5.
[90] Pepe, *Storia della CGL*, 2: 42–3.

endowed with the comprehension that the parties involved have. [The arbitration commissions] are in a far better position to act justly.[91]

In accordance with the LIT's basic public–private distinction, Ferraris not only underscored the superiority of independent syndical practice but called upon the state to refrain from engulfing the autonomous realm of production within its institutional orbit:

The state should allow our organs of pacification to evolve freely. It should allow them to develop according to the exigencies of industrial life. It should let them profit from their autonomy and independence. The theoreticians of social legislation should not be permitted to drape over industry a leaden cloak of legislative requirements, regulatory norms, ministerial directives, and bureaucratic circulars. Industry and labor are life. The state should allow this life to evolve freely, without pretending to make itself master from the very outset over all phenomena, regulating them according to its pleasure.

Fear that industry would be bureaucratized by the state was a predominant theme in the LIT bulletin. Just as it had polemicized against any intrusion by workers' syndicates upon managerial authority, it railed against the quagmire of "obligations and fetters which tend to bureaucratize our industries on the model of the great state apparatus";[92] against "that useless, dangerous bureaucracy which, as it sucked up the state, tends now to envelop our industrial liberty within its tentacles."[93] Besides the liberal public–private distinction, the LIT invoked the same productionist stance against state intervention that it had utilized against workers' syndicates: only by allowing the industrialist unlimited freedom to order the factors of production according to the optimality formula could new wealth be generated which might gradually help finance the growing fiscal burden resulting from the various new forms of social legislation.

Although the CGL generally supported the extension of social legislation, there were occasions when it too shared the LIT's resentment against the imperious manner in which such projects were imposed. Once the two organizations actually joined forces in opposing a state-administered maternity fund whose cost was to be borne directly by management and workers, with no direct contribution made by the state. In a joint resolution the CGL and the LIT asserted that "if the state intends to pursue the path of social legislation and institute a

[91] *BLI* 8 (1914): 5–6.
[92] *BLI* 3 (1909): 7.
[93] *BLI* 5 (1911): 2.

system of social insurance, it cannot purely and simply limit itself to commanding but must also 'do.' "[94] The CGL shared the LIT's view that maternity was an issue that concerned the collectivity as a whole, having "no special reference to industry." Rigola, head of the CGL, called the project "an atrocious joke," arguing that its administrative cost would absorb the better part of the fund, since "no bureaucracy is as weighty, as slow, and as costly as that of the state."[95]

The LIT constantly argued that since it was largely through industry that the state obtained the revenue necessary for the administration of social programs, its needs and exigencies had to be respected, and that social legislation should not be an opportunistic response to the "clamoring of the piazza" or be slavishly copied from abroad to demonstrate that Italy had caught up with the more-advanced nations. In a lengthy but characteristic statement of the LIT's position, Craponne claimed:

The duty of the state is not to yield to the clamoring of the piazza, but rather to choose with clear criteria the route which can lead the Nation to greatest prosperity. Much of the social legislation is indissolubly tied to an augmentation of national wealth which has provided the primary basis for bettering Italian conditions over the past thirty years. The tendency of our political leaders, unfortunately, has been that of placing ever heavier burdens on the free exercise of the industrialists' activity.

We do not and have not opposed a priori all that which is called social legislation. We simply ask that these programs be adapted to the special conditions of Italy and not follow the all too frequent method of justifying legislative reforms in this area with the no less frequent refrain of the Minister who each year presents these legislative projects: "It is a question of a reform which has for some time been applied abroad and will serve finally to put Italy on the same level as the more-advanced nations."

No! The progress of our country will not be obtained by legislative projects but through our activity. We can say it proudly, we industrialists: it is our activity which has given to Italy and to the state the means with which to be able to fulfill these new functions. Does the government think that in the final analysis the free development of our energy is merely in our narrow interest and not in the interest of the entire Nation? Does the government recognize that the full development of our industry signifies the growing welfare of the entire society? Has the government understood that what our industry earns is distributed in a thousand diverse ways, directly and indirectly, through state agencies to raise the condition of the whole social body?

[94] Abrate, *Lotta sindacale,* p. 129.
[95] Ibid., p. 128.

Economic life in Italy is still in formation. Our industry does not have a skeletal structure strong enough to sustain the same weight as that of English or German industry, both older and placed in better natural conditions. It is still, one can say, in its youth. One should not impede its growth with constrictive fetters. At a minimum – if one is searching for foreign models as a guide for governmental action – what should be recognized is all that has been done abroad to favor and promote the flowering and growth of industry, along with the betterment of workers.[96]

According to the LIT, social legislation should be enacted on the basis of a clear and systematic inventory of both needs *and* capacities. Free as much as possible from bureaucratic formalism, it should be guided by the optimality formula, "achieving the maximum effect with the minimum force."[97] Not surprisingly, the LIT's preferred initiative in this area was the one most directly related to the needs of production: raising the level of professional (vocational) education. "That which the government spends for so much bureaucracy, a harmful encumbrance and useless to all, could be better spent in raising the value of our workforce, a more effective means than any other."[98]

Such was the general ideological position of the LIT: its functionalism, its liberal–technocratic productivism, its vision of industrial relations and the state. Compared to the earlier "dependent" industrial attitudes, the LIT proudly trumpeted the centrality of industry in national development and the need for autonomously rationalized syndical relations and freedom for industry to develop as a distinctive, self-directed sphere with a minimum of state constraints. Yet within this vision lurked unrecognized contradictions. On the one hand, its technocratic bias called for an institutionalization of relations with the workers' movement so that "impulsive" agitation would be restrained by structured, conciliatory practice, thus ensuring the continuity of production. On the other, its liberal bias against the "monopolistic" recognition of any one of the workers' syndicates (even the one most favorable to this institutionalization) and its often overly combative posture in labor conflicts tended to negate the very conditions through which regulatory practice might have been established.

Instead of enlightened co-optation, oriented toward enlisting the cooperation of a potential "institutional partner," the LIT tended to

---

[96] *BLI* 2 (1908): 3; 3 (1909): 4; 4 (1910): 4, 5.
[97] *BLI* 3 (1909): 4.
[98] Ibid.

remain in a conflictual stance, naively believing perhaps that a protracted armed truce would necessarily evolve into conciliatory practice. Moreover, although the LIT posited a strict separation between political and economic activity, it is difficult to imagine how the sum total of worker demands could be contained within the limits of syndical practice alone, given the existence of the Socialist Party and the state's commitment to extend social reforms. The LIT recognized and indeed feared the manifestly political orientation of the reformist CGL, "which, in contrast to the revolutionary syndicalists, does not shun parliamentary action or assume toward the state an attitude of sterile and negative opposition."[99] Yet the LIT took no political measures of its own, such as entering into party alliances, to counter the growing force of the organized workers' movement. As we shall see, even when other sectors of the bourgeois bloc indicated a readiness to enter the political arena, the LIT preferred to remain within its narrow syndical orbit.

Finally, the LIT never considered the possibility of a profound contradiction between its functionalist–technocratic vision of productive relations and its "inherited" traditional liberalism or whether such liberalism, in fact, was a requisite political vehicle for the realization of its overriding productivist aspirations. It should be clear by this point that no antiliberal, corporatist, or manifestly authoritarian political positions had been advanced by the LIT. And yet the LIT's productivist critique of the actual functioning of the liberal regime, as opposed to some ideal type, prefigured what would become key elements of a new, antiliberal, technocratic assault on the liberal state in the post–World War I period: its humanistic dilettantism, lack of specialized competence, and bureaucratic parasitism; its incapacity to allow for the direct representation of organized interests; its proclivity to respond more to mass pressure than to the objective exigencies of the nation. In other words, between the LIT's outspoken productivism and its negative appraisal of the liberal state's actual performance, a curious void was laid bare regarding what specific political restructuring would be necessary either to rectify the existent regime and make it more responsive or to replace it with another regime type, one perhaps more closely modeled on the functionalist and hierarchical pattern of productive relations. At this time, however, the LIT

[99] *BLI* 2 (1908): 10–11.

provided no clue as to how this void might be filled; it chose instead to shun political activity as such, entrenching its position in civil society through syndical practice.

Political activity

In the Introduction, we touched on the passive nature of the Risorgimento. Occurring after feudalism had already been dismantled, yet before capitalism had taken an industrial turn, Italian unification was led by a moderate aristocratic–bourgeois alliance. Pressured neither from the extreme Right (to restore a pre-1789 order) nor from the extreme Left (a Socialist workers' movement), the Moderates had little need to create such political structures as national parties or interest associations. The narrowly based administrative state they founded directly reflected these class interests and guided from above what never had to be organically represented from below. In the place of representative and integrative structures, the politics of *trasformismo* served to mediate between a narrow range of upper-class interests. In time, a relatively autonomous and long-tenured political class of lawyers, by profession well suited to act as personal brokers, became the custodians of the state, a liberal *partito di governo* which clientelistically tutored interests that needed no direct representation.

Industrialists, as a distinctive class fragment, were late-joining members of the bourgeois bloc, initially dependent upon the state for the promotion of their interests and willing to accept a subservient position in relation to agrarians, merchants, and professionals. By birth, they tended to come from humbler origins,[100] sometimes beginning as workers or artisans. Also, by virtue of their practical or technical education, they were isolated from the prevalent humanistic bourgeois culture. Even though they were junior members of the bourgeois bloc, and at times exhibited some degree of animosity toward their "parasitic" seniors, there was no compelling need, nor were there any existent institutional channels, for them to challenge the traditional bourgeois political equilibrium. Autonomous political action might have involved costs and risks disproportionate to the relative security of dependency. It probably would have necessitated the formation of a national political party and an attempted hege-

---

[100] Einaudi, *Condotta economica*, p. 17; Craponne, *Italie au travail*, pp. 24–6.

mony over other classes and class fragments within an institutional framework stacked against such an initiative and within a political culture hostile to or inexperienced in mobilization. Moreover, it would have risked linking the fortune of industry to the success or failure of such autonomous political action.[101]

In the Introduction, we made reference to Paolo Farneti's study of the *classe politica* from unification to 1914, a study that indicated, in relation to France and Germany, a disproportionately high percentage of lawyers and a disproportionately low percentage of industrialists.[102] Personal memoirs, as well as public statements made by industrialists, suggest a profound sense of isolation from both the larger bourgeoisie's humanistic culture (including its traditional prejudice against productive or commercial endeavor and its tendency toward the oratorical and abstract) and the *classe politica*, the "lawyers and professors," who bore the worst traits of that culture.[103] Even here, the stature and background of Gino Olivetti as an associational leader are highly significant. A lawyer and an "intellectual," as well as thoroughly versed in technicocommercial matters, Olivetti may be seen as a "cultural mediator" between the productive and humanistic realms, a role that few industrialists themselves could have played, given their "philistine" backgrounds and discomfort in the very presence of "lawyers and professors." When they did participate in political bodies, industrialists tended quickly to lose patience with, as Ettore Conti called them, "a class of Ciceros neither born nor made" (his motto, as he was proud to point out, was *faire sans dire*).[104] Reviewing oral and written statements produced by industrialists, one is immediately struck by their frequent self-description as a *borghesia produttrice* or a *borghesia del lavoro*, terms intended to set them apart from the traditional and, in their eyes, largely parasitic *borghesia*. Institutions were never created in Italy that might have integrated the humanistic and technicoproductive sectors into a relatively homogeneous *classe dirigente* (as, e.g., had been partially accomplished in France through the *grandes écoles*), and hence the two persisted as heterogeneous, if not actually antagonistic, class fragments; the one

[101] Farneti, *Sistema politica*, pp. 183–5.
[102] Ibid., pp. 245–8.
[103] On Olivetti see Caizzi, *Gli Olivetti*, p. 48; on Agnelli see Castronovo, *Agnelli*, p. 155; on Rossi see Baglioni, *Ideologia della borghesia industriale*, pp. 244–6. For the observations of Craponne see his *Italie au travail*, pp. 24–6.
[104] Ettore Conti, *Dal taccuino di un borghese* (Milan: Garzanti, 1971), p. 29.

"producing," the other "governing." Although it is certainly true that industrialists maintained clientelistic relations with politicians, these relations were more on the order of professional procurement than what might be called "organic" (i.e., where the bonds between representative and represented are based on a strict commonality of outlook, interest, and necessity).

So long as the state concerned itself only with the common affairs of the enfranchised upper classes, and so long as industry constituted a quantitatively minor fraction of the national product, such dependent, clientelistic relations were still viable. However, with the changes in state policy initiated by Giolitti, wherein the state now presumed to mediate, transform, and alchemize not only the heterogeneous bourgeois interests but those of workers as well, and with the simultaneous industrial "takeoff," leading to greater social differentiation and the formal organization of interests, industrialists were literally driven from political dependency toward greater autonomy.

We have already mentioned that at the local level, in Turin, the traditional mercantile and professional elite was being successfully challenged by an "industrializing bloc" composed of the "new" industrialists and reform Socialists, both interested in a *promozione municipale* of rapid industrial growth, vocational training, improved social-service facilities, and modernization of the city's infrastructure. In 1902, these industrialists had already set themselves aside from the older leadership in the local Unione Liberale Monarchica by calling for a new program of "efficiency" in the municipal administration and a "struggle to the end" against the "do-nothings." By 1905, they had formed a *commissione permanente* which made specific recommendations to the municipal administration as to the *capitale fisso sociale* necessary for Turin's whole-scale transition to a major urban–industrial center: those essential local initiatives needed to create a modern infrastructure (communication, transportation, energy, education, and housing) and a consequent lowering of production costs. Composed of such individuals as Dante Ferraris, Giocomo Bosso, and Emilio Remmert, all of whom would soon assume prominent positions in the LIT, the *commissione permanente* not only was instrumental in promoting such infrastructural programs as a reduction in the price of energy for industrial use to cost from the municipal electric company but also was successful in getting the city council to diminish and gradually abolish taxes on raw materials, thus again lowering production costs.[105] Through the *promozione municipale,* the city administration became, according to *La Stampa,* "a great company in the service of the city's future." Never before had "our city a happier hour in the development of the public economy, in the marvelous growth of business, and in the stupendous production of its factories. Today much work is done in Turin, much is produced, much is earned. It is absolutely necessary that the city administration be capable of favoring such an ascendant movement."[106]

With the support of Alfredo Frassati – publisher of Turin's *La Stampa,* ardent Giolittian, and a major power broker in the city's liberal politics – industrialists began to win elective seats on the municipal council (by 1906 they would number twelve of the fifty-seven liberal majority).[107] The Società Promotrice, as opposed to the syndical LIT, assumed a greater political role, becoming "the political center of the liberal Turinese bourgeoisie."[108] Composed of the same general membership as the LIT, the formally divergent orientations of the two industrial associations represented more a functional differentiation (the one political, the other syndical) than any real conflict of views. Yet they also differed in scope and outreach, the Società Promotrice confined to local politics, and the LIT oriented from the outset toward developing into a national syndical association. Political success at the local level had little direct impact at the national level, given the institutional framework of the liberal state (a "federation of localisms" controlled from the top by the strong hand of the prime minister). Although initial productivist aspirations could be partially satisfied through municipal reforms, the central questions affecting industry (e.g., tariffs, social legislation, fiscal policy) were national in scope and not subject to the same relation of forces as existed in the local politics of Turin. Each city had its own separate liberal association, and these were not aggregated into a national liberal party. Control over one such local association was relatively unimportant, and the generalization of control throughout Italy, given the structure of traditional liberal politics and the geographical confinement of industry to the northern industrial triangle, was virtually impossible.

Not only was political activity in the prewar period confined to the

---

[105] Castronovo, *Economia e società,* pp. 180–9.
[106] Ibid., pp. 182–3.
[107] Ibid.
[108] Abrate, *Lotta sindacale,* p. 44.

local level, compared to the national reach of syndical activity, but the very basis of such politics was more technicoproductivist and administrative (e.g., the *promozione municipale*) than mobilizational. Industrialists indeed had moved from dependency toward more autonomous representation of their own interests, but they had yet to even think of a transition from autonomy to hegemony. Thus, one may note that the organizational development of the LIT, unifying the industrial class along "prepolitical" lines and consolidating its influence in civil society, left unchallenged the traditional liberal constellation at the national level, a political constellation no longer organically based on any one class bloc (as it had been originally), or on any party or interest-group structure, but entirely on the capacity of a great leader to mediate between increasingly contradictory interests.

As suggested earlier, by 1911 the structurally amorphous Giolittian regime had begun to show signs of internal collapse. *Trasformismo* had been stretched to the point of rupture by strategically necessary, though objectively improbable, attempts at containing autonomously organized groups within the traditional liberal institutional framework through a series of contradictory preemptive concessions. The most daring of these were the Libyan War (to satisfy the Nationalists) and universal suffrage for men and nationalization of life insurance (to satisfy the Socialists). The Socialists, except for a minority reformist faction (expelled from the party in 1912 by "revolutionaries" led by Mussolini), reacted to the Libyan War by moving to the Left and effectively cutting all ties with Giolitti, while the Nationalists only became more extreme in their imperialist aspirations. Universal suffrage, rather than serving as the conservative force Giolitti imagined, the ultimate step in his reformist program, effectively undercut the capacity of the partyless and divided liberals to retain a workable parliamentary majority, while allowing mass parties finally to enjoy the political weight that their numbers warranted. Thus, in the elections of 1913, Socialists increased their parliamentary representation from 41 to 78 seats, while the heterogeneous liberal majority decreased from 370 to 318 seats (and of these, one-third had been elected only with the support of moderate Catholics under the terms of Giolitti's pact with Count Gentilioni).[109]

Coincident with this deteriorating political situation, Italy had en-

---

[109] Carocci, *Giolitti*, p. 157; Leoni, *Partiti politici*, p. 240; Mack Smith, *Italy*, p. 283.

tered a period of economic decline that would not improve until the outbreak of war. The industrial expansion and general prosperity that had afforded a margin for Giolitti's earlier reforms had ended by 1908, and in the ensuing period (1908–13) the annual average rate of growth in total industrial output fell from 6.7 to 2.4 percent (some key sectors: metalmaking, from 12.4 to 6.1 percent; machine manufacturing, from 12.2 to 2.0 percent; chemicals, from 13.7 to 1.8 percent).[110] Thus, an extreme contradiction emerged between Giolitti's political imperatives and the economic capacity of the nation. At the very time when Giolitti, for political reasons, was driven toward demanding still greater concessions from the industrialists, the latter, already critical in principle toward subjecting production to "political speculation" and now incapable of bearing additional burdens because of the economic downswing, moved to open opposition. Giolitti's earlier pronouncements on the neutrality of the state in labor conflict and on the state's essential function of maintaining order and protecting property now appeared to be negated by a practice ever more oriented toward political survival, of dominating from above those forces and interests that could no longer be mediated and reconciled.

The CIDI in June 1911 opposed Giolitti's nationalization of life insurance on the grounds that the state had no constitutional right to expropriate at will a given branch of industry. This, in their view, represented a dangerous precedent that might be applied to other branches as well, if and when politically expedient.[111] Its condemnation of the state's "dangerous and useless interventionism" was based, as we have seen, on a commitment to economic liberalism, and its opposition to the nationalization of life insurance was shared by leading liberal economists of the day (Einaudi, Pantaleoni, De Viti de Marco) and by liberal–conservatives led by Sonnino and Salandra.

The most dramatic confrontation, however, between industrialists and Giolitti occurred during the Turin automobile strike of 1913. After its defeat in the previously mentioned strike of 1912, FIOM was thoroughly reorganized under the leadership of Bruno Buozzi, who, in February 1913, presented the *consorzio* of auto producers with a

---

[110] Gerschenkron, *Economic Backwardness,* pp. 72–89.
[111] *BLI* 5 (1911): 8.

list of demands calling for salary increases, shorter working hours, and reinstatement of concessions lost in the ill-fated 1912 contract.[112] Having received an unsatisfactory response from the *consorzio,* FIOM declared a strike on 19 March. Unlike the strike a year earlier, this time thorough preparations had been made, including a sizable strike fund filled with contributions from other workers' syndicates in Italy and abroad (the German metalworkers alone sent 100,000 marks). In May, another industrial *consorzio* was formed, that of the metalmaking and machine-manufacturing sectors, whose leaders feared that possible concessions granted by the automotive *consorzio* might be generalized to these sectors as well. The two industrial *consorzi* then entered into an agreement to take common action by announcing a lockout in all member firms beginning 26 May.

While FIOM and Giolitti were interested in keeping the conflict limited to the automotive sector, though for different reasons, the industrialists deliberately chose to expand the conflict as a show of syndical strength, and also to eliminate the financial support that autoworkers were receiving from their counterparts in these other sectors. Such a generalized lockout had been successful in England and in Germany, so the strategy was adopted in Turin.

After government-sponsored attempts at mediation failed, Craponne and Ferraris, representing the LIT and the *consorzi,* were summoned to a meeting with the prefect, who informed them – on behalf of Giolitti – that if the lockout were effected, public authorities would not protect the factories from possible worker violence and that such instructions were to be made public. At the same time, Craponne, French by birth, was threatened with deportation as a "foreign subversive." Recently, Giolitti had intervened in a Milan general strike led by revolutionary syndicalists, arresting their leaders (Bacchi and Corridoni). Through a somewhat farcical display of "neutrality," he now attempted to counterbalance this action by moving against Craponne, depicted as a "syndical extremist." The semiofficial *Tribuna* of May 27 declared:

We must deplore the fact that the major initiator and counselor of this device is a foreigner. Italy is open to capitalistic initiatives by citizens of all nations, but these, coming to our country and establishing industries, must beware of

---

[112] On the strike see *BLI* 7 (1913): 6; Abrate, *Lotta sindacale,* pp. 96–102; Castronovo, *Economia e società,* pp. 312–18; Spriano, *Torino operaia,* pp. 231–5.

provoking agitations whose effects may go beyond the immediate question and become political. The hospitality which M. Craponne enjoys in Italy ought to impress him with obvious considerations: just as we cannot permit syndical agitators and foreign anarchists to come to Italy and incite or embitter workers' agitations, we cannot any the less permit foreign capitalists to play the same game.[113]

Faced with these threats, the lockout was suspended, Craponne resigned as president of the LIT, and the three-month strike was ended on terms favorable to FIOM. As if to emphasize the personal mediation of Giolitti, the agreement was signed, not in the "official" office of the prefect, but rather in the office of Frassati, editor of *La Stampa*. The animosity vented toward Giolitti on the part of industrialists was almost as great as that which would follow the famous occupation of the factories in the postwar period, and such criticism was based precisely on the same two grounds: (1) the refusal on the part of the state to protect property and (2) intervention in a labor conflict in favor of the workers, rather than remaining neutral.

Olivetti pointed out that in other countries where the general lockout had applied, no government leader or major newspaper had accused industrialists of being "syndical subversives." Rather, such action was recognized as a legitimate counterpart to the strike so long as it was strictly confined to the syndical arena. To Olivetti, the state's action had violated the very basis of liberalism, because protection of property, a constitutional right, was now made contingent upon the renunciation of a legally permissible syndical action and upon acceptance of a state-imposed settlement. Giolitti's action had violated his earlier commitment to unfettered syndical freedom and the neutrality of the state. Now, according to Olivetti, "the Government will become the absolute arbiter of all conflicts; no longer will the respective forces of industrialists and workers decide the victory. It will be uniquely governmental action, intervening and imposing its will, regulating the fortunes of industry and of the workforce according to its judgment."[114]

The irony of the LIT's falling victim to the Giolitti of 1913 by following the invocations of the Giolitti of 1901 was not missed by the highly regarded Communist historian Paolo Spriano:

[113] *BLI* 7 (1913): 6.
[114] Ibid.

Giolitti showed in this case the firmness that had marked his previous relations with intransigent industrialists. He had even gone beyond that by favoring the strikers and breaking that neutrality which had been his proclaimed maxim in labor conflicts; by placing himself, in practice, against the very line he himself had expounded a decade earlier regarding workers' and industrialists' syndicates, a line of reciprocal self-defense. Paradoxically, one might say that Craponne was chased from Italy by the honorable Giolitti when he himself had followed a Giolittian orientation![115]

Olivetti, embittered by Giolitti's high-handedness, could not refrain from ending his article in the LIT bulletin with a thinly veiled threat, all the more revealing, perhaps, in light of events to come:

The Government should not however believe that because today industrialists have had to bend before its imposition, faced with the unique and supreme necessity of not sacrificing the life of their beloved and trusted leader, they will not indelibly record the affront they have endured or will voluntarily submit to intimidation by such methods. That would be a wish the Government should not seriously nurture.[116]

Within ten months, however, Giolitti would resign from office, his precarious majority undercut by the radicals' movement to opposition after learning of Giolitti's electoral deal with the Catholics. With his resignation, and the assumption of office by the conservative Salandra, the prewar era of democratic reform had come to an end, replaced by a new, so-called *politica nazionale:* an alliance of all "constitutional" forces against the Socialists, based on Sonnino's earlier conception of a conservative–authoritarian *blocco liberale* mobilized against the "subversives."

Politics in Turin reflected this general trend. In the national elections of October 1913, the first held under universal male suffrage, Socialists were victorious in three of the city's five electoral districts.[117] Within a climate of increased class conflict and political polarization, the "red week" broke out in June 1914. While in Italy's rural regions, especially Emilia–Romagna, the movement assumed the character of a peasant *jacquerie,* the industrial cities were subjected to a national general strike, called in response to the government's repression of an antimilitarist demonstration in Ancona. Turin was the scene of violent clashes between the police and workers, leading

[115] Spriano, *Torino operaia*, p. 233.
[116] *BLI* 7 (1913): 6.
[117] Spriano, *Torino operaia*, pp. 264–82.

to a state of alarm among the "forces of order." Even the traditionally calm and reformist *La Stampa* commented on 11 June:

The general strike passed like a cyclone over Turin and over all Italy with its procession of bloody tumult, of criminal excess, of pillage and violence without precedent. It is certain that the general strike of 1914 was more sinister and graver than its ill-famed predecessor of 1904. Revolutionary Socialism has the Commune within its grasp. Everyone should take his proper post of battle.[118]

Shopkeepers and other sectors of the petite bourgeoisie, already swept up in the growing tide of patriotism and anti-Socialism brought on by the Libyan adventure, constituted a Comitato Permanente per la Difesa dell'Ordine.[119] Against the backdrop of the previous Socialist electoral victory and the alarm signaled by the general strike, a bloc of liberal, clerical, and Nationalist forces dealt a decisive blow to the Socialists in the local election of 14 June 1914, polling 39,883 votes to the Socialists' 26,781.[120] Though the LIT, remaining formally apolitical, did not participate in the election, the industrialists played a conspicuous role in the reorganization of the Unione Liberale Monarchica and added five of their number to the city council.[121] By no means the avant-garde of this conservative drift, which was more a reflection of the entire bourgeois bloc, industrialists nevertheless ended their prior status as a passive element within this bloc, emerging – as they had never done under Giolitti – as an active political force.

This is not to say that the industrialists were making their bid for class hegemony, or even that their new political involvement was selectively organized behind one specific party as opposed to another. Rather, because the bourgeoisie as a bloc faced a common threat in the Socialists, the nominal distinctions between liberal–democrats, liberal–conservatives, and Nationalists gave way to a higher political unity. Nothing better illustrates this new conservative unity than the special election held in Turin's fourth *collegio* (electoral district) on 28 June 1914 to fill the parliamentary seat left by the death of Pilade Gay, a Socialist. Though the Nationalists had little mass following in Turin, nor were many industrialists counted among their ranks,

---

[118] Ibid., p. 277.
[119] Ibid., p. 275.
[120] Ibid., p. 278.
[121] Castronovo, *Agnelli*, p. 74.

Giuseppe Bevone emerged victorious as the candidate of the "constitutionalists," supported even by Giolitti and *La Stampa*. A year earlier – before the October 1913 national elections and the red week – such a candidacy would have been unlikely, if not absurd.

The relationship between Turinese industrialists and nationalism was complex and not given to easy schematization, especially because economic and political nationalism had not been coterminous until 1913–14, when Alfredo Rocco, future minister of justice under Mussolini and a major architect of the corporatist state, imposed his integral theoretical direction upon what previously had been a rather amorphous literary–patriotic movement composed largely of *déracinés* intellectuals. Economic nationalism, though much in favor during the long depression of the 1870s–90s, had been largely undercut by the upward turn in world trade at the turn of the century, which, it will be recalled, provided the basis for Italy's takeoff and relative prosperity during the early Giolitti period. However, with the downward turn of the business cycle in 1911, even as liberal a group as the LIT began to turn its attention to provisions already adopted in Germany, France, and England to protect domestic markets through tariff measures and consumer campaigns favoring the "national product" (where private consumers and the state were encouraged to purchase only domestically produced commodities, thereby "defending" the national labor force against unemployment).[122]

In 1912, the CIDI launched such a campaign, openly supported by the CGL, which was understandably preoccupied by the growing level of unemployment. Rinaldo Rigola, its leader, said that sustaining national production was "not just an interest but a duty of civil education to which workers' organizations could not fail but respond. In this sense, but in this sense only, we too are nationalists."[123] Although members of the CIDI (Olivetti, Agnelli, Bocca, Ferraris) participated in the protectionist Comitato Nazionale per le Tariffe Doganali ed i Tratti di Commercio, sponsored by the Milan-based Associazione fra le Società Italiane per Azione (ASIA; founded in 1910 by financial and industrial interests, including many members of the CIDI), the CIDI itself, as a syndical body, declined to take a position on protection for fear of having its unity split by groups

---

[122] Abrate, *Lotta sindacale*, pp. 133–4.
[123] Ibid., p. 133.

with competing tariff interests. Rather than concentrate on tariff protection, the CIDI concerned itself more with promoting legislation designed to give preference to Italian products, a measure that, although protective, would not likely find opposition among the membership.[124] Despite these conjunctural nationalist tendencies, the CIDI never made protection, in any form, part of its general program.

In contrast with the ad hoc measures noted above, the emergence of Alfredo Rocco as theoretician of the Nationalist movement in 1913–14 would mark the beginning of Nationalism as a distinctive, rigorously conceived doctrine based on (1) the total rejection of economic and political liberalism rooted in an "atomistic, cosmopolitan, and materialistic conception of the state"; (2) the promotion of a "national solidarity of producers" by means of juridically incorporating and "disciplining" syndicates within the state; and (3) a program of principled protection and military preparation for an imperialist foreign policy.[125] Like the LIT, Rocco stressed productivism and functionalism, though he linked these to corporatism, which, of course, the LIT had always condemned in favor of liberalism. Rocco fused the problem of production with Corradini's notion of Italy as a "proletarian nation." Not only must production be given preference over distribution, but production itself must be considered from the standpoint of Italy's struggle against exploitation by the "plutocratic nations," meaning protection of the domestic market and conquest of new colonial spheres.[126] In place of the Socialist concept of class struggle, Rocco substituted the concept of functionalism:

> The accusation that the Socialists make against the bourgeoisie, that of being a class inexorably separated from, if not an enemy of, the proletariat, is erroneous because the bourgeoisie is not a closed class, as was the nobility under the *ancien régime*. It is, more than a class, a social function to which all can be admitted and from which he who has been admitted can be removed. It is like an immense canal, open above and below.[127]

Less concerned, no doubt, with the doctrine's philosophical grounding, the state-supported industrial sector (steel, shipbuilding, armaments) fully recognized the utility of such concrete proposals as

---

[124] Ibid., p. 144.
[125] Franco Gaeta, *Nazionalismo italiano* (Naples: Edizioni Scientifiche Italiane, 1965), pp. 118–19.
[126] Alfredo Rocco, *Scritti e discorsi politici*, 3 vols. (Milan: Giuffre, 1938), 1: 14.
[127] Ibid., pp. 22–3.

principled protection and aggressive imperialism (especially if these could be tied to the patriotism aroused by the Libyan War) and of the anti-Socialism common to all "constitutionalist" forces during the troublesome 1913–14 period. These interests were scarcely represented within the CIDI, which was composed mainly of export-oriented manufacturers. Nothing in the CIDI's literature suggests any sympathy toward the Nationalist program. On the contrary, much of the program could be considered objectionable (e.g., its etatism, principled protectionism, corporatism, and imperialism). The CIDI had expressed little interest in the Libyan invasion, nor would it assume an interventionist position with respect to World War I. Italian industry in general, with the notable exception of the state-supported sector, had been traditionally opposed to colonial adventures, seeing in them a drainage of capital that otherwise might have been productively invested.

Nevertheless, the new president of the LIT, Dante Ferraris, would be instrumental not only in raising funds through which the Nationalist weekly *Idea Nazionale* was transformed into a daily but also in contributing to the Unione Nazionalista Torinese and actively supporting Bevione's candidacy in the 1914 special election.[128] Given the present state of documentation, it cannot be established to what extent LIT leadership concurred or differed with such action, other than noting that it was clearly at odds with the public position of both the organization and certainly its general secretary, Olivetti. League members were free to pursue their political interests outside the association's structure, and in this case it would appear that the Nationalism of Ferraris was connected more with his personal holdings than with his official position in the LIT. Indeed, in none of Ferraris's LIT-related speeches or articles can the slightest trace be found of political Nationalism. Aside from being a vice president of Fiat, Ferraris had extensive investments in the armaments sector[129] and, consequently, might have been more than willing to support the Nationalist program for obvious instrumental reasons.

After the outbreak of war, however, when military contracts were of interest to the automotive and machine-manufacturing sectors, whose civilian market had slackened, Fiat, as well as the *consorzio* of

---

[128] On Dante Ferraris see all works cited in this chapter by Valerio Castronovo.
[129] Castronovo, *Economia e società*, p. 334.

Turinese automakers, also contributed to Ferraris's *Idea Nazionale* fund (the contributions were actually made directly to the personal account of Ferraris, not to the journal). Ferraris abruptly terminated his affiliation with *Idea Nazionale* in October 1915, when the journal began to attack viciously the "German" Banca Commerciale, to which he and his associates were tied. By then, *Idea Nazionale* had entered into binding relations with the armament, shipbuilding, steel-producing giant Ansaldo (of which Alfredo Rocco became a share-holder and legal advisor) and its "Italian" Banca di Sconto (financed, in part, with French capital through the offices of the French govern-ment, eager to replace German economic influence in Italy, especially the potent Banca Commerciale).[130] Ansaldo, major backer of *Idea Nazionale* and, later, Mussolini's *Il Popolo d'Italia,* was never an active participant in either the prewar CIDI or the postwar Confin-dustria. By its repeated attacks upon the Banca Commerciale, to which the major share of Italian industry was directly or indirectly bound, Ansaldo had become somewhat of a pariah in the associated industrial community.

As for contributions to Mussolini's newspaper during the prewar period, there is an unconfirmed report by Filippo Naldi, former direc-tor of the journal *Il Resto del Carlino*, that in November 1914 a number of industrialists – Esterle (Edison), Agnelli (Fiat), Bruzzone (Unione Zuccheria), and Perone (Ansaldo) – paid some of the initial expenses. However, due to the divergent interests represented, as well as Mussolini's very credible revolutionary stature at the time, this contribution, if indeed it was made at all, has come to be interpreted as an attempt to exacerbate the divisions within the Socialist camp.[131]

During the ten months between the outbreak of the war and Italy's belated entry, the economy was subject to unprecedented strain. Few European nations were as dependent upon international trade as Italy, which lacked vital raw materials, investment capital, and a domestic market capable of absorbing its manufactured goods. The immediate disorientation of Italian industry was well recounted by Olivetti:

---

[130] E. Galli Della Loggia, "Problemi di sviluppo industriale e nuovi equilibri politici alla vigila della primo guerra mondiale: la fondazione della Banca Italiana di Sconto," *Rivista Storica Italiana* 82 (Dec. 1970): 833.
[131] Brunello Vigezzi, *L'Italia di fronte alla prima guerra mondiale* (Naples: Ricciardi, 1966), p. 949.

At the beginning of August a destructive wind blew upon our economy and enveloped everyone in one shot: producers, consumers, industrialists and workers, the government and governed. The decree of 4 August, that decree which broke all normal economic relations, not only foreign but also domestic, was perhaps least opportune. . . . In the early days of August, credit, the great current that carries the blood of economic life, ceased to function. The consumer, frightened by the danger of a catastrophe, closed himself off. The suppliers, also fearful of tomorrow, often refused to execute their contracts. International exchange was brought to an immediate and complete stop. How and for whom could one produce under such conditions? Factories closed and unemployment began to constitute a terrible spectre for the nation and the government.[132]

Within the belligerent countries, credit and exchange institutions could no longer function without government supervision; export prohibitions were placed on raw materials and combustibles; shipping and land transportation were subjected to military needs. In a matter of weeks after the outbreak of war, the price of coal in Italy tripled; coal and other raw materials had to be sought from more distant, neutral countries at higher cost and transportation charges (aside from outright seizure by belligerents of materials declared "contraband of war").[133]

Due to this change in the conditions of production during Italy's ten-month neutrality, the LIT's position of fundamental opposition to state intervention was greatly modified. "Italian industry cannot live without credit, cannot produce without raw materials, and cannot continue to produce if it is improbable that its product will be sold." Industry faced "problems so formidable" that "the work of an Association cannot be sufficient."[134] Only the state had the means to provide new sources of credit, to subsidize the purchase, transport, and allocation of raw materials, to negotiate directly with governments in a situation where previously privately negotiated trade was now processed by governmental agencies.

By now the solution to such problems is no longer even minimally within the possibility of private initiative. We are in a time when only state action can be effective. To the state we are now constrained to turn more often, asking it to at least put us in such a condition that our private initiative may usefully operate. In international commerce, private individuals no longer negotiate and contract, only governments. Even for Italy this is so, and for that reason

---

[132] *BLI* 9 (1915): 1; Abrate, *Lotta sindacale*, pp. 147–8.
[133] *BLI* 9 (1915): 1.
[134] Ibid., pp. 2–3; Abrate, *Lotta sindacale*, p. 149.

we must turn to the state as the guardian of our interests, hoping for vigilant and active direction, which, under the circumstances, only it can provide.[135]

LIT leadership, which previously had assumed no governmental role, was called to Rome for consultations with the Ministries of Agriculture, Industry, and Commerce; Finance; and Foreign Affairs. Thereafter, according to Mario Abrate, "action of the LIT was directed at the maintenance of continuous contact with governmental authorities, soliciting provisions, advising, and suggesting new directions for state action."[136] The major concern was not advocacy of Italy's actual intervention in the conflict but that in this difficult, war-related situation, industry continue to function. Cautious empiricists that they were, however, LIT leaders recognized the possibility of imminent intervention and thus advocated "preparation" so that Italy would not find itself ill prepared for combat. The industrial association publicly stated that it "has not, and ought not to, take a position between the various tendencies which agitate the nation at the present moment, but it cannot fail to concern itself with whatever possibility the future might have reserved for us."[137] It is true that "preparation" injected a new breath of life into Turin's depressed industries, as military contracts, both domestic and foreign, began to lift the city out of the desperate situation it had found itself in at the immediate outbreak of war. Yet, as Spriano observes, the Turinese industrialists showed little inclination to "pass from this level to the adventure of war."[138] Turin had been the most neutral of all Italy's major cities, the least receptive to the so-called *radioso maggismo* of the Nationalists.[139]

There can be no doubt as to the position of Olivetti, to whom the war was a "monstrous phenomenon," a "brutal destruction of men and riches," a flame which destroyed the liberal "world of yesterday," whose "vision of universal peace, emergent from the freedom of international commerce, seemed to unite nations in a solid network of ever tighter and less-soluble ties: a structure thus alive with light and full of promise." Olivetti fully shared the view of Einaudi, who saw in the war a potential for the collectivization of society and state

---

[135] *BLI* 9 (1915): 2–3.
[136] Abrate, *Lotta sindacale*, p. 150.
[137] *BLI* 9 (1915): 2–3.
[138] Spriano, *Torino operaia*, p. 299.
[139] Ibid., p. 299; Abrate, *Lotta sindacale*, pp. 151–3.

control over industry due, not to the "enactment of a prearranged plan on the part of a Communist legislator, but determined by the iron, yet at the same time disorderly, logic of state intervention to ensure equal sustenance to all."[140]

Much as Olivetti personally regretted the altered situation, he did not fail to recognize that a new political course for industry would have to be chartered. Given the incapacity of industry to advance its own interests without the help of the state and the greater economic role the state would necessarily play in a "mobilized economy," a condition of potential dependence developed such that industry could emerge either mastered or master. The original conception of the LIT – based on a neutral, noninterventionist state in which interests competed at the prepolitical level of civil society through associational self-defense – had already showed signs of inadequacy during the Giolitti years. Certainly now, in the war-imposed situation, the state could no longer be conceived of as an abstraction, a phantom, a force external to the vital interests of industry. In an otherwise innocuous book review in the LIT's bulletin, unfamiliar rhetoric appeared, such as "rising to the height of the state, identifying with it," as well as the suggestive claim that "to invoke the state is ridiculous when one has not the strength to conquer it."[141] Collaboration with the state could never take place in a vacuum. As the historian Mario Abrate perceptively noted: "From the viewpoint of the CIDI, a close collaboration with the state could not help but lead to the attempt, open or subterranean, to master it, insofar as a strict dependence upon the state, in the manner that political power was expressed in Giolittian or post-Giolittian democracy, was inconceivable in the long run and perhaps objectively impossible."[142]

The war thus led to a process of politicization that would lead eventually to direct associational participation in electoral activity and parliamentary politics. However, one must note that from 1915 to 1919 these forms of political life were largely eclipsed. The state, through its war-based "emergency powers," ruled by decree. Thus, the focal point of interest politics was no longer Parliament, now little more than a vestigial organ, but the state ministries, especially the Ministry of War with its Comitato di Mobilitazione Industriale. The

[140] Einaudi, *Condotta economica,* p. xxxix.
[141] *BLI* 9 (1915): 4.
[142] Abrate, *Lotta sindacale,* p. 153.

formative political experience of the *class industriale* would take place within the context of a "precorporatist" wartime state, not within a parliamentary, democratic arena. Although industrialists would derive major benefits from this new "administrative state" and would become habituated to the continuity of production which this state guaranteed, such experience ill prepared them for the intensified electoral battles and explosive labor unrest that would reemerge with the war's termination.

2. The First World War: a precorporatist experience

The transition to a "mobilized" institutional framework necessitated a basic restructuring in the relationship between the CIDI and the state. The CIDI believed itself faced with the choice of either overtly entering the political process and exerting its influence over the state or, by default, running the risk that industry might become the supine object of unmediated governmental control. Although the CIDI was instrumental in the very conception of the Central Committee of Industrial Mobilization, the state agency charged with economic coordination, the CIDI saw its influence gradually undercut by the burgeoning state bureaucracy, which progressively absorbed its associational functions and co-opted its membership while dispersing its leadership.[1] The CIDI and its affiliated organizations had been very much creatures of the liberal Giolittian era. Within the new mobilization context, they had seemingly lost their formative raison d'être: the state repressed syndical conflict, the state tutored individual industrial interests, and the state mediated between diverse sectors. Rather than domination of the state apparatus by the CIDI, the war mobilization led to an unanticipated regression to a preassociative, clientelistic phase similar to that preceding the Giolittian period, where lines of interest ran vertically from individual firms to the state, unmediated by any autonomous intersectoral body acting in the generic name of industry.

The general eclipse of associational activity during the war is reflected in the reduced scale and frequency of speeches and bulletins published by the CIDI and its member organizations, key sources for the hermeneutic approach which informs the other chapters of the present study. Given this lacuna, for the war years it is impossible to pursue an association-based textual analysis as the principal method. Instead, our attention will be directed toward those structural and institutional modifications characterizing wartime Italy and, more

---

[1] Abrate, *Lotta sindacale*, p. 205.

specifically, the effect these had upon productive relations. Further-more, we shall consider ideological responses to the changed social context (e.g., the corporatism of the Nationalists and the productiv-ism of Mussolini), ideologies specifically directed toward the enlist-ment of industrial support. Such an analysis should afford the reader some preliminary understanding of the industrialists' subsequent re-sponse to the crisis-laden period following the war, when the "precor-poratist" controls were lifted and they were once again, with a return to the liberal system, challenged at the productive and political levels. Furthermore, such an analysis will shed some light on the industrial-ists' initial reaction to corporatism as an alternative regime type to liberalism.

Treating the war as a "precorporatist" experience is admittedly novel, but existing political nomenclature is patently inadequate should one attempt to categorize the organizational basis of the war-time state. "Liberal" it certainly was not, if by that one envisions a regime whose political center is a popularly elected legislature, which guarantees basic political and syndical rights, and where the state neither formulates, regulates, nor coordinates economic activity but leaves it to the voluntaristic "free play of interests."[2] The term "inter-ventionist state" (in the sense of intervening both in the economy and in the war itself) is too vacuous to be of any analytic value, since it cannot specify either the scope or the modality of generically distinct forms of intervention. Nor is the unqualified term "corporatist" fully appropriate, if by that one envisions a regime informed by an antilib-eral ideological and juridical conception, whose civil society is hierar-chically organized and "framed" (*inquadramento*) within an all-inclusive system of unitary, compulsory, noncompetitive, and func-tionally differentiated associational bodies subordinated to state au-thority.[3]

Despite the absence of a fully articulated corporatist ideology and institutional framework, however, one can identify in the wartime state structural trends which prefigured, and historical experiences which preconditioned, subsequent corporatist development. This is

---

[2] For my distinction between liberal and corporatist organization I have drawn freely from the distinction made between pluralism and corporatism by Philippe Schmitter in "Still the Century of Corporatism?" *Review of Politics* 36 (Jan. 1974): 85–131.
[3] Ibid.

certainly not to suggest that "state corporatism"[4] was the only con-
ceivable outcome of the war, but merely that an alternative regime
form was "in the making," available for future appropriation and
development should the reconstituted liberal regime fail to adequately
resolve its own inherent weaknesses, much less deal with the manifold
conjunctural problems related to postwar reconstruction.

At the structural level, one might note that (*a*) the state formulated
and directed all essential economic activity through a nexus of functionally specific, employer–employee committees appointed and coordinated from above; (*b*) productive relations were "disciplined" at
the factory level by placing plants under military authority and by
juridically establishing a state-certified, occupational hierarchy and
compulsory chain of command whose violation was subject to specified military–penal sanctions (e.g., desertion and insubordination); no
form of syndical agitation was permitted, and all sources of conflict
were to be resolved by compulsory arbitration; (*c*) the public sphere
was fully subordinated to state authority, losing its independent status
as a mediator between the state and civil society (censorship was
rigorously applied, while the state attempted to mobilize public opinion directly).

As for historical preconditioning, one might bear in mind (*a*) the
precedent of dissolving political liberalism (i.e., the substitution of
executive for legislative power, the abrogation of constitutionally
guaranteed individual and associative liberties) under crisis conditions
in the name of "order" and "national unity" against foreign and
domestic "enemies"; (b) the belief, based upon the war mobilization,
that the state could "discipline" all of civil society and render nonantagonistic, through juridical reconstruction and institutional rearrangement, sources of social cleavage (class struggle, in particular),
and could "hierarchize" the social collectivity according to a presumed gradation of "competencies" and "capacities."

Although the term "precorporatism" was not used as such in contemporary discourse, and is treated here as a purely analytic construct, we shall see that determinate sets of actors not only were
conscious of a corporatist alternative (or, rather, competing corporat-

---

[4] Ibid. For my distinction between precorporatism and state corporatism I have drawn
freely from Schmitter's distinction between societal and state corporatism, except
that I am suggesting a definite historical sequence between the two types in Italy for
the period specified.

ist alternatives) arising immediately from the war experience but actively promoted such an outcome.

Italy's intervention: an authoritarian precedent

As is well known, Italy was not obligated to enter the war by treaty commitments or in response to military attack. After bargaining with both sides, it entered the conflict on the side of England and France, who promised greater territorial spoils with which the liberal–conservative government of Salandra might realize Italy's "sacred egoism." Knowing that the Giolittian parliamentary majority was opposed to intervention, as was "public opinion" (based on prefectoral reports specifically solicited on the subject of intervention before the Treaty of London was signed in late April 1915),[5] the government embarked upon what Salvemini termed a "pre-fascist *coup d'état*"[6] and what Richard Webster analyzed as the culmination of a post–red week (June 1914), conservative–Nationalist involution, definitively terminating the "Giolittian experiment" by resolving domestic contradictions through war:

A successful war, undertaken at just the right moment, could unseat Giolitti, give the conservative government authority and force to suppress the Reds, and open new horizons for Italian imperialism. It would lessen the role of parliament, while adding new lustre to the military traditions of the monarchy.[7]

"Radiant May" demonstrations were staged by the government and interventionist forces; the poet D'Annunzio was recruited from a hideout in southern France (where he sought refuge from his Italian creditors) to address mass rallies and revive sentiments of Italian heroism. According to Salvemini:

In May 1915, for the first time in Italian public life, the "anomaly" of pseudo-revolutionary manifestations was seen, favored – nay even prompted – by the men in power to force the hand of Parliament. In May 1915, Salandra and Sonnino and the "interventionist" groups carried out an active and proper *coup d'état* against the parliamentary majority. Italy had a dress

---

[5] Thayer, *Italy and the Great War*, pp. 307–12.
[6] Gaetano Salvemini, *The Origins of Fascism in Italy*, trans. Roberto Vivarelli (New York: Harper & Row, 1973), p. 108.
[7] Richard Webster, "From Insurrection to Intervention," *Italian Quarterly* 5 (1961–2): 62.

rehearsal of the other *coup d'état* which in October 1922 was to be the March on Rome.[8]

A mobilized economy and the adoption of antiliberal measures were in no sense peculiar to Italy. In varying degrees, all the belligerents so acted. The Great War, as it was called, was after all the first "total war," where the "home front" became an integral part of the military effort, where resources, production, labor, intellectuals, and public opinion were all mobilized.

This said, however, differences in the Italian case must be noted. Whereas in other Allied nations, parliaments maintained legislative authority (declaring war, enacting restrictions on civil liberties, appropriating state funds), in Italy parliamentary authority was undercut and such measures were enacted by executive fiat with little parliamentary or popular support.[9] As Salvemini observed: "The governments of France and England had entered the war with the unanimous, or almost unanimous consent of their peoples. Italy never experienced any *'union sacrée.'* "[10] After the neutralist parliamentary majority had been presented with a diplomatic fait accompli and had been verbally and even physically intimidated by Nationalist thugs (with official connivance), it voted to give the government full powers "in case of war."[11] Thereafter, the legislative body went into political hibernation, meeting less frequently and occupying itself largely with ceremonial matters. Parliament, according to Dennis Mack Smith, "was in fact of no great importance during the war, and government by decree was more extensively adopted than in other belligerent countries."[12] Though a salaried deputy, Giolitti did not bother to attend a parliamentary session until November 1917.[13] In his memoirs, he, too, noted that "the governing powers had in fact suppressed the action of the Italian Parliament in a way that had no parallel in other allied countries"; that "all discussions of the budget, all control over state expenses had been suppressed"; and that "Parliament was kept in the dark as to financial commitments."[14] Similarly, Giuliano Procacci ob-

[8] Salvemini, *Origins of Fascism*, pp. 107–8.
[9] Roberto Vivarelli, *Il dopoguerra in Italia e l'avvento del fascismo* (Naples: Istituto Italiano per Gli Studi Storici, 1967), p. 40.
[10] Salvemini, *Origins of Fascism*, p. 108.
[11] Mack Smith, *Italy*, pp. 296–305.
[12] Ibid., p. 308.
[13] Ibid.
[14] Procacci, *History of the Italian People*, p. 405.

serves that the state "went through a process of profound change," becoming "a more authoritarian state in which executive power systematically prevailed over the legislative." Ministers were even appointed by decree without the formal approval of Parliament.[15]

A second important difference between Italy and other combatants concerned the position of principled opposition to the war assumed by the Socialist Party (as well as the CGL and a majority of the revolutionary syndicalists). No French *union sacrée* or German *Burgfrieden* for them, they remained faithful to the cause of proletarian internationalism though their counterparts elsewhere became national patriots and voted for war credits. At the international congresses of Zimmerwald in 1915 and Kienthal in 1916, the Italian delegation was the only one representing an official Socialist Party and not a dissident faction. No less than Lenin, although critical of the reformist nature of the Italian party, praised it for not having committed a "similar deceit" to that of the opportunists, renegades, and pseudo-revolutionaries who supported the war.[16]

Besides the Socialists, the Catholics also opposed the war. Pope Benedict XV's characterization of the conflict as "useless carnage" received great publicity and was much deplored by the Allies.[17] In sum, the two popular movements, which after the war would overturn the amorphous and internally divided liberal parliamentary majority, had been alienated from and critical of the war effort.

Thus, although it is true that illiberal or even objectively authoritarian policies were also put into practice in other belligerent nations, such measures had generally been enacted by parliamentary norms, by parliamentary majorities, and with undeniable popular consent. These nations had, in a sense, freely willed their own wartime unfreedom. In Italy, however, not only were these measures objectively authoritarian but so too were the modus operandi and institutional framework; that is, against the parliamentary majority, in violation of parliamentary norms, and despite popular disapproval, executive power had committed the nation to the war and had erected an authoritarian state.

This is not to say that the "interventionists" were a homogeneous

[15] Ibid.; Procacci, "Appunti in tema di crisi dello Stato liberale e di origini del fascismo," *Studi Storici* 6 (Jan. 1965): 231–2.
[16] V. I. Lenin, *Sul movimento operaia italiano* (Rome: Riuniti, 1970), p. 13.
[17] Mack Smith, *Italy*, p. 311.

reactionary bloc whose constituent elements all supported Italy's entry into the conflict for similar reasons. There were dissident Socialists and revolutionary syndicalists who invoked the memory of the Commune or saw the war as a revolutionary opportunity. There were liberal–democrats who, for idealistic reasons, wanted to defend "the cause of freedom" against the invader of Belgium. Yet these remained subaltern elements under the hegemony of the conservative–Nationalist coalition, which initially had been oriented toward intervention on the side of their spiritual brothers, Austria and Germany, but whose practical imperialist aspirations were better served under terms offered by England and France. It was this conservative–Nationalist coalition which, in fact, had effected the coup from above. Left to their own resources and devices, the "Left" and liberal–democratic elements would never have been able "from below" to commit the nation to war, much less realize their idealistic or revolutionary aspirations.

Whereas the preponderance of scholarly study on the origins of Fascism concentrates on the multidimensional postwar crisis, it is our view that the intervention and formation of a wartime state, although not necessarily "predetermining" the outcome of that crisis, "preconditioned" the range of possible outcomes by creating an authoritarian precedent and offering an alternative regime type to the weakened and perhaps historically inadequate form of Italian liberalism after the war.

The parallels between the crisis-laden 1913–15 period and the still more chaotic 1919–22 period are striking, as are their respective authoritarian resolutions. The 1913–15 period witnessed intense class conflict that was not satisfactorily resolved within the liberal institutional framework. The capacity of the state to broker social compromises had collapsed. At the same time, respect for the rights of property and the maintenance of civil order had been put to the question. The weak governmental response to the factory occupations in northern industrial cities and to the "monopolistic" control by "red leagues" in rural communes, characteristic of the 1919–22 period, had obvious precedents in the 1913–15 period and had similarly led to a weakening of the Giolittian "experiment" and consequent proclivity toward an authoritarian solution. Had not Giolitti, who would later "permit" the factories to be occupied and "force" industrialists to accept the principle of "worker control," been the very same prime minister who told the LIT that Turinese factories would not be protected if it declared a general lockout and who compelled it to give in to workers' demands at the risk of seeing its leader Craponne summarily expatriated? Had not the breakdown of civil order experienced during the red week of 1914 evoked sentiments for a "strong state" and anti-Socialist "squadrist violence" (with official condonation) similar to those following the 1919–21 *biennio rosso*?

Similarly, the postwar mobilization of property owners and local Fascists in the red belt of Emilia–Romagna against Socialist-dominated local governments and red leagues had roots in the 1913–15 period. After the introduction of universal male suffrage in 1912, the province of Bologna was effectively in Socialist hands: six out of eight provincial *collegi,* two-thirds of the *comuni* (municipalities).[18] In an attempt to break the "labor monopoly" of the red league of Molinella during the fall of 1914, property owners and their "recruits" pitted themselves in open battle against the league, leaving five dead and many wounded. The conservative and Nationalist press seized upon the *fatti di Molinella,* blaming Giolitti for having "depressed the bourgeois army and armed the army of the so-called proletariat."[19]

Moving from considerations of class conflict to politics, during the 1913–15 period a process of fragmentation similar to that which occurred during the postwar period was taking place. Just as he would do in the summer of 1921, Giolitti, unable to dominate the heterogeneous parliamentary majority which he himself had alchemized into an electoral bloc, voluntarily took one of his famous "political vacations," leaving the liberal–democratic forces divided and leaderless in the face of a minoritarian "opening to the Right." The Socialists in both periods had achieved significant and "threatening" electoral gains at the local and national levels; at the same time, however, they were racked with immobilizing schisms, unable to speak with one mind and impose the full measure of their electoral weight. As during 1921–2, when the party split first to the Left (with the Communists leaving to form an autonomous party) and then to the Right (with minimalists splitting from maximalists, and the CGL declaring itself independent from each splinter party), so too in 1912,

---

[18] Vegezzi, *L'Italia di fronte alla prima guerra,* pp. 42–3.
[19] Ibid., p. 964.

when the previously dominant reformists were expelled from the Socialist Party and the revolutionary syndicalists left the CGL to form their own national confederation. Italy's major political forces – liberals, Socialists, and, to some degree, Catholics – had become internally fragmented and mutually antagonistic. This led to a situation in which the liberal political system lost its capacity for mediation and integration, a stasis of the parliamentary process, and a resultant opening to the Right in the 1913–15 period as interventionism and in the 1919–22 period as Fascism. Thus, these extraparliamentary, authoritarian outcomes might be viewed as attempts to resolve from above determinate sets of contradictions broadly associated with the perpetuation of bourgeois rule within a context of heightened class conflict and eclipsed liberal hegemony: the lack of an affirmative, universal ideology with which to generate consensus; the breakdown of traditional linkages between the representatives and the represented; decreased capacity to both preempt mass demands and extract distributional rewards; parliamentary immobility and public policy stasis; a breakdown of civil order; production discontinuities; threats to private-property prerogatives.

Yet if, as has been suggested, both authoritarian outcomes were related to the problem of maintaining bourgeois rule under crisis conditions, one would want to examine very carefully precisely which bourgeois interests self-consciously backed these initiatives. In a suggestive essay on the crisis of the liberal state and the origins of Fascism, Procacci sees in the intervention and Fascism the reconstitution of a *blocco di potere di tipo prussiano* that had originally formed during the 1880s but had been replaced under Giolitti by a new, unstable power bloc based on a social compromise between the workers' movement and the *borghesia produttiva*.[20] Unfortunately, Procacci never fully specifies what he means by, or who he includes within, this "Prussian power bloc," although presumably he was influenced by Gramsci's analysis of the industrial–agricultural protectionist bloc formed during the Crispi era, as well as by Marx and Engels's earlier writings on the Bismarckian industrialist–Junker coalition. Procacci's ambiguity is unfortunate, as divergent industrial interests, or even the same interests in different developmental stages, could be subsumed under either the "Prussian" or "Giolittian" con-

---

[20] Procacci, "Appunti in tema di crisi dello Stato liberale," pp. 221–37.

figurations. In any event, Procacci at one point admits that the intervention could not be understood as the result of pressure exerted generically by the industrial class, noting the strident interventionist attack against the so-called *germanofili* firms associated with the "German" Banca Commerciale.[21]

Procacci's analysis, however, is helpful precisely because it does not crudely reduce the intervention to the naked class interest of the industrialists but rather focuses attention on the intervention as a profound transformation of political alliances and state forms. As we have seen, there were accumulated resentments against the Giolitti experiment by both industrialists and landowners. Furthermore, after the red week and spectacular civil unrest of 1914, the middle classes, whose patriotic sentiments had been aroused by the Libyan invasion and by Nationalist propaganda, were mobilized (as we saw in Turin) for the "defense of public order."

However, there is quite an inferential leap, all the more striking in the absence of group-specific historical treatment, between disaffection from the Giolittian experiment and, as Procacci would suggest, purposive, calculated, and self-conscious support for a manifestly authoritarian regime, *di tipo prussiano* or any other. Certainly disaffection from Giolitti and heightened concern for civil order among a broad spectrum of disaggregated bourgeois and petit-bourgeois groups were, in retrospect, conducive to an authoritarian initiative. This is not to say, however, that *at the time* these groups subjectively perceived the situation in such terms or that they inclusively played an active role in, desired, or even supported the particular authoritarian coup that did take place.

Rather than having resorted to a somewhat dubious allusion to Prussian-like forces, Procacci might have expanded upon his far more suggestive discussion of the contradictions and inherent weaknesses of the liberal–democratic regime symbolized in the very person of Giolitti, a leader who by 1914 had exhausted his capacity for transformist acrobatics, becoming an object of intense political ridicule on the Left as well as the Right. By 1914, both Giolitti and his regime no longer had a base in the country (as opposed to Parliament), indicating that the sharp analytic divide between his and a "reconstituted" power bloc, in fact, was blurred historically by an intervening phase

[21] Ibid., p. 229.

of political degeneration and uncertainty. In short, by 1914 there was no real and perceived choice between two competing options (one liberal–democratic, the other authoritarian) upon which determinate groups purposively acted. Rather, a conservative trend common to all components of the bourgeoisie and petite bourgeoisie developed in reaction to the felt inadequacies of the Giolittian regime, a trend reflected in the Salandra government's *politica nazionale*. Yet, even here, a further distinction must be made between this broadly based conservative drift regarding essentially domestic policy and generalized support for an interventionist foreign policy. No such commonality of view was to be found regarding the intervention, nor were there generalized perceptions on the part of these actors that the intervention constituted an instrumental means of resolving domestic conflict.

If the intervention is properly seen as an authoritarian coup, then it was a coup conceived, initiated, and directed by executive power. It is here that the intervention must be distinguished sharply from Fascism, since Fascism, despite official connivance, emerged as a truly autonomous force with a distinctive mass base.

In March 1914, Giolitti, unable to dominate his heterogeneous and rapidly disintegrating majority, resigned as prime minister and advised the king to appoint Salandra. Salandra possessed neither his own parliamentary majority nor manifest popular support, for new elections were not held. His relations with Parliament were strained, particularly after the repressive measures he introduced in the wake of red week, yet his survival was dependent upon unenthusiastic and eroding support from Giolitti's majority. Had it not been for the intervention, used by Salandra as a deliberate means for maintaining political power and redirecting domestic and foreign policy, the new government – as Giolitti fully expected – would have been short-lived.[22]

After the Battle of the Marne and news of Russian victories in the Carpathians, Salandra and his foreign minister Sonnino believed that a quick Entente victory was in sight. Accordingly, in April, after satisfactory territorial concessions were made, the government signed the Treaty of London, committing Italy to fight by the end of May. During the course of negotiations, the government was not in consultation with Parliament or with extraparliamentary political and eco-

---

[22] Thayer, *Italy and the Great War*, p. 320.

nomic groups; single-handedly, it decided upon intervention. Such a quick operation could both ensure public order and silence the Socialists while rendering the executive independent from an internally divided and hostile parliamentary majority. Territorial acquisitions would further add to executive prestige at the expense of the "neutralist" and "renunciationist" legislature.

This is not to say that the executive coup took place in a vacuum, oblivious to pressure on public opinion exerted directly by the interventionist press and indirectly by particular industrial groups that stood to profit from war production. Yet these, as well as liberal–democratic, Socialist, and revolutionary-syndicalist interventionist elements, never constituted an actual conspiratorial entity in their own right. At best, they effectively served as vehicles to marshal popular support after the decision to intervene already had been made by the executive, when the neutralist Parliament had to be intimidated into submission through officially choreographed Radiant May demonstrations.

In the previous chapter, we observed that although specific sectoral interests were interventionist as a matter of self-interest, the CIDI took no such position. Instead, it advocated "economic preparedness" for whatever decision might be taken. Rather than seeing in the intervention an opportunity to resolve domestic problems, a view that certainly was at odds with the stated position of Gino Olivetti, the CIDI saw in the intervention process a total disregard for the "preparedness" they had invoked. No mobilization plan had been formulated, and no preparatory study of existing credit, raw materials, and transportation facilities had been made. In negotiating the Treaty of London, the government had requested financial assistance from the Allies for only several months and had not even asked for special help with vital raw materials. Having called Nitti a pessimist for thinking that the war might last beyond the winter of 1915, Salandra brazenly committed Italy to a war that would cost the state twice the sum of all governmental expenditures from 1861 to 1913.[23] The CIDI accepted the intervention as a fait accompli; without any pseudoheroic references to Radiant May, it offered its technical expertise to the war effort.[24]

[23] Mack Smith, *Italy*, pp. 307–13.
[24] *BLI* 9 (1915): 5.

Generally speaking, it is true that the CIDI had grown increasingly estranged from Giolitti, based on its perception of his disregard for the "objective necessities" of rapid industrialization (productivism), his deviation from classic liberalism (public–private, state–civil society distinctions), and the opportunistic violation of his own, self-stated syndical policy. As an organization, the CIDI had attacked Giolitti for his high-handedness during the 1913 automobile strike and his nationalization of life insurance. Individual members of the CIDI were sufficiently shocked by the 1913 Socialist electoral gains, the red week, and the increase in violent class conflict – which they, rightly or wrongly, along with the bourgeois bloc in general, attributed to Giolitti's policies – to support liberal–nationalist electoral coalitions against the Socialists in local elections. One might even say that the CIDI, in some sense, was swept up – though certainly was not the advance guard – in the previously described 1913–15 conservative drift.

And yet, despite all this, the CIDI indicated no manifest support or sympathy for Salandra and Sonnino, the presumed "authoritarian alternative" to Giolitti; nor is there anything in its literature indicating a willingness to go beyond a generalized state of disenchantment with liberal parliamentary government toward the pursuit of any specifically authoritarian course.

The industrial mobilization

Despite the fact that Italy actually entered the war nine months after the conflict had already begun, no general plan or specific vehicle for industrial coordination had been established by the state. In his famous study of the war economy, Einaudi noted that in Italy no comprehensive schema for industrial mobilization had been developed (as in Germany), nor were ad hoc measures (as in England and France) quickly put into effect.[25] Yet from the outbreak of hostilities in August 1914, the CIDI had been one of the more active consultative bodies to be found in Rome. Even before Italy's entry into the

---

[25] Einaudi, *Condotta economica*, p. 62. See also a special double issue of *Italia Contemporania* devoted to the Italian economy during the First World War: no. 146/147 (June 1982). On Germany, see Gerald Feldman, *Army, Industry, and Labor in Germany: 1914–18* (Princeton: Princeton University Press, 1966).

war (May 1915), the CIDI had established a permanent consultative committee within the Ministry of Agriculture, Industry, and Commerce to advise the government on questions relating to industry and the "organization of national production."[26] In addition to assuming a more "official" role vis-à-vis the state, with Italy's actual intervention in the conflict the CIDI began to assume a more authoritative posture with respect to members firms, issuing directives on their national responsibility in matters concerning production and employment. For example, member firms were instructed, in case of a productive diminution, to avoid laying off workers by reducing working hours and increasing shifts; in case of a productive upturn, members were to hire new workers rather than augment working hours, giving preference to families of drafted workers.[27]

Olivetti immediately devoted himself to the study of industrial mobilization, recognizing – as did such diverse observers as Lenin and Lysis (Ernest Letailleur) – the technical superiority of the highly rationalized German model.[28] Though an economic liberal by faith, Olivetti was led to believe that the war presented an exceptional situation wherein production would have to be centrally coordinated and individual entrepreneurial prerogatives sacrificed, even "if we had been the first to sustain that in normal times industrial freedom should be left full and complete, because under the stimulus of competition productive progress can be refined and rendered more efficient." Strikes would have to be prohibited and compulsory arbitration imposed, since productive relations "were no longer so much between workers and industrialists, as between workers, industrialists, and the state," and also since the "function of industry" had become in war a "public function," subject to centralized public regulation.[29]

Though Olivetti recognized the necessity for "rationalized planning" and the "public" coordination of industry, he lost none of his characteristic skepticism regarding the competence of the state bureaucracy to initiate and administer policy effectively in its own sphere, much less assume a directive role over industry. It should be underscored, therefore, that for Olivetti "public" and the "state" were not coterminous; though coordinating bodies, or mobilization

[26] Abrate, *Lotta sindacale*, p. 160.
[27] Ibid.; *BLI* 9 (1915): 5.
[28] Abrate, *Lotta sindacale*, p. 33. On Olivetti's analysis of the German mobilization see *BLI* 9 (1915): 6–7.
[29] Abrate, *Lotta sindacale*, p. 161.

committees, would assume a juridically specified, public function, they were to be composed of nonstate personnel and operate beyond the boundaries and norms of the traditional state apparatus. De jure, any "public" entity ultimately would be invested with and accountable to state authority; de facto, what Olivetti had in mind was a functional division of competence between the state (here represented by the military) and "public" mobilization committees. The former would determine military strategy and war-related needs; the latter would initiate and coordinate productive policy aimed at satisfying such needs. Thus, while central and regional mobilization committees were to be formally subjected to military jurisdiction, in fact they were to be autonomous loci of productive authority. What this meant, in essence, was a form of private industrial self-regulation endowed with publicly sanctioned compulsive power. Naturally – or so it was thought – the CIDI would assume a central role in this project, being the only interregional and intersectoral industrial association and, by now, a valued ministerial consultant.

With the decrees of 22 August and 26 September 1915, a central mobilization committee based in Rome and seven regional committees were created. Not surprisingly, they were modeled on Olivetti's suggestions, and the CIDI expressed its "ardent satisfaction" that its recommendations had been accepted.[30] Although these committees were supposed to be composed of equal tripartite representation (civil, industrial, labor), industrialists were often selected also as civil representatives, allowing them to dominate the new organisms. Of the five civil (as opposed to industrial) representatives on the Piemontese regional committee, for example, four were closely identified with the LIT (Gino Olivetti, Emilio De Benedetti, Giuseppe Garbagnati, and Enrico Bonelli).[31]

This mobilization structure was charged with four essential tasks: (1) coordinating industrial production with military needs; (2) determining what factories were to be declared "auxiliaried"; (3) resolving syndical controversies; and (4) authorizing resignations, firings, and transfers of personnel from one firm to another.[32] As for indus-

[30] "Problemi industriale di guerra," presidential address to the LIT general assembly, 16 May 1916, complete text at HAUIT
[31] Abrate, Lotta sindacale, p. 163.
[32] On the functions of the mobilization committees see Abrate, Lotta sindacale, pp. 162–3; Alberto Caracciolo, "La grande industria nella prima guerra mondiale," in A. Caracciolo, ed., La formazione dell'Italia industriale (Bari: Laterza, 1971), p. 176.

trial coordination, the preexisting network of private industrial associations served, at the outset, as a ready-made, "deputized" form. Sectoral associations were authorized to allocate governmental orders among their member firms (usually proportionate to plant size).[33] Intersectoral associations, like the LIT, served as distributors of raw materials and were authorized to process export licenses as well.[34] With the unanticipated long duration of the war, however, a major structural transformation would take place. The privately based, "public" structure, fruit of the CIDI's initial influence and the state bureaucracy's initial unpreparedness, eventually was encapsulated within, and thus displaced by, a proliferation of newly created entities and hierarchies generated by the state bureaucracy, such that direction no longer emanated from industrial associations, but rather from ministerial command posts.

Before examining the CIDI's response to this structural transformation, a description of war production itself is necessary. Under the abovementioned decrees, mobilization committees could declare "auxiliaried" any private factory that, by virtue of its product or plant, might contribute directly to the production of war material. In such cases, all factory personnel (owners, managers, supervisors, and workers) passed under military jurisdiction, and the existing factory hierarchy was reinforced with coercive public power through the introduction of military codes of discipline and penal sanctions. Should industrialists have refused to cooperate, their factories would have been requisitioned. However, the advantages associated with being auxiliaried made recourse to such drastic action unnecessary; indeed, many requests for auxiliaried status had to be rejected (230 in Turin alone). In the first place, factory discipline, hitherto a contentious subject, was rigorously enforced; strikes and agitations were prohibited, workers could not voluntarily refuse to obey orders or leave their posts for any reason, questions of salary and working conditions were removed from negotiation at the factory level and arbitrated by industrialist-dominated mobilization committees. Stiff military punishment, ranging from immediate transfer to the front to prolonged incarceration, was applied to insubordinate workers. Armed troops were stationed within and outside factory gates; covert

---

[33] Einaudi, *La condotta economica*, p. 174.
[34] Abrate, *Lotta sindacale*, pp. 165–70.

"secret agents" and labor spies were employed to weed out "subversives." Absenteeism quickly dropped from 8.4 to 4.9 percent. Second, significant economic advantages were associated with auxiliaried status: preferential treatment was afforded in the allocation of scarce raw materials, in the provision of credit and advances for procurement orders, and in access to transportation and communication facilities. Furthermore, the workforce of auxiliaried factories was exempted from military service, guaranteeing occupational stability and limited turnover.[35]

The most immediate consequence of the mobilization was a pronounced and "pushed" speculative attitude which pervaded Italian industry. Einaudi observed that the war did not abolish the entrepreneurial desire for profit, it merely rendered profit independent from cost.[36] As the parliamentary commission that would later study the war economy noted, little official attention was given to the proprieties of bookkeeping or rigorous in-plant supervision of auxiliaried factories. It was deemed repugnant by the responsible officials to "impose direct accounting and technical controls upon private industry on matters pertaining to the inspection of its technical functioning and above all on the effective cost of its products." Such officials wished to "avoid interference which might disturb the freedom of industrialists in the technical functioning and accounting of their firms . . . in the hope that maximum production might be thus attained, and of directing the entire industrial organism toward solving the problem of armament, with the purpose of attaining the maximum effect with means which were indubitably scarce at the outset."[37]

This remarkable respect for private initiative was less the arbitrary whim of minor officials, easily corruptible, than explicit ministerial policy established by General Dallolio:

With the powers conferred upon it, the government might then have assumed the administration and technical direction of the factory, substituting itself for the industrialist. Now, there is no need to delude oneself. Because it must follow state accounting laws and because of its inevitable bureaucratic

---

[35] On auxiliaried factories see Castronovo, *Agnelli,* pp. 111–14; Clough, *Economic History,* pp. 184–5; Einaudi, *Condotta economica,* pp. 102–13; Pietro Grifone, *Il capitale finanziario in Italia* (Turin: Einaudi, 1971), pp. 22–43.

[36] Einaudi, *Condotta economica,* p. 60.

[37] Ibid., p. 63.

functioning, the government is fatally a slower and perhaps even a less efficient industrialist than private individuals, such that in its hands production, rather than increase, probably would diminish and be more costly. There would thus result, in the early period, a consequence diametrically opposed to that desired.

The general instructed his staff, military and civilian, to grant industrialists complete freedom of action over production and to concentrate instead on formulating military needs.[38]

Despite the "militarization" of factories, with its sharp limitations on civil liberties, General Dallolio was aware that violent worker reaction was always a distinct possibility. Both the Socialist Party and the CGL had opposed the war and were ill disposed toward voluntarily accepting the new productive order, especially the denial of their full political and syndical rights. Hence, the general promoted a number of preemptive social-reform measures (hygienic services, compulsory accident insurance, pensions) in auxiliaried factories and encouraged industrialists to be conciliatory in granting salary increases, lest "latent worker movements be transformed into regrettable and dangerous agitations."[39] In short, the general felt that repression alone could not ensure social peace; some concessions would have to be granted.

The extent of such concessions, however, was limited by the political isolation of the workers' leadership. Parliament, where Socialists carried some weight, was eclipsed; the mobilization structure and restrictions on political and syndical liberties all had been effected by executive decree. Because they had opposed, and continued to oppose, the war on principle, Socialist and CGL leaders were precluded from occupying cabinet or high administrative offices, which their counterparts enjoyed in France (the French Socialist Party sent Jules Guesde and two other leaders into the cabinet; Leon Jouhaux, general secretary of the CGT, became a "commissar of the nation").[40] Unlike German trade unions, which used support for the war effort to increase their organizational significance, baldly extracting political (suffrage reform) and syndical (union recognition, collective bargaining) concessions,[41] the Italians sought only to conserve those gains that had previously been obtained.

[38] Ibid., pp. 102–4.
[39] Abrate, *Lotta sindacale*, p. 191.
[40] Val Lorwin, *The French Labor Movement* (Cambridge: Harvard University Press, 1954), pp. 47–9.
[41] Feldman, *Army, Industry, and Labor in Germany*, p. 207.

Whereas in France and Germany workers had gained the right, under their respective mobilization programs, to legally recognized representation within the factory (in the face of strong opposition by industrialists),[42] in Italy no such action was taken and industrialists enjoyed unlimited managerial authority. True, the *commissione interna* was tolerated in those sectors where it had been adopted before the war, yet these bodies led a difficult existence and had no impact on the militarized plant hierarchy and no autonomous input into the regional mobilization committees.[43]

Distinguishing, in principle, support for the war from defending the material condition of the working class, the CGL and its constituent federations did send representatives to serve on the central and regional mobilization committees. Yet that very public distinction, as well as the inequitable composition of these bodies, meant that syndical representatives would always negotiate from a position of relative weakness.

Nevertheless, it should be noted that the industrialists chose not to take full advantage of their relative strength and to rely solely on the coercive power of the state to discipline workers into compliance with their directives. Olivetti had not broken with the private, conciliatory syndical practice of the prewar period; he was keenly aware that labor relations in the postwar period, when disciplinary controls would be lifted, might be greatly conditioned by the attitude assumed by industrialists during the mobilization.

In Turin, despite the fact that the LIT dominated the regional mobilization committee, industrialists elected not to use this body as an instrument of class control. The LIT specifically requested that labor representatives be freely chosen from those syndicates that had represented workers in negotiations during the prewar period (in particular, FIOM). During the first year of the war, not one order concerning labor conflict had to be issued from the regional committee. All significant conflicts and contract negotiations were dealt with privately, outside the compulsive mobilization framework, even the important renewal of the contentious automobile contract, which gave workers salary increases of 50–75 percent, established the principle of "minimum salaries" and supplements for overtime, night work, and holiday hours, and even provided that the *consorzio* would

---

[42] D. W. Brogan, *The Development of Modern France* (New York: Harper, 1940), p. 531.
[43] Spriano, *Torino operaia*, pp. 469–71.

pay 1,000 lire weekly to FIOM for distribution to the families of workers under arms.[44] Olivetti counseled industrialists to concede all that was possible in the hope of avoiding any resort to compulsory arbitration, a practice that he disapproved of in principle and feared might be continued, if extensively used, later when the war was over. He also believed that a conciliatory attitude, and generous salary concessions, might of course contribute to the maintenance of public order and the continuity of production.[45]

It should not be forgotten, however, that during the wartime productive boom, salary concessions – so seemingly generous – were rarely commensurate with corporate earnings, and the rate of profit in key sectors rose to unprecedented levels. Given such profit margins, salary concessions were a relatively small price to pay for intensified productive rhythm and increased output. Numerous observers have dispelled the myth of widespread worker enrichment during the war.[46] While it is true that some highly privileged categories (e.g., autoworkers) significantly improved their material situations, average real wages actually declined from an index of 100 in 1913 to 64.4 in 1918, although nominal wages increased from 100 to 170.6. In all but a few cases, salary increases never succeeded in keeping pace with the increase in the cost of living (which rose from an index of 100 in 1913 to 264.1 in 1918).[47]

Another indication of the CIDI's conciliatory attitude was its position on social legislation. It will be remembered that in the prewar period the CIDI consistently had been critical of attempts to extend the scope of such legislation, arguing it would siphon off necessary investment capital and undermine individual responsibility and parsimony in the worker. Partially in response to incongruities resulting from compulsory social insurance instituted in auxiliaried factories and voluntary programs available in the others, and partially in an attempt to preempt demands that might be advanced by workers' syndicates in the postwar period (when their full political weight might be brought to bear), the CIDI in July 1917 called for a complete system of social insurance based on a triple contribution by industrialists, workers, and the state.[48]

---

[44] Abrate, *Lotta sindacale*, pp. 176–7; Spriano, *Torino operaia*, pp. 348–9.
[45] Abrate, *Lotta sindacale*, pp. 178–80.
[46] Einaudi, *Condotta economica*, pp. 118–19; Spriano, *Torino operaia*, pp. 376–91.
[47] Cesare Vannutelli, "Occupazione e salari," in *L'economia italiana dal 1861 al 1961* (Milan: Giuffre, 1961), p. 570.
[48] Abrate, *Lotta sindacale*, pp. 171–6.

Most revealing of the CIDI's moderation, especially in light of the "reactionary" attitude toward labor Italian industrialists allegedly harbored, was its position during and after the worker uprising that took place in Turin during August 1917. Objective factors leading to mass discontent included a general fall in real wages, food shortages, and price increases. The critical subjective factor, however, was the February Revolution in Russia and a wellspring of mass sympathy for Lenin in his subsequent struggle against the Kerensky government.[49] The prefect of Turin transmitted the following flier to Rome as representative of the growing mood:

Comrades, our comrades in Russia, in an admirable example of proletarian force are carrying out the work of justice. If all other peoples would do likewise, war would cease. Let us imitate them, comrades. Proletarian soldiers, when they tell you that the proletariat hates you, give them the lie. What we are doing is for the common good. Follow the example of your Russian comrades. Don't be parricides. Unite with us in the cause of peace and freedom.[50]

When, in August, an official Menshevik delegation that had been touring Allied nations promoting Kerensky's program arrived in Turin, they were greeted with cries of "Viva Lenin!"

The spark that ignited the powder keg though was a critical shortage of grain, forcing the city's bakeries to close. Workers spontaneously refused to enter the factories, shouting: "We haven't eaten. We can't work. We want bread!" This led to the sacking of stores, the erection of barricades in the streets, bloody clashes with police and soldiers, and finally to the loss of fifty lives with hundreds more wounded; in all, one of the most dramatic and violent clashes in Italian labor history. Widespread arrests of Socialists and anarchists took place, and 177 exempted workers immediately were sent to the front. The alleged "leaders" of the uprising were tried before a military court a year later.

While local authorities, the prefect in particular, had been requesting additional security forces since March, demanding that Turin be declared a "war zone," the LIT instead had been requesting increased state assistance to workers to relieve the mounting pres-

[49] On the August 1917 uprising in Turin see John Cammett, *Antonio Gramsci and the Origins of Italian Communism* (Stanford: Stanford University Press, 1969), pp. 44–62; Einaudi, *Condotta economica*, pp. 114–15; Spriano, *Torino operaia*, pp. 393–431.
[50] Cammett, *Antonio Gramsci*, p. 51.

sure.[51] Both before and after the uprising, the CIDI refused to identify itself with the manifestly repressive position assumed by the prefect, who referred to the incident only as an "unfortunate episode." Olivetti went so far as to deliver a deposition at the trial of the uprising's leaders supportive of their acquittal, emphasizing such causative factors as war-related hardships and particularly food shortages.[52]

From what has been said concerning the practice of industrialists during the mobilization, a paradox immediately becomes apparent: on the one hand, the CIDI itself had initially conceived the mobilization structure, which was, so to speak, its idea; on the other, the industrial association was curiously hesitant in trying to take it over. No clear explanation for this is to be found in the association's publications or internal communications. Lacking this, the only logical interpretation, and one indirectly supported by the documents, would be based on a residual liberal antipathy felt by the CIDI leaders toward coercive and collectivized economic control and would emphasize the CIDI leaders' suspicion that during the war such control would not lead to optimal utilization of resources and productive facilities and their fear that after the war such control, if institutionally extensive, might continue. Moreover, these forms of state intervention would be especially threatening in the postwar period, when political and syndical restraints on the working class would be lifted, for then workers might bring their political influence directly to bear on those inroads the state had carved for itself within the private sector, politicizing production and thereby undermining individual initiative and managerial authority. Whatever the reason for its hesitation in attempting to master the mobilization structure, the consequences of not doing so were doubly detrimental for the CIDI and for Italian industry in general. First, it provided the state bureaucracy with an open opportunity to engulf the mobilization structure in its own right, progressively reducing it to a passive administrative conduit for policy decisions made at the ministerial and subministerial levels. Second, it undercut the CIDI's intersectoral functions of mediating and aggregating divergent interests. Such interests, in the absence of a CIDI-dominated mobilization structure, separately sought direct clientelistic relations with the expanding state bureaucracy.

[51] Spriano, *Torino operaia*, p. 405.
[52] Abrate, *Lotta sindacale*, p. 180; Spriano, *Torino operaia*, pp. 435–6.

The result was beneficial neither for the CIDI nor for state development. The CIDI and its constituent associations were no longer vital institutional foci: their key functions were appropriated or rendered superfluous by the mobilization structure, and their leadership was dispersed and co-opted within the growing maze of specialized bureaucratic entities. Unlike the United States, where the less statist, more self-regulatory mobilization apparatus actually encouraged the growth of trade associations,[53] in Italy the mobilization structure discouraged such growth. No longer fearing class antagonists, either in the syndical or political arenas, individual and progressively atomized industrialists manifested little collective consciousness. It is interesting that references to the *classe industriale* or to an "industrial interest" generically distinct from other classes and interests are not to be found, or rarely, in industrial literature of the period. Hence, it is not surprising that associations which would have reflected such concerns seemed to have lost their salience, as lines of political influence ran directly from individual firms to various parts of the state apparatus, unmediated by any private collective agency acting in the name of industry.

The state, though vastly inflated in quantitative terms, was hardly "strong" qualitatively, if by that one means the capacity to conceive and impose an internally consistent, unitary direction upon national life, subordinating private interests to the public interest.[54] An amorphous web of overlapping jurisdictions developed, each jealous of its separate authority and prerogatives. Einaudi notes that there was little coordination between diverse administrations of the state, even subsections of the same ministry.[55] Procacci speaks of an uncoordinated series of "fiefs" and "water-tight compartments," recalling Gramsci's description of "autocrats multiplying by spontaneous generation," each "doing, undoing, knitting, destroying."[56]

It was only after this imposing, state-dominated mobilization structure gradually showed itself so dysfunctional and irrational in its totality, so incapable of providing a coherent, responsive, and predictable direction to the general economy, that its constituent parts began

[53] Grant McConnell, *Private Power and Public Interest* (New York: Random House, 1970), pp. 60–3.
[54] Procacci, "Appunti in tema di crisi dello Stato liberale," p. 233.
[55] Einaudi, *Condotta economica*, p. 128.
[56] Procacci, *History of the Italian People*, p. 406.

to appear less as opportune vehicles for state favors and largess than as counterproductive bureaucratic impediments, making rational calculations impossible and frequent trips to Rome, wandering from agency to agency, a much-lamented necessity for industrialists.[57] By the end of the war, a general antipathy toward the *bardatura di guerra* (war-imposed constraints) was characteristic of a broad spectrum of industrialists, who invoked quite explicitly the rapid return to a "free economy." The only conspicuous exception to this position, predictably enough, was the state-dependent sector.

The CIDI reacted bitterly against the progressive bureaucratization of the central and regional mobilization committees, structures they had originally intended as agile and efficient organs of self-regulation, free from superfluous layers of administrative fat and relatively autonomous from the existing state apparatus:

That organism which had been conceived according to practical criteria of speed and equity slowly became transformed into a bureaucratic body in which the reign of the circular, the regulation, and the service warrant came to dominate that which should have been the guiding principle of the mobilization committee: practical good sense in applying necessarily generic directives imparted from the center, rapid adaptability to the industrial necessities of the place and the moment.[58]

The CIDI was alarmed by the continuous proliferation of new administrative bodies and competing hierarchies, which, on the one hand, locked the mobilization committees securely within the state apparatus and, on the other, sapped the committees of their vital functions. According to Mario Abrate:

The regional committees were loaded down with congeries of regulations which, little by little, deprived them of executive functions, that is, active powers attributed to them, reducing them to "a new source of bureaucratic formality, ill-adapted to follow the swift rhythm, the nimbleness, and the necessities of industry." Too many were the cases where the committees were obliged to limit themselves to obeying or referring "to higher authorities." What had been conceived of as almost industrial organisms, propellers and coordinators of productive energy, had become the "simple administrative service of a ministry for whom only one task was reserved, that of discussing economic questions."[59]

---

[57] Einaudi, *Condotta economica,* p. 234.
[58] Abrate, *Lotta sindacale,* p. 167; *BLI* 11 (1917): 1.
[59] Abrate, *Lotta sindacale,* p. 167.

The related phenomena of irrational bureaucratic growth and technical incompetence were prevalent themes in the industrialist literature during the later war period, themes at times echoed by nonindustrialists as well. Luigi Albertini of the *Corriere della Sera* wrote: "between the Ministry of Transport, Ministry of Commerce, Special Ministerial Committee on Consumption Policy, General Commissariat for Food Services, Director of Provision Services, one can no longer find one's bearings."[60] Ettore Conti, a future president of Confindustria who served during the war in a number of administrative agencies and headed the interministerial committee charged with eventually dismantling the mobilization apparatus at the war's end, noted in his diary:

The facility of the bureaucracy to expand itself [*gonfiarsi*] beyond the necessities for which it had been created is amazing. There are cases in which an office of four was instituted with the assignment of tasks that in private industry would require only two people. But the four felt the need for special lodging, then for a doorman, then a typist, then a telephone operator, and almost immediately an archivist and a head of personnel. To accommodate the many requests for placing draft-aged sons of influential fathers in desk jobs, the number of personnel increases still further; they then ask for a second suite, and so on.[61]

Emilio De Benedetti, president of the Società Promotrice, complained that the government had not taken sufficient account of the expertise of individual industrialists, and still less that of "efficient, hardworking and intelligent associations." While in other belligerent nations men of proven competence were chosen to administer the industrial mobilization, in Italy this task was entrusted to military personnel, politicians, lawyers, and bureaucrats, all of whom lacked sufficient technical training and practical experience to handle the task:

Why in Italy was there not adopted the same system that in the Allied and enemy nations gave such good results? Why was no attempt made to place in managerial positions the man or men most qualified? Especially where it was and is necessary to resolve industrial problems, practical problems of organization and production, it was natural and evident that one ought to take advantage of the efforts of those who knew these problems, and knew them from practice. Instead, those selected were military men, professors, bureaucrats, politicians, in all every kind of person – some of high quality,

[60] Caracciolo, "Grande industria," p. 180.
[61] Conti, *Taccuino*, p. 107.

some intelligent – yet men who lived far from the formidable problems they had to resolve. The industrialists, even though they had given the best evidence of what they were able to do, creating from nothing a war industry, overcoming obstacles and difficulties, were rarely consulted and much less listened to.[62]

Even industrialists who remained outside the associational fold, like the "Socialist" Camillo Olivetti (manufacturer of typewriters and precision electrical equipment), joined the chorus. Olivetti noted that in Germany, "militaristic nation *par excellence*," industrial mobilization had been entrusted to a "true and great industrial organizer like Rathenau," not to soldiers and politicians.[63] Olivetti was especially enraged with the corrosive effect that bureaucratic corruption and clientelism was having on industry, all too willing, in his view, to accommodate itself to such norms. He was shocked, after having made a deliberate attempt to conserve precious metals, at the difficulty he encountered in convincing mobilization authorities – who reacted to his entreaties "with evident stupor" – to reappropriate the excess that he had been allocated.[64] Incensed, he repeated the by now almost ritualistic industrialist *j'accuse* against the incompetent, corrupt, lawyer-dominated *classe dirigente:*

Unfortunately, in Italy we do not have a real *classe dirigente*. We have a *clique dirigente* composed of a heterogeneous rabble of politicians, for the most part lawyers, who possess neither capacity nor intelligence nor honesty, who have led the country to the present disastrous condition prepared by a half century of misgovernment whose effects the war has only made more evident.[65]

Nevertheless, what is striking about such criticism of weak political leadership and unconscionable bureaucratic incompetence is its relative tardiness, becoming conspicuous only at the end of the second year of the war. Although it is true that the process of bureaucratization had been gradual, and perhaps had not reached a critical threshold before the spring of 1917, it might also be surmised that industrialists, during the earlier period, had been sufficiently content with particularistic clientelistic advantages and lucrative profits to overlook inherent incongruities in the mobilization structure until the structure began to actually break down in individual cases.

---

[62] Speech delivered 18 Apr. 1918, text at HAUIT.
[63] Caizzi, *Gli Olivetti,* p. 77.
[64] Ibid., p. 71.
[65] Ibid., p. 106.

Industrialists, as a class, by no means dominated or directed the mobilization structure. However, lamentation about not being consulted or listened to notwithstanding, individual industrialists did manage to penetrate the apparatus at key points, such as being officially designated *capo gruppi* for particular branches of industry with allocative authority over their direct competitors. In other cases, military inspectors were "procured" as outright exponents of specific interests (e.g., the famous case of Colonel Ricaldoni, who, as an advocate of the Perrone brothers, managed to overcome civilian opposition to the installation of the Ansaldo hydroelectric steelworks in the Val d'Aosta).[66] Einaudi spoke of the power wielded by the best-organized groups in their respective sectors and condemned the corruptive effect this was having on the economy in general, as well as on those very private groups. Managerial recruitment, he observed, became less a matter of professional than *political* competence:

Decisive weight was given in such choices to their ability and astuteness in obtaining licenses, privileges, favors, tax exemptions, allocations of raw materials at favorable prices, legal limitations on the number of participants in productive and commercial *consorzi*. The industrialists, managers called on basis of their competence to direct state economic services and to collaborate toward their success, realized that the power of the state, which is coercion, could be used to eliminate bothersome competition, to impede the entrance of newcomers to established markets, to procure large profits for the participants of privileged groups.[67]

A tendency toward unprecedented concentration lay behind this emergent symbiosis between large-scale corporate interests and the state. Such concentration, in part, was a response to objective conditions: the magnitude of procurement orders and allotment of generous contract advances, the difficulty of obtaining adequate materials and combustibles from abroad. All these factors encouraged major firms to seek horizontal alliances and to construct "full-cycle" production facilities by vertically integrating raw-material extraction and processing, foundry, machine-tool, and production components. Concentration was also encouraged by state fiscal policy that, on the one hand, limited the distribution of dividends to 8 percent of corporate earnings and, on the other, exempted from war-profit taxes investments made in plant expansion, modernization, and other forms of

---

[66] Caracciolo, "Grande industria," pp. 186–7.
[67] Einaudi, *Condotta economica*, p. 407.

capital improvement. The former led to an accumulation of forced savings, while the latter provided a vehicle whereby such savings necessarily would be channeled into nontaxable plant investment.[68]

As in other belligerent nations, Italy experienced a dramatic increase in public consumption. While private consumption rose from 79,518 million lire in 1913 to 84,632 million in 1918, public consumption rose from 3,996 million lire to 21,990 million, after having reached a high of 31,778 million in 1917. Per capita public consumption rose from 107 to 585 lire, after having reached 841 in 1917.[69] This massive public expenditure was regulated by ambiguous contractual norms and notoriously lax administrative procedures. Mobilization administrations did not have to submit their accounts for the purchase of supplies to the scrutiny of the state's own general accounting office, the Court of Accounts. A Consultative Commission for the Revision of Prices eventually was created to oversee this operation and belatedly managed to effect considerable savings (203 of 405 contracts submitted to it from January 1917 to April 1918 were rejected).[70]

Not only did the war create a seller's market in relation to one large and vulnerable customer, the state, but commodity prices bore no rationally calculated relation to productive costs (which went largely unsupervised). Consequently, those sectors most directly related to the war effort enjoyed unprecedented rates of profit. While the average rate of profit rose from 4.26 to 7.75 percent, declared profits (regarded with some measure of suspicion by Italian economists) in the war-related sector rose sharply: steel, from 6.30 to 16.55 percent; automotive, from 8.20 to 30.51 percent; shoes, from 9.3 to 30.51 percent; cotton, from −0.94 to 12.77 percent; chemicals, from 8.02 to 15.39 percent; rubber, from 8.57 to 14.95 percent.[71]

Expansion and concentration were most conspicuous in heavy industry. Italian artillery had increased sixfold during the course of the war; at the time of the armistice, Italy had 7,709 pieces of artillery to 11,608 for the French, 6,690 for the United Kingdom, and 3,308 for the United States. In 1915, the Italian army had 3,400 trucks and

---

[68] Caracciolo, "Grande industria," p. 189; Clough, *Economic History*, pp. 185–90; Grifone, *Capitale finanziario*, p. 30; Salvemini, *Origins of Fascism*, p. 35.

[69] Romeo, *Breve storia*, p. 115.

[70] Clough, *Economic History*, pp. 184–5; Einaudi, *Condotta economica*, pp. 125–8.

[71] Romeo, *Breve storia*, p. 116.

buses, but at the end of the war it had 27,400, after exporting 1,867
in 1917. In January 1915, there were only 60 workers in aviation
manufacture; four months later there were 1,500. By June 1917, 16
planes and 21 motors were being turned out daily; and in 1918,
6,523 planes and 14,820 motors were produced.[72]

Ilva, Italy's "steel trust," had seen its capital holdings rise from 30
million lire in 1916 to 300 million lire in 1918. Beyond absorbing
smaller firms in the steel sector, it entered shipbuilding, munitions,
and automotive manufacture. Ansaldo, which began in shipbuilding,
increased its capital holdings from 30 million to 500 million lire (and
its workforce from 4,000 to 110,000 employees), developing its own
iron mines, hydroelectric plants, and steel-producing facilities. Additionally, it began to manufacture dynamite, automobiles, bicycles,
and telephones. Fiat, which saw its capital holdings increase from 17
million to 200 million lire, jumped in rank from Italy's thirtieth
largest firm to its third largest, immediately behind Ilva and Ansaldo.
Though it developed its own steel-producing and toolmaking capacity, Fiat retained its essentially vertical character, emphasizing automotive production.[73]

Yet even among these giants of heavy industry, there were significant differences of interest which persisted throughout the war and
became more evident after the armistice. First, Ilva and Ansaldo, even
before the war, had been key elements in the state-dependent sector;
without protection and subsidies, they could not have survived. Fiat,
on the other hand, had always competed well in international markets
and was one of Italy's major exporters before, during, and after the
war (before the war, automobiles represented 40 percent of Italy's
total machine-manufacturing exports; during the war, 46.7 percent;
in the immediate postwar period, 54.5 percent; and by 1924, 65
percent).[74] Ilva and Ansaldo had given conspicuous support to the
Nationalists, who advocated principled protection and an aggressively imperialistic foreign policy, whereas Agnelli, head of Fiat, was
a pronounced "Wilsonian" who actually coauthored a book in 1918
proposing a "European Federation," modeled on the British Com-

[72] Clough, *Economic History*, pp. 182–3.
[73] Castronovo, *Agnelli*, pp. 152–3; Clough, *Economic History*, pp. 204–7; Romeo, *Breve storia*, pp. 121–3.
[74] *L'industria italiana* (Rome: Confederazione Generale Fascista dell'Industria Italiana, 1929), p. 135.

monwealth and the United States, that might "overcome the concept of nationality." Agnelli called for the "transformation of national markets into a continental market," giving European industry "the same gigantic impulse which American industry experienced after the Civil War," a position, needless to say, diametrically opposed to the *industria nazionale* promoted by Ilva, Ansaldo, and the Nationalists.[75]

Second, Agnelli had been one of the major proponents of associational development in industry, from the founding of the LIT in 1906, through the constitution of the CIDI in 1910, to Confindustria in 1919. In contrast, the leadership of Ilva (Max Bondi) and Ansaldo (the Perrone brothers) had shown comparatively little interest in aggregative industrial associations, pursuing instead direct clientelistic relations with the state.

Third, a source of cleavage was based on antagonistic bank affiliations and Ansaldo's brazen, though unsuccessful, attempt to monopolize Italy's financial structure, as well as the machine-manufacturing sector. Ansaldo and "its" Banca di Sconto had consistently attacked the predominant financial power of the "German" Banca Commerciale, which was affiliated with both Ilva and Fiat. By attempting to buy a majority of their stocks, Ansaldo sought to capture Fiat and the Banca Commerciale, thereby enabling it ultimately to control investment credit and to undermine the dominant position of Ilva in steel production and Fiat in machine manufacturing.[76] Thus, even among the most concentrated, influential, and presumably cohesive components of heavy industry, there was no commonality of view or coordination of policy; each firm separately pursued its own particular interest.

In the associational vacuum created by the mobilization, the *classe industriale* was reduced to a disaggregated collection of atomized interests, each vertically connected to the state apparatus but horizontally unbound by any class-specific ties. Individual industrialists might very well have "colonized" proximate sections of the mobilization infrastructure, exploiting these to their own advantage against com-

[75] Valerio Castronovo, "Il potere economico e il fascismo," in Guido Quazza, ed., *Fascismo e società italiana* (Turin: Einaudi, 1973), pp. 55–8; Castronovo, *La stampa italiana dall'unità al fascismo* (Bari: Laterza, 1970), pp. 242–6, 260–3; Vivarelli, *Dopoguerra*, p. 234.

[76] Castronovo, *Agnelli*, pp. 149–51; Romeo, *Breve storia*, p. 125.

petitors, but the industrial class, as such, exercised no hegemony. If anything, it emerged from the war as a weakened collective entity, its sense of unity and capacity for self-defense anesthetized by the precorporatist tutelage of fragmented interests and the disciplining of labor. In sum, the industrial class emerged from the war ill prepared for the dramatic syndical and political battles to follow.

War-inspired productivism

During the course of the war, production assumed a universal centrality independent from, and not reducible to, its relation to any specific mode of production, capitalist or Socialist. Such "imperatives" as management, mechanization, hierarchy, and discipline were treated by a variety of authors spanning the political spectrum from Communists to Fascists. Before proceeding with Italian productivist thought emanating from the war, we shall briefly review productivist currents elsewhere in Europe to give some sense of the sensitivity of the epoch to this question and to indicate that even Mussolini's "fetishism" with production was neither unique, original, nor necessarily reflective of a "reactionary" mentality.

Lenin's flirtation with Taylorism is well known, and his economic advisors Milyutin and Larin explicitly modeled the early Soviet economy along industrial-planning concepts developed by the architects of Germany's mobilization, Rathenau and Moellendorff. As Charles Maier observes, "continuing into the twenties, industrial trusts under Bolshevik command served as a flexible framework within which to reorganize a shattered economy."[77] Writing in *Izvestia* (28 April 1918), Lenin went so far as to suggest that the central task of Socialism was to liberate the objective productive apparatus and techniques of capitalism from their exploitative fetters:

The Taylor system, the last work of capitalism in this respect, like all capitalist progress, is a combination of the subtle brutality of bourgeois exploitation and a number of the greatest scientific achievements in the field of analyzing mechanical motions during work, the introduction of the best system of accounting and control, etc. The Soviet Republic must at all costs adopt all that is valuable in the achievements of science and technology in this field. The possibility of building socialism will be determined precisely by our success in combining Soviet government and soviet organization of adminis-

[77] Maier, "Between Taylorism and Technology," p. 50.

tration with the modern achievements of capitalism. We must organize in Russia the study and teaching of the Taylor system and systematically try it out and adapt it to our purposes.[78]

In Germany, Karl Korsch, writing in the aftermath of the "November Revolution," suggested that in the transitional stage between capitalism and a socialized economy, productivity ought not to be sacrificed, even if this meant actually increasing the salary and technical authority of the industrialist while "universalizing" the range of private interest until "worker capitalism" replaced "proprietary capitalism."[79] Speaking of the necessity for hierarchy and discipline in the workplace, themes generally associated with Fascism, Korsch approvingly cited Lenin on the "absolute necessity" for "subordination without objection of hundreds and thousands to a single will."[80]

Such a conception of the workplace had informed "really existing socialism" from the very beginning. Putting aside mystification regarding the higher end to be realized, "building socialism" served as little more than a substitute Protestant ethic, yet one far more severe and less concerned with the subjects themselves than "bourgeois conceptions." Clearly, Gino Olivetti's words on the technical imperatives of managerial authority, seen by some, mistakenly, as proto-Fascist, pale by comparison to Soviet pronouncements on the subject. Olivetti, as we shall see in the next chapter, used rather effectively the theory and practice of labor relations in the Soviet Union to counter the factory council concept developed after the war by Gramsci and others, a concept and practice grounded, or so they thought, on Leninism.

In France in 1918, the reformist CGT explicitly rejected a revolutionary program or even militant class struggle in order not to jeopardize production during the period of reconversion. Only through class collaboration could a high level of productivity be maintained, thus avoiding widespread unemployment and a fall in wages.[81] Even more integrally productivist was Lysis (Ernest Letailleur), whose *Vers la démocratie nouvelle* was immediately translated into Italian with a foreword by the "Bernsteinian" Socialist Ivanoe Bonomi. Calling for

[78] Ibid., p. 51.
[79] Karl Korsch, *Consigli di fabbrica e socializzazione*, trans. Giorgio Backhaus (Bari: Laterza, 1970), pp. 34–5.
[80] Ibid., pp. 59–60.
[81] Renzo De Felice, *Mussolini il rivoluzionario* (Turin: Einaudi, 1965), p. 408.

a "new socialism," his thoughts prefigure Mussolini's rather-derivative productivist writings. Lysis referred specifically to four "necessary" and "absolute" principles for industrial progress and social betterment, principles that were to apply equally to all regimes, democratic or authoritarian:

And these are: *stability*, continuity in the functions, without which no one can perfect himself or give the measure of his true value or undertake lasting work; *initiative and responsibility*, without which the individual remains a mediocre producer according to the law of minimum effort; *competence*, evident principle according to which everyone ought to be in his place and occupy only the function for which he is capable; and finally *hierarchy*, necessary because each organism includes consignments of unequal measure, some commanding, others obeying.[82]

Lysis attacked the technical incompetence of liberal–democracy, based as it was on universal male suffrage within a territorial district ("an insult to good sense"); in its place he advocated functional representation. He recognized the specialized competence of industrialists: "that which ensures a monopoly in the firm to the *padroni* is not the possession of capital – a revolution might cut that from them in an instant – but rather the experience and the necessary cognitions which the proletariat lack."[83] Thus, it would be counterproductive and even "reactionary" to be opposed to capitalism: "if capitalism, in the moment we cross, is an indispensable factor of progress, not only would we be reactionary in paralyzing its function, but we would fall short of our duty and would act against our very interest."[84] To sustain and encourage capitalism, however, was not to tolerate its "abuses and deficiencies"; rather, one must distinguish "healthy capitalism from parasitic and harmful capitalism."[85]

This necessarily brief sample of European war-inspired productivism is intended to suggest a widespread concern for the "universal imperatives of production" which the war had heightened. No longer was political discourse centered on "man as citizen" in the tradition of bourgeois natural law (the basis of political liberalism), but increasingly on "man as producer" (the basis of both corporatism and Socialism). The very term "producer," although it had never fully

---

[82] Lysis, *Verso la nuova democrazia*, trans. Carlo Rasponi (Florence: Bemporad e Figlio, 1919), p. 72.
[83] Ibid., p. 272.
[84] Ibid., p. 280.
[85] Ibid., p. 281.

disappeared from the popular vocabulary, suddenly reemerged during the war in its characteristic *saint-simonian* sense (i.e., the essential distinction between "productive" and "parasitic" societal elements). With such connotation it was employed by a diverse collection of contemporary actors, including Lenin, Korsch, Gramsci, Lysis, Mussolini, Rocco, and Rossoni. To be sure, left-oriented and right-oriented members of this partial list were in clear disagreement as to precisely which specific elements or classes were indeed fish or fowl; yet, at the conceptual level, the distinction remained remarkably constant.

Economic liberalism, based on the free play of individual and atomized interests, had long been on the wane. Yet the war, through its "total" mobilization of society and particularly productive activity, its explicit recognition of organized, hierarchical, and structured constellations of interest, and its alternative model of an "associative economy" (a term much used in Europe during the war), had seemingly rendered this classic conception hopelessly anachronistic. Hereafter, economic liberalism would lose its doctrinal clarity, coming to mean in the 1920s merely the defense of private interests against state intervention (a direct reaction to the experience of wartime controls) and, paradoxically, in the 1930s, a pragmatic, nonideological rationale for piecemeal, state intervention to correct the self-destructive tendencies of unregulated capitalism (e.g., the New Deal).

From this general discussion of war-inspired European productivist literature, we turn our attention once again to the Italian case. We shall consider the position of the Nationalists and then Mussolini, each of whom made conspicuous bids for industrialist support in their distinct, if at times convergent, programs for postwar reconstruction.

Of the two positions, that of the Nationalists led to a more rigorous and articulated doctrinal development and would, in fact, eventually serve as the theoretical and juridical underpinning of the *stato fascista*. Though the Nationalists, as an autonomous intellectual and political force, lacked the mass base and practical strategic acumen of Mussolini, who they initially regarded with a good deal of suspicion, they possessed an ideological richness that the Fascists lacked and a juridical–institutional framework without which the Fascist transition from an inherited, inadequate liberal regime to the construction of a viable, alternative state form would have been problematic if not impossible. To leap momentarily into material which will be dealt with in subsequent chapters, it should be noted that during the critical juncture (1925–7) when the juridical–institutional groundwork of the "regime" was laid, and the Fascist Party was uprooted as an autonomous force and sacrificed to the state, the Nationalist Alfredo Rocco was minister of justice (and architect of the fundamental *leggi fascisti*) and the Nationalist Luigi Federzoni was minister of the interior (and state "enforcer" against recalcitrant Fascists). As Franco Gaeta, author of *Nazionalismo italiano,* suggests, it was one thing to smash and repress democratic and Socialist opposition with the methodical use of force and quite another to create the juridical–institutional framework that rendered such a "counterrevolution" permanent.[86]

To Alfredo Rocco, leading theoretical light of the Nationalists, the war had made inevitable a definitive "state-corporatist" outcome, in contrast to the tentative and semiarticulated "precorporatist" mobilization. The war, Rocco argued, had further impelled two interrelated trends, productive concentration and syndicalization, to such an extent that they no longer could be contained within the framework of the liberal state. Corporatism, in this sense, would arise from the same basis as Communism, except here, of course, the liberal state would be replaced by a more stable "counterrevolutionary" order in which socialized workers would no longer be under the demagogic influence of "agitators" and "political speculators" but contained in compulsory, unitary syndicates "disciplined" by the state.

Before proceeding with Rocco's analysis, it will be revealing to take brief note of a youthful (1916) and somewhat mechanistic statement by Gramsci to illustrate the analytic commonalities between Communist and corporatist perspectives, if not thereby to appreciate better the differences in the postulation of ultimate outcomes: Communist revolution or corporatist counterrevolution. Here we find Gramsci expressing his admiration for the industrialists who, like Marx's "unknowing gravediggers," organized large-scale production, socialized workers, and thus created the necessary conditions for their own undoing:

For these men I have a profound admiration; they are the dominators of our epoch, the kings much more powerful and more useful than kings of times past and even our own. It is they who uproot the ignorant and unmanageable masses and thrust them from their supine, somnolent, and bucolic tranquility

---

[86] Gaeta, *Nazionalismo italiano,* pp. 154–5.

into the incandescent crucible of our civilization. . . . Agnelli constructs factories and necessarily the workers become Socialists. At a certain point, the bourgeoisie will be incapable of containing the economic forces which they themselves stirred up, and then will happen that which must happen.[87]

Rocco, whose admiration for the industrialists certainly was not less than that of Gramsci, envisioned as an alternative to both unviable liberalism and insurgent Communism (1) the replacement of the liberal *borghesia politica* by the *borghesia produttiva* as the new *classe dirigente* and (2) the construction of a corporatist state modeled on the discipline and compulsive hierarchy of productive relations. To return to Rocco's analysis of concentration and syndicalization:

What has the war shown us? It has shown us that in the organization of production the small- and medium-sized firms are destined to disappear and give way to large industrial enterprises. . . . The concentration of production has been manifested in a miraculous way and we have seen colossal enterprises constructed which before the war did not exist in Italy. . . . This phenomenon of the concentration of production has come up against another phenomenon which had important manifestations even before the war: the organization of labor. On the one hand, the enterprises are concentrated, and on the other, the workers organize themselves ever more effectively. The producers unify not to combat the workers but rather to produce better and at lower cost. Yet by the very fact of their organization they come to find themselves in confrontation with the workers' organizations.[88]

Rocco's corporatist solution to this impasse was the creation of national cartels for each branch of industry that would, by their very scale, realize the greatest productive potential, while avoiding "useless" domestic competition, thus allowing Italian industry to better compete in world markets.[89] At the same time, syndicates would be restructured, losing their status as "organs of class self-defense" and becoming "integral"; that is, they would include, in one unitary sectoral body, "all the elements of production: organizers, managers, manual workers, united together in indissoluble ties of common interest."[90]

Recognizing that this "natural" collaboration would not occur spontaneously, because of the influence of "professional agitators" over the masses, the state would "energetically intervene" and construct these structures from above: "In the integral syndicate the

[87] Castronovo, *Agnelli*, p. 127.
[88] Rocco, *Scritti*, 1: 382.
[89] Ibid., p. 515.
[90] Ibid., p. 490.

intolerable antagonisms of class, isolated from the political agitation of professional demagogues, find an automatic resolution and discipline. To ensure this, in any case, the state ought to energetically intervene."[91] Any residual distributional conflict remaining unresolved within the integral syndicate would be adjudicated by specially created labor courts, rather than permitting open class struggle or autonomous class self-defense.[92]

This intervening state, quite obviously, would no longer be the liberal state, for the liberal state was incapable of so acting, reflecting as it did the amorphous congeries of antagonistic and imperfectly organized interests. The intervening state, for Rocco, was the integrally corporatist state, organically and hierarchically constructed on representational structures reflecting functionally interdependent interests:

The state – one need not forget – today is still that which resulted from the French Revolution, the liberal state whose organs, except for the head of state in a monarchic regime, are the expression of the incoherent will of amorphous and unorganized multitudes, the sum of individuals incapable of realizing anything other than their single interests. These organs are by definition incompetent, and even if their personnel are changed, they are destined to be incompetent to fulfill economic functions for which technical and spiritual preparation is necessary, preparation that they do not possess and are incapable of possessing. The men may be excellent, but it is the organism that cannot function because of its natural ineptitude. I do not wish to "mortgage" the future. I believe instead that the inevitable development of economic organization will lead to a transformation of production that cannot help but have repercussions on the state organism. The phenomenon, which predated the war but which the war enormously accelerated, of industrial concentration is the parallel phenomenon of the syndical organization of the two elements of production, industrialists and workers, and will probably prepare, with other forms and greater fullness, a return to the corporatist organization of production. . . . The organization thus created will necessarily assume a national function and a public character; it will be automatically transformed into an organ of the state. In that moment, the separation between the state and the productive enterprises will diminish, not through the absorption of the one by the other, nor by the subordination of the former to the latter, but instead by natural coordination and connection. The state then will have acquired a competent organ to exercise the productive function, which it will direct according to the exigencies of the supreme economic and political interests of the nation.[93]

[91] Ibid.
[92] Ibid., p. 504.
[93] Ibid., pp. 506–7.

Parliament, in the long run, would be replaced by an integrally corporatist chamber; in the short run, Rocco proposed transforming the
Senate into a professionally elected corporatist body with greater
legislative authority than the "oppressive and demagogic" popularly
elected Chamber of Deputies.[94]

In broad outline, such was the conservative corporatist schema of
Alfredo Rocco. By no means was it the only corporatist position to
emerge from the war, despite the fact that it did eventually become
the acknowledged juridical–institutional basis of the Fascist state. As
we shall see later, from the revolutionary syndicalists (e.g., Alceste De
Ambris, author of D'Annunzio's corporatist constitution of Fiume;
Edmondo Rossoni, head of the Fascist labor syndicates) there
emerged competing "left-corporatist" conceptions, based on a "state-
syndicalist" model in which the state, rather than constituting an
autonomous disciplinary force over and above the syndicates, would
be no more than the sum total of all national syndical associations,
units that would initiate and execute all state functions. In contrast
with Rocco's "statalization of the syndicate," they proposed the "syndicalization of the state"; the former a "top–down" concept, the
latter "bottom–up."

In a suggestive, if polemical, description of the etatist bias of
Rocco's syndicalism, Piero Gobetti, a young Turinese liberal who
would die at the hands of Fascist thugs, compared such "syndicalism
without struggle" to "Hegel without the dialectic" and "public law
without politics." For Gobetti, Rocco's work reduced social praxis
simply to "an administrative measure"; his national syndicates were
a juridical invention, the "seedbed for new clients."[95]

Who were these "new clients" to whom the Nationalist program
was addressed? Alfredo Rocco and Enrico Corradini, the two principal
Nationalist spokesmen, made overt appeals to the *borghesia produttiva*. They called for this bourgeois fragment to end its "traditional pri-
vatism," to become conscious of its "public function," and to replace
the parasitic and incompetent *borghesia politica* and become the new
classe dirigente. "You are the organizers," said Corradini, "you are the
borghesia produttiva, which means that you are the contractors of the
modern world." The liberal state was "bureaucratic and parliamen-

---

[94] Ibid., p. 482.
[95] Gaeta, *Nazionalismo italiano*, pp. 31–2.

tary, a despotic and incompetent bureaucracy and a dominating parliamentarism devoid of any preparation, always treating the affairs of industry, during peace and war, with profane hands."[96]

Instead, popular sovereignty should give way to a "government of the most capable," and the state should be transformed into "an administrative office of the producers."[97] Rocco, echoing a refrain characteristic of industrialist-authored literature, attacked the bureaucratic incompetence of the wartime state, noting that in Italy, unlike Germany, industrialists were not sought after by the government to contribute their expertise and counsel to the mobilization effort.[98] Similarly, he repeated the long-standing equation between the interests of industry and the national interest, as well as the primacy of production over distribution. Above all, Rocco said, industrialists performed "a most important and vital national function," acting not so much to enrich themselves as to "render the nation more prosperous."[99]

Profit, according to Rocco, was not

a gift that the collectivity gives to the organizers of production, nor "theft" that the former endures. Rather, it is compensation that the collectivity pays to those who manage production on its account. To reduce it to a question of giving and receiving between two categories of individuals is to mentally suppress the nation and to reveal an incapacity to understand the phenomena of social life from a truly social point of view.[100]

As for the primacy of production over distribution:

It is therefore clear that to augment the well-being of the Italian people it is not so much necessary to distribute the wealth and income of the Italian nation differently as to augment it globally. Produce more and then work more, that is the program of nationalism ... work, work, work, produce, produce, produce; that is the secret of the incessant and unlimited betterment of the nation and of single citizens, among these, principally, the workers.[101]

From the organic corporatist productivism of the Nationalists, we turn to the derivative and eclectic productivism of Mussolini. Musso-

---

[96] Enrico Corradini, "Discorsi di guerra agli uomini d'affari per una coscienza di classe borghesia produttiva," reprinted in Cafagna, *Il nord*, pp. 465–6. See also Corradini, *Il regime della borghesia produttiva* (Rome: n.p., 1918).
[97] Vivarelli, *Dopoguerra*, pp. 255–8, 588.
[98] Rocco, *Scritti*, 1:571–2.
[99] Ibid.
[100] Ibid., p. 48.
[101] Ibid., pp. 515–16.

lini, it will be remembered, was expelled from the Socialist Party because of his interventionism, founding the journal *Popolo d'Italia* in November 1915 with the help of contributions allegedly made by industrialists, but also by French Socialists.[102] He had assembled around him a group of dissident Socialists, revolutionary syndicalists, anarchists, and Republicans. The journal soon became one of the leading organs of "left-interventionism" and bore the subtitle *A Socialist Daily*.

However, dating from the tragic Italian defeat at Caporetto in October 1917, Mussolini gradually began to distance himself from left-interventionism, remaining apart from the constitution of the Italian Socialist Union (May 1918) and the reconstitution of the Italian Union of Labor (Unione Italiana del Lavoro; UIL) in June 1918, organizations through which the left-interventionists sought to participate in postwar international conferences on equal footing with the official Socialist Party and the CGL, as well as affirm their Socialist character in contrast with the right-interventionists.

The most obvious moment of this disengagement on Mussolini's part came on 1 August 1918, when the subtitle of *Popolo d'Italia* was changed from *A Socialist Daily* to *A Daily of Combatants and Producers*. This change was motivated by three principal factors: (1) Mussolini's growing financial ties with Ansaldo, which had matured during the summer of 1918, after a series of meetings in Genoa; (2) the influence of French syndical writings and Lysis's productivism upon Mussolini, who was in the process of developing a program for postwar reconstruction; and (3) a conscious attempt on the part of Mussolini to broaden his social base through invoking such formulas as "productivism" and "trenchism." With the former, he sought to open himself to industrialists without renouncing the interest of workers; with the latter, he hoped to reach the masses uprooted by the war and no longer necessarily loyal to traditional class, religious, and regional identifications and structures.[103]

From the very first of his many productivist writings, even those preceding the definitive "change" of 1 August 1918, Mussolini echoed such themes as discipline within the productive hierarchy, the historical role that capitalism had yet to play, the "function" of the

---

[102] De Felice, *Mussolini il rivoluzionario*, p. 302.
[103] Ibid., pp. 413–18; Castronovo, *La stampa*, pp. 260–3.

industrialist, and the immediate postwar necessity of increased production:

It is not a question of appropriating goods but rather of producing them without interruption. It is not a question of equalizing men in the sense of *aplatir* but of strongly establishing hierarchies and social discipline. [1 May 1918]

The syndicalism which appears today a method, a tendency – and not a "State" to be realized in some distant tomorrow according to the dogma of a church – says one word strongly: discipline. . . . That is, coordination, harmony, necessary hierarchy. Either this or chaos. . . . Discipline ought to be accepted. The manual worker ought to obey the architect. Discipline ought to be, when necessary, imposed. [12 June 1918]

To defend producers signifies permitting the bourgeoisie to fulfill its historical function; there are still two continents almost intact which await to be overturned by the turbine of modern capitalist civilization. [1 August 1918]

The essential thing is "to produce." This is the "beginning." . . . It is necessary to exalt the producers, because upon them depends the more- or the less-rapid postwar reconstruction. You disorganize production and you prepare a pitiful postwar situation for those who return from the trenches. . . . There are capitalists who have a sense of their historical function and who "dare"; there are workers who understand the inescapability of this capitalistic *processus,* seeing the mediate and immediate benefits they can draw from it. Yes, produce, produce, produce. . . . It is in the interest of the worker–producer to carry the capitalist economy to its extreme expression, multiplying it in intensity and in extension. [18 August 1918][104]

None of these themes, taken separately, were original, nor did they, taken together, constitute a new theory of society or suggest a coherent, alternative regime form. From Lysis he borrowed such concepts as hierarchy, competence, and the remaining historical function of capitalism. Although Mussolini would speak of a collaborationist *sindacalismo nazionale,* it would appear that the source behind this concept was not the Nationalist writings of Rocco and Corradini,[105] since no mention is made of an explicitly corporatist framework – hallmark of the Nationalists – in which such syndicates would be contained and function. Rather, it was to the French syndicalists of the CGT that Mussolini turned his attention. Beginning in April 1918, *Popolo d'Italia* made a series of explicit references to articles that had appeared in *Bataille Syndicaliste* on the subject.

104 De Felice, *Mussolini il rivoluzionario,* pp. 492–3.
105 Vivarelli, *Dopoguerra,* pp. 270–5.

In France, the productivist–collaborationist thesis had been proposed even before the outbreak of the war by Alfred Merrheim. During the war, it had been expounded by Victor Griffuelhes and Leon Jouhaux and had been incorporated in the CGT program emanating from the Congress of Lyon (September 1919), which called for both collaboration and nationalization.[106] To be sure, the French syndicalists employed a more militant, class-specific vocabulary than did Mussolini, speaking of "workers" and "capitalists," as well as "producers," and unlike Mussolini, they explicitly called for the nationalization of certain sectors. Nevertheless, it was as "men of the Left" that they argued for collaboration in the name of higher productivity; only through higher productivity could worker *revendications* be satisfied in the immediate postwar reconversion. If a productive crisis were brought on by militant action, unemployment and a drop in salaries would befall the workers. As *Bataille Syndicaliste* explained on 11 September 1918 (translated shortly thereafter by *Popolo d'Italia*):

The purpose of this journal ought to be that of defending the interests of the producing class and of aiding and activating indispensable industrial and commercial development. When the working class demands better conditions of life, it expresses a theory of progress, since this *revendication* can become a reality only insofar as there is progress in economic development. . . . Just as a nation having a working class of an inferior moral level cannot develop itself intensively, it is impossible for a working class to conquer superior conditions of life in a nation of scarce or minor development. . . . The formula for the working class ought to be the maximum of production with the minimum of working hours for the maximum of salary. For the *patronat*, the maximum development of plant machinery for the maximum yield with the minimum of general expenses. These two combined formulas ought to ensure a greater capacity to consume for the whole nation.[107]

Similarly, on 9 November 1918, Mussolini wrote:

It is a question of creating and "activating" a convergence of economic forces through which the maximum productive potentiality will correspond to the maximum well-being for the working masses. In turn, this augmented well-being reflects back upon productive potentiality. It is necessary to convince oneself that the two economic forces, *produttori borghesi* and *produttori proletari*, condition each other with a mathematical rigidity. An insufficient

---

[106] De Felice, *Mussolini il rivoluzionario*, pp. 405–8; Vivarelli, *Dopoguerra*, pp. 272–4.

[107] De Felice, *Mussolini il rivoluzionario*, p. 405.

bourgeoisie, retrograde and fearful, has its necessary antithesis in an uncultivated, degraded, and impoverished proletariat. . . . Conflict can arise between
the two forces with respect to the division of profits, but the common interest
of the two forces is that there be profits, and these are obtained only with the
initiative, audacity, and foresight of the *produttore borghese* united with the
discipline, diligence, and sense of responsibility of the *produttore operaio*.[108]

Once again, with reference to a productivist article appearing in
Bataille Syndicaliste, Mussolini eight days later reduced his concept
of *sindacalismo nazionale* to its "essential terms." These were:

No political revolution, no extremism, no expropriation, and not even class
struggle if the heads of the enterprise are intelligent. Intense and harmonious
collaboration between industrialists and workers in production; satisfaction
of the just demands of organized labor. These are the bases of *sindacalismo
nazionale*.[109]

In the same article, Mussolini made reference to a distinction between
"destructive" political Socialism and "creative" *sindacalismo nazionale*:

There are, on one side, the professional bourgeois of Socialism who, experi-
menting with their thesis, would not stop from sharpening the economic and
social crisis provoked by the war and who would necessarily hurl European
society into total chaos. There are, on the other side, the organizations of the
working class which reject the confused and stupid "anticipations" of Socialist politics, inasmuch as they sense that capitalism still has a function to fulfill
and that the advent of the proletariat ought to come from the base, not from
the top through decrees issued by a political government of card-carrying
Socialists. Faced with this antithesis that is so clearly delineated, between
political Socialism and the working masses, our line of conduct is clear.
Combat without respite the political party which continues its sordid speculation to the detriment of the working class, and support, as the French syndicalists say, the just *revendications* of the organized proletariat.

This distinction between Socialism and the syndicates was essential
not only at the somewhat abstract level of productivism (i.e., those
forces which had an interest in disturbing the productive process, as
opposed to those who had an interest in its continual expansion)
but, even more significantly, at the political–strategic level, since the
syndical unity that Mussolini envisioned and actively promoted was
not restricted to interventionist syndicates like the UIL (which had a

[108] Vivarelli, *Dopoguerra*, pp. 270–1.
[109] De Felice, *Mussolini il rivoluzionario*, p. 493.

limited base in the working class) but extended to the CGL as well. In short, if the CGL could be severed from the Socialist orbit, not only would Socialism be neutralized as a political force but Mussolini would have an opportunity to extend his base from the left-interventionists to the full spectrum of the organized working class. As we shall see, such a project did not end with the coming to power of Fascism. Even after the March on Rome, Mussolini repeatedly sought an accommodation (albeit one-sided) with the CGL, acutely aware of the limited extension of the Fascist syndicates. This accommodating attitude toward the CGL was always in marked contrast with Mussolini's uncompromising opposition to the Socialist Party.

Coincident with the development of this productivist position was Mussolini's outspoken support of the CGL's "autonomist" wing (Rigola, D'Aragona, Bianchi), who, as pragmatic reformists, were increasingly alienated from the maximalist leadership of the Socialist Party, and who gave signs of bringing to life an actual labor party. Significantly, *Popolo d'Italia* on 12 January 1919 carried an interview with D'Aragona in which the leader expressed his disagreement with the wing of the CGL tied to the Socialist Party which rejected any accord with interventionist syndicates like the UIL.[110] D'Aragona argued that such matters had to be approached from a syndical, and not a political, perspective, one free from a priori acrimony.

On several occasions, Mussolini suggested that the French CGT was the model that the Italian CGL ought to follow, for they had transcended the "apocalyptic and mystic" syndicalism of Sorel, laying bare the basis for a syndicalism that was "pacific and pragmatic," that "took into account new facts," and that "based itself on reality."[111] Mussolini applauded the essay "Les travailleurs devant la paix," written by Jouhaux, in which the CGT leader called for the constitution of a National Economic Council that would formulate economic policy and be composed of the various categories of producers and consumers.[112]

A month later (30 March 1919), Mussolini called for the creation in Italy of National Councils, explicitly copying the idea from Kurt Eisner, "the major author of the German revolution." Such bodies

---

[110] Ibid., p. 495.
[111] Ibid., p. 494.
[112] Ibid.

"overcome the dilemma: either a parliament or a soviet"; for although the Parliament remained, parallel to it arose a new system of
direct, functional representation. However, such a project called for
the constitution of a new state, as the traditional one "could not
contain it."[113]

Although at first glance this political reconstruction appears markedly similar to the short-term solution proposed by the Nationalists
(one popularly elected chamber, one corporatist one), it should be
noted that during this early productivist period of Mussolini, no
programmatic references to corporatism were made. The construction
of a new state form based on functional representation, though also
supported by Nationalists, in Mussolini's development was derived
from French syndicalist and German Socialist sources. In fact, Mussolini's proposals were not all that far from positions taken by the CGL,
which, at the end of 1918, had called for the creation of syndically
composed bodies to which would be transferred parliamentary authority over economic legislation. In May 1919, the CGL called for
a constituent assembly "with election by professional category" to
construct a new republican form of government.[114]

The idea that functional representation would be more competent
to deal with economic and "technical" matters than territorial representation developed a broadly based following during the closing
months of the war and well into the postwar period. The Republican
Party in 1918 proposed the "transformation of national representation with the institution of regional assemblies elected by professions
and trades by local interests, and of a national assembly for general
policy and common legislation."[115] Even the somewhat bizarre,
youth-oriented Futurist Program of 1918 suggested a technical and
functional transformation of Parliament:

Transformation of Parliament through an equal participation of industrialists, agriculturalists, engineers, and *commercianti* in the Government of the
Nation. The minimum limit of age for office will be reduced to 22 years. A
minimum of lawyer deputies (always opportunists) and a minimum of professor deputies (always retrograde). A Parliament emptied of numbskulls and
rabble. Abolition of the Senate. If this rational and practical Parliament does

---

[113] Alberto Aquarone, *L'Organizzazione dello Stato totalitario* (Turin: Einaudi, 1965),
pp. 3–4.
[114] Einaudi, *Condotta economica*, p. 310; De Felice, *Mussolini il rivoluzionario*, p.
517.
[115] De Felice, *Mussolini il rivoluzionario*, p. 442.

not bear good results, we will abolish it to arrive at a technical government without Parliament, a government elected through universal suffrage. We will replace the Senate with an Assembly of Control composed of twenty youths not yet 30 years of age, elected by universal suffrage. Instead of a Parliament composed of incompetent orators, moderated by a Senate of moribunds, we will have a Government of twenty technicians stimulated by an assembly of youth not yet thirty.

Finally, the newly formed Catholic Party (Popolari) in 1919 called for "representation by class, without exclusion, within the public organs of labor at the Commune, Province, and State levels," and a "Senate elected with prevalent representation of the corps of the nation (Academic Corps, Communes, Provinces, Organized Classes)."[116] Parenthetically, we might note that this broadly based concern for political reconstruction was itself an obvious indication that the traditional liberal institutional framework had lost a good deal of its legitimacy, and that a simple return to the status quo ante was unlikely to succeed.

The actual formation of the Fasci di combattimento will be treated later. Here we will conclude the discussion of Mussolini's productivism by noting its affinity, not to the corporatism of the Nationalists, but rather to the stream of anti-Bolshevik Socialist thought that prevailed in western Europe during 1917–19. As De Felice suggests, it would be wrong to judge as essentially conservative either Mussolini or "Fascism" during this early period. Despite the "classic" form it would eventually assume, Fascism in Italy emerged as a phenomenon of the Left, in terms of both its original membership (principally dissident Socialists, revolutionary syndicalists, anarchists, and Republicans) and its initial program (e.g., an eight-hour working day, minimum wages, participation of workers in the technical functioning of industry, transfer of the responsibility for operating industry and public services to such proletarian organizations as were morally and technically qualified, a heavy and progressive tax on capital that would take the form of partial expropriation, revision of all war supply contracts, and confiscation of 85 percent of war profits). True, the social composition of its membership and its program would change fundamentally in a rightward direction during the following three years, yet Fascism's ultimate point of arrival was hardly the result of a unilinear trajectory immanently determined from its point

[116] Leoni, *Partiti politici*, pp. 250–1.

of departure. Its rightward drift was as much due to the failure of Fascism's initial aspiration to establish a mass base on the Left as to the "gravitational force" exerted by liberal and conservative elements eager to "instrumentalize" Fascism against the postwar wave of working-class insurgency. Mediating these opposed pushes and pulls, of course, was the opportunism of Mussolini, without whose political acumen Fascism, an unruly, heterogeneous, locally based movement, never would have become a dominant political force.

Productivist programs and the industrialists

In the previous discussion, we tried to suggest how in Italy, as in other European nations, the primacy of production, the hierarchical nature of industrial relations, and the directing "function" of the industrialist himself had assumed an unprecedented centrality in public discussion and political speculation. Moreover, in contrast with the prewar period, this wave of productivism was less the product of actual industrialists, or industrial "experts" like Taylor, than of political actors who sought to predefine the institutional basis for a postwar reality.

Naturally, the response of all industrialists to such productivism was not uniform but depended on individual patterns of prewar development, individual reactions to war mobilization, and individual perceptions of postwar imperatives. Although the full scope of this industrialist response necessarily must await detailed analysis by sector and plant size, we shall attempt roughly to delineate two distinct responses: that of the large-scale, state-dependent sector and that of the industrial associations we have been studying thus far.

One should be aware of the obvious limitations of such a strategy, which, for want of better source material, we are compelled to adopt. First, other positions, hitherto unacknowledged in scholarly analysis or in the contemporary literature (e.g., the response of unorganized, small-scale producers), might have existed. Second, as far as the positions taken by industrial associations are concerned, one must note that the very nature of an organizational decision tends to mask internal conflict that might have preceded or followed its formal adoption, as well as obfuscate possible differences of interest between the association, as an independent entity, and its membership. With these cautions noted, we shall proceed.

The origins of the state-dependent sector have been dealt with in the Introduction, where it was suggested that from the outset – unlike those interests which tended to join associations – firms in this sector were dependent upon protection, subsidies, and government contracts for their very existence. Instead of seeking horizontal solidarity with other sectors, the major enterprises of this sector sought direct, vertical links with the state.

Firms in the steel sector initially had been founded as large-scale enterprises and had shown a marked proclivity for concentration even before the war (e.g., the formation of the Ilva "steel trust" in 1911–12). They had developed a productive capacity in excess of what the peacetime domestic market could absorb, yet produced at prices so high (lacking, among other factors, domestic sources of iron and coal, as well as little competitive incentive for technical innovation) that their products could never find an outlet in exports (Italian steel in 1914–15 was 140–50 lire per ton, as against 75 in England, 80–5 in the United States, and 100 in Germany).[117] Hence, they supported what was referred to as an *economia nazionale* program rather than economic liberalism: large military appropriations, intervention in the war, and a foreign policy of aggressive imperialism.

Ansaldo, Italy's largest shipbuilder, started initially in the *meccanica*, or machine-manufacturing, sector, producing locomotives as well as ships. Due to the high cost of steel and competition from steel interests which began to expand into shipbuilding, Ansaldo developed its own steelmaking capacity, ultimately becoming a large steel producer in its own right. In the decade preceding the war (1903–13), it had concentrated on warship construction, its annual average tonnage reaching 8,386.6, compared to 1,588.1 for the period 1894–1903. As a historian of Ansaldo's development put it: "The warship, complete and ready for action, represented on the eve of the European conflict the principal production of Ansaldo, together with artillery. From a generically *meccanica* industry it had become, by successive stages, a typical armament industry which had as its principal client the State."[118] Headed by the notorious Perrone brothers, Ansaldo was the most aggressive proponent of Nationalism, pursuing even domestically a self-interested "purification" of the Italian economy of for-

---

[117] Romeo, *Breve storia*, pp. 81–5.
[118] Della Loggia, "Banca di Sconto," p. 833.

eign (German) influence. We have already noted Ansaldo's speculative actions against the Banca Commericiale and Fiat. During the war, the Perrone brothers became somewhat ludicrous in their calculated patriotism, accusing even Dante Ferraris, then president of the LIT and a vice-president of Fiat, of being party to a "true and earnest mechanism of sabotage in favor of Germany" in a confidential note sent to the minister of the treasury.[119] After having received similar communications, Orlando, the last wartime prime minister, actually referred to the Perrone brothers as "maniacs who see Germans, defeatism, and betrayal everywhere."[120]

While the two giants Ilva and Ansaldo were in perpetual conflict over sources of investment capital and competed in overlapping markets, they shared a common interest in Nationalism. In the public eye, both had been objects of severe criticism owing to their "artificial" and "parasitic" nature, as well as their corruptive political influence. Nationalism provided a legitimizing vehicle for their material interests (i.e., protection, subsidies, military appropriations), as well as an ideological cover to be employed against liberal and Socialist critics (ever more necessary in an emergent context of universal suffrage and mass entry into politics).

Creating an identity in the public consciousness between the controversial interests of this sector and the national interest necessitated, in the first instance, an unprecedented attempt to manipulate the press through the outright acquisition of major newspapers and selective "contributions" to others; and, in the second, financial backing of avowedly Nationalist groups and their respective publications.

Ansaldo, which before the war owned *Secolo XIX* of Genoa, took control of the influential Rome daily *Il Messaggero;* Ilva acquired controlling interest in *Il Secolo* of Milan, *Il Mattino* of Naples, and *La Nazione* and *Il Nuovo Giornale* of Florence.[121] A parliamentary commission studying war expenses discovered that between November 1917 and October 1919 alone, Max Bondi of Ilva had spent more than five million lire on press-related "publicity."[122] We have already noted the interpenetration between Ansaldo and Nationalist leadership (Alfredo Rocco was a shareholder and legal advisor of Ansaldo;

[119] Castronovo, *Agnelli*, pp. 141–2.
[120] De Felice, *Mussolini il rivoluzionario*, p. 414.
[121] Castronovo, *La stampa*, pp. 242–4; Romeo, *Breve storia*, p. 124.
[122] Castronovo, *La stampa*, p. 277.

Idea Nazionale was the primary vehicle through which Ansaldo publicly attacked the "German" Banca Commerciale), as well as Ansaldo's contributions to *Popolo d'Italia,* matched in subsequent months by Ilva.[123]

Of greater significance for our purpose, however, than more or less predictable attempts at mobilizing the press behind programs of necessary state support was this sector's interest in productivism, especially during the closing months of the war, when structural weaknesses resulting from ill-considered expansion, problems relating to peacetime conversion, disturbances of civil and productive order, popular anger over war profits, and public debate regarding the future of state-dependent industry had already begun to take place. It was then that support for a particular form of productivism, contained within the more general Nationalist schema, became materially and ideologically necessary. This type of productivism would feature a collective national interest in the continued existence and further development of concentrated, large-scale industry: militarily (national defense, future colonial expansion), productively (the higher rationality of self-sufficient, large-scale units, the irrationality of "superfluous competition"), and socially (protecting "national labor," provision of employment for hundreds of thousands of workers). This was a form of productivism which, furthermore, called for the construction of a "strong state," dominated by the "competent" *borghesia del lavoro,* impervious to "defeatist" and "anti-Nationalist" demagoguery, and organized according to the same functional and hierarchical principles as production. This was a state which might, on the one hand, further the "cartelization" and "rationalization" of industry, while, on the other, "discipline" the consequently concentrated industrial workforce, containing it in compulsory "statalized" syndicates. In a word, this was the corporatist productivism of Alfredo Rocco, exponent of a new *economia associativa.*

As for the productivism of Mussolini, it would appear that the support given by Ansaldo and Ilva was based less on its ideological articulation per se (which, compared to that of Rocco, covered fewer of their sectoral needs) than on the political stature of its author, that is, the enlistment of a bona fide left-wing force against the "reds" and "defeatists" and in support of class collaboration, factory discipline,

---

[123] Ibid., p. 268; Castronovo, "Potere economico," p. 56.

and aggressive imperialism. The Nationalists had been identified only with the right-interventionists; Mussolini represented an opening toward the eventual co-optation of the left-interventionists and returned veterans, the missing mass base for a viable Nationalist program.

This is not to say that the formulations of Rocco and Mussolini were simply reflective of mercenary solicitations. In fact, both men had initially developed their productivist principles independent of direct industrialist interest: Rocco having conceived his corporatist schema in the prewar period before his affiliation with Ansaldo; Mussolini deriving his productivism from left-wing sources previously cited.

Rather, there was an "elective affinity" between ideology and material interest; once bonds were created, however, a gradual accommodation of the former to the latter occurred, never reaching, to be sure, a condition of pure subservience but nevertheless becoming increasingly apparent throughout the postwar period. As essentially political actors, without self-sufficient organizational bases, Mussolini and Rocco were dependent upon financial backing; this imposed objective parameters, quite apart from their separate spontaneous or induced proindustrialist sentiments, within which they had to function so long as such support was necessary. To anticipate, this is not to imply a generic or global proposition regarding the dependency of Fascist groups upon determinate industrial interests but rather to suggest a sequential progression wherein such groups, lacking sufficient material resources at the outset, were constrained to appear as if they were available instruments for "threatened" industrialists (among other sets of "threatened" actors). Once in power, however, and especially after a Fascist regime had been constructed, extractive and distributional resources became available to Fascist leadership directly from its control of the state, minimizing the earlier dependency relation and allowing for a degree of autonomy unacknowledged in many classic interpretations of Fascism, such that the initial "masters" became dependent clients of the reconstructed state, operating within political and economic parameters actually set by their former "agents" (i.e., post-1926 Fascism; post-1936 National Socialism).

In our analysis of relations between the state-dependent sector and the productivisms of Mussolini and Rocco, we have indicated specific patterns of material support and programmatic political interest. This is not to suggest that among the four elements – Ansaldo, Ilva, Rocco, Mussolini – there existed intersubjective bonds or that they formed in aggregate a compact homogeneous bloc. We have already noted the intense rivalry between Ansaldo and Ilva, which, in fact, precluded joint action, despite a higher commonality of sectoral interest. Similarly, the relationship between Mussolini and Rocco was one of mutual suspicion arising from the "leftist" background of the former and the characteristic conservatism of the latter (and, consequently, differences between their respective followers). Programmatic coordination between Fascists and Nationalists did not occur until after Mussolini was in power and two further interrelated exigencies had to be met: first, that of conceptualizing a new and organic juridical–institutional framework which might render permanent authority relations that had previously been based on a tentative melange of residual liberalism, arbitrary repression, and unstable mass support (i.e., the transition, impelled by the Matteotti crisis of 1924, from "liberal Fascism" to "nonintegral corporatism"); second, that of framing the previously autonomous institutions of civil society – enterprises, syndicates, parties, associations – within this reconstructed institutional framework.

We turn our attention now to the second and more diffuse constellation of industrial interests, namely, that of the industrial associations. A comparison between the prewar productivism articulated by these associations and the war-induced productivism espoused by nonindustrial political actors (i.e., Rocco and Mussolini) would indicate that essentially nothing new had been added by the latter regarding productivism proper. What had changed, and changed significantly, was its politicization, its placement within a new context of juridical–institutional reconstruction, its direct linkage with the steering attributes of the state.[124] It will be recalled that earlier associational productivism had been placed within the context of a liberal–technocratic worldview, such that production had been conceived as a private, autonomous, and self-directed realm, following its own intrinsic logic of optimality and formal rationality. Grounded in the public–private, state–civil society distinctions of classic liberalism, this productivism anticipated an emergent pattern of institutionalized class struggle and syndical regulation. But this was to be consensual

---

[124] On "steering" see Habermas, *Legitimation Crisis*, pp. 33–92.

and develop spontaneously from the free play of organized interests, not a compulsive system imposed by the state according to some abstract doctrine. Within this liberal–technocratic worldview, productivism had been less an intended model for state and societal reconstruction than a specific, circumscribed programmatic orientation to function within the existent liberal system. Ideologically, it was to supplement liberalism, not replace it, serving to compensate perhaps for the limited penetration of market legitimation in Italy during an epoch of belated "takeoff" and unprecedented technological transformation. Gino Olivetti often hinted at "Weberian" comparisons with the industrially more advanced nations, in particular, the United States, noting the nongeneralized nature of the capital nexus in Italy and the lack of a "Protestant ethic" in Italian culture (i.e., self-discipline, a secularized vocational ethos, renunciation of immediate gratification),[125] two elements that might otherwise have provided legitimation for industrial capitalism, notwithstanding factors relating to the actual ordering of productive relations. Lacking the material and cultural supports found elsewhere and faced, moreover, with a workers' movement that from the outset challenged the existent hierarchy of factory relations, the associations' ideology had to be grounded in the productive process itself.

In making the distinction between the state and the realm of production, the associations hardly acknowledged the specific supports that the liberal state contributed to the reproductive capacity of industry (i.e., the system of civil law guaranteeing the rights of private property; the provision of education, communication, and transportation services; the promotion of domestic interests in international markets through trade and tariff policies). Their conception of the nightwatchman state simply took these supports as a given. However, with the outbreak of war, and the disruptive effects it had upon Italian industry, the associations tentatively modified their antistatist position and their resistance to state intervention, specifically invoking state aid to complement the now ineffectual efforts of private initiative in maintaining production under such difficult and unusual circumstances. Yet never did such a war-induced reappraisal of the state's role go so far as to entertain a permanent and structural state presence in the economy, in terms of either "protecting the market

[125] Ibid., pp. 75–7.

from its own destructive tendencies" or replacing the spontaneous working of economic forces by a centralized state steering of the productive system (two interrelated phenomena which Habermas identifies as characteristic of "organized," rather than "liberal," capitalism).[126]

In stark contrast to the state-dependent sector, whose prewar development and wartime experience oriented them toward an antiliberal, corporatist postwar reconstruction, the associations' prewar development and wartime experiences oriented them toward a characteristically liberal, anticorporatist postwar reconstruction, one in which the mobilization apparatus would not be extended and developed into a new state form but quickly dismantled and the economy purged of all *bardatura di guerra*. Such an orientation was based not only on longstanding ideological principles, as significant as these might have been in interpreting and evaluating empirical experience, but even more directly on their immediate reaction to the mobilization structure. In their eyes, the mobilization simply reconfirmed an enduring faith in economic liberalism, for experience had once again shown that the state was a poor economic coordinator. Although the precorporatist wartime state had guaranteed managerial authority and had prevented production discontinuities due to labor agitation, the price paid for these net gains had been disproportionately high: state control over all the vital factors of production and contracting out to private producers, as passive agents, productive quotas that had been bureaucratically formulated and were irrationally administered.

Though individual firms had been successful in penetrating the mobilization structure and in momentarily exploiting such privileged status, the misallocation of resources, the production delays, and the administrative bottlenecks that came to characterize the mobilization effort all were perceived by a broad spectrum of industrialists as prima facie proof of the state's incapacity for economic management.

We have seen that the CIDI encouraged its membership not to exploit fully the coercive potential guaranteed in the mobilization provisions, counseling them rather to privately come to terms with workers' syndicates outside the arbitration framework of regional mobilization committees. Though it is true that the mobilization "stick" was always

---

[126] Ibid., pp. 53–9.

available should the conciliatory "carrot" prove ineffective and that the repressive institutional context foreclosed options that workers' syndicates might otherwise have exercised, the CIDI, nevertheless, did make a sincere effort to remain faithful to its earlier liberal–technocratic orientation: private and voluntaristic cooperation between organized capital and organized labor and the granting of material incentives in return for increased managerial authority.

Toward the end of the war, when social unrest and radicalism inspired by the Russian Revolution began to surface, the CIDI maintained this conciliatory policy (e.g., its moderate behavior in the 1917 Turin uprising). A number of firms, like Fiat and Pirelli, actually initiated profit- and stock-sharing programs during this period, hoping to instill in the workers a sense of loyalty to the enterprise, a sense that they had a tangible interest in production.[127] Such a co-optive strategy, interesting enough, was resisted by both the CIDI and the CGL. To the CIDI these programs might lead to conflicts of interest between workers and nonsalaried shareholders, and perhaps lead as well to attempts on the part of workers to influence the technical and financial management of the factory, thus compromising the unitary and absolute basis of managerial authority and opening the door to ill-conceived projects of "worker control." Questions of distribution had to be clearly delimited from questions of production; the CIDI underscored the distinctive functions of industrialists and workers, recommending that "accord between industrialists and workers, capital and labor, ought to be found in areas other than in the invasion of their reciprocal functions." Further:

We are convinced that industrialists and workers fulfill two diverse functions in the field of production: that is, the directive function of the former, the executing function of the latter. It is that way by the very nature of things. Even in Russia, where the new regime appeared in the first moment willing to sweep away every trace of the industrialists, today the government looks to them, beckons them to resume their functions and reorganize production.[128]

The national council of the CGL, meanwhile, put workers on notice against "such illusory forms of betterment," insisting that they focus their attention on hours and wages.[129]

---

[127] Franco Catalano, *Potere economico e fascismo* (Milan: Lerici, 1964), pp. 98–101; Abrate, *Lotta sindacale*, pp. 184–5; Castronovo, *Agnelli*, pp. 159–60.
[128] *BLI* 12 (1918): 1.
[129] Catalano, *Potere economico*, p. 101.

Other less dramatic gestures were made by individual firms, eager to gain acceptance of the existent productive hierarchy from their workers. Agnelli of Fiat, for example, who was known to tour his factories and talk with the workers, initiated a suggestion-box procedure whereby employees who contributed ideas toward improving productive techniques were awarded bonuses, delivered personally by the "Napoleon of the European automobile industry" (as Samuel Gompers referred to Agnelli). Moreover, notices were posted on Fiat factory walls encouraging employees who felt that they possessed skills meriting a position of greater responsibility to consult the management. Agnelli made a self-conscious effort to have his workforce believe that within the Fiat hierarchy there was ample opportunity for upward mobility, affirming that "in Fiat factories one can find more easily than outside even the executives it needs."[130]

Such conciliatory efforts were private in nature, outside the context of the mobilization structure. The CIDI, as we saw in the previous chapter, had always been skeptical of "abstract theories" of class collaboration and legislated labor practice, doubting that the intrinsically conflictual nature of such relations could be resolved in any way other than free syndical practice, mutual accommodation, and private conciliatory efforts. Therefore, it should come as no surprise that no support for such Nationalist concepts as compulsory cartels, compulsory syndicates, principled protection, and imperialism can be found in any association publication. Nor were such corporatist fictions as "just prices" and "just wages," removed from the free play of market forces, taken seriously. To Rocco, profits and salaries were abstract concepts, "compensations" that the "collectivity" rendered to those who direct and execute productive functions, compensations calculated not according to the "mechanical" and "hedonistic" principles of liberal economics but according to productive and ethical standards derived by the state. Similarly, private initiative, so fundamental to the CIDI's liberal–technocratic productivism, was for Rocco not a cardinal principle but rather a contingent vehicle "appearing to be the most suitable instrument for intense production."[131] Rocco harbored no principled opposition to "state initiative" as such, as opposed to "private initiative," and did not exclude the possibility that the for-

---

[130] Castronovo, *Agnelli*, p. 117.
[131] Rocco, *Scritti*, 1: 656.

mer might eventually intrude upon or even substitute itself for the latter, should "national contingencies" call for it. To anticipate, this was precisely one of the fundamental conflicts that would engage industrialists and the state under Fascism.

The *Rivista delle Società Commerciale,* soon to become an official organ of the newly formed Confindustria (and to be edited by Gino Olivetti), well reflected the association's enduring liberalism and suspicion of corporatism. In a review of Rathenau's *New Economy,* which it observed had found little response among industrialists but had found a "following especially among our Nationalists, always disposed to assign major economic attributions to the state," the journal frontally assaulted any notion of compulsory cartels and syndicates, pointing out the past failures of state intervention:

It is the free spirit of initiative and not coercive labor which ought to be the decisive factor in economic reconstruction. With coercion and with the economic order yearningly suggested by Rathenau and his followers, one runs the risk of having as great, if not greater, dissipation of energy than that lamented in the existing system of economic organization. . . . Today compulsory labor and obligatory syndicates would have no other effect than augmenting the meddling of the state in production and would complicate industrial relations precisely in that period requiring a major elasticity of movement and a major rapidity of action so as to confront the extremely varied and complex situations that present themselves in this period of adjustment following the war. . . . Obligatory syndicates, moreover, suppressing the competition between firms, would come to annul the efficiency of that factor which, ensuring the highest quality at the lowest cost, might protect the consumer from a rise in prices. The experiments undertaken during the war and during the armistice demonstrate clearly, even to the most fervent supporters of state intervention, how with obligatory *consorzi* and with the meddling of the state in the running of enterprises, the economic crisis of the postwar period is not resolved but sharpened to the advantage of the privileged few, directly or indirectly through the actions of an inept and malevolent bureaucracy.[132]

The CIDI was certainly no less productivist than it had been in the past. For Olivetti, the level of salaries and employment generated by wartime stimulation and closed international markets could only be maintained, once war contracts were terminated and international markets reopened, with "the maximum yield per worker and the maximum perfection of the productive apparatus."[133] This, however,

---

[132] *Rivista delle Società Commerciale,* 30 May 1920.
[133] Abrate, *Lotta sindacale,* p. 184.

could only take place within a liberal, competitive context, freed from the constraints of state intervention. Nothing but skepticism was vented by the CIDI toward war-inspired schemes, domestic or foreign, of an *economia associata*.

If anything, by the end of the war industrialists (except for the state-dependent sector) manifested what Einaudi referred to as a "revolt against the *collettivismo bellico.*"[134] Beyond complaints of a general coordinative nature mentioned earlier, particular concern was focused on the government's failure to make any tentative plans for the immediate postwar period regarding the extension of inter-Allied agreements covering credit, exchange rates, and the supply of raw materials. In England, France, Germany, and Austria, special ministries had been created to deal with the transition to a peacetime economy, whereas in Italy, as Emilio De Benedetti argued, such considerations "remained in a state of offensive inertia." The most pressing problem was the provision of raw materials, yet little initiative in this area could be taken by private individuals so long as the state retained exclusive control. Private individuals, said De Benedetti, had no way of even knowing "the real state of things" upon which they could rationally plan, since "governmental policy has broken those relations which existed before the war between producers of raw materials and their buyers."[135] According to Dante Ferraris:

The Government has never let any occasion go by without saying one must produce, produce, produce; the salvation of the nation resides only in production. But I ask: what can we, heavy creditors of the state, produce? With what raw materials, if these raw materials are not guaranteed, and at what price, if we do not as yet know what prices we will have to pay for such materials?[136]

Ferraris called for an end to government controls and a rapid transition to a free economy. Whatever coordination would be necessary in the interim (e.g., the supply of raw materials) should be left to private industrial *consorzi* and *sindacati*, operating under state supervision:

The war has clearly demonstrated, if this were really necessary, that the state is not a good buyer or a good distributor. For a rapid return to an economy of peace, the best thing might be an immediate concession of freedom – the

[134] Einaudi, *Condotta economica*, p. 233.
[135] Speech by Emilio De Benedetti, 18 Apr. 1918, text at HAUIT.
[136] Speech by Dante Ferraris, 8 Dec. 1918, text at HAUIT.

fullest freedom – to our industries, cutting all the fetters and stumbling blocks which now constrain them. But since this is not yet possible, one ought to at least substitute for the functioning of the state the functioning of industrial *consorzi* and *sindacati*, which might freely, under state supervision, provide for the supply and distribution of raw materials.[137]

Such a statement was significant not only in its call for an end to state controls but also in its explicit suggestion that private industrial associations, as autonomous bodies, should resume the mediating and aggregating functions that had been appropriated by the state during the course of the war, reestablishing those horizontal, interclass bonds that had been short-circuited by direct lines of interest between individual producers and the state. We shall return to this point in our concluding remarks regarding lessons that industrial associations learned from the war experience.

With the armistice in November 1918, the campaign against state controls picked up considerable momentum, as industrialists were thwarted in their attempts at reconversion by such continuing problems as lack of raw materials; administrative tie-ups in the granting of permits, licenses, and so on; and difficulties in importing necessary machinery. Einaudi noted the existence of large manufacturing establishments with millions in back orders that remained closed because necessary foreign-made machines could not be introduced, machines paid for as much as a year earlier but blocked by the foreign exchange office, fearing a worsening of the commercial balance:

Now there are pieces of machinery, precision goods covered by patents, which are not and cannot be fabricated in Italy, import authorization for several dozen of which had been requested. After infinite solicitations, only a half-dozen or fewer were granted, provoking hilarity among foreign producers and ferocity among Italian consumers, at the same time hampering industrialists from keeping factories in operation which give work to many people and produce items necessary for consumption. The general conviction among industrialists is that it is impossible to introduce the smallest things into Italy without having to make repeated trips to Rome, preceded by letters to deputies and senators. They do not yield, except after repeated and urgent requests, and even then orders are reduced at random to half, a tenth, making it often impossible to meet the need for which those concerned had made the initial request.[138]

---

[137] Ibid.
[138] Einaudi, *Condotta economica*, p. 239.

As for the manner in which industrialists were forced to adapt themselves in dealing with the state bureaucracy, Einaudi gives a graphic description:

While industrialists shuttle between Turin and Rome, between Milan and Rome, between every large and small industrial center and the capital, and while those who have responsibility for running industry and giving work to thousands of laborers are in a state of anxiety due to raw materials which do not arrive, due to licenses to import coal requested months ago which never arrived, they come to approach intermediaries, without skill or position, from elderly coffee-waiters to types who have never had anything to do with commerce, who offer ready permission to import coal or raw material if an adequate price is paid. . . . For settlement of such affairs, an intermediary is necessary, a man used to ministerial staircases and the corridors of government offices.[139]

The culmination of this revolt against *collettivismo bellico* occurred at the end of January 1919, during a postwar industrial congress held at Bergamo. There the most severe language yet was used against

the government which does not keep its promises, which impeded with its fetters the movement of those who would have the will to act, which causes markets to be lost that Italian producers had succeeded in conquering, which prepares disasters for the country by saddling industry with ever greater burdens. Instead of giving freedom to industry, it devises monopolies which then it does not know how to administer, and while it fails to provide, it prevents private concerns from providing for themselves, such that for several months we ran the risk of finding ourselves without oil and coal, almost like during 1917 and 1918.

After enumerating specific failings of the war-imposed constraints on industry, an appeal was made for the full-scale dismemberment of the mobilization apparatus and the immediate dismissal of its officials – professors, counselors, soldiers, and lawyers – "whom we have tolerated too long. Those who work are tired of being commanded by scribblers of file cards. Industrialists and workers are capable of coming to terms among themselves." With the end of the war, "no one any longer feels obliged, now that the enemy is defeated, to remain subordinate to those superior only in conceit and incompetence."[140]

From the foregoing discussion, it should be clear that unlike the state-dependent sector, which had a vested interest in preserving and

[139] Ibid., pp. 239–40.
[140] Ibid., pp. 235–7.

expanding the state's economic role, the position of industrial associations was one of total opposition to continued state intervention and
impatient insistence on a rapid return to an unregulated economy.
Imposed labor peace was too high a price for enduring what they
viewed as an irrational, bureaucratic, and compulsive economic
framework, one that allowed for neither calculation nor efficient
performance. True, managerial authority had been guaranteed, and
managerial authority was a basic element of their productivism. Yet
managerial authority had always been justified with reference to the
optimality formula ("to achieve the maximum effect with the minimum force"), which applied, as well, to all economic action. Based on
this criterion alone, and quite apart from their traditional liberalism
(public–private, state–civil society distinctions), they pragmatically
rejected contemporary conceptions of a compulsively coordinated
economy under state direction. Rather than let such a half-baked
structure continue, they were more than ready to sacrifice controls
which had been placed on labor – the one net benefit of the mobilization – and resume the free, unrestrained syndical practice that preceded the war.

Precorporatism and lessons learned from the war

The war experience had taught associational leadership two basic
lessons that would orient their conduct during the immediate postwar
period, as well as under the Fascist regime itself. The first, more
confirmation of a long-standing view, was that the state was an
inherently incompetent economic manager: that its personnel, its
action-orienting norms, and its decision-making criteria were arbitrary, formalistic, and insensitive to the complexity, pace, and reac-
tive–adaptive exigencies of production; that centralized state decision
making was intrinsically inferior to the optimality resulting only from
the free play of private interests characteristic of a liberal economy.
The second lesson, based paradoxically upon the first, was the structural need for a potent, autonomous, and national class association
to coordinate the common interests of industry and to contain the
fragmentary excesses reflective of individual firms maximizing their
narrow interests at the expense of the class as a whole.

One might, at first glance, imagine that centralized economic management would bolster the collective bonds of industry compared to

the situation in a necessarily less cohesive liberal economy, that somehow global coordination of the whole would automatically lead to
greater coordination and associability among the constituent parts.
Such a view is mistaken on two counts. First, it fails to consider
associative needs engendered in a liberal economic system (specifically, organized class defense through syndicates, as well as representation of the group's collective interests in political confrontation
with the collective interests of other organized groups and the state
itself). Second, such a view fails to allow for the fragmentation of
horizontal class bonds inherent in the peculiarly vertical structuring
of a corporatist order.

Although an extensive discussion of corporatism is beyond the
scope of the present study,[141] a number of general heuristic observations pertaining to the effect of corporatist organization on patterns
of class solidarity is in order to place in better focus the decidedly
negative impact that precorporatist mobilization had upon the CIDI,
confirming at a practical, experiential level the skepticism which the
association had already manifested toward corporatism before the
war from a more abstract, ideological perspective.

Corporatism had been viewed by its theorists and practitioners as
the historical supercession of both "liberal individualism," brought
about with the French Revolution's destruction of traditional guilds
and corporations, and the divisive, debilitating effects of class struggle, viewed as a degenerate political phenomenon where syndicates,
"natural" expressions of functional interests, are misdirected into
conflictual, rather than collaborational, relations.

To overcome individualism and class conflict, the corporatist state
formally restructures civil society along functionally specific, interclass lines into predefined productive "categories," each separately
"framed" within a distinct, hierarchically organized "corporation"
that is vertically linked, as a self-contained unit, to the state coordinating apparatus that integrates from above these functionally differentiated corporations into a functionally interdependent whole. The
potential for conflict is reduced by compelling everyone to join the
official, vertically based, unitary, interclass network and preventing
the spontaneous or voluntary formation of horizontal, intraclass link-

---

[141] For an excellent discussion of corporatist literature, see Schmitter, "Still the Century of Corporatism?"

ages. This is accomplished by making membership in the juridically sanctioned corporations obligatory for all who are occupationally involved within each specified category, while at the same time proscribing the formation of autonomous, competitive, intraclass associations that might cut across these "vertical pillars," horizontally aggregating whole strata. Because autonomous action of a syndical nature (e.g., strikes, lockouts, boycotts, slowdowns) or a political nature (competitive party mobilization, demonstrations, publications) is forbidden, privileged property-holding classes are defended by the state against challenges from below, despite the fact that they, in turn, are constrained to sacrifice some measure of their own autonomy, their own political and economic initiative.

What consequences would such corporatist restructuring have upon the industrial class? Insofar as autonomous associations had been developed, these would become superfluous, as their primary functions would be assumed by the state. But at what cost? Obviously, the property order and managerial authority would be protected from challenges which otherwise might have been initiated from below, by no means a negligible guarantee, especially in a case like Italy, with its history of social unrest and challenges to managerial authority. Yet at the same time, industrialists' capacity to defend property and managerial prerogatives from above, from the state itself as an independent compulsory force, could be significantly undercut. Individual firms might retain the ability to affect state policy regarding their specific sectors through clientelism, but the industrial class as a collective entity would no longer possess the unified organizational resources to influence intersectoral, macroeconomic state policy, now oriented toward coordinating and "steering" the economy as a whole. The industrial class would thus lose its ability to prevent an increasingly independent state from progressively fragmenting the class into watertight compartments and directing economic policy according to its own criteria and needs, however near or far these might or might not be in relation to the expressed criteria and needs of the industrialists themselves.

A second order of problems concerns the transition from a "tentative" or "emergency" precorporatist system (e.g., the war mobilization) back to a liberal, parliamentary one. This involves the freeing of civil society from the state's compulsory domination and the consequent return to liberal competitiveness, where obstacles to autonomous, intraclass action are lowered, if not formally eliminated, and the coercive force of the state is no longer used to protect propertied classes from lower-class groups, which may now freely challenge existing property and authority relations so long as they remain within liberal constitutional limits. Although these "limits," as suggested earlier, are biased in favor of the propertied classes, they are insufficient, in and of themselves, to conserve the status quo once universal suffrage has been introduced and legal restrictions against mass mobilization have been abrogated.

In such a context, the industrial class, its capacity for syndical self-defense and interest aggregation debilitated by previous corporatist structuring, would be highly vulnerable to challenges from below, lacking the requisite structures and intersubjective cohesiveness, both within the class itself and in relation to other bourgeois fragments similarly incapacitated, to maintain the menaced order. In this situation, three outcomes would appear possible: some form of social revolution, the reconstruction of a liberal equilibrium, or the reversion to a more permanent form of corporatism.

Assuming that a viable liberal outcome would be the preferred alternative, it would seem that the rapid reconstitution of inter-sectoral associational bonds would be imperative. Lacking this, as a first step, there would be no collective basis for competitive action in the economic and political spheres. This would be a necessary but not sufficient condition for the resurrection of bourgeois dominance within a viable, reconstituted liberal order. Also necessary would be the reconstitution and repoliticization of a unified bourgeois bloc capable of collectively reimposing its hegemony over other classes. Hypothetically, then, besides resuming functions of syndical self-defense and interest aggregation, industrial associations in this new context would be expected to assume a multifaceted political role, including such activities as meshing the interests of industry with those of other bourgeois fragments, participating in electoral mobilization and placing their representatives in public office, contributing to the articulation of a new "political formula" (ruling ideology), and appropriating coordinative economic functions that the state still possesses but gradually relinquishes.

These heuristic observations on corporatist organization, patterns of industrial associability, and problems relating to the transition from a corporatist to a liberal order are intended to conceptually approximate and identify determinate relations and sequences that will be treated historically in this and subsequent chapters.

As stated at the outset, the mobilization was not corporatist in the fully articulated institutional and ideological sense but could be categorized as precorporatist insofar as the state attempted to formulate and direct economic policy, not through Parliament, but instead through a nexus of functionally specified, vertical hierarchies coordinated from above, and insofar as class relations were "disciplined" through state policy on labor activity, compulsory arbitration, *and* political expression, all restricting the capacity for autonomous syndical and political initiative.

This structure, initially conceived of by the CIDI in vastly different form, came to leave little institutional space for the CIDI. Whether the CIDI's loss of initial influence was due to some inherent tendency on the part of the state bureaucracy to superimpose itself over all autonomous associational entities, was due to the strategic failure of the CIDI in confronting such a tendency, was due to a deliberate choice on the part of its leaders not to have industry directly identified in the eyes of the workers with a manifestly repressive labor policy, or was due to some indeterminate combination of all these is an open historical question that cannot be answered conclusively on the basis of available evidence.

If, however, the cause of this associational eclipse is in question, the outcome is patently clear: the industrial class, as a collective entity, was weakened in two senses.

From above, the state had undermined the internal cohesiveness of the class. On the one hand, the state became an independent locus of compulsory intersectoral coordination, predefining and predetermining the conditions under which individual firms would operate. On the other, the very construction of a market situation characterized by one large and vulnerable consumer (the state) counterposed to multiple producers encouraged a pronounced proclivity for self-seeking, clientelistic strategies on the part of individual firms, each striving, at the expense of others, to monopolize state contracts in their original sectors, as well as expanding into new ones, however improbable the long-term possibilities for postwar survival, in the hope of still greater short-term gain. For the associational motto put forth earlier by Olivetti, All for One and One for All, came to be substituted *Enrichissez-Vous, C'est le Moment Supreme*. As the historian Valerio Castronovo observes: "The war, to be sure, far from cementing solidarity in the industrial front, had given rise to open rivalries and animosities which could not have been more profound and venomous."[142]

From below, the state, through its repressive labor policy, had anesthetized the industrialists' collective capacity for syndical defense, such that it was not until the middle of 1920 that they effectively began to marshal their forces and hold the line against a series of successive concessions they had previously granted. While they publicly stated that these were yielded out of "enlightenment," they privately admitted that the real reason was "imperfect organization and lack of discipline among the industrialists."[143] In contrast, workers initially had shown far greater syndical strength, which was in part a reaction against the repressive policies they had endured during the war and in part a product of success in the early encounters. Membership in the CGL rose sevenfold, from a prewar level of 321,000 to 2,200,000 by the end of 1920, and had extended into new categories (e.g., private office workers and state functionaries). Though it is true that in the climate of labor insurgency following the war, labor confederations everywhere experienced a dramatic rise in membership, the increase in Italy was proportionately greater than that of any other European nation (e.g., France, from 1,000,000 to 2,400,000; Germany, from 2,500,000 to 8,000,000; England, from 1,572,391 to 4,317,537).[144]

Reflecting upon the loss of associational influence, the fragmentation of the industrial class, and the growing wave of resentment against the *collettivismo bellico*, leadership during the latter part of 1918 began to consider corrective steps to be taken after the war. Dante Ferraris, while critical of the government for its "mistaken politics," did not hesitate to pin some responsibility on the industrialists themselves, who, "through the exercise of personal influence, the promotion of single interests or those of determinate groups," had overlooked the necessity of making "some momentary personal renunciations" in favor of collective bodies which might have otherwise

---

[142] Castronovo, *Agnelli*, p. 164.
[143] For a public expression see *L'Informazione Industriale*, July–Sept. 1919; for a private view see Abrate, *Lotta sindacale*, p. 233.
[144] Angelo Tasca, *Nascita e avvento del fascismo*, 2 vols. (Bari: Laterza, 1974), 1:115.

exercised adequate influence upon the government.[145] Olivetti began to reflect upon the prospect of forming a national association "possessing such intrinsic strength as to contain the heterogeneous impulses arising from the various productive sectors."[146]

In the view of such classic anti-Fascist scholars as Salvemini, Tasca, Guerin, and Rossi, the formation of Confindustria, occurring two weeks after the formation of the Fasci di Combattimento (8 April 1919), was a reflexively defensive response by industrialists to the wave of strikes and civil unrest that inundated Italy during the spring of 1919; even more recently (1968), Procacci, in a much acclaimed work, refers rather simplistically to Confindustria as nothing more than a "counter-revolutionary general staff."[147]

Certainly the eruption of unfettered worker initiatives during the 1919–20 *biennio rosso* contributed to the reciprocal growth of Confindustria, just as in the prewar period the formation and extension of industrial associations had been in response to syndical struggle initiated by workers. Two further points, however, must be acknowledged. First, the formation of Confindustria was not an impulsive, automatic, and direct "counterrevolutionary" response to the events of spring 1919 but rather had been a long-standing organizational goal (the "formation of a truly national organization" had been discussed as early as 1906–8, when the LIT began to expand outward from Turin to the provincial and the regional levels). Moreover, Confindustria had been in the project stage as early as December 1918, before the "red wave" had even begun. Second, the classic view of Confindustria as merely a negative response to postwar labor unrest fails to account for the independent effect that the precorporatist mobilization had upon the industrial class and upon industrial associations, as well as the positive role that Confindustria was to play in terms of reconstituting fragmented industrial interests into a collective whole and serving as a political vehicle for direct industrialist participation in a reconstituted liberal state.

It would appear that behind the initial conception of Confindustria lay an unrealized hegemonic project that went well beyond syndical defense, the major function of prewar associations. It entailed an overall political restructuring of the entire bourgeois bloc, such that

---

[145] Abrate, *Lotta sindacale*, p. 201; also see n. 136 above.
[146] Abrate, *Lotta sindacale*, p. 206.
[147] Procacci, *History of the Italian People*, p. 412.

the *borghesia produttiva* would finally assert its dominance over the *borghesia politica*. First, a superconfederation was to be formed composed of employer associations from industry, agriculture, banking, and commerce to coordinate their common interests and assert themselves as a unified bloc.[148] Second, an autonomous "economic party" was to be formed, situated within the heterogeneous liberal orbit, that would be a vehicle through which associational leaders would be elected to Parliament and a political focal point around which the "organized interests" of the bourgeoisie might exert their influence upon the various liberal factions, pressuring them programmatically to respond to their articulated needs. As it turned out, both these initiatives failed. Industrial leadership could not convince the other employer groups to form a superconfederation, and each group gave rise instead to a separate national confederation. A Partito Liberale Economico, as we shall see, was founded, but it was ultimately successful only in getting a limited number of associational leaders elected to Parliament and had little effect on the traditional pattern of personalistic, fragmentary, and insular politics among parliamentary liberals, who were unconnected to any organic class interest or mass base in the country.

The actual project for the constitution of Confindustria had been finalized by Olivetti and Ferraris during the closing days of 1918, and on 3 January 1919, notice was given to the various existing organizations of the imminent formation of "one unique and potent organization to coordinate the associative forces of Italian industry."[149] Unlike the CIDI, this confederation would be truly national in scope and have its headquarters in Rome, the political capital, rather than Turin. Symbolized in this very choice was a definitive break with the formally apolitical character of prewar associations, an orientation, as we saw in the previous chapter, that had already been undermined by the internal collapse of the Giolitti experiment in 1913–14, when these associations began the transition from political dependency to autonomy.

Already in 1918, associational leaders had expressed the view that industrialists would have to play an increasingly political role. On the one hand, their "relative weight" within the bourgeois bloc had

---

[148] Sarti, *Fascism and Industrial Leadership*, pp. 11–12.
[149] Abrate, *Lotta sindacale*, p. 206.

greatly increased, accelerated by the "pushed" nature of wartime expansion; on the other, the state still controlled too many economic functions vital to the needs of industry to be entrusted to "professional politicians" of the *borghesia politica,* who had shown themselves ineffective in fulfilling the needs of industry during the prewar period of transformist accommodation, as well as in performing the economic tasks that they had entrusted to themselves during the war.

Emilio De Benedetti maintained that the presence of industrialists "in the state, that is, in political life, in Parliament, and in the Government," was a necessary consequence of the important economic functions which the latter still controlled.[150] The industrial class, De Benedetti claimed, had become conscious of its political responsibilities; it had "experienced a psychological transformation because it has understood the importance of its function not only in economic life but also in the public life of the nation." Now industrialists "considered it their duty not to leave public affairs entirely within the hands of politicians, theoreticians, and functionaries, and not to leave to the judgment of these the vitally important decisions concerning the economic life of the state and the formation of trends which affect the public spirit."[151] It may be recalled that Dante Ferraris, noting the state's poor performance in performing the economic functions it had assumed, called for the appropriation by industrial associations of such tasks as the acquisition and supply of raw materials.

With the creation of Confindustria, a new hegemonic pretension characterized public statements made by its leadership, the conviction that industrialists were no longer junior partners of the bourgeois bloc but should have political weight commensurate with their economic and technical stature. Olivetti, perhaps engaging in implicit self-criticism, observed:

In reality, the industrialists – and this is their greatest mistake – have until now abstained from taking an active part in public life. They have directed nothing, not even exercising their influence in those new areas of state activity in which their competence might have been truly useful.[152]

In his inaugural address as first president of Confindustria, Ferraris put the matter far more emphatically:

[150] *L'Informazione Industriale,* 22 July 1920.
[151] See n. 135 above.
[152] *L'Informazione Industriale,* July–Sept. 1919.

Scattered until now into usually autonomous organizations, the industrialists have not asserted themselves as a ruling class. They have fought for the future of their industries on economic grounds but have been absent from public life as a tightly organized group with an active and united leadership. New times now summon industrialists to play a larger role in public affairs.[153]

Remarking on the formation of Confindustria, Ettore Conti, himself a future president of the confederation and a senator by recent appointment, suggested that the new body "ought to be a showcase in which industrialists put forth their best men, placing them in view for eventual government service."[154] No doubt Conti had in mind the fact that Ferraris, president of Confindustria barely two months, became in June 1919 minister of industry in the newly formed Nitti government, while Gino Olivetti, general secretary of Confindustria, was elected to Parliament in November 1919, heading the ticket of the Partito Liberale Economico.

Associational leadership had become cognizant of the debilitating effects of precorporatist mobilization on the industrial class, and thus they entered the postwar period with programmatic aspirations clearly oriented toward overcoming these weaknesses and actively participating in the renewed liberal, competitive context as a nationally organized, autonomous, and potentially hegemonic force. Particularly striking, in light of events to follow, was their manifest rejection of dependency either on state tutelage or on political leadership by exogenous forces of whatever label. Initiative, both syndical and political, was to emanate from within the associative structure; Confindustria was to become the focal point around which industry and other segments of the *borghesia produttive* would aggregate their common interests and jointly, as an organized bloc, challenge the traditional political dominance of the parasitic, ineffective, and incompetent *borghesia politica*.

Though associational leadership spoke of industrialists becoming conscious of their public function, of ending their customary estrangement from political life, and of having their interests organically represented before the state, they did not propose any radical restructuring of the liberal state or construction of an *economia associata*. Having suffered the negative consequences of a command economy and precorporatist mobilization, industrial leadership invoked,

[153] Sarti, *Fascism and Industrial Leadership*, p. 18.
[154] Conti, *Taccuino*, p. 148.

rather, the rapid return to a free economy and prepared for political and economic action within the context of a liberal parliamentary system, penetrating the liberal party factions from within in the hope of transforming this amorphous, internally divided, and unrepresentative bloc into a unified expression of the *borghesia produttiva*. Rather than further rationalizing or giving institutional permanence to the economic functions which the wartime state had assumed, associational leadership sought to depoliticize production and return it to the status of a private and autonomous realm within civil society. In this sense, their interest in politics was not of a transformative nature but was that of traditional liberals. The Nationalists, however, sought to impose upon the state a new compulsive form modeled on the hierarchical order of productive relations. This difference should be firmly kept in mind when considering the rise of Fascism and the industrialists' attitude toward corporatism under Fascism.

3. The postwar crisis and the rise of Fascism

Before moving directly to an analysis of the industrialists and the rise of Fascism, we shall briefly examine the general context in which this relationship developed. This entails an analysis of the postwar crisis that led to the collapse of the liberal system and the subsequent rise of Fascism. It is our central contention that the predominant problem confronting postwar Italy was the legitimation of political authority. The ascension to power on the part of the Fascists (or, more precisely, on the part of Mussolini within the framework of a coalition government) may be understood less as prima facie proof of Fascism's invincibility as a political force than as evidence of the political incapacity of the bourgeoisie, the *classe dirigente,* to reconstitute a viable and legitimate regime in its own right upon the organizational and ideological basis of traditional Italian liberalism.

Even without the war and the severe conjunctural problems associated with the postwar crisis, Italian liberalism would still have had great difficulty adapting to the advent of mass politics. In Chapter 1, we observed that by 1911 the structurally amorphous Giolittian regime had already shown signs of internal collapse. In Chapter 2, we noted a marked conservative–authoritarian trend characterizing the 1913–15 period, prefiguring, in many respects, the crisis pattern to emerge once the war had ended.

What we have described as a precorporatist regime drew its legitimation from the fact that the nation was under arms, no matter how much this might have been a calculated attempt on the part of certain interests to resolve from above domestic contradictions threatening from below. What would be the basis for legitimation once the war "emergency" ended? How would the bourgeoisie legitimate its rule when the executive was stripped of its authority to govern by decree, when the precorporatist superstructure was dismantled, when free and unrestrained syndical practice reemerged, and when elections no longer could be "made" (as in the old days of restricted suffrage,

single-member constituencies, limited party development, partial prefectoral intervention, and generalized corruption)?

The specific form of the legitimation crisis befalling the liberal
regime, however, was more than simply a culmination of those long-
term weaknesses of organization, penetration, and ideology which we
have treated thus far. Certainly, it is clear that there had been a
degenerative trend of long standing, that is, the liberal regime's growing incapacity to simultaneously cultivate a mass base and effectively
mediate among an expanded range of strata and groups which were
developing their own associational structures. These associations progressively short-circuited the traditional framework of *trasformismo*
by autonomously advancing their own interests rather than remaining
dependent upon tutelage and compromise imposed from above. No
political adaptation or reconstruction had been developed to accommodate the entry of organized groups into national political life.
Instead of lessening social conflict and promoting stability, as some
liberal observers had initially predicted, organized groups gradually
undermined the traditional modus operandi (which was based, as we
have seen, on a deliberate papering over and intentional nonrecognition of differences grounded in programmatic principles and interests). In such a context, formally organized interest groups did not, as
pluralists tend to suggest, spontaneously give rise to a new constellation of homeostatic competitiveness. At the structural level, one might
say that the liberal regime became increasingly predisposed toward a
generalized crisis, unable to convert through its unaltered institutional
mechanisms new sources of demands into effective and legitimate
public policy.

This generalized crisis reached its most acute stage during the turbulent postwar period; at the very time when demands were greatest
upon the liberal political system, its institutional and ideological reserves were at their lowest. To understand the problem in its totality,
however, one must cumulatively add to the dynamic of long-term
institutional degeneration the problems specific to the postwar era –
in other words, to the problems of structure, the problems of conjuncture. It was this concatenation of structural and conjunctural problems, of systemic debilitation and cumulative "overload," that characterized the postwar crisis.

Regarding the postwar conjuncture, we shall briefly note economic,
social, and political dimensions of the crisis. Furthermore, we shall

chronologically distinguish between two bienniums. The first was the so-called red biennium *(biennio rosso)* of 1918–20, characterized by dislocating inflation and spectacular mass agitation (including the sacking of stores, food riots, strikes, and factory and land occupations). The second was a biennium of reaction, 1920–2, characterized by economic depression, a marked diminution of mass agitation, yet a deepening political crisis culminating in a conservative–authoritarian orientation that we shall identify as "liberal–Fascism." This periodization is critical in differentiating an early moment of class conflict from a later moment of political crisis and regime substitution, suggesting that factors relating to the constitution of a viable and legitimate bourgeois regime in the "postthreat" period cannot be simplistically reduced to the level of class struggle or even class equilibrium but must be sought after at the far more subtle and ultimately "overdetermining" level of political contradiction. We shall return to this point after a specification of the economic and social dimensions of the crisis.

The economic crisis

The economic crisis which befell Italy during the postwar period was substantially similar in form to difficulties experienced by all other major belligerents: the creation of a bloated, war-related productive capacity, enormous state deficits, and unprecedented rates of indebtedness and inflation. Yet the resources which Italy could bring to bear upon the resolution of such problems were relatively limited: it was the last of the major belligerents (excepting Russia) to have industrialized, it possessed the lowest level of available capital, and it had the poorest endowment of vital natural resources. A marked dependence on imported raw materials had always typified the modern Italian economy. Imports had been partially paid for by an expanding, though never equivalent, capacity to export finished goods, and partially in the form of emigrant remittances and tourist expenditures. A necessary condition for the continued success of such a pattern was world peace and a high level of international trade, a condition that the war had ended. Tourism, of course, was curtailed during the war and only gradually recovered during the 1920s; emigration, Italy's historic safety valve, also dropped sharply during the war, only to be subsequently limited by restrictive quotas enacted in the United

States. International trade had been replaced by stringent import–export controls during the war, followed thereafter by a universal drift among all industrial nations toward protection.[1]

In 1914, exports covered 75 percent of imports; by 1918, this had dropped to 20 percent. Not only did the volume of imports remain large while that of exports dropped, but the prices of imports rose faster and higher than the prices of exports.[2] Using 1913 as an index (1913 = 100), the price of coal had risen to 1666.0 and cast iron to 1036.3 in Italy, while in England the indices were respectively 204.0 and 191.0.[3] At the same time, freight and insurance rates soared; the cost of sending a ton of wheat from Buenos Aires to Genoa went from 8 gold lire in January 1913 to 279.2 gold lire in May–October 1918. These factors had a staggering effect upon Italy's commercial balance, which went into an alarming deficit. The nation went heavily into debt but was unable to continue buying abroad because credits extended to it while the war was still raging were cut off soon afterward (credits Italy owed England and the United States amounted to 20.6 billion gold lire as of October 1920, a sum greater than Italy's internal debt).[4]

State expenses from 1913–14 to 1918–19 increased from 2.5 billion lire to 30.9 billion lire, while the state deficit grew from 214 million lire to 23.3 billion lire. Despite the fact that new taxes were levied (on war profits, capital, and inheritance), these were poorly administered and the government was able to pay for an ever smaller percentage of annual expenditures, that level falling from 93.9 percent in 1914 to 29.8 percent in 1918.[5] Fiscal policy, during and after the war, never confronted this glaring discrepancy but instead postponed the day of reckoning by, on the one hand, dramatically increasing the level of public debt (15,219.8 million lire in 1914 to 95,017 million lire in 1921)[6] and, on the other, printing paper currency far in excess of held reserves. The value of lire in circulation rose from 2.2 billion in June 1914 to 11.7 billion in January 1919, to

---

[1] Clough, *Economic History*, p. 170; Romeo, *Breve storia*, p. 127.
[2] Clough, *Economic History*, p. 192.
[3] Ibid., p. 193; Romeo, *Breve storia*, pp. 128, 444–5; Vivarelli, *Dopoguerra*, p. 387.
[4] Paolo Spriano, *L'occupazione delle fabbriche* (Turin: Einaudi, 1964), pp. 40–1.
[5] Federico Chabod, *L'Italia contemporanea* (Turin: Einaudi, 1961), pp. 28–9; Clough, *Economic History*, pp. 196–7.
[6] Chabod, *L'Italia contemporanea*, pp. 28–9; Clough, *Economic History*, p. 196; Spriano, *Occupazione*, pp. 40–1.

12.3 billion in June 1919, to 20.4 billion in December 1920. The percentage of this currency in circulation actually backed by reserves fell from 44.6 percent in December 1914 to 10.1 percent in December 1920.[7]

The progressive weakening of the lira was not readily apparent during the course of the war, as inter-Allied credit and exchange accords kept currencies relatively stable. However, when these accords were terminated, the lira plunged against the dollar and pound sterling (lire/dollar: 6.34 in 1918, 13.06 in 1919, 28.57 in 1920; lire/sterling: 30.37 in 1918, 50.08 in 1919, 99.96 in 1920).[8] This fall in the value of the lira both home and abroad, coupled with an expansion of the money supply and a heavy demand for scarce consumer goods, triggered the disintegrating inflation of 1919–20. This inflation, in turn, was the material force behind the mass insurgency of the *biennio rosso,* as well as the deepening crisis of state finance. The price index (1913 = 100) shot up to 412 in 1918, 450 in 1919, and 590 in 1929, while real wages (1913 = 100) were 54.6 and did not show improvement over the 1913 level until late 1920, when they rose to 114.4. By that time, however, labor disorders and rising unemployment had offset whatever marginal gains had been made in the statistical relationship between prices and wages.[9]

In order to cushion the impact of this inflationary spiral, the state assisted both producers and consumers. It made coal available to the large steel firms at low cost while at the same time subsidizing cooperatives. The most significant measure in this regard was the so-called political price of bread, wherein the government maintained the consumer price of bread constant – compared with the steep price rises in all other commodities – by paying the difference between the inflated price of grain and the stabilized price of bread. Having been enacted in the hope of quelling mass unrest evoked by sudden price increases, the measure became transformed from a temporary expedient into one of the major fiscal and political problems of the postwar period. On the one hand, the political price of bread was viewed as a

---

[7] Felice Guarneri, *Battaglie economiche tra le due grandi guerre,* 2 vols. (Milan: Garzanti, 1953), 1:43; Luigi Salvatorelli and Giovanni Mira, *Storia d'Italia nel periodo fascista,* 2 vols. (Verona: Mondadori, 1972), 1:35; Vivarelli, *Dopoguerra,* 494–5.

[8] Clough, *Economic History,* pp. 196–7; Guarneri, *Battaglie economiche,* 1:2; Spriano, *Occupazione,* p. 40.

[9] De Felice, *Mussolini il rivoluzionaria,* p. 434.

"conquest" of the working class by the state, not to be tampered with in the new context of social unrest and mass politics; on the other, the measure was wreaking havoc with the already precarious condition of state finances. During the summer of 1919, the treasury was losing 200 million lire per month to maintain the political price of bread, and by the spring of 1920, the loss had risen to 500 million lire per month.[10]

The state's fiscal crisis was one of the significant postwar political contradictions we shall deal with shortly, namely, the systemic necessity for a program of economic reconstruction oriented toward deflation, then stabilization, so that capital could be accumulated, investments encouraged, and productivity increased, versus the political incapacity to institute such austere, unpopular measures, given the organizational strength of the Socialist and Catholic parties (mass parties with affiliated syndical confederations), as well as the new electoral imperative, common to all parties, to appeal to the broadest spectrum of voters. In March 1920 the Chamber (or lower house of Parliament) unanimously decided to continue the bread subsidy "simply because no one dared antagonize the voters, even though they knew that this would ruin the country's balance sheet."[11] Nitti, then prime minister (and a professional economist by training), grew increasingly alarmed at the burgeoning state of the budget: either state expenses would have to be reduced (which meant cutting the bread subsidy) or the government would have to continue printing more money, thus further aggravating inflation. With a decree/law issued on 4 June, Nitti lowered the bread subsidy without consulting Parliament. This led to violent demonstrations in the country and unanimous opposition in Parliament to his continued tenure as prime minister. On 9 June Nitti withdrew the decree/law and resigned from office. The political price of bread, for the moment, could not be touched.[12] Only much later, in February 1921, when the militant days of the *biennio rosso* had given way to the contrasting mass demoralization and passivity of the second biennium, was Giolitti, then prime minister, successful in abolishing the measure with little more than limited and formal opposition.

By the third quarter of 1920, the inflationary bubble began to burst

[10] Clough, *Economic History*, p. 204; Salvatorelli and Mira, *Storia*, 1:24.
[11] Mack Smith, *Italy*, pp. 331–2.
[12] Salvatorelli and Mira, *Storia*, 1:144.

due to internal dynamics culminating in increasing underconsumption and also to an international recession which began in the United States during the spring and spread rapidly to the principal European markets.[13] Italian national production fell 40 percent in relation to 1919; unemployment, which at the end of 1920 stood at 100,000, rose to 400,000 by the middle of 1921 and surpassed 600,000 by the end of the year.[14] Particularly hard hit were the firms that had become overcapitalized and bloated in productive capacity during the war. The two giants of the state-supported sector, Ansaldo and Ilva, both failed during 1921, precipitating a crisis in the financial sector as well. Ansaldo pulled down with it its interconnected Banca di Sconto. Fiat, the third largest firm, had been constructed on a far sounder financial base and had been particularly successful in rapidly shifting its production to peacetime commodities. Yet even the giant Turinese automaker, which exported a high percentage of its output, was forced to lay off thousands of workers as its foreign sales were increasingly undercut by the growing drift toward protection.[15]

The social crisis

The postwar inflation and subsequent depression had a profound impact on the social stability of Italy, though it would be crudely reductionist to maintain that economic factors alone were the sole determinants of the mass agitations that characterized the *biennio rosso* and their subsequent ebb during 1921–2. This would neglect popular attitudes, including an inflation of expectations generated during the war regarding the future. In Italy and elsewhere the populace had been led to believe that wartime sacrifices would find compensation in a new and more just social order. Throughout the war, government propaganda had promised soldiers that fundamental social change would greet their return from the front.[16]

Nor were unredeemed war promises the only basis for mass unrest. When considering the spectacular agitations of the *biennio rosso*, one must not lose sight of the generalized international context of massive

[13] *CGII Annuario 1922.*
[14] Paolo Alatri, "La Fiat dal 1921 al 1926," *Belfagor* 29 (Mar. 1974): 298–9.
[15] Ibid., p. 298; Castronovo, *Agnelli*, pp. 282–6.
[16] Salvemini, *Origins of Fascism*, pp. 120–1.

strikes and revolutionary and counterrevolutionary rhetoric of which it was part. Everywhere in the West, both in Europe and in the United States, there had been talk of a "red wave." A plot of Italy's statistics on the number of strikes and the number of personnel directly involved in labor conflicts, however, indicates a steep increase for the period 1919–20, followed by an equally dramatic decrease for the period 1920–1. In fact, the first six months of 1920 represented the peak in Italian postwar labor conflict, when Italy experienced roughly twice the number of strikes (1,769,000) as it did during the last six months of 1919 (877,000).[17] Moreover, as one would expect, *after* 1920 the number of workdays lost due to labor conflict reflects the downward slope of the second biennium (1920: 16,398,227; 1921: 7,702,670; 1922: 6,586,235).[18]

Strike statistics alone do not reveal the full scope and intensity of social unrest which set Italy apart from the rest of Europe during the universally turbulent years of 1919–20. The data for Italy are limited to those categories of workers directly involved in specific instances of labor conflict; they do not include the massive number of additional individuals involved in sympathy strikes and general strikes, to say nothing of other forms of collective action such as food riots, looting, land seizures, factory occupations, and political demonstrations.[19]

The wave of social unrest that began during the spring of 1919 was due primarily to a steep rise in the cost of living, especially the price of food. The first manifestation was a dramatic rise in the number of strikes, as workers demanded higher wages to offset inflated prices. The number of strikers in industry and agriculture – 22,280 in January, 40,103 in February, 68,820 in March – climbed to 87,449 in April and then leaped to 309,026 in May.[20] During this period, even groups not traditionally given to such action (e.g., magistrates, teachers, public officials, even priests) resorted to the strike out of desperation.[21] Economic strikes of one category often provoked soli-

---

[17] Ibid., p. 251.
[18] Carmen Haider, *Capital and Labor under Fascism* (New York: Columbia University Press, 1930), p. 24.
[19] Salvemini, *Origins of Fascism*, pp. 173–4, 184–98; Vivarelli, *Dopoguerra*, pp. 385–454.
[20] Salvemini, *Origins of Fascism*, p. 186.
[21] Vivarelli, *Dopoguerra*, pp. 411–13.

darity strikes among other groups, through which workers' syndicates endeavored to force employers to agree to terms demanded by the original strikers.[22]

On 11 June, food riots and looting began in La Spezia and rapidly spread to other towns. Police and troops rarely intervened, and shopkeepers sought the protection of the local Camere del Lavoro, to whom they were constrained to consign their keys and ask for assigned guards. Meanwhile, in Turin and Milan general strikes were called on 13 June to commemorate Rosa Luxemburg's death. That evening in Turin 20,000 people gathered in the center of the city, chanting "Death to the king." Intermittent clashes took place between police and demonstrators, leading ultimately to a police raid on the Camera del Lavoro.[23]

Numerous other incidents occurred throughout the rest of June, less ominous in nature than the above, until 30 June, when a new wave of food riots and looting convulsed the entire country. Beginning at Forlì, in Romagna, they quickly spread throughout the whole peninsula. Unlike the earlier food riots, looting, and general strikes, this wave of unrest crippled Italy's major cities as well. According to Salvemini, "It seemed in those days that a revolution on the Russian pattern was going on and that nothing could stop it."[24] Local soviets sprang up in Tuscany and Liguria.[25]

In fact, however, these outbreaks were little more than a spontaneous reaction to the steep rise in prices; no political force, not even the maximalist wing of the Socialists, attempted to channel the excitation toward a revolutionary goal. A sympathetic observer, Pietro Nenni, described the events as "tumultuous, anarchoid, bereft of direction or overall concepts and clear and precise objectives."[26] Salvemini and Vivarelli underscore the absence of any Socialist initiative either in inciting these disruptions or in encouraging their escalation.[27] Quite to the contrary, Socialist organizations and syndical organs actively sought to break the wave of unrest and reestablish order. In many cases, the Camera del Lavoro represented the only authority respected by both

[22] Salvatorelli and Mira, *Storia*, 1: 77; Salvemini, *Origins of Fascism*, p. 187.
[23] Maier, *Recasting Bourgeois Europe*, pp. 117–19; Salvemini, *Origins of Fascism*, p. 189.
[24] Salvemini, *Origins of Fascism*, p. 207.
[25] Salvatorelli and Mira, *Storia*, 1: 85; Maier, *Recasting Bourgeois Europe*, p. 117.
[26] Maier, *Recasting Bourgeois Europe*, p. 117.
[27] Salvemini, *Origins of Fascism*, pp. 206–21; Vivarelli, *Dopoguerra*, p. 414.

protesters and shopkeepers, in contrast with the organs of national and local government, which were noteworthy only in their absence.[28] Shopkeepers who wanted to avoid being looted attached placards to the fronts of their shops saying, "I have given over my keys to the representatives of the people," or "Merchandise has been placed at the disposal of the Camera del Lavoro."[29] Local authorities, overwhelmed by the magnitude of the uprisings and under Prime Minister Nitti's orders to avoid violence, could do little more than impose price slashes of 50 percent on essential goods. Nitti gave official sanction to such emergency measures with a decree on 6 July.[30]

During the summer of 1919, there followed an international general strike to protest military intervention against Russia and Hungary on the part of the Western powers, and a wave of land occupations which began in Lazio and quickly spread southward to Calabria and Sicily. The authority of the state, which appeared absent during the food riots and looting, was called into question still again. The international general strike, billed by the Socialists and the CGL as the *scioperissimo*, the supreme strike, the coming of the "great hour," largely fizzled out and greatly demoralized Italian workers. However, Nitti was sufficiently alarmed in its wake that he instructed local prefects to make contact with patriotic volunteers (including Fascists) who might cooperate in the "maintenance of public order" and repression of the violence and revolutionary attempts. Nitti reacted to the land occupations in the same manner as he did to the earlier looting and food riots, refusing to use troops against those who violated private property. Treating the land occupations as a fait accompli, he issued the Visocchi decree on 2 September, which granted prefects the power to legitimate the temporary occupation of uncultivated or poorly cultivated lands (within the next four years, committees of experts and arbitrators were to decide whether the occupation should become permanent and what indemnity should be paid to the old owners). Bourgeois opinion was outraged at the government's weak showing and Nitti was charged with being an accomplice of "rural bolshevism."[31]

---

[28] Vivarelli, *Dopoguerra*, pp. 415–16; Salvatorelli and Mira, *Storia*, 1: 85.
[29] Salvemini, *Origins of Fascism*, pp. 206–7.
[30] Maier, *Recasting Bourgeois Europe*, p. 117.
[31] Einaudi, *Condotta economica*, pp. 283–309; Vivarelli, *Dopoguerra*, pp. 418–34; Salvemini, *Origins of Fascism*, pp. 226–7.

With the coming of 1920, an unprecedented burst of *scioperomania* (strike mania) inundated the country. During the first half of the year, the number of strikers for economic reasons jumped to 1,769,000, compared to 877,000 for the second half of 1919. Data are not available for solidarity strikes, general strikes, street riots, etc., though these increased in like proportion according to Salvemini.[32]

One of the more alarming aspects of this new wave of strikes was the participation of key categories of public-service workers, many of whom (railwaymen and employees of the postal, telegraph, and telephone services) had never struck during 1919 for higher wages or participated in the July international general strike. Railway workers, whose national union had fallen into the control of revolutionary syndicalists and anarchists, struck fifty times between January and June 1920, sometimes holding up trains conveying troops summoned to restore order at various hot spots, as well as trains thought to be carrying ammunition destined for use against Soviet Russia.[33] In bourgeois circles not only was there general resentment against the inconvenience caused by interruptions in the functioning of governmental services, but particular rage was directed toward public-service personnel who joined in general strikes, leaving entire cities virtually paralyzed. As early as January 1920, voluntary associations for the maintenance of public order and public services began to form in various cities. The bourgeoisie began to pass from a state of defensive endurance to one of offensive counteraction; if the state were to relinquish its authority, functions, and obligations, they would assume responsibility for such burdens themselves.[34]

The great industrial conflicts of 1920 will be treated later. Here, we would merely point out that the industrialists, through their powerful national organization, Confindustria, had shown themselves a more compact and powerful force than their worker adversaries. With little or no help from the government (in stark contrast to labor policies followed in other capitalist countries at the time) and without resorting to the solicitation of "white guards," they almost single-handedly weathered a concerted series of worker initiatives and assumed a directing role in the restoration of public order and public services through volunteer committees.

[32] Salvemini, *Origins of Fascism,* p. 251.
[33] Ibid., p. 252.
[34] Salvatorelli and Mira, *Storia,* 1:131.

This action, worker demoralization resulting from unsuccessful initiatives, and the depressing effect of high unemployment brought on by the downward business cycle marked an end to the turbulent postwar industrial radicalism. During the first quarter of 1921, the number of strikes compared with the same period in the preceding year fell from 493,914 to 148,796, and the number of working days lost fell from 6,268,900 to 1,644,250, a decrease of approximately 70 and 74 percent respectively. Writing at the end of 1920, Mussolini observed: "Within the last three months the psychology of the working masses has been profoundly modified." In February 1921, Giolitti lifted the political price of bread with only formal and rather spiritless opposition on the part of Socialist deputies, whereas Nitti had been turned out of office seven months earlier for having dared touch this "working-class conquest."[35] Industrialists, as we shall see later, clearly perceived in 1921 that the threat of "Bolshevism" had passed and that class relations, though not a stable government, had been restored in their sector.

The situation was far different in the agrarian sector. Charles Maier notes that Italy was distinct in having had to face widespread rural unrest in addition to other sources of social conflict which were common to the other major powers.[36] Agrarian radicalism had deep roots in the Po Valley, and particularly in the red belt of Emilia–Romagna, dating back to the nineteenth century. Here it was not a question of red cities surrounded by a white countryside, but almost the reverse. Unlike the land occupations in the south during 1919, peasant agitations in the north were less spontaneous than syndical in nature. In this region the organization of agricultural labor exceeded that of any other country in Europe.[37] The National Federation of Agrarian Workers (Federterra) had organized the *braccianti* (landless salaried laborers) into red leagues, which, in conjunction with locally based Camere del Lavoro and Socialist town administrations, virtually monopolized the various factors of agricultural production. By the fall of 1919, the Federterra had more than doubled its wartime membership and reached 457,000; membership would double again in less than a year.[38] During 1920, strike days lost would quadruple

[35] Tasca, *Rise of Fascism*, p. 90.
[36] Maier, *Recasting Bourgeois Europe*, p. 47.
[37] Ibid.
[38] Ibid., p. 49.

from 1919's already impressive total of 3.5 million. Against Federterra's offensive of 1919–20, the agrarian bourgeoisie's reaction, in
Maier's words, was "fragmented and ineffective."[39]

In his account of the rise of rural Fascism, Adrian Lyttleton suggests that agrarians gave their unqualified support to the Fascist
movement, in contrast to the industrialists, "because the agrarians
never had an organization of their own comparable in efficiency to
the Confindustria. The rise of employer organizations in agriculture
roughly paralleled the same process in industry, but with important
differences. The farmers and landowners were more individualistic
and more backward-looking in their attitude to labor relations, and
many showed scarce interest in association."[40] While success in de-
feating or containing the effects of strikes had contributed to Confindustria's growing influence upon both individual industrialists and
public policy during 1920, the numerous defeats suffered by agrarians
were blamed upon the moderate and ineffective policies of the newly
formed Confederazione dell'Agricoltura. Added to syndical defeat
was electoral defeat. In contrast to the Socialists' relatively poor
nationwide showing in the fall 1920 local elections (compared to their
spectacular success in the November 1919 national election), they did
particularly well in the northern rural regions. In Emilia, for example,
the Socialists took 223 of the 290 communes. Unlike in the urban
industrial centers, here an entire way of life appeared to be at an end
as both economic and political power passed into the hands of the
basso popolo, taking with it the traditional social prestige that the
rural bourgeoisie had always enjoyed. According to Maier, "A hundred reminders pressed home the fragility of bourgeois attainments:
red flags flying over medieval city halls; public transportation interrupted for days at a time, and carriers bedecked with red flags when
they were operating; negotiating from a position of weakness with
powerful labor unions backed by Socialist town councils."[41]

Given all this, it should come as no surprise that a Fascist attack on
the Socialist town administration of Bologna in November 1920
would transform the "Fascist movement" from a rather insignificant,
middle-class, urban phenomenon into a national political force as the

[39] Ibid., p. 175.
[40] Adrian Lyttelton, *The Seizure of Power: Fascism in Italy, 1919–29* (New York:
Charles Scribner's Sons, 1973), p. 214.
[41] Maier, *Recasting Bourgeois Europe*, p. 177.

spearhead of an agrarian reaction. At this no one was more bewildered than Mussolini, who had written that Fascism seemed destined to remain an urban force. A few weeks after the attack at Bologna, a similar operation was executed by the Fascists in Ferrara, followed in turn by "punitive expeditions" against Socialist town administrations and workers' organizations throughout the Po Valley. In November 1920, all twenty-one municipalities had in local elections passed into Socialist hands; toward the end of April 1921, only four were Socialist, and it was not long before the town administrations of these too were dissolved or their leaders forced to resign. With good reason, the liberal paper *Giornale d'Italia* referred to agrarian Fascism as a *jacquerie bourgeoise*.[42]

With official complicity, punitive expeditions developed into full-scale military operations until, one by one, all centers of Socialism had been decimated in the northern rural regions. A detailed description of this process is beyond the scope of the present chapter but may be readily found in the classic studies of Tasca, Salvemini, and Salvatorelli and Mira.

Here we would note only that both the theater and nature of social conflict substantially changed with the coming of the second biennium. From basically urban–industrial areas, the vortex had shifted to the northern rural zones and from offensive action on the part of the workers' organizations to their rather ineffectual self-defense in the face of Fascist violence. At no time between the fall of 1920 and the fall of 1922 (when Mussolini came to power) did the working class, industrial or agricultural, launch any significant attacks or even make any credible threats against the bourgeoisie. Victory, at the level of naked class struggle, had been won by the latter. Transforming that victory into a stable and legitimate political order, however, was another matter.

The political crisis

Having taken a quick historical sweep of the period under consideration, we now move toward an analysis of the political crisis. We may note at the outset that although the question of class dominance had been settled by the end of the *biennio rosso*, the political crisis,

---

[42] Tasca, *Rise of Fascism*, pp. 82–130.

rather than finding resolution, became increasingly severe. If anything, the governments of the second biennium were less stable and comported themselves with less resolution and authority than those of the earlier period. To comprehend this somewhat unusual phenomenon, we must now focus our attention on the profound political transformations that characterized postwar Italy, as well as the inability of the unreconstructed institutional structure and traditional modus operandi to deal with them.

The liberal state that emerged from the Risorgimento had been erected upon a rather limited social base, and it had never been intended to function under conditions of mass mobilization. This had been discouraged by limitations on suffrage, methods of corruption and intimidation practiced by prefects in single-member districts, and pervasive voter apathy.[43] Given such conditions, conflicts emerging within the small, politically active class could be solved through *trasformismo* without recourse to forming national political parties with organizational bases extending beyond Parliament.

These conditions had profoundly changed in the postwar period, and for the first time the liberal state had to bear the full brunt of mass mobilization. In 1912 the vote was given to all males who had done military service, yet the electoral system was based on single-member districts, which, through the machinations of the prefects, still ensured a liberal majority. Thus, in the 1913 national elections the underrepresented Socialists were held to fifty-two seats; Catholic politicians, with little hope of gaining majorities in many districts, came to terms with Giolitti rather than form a separate political party. By 1919 the franchise had become virtually universal for males, and proportional representation had been adopted.

The November 1919 national election, which Nitti conducted with uncharacteristic fairness, definitively ended the liberals' parliamentary majority. The prime minister had optimistically predicted the return of a sizable "constitutionalist" majority and the capture of no more than sixty seats by the Socialists. However, the "constitutionalist" parties (liberals, radicals, Nationalists) retained only 239 of their former 410 seats, while the Socialists increased their total from 52 to 156, becoming the largest party in Parliament as well as in the country. The Catholics, who had no party in 1913 (though 29 deputies

[43] Lyttelton, *Seizure of Power*, p. 8.

were designated as "clericals"), formed the Partito Popolare in 1919 and won 100 seats. Thus, the two mass parties, with 256 seats out of 508, undercut the traditional majority, without which the liberals could not effectively govern.[44]

While the French elections of 1919 demonstrated a high degree of bourgeois cohesion in the form of the Blocco Nazionale, the November 1919 Italian election, as Charles Maier suggests, indicated a shocking state of "bourgeois disarray."[45] In Italy, where liberals were under far greater systemic pressure to unify, they were internally divided, fighting each other, and rehashing old squabbles: interventionists against neutralists, liberal–democrats against liberal–conservatives. Following the traditional practice of clientelism and cultivating a personal following, each of the major liberal leaders – Giolitti, Nitti, Salandra, Orlando – advanced an alternative election program suited to his own tactical position. Furthermore, no effort was made to aggregate the myriad autonomous, locally based liberal associations into one unified national liberal party, or even band together into a national electoral bloc that could run as one list. Within the "liberal area" there were twenty-six separate lists, based more upon regional and personal following than substantive programmatic difference.[46] The prefect of Milan, writing to Nitti about the city's four separate liberal lists, complained that "the said parties are divided, distinct, in multiple gradations that represent no diversity of program but only of personal ambition."[47]

Moreover, proportional representation in Italy encouraged a trend all too familiar in the political science literature on that type of electoral system: the entrance of interest groups directly into the political arena rather than bargaining and compromising within the party structure. Industrialists, for example, formed a Partito Liberale Economico; landowners, a Partito Agrario Nazionale. Of course, there was no real party system in Italy, so these groups could not very well have had their interests aggregated in as yet undeveloped structures. Nevertheless, proportional representation gave them greater incentive to pursue their own sectoral, particularistic interests

[44] Leoni, *Partiti politici*, pp. 257–61; Salvemini, *Origins of Fascism*, p. 232; Maier, *Recasting Bourgeois Europe*, pp. 128–34.
[45] Maier, *Recasting Bourgeois Europe*, pp. 91–134.
[46] Leoni, *Partiti politici*, pp. 257–9.
[47] Maier, *Recasting Bourgeois Europe*, p. 124.

rather than to form a united class bloc that might have better shored up the crumbling facade of bourgeois hegemony. Here the disaggregating effect that precorporatist mobilization had upon the internal cohesion of the bourgeoisie, plus the growing disdain that the *borghesia produttrice* felt toward the "incompetent" *borghesia politica,* found full institutional expression. Interest groups substituted themselves for political parties, short-circuiting the traditional relationship between the represented and their representatives.

Had the *borghesia produttrice* the requisite time, historical experience, and overall capacity to assert their dominance over the divided *borghesia politica,* the fragmented liberal party might have been reconstituted upon an organic class base rather than appear as an increasingly artificial and superseded nineteenth-century relic, fit more for a museum of political anomalies than competition against mobilized mass parties and the defense of class interests. As it turned out, no such transformation occurred and the bourgeois bloc crumbled internally at the same time it was facing unprecedented external challenges from below. This description of the rather pitiful state of the bourgeoisie as a *classe dirigente* is not a mere post factum judgment; the problem was recognized at the time by industrialists, agrarians, politicians, and publicists alike, who sensed that their world was beginning to fly apart while they lacked the political acumen to assess the gravity of the crisis and lacked the necessary structures to keep that world intact. Revealing, in this regard, is the following comment by Nitti: "Italy is on its way to becoming a big Nicaragua. And that because of the will and work of the classes that claim to be in charge. This stupid and idiotic bourgeoisie does not have the slightest sense of the mortal danger we are in and works happily to speed up the catastrophe."[48]

Given the political transformations Italy experienced during the postwar period, bourgeois hegemony could only have been preserved with the formation of a national liberal party that better reflected the interests of the *borghesia produttrice,* as well as reassured fragments of the petite bourgeoisie suffering from status paranoia. Such a party might have been a focal point of "positive aggregation" for the various bourgeois fragments and also for those petit-bourgeois fragments usually incapable of autonomous political direction which generally adhere to bourgeois parties.

In the vacuum created by the absence of such a party, Fascism

---

[48] Ibid., p. 121.

subsequently emerged as a "negative aggregation," drawing to it, for
want of a viable alternative, debilitated bourgeois and petit-bourgeois
fragments. They looked to Fascism as a "next best" solution, one that
might, for so long as necessary, conserve minimal conditions for their
social reproduction. The critical alternatives, to invoke our periodization again, were not liberalism and Socialism, for Socialism was no
longer a real possibility in anyone's calculus by 1921. The alternatives
rather were between a bourgeois order no longer capable of sustaining itself within the framework of traditional liberalism and one
buttressed by a new political force that no one fully comprehended,
yet that appeared by 1922 to have become a more robust and plebe-
ian form of liberalism. Fascism, in the eyes of many liberals, would
add young blood and energy to liberalism and, if properly channeled,
might help renovate the liberal state and restore its authority. This
convergence between liberalism and Fascism we shall refer to as
"liberal–Fascism"; we will return to it in the concluding portion of
the present chapter.

Bourgeois disunity and the failure to constitute a national liberal
party became, as one Italian specialist put it, "the banana peel upon
which the liberal state slipped."[49] According to Maier, the "crisis
within liberalism became the crisis *of* liberalism."[50] The liberals' disunity and lack of a mass base were weaknesses that certainly did not
escape Mussolini, who as early as October 1919 observed: "The
liberals are a tendency more than a party. Many officers, few soldiers,
no mass of people."[51]

Relative to the liberals, the Socialists and the Partito Popolari appeared potent indeed, possessing national organizations as well as affiliated trade-union confederations and cooperatives. The Socialists
had 3,000 sections and by 1921 controlled 2,162 of 8,000 communes
and 26 of 69 provinces. The CGL had a membership of 2,400,000.
The Popolari had 2,700 sections, controlled 1,630 communes, and
possessed a vast network of rural banks and cooperatives. Its trade-
union confederation, the Confederazione Italiana dei Lavoratori, had
a membership of 1,161,238, most of whom were agricultural
workers.[52]

[49] Alberto Giovannini, *Il rifiuto dell'Aventino* (Bologna: Il Mulino, 1966), pp. 6–39.
[50] Maier, *Recasting Bourgeois Europe*, p. 134.
[51] Mussolini, *Scritti e discorsi* (Milan: Ulrico Hoepli, 1935), 2:41.
[52] Chabod, *L'Italia contemporanea*, p. 46; De Felice, *Mussolini il fascista*, 1:426;
Leoni, *Partiti politici*, p. 251; Salvemini, *Origins of Fascism*, p. 139.

Neither party, however, lived up to the true potential that their relative organizational strength would suggest. They could act as a negative force, hampering the liberals and stalemating Parliament, but could not, singly or jointly, constitute an alternative hegemonic force capable of fundamentally transforming national political life. In true Italian fashion, both parties were congenitally marked by factionalism and localism. On principle, all Socialist factions refused to participate in or support a "bourgeois government" (except for the reformists during the fall of 1922, when it was too late). Unable to bring about a revolution and unwilling to make effective use of their representational strength through a parliamentary strategy, the Socialists acted in such a way as to destabilize the liberal state with no strategic plans or sense of responsibility regarding what would follow its demise or how they might assume the role of a new *classe dirigente* and guide the transition to a new order. Typical of this attitude were the remarks of the Socialist deputy Claudio Treves, who before the Chamber admitted his party's helplessness: "This is the crux of the present tragic situation: you can no longer maintain your existing social order and we are not yet strong enough to impose the one we want."[53]

The Popolari were split between an almost Marxist, radical wing led by Guido Miglioli and the more conservative clerical establishment. Mediating between the two was the party's secretary, Don Sturzo, a Sicilian priest who leaned toward the Left and prevented the party from becoming the conservative force that many observers initially expected. Like the Socialists, the Popolari lacked an affirmative conception as to how the liberal state would be transformed or what role they were to play within it. They too were debilitated by factionalism and by their obstinate suspicion of the historically anticlerical, liberal *classe dirigente* that had monopolized political life since the time of Cavour.[54]

Both mass parties lacked discipline and a cohesive national structure. Their distinctively local roots allowed for the systematic, one-by-one destruction of these bases by the far less numerous Fascists during 1921–2, with no coordinated defense ever attempted. Worse still was the fact that these two mass parties refused to reach any accord whatsoever, though they jointly commanded a parliamentary

[53] Tasca, *Rise of Fascism*, p. 73.
[54] Mack Smith, *Italy*, p. 326.

majority and appealed, in large measure, to the same working-class constituency.

Many aspects of the political crisis can be traced either directly or indirectly to the stalemated composition of the Parliament, central organ of the liberal state. In any liberal regime, it is hard to imagine a government effectively functioning without either a workable majority or a sufficiently broad consensus among diverse parties to allow for compromise coalitions. In Italy both these conditions were lacking, denying the various prime ministers the possibility of initiating decisive action (including repression) which might have more adequately dealt with the nation's conjunctural problems. Instead, there were a succession of weak governments and public-policy stasis; the consequent ineffectiveness of the liberal regime, in turn, led to a further erosion of its already precarious legitimacy.

Loss of a parliamentary majority (and thereby loss of parliamentary control) was perhaps the most telling institutional manifestation of the crisis in bourgeois hegemony, for under conditions of liberalism it led to a paralysis of the state. Though the proletariat had already lost at the level of direct class conflict, its continuing numerical strength in Parliament foreclosed the possibility that any government might initiate sweeping fiscal programs at their expense or undertake repressive measures – actions which a bourgeois government sometimes has to take, and indeed did take elsewhere during this period – while at the same time surviving a vote of confidence.

As noted earlier, the liberal state had already entered the postwar period in a distinctively weakened condition, due to the particular circumstances under which Italy had entered the conflict. Furthermore, it had placed all of its prestige behind the obstinate insistence on territorial claims in the Adriatic (beyond the terms of the Treaty of London, which the United States did not sign nor President Wilson respect), only to have these frustrated in Paris in a ludicrous and demeaning fashion.[55] Possessing neither a working Parliament nor a monopoly over the legitimate use of violence, the state lost control not only over civil society but over its own constituent organs and personnel. The authority of the state was openly challenged by groups of the Left and the Right who disrupted civil order with impunity, as well as by civil servants and military officers who only selectively

---

[55] Ibid., p. 314; Salvemini, *Origins of Fascism*, p. 184; Vivarelli, *Dopoguerra*, pp. 342–84.

followed directives from Rome, at times brazenly and seditiously violating them. Basic state functions were either not executed or performed inadequately. Whereas other bourgeois governments had actively come to the defense of property and the capitalist order, in Italy the bourgeoisie stood naked. When it was needed, the government was either absent or paralyzed. Few could argue with Mussolini when three weeks before the March on Rome he declared:

By now the liberal state is a mask behind which there is no face; a scaffolding behind which there is no building. There are some forces, but behind these no longer any spirit. All those who should be supported by this state feel that it has touched the extreme limits of shame, of impotence and ridicule.[56]

The rise of Fascism

In terms of our periodization, Fascism became a major force in Italian political life only at the tail end of the *biennio rosso*, becoming a mass movement and later a political party during the second biennium when the Socialist impetus had already subsided.[57] The founding rally of the Fasci di Combattimento at the Piazza San Sepolcro in Milan, later reconstructed as an epochal benchmark, went largely unnoticed by Mussolini's own admission. On that day in March 1919, Mussolini's intentions for the new movement were rather limited: to prevent the dispersion of the "interventionist Left" and to constitute a new center of attraction in relation to the working class.[58] The original Fascist program reflected these intentions, as well as the social composition of the founding nucleus, mainly renegade Socialists and revolutionary syndicalists who had supported the war. While it stressed nationalism, to the dismay of the Nationalists it also called for distinctively left-wing reforms, including a compulsory law for the eight-hour workday, minimum wages, participation of workers' representatives in the technical management of industry, transfer to morally and technically qualified proletarian organizations the responsibility for operating industries and public services, a heavy and progressive tax on capital that would take the form of partial expropriation of all kinds of wealth, confiscation of all the properties belonging to religious congregations and abolition of all the revenues of episcopal

[56] Mussolini, *Scritti*, 2:353.
[57] Tasca, *Rise of Fascism*, p. 300.
[58] De Felice, *Mussolini il rivoluzionario*, p. 500.

sees, which "at present constitute an enormous burden on the nation while serving as a prerogative for a few privileged persons," revision of all contracts for supplying war material, and confiscation of 85 percent of war profits.[59] Against the "internationalist" Socialists, who had "betrayed the Patria," they sought to compete for the same working-class constituency, and returned veterans as well.

It is sometimes forgotten that during the first year of its existence, the movement supported all the spontaneous mass initiatives of the *biennio rosso,* often berating the Socialists for not being sufficiently militant.[60] In March 1919, Mussolini supported the first occupation of a factory that Italy had ever witnessed, initiated by the newly constituted UIL, a trade-union confederation founded by interventionist revolutionary syndicalists. During this action against the Franchi-Gregorini metalworks in Dalmine, which had threatened to lock its gates rather than give in to UIL demands, workers carrying the national flag forced their way into the factory and continued production. Mussolini heaped praise upon this "productivist strike" in *Popolo d'Italia.*[61] Occasionally, local *fasci* went further. At their first meeting, the Ligurian Fascists praised the refusal of the seamen's union to transport supplies to White Russia, causing some Nationalists to walk out in disgust.[62]

However, all attempts at cultivating a working-class base and drawing the proletariat away from Socialist institutions met with failure. When Mussolini was a candidate in Milan during the November 1919 national election, he received only 5,000 of the 270,000 votes cast. From this point on, though not in perfectly linear fashion, Fascism began to move to the Right. Over the next two years its composition would change, as many Socialists, revolutionary syndicalists, anarchists, and republicans dropped out of the movement, replaced by bourgeois and petit-bourgeois elements who were disaffected from the "constitutionalist" bloc.[63] At the same time, the Fascist program would be gradually stripped of its radical demands, replaced by more-conservative formulations reflective of the growing convergence between Fascists and liberals.

[59] Ibid., p. 501. For an English text of the Fascist program see Charles Delzell, ed., *Mediterranean Fascism* (New York: Harper, 1970), pp. 13–14.
[60] Salvemini, *Origins of Fascism,* pp. 214–15.
[61] De Felice, *Mussolini il rivoluzionario,* p. 503.
[62] Lyttelton, *Seizure of Power,* p. 68.
[63] De Felice, *Mussolini il rivoluzionario,* pp. 505–6.

The 1920 program still called for worker representation in management, but "restricted to matters regarding personnel," no longer "the technical management of industry"; confiscation of 85 percent of war profits was narrowed to those profits left "unproductive"; the "great value of the *borghesia di lavoro*" was recognized. By 1921, the program would advocate the disciplining of "the disorderly struggles between classes and occupational interests"; reducing the economic functions of the state ("the return to private enterprise of those industrial plants whose management by the state has proven unsatisfactory"); the "termination of the monopoly of the post and telegraph system so that private initiative can move into this field and eventually replace state control"; the return to fiscal conservatism ("balancing the budgets of the State and local public agencies to be achieved through rigorous economies in all parasitical and superfluous bodies"); the "rigid safeguarding of the taxpayers' money, eliminating every subsidy or special favor on the part of the State or any other public agency to consortiums, cooperatives, industries, clienteles, and other entities which even though they may be incapable of managing their own affairs are not indispensable to the nation"; opposition "to the kind of financial and tax demagoguery that discourages initiative and sterilizes the very sources of saving and national productivity"; and the social utility of private property ("the National Fascist Party is in favor of a regime that encourages the growth of national wealth by spurring individual initiative and energy which constitute the most powerful and fruitful element in economic production, and it absolutely repudiates the motley, costly, and uneconomic machinery of state control, socialism, and municipalization").[64]

Until November 1920, however, the Fascists were a rather small, inconsequential, urban movement whose sporadic attacks against Socialist demonstrations had but marginal significance in national politics. Mussolini ended that total state of isolation in which he found himself after the November 1919 election by identifying himself with D'Annunzio's occupation of Fiume, but it was not until the outbreak of rural Fascism in the Po Valley that the movement began to expand numerically and acquire an unsuspected mass base, becoming a political force of national importance.

Mussolini's insertion into national politics occurred between the closing days of 1920 and the spring of 1921 and was the result of a

---

[64] Delzell, *Mediterranean Fascism*, pp. 14–37.

trade-off with Giolitti. Mussolini attained for the Fascists inclusion in the anti-Socialist Blocco Nazionale, whose electoral support enabled the movement to emerge from the May 1921 election with thirty-four seats in Parliament and entry into the centrist "constitutionalist" inner sanctum, where all effective political compromise and brokerage traditionally took place. Giolitti secured Mussolini's neutrality before forcibly evicting D'Annunzio from Fiume and hoped to domesticate and absorb the emergent political force as a subordinate element within his Right-Center coalition.

Once in Parliament, however, Mussolini declared his independence from Giolitti, and while Fascist violence was raging in the periphery, he sought to solidify his position in Rome by reassuring potential allies and dividing known enemies. Characteristic of this new, more moderate Mussolini was his first speech in the Chamber of Deputies. To the liberals, he affirmed his anti-Socialism, he called for a return to the "Manchestrian" state, and he underscored the historical viability of capitalism. He appealed to the right wing of the Partito Popolari and the Vatican by claiming his opposition to divorce, his support for school reform, his intolerance for anticlericalism, and his hope that church–state relations could be finally resolved. "I affirm here and now that today the Latin and imperial tradition of Rome is represented by Catholicism." Finally, he raised the possibility of a change in the Fascists' attitude toward the CGL, if the confederation would break from the Socialist Party, praising its realism and technical competence.[65]

Mussolini, however, was faced with two threatening contradictions, and only his great skill at mediating both made possible the eventual political success of Fascism. The first was a growing schism during 1921 between what Gramsci and others referred to as *i due fascismi* (the two Fascisms): the blindly reactionary rural Fascism supported by large landowners who had no sense of politics other than *squadrismo* and the urban, middle-class movement of which Mussolini was part, increasingly inclined toward becoming an aggregating national "middle party" and coming to power through constitutional means.[66] The second, related contradiction concerned a precarious balance between terror and politics which Mussolini had to

[65] Ibid., pp. 22–7; Mussolini, *Scritti*, 2:163–88.
[66] De Felice, *Mussolini il fascista*, 1:12–20; Antonio Gramsci, *Socialismo e fascismo: "L'Ordine Nuovo,"* 1921–22 (Turin: Einaudi, 1971), pp. 297–9; Lyttelton, *Seizure of Power*, pp. 54–5.

maintain vis-à-vis the liberal bourgeoisie: on the one hand, Fascism had to remain an armed force, ready to help reestablish civil order should the need arise; on the other, Mussolini had to demonstrate that it was a *disciplined* force which he alone could dominate and prevent from becoming a greater liability, with its excess brutality and at times senseless disruption of civil order, than an asset.

Both these contradictions exploded during the spring of 1921 and threw the movement into a state of internal crisis from which few observers thought it would emerge intact. This crisis was precipitated by an increasing wave of violence by the provincial *squadristi*, which began to alienate public opinion, no longer fearing "Bolshevism" and concerned that Fascism might become a major obstacle to a return to normalcy and social peace. Mussolini, sensing this drift, attempted for the first time – and certainly not the last – to control squadrism. Given the loose organizational structure of the movement, however, no discipline could be imposed from the center. As Lyttleton suggests:

The movement of provincial *squadrismo*, although originally encouraged from the centre, was a "chaotic ensemble of local reactions." The speed and nature of its development was neither foreseen nor entirely welcomed by Mussolini and the national leadership. *Squadrismo* soon revealed itself as a Frankenstein monster, uncontrollable by its inventors.[67]

Sensing strong parliamentary sentiment for a formal truce between Fascists and Socialists, especially with Bonomi's ascension to power in July 1921, combined with the need to demonstrate that Fascism could be controlled by him and play a constructive, rather than a totally negative, role, Mussolini began negotiations which would lead to the "pacification pact" and moderated the tone of *Popolo d'Italia* to prepare Fascists for its signing. On 13 July, for example, he wrote:

Until now we have used strong remedies to mend the ways of the Italian working people. But an able physician knows how to adapt the medicine to the course of the sickness. To speak of an Italian working class that now goes Bolshevist is absurd. Everyone knows that the mentality of the workers as a whole is basically different from what it was two years ago. . . . If we intend to remain always on the level of violence, this will show that we possess no truth, but we are only a negative phenomenon. I once was ready to consent to the use of violence. But now, for national reasons, and above all for human reasons also, I am against it.[68]

---

[67] Lyttelton, *Seizure of Power*, pp. 54–5.
[68] Salvemini, *Origins of Fascism*, p. 335.

Eight days later an incident at Sarzana compelled Mussolini to hasten the pace of this conciliatory process. A punitive expedition of six hundred *squadristi* was repelled by the police, the *arditi del popolo,* and workers. Not only were the Fascists repelled, they were literally chased out of town, leaving behind eighteen victims, some impaled on pitchforks and stabbed with gardening knives. It appeared as if a civil war were beginning which might now find the Fascists isolated. Rather than protest by breaking off the negotiations in progress, Mussolini sought to have the pact signed as quickly as possible.[69]

When the pact was signed on 3 August, the provincial Fascists began to rebel against Mussolini's leadership. As De Felice points out, *squadristi* had nothing to gain and everything to lose from pacification: the end of their local power, status, and material support. Condemned to obscurity and inaction, possibly liable to stand trial for their criminal acts, they would in no way countenance a betrayal of *their* "revolution."[70] Aligned with the provincial leaders were the agrarians and the Fascist syndicalists who feared that without intimidation, the Socialist syndicates and leagues might return from the dead. Regional conferences were held and resolutions voted rejecting the pact.

However, the crisis ended in November 1921 at the Fascist national congress. Mussolini's opponents were divided among themselves, no alternative leader emerged, and no consensus was reached over the movement's future orientation. A compromise was struck, but clearly in Mussolini's favor: he agreed to repudiate the pacification pact, yet the movement was transformed into a party. The more centralized, hierarchical party structure gave Mussolini, now Fascism's undisputed Duce, significantly more power, especially in relation to the provincial leaders. Although he may not have fully realized it at the time, the continued existence – even if a bit more muzzled – of seemingly mad, recalcitrant elements gave Mussolini some degree of leverage over the liberals before the March on Rome and afterward: if he were afforded greater power, it was thought, he would be in a stronger position to keep the violent *squadristi* in check. The transformation from movement to party also enabled Mussolini to insert Fascists in the Right-Center area of Parliament, programmatically close to the liberals, one wing of the Popolari, and the Right in general.

Nevertheless, *squadrismo* continued to run the risk of alienating

[69] De Felice, *Mussolini il fascista,* 1:139.
[70] Ibid., p. 146.

public opinion when it became particularly odious. To counter this, Mussolini tailored Fascist programmatic announcements to reassure the liberals and the world of business, stressing a return to the "Manchestrian" state and the value of private initiative, hierarchy, fiscal conservatism, and productivism. The financial program written in January 1922 was particularly well received, drawing praise from none other than Luigi Einaudi, then economic specialist of the *Corriere della Sera,* who contrasted it to the "empty muddle of commonplaces" pumped out by the "so-called liberals, Popolari, Socialists, and Communists." The bases of the Fascist program, to Einaudi, were "none other than the old immortal principles of liberalism, but it is a pleasure, in any case, to see them repeated by bold youths."[71] In an article entitled "Which Way Is the World Going?" Mussolini claimed: "It may be that in the nineteenth century capitalism needed democracy; now it can do without it. . . . Democracy in the factory lasted only as long as a bad dream. What has happened to the German *Betriebsrate* and the Russian factory councils?"[72]

Mussolini placed Fascist deputies in the Parliamentary Economic Alliance, which was led by none other than Gino Olivetti of Confindustria, and appropriated major elements of the alliance's program in the September 1922 Fascist economic program. Once again, Einaudi was full of praise in the *Corriere della Sera:*

This newspaper, which, without pretending to guide any party, places its point of honor in the stirring of ideas, is pleased that a party, whatever be its name, has returned to the old liberal traditions and has drunk once again from the immaculate source of life of the modern state, and wishes that it not degenerate and that it agree to seriously implement the liberal program without contaminating it with impure contacts.[73]

The announcement of the decidedly liberal economic program of the Fascist Party was followed by Mussolini's speech at Udine later in September, where, once again, the theme of stripping the state of all economic functions was stressed. "Enough of the railwayman state, with the postman state, with the insurer state. Enough of the state in business at the expense of the Italian taxpayers, aggravating and exhausting finances of the Italian state."[74]

[71] Ibid., p. 242.
[72] Lyttelton, *Seizure of Power,* p. 75.
[73] De Felice, *Mussolini il fascista,* 1:332.
[74] Mussolini, *Scritti,* 2:320.

Mussolini's astute mixture of liberalism and violence effectively neutralized many moderates who would have opposed him had he represented *only* violence or had he mixed violence with the primitive leftism of the original Fascist program. Suspicions continued, to be sure, and no one thought of a cabinet dominated by Fascists, much less a government presided over by Mussolini; yet there was a growing consensus among liberal politicians, and the borgeoisie in general, favoring Fascist participation in a future cabinet. For example, this was the position of Luigi Albertini, editor of the *Corriere della Sera:* Fascism must be constitutionalized before it was too late; it was time for violence to end; participation in government would make Fascism "responsible." In substantial agreement with Albertini were all the major liberals: Giolitti, Nitti, Salandra, and Amendola.[75] Mussolini shrewdly took advantage of this sentiment and entered into separate negotiations with Giolitti, Nitti, Salandra, Orlando, and Facta regarding the terms under which the Fascists would enter their respective potential cabinets, knowing full well that he stood no chance of coming to power in this manner but nevertheless could keep these leaders divided and neutralized while he was actually planning the March on Rome.

Timing was of the utmost importance, however, for two related reasons. First, Mussolini feared that the *squadristi* might get completely out of hand, undercutting his stature as a Right-Centrist, as well as disillusioning those who thought him capable of disciplining his followers.[76] Second, such violence might in turn lead to greater cooperation between the Socialists and the Popolari, who jointly might then support another Giolitti ministry, this time pledged to uphold legality. Mussolini feared the second possibility more. During the course of a 16 October meeting in Milan with Fascist leaders who were asking for more time to plan the March on Rome, Mussolini said, "we need to activate the masses to create an extraparliamentary crisis and come to power. We need to impede Giolitti's coming to power. As he fired on D'Annunzio, he would fire on the Fascists."[77] Speaking to Cesare Rossi that same day, Mussolini again aired the same preoccupation. "If Giolitti returns to power, we are screwed [*fottutti*]. Remember that at Fiume he bombarded D'Annunzio. The

[75] Barie, "Luigi Albertini," p. 532.
[76] De Felice, *Mussolini il fascista*, 1:305.
[77] Ibid.

others did not wish to understand that. . . . but I have taken a stand. Within a month all the preparations must be finished."[78]

We need not go into detail concerning the March on Rome itself. Instead, we shall conclude this treatment of the rise of Fascism by briefly placing the event in context. Looking retrospectively at the epoch of Italian Fascism, one is tempted to say that "Fascism" came to power on 31 October 1922. Although such a statement is to some degree formally correct, it misleadingly suggests a moment of clear demarcation between the liberal regime and the Fascist regime in institutional structure and in subjective recognition. As we shall see, the "Fascist regime" was a long time in the making, especially when compared to the German experience of 1933. What emerged on 31 October 1922 we shall call, for want of better words, "liberal–Fascism," a hybrid, unstable, and transitory regime type under which the formal juridical–institutional framework of the liberal regime was conserved (i.e., party and syndical pluralism, competitive elections, freedom of the press, freedom to strike, etc.) and under which political control and repression were executed selectively and informally without recourse to special legislation or a new constitution.

Furthermore, as Maier suggests, there was no sense of an "epochal breaking point" in public opinion either on the part of Socialists, who called for no mass demonstrations or general strikes, or on the part of liberals, who thought that Mussolini would be replaced after a brief interlude.[79] Certainly no one thought that "Fascism" – whatever that might have meant – had come to power: Mussolini headed a coalition government consisting of three Fascists, two Popolari, four liberals, the philosopher Giovanni Gentile, and two military ministers. Had it not been for the right-wing Fascists, even Gino Baldesi of the CGL would have entered the cabinet as minister of labor. Liberals and industrialists thought they had neutralized the March on Rome as a "revolutionary phenomenon" by having Mussolini become prime minister through correct constitutional procedure. Albertini went so far as to say, "Once he is at Rome, he will be much more subject to influence."[80] Given the rather moderate composition of the government, which greatly displeased the rural Fascists, who demanded an all-Fascist cabinet, and the patently liberal economic policy to follow, it appeared – for a time – that Albertini might have been correct.

[78] Ibid., pp. 304–6.
[79] Maier, *Recasting Bourgeois Europe*, p. 324.
[80] Lyttelton, *Seizure of Power*, p. 96.

We suggested that the political crisis of postwar Italy found its resolution in a hybrid regime which represented a growing convergence between liberalism and Fascism. Having dealt with one side of this partnership, the growing liberal coloration which the Fascists assumed in 1921–2, we turn now to the liberals.

We noted that in response to the red wave, practically all the Western nations experienced a conservative shift such that strikes, mass demonstrations, and demands for social justice were met with rigorous and usually repressive state action. This was not the case in Italy, because of the liberals' political weakness, as revealed in their inability to constitute a strong, stable government with which to conserve the bourgeois order and promote economic reconstruction. Only by extraparliamentary means, therefore, could action be taken similar to that legitimately initiated elsewhere. Above all, this meant finding a counterforce that could stand up to the ascendant force of Socialism and "neutralize" the locally based strongholds of the Socialists and Popolari so that at the national level the political balance might once again shift back to the traditional liberal center.

Though some degree of liberal sympathy toward Fascism can be traced back to the early days of the *biennio rosso*, when Blackshirts confronted Socialist demonstrators in the streets and numbered among the "volunteers" in the various committees for the maintenance of public order, it was not until the outburst of rural Fascism during the fall of 1920 that Fascism became a national political force, worthy of attention, as it "liberated" northern rural zones from Socialist and Catholic dominance. Such liberal spokesmen as Albertini, relatively hostile toward Fascism until then, would refer to the first punitive expedition in Bologna as a "sainted reaction."[81] Although liberal spokesmen such as Albertini would at times criticize Fascist methods, particularly when the dosage appeared disproportionate, there was widespread appreciation of their practical results.

Concern that the Fascist movement might self-destruct before fulfilling its "mission" was voiced during the summer of 1921, when the Fascists were in a state of internal crisis. The liberal–conservative *Giornale d'Italia* of 19 August stated:

We are not impatient for the development of the crisis in fascism; on the contrary, we have criticized Mussolini for wanting to bring it on. In our view, as we have often said, fascism has only a temporary function, but for precisely

81 De Felice, *Mussolini il rivoluzionario*, p. 662.

this reason it must be liquidated only gradually, when it becomes superfluous.
. . . The premature crisis of fascism is very harmful, and its immediate disintegration would be ever moreso, since it would weaken national and conservative political forces and leave the ultra-democratic forces in control of the country's destiny. Hence, it would be a mistake for the fascists to break up their forces now and leave the ground open for unfettered democracy in which the socialists would be the real masters.[82]

By 1922, when the liberal coloration of Fascist Party programs was universally praised in the bourgeois press, it was thought – as De Felice put it – that Fascism might be "liberalism of the masses."[83] Though programmatically adhering to traditional liberal doctrine, Fascism had roots in the popular classes, bringing to liberalism new blood and determination, while helping to reestablish the traditional order.[84] In March 1922, Albertini called for a government with "Fascist resolution and liberal spirit."[85] On 24 September 1922, Salandra proclaimed himself an "honorary Fascist," saying that only advanced age kept him from joining the party and donning a black shirt.[86]

Significantly, when a national liberal party was finally formed (Partito Liberale Italiano) at Bologna on 8–10 October, affinity with Fascism was manifest in attire (khaki shirts), speech, and program. A motion to add the adjective "democratic" to the official name of the party was roundly defeated. The new party secretary, Giovannini, admonished the assembly to "reject that democracy which has trafficked with Socialism, that democracy which has poisoned the country, prostituting it to Socialism." Amadeo Sandrini, a member of Salandra's faction, stated: "In Fascism I see the principle that unites us. Let there be an association, a collaboration between us and them." The party program, like that of the Fascists, called for restoring the state's authority, stripping the state of all economic functions, privatizing the public services, balancing the budget and revising "demagogic" fiscal policy, reducing public expenses and the number of state employees, promoting private property and individual initiative, and including in public education preference for "collaboration between social classes in opposition to the principle of class struggle." Commenting on the congress, *Il Secolo* wrote: "It is difficult to deny

---

[82] Tasca, *Rise of Fascism*, pp. 154–5.
[83] De Felice, *Mussolini il fascista*, 1:226.
[84] Castronovo, *La stampa*, pp. 318–20.
[85] Ibid., p. 320.
[86] Paolo Alatri, *Le origini del fascismo* (Rome: Riuniti, 1971), p. 348.

to the liberals at Bologna the attribute of conservatives, or even, if one wished, of reactionaries."[87]

Nitti, a liberal–democrat, speaking on 20 October, argued that the budget had to be balanced, strikes in public services made a criminal offense, all reforms likely to impede production or discourage investment of capital abandoned, and demagogic fiscal legislation dropped. He added: "Democracy exists, socialism exists, but fascism too exists as an ethico-social phenomenon and has developed to such an extent that no statesman can neglect it. . . . We should utilize all live forces and welcome the idealistic part of fascism, which has been the cause of its progress."[88]

Alberto Bergamini, editor of *Giornale d'Italia* and a close friend of Croce and Salandra, wrote on 6 October: "We are sincere friends of the Fascists." After the March on Rome, on 30 January 1923, he wrote that he was proud to have supported the movement which brought Mussolini to the government, that he had no regrets. Finally, on 24 February 1923, he wrote:

Between Fascism and the Liberal Party there is developing a system of relations which could not be more amicable. . . . We believe that one ought to look forward to an even closer tie than at present and an understanding which would permit the establishment of reciprocal collaboration on firm bases. The principles that inspire the two parties are identical, and we liberals can claim the honor of having been, so to say, pre-Fascists when it was fashionable to be democrats.[89]

At the time of the March on Rome, and for some time thereafter, liberals deluded themselves that they still were in ultimate control and that they had domesticated Mussolini. During this period Croce saw no essential contradiction between liberalism and Fascism; he felt that Fascism could not last, because it reflected no "idea." Actually, as late as June 1926, when the juridical framework for a distinctively Fascist regime was already being laid, Croce told a friend that he was sure the liberals could overturn Mussolini when the time was right, and in the meantime "he is our prisoner."[90]

[87] Ibid., pp. 209–11; Giovannini, *Il rifiuto*, pp. 77–135; Leoni, *Partiti politici*, pp. 287–91; Maier, *Recasting Bourgeois Europe*, pp. 341–3.
[88] Tasca, *Rise of Fascism*, pp. 275–6.
[89] Alatri, *Origini*, p. 105.
[90] Alastair Hamilton, *The Appeal of Fascism* (New York: Avon, 1978), pp. 69–77; Denis Mack Smith, "Croce," *Journal of Contemporary History* 8 (Jan. 1973): 49.

Industrialists and the rise of Fascism

Having treated the multiple postwar crises which found their tentative resolution in Mussolini's ascension to power, we turn now to the industrialists' role in this process, the particular problems they faced, and their specific relation to the rise of Fascism.

Before beginning the analysis, however, some preliminary remarks are in order regarding the traditional Marxist view of Fascism as the instrument of the industrial bourgeoisie, a view shared by both Communists and Socialists.[91] Illustrative is Turati's confrontation with Mussolini in the Chamber on 19 November 1922: "The Confederation of Industry – which swaggers at being the real victor, of having decisively influenced the highest spheres in its triumph – is today there at the bench of government through interposed persons. Honorable Mussolini, I see the pointed and Semitic nose of Honorable Olivetti emerging all too visibly from behind your shadow."[92] Two reasons are typically cited for such instrumental use of Fascism on the part of industrialists: the need to impede the advance of a well-organized, revolutionary proletariat and the need to terminate Giolitti's "demagogic" reforms (worker control, tax on war profits, registration of stocks in the bearer's name, etc.).[93] Both reasons are without substance. As for the latter, we have already noted and will see once more that Giolitti's reforms already had been administratively nullified, though not formally revoked, by the end of 1921. As for the former, we have seen that the proletariat had already been defeated by the end of the *biennio rosso;* it was unsuccessful in defending its previous "conquests" (e.g., the political price of bread), to say nothing of preserving its organizational integrity, *before* Mussolini came to power. The image of the bourgeoisie – or at least the industrialists – with their backs to the wall and turning to a "white guard" is simply fallacious. Mussolini, as well as bourgeois publicists and the industrialists, noted a return to mass tranquility by mid-1921. Tasca, who early in his classic study *The Rise of Fascism* claims that the September 1920 factory occupations gave the industrialists a "psychological shock" which "explains their fury and guided their

---

[91] For Comintern's interpretation of Fascism see Franklin Adler, "Thalheimer, Bonapartism and Fascism," *Telos* 40 (1979): 101–8; John Cammett, "Communist Theories of Fascism," *Science and Society* 31 (1967): 149–63.

[92] Rossi, *Padroni del vapore*, p. 44.

[93] Ibid., pp. 28, 73.

successive steps," implicitly concedes in his concluding remarks that Fascism was due less to the actions of industrialists than to "the landowners' offensive in the form of military action and territorial conquest," to the economic crisis of 1921, to the complicity of state personnel, to the discrediting of Parliament, to the political acumen of Mussolini, and, "most important," to the "socialists' feebleness and mistakes, which were the direct cause, not of fascism itself, which appeared in every country after the war, but of its success in Italy."[94] Nor is the "delayed-reaction" hypothesis of the liberal historian Federico Chabod any more convincing: that "fear" is often retrospective, "reaching greatest intensity after the objective danger has already passed."[95] Given the widespread recognition that the "Bolshevik threat" had already passed by mid-1921, as well as the failure to cite any specific "fearful utterances" on the part of industrialists during the entire period of the second biennium, Chabod's formulation, in contrast to his characteristically astute analysis, appears devoid of substance.

As we suggested earlier, in the most general sense, the postwar crisis was one of bourgeois hegemony; that is, in securing and maintaining the consent of other classes and class fragments within the organizational framework and ideology of liberalism. Responding directly to such a situation, Fascism emerged as a distinctive political force, *not* as the mere sectoral agent of the industrialists, but rather as a negative aggregation, filling the vacuum created by the incapacitated bourgeoisie as a *classe dirigente.* Ironically enough, in light of their reputed responsibility for Fascism, the industrialist sector had less need to use Fascism as an instrument than any other sector. They had quite successfully overcome working-class resistance and shifted public policy in their favor before the March on Rome, and they had done so without recourse to the Blackshirts. This success, however, was *merely sectoral;* it did not, in and of itself, preserve the universal conditions under which the fractured and debilitated bourgeoisie could maintain its political domination. Therefore, the essential relationship between industrialists and Fascism is not to be found, as has often been claimed, in their specific status as *industrialists* but rather in their generalized status as *bourgeois;* that is, as members of a larger class no longer capable of maintaining its traditional form of political rule.

[94] Tasca, *Rise of Fascism,* pp. 80, 324.
[95] Chabod, *L'Italia contemporanea,* p. 52.

As was the case in the 1913–15 drift toward conservatism, the industrialists were hardly the vanguard element but participated as members of the larger bourgeois bloc. At the sectoral level, rather than the class level, Fascism was so linked to the agrarians that the Comintern's first statement on the new phenomenon read: "The fascists are primarily a weapon in the hands of the large landowners. The industrial and commercial bourgeoisie are following with anxiety the experiment of ferocious reaction which they regard as black bolshevism."[96] Eighteen months after the March on Rome, both Gramsci and Togliatti maintained that the industrialists "were rather diffident toward the new regime."[97] A similar judgment was cast by Cesare Rossi, Mussolini's closest lieutenant at the time of the March on Rome, and someone who actually participated in discussions with Confindustria leaders during the closing days of October 1922:

The majority of industrialists were dominated by a diffuse diffidence toward Mussolini's initiative for three motives: the primitive leftist character of Fascist postulates, which disturbed the sleep of the rich and supporters of social conservation; the preoccupation that *squadrismo* might provoke reactions in the factories where strikes were already taking place by will of the Socialists; and the absolute nonexistence at the workplace of any nucleus of Fascist workers on whom they could rely. . . . While it is historically verified that it was the agrarians who decided the development of Fascism, above all in the field of national politics, it was vice versa with the industrialists, who in aggregate and in their syndical associations remained estranged and uneasy spectators.[98]

Finally, a word about financial contributions on the part of industrialists is in order, since it has generally been presumed by a wide spectrum of historians (e.g., Salvemini, Tasca, E. Rossi, Alatri, Rapaci, and Salvatorelli and Mira) and accepted as axiomatic that industrialists were the primary bankrollers of Fascism. No documentation was ever put forth to verify this claim. In part, this was due to the obvious technical difficulties involved in tracking down such sources; in part, this was also due to the skepticism that such contributions were intentionally well "laundered" to begin with. To date we have no comprehensive and definitive study on the subject, though De

[96] Jane Degras, ed., *The Communist International, 1919–43, Documents,* 3 vols. (London: Frank Cass, 1971), 1:376.
[97] Palmiro Togliatti, *La formazione del gruppo dirigente del partito comunista italiana nel 1922–24* (Rome: Riuniti, 1962), pp. 53–4.
[98] *Il Tirreno,* 16 Nov. 1955; Piero Melograni, *Gli industriali e Mussolini* (Milan: Longanesi, 1972), pp. 18–19.

Felice has taken the first tentative step with an analysis of contributions recorded by the administrative secretary of the Fascists, Marinelli. De Felice concludes that agrarian contributions were greater than those of industrialists; that unlike agrarians, industrialists never collectively contributed funds through their associations before the March on Rome but gave on an individual basis (usually to remain on good terms with local Fascists rather than assist the movement to assume the reins of government); and that the bulk of the industrialists' contributions were made after, not before, the March on Rome (4,125, 750 of 5,919, 975 lire).[99]

Initial postwar orientations

Confindustria entered the postwar period with a liberal–technocratic, productivist orientation substantially similar to the one characterizing its prewar development. Just as associational leaders had argued earlier that rapid economic development could take place only if industrialists were allowed to fulfill their "function" unhampered by bureaucratic state intervention, they would now argue that postwar reconstruction was dependent upon the same conditions. A new wave of Taylorism inundated industrial publications with the translation into Italian of the author's principal work in 1915, and a general concern with "rationalization" was similarly in evidence, stemming from productive innovations that had been undertaken during the mobilization. As one Confindustria publication put it, "after the war we are all a little *americanizzati* and *germanizzati*."[100] On the basis of the prewar optimality formula (to achieve the maximum effect with the minimum force), and because of the growing expense of raw materials and labor (the relative equalization of Italian salaries with those of the major European powers and the consequent loss of Italy's competitive advantage due to "cheap labor"),[101] Confindustria encouraged technical innovation and greater mechanization. Thus, the eight-hour day and minimum salaries were conceded in exchange for increased Taylorization and the recognition of absolute managerial authority in many of the major postwar labor contracts.

---

[99] Renzo De Felice, "Primi elementi sul finanziamento del fascismo dalle origine al 1924," *Rivista Storica del Socialismo* 7 (May 1964): 223–441.
[100] *Rivista delle Societa Commerciale*, 31 July 1919.
[101] *L'Italia Industriale*, July 1919.

Similarly, Confindustria leaders anticipated a return to the syndical practice which had begun to develop in the prewar period; that is, the containment of spontaneous and "impulsive" unrest through the growing regulation and institutionalization of labor relations on the part of worker and employer syndicates, each disciplining their respective memberships and responsible for the faithful execution of negotiated contracts. Here, the traditional state–civil society distinction was reasserted: production was considered an autonomous realm and syndical practice was to be apolitical, such that the outcome of syndical competition would be a function of the intrinsic organizational strengths of the associations involved, not their ties to exogenous political forces which might seek to secure through state intervention that which could not be otherwise won. The state was expected to remain neutral in labor contract negotiations, "neutral," of course, presupposing the preservation of public order and defense of private property.

As was the case earlier, the trendsetter in actualizing these orientations was the machine-manufacturing sector, in particular the automotive industry, with Fiat the undisputed leader. In his biography of Agnelli, Valerio Castronovo writes of Fiat's "new system of labor organization, more uniform and rigorous, where the norms of 'efficiency' and 'rationality' cojoined with a change in the internal composition of the workforce transformed Fiat into a new, lucid productive machine, where implements and rhythmic syncopations were regulated from above through the mediation of a new group of managers, a staff of engineers and department heads who were on the road to a general renovation."[102] Construction was begun on the new Lingotto factory, the first in Italy built with reinforced concrete and recognized by a visiting National Association of Manufacturers delegation as "the most perfect American-styled factory." This plant, more than two kilometers long, contained assembly lines so well integrated that the velocity of production was 80 percent faster than Fiat's prewar rate.[103] Even within the context of industrially advanced Turin, it seemed even to observers like Gramsci and Gobetti as if Agnelli had hurled the city into a disarming americanesque age of technological modernism.[104]

---

[102] Castronovo, *Agnelli*, p. 326.
[103] Ibid., pp. 226–7, 341.
[104] Ibid., pp. 339–48.

A school (Scuola Allievi Fiat) was created to train employees and their dependents in the so-called *scienza del lavoro*, a private health-care system was established, recreational facilities and day-care centers were constructed, and a YMCA was transplanted from America.[105] Class collaboration was conscientiously stressed by management; both labor and capital had a common stake in increased productivity. Workers were to be depoliticized, their everyday existence (work and leisure) was to be organically integrated into the enterprise, and their identity and loyalty were to be tied to Fiat. As Mario Fassio, a Fiat executive argued, management had to "divert the worker from the world of politics by transporting him to an economic–professional one, and there train his mind through the study of problems concerning the economy, work, and the science of production. There he would find the appropriate path for his rapid economic and professional growth."[106]

This co-optive approach to labor on the part of Fiat was not so naive as to envision the supersession of trade unions. All industrialists who had participated in the formation of *sindacati padronali* recognized that, for better or worse, syndicates were a permanent fixture of labor relations. They could, however, become "institutional partners," jointly cooperating in expanding productivity and maintaining social peace. From the industrialists' perspective, this was contingent upon two factors: first, the recognition, on the part of workers' syndicates, that the technical hierarchy of production was a domain in which management was to exercise absolute and undivided authority; and second, that politics was to be kept outside the factory and not intrude upon syndical relations. As Agnelli told reporters in an interview, "We want syndicates. Only they must concern themselves strictly with problems inherent in the lives and needs of workers. If politics enters, *addio*.... Believe me, syndicates we want, but apolitical."[107]

In the hope that they might ensure the tranquility necessary to renovate their plants and further rationalize production through the adoption of "scientific management" (Taylorism), industrial associations opened the postwar period with a manifestly conciliatory attitude toward workers' syndicates, the CGL in particular. Once again,

[105] Ibid., pp. 332–3.
[106] Ibid., p. 330.
[107] Ibid., p. 337.

the Turinese industrialists led the way, being the first to concede the eight-hour day, minimum salaries, increased wages, cost-of-living adjustments, and broader acceptance of the *commissione interna*.

The model contract, in this regard, was one concluded between FIOM and AMMA (Associazione Metallurgici Meccanici e Affini) led by Agnelli. Negotiated during February 1919, this pact largely continued the prewar Turinese approach of yielding material concessions in exchange for the recognition of absolute managerial authority and a guaranteed period of industrial peace. The similarities between the new pact and the ill-fated contract negotiated between FIOM and the automobile *consorzio* in December 1911 are striking: both took place during periods of radical technological transformation when industrialists wanted to avoid, at all costs, any interruption of production; both stipulated the deposit of a "caution" by each worker of a week's salary; and both established a binding process of conciliation, leading ultimately to intervention by the CGL and Confindustria before a strike or lockout could be declared.

As in 1911, the agreement had been quickly reached between the leaders of the two opposing syndical bodies, but as Giuseppe Maione notes, these leaders would soon find themselves "before an unforeseen phenomenon which neither desired: the rise of a workers' rebellion that had the force to upend all the conditions of accommodation which in this 'delicate' period of economic reconstruction seemed necessary and auspicious."[108] Once again, FIOM proved to be an unreliable partner, incapable of controlling its rank and file. For a month, FIOM had launched a major propaganda campaign to sell the pact to its members. It stressed the historical significance of the "conquest" of the eight-hour workday ("the greatest accord which had been stipulated in any country of the world"), as well as the need "to demonstrate to the industrialists that we are worthy of that which has been conquered." Unfortunately, the truce that the industrialists had considered the fundamental condition of the pact, and which FIOM leaders had accepted, was broken within a month by spontaneous worker agitations.[109] Only in part were these caused by the felt inadequacy of the monetary concessions relative to the uncontrolled inflation and steep price increases. The primary motive, and one that would become paramount in the months to come, was the perceived

---

[108] Giuseppe Maione, "Il biennio rosso," *Storia Contemporanea* 1 (Dec. 1970): 828.
[109] Ibid., pp. 829–32.

inadequacy of syndicates per se in relation to the revolutionary aspirations of the workers. Syndicates could not serve as transformative vehicles, capable of fundamentally altering the very structure of capitalist enterprises; instead, by their very nature, they tended to seek reformist accommodation, as a subordinate element, within that framework. Unlike the syndical leaders of industry and labor, who basically shared a common "realistic" view of industrial relations, the rank and file clearly had a different agenda. Partial concessions by the industrialists only stimulated more extreme criticism over the very nature of capitalist organization: not increase in piecework rates, but abolition of piecework itself, which set worker against worker; not submission to or cooperation with the existing factory hierarchy, but the end to all hierarchy and creation of worker self-management. It was in this atmosphere of spontaneous worker demands, revolutionary in essence, and of worker estrangement from reformist syndicates that Antonio Gramsci's writings on factory councils began to unfold in the pages of *Ordine Nuovo*.

A detailed analysis of why the demand for worker self-management was more intense in Italy (and particularly in Turin) than elsewhere is beyond the scope of this study. Certainly, the Bolshevik revolution was a significant factor; one need only recall the shouts of "Viva Lenin!" which greeted the visiting Menshevik delegation during August 1917 in Turin. Also of relevance was the generalized reaction everywhere against war-imposed discipline once the conflict had ended, when previously mobilized populations expected the immediate realization of promises that had been made by various government propaganda offices for a more just and equitable social order. Liberal observers like Max Weber and Luigi Einaudi separately noted that the previously "compulsive" nature of capitalist organization appeared to be breaking down, as was the old "willingness to work" which went along with it. Gone were the days, so they thought, that *padroni* could play the role of *Herr in Hause;* in the popular consciousness, the age of the "absolute sovereignty of the *imprenditore* in the factory regarding relations between labor and capital" was superseded and replaced, in the words of Einaudi, by a "type of rule by consensus."[110]

[110] Max Weber, *Economy and Society,* 2 vols., ed. Guenther Roth and Claus Wittich, trans. Ephriam Fischoff (New York: Bedminster Press, 1968), 1: 153; Einaudi, *Condotta economica,* p. 407.

The most revolutionary manifestations of this phenomenon were the factory council movement in Italy and the *Räte* movement in Germany. Yet even reformists began to speak of a "new role for labor," and through the efforts of interventionist trade unionists who had assumed governmental or quasi-governmental tasks during the war, an International Labor Office (ILO) was created as an official organ of the League of Nations. Indeed, one entire section of the Treaty of Versailles (Part XIII, Articles 387–427) was devoted to the subject of labor, setting forth the institutional framework of the ILO, whose "guiding principle" was that "labor should not be regarded as merely a commodity or article of commerce." Specifically mentioned in the treaty were "methods and principles for regulating labor conditions which all industrial communities would endeavor to apply," among which were the eight-hour day, the right to free associations, the abolition of child labor, the principle of equal pay for women, and provision for a system of inspection to ensure that laws and regulations were followed. Although it is true that the ILO would prove to be little more than a consultative forum and data-collection agency, the mere existence of such a body and the formal recognition of labor's rights in the Treaty of Versailles were indicative of the changed valuation of workers.

Yet not even the German *Räte* movement commanded the same mass support as the Italian factory council movement, nor did it drain so much legitimacy from the traditional workers' syndicates. In Turin the movement found its vortex; here the most politically conscious and technically qualified labor force in Italy joined forces with the most penetrating and imaginative group of Marxist intellectuals, the *ordinovisti* led by Gramsci. Together, they sought to make Turin Italy's Petrograd.

Cognizant of the Turinese workers' revolutionary aspirations and their growing disaffection from the traditional syndicates, Gramsci maintained that a new transformative agency had to be developed that would both prefigure the future Socialist state and prepare the workers technically and politically, in the interim, for eventual self-government.[111] He argued that this new agency already existed in embryonic form in the *commissione interna*. By transforming the

---

[111] On Gramsci's concept of factory councils see his *L'Ordine Nuova*, pp. 10–13, 27–31, 31–4, 44–8, 131–5, 146–54.

commissione interna into a *consiglio di fabbrica* (factory council), workers could transcend their subaltern status in the productive process, experience themselves as self-directed subjects, and challenge the capitalist system in its most fundamental cell, the workplace. "Today the *commissioni interne* limit the power of the capitalist in the factory and perform functions of arbitration and discipline. Developed and enriched, tomorrow they will be organs of proletarian power which substitute themselves for the capitalist in all his practical functions of direction and administration."[112] Syndicates could not play this transformative role, because they were fully integrated within the capitalist framework. At best they were defensive and competitive organs that saw the workers only as wage earners, not producers. The syndicate, Gramsci argued, represented the affirmation of capitalist legality; the factory councils, its negation.[113]

So much for Gramsci's theoretical justification for factory councils; without doubt, his concept of prefigurative and transformative structures holds an important place in the development of Marxist thought, suggesting an active, practical transcendence of economism and fatalism. Less impressive, however, were Gramsci's political judgment and tactical acumen regarding the immediate situation in postwar Italy. Perhaps his greatest error was the misperception that industrialists had become mere speculators, parasites, and dead wood, that they had lost the capacity to administer their factories effectively and maintain class unity.[114] One would have thought that after the Turinese industrialists dealt the working class in general, and the factory council movement in particular, a stunning defeat in April 1920, overcoming the longest and most compact general strike yet to have occurred in Italy, Gramsci would have reconsidered their imminent demise. There was indication of this in his commentary on the April 1920 defeat; he wrote that the industrialists had conducted themselves with "extreme ability," that they constituted themselves as a "block of steel" against the proletariat, and that "one word of order beamed from Confindustria found immediate actuation in every single factory."[115] Yet three months later, Gramsci returned to his original

---

[112] Ibid., pp. 10–13.
[113] Ibid., p. 133.
[114] Ibid., pp. 13–19, 48–51, 78–88, 154–64, 169–76, 324–7.
[115] Ibid., pp. 108–22.

caricature; after the factory occupations, he claimed that the industrialists had "become a sack of potatoes, an aggregate of inepts and imbeciles, without political capacity, without internal force."[116]

So extreme was Gramsci's critique of the syndicates that the *ordinovisti* never encouraged the factory councils to duplicate "reformist" concerns for such things as salaries, full employment, working hours, and so on. Thus, when the revolutionary tide had ebbed, the councils appeared to have lost their raison d'être, since they were concerned only with offensive, not defensive, action, with fomenting revolution, not preventing reaction. Nor was the uniqueness of Turin fully comprehended. It was only really in Turin that the councils took root; the projected universality of the council form was never realized in the rest of the northern industrial triangle, much less elsewhere on the peninsula. Finally, Gramsci tended to view the Italian situation in Russian terms, showing little of his later comparative insights concerning fundamental differences between the "eastern state" and the "western state." In contrast with his mature prison writings, here Gramsci suggested that the Russian model could and should be exported and copied. In June 1919, he maintained that Italian Communists should emulate the Russian experience, thus "saving time and work." In August 1919, he stated that Italian conditions were "not much different" from those in Russia. Political forces and sequences in Italy were placed in direct and unmediated relation to those in Russia: in November 1919, Gramsci stated that the Popolari were to the Socialists as Kerensky to Lenin; again in November 1919, he maintained that Italy was in the same condition as Russia during September 1917. Hence, Italy was in a revolutionary situation, and an Italian equivalent to the soviets had to be found. This Gramsci would discover in the factory council; an Italian October, however, never came.[117]

The initial industrialist response to worker unrest and mass agitation was rather bland. This was due, in part, to the debilitation industrial associations had experienced during the mobilization, but equally important was their fear of further exacerbating the insurrec-

[116] Ibid., pp. 171–2.
[117] Ibid., pp. 51–3; Gramsci, *Socialismo e fascismo*, pp. 260–2; Franklin Hugh Adler, "Factory Councils, Gramsci and the Industrialists," *Telos* 31 (spring 1977): 67–90; Massimo L. Salvadori, *Gramsci ed il problemma storica della democrazia* (Turin: Einaudi, 1970), pp. 75–204, 367–98.

tionary climate, particularly in the period from spring 1919 (food riots, looting, general strikes, land occupations) till spring 1920, when in reaction to the April general strike, they first began to show their strength. Indiscipline was passively tolerated in the factories, as were abuses of power by the *commissioni interne* (which were only supposed to see that labor pacts were respected and that grievances were promptly transmitted to management, both functions to be performed after working hours). Though not formally recognized by industrialists, factory councils began to form spontaneously during the summer of 1919. No attempts were made to suppress the new bodies. Sensitive to the rather volatile state of public opinion, wherein they were disparaged daily as speculators, sharks, and exploiters, industrialists and their associations maintained a rather low profile until labor agitation, focused on authority relations within the factory, surpassed their limits of tolerance and, of course, until they had marshaled their organizational forces to the point of once again being able to confront the workers' movement with some confidence of victory.

When food riots spread to Turin in early July 1919, and five hundred shopkeepers consigned their keys to the Camera del Lavoro, the LIT sent a rather mild note to the various labor organizations complaining about the "too frequent disturbances" of work and public order, which, if continued, might force them to "take measures that they think necessary."[118] This is not to say that the industrialists were untroubled by the situation; rather, they were as yet too inhibited to react in a more forceful manner. No longer could the state be relied upon as a repressive force, as it had been during the war mobilization and, one should add, as it continued to be in the other capitalist nations during the immediate postwar period. Nitti, it will be recalled, had expressly instructed the prefects to refrain from acting against food rioters. During these days it appeared as if the Camera del Lavoro had become the legitimate seat of public authority.

Apprehension was much in evidence at the 29 July meeting of Confindustria's delegate council, presided over by Gino Olivetti. In Alessandria, the Camera del Lavoro had dispatched a corps of red guards to a textile firm, which was ordered to pay a monthly tax to the syndical body. Another firm in central Italy was forced to consign

---

[118] Abrate, *Lotta sindacale*, p. 213; Maione, "Biennio rosso," *Storia Contemporanea* 1 (Dec. 1970): 849.

an automobile to a band of red guards, who, after using up its gasoline, returned for a refueling. This time the firm refused to cooperate unless authorization was given by the police, and astonishingly enough, the workers returned with a requisition order from the Camera del Lavoro bearing the official stamp of Pubblica Sicurezza. Complaints were voiced that, in reality, power had passed from local authorities into the hands of the Camera del Lavoro. It was one thing for the Camera del Lavoro to make such pretenses, quite another for local authority to yield. So spoke Olivetti.[119]

Still again, during July 1919, industrialists were passive. Faced with the international general strike protesting Allied intervention in Russia and Hungary, Confindustria instructed its member associations to take no countermeasures. Should the so-called *scioperissimo* prove threatening, industrialists were to close their factories immediately.[120]

Had the industrialists' knees terminally buckled before their proletarian executioners, as Gramsci thought? Publicly, they proclaimed that concessions and moderation were signs of enlightenment; privately, they admitted to "imperfect organization" and "indiscipline."[121] Yet one ought not simply to conclude that "enlightenment" was just an ideological cover to mask internal weakness. Olivetti still maintained faith that Confindustria and the CGL, through negotiation and compromise, could reconcile their programmatic differences and shunt the dramatic discharge of postwar class conflict back within the framework of "industrial legality." To accomplish this, the respective syndical bodies would have to better discipline their members, while revolutionary forces, of which *L'Ordine Nuovo* was the purest expression, would have to be vigorously confronted.

These concerns were reflected in Olivetti's editorial "In tema di economia capitalistica," written for the inaugural issue of Confindustria's journal *L'Italia Industriale*. His target was the "new Socialist publications" which advocated "a type of urban–industrial communism" and called for an "Italian reproduction of Russian sovietism." These advocates, Olivetti argued, had misunderstood enlightenment for weakness. For years, rather decades, the eight-hour day and minimum salaries had been the major revendications of the working class.

[119] *L'Italia Industriale*, July 1919.
[120] Abrate, *Lotta sindacale*, p. 213.
[121] Ibid., p. 233.

Now that the Italian industrialists had taken the "daring step" (indeed, "too daring, according to many, including nonindustrialists") of conceding them without a strike, proof that the present capitalist regime was capable of cooperating with organized labor and satisfying its fundamental demands, these new "organizers" mistakenly perceived this as terminal weakness, proclaiming the imminent collapse of capitalism: "Industrialists conceding without strikes reforms which had been a distant, remote dream on the part of organized labor for decades? This certainly had to be because they felt the moment near to abandon their factories and seek with concessions, *in articulo mortis*, to prolong their agony." Instead, Olivetti argued, Italian industrialists chose to place themselves in the vanguard. "Italy, a country without combustibles and raw materials, a country industrially young and hardly strong, has set an example with these reforms which even today are not as extensively and thoroughly applied in the United States, England, France, or even Germany." Not only were these reforms "daring," but as Olivetti explicitly noted, they signaled a concrete programmatic convergence between the organizational forces of labor and capital.[122]

The ideological duel had begun between Olivetti and Gramsci, theoreticians of their respective classes. Olivetti, from the very outset, perceived the factory councils as institutions that had to be combated at all costs. On the one hand, they threatened to undermine the continuing institutionalization of class conflict by competing with labor syndicates for the primary allegiance of the rank and file. On the other, they threatened the orderly development of the productive process by challenging ever more strongly the hierarchical factory structure, over which managerial authority had to be absolute.

Rather than deal with factory councils as an abstraction – as a prefigurative and transformative structure that might ease the transition to Socialism – Olivetti, with characteristic empiricism, set out to conduct a comparative case study on how factory councils in Germany and Russia *actually functioned* and to what degree they had, in fact, replaced unitary factory hierarchy with worker self-management. Here, indeed, Olivetti would attack Gramsci's conception at its weakest point by demonstrating in both cases that factory councils had little more effective authority, *and in Russia a good deal*

---

[122] *L'Italia Industriale*, July 1919.

less, than the Italian form of the *commissione interna,* and that in both cases managerial authority over the actual productive process remained unitary and absolute. Of the two cases, that of Russia had far greater ideological bearing, for if in the homeland of Communism – the one existing proletarian state, the source and model behind Gramsci's concept of factory councils – workers lacked self-government within the factories, then this self-government must be mere myth, incapable of realization. In this regard, Olivetti would continually point to the "steps backward" in Russian practice to attack the theoretical adequacy of Communism, in his view a *concezione orientale* outside the logic of Western rationality. Just as he would now attack the idea of worker self-government by showing that the Russians had simply replaced one unitary hierarchy with another, he would later argue, once the New Economic Policy (NEP) was instituted, that the role of the industrialist was obviously indispensible if an adequate level of production were to be maintained.

Olivetti's study on factory councils was presented to Confindustria's delegate council on 7 March 1920 and was published shortly thereafter in various industrial journals.[123] Concerning Russia, Olivetti noted that with the decree of 3 March 1918, which nationalized firms previously private but acting under state control, the deliberative faculties of factory councils had been sharply reduced in favor of one-man management. "This limitation of the factory council's power under nationalization, in contrast with what it had been under private management, amply demonstrates that even in Communist opinion, the directing and disciplining power of any firm whatsoever, however composed, can only be unitary." Now that the councils "had even lost the right to present their demands directly to the management of the factory," they constituted little more than "simple mutual-benefit and recreational clubs." The German *Betriebsrate,* Olivetti argued, was substantially similar to the Italian *commissione interna,* though they had the additional right to inspect the firm's accounts and send delegates to participate in corporate board meetings. However, they had no deliberative function that could influence the productive process itself, except in seeing to it that the labor contract was properly respected.

---

[123] Ibid., Apr. 1920; *L'Informazione Industriale,* 18 Mar. 1920.

Both these systems thus have not misunderstood that which is the prime necessity of any productive system, and that is the unity of command or direction, so that there may exist in the firm a continuity of plan and quickness of decision which can only come from he who has complete understanding of all the various aspects of productive organization. Without this, no economic regime – no matter to whom belong the profits and to whom go the benefits – would be able to exist. It is not possible to misunderstand this necessity. It is not possible, without throwing the firm into disorder, to establish two powers within it, opposed to one another, in such a manner as to break the unity necessary for direction. It is for this reason, faced with the Russian and German systems, that one might welcome one or the other on the basis of Communist or anti-Communist political conviction, but not intermediate solutions which do not divide the factory into tasks but, rather, [divide] the authority to direct into diverse sources of power.

Olivetti pointed out that in Italy, without the need of laws, doctrinal principles, or even the Socialists in power, the *commissione interna* had been allowed to function. Those who would transform it into a factory council confused two distinct problems: production and distribution. Production must always follow the same logic. Governed by an objective technical imperative, as well as the laws of economics, it is oriented toward one end: to produce the maximum effect with the minimum cost.

Once wealth has been produced, its division can be discussed. On this point one could admit to a diversity of conceptions in which not only economic laws but also political considerations have their influence. But a confusion between the two problems is not possible without leading to a complete subversion of the most economic, and therefore the most socially useful, organization of production.

Finally, Olivetti dealt with the consequences that factory councils would have for syndical practice. Factory councils would be autonomous organs, not anchored in any responsible labor organization. How then could binding agreements be reached?

If one examines the Italian conceptions put forth in this regard, the councils are organs antithetical to syndical organizations. They are only elective expressions of the majority of workers in one factory, mandated by them, revokable at any moment, such that they could not represent before the industrialists and their organization a body with which, as with labor syndicates, one could come to agreements having even relative generality and continuity. The members of the factory councils would not represent an entity distinct from the workers of each single factory, but only those workers, and are therefore but the expression of an always changeable will of the mass at any given moment. If the mass changes its will and changes the members of the council, no organ would exist which might intervene in order to have agreements reached with the council respected. Thus, a state would develop where labor accords would be rather difficult, whereas in fact today they take place between industrial and labor syndicates; that is, two organs that assume obligations, even if only relatively, guaranteeing compliance. . . . With factory councils, this would no longer be possible.

After Olivetti's presentation, the delegate council discussed the dangers inherent in giving any recognition to factory councils and adopted a resolution drafted by Olivetti, similar to one adopted three weeks earlier by the LIT, pledging resistance and instructing member organizations to await instructions from Confindustria. Circulars to this effect were dispatched from the Rome office, ordering firms to maintain strict discipline in their factories and to see that labor contracts were rigorously observed and, in particular, that the *commissioni interne* stayed within the narrow limits of their assigned functions. All agitations were immediately to be reported to Confindustria and not overlooked for *"amor di pace"* or *"di quieto vivere."* However, no "provocative" action was to be taken by industrialists; "resistance ought not be reaction."[124]

Though the industrialists were still too cautious to launch counteractions, a marked change was evident among them during March 1920. That optimism with which they had entered the postwar period now turned to rage against both workers and the Nitti government, which had taken no actions against urban rioting, land occupations, or strikes among public-service personnel. At the same meeting of the delegate council where Olivetti presented his study on factory councils, Confindustria's president, Giovanni Silvestri, insisted that the government meet "the necessities of the moment," that it remember it was "the emanation of a bourgeois individualist regime," whose defense should be "its prime task." Reflecting the long-standing disaffection of the *borghesia produttrice* from the *borghesia politica*, Silvestri's condemnation of the liberal politicians reached unprecedented intensity. "Our political parties are vile in the infamy of their conduct." "It is necessary that we now yell in a great voice to the government, enough! Put on the brakes, and if it is still possible, arrest your fatal descent. Today we have done our duty; now you

[124] Confindustria Circulars, Confindustria Library, Rome: P.N. 3346, C. 84, 14 Mar. 1919; P.N. 3504, C. 88, 29 Mar. 1920.

do yours."[125] Silvestri's speech, in turn, was followed by another unanimously passed resolution proposed by Olivetti, calling on the government to "abandon old weaknesses, old methods, and old tolerances by bringing new men and methods to the direction of the state."

What had precipitated this new mood of pronounced belligerence, so discernibly in contrast with the industrialists' earlier optimism? Beyond Nitti's "permissiveness" in dealing with disturbances of public order and strikes in the public services, they were more immediately preoccupied with indiscipline in the factories, which now reached alarming proportions (e.g., from October 1919 to March 1921, Fiat averaged three labor disputes per day, not counting national and political strikes),[126] heightened strike activity, and factory occupations.

Already in November there had been a premonition of things to come. Nitti decided to declare 4 November a national holiday to commemorate the war victory. The LIT, foreseeing worker hostility toward any such celebration, nevertheless instructed its member firms to close their factories that day. Spurred on by *L'Ordine Nuovo,* the Turinese workers decided to abstain from work on 7 November to celebrate the Bolshevik revolution (against orders from FIOM, which were followed in all the other major cities, including Milan and Genoa). Both AMMA and the LIT called special meetings to discuss how they would respond to this action, in clear violation, so they thought, of the previously negotiated AMMA–FIOM contract. At the AMMA assembly, Agnelli spoke of the "very grave difficulty in which industry found itself because of the changed relations with the workers" and declared that the situation would have to be met "with maximum prudence but not minor firmness." Opposing those who demanded an immediate lockout, Agnelli counseled caution, since the national election was to take place later that month. He warned the assembly that nothing should be done "to alienate public opinion from the industrialists' cause," especially since Olivetti was running on the newly formed Partito Liberale Economico list. It was indispensable to choose "a more opportune moment," one in which the whole question of factory discipline would be at issue, before taking forceful action.

---

[125] *L'Italia Industriale,* Apr. 1920.
[126] Giuseppe Maione, "Il biennio rosso: lo sciopero delle lancette," *Storia Contemporanea* 3 (June 1972): 269.

It was thus decided merely to insist upon the rigorous application of the labor contract, imposing a penalty for the hours not worked. When the penalty was applied, on 17 November, the workers went out on strike. The matter was ultimately arbitrated in the workers' favor by the prefect of Turin, who held that the workers' abstention on 7 November should be considered a "political strike," permitted under terms of the contract. Olivetti felt it best "not to insist too strongly on this question of incidental character, while preparations should be made for a vaster battle concerning the essential question of order within the factory, an issue of interest not only to the machine-manufacturing firms but to all industries in all regions." For his part, Agnelli, not wanting a strike based on so narrow an issue to be in effect during the election, expressed his hope that "the new Chamber might yield a government more authoritative and strong."[127]

December saw a worsening of the situation in terms of public order and factory discipline. On 2 December, a national general strike was called by the Socialist Party and the CGL to protest beatings inflicted on Socialist deputies who had created an uproar by walking out of a royal sitting shouting "Long live Socialism." Though the Socialist Party and the CGL called for disciplined action, mass response, especially in Turin, was spontaneous and violent. A false rumor had spread that two Turinese Socialist deputies were on their deathbeds in a Rome hospital. Workers poured out of the factories and gave chase to policemen, who were insulted and forced to surrender their weapons. Directives from the national organizations to maintain discipline and return to work on 4 December were disregarded. Before returning to work on 5 December, workers from Fiat adopted the following resolution, indicative of the growing distance separating the national organizations from the rank and file, who felt greater loyalty to their "real" representatives, the factory councils and *commissioni interne:*

The workers of the Fiat foundry, meeting in assembly on 4 December, protest the conduct of the leaders of the national proletarian organizations because, after having declared a general strike of indeterminate duration, they broke off this mass action before convening the real representative organs (that is, factory councils and *commissioni interne*). . . . [The workers] resolve to work

---

[127] Abrate, *Lotta sindacale,* pp. 220–4; Maione, "Biennio rosso," *Storia Contemporanea* 1 (Dec. 1970): 870–1.

tomorrow, 5 December, [and serve] notice that it will no longer be possible to place the masses before the rifles of the *carabinieri* and then break off every impulse of just revenge when the masses prepare themselves to check the violence of constituted authority.[128]

Within the factories, *commissioni interne* by secret vote were being transformed into factory councils and attempting to augment their functions. Industrialists were bound by associational discipline not to recognize or tolerate the councils, but there was little they could do because these councils considered themselves "proletarian institutions" and neither sought nor needed legitimacy from the *padroni*. When, in February 1920, the LIT questioned the Rubber and Chemical Workers League about notices that were being circulated at the Michelin plants announcing factory council elections, they were told in response that the "Lega Industriale has nothing to say with regard to contracts in force, since the modification, created with political and economic criteria by will of the workers, is a clearly Communist contribution."[129]

Addressing a 9 December meeting of AMMA, Agnelli said there were three possible courses of action to take: accept these innovations, seek to control them, or oppose them vigorously ("in battle"). In his opinion, the first alternative was to be discarded immediately; the second involved the danger of getting embroiled in long-winded discussions "even more difficult because the masses no longer have strong and mandated representation, and that, in any case, these always finish with concessions." Only the third alternative remained, but before this course could be followed, sufficient organization and preparation were necessary. For the moment, they could only insist upon the rigorous application of existing contracts, "to resist, but to avoid provocations and pretexts."[130]

With the coming of 1920, strike activity reached unprecedented proportions. During the first half of the new year, the number of workers engaged in strikes for economic reasons (i.e., excluding general strikes and solidarity strikes) rose to 1,769,000, compared to 877,000 for the second half of 1919.[131] These included large national strikes by category, as well as public-service strikes which had a direct

---

[128] Maione, "Biennio rosso," *Storia Contemporanea* 1 (Dec. 1970): 872–3.
[129] *L'Informazione Industriale*, 26 Feb. 1920.
[130] Abrate, *Lotta sindacale*, p. 226.
[131] Salvemini, *Origins of Fascism*, p. 251.

effect upon industry. Agnelli warned the prefect of Turin on 20 January that the railway strike might provoke a suspension of all work in the city's factories. As for the labor scene in general, the director of Fiat warned that "a violent crisis will soon burst forth," though he would not induce it.[132] The major concern of the industrialists, however, was not the strikes having to do with salary demands, as inconvenient as these were, but rather the revolutionary character that the whole thrust of labor agitation was assuming: obstruction, factory councils, occupations. When mention is made of "the occupation of the factories," one immediately thinks of the massive September 1920 phenomenon that engulfed the entire industrial triangle. However, there were a number of significant occupations during the first three months of the year, and it was these, more than any other single factor, which caused industrialists to change fundamentally their tactics from passive resistance to direct action.

Mention was made earlier of the occupation at Dalmine in March 1919, led by Edmondo Rossoni's UIL. Perhaps because the UIL was a "Nationalist" syndicate and flew the tricolor rather than the red flag over the Franchi-Gregorini plant, little attention was given to the incident either in industrial publications or in the national press. Of all major Italian newspapers, only Mussolini's *Popolo d'Italia* gave it substantial coverage, calling it a *sciopero produttivo*.[133]

Far greater concern was evidenced during the early 1920 occupations of the Mazzonis cotton factories in Piemonte (Turin, Favria, Torre Fellice, Luserna S. Giovanni) and the steelworks of Genoa and Sestri Ponente in Liguria. Baron Mazzonis, head of the family firm, was one of the more reactionary Piemontese industrialists and had refused to join any industrial association or recognize any labor syndicate.[134] On 9 January, a young woman worker refused to work overtime, encouraged others to do likewise, and was consequently fired. This brought on the refusal of the entire department where she worked to continue production until the woman was reinstated. In turn, they were all immediately fired. At this point, the Federazione Operai Tessili (FIOT), the national textile workers' syndicate, inter-

---

[132] Abrate, *Lotta sindacale,* p. 248.

[133] Ferdinando Cordova, *Le origini dei sindacati fascisti* (Bari: Laterza, 1974), p. 16.

[134] On the Mazzonis case and for the quotations in the following paragraphs, see Abrate, *Lotta sindacale,* pp. 249–53; Einaudi, *Condotta economica,* p. 319; Maione, "Biennio rosso," *Storia Contemporanea* 3 (June 1972): 250–5.

vened and declared a strike on the basis of four demands: the firm's recognition of FIOT, application of the nationally negotiated contract for that category, reinstatement of all workers fired, and back pay for workdays lost because of the conflict. The baron refused all these demands, whereupon FIOT asked the Camera del Lavoro of Turin for its solidarity. When it appeared that the Camera del Lavoro was about to extend the strike to all other factories in the city, the prefect intervened, inviting Mazzonis to the prefecture for a private meeting in the hope that he might be able to use his office as a vehicle for arbitration.

Mazzonis met with the prefect but refused to countenance any outside agency intervening in the private affairs of his firm. Invoking a wartime decree still in effect, the prefect referred the case to a Conciliation Commission, composed of a judge and representatives of labor and capital. The commission found in favor of the workers on one of the demands: that an industrialist could not refuse to apply national contracts which had been freely negotiated by associations representing both parties. When the prefect asked Mazzonis to comply with the recommendations of the commission, the baron rather haughtily told him to attend to his own profession and not meddle in areas outside his competence. Under mounting pressure from Nitti to prevent the entire city from being embroiled in an imminent general strike, the prefect then ordered Mazzonis to comply with the commission's recommendations. Once again, the baron refused.

Meanwhile, the Mazzonis workers, exasperated by the prolonged strike and the intransigence of management, forced the factory gates and resumed production under the direction of a factory council, a move actually copied from the example set by Ligurian workers several days earlier. Red flags were hoisted over the factory and red guards patrolled the gates. Nitti quickly telegraphed the prefect to do something so that such action would not spread to Turin's other factories, but to act with caution so as not to provoke the workers. On 2 March, the prefect issued a decree requisitioning the Mazzonis factories and placing them under the direction of Turin's labor inspector, who immediately granted all four labor demands, which were to be binding for the present and the future. After fifty days of strike, normal production was resumed under state control. Finally, on 9 April, the requisition was revoked and the factories were returned to the outraged Baron Mazzonis.

Not only was the baron enraged, but Luigi Einaudi, writing in *Corriere delle Sera* on 3 March, called the prefect's action wholly illegitimate. No law, after all, compelled Mazzonis to belong to an industrial association or, for that matter, to recognize a labor syndicate; therefore, he could not be bound to contracts negotiated separately by such bodies. The noted liberal economist particularly resented the corporatist implications of such public policy. "We live in an epoch where men, wearied of modern contractual liberty, wish a return to a type of state or fetters typical of the Middle Ages."

Gino Olivetti, as an associational leader, was placed in a difficult predicament. The Mazzonis case, as a precedent, might lead to further incursions of state authority, threatening the contractual and even managerial autonomy of industrialists. Yet, since Mazzonis had chosen to remain outside the organizational fold, there was nothing for the LIT or Confindustria to do except complain and vote resolutions of protest. Commenting on the Mazzonis case, Olivetti attempted to deal with the principles at issue and not defend the conduct of Mazzonis, "who had closed himself off in a manner not very sympathetic." While defending the principle of individual liberty, Olivetti criticized as simply anachronistic the nonrecognition of workers' and industrialists' syndicates. "When the whole economic sphere is organized, when the order based on individualism had been replaced by one based on classes, the individual ought to seek the protection of his liberty, not in isolation, but in the solidarity of his class." What had befallen Mazzonis should be seen as an example by those who chose to remain apart from Confindustria, for had he been an association member, "all that happened could have been avoided."

Paralleling Einaudi's argument, Olivetti maintained that the prefect clearly had exceeded his authority; no law compelled an industrialist to recognize syndical associations, apply contracts negotiated by them, or accept the recommendations of consultative conciliatory agencies. The "intervention of political authority in Turin was executed in a manner absolutely contrary to the law which it is charged with enforcing." Mazzonis's conduct, while regrettably negative, was perfectly legal; those who violated the law were the workers who violently invaded his factories, his private property. The prefect, wanting to end this illegal occupation, could have found less "absurd" means than holding the property owner responsible and requisitioning his factories. Regarding the law and public policy, the gravest consequences might follow from this precedent, since "no industrialist can now be sure that the law is what it is, and not instead what the prefect wills."

Olivetti then moved on to the manner in which the prefect's decision was executed. Not even during the war, he argued, had requisitions without indemnity ever taken place, as if, in any case, requisition were a proper means by which to settle a labor dispute. Most outrageous, however, was the fact that a government bureaucrat, with no responsibility whatsoever for the future of the firm, was placed at its head for an indeterminate period of time, making administrative decisions and accepting contractual obligations in the firm's name:

We do not know if the government was in full knowledge or if it had approved this whole series of errors. We believe it did not, because this would mean that it lacks the courage either to apply or to modify the law. It could also mean that the Italian industrialists will have to find other ways to oppose these illegal forms of intervention, which might serve to easily resolve a difficult local situation, yet lead to much greater injury to the national economy. What industry would ever be able to survive if, faced with the resistance of an industrialist to concede workers' demands, the state intervenes by requisitioning, having others pay what it wills, and later returns the firm after perhaps having ruined it? Ruined it, that is, on its account. There are plenty of examples: railroads, the postal and telegraph system, arsenals, munition works! Continue, even socialize . . . the state industries go so well.[135]

While the Mazzonis conflict was unfolding in Piemonte, in Liguria a salary dispute in the steelmaking sector led to worker vandalism (the breaking of windows at Ansaldo), obstructionism, and finally occupation, complete with red flags, after the firms decided to shut down the factories. The dispute was finally settled with the help of the CGL.[136]

The worsening labor relations, and more immediately these early 1920 occupations, account for the belligerence manifested in the aforementioned Confindustria meeting where Olivetti presented his study on factory councils, Silvestri spoke of politicians being "vile in the infamy of their conduct," and a resolution passed calling for the government to abandon "old weaknesses, old methods, and old tolerances." Significantly, no mention was made of the fact that Dante

---

[135] L'Italia Industriale, Jan. 1920.
[136] Maione, "Biennio rosso," Storia Contemporanea 3 (June 1972): 257–8.

Ferraris, first president of Confindustria, was actually minister of industry in the "weak-kneed" Nitti government, although his apparent inaction would later lead to cynicism toward "industrialists-turned-politicians."

Meanwhile, in the agricultural sector, a strike in the Po Valley involving 60,000 peasants led to land occupations, the burning of landowner's houses, and armed battles between rural red guards and landowner-led volunteers. As Giuseppe Maione suggests, the time had come for a bourgeois counteroffensive:

The first months of 1920 passed in a crescendo of agitations. From 16 February to 20 February, there were grave incidents at Sestri, on the 28th there was the occupation of Mazzonis which terminated on 3 March and was immediately followed by the occupation of the Mussa factory in Asti. On 2 March the long chemical workers' strike ended, but the same day the peasant strike began. Outside Piemonte the general strikes of Naples in February, of Milan following the massacre of some anarchists, of Terni, Treviso, Palermo, Bologna, and Naples once again in March, had an echo no less profound. These had been enough to dispel any illusion of social tranquility, but there was need of someone who might assume the initiative of organization and reaction, and it was the Piemontese industrialists, with Agnelli in the lead, who gave life to the counteroffensive.[137]

The time had ripened for a definitive showdown between industrialists and workers over the general question of factory discipline, as well as the specific issue of factory councils. How else can one understand why a rather innocuous dispute in a Fiat factory over clock hands quickly developed into a massive general strike, including, at its peak, half a million workers and affecting a regional population of four million?[138] To both sides, the central question was who would control production. According to Gramsci:

The April Turinese movement was in fact a magnificent event in the history not only of the Italian proletariat but of all Europe, and, we may say, the world. For the first time in history, there was a case in which the proletariat undertook a struggle for the control of production without having been impelled into action by hunger or unemployment. What is more, it was not only a minority, a vanguard of the working class, but the entire mass of Turinese workers who descended into battle, incurring privations and sacrifices till the very end.[139]

[137] Ibid., p. 269.
[138] Gramsci, L'Ordine Nuovo, p. 177.
[139] Ibid.

Yet Gramsci admitted that "the Turinese working class was dragged into battle; it did not have the freedom of choice."[140] It was the *padroni* who took the initiative. The industrialists, who had been waiting and preparing for such an incident to present itself, seized upon the opportunity to contain the movement toward factory councils that had been undercutting their managerial authority and blocking further development of institutionalized syndical practice. "The purpose of this battle," said Agnelli, "is to resolve the question of the *commissioni interne*. And for that reason, either the industrialists will succeed in containing them in their proper functions or they will have to renounce their very autonomy."[141] According to Olivetti:

In substance, it was the objective of the industrialists to establish clearly that *during working hours, one works and does not discuss, and that in the factory directive authority can only be unitary.* That necessarily led to depriving factory councils of all authority and to the resumption of technically disciplined hierarchy, an imperative of production. At the same time, these affirmations of the industrialists were not directed against the labor syndicates, which indeed had everything to gain from the elimination of these new extremist organs counterposed to them no less than to the industrialists, but were directed rather against the attempt to install in larva form a sociopolitical Soviet regime.[142]

Admitting that the specific targets of the industrialists' initiative were factory councils, Olivetti suggested that they were left with no other choice. For months, they had tried to deal with the related issues of indiscipline and violations by the *commissioni interne* of their contractually stipulated functions. Passively industrialists had waited for the spirits of workers to calm; ineffectually they had enlisted the support of the CGL and particularly FIOM. By the end of March, neither of these approaches were any longer tenable, as "extremist elements" (the *ordinovisti*) had successfully incited the workers toward greater revolutionary fervor and had weakened the syndicates to the point of "no longer being able to control the masses." Now the industrialists would take matters into their own hands, waiting for the first opportune moment.[143]

On 13 March, the government announced that daylight saving time, which had been adopted during the war and then dropped,

[140] Ibid., p. 110.
[141] Castronovo, *Agnelli*, p. 226.
[142] *L'Italia Industriale*, May 1920.
[143] Ibid.

would be reinstituted starting 21 March. Since this was perceived by some categories of workers as a throwback to the resented mobilization discipline, noncompliance was threatened. The LIT met on 19 March to consider the matter and decided to follow standard procedure: an agreement was to be negotiated with the Camera del Lavoro, as the local intersectoral syndical representative of labor, and then rigorously applied. Spontaneous acts of indiscipline, after such bilateral syndical agreement had been reached, were to be met with "a forceful demonstration to stem the continuous pretenses of the workers." Once again, Olivetti counseled that industrialists should not provoke the workers but "should instead adopt a decisive and severe posture as soon as the workers gave them cause."[144]

At an AMMA meeting the next day, Agnelli, frustrated that a policy of passive tolerance had only encouraged greater indiscipline and angered by "a series of facts which has by now rendered the industrial situation intolerable and has completely undermined management in the face of the working masses," recommended initiating a lockout. Others rejected this idea, preferring to provoke a strike through the rigid application of the labor contract, then closing the factories until workers agreed to respect the pact. Meanwhile, Olivetti claimed to have information from Rome that the government's attitude had "changed in relation to what it had been during the past four or five months," and it was now "more decisively favorable to the protection of industrial property." Thus, industrialists could feel reassured that the state would at least be neutral, if not supportive, with regard to whatever action they might take. Yet public opinion also had to be considered, and it was decided that if forceful action were to be taken, this had to be done in reaction to a problem that might elicit the most sympathy toward the industrialists' position. The machine-manufacturing sector, known to have the most undisciplined and troublesome workforce, would begin by rigorously applying the existing contract and, as soon as workers violated the pact, a general lockout would immediately follow. So confident were they that their calculations were in order, that Agnelli, Olivetti, and De Benedetti visited the prefect and told him to prepare for an imminent *serrata generale* (general lockout).[145]

---

[144] Consiglio Direttivo, LIT, meeting of 19 Mar. 1920, HAUIT.
[145] Abrate, *Lotta sindacale,* pp. 260–1; Castronovo, *Agnelli,* pp. 224–5.

Fiat decided to formally comply with the government's directive concerning daylight saving time by having the factory clocks set accordingly, though the normal workday would be followed as if the clocks had never been changed. On the morning of 22 March, the head of the Industrie Metallurgiche section began to alter the clock hands. The *commissione interna*, mistakenly believing that daylight saving time was to be put in force, protested. When the director attempted to explain Fiat's policy (admittedly, quite incredible), the *commissione interna* was unconvinced and ordered the hands to be set back to normal time. At that point, the issue was no longer merely one of clock hands but the *commissione interna*'s overstepping its authority. They were immediately fired, whereupon the rest of the workers laid down their tools and refused to continue until the members of the *commissione interna* were reinstated. Management offered to reinstate the fired workers, providing they be dismissed from the *commissione interna* and not be eligible to serve again for a certain period of time. Negotiations concerning how long this interval should be dragged on till the next day, when workers, losing patience, occupied the factory. On 25 March, the police entered through a rear door and ejected the workers, who put up no resistance but marched instead to the Camera del Lavoro. Responding to the occupation, management had returned to its original position of firing members of the *commissione interna* outright. However, privately AMMA tried unsuccessfully to reach an agreement with FIOM (which had not yet intervened in the conflict) "above the masses." On 26 March, the workers returned to the factory but then began a sit-down strike which was extended to all machine-manufacturing factories in Turin. When the workers arrived at the factories on the morning of 30 March, they found that the gates were locked and protected by the police.[146]

Negotiations continued for several days, but the inexperienced members of the *commissioni interne,* finding themselves in water above their heads, asked Buozzi of FIOM to step in as their negotiating agent. Though Buozzi asked for complete freedom to negotiate from the *commissioni,* he was forced to submit each tentative agreement to them for approval. Mutual suspicion between FIOM

---

[146] Abrate, *Lotta sindacale,* pp. 260–3; Einaudi, *Condotta economica,* pp. 323–5; Maione, "Biennio rosso," *Storia Contemporanea* 3 (June 1972): 275–80.

leadership and the *commissioni* made it impossible for the workers to present a united front, while the rank and file themselves were divided upon what to do, as indicated by a referendum held on 9 April either to continue the strike or to return to work on terms negotiated by Buozzi (but rejected by the local directive council of FIOM and the *commissioni*). Fewer than half the workers even voted, and those who did gave an inconclusive response (6,196 favorable to the accord, 5,397 against). Finally, on 14 April, the Camera del Lavoro called for a general strike.[147] This April general strike, in terms of scale and duration, was the most notable moment of labor solidarity yet experienced in Italian history. In Novara, 300,000 peasants joined the action, while railway workers throughout the country prevented troop-carrying trains from arriving in Turin. The city was virtually paralyzed, as transportation and other public-service workers joined the action.

Industrialists reacted by organizing and subsidizing a Comitato di Organizzazione Civile that hired "volunteers" to maintain order, run essential public services, and plaster handbills all over the city bearing such slogans as "In the factory one works, one doesn't discuss" and "In the factory there must be one authority only." As Mario Abrate notes, "without recourse to a corps of black or white guards, industrialists succeeded in removing the threat of paralysis that weighed upon Turin and that would have definitely led to concessions on the syndical front."[148] Since the volunteer organization was open to all "who love Italy and stand with the parties of order, without regard to political tendency," it should be no surprise that Fascists figured in their ranks (though in small number, as at this time the Fascists had a very limited following in Turin).[149] However, the industrialists always maintained firm control over the organization, which was committed to the preservation of order and legality, an orientation hardly compatible with *squadrismo,* which, in any case, occurred in Turin only after the March on Rome and, at that time, met with sharp protest on the part of the Turinese industrialists.

The workers' fate was sealed on 20 April, when the CGL and the Socialist Party refused to extend the general strike to the national

---

[147] Maione, "Biennio rosso," *Storia Contemporanea* 3 (June 1972): 280–7; Abrate, *Lotta sindacale*, p. 263; *L'Informazione Industriale,* Apr. 1920.

[148] Abrate, *Lotta sindacale*, p. 268.

[149] Ibid., pp. 266–9.

level. Both organizations, though they had formally approved the concept of factory councils, which had strong mass support, had grown increasingly hostile toward the *ordinovisti* council concept, wherein the councils were autonomous from party and syndicate. To Serrati, the councils were too much in the revolutionary syndicalist tradition; while to Bordiga, they were essentially reformist and corporatist. As Gramsci commented bitterly:

The Turinese proletariat was isolated from the rest of Italy. The central organs would do nothing to help, not even publish a manifesto to explain to the Italian people the importance of the Turinese workers' struggle. *Avanti!* refused to publish the manifesto of the Turinese section of the party. The Turinese comrades caught from everywhere the epithets "anarchist" and "adventurists." At the time, there was supposed to be in Turin a meeting of the Socialist Party's national council. This meeting, however, was transferred to Milan, because a city "overwhelmed" by a general strike seemed ill fitted to serve as a theater for Socialist discussions.[150]

D'Aragona, secretary of the CGL, arrived in Turin on 21 April and quickly reached a settlement with Olivetti on the latter's terms. It appeared that with the defeat of the factory councils, the traditional primacy of syndicates might be reestablished. Buozzi, speaking at the FIOM national conference on 23 May, criticized the Turinese movement and called for syndical discipline. So taken were the industrialists by this speech that it was fully reproduced in the Confindustria bulletin.

We are all in agreement with regard to the constitution of factory councils, but they must be constituted so as to function in a bourgeois regime. Expropriate? Raise a red flag above the factory? Strike for the conquest of factory control? And then? We have seen what a pitiful end certain experiments have had. The time has come to find our bearings and reenter reality. In Turin the industrialists wanted a battle, not against the factory councils in and of themselves, but rather against the abuses they had generated, because they understood that workers wanted to attribute functions to them irreconcilable with the regime in which we live, and they won while we have been turned backward. . . . Factory councils, okay, but disciplined by the Federation. Without discipline no good can be done.

In a similar vein, Giuseppe Bianchi was also quoted as having written in *Battaglie Sindacali*, organ of the CGL: "In the factory either the *padrone* commands or the workers. Joint command is impossible.

[150] Gramsci, *L'Ordine Nuovo*, p. 180.

Factory control understood as an immediate possibility, beyond the interference of universal economic laws, is rubbish."[151]

It appeared, at least for a while, that the industrialists had won the ideological battle, that revolutionary aspirations had given way to common sense. Giolitti replaced Nitti as prime minister in June, and there was widespread optimism, even among his former adversaries, that at last there was a chief of state who could dominate national politics and give firm direction to economic recovery. Agnelli telegraphed Giolitti: "I feel the duty to express full faith in the one man who can solve the grave crisis which the country faces." Toeplitz, head of the Banca Commerciale, placed at Giolitti's disposition "every capacity and faculty of the Banca . . . for the program of financial reconstruction the government proposes."[152] Little did anyone know that new and more-massive factory occupations were but two months away.

The occupation of the factories

At the very same FIOM national conference (20–25 May 1920) where Buozzi bitterly attacked the Turinese workers' movement, it was decided to present the industrialists with a schedule of salary increases made necessary by the dramatic rise in the cost of living. There was to have been, on the average, an increase of 40 percent over prevailing wages.[153] Delivered to the Milan-based Federazione Nazionale Sindacale degli Industriali Meccanici e Metallurgici (the national federation of which AMMA in Turin was a member), these demands were rejected out of hand. Industry, it was claimed, was in no condition to augment salaries. The first meeting between the two syndical bodies took place on 29 July; no progress was made beyond a restatement of their respective positions. Another series of meetings was held between 10 and 13 August, but once again the industrialists, represented by Eduardo Rotigliano of Ilva, were intransigent and the talks broke down. According to Buozzi:

When the workers' delegation finished their refutation of the claims made by the industrialists' delegation, their head, Rotigliano – then a Nationalist, later a Fascist – ended the dispute with the provocative declaration: "Further

---

[151] *L'Informazione Industriale*, 3 June 1920.
[152] Castronovo, *Agnelli*, p. 231.
[153] Abrate, *Lotta sindacale*, p. 284; Spriano, *Occupazione*, p. 26.

discussion is pointless. The industrialists are against the concession of any increase whatsoever. Since the end of the war, they have continually lowered their pants. It's enough now and you can start."[154]

FIOM called a special meeting on 16–17 August with representatives of the CGL and the Socialist Party, where it was unanimously agreed to begin, starting 21 August, obstruction in all the factories. After the moral and material exhaustion of the disastrous April general strike, it was felt that obstruction was the only means of pressuring the industrialists whereby workers could still draw a salary sufficient to sustain the action. It was further decided that should this obstruction be met with a lockout, the workers would proceed to occupy the factories.

The prefects of Turin, Milan, and Genoa sent alarming reports to Rome on the situation in their cities, fearing that intransigence on the part of the industrialists would precipitate another wave of civil strife. Camillo Corradini, undersecretary for internal affairs, replied: "It is necessary to establish contacts with all the most authoritative industrialists to persuade them not to precipitously make decisions that might have grave consequences on the future development of the movement."[155]

Arturo Labriola, minister of labor, called representatives of both parties to Rome, offering to mediate the dispute. Buozzi accepted, willing to suspend obstruction if the industrialists were willing to resume negotiations, but Jarach and Rotigliano refused, maintaining that such government intervention would be "neither useful nor practical."[156] In contrast with Jarach and Rotigliano, Buozzi had shown great flexibility; he went so far as to suggest that FIOM might accept the industrialists' position if they could demonstrate with relevant data (costs, profits, etc.), rather than simply maintain, that industry was in no position to grant salary increases.[157] Such information, however, was forthcoming neither to FIOM nor to the government.

During the workers' obstruction, production fell to 10 percent of normal output. In Turin, Agnelli and AMMA were dissatisfied with the intransigence of the national federation; they believed some concessions, "more of form than substance," could have been given to

[154] Ibid., p. 43.
[155] Ibid., p. 50.
[156] Ibid.; Abrate, *Lotta sindacale*, p. 289.
[157] Castronovo, *Agnelli*, p. 241.

prevent a breakdown in the negotiations. Yet obstruction could not be tolerated. Therefore, it was decided to close single factories where production had fallen the most, since "a general lockout would put the government and public opinion against the industrialists, who have need of both." The poorly led national federation, despite pressure from Turin, never formulated an organizational response to obstruction until it was too late, until, that is, factory occupations had already begun, triggered by a decision of the Romeo automobile plant in Milan, independent of any association agreement or consultation, to declare a lockout on 30 August.[158] Within a week, factories of every sector would be occupied throughout the peninsula by more than 500,000 workers (150,000 in Turin alone).[159]

The obvious question is why were the industrialists so intransigent? One purported explanation is that industrialists welcomed the illegal seizure of the factories as a means of forcing Giolitti to commit the army and the police against the workers, thereby abandoning his policy of neutrality in labor conflicts.[160] There is little evidence to sustain such a hypothesis, which, in our view, underestimates the industrialists' long-standing horror at such forms of revolutionary action, especially when the industrialists had no reason to believe that Giolitti would either be neutral or act in their favor. Spriano, to the contrary, supports Labor Minister Labriola's judgment that the industrialists were more concerned with the government's fiscal policy than with workers, and doubts "that the industrialists would have wished to saddle the government with the necessity of using force, obliging it to almost take a position against the workers."[161]

That the industrialists' intransigence was due to Giolitti's fiscal policy has been argued more recently by a number of Italian historians of divergent political perspectives.[162] Like virtually all fragments of the bourgeoisie, industrialists had supported Giolitti's return to power in the hope that he might dominate national politics as he had done in the prewar era, thereby laying the groundwork for economic reconstruction and a return to social stability. Now that a seemingly

---

[158] Abrate, *Lotta sindacale*, p. 290–5; Castronovo, *Agnelli*, p. 243.
[159] Spriano, *Occupazione*, pp. 63–7, 96.
[160] Sarti, *Fascism and Industrial Leadership*, p. 27.
[161] Spriano, *Occupazione*, pp. 49–51.
[162] Abrate, *Lotta sindacale*, p. 285; Castronovo, *Agnelli*, p. 245; Carlo Vallauri, "L'attegiamento del governo Giolitti di fronte all'occupazione delle fabbriche, I," *Storia e Politica* 4 (Mar. 1965): 51.

strong government had finally replaced that of Nitti, industrialists did not want to openly attack it. Though they realized that Giolitti's fiscal legislation directed against the wealthy was a device by which he could later credibly abolish the political price of bread, industrialists were more concerned about the short-term effects such legislation would have upon investments and net gains. In July, De Benedetti, president of the LIT, had met with Giolitti, who reassured him that "if the measures would have to be maintained for political reasons, in their application account would be taken of the observations made, and the collaboration of industrialists and bankers would be accepted in drawing up the legislation."[163]

Some means, however, would have to be found to apply pressure on Giolitti, who typically responded more to momentary pulls and pushes in the immediate political situation than to principled, doctrinally based programs. As Vallauri suggests, resisting the workers' obstruction to the limit might force the government to intervene, as it did in the past, and offer public-policy concessions (e.g., tariff reform, subsidies, tax adjustments) in exchange for partially granting the workers' demands.[164] Similarly, Castronovo notes that "the conflict even at its most crucial state, between 28 August and 1 September, did not seem to leave these confines: of a 'strike' by the industrialists to dismantle Giolitti's fiscal legislation, or of an unlimited defense of certain groups, if not a precise political pressure masked by economic and syndical pretenses."[165]

As Oscar Sinigaglia, one of Italy's leading industrial engineers, would write in October 1920, no one could have believed that industry, which generally had been operating at full capacity, was incapable of yielding a penny in salary increases.[166] This, he argued, was why industrialists refused to release any relevant data to support their unequivocal position. At best, such a stand was based, not on the actual state of industry, but rather, as Agnelli put it, on the "uncertainty of the immediate future." That "uncertainty" had less to do with the immediate salary picture than how and to what degree Giolitti's fiscal program might be put into effect.

---

[163] Abrate, *Lotta sindacale*, p. 282.
[164] Vallauri, "L'attegiamento del governo Giolitti, I," p. 51.
[165] Castronovo, *Agnelli*, p. 282.
[166] Oscar Sinigaglia, "Nuovi rapporti tra capitale e lavoro," *Vita Italiana*, Oct. 1920, reprinted in Lucio Villari, ed., *Il capitale italiano del novecento* (Bari: Laterza, 1972), pp. 107–8.

Yet the industrialists were not a monolithic bloc. The same divisions which we traced earlier between the state-supported sector and the competitive sector arose once again. All those who have written on the conflict in question have noted a far greater intransigence on the part of Ansaldo and Ilva during the conflict and afterward. The state-supported sector had been the object of much of the postwar criticism against "speculators" and "profiteers"; Giolitti's fiscal legislation, as well as his proposed investigation of war contracts, would have hit them the hardest. Indeed, against this sector syndical leaders had their strongest case: how could industries that owed their very survival to the Italian taxpayers refuse to open their books for inspection? Already before the 16–17 August negotiations, Ansaldo had declared a lockout on 22 July, alleging "financial impotence" to pay its workers and thereby hoping to create a sense of economic alarm at precisely the moment Giolitti's fiscal legislation was before Parliament.[167] One should not forget that Rotigliano, the belligerent negotiator, was an executive of Ilva, and that Romeo, which precipitated the occupations by independently declaring a lockout, was tied to Ansaldo's Banca di Sconto. Moreover, representatives of the state-supported sector tried to defeat acceptance of the occupation settlement negotiated by Olivetti and Conti. On 19 September, *Idea Nazionale*, subsidized by Ansaldo, would carry an article entitled "Story of the Industrialists' Capitulation" that bitterly attacked Olivetti and Conti, as well as the Banca Commerciale, which had allegedly been responsible for the "capitulation" to favor "German interests."[168]

That industrialists did not take Arturo Labriola's offer to mediate seriously is not surprising. The Labor Ministry had just been created upon Giolitti's return to power; no government ministry had ever served as a mediating agency, so there was no precedent other than mediation by the prefect at the local level. To many, creation of a Labor Ministry was more of a symbolic than substantive action; that the post of labor minister had first been offered to Turati and then to Labriola, the revolutionary syndicalist who led the 1904 general strike, indicates that Giolitti himself never intended for the new ministry to be viewed as an impartial mediator. In early July, Labriola had introduced legislation that would have provided greater state subsid-

[167] Castronovo, *Agnelli*, p. 238.
[168] Vallauri, "L'attegiamento del governo Giolitti, I," p. 53; Spriano, *Occupazione*, pp. 130, 209.

ies for cooperatives, organs – Labriola explained – that might ease the transition from capitalism to Socialism. Speaking in the Chamber on 6 July, Labriola referred to the cooperative as "an economic form which we all encourage and look forward to above all because in it we see the germ of the new economic organ of society." As for another transitional form, factory councils, Labriola said, "As for myself, I look upon these solutions with major sympathy. . . . We live in a workers' democracy in a time and in a phase of workers' democracy wherein workers themselves execute an ever greater influence on industry and labor. We naturally desire that this process terminate in the creation of new institutions."[169] While the occupations were in progress, Labriola gave interviews to foreign journals, suggesting that it was official policy to create new institutions that might prove useful in the transition to Socialism. When criticized in the Senate by Dante Ferraris for making such statements, Labriola replied, "Socialist I entered a coalition cabinet, Socialist I remain."[170] Small wonder the likes of Olivetti, Conti, and Agnelli were not prepared to take the new labor minister seriously.

What of the industrialists' perception, or misperception, of Giolitti? Giolitti had indicated a willingness to be flexible in the administration of his fiscal measures but gave no concrete commitments. He advised industrialists to make salary concessions, warning them that in no case could they count upon the state to intervene in their behalf against the workers. Mario Abrate, on the basis of some rather sketchy evidence, has tentatively suggested that Giolitti had initially indicated to Agnelli that the government would so intervene. Until more evidence is forthcoming, this hypothesis must be questioned, since it flies in the face of all prefectural communication, as well as the public statements of both Agnelli and Giolitti. On the floor of the Senate, Giolitti claimed:

The industrialists told me when I passed through Turin before the conflict broke out that they intended to proceed with a lockout; this was no secret, as it had been repeated to me by many other persons who were not industrialists. I counseled them against this in every way. Since I knew perfectly well that a mass of several hundred thousand workers could not be dealt with by force, I declared to these industrialists that they could not in any way count on the intervention of public force. I declared this in a formal manner; thus

---

[169] *Atti Parlamentari*, Camera, 6 July 1920, pp. 2942–4.
[170] *Atti Parlamentari*, Senato, 26 Sept. 1920, pp. 1667–720.

no one can be grieved if the government fails in something which it had in no case promised to do.[171]

As for Agnelli, on 5 September he published a letter in *La Stampa* to the same effect:

At the outset of the conflict, being our duty as industrialists to call upon the head of government and hear his point of view, it was clearly declared to us that this was a private matter and that it was a consistent principle of political authority not to intervene.

There is some indication that Giolitti and Agnelli reached some private understanding *during* the conflict, as Agnelli became the most conciliatory of all the industrialists – he also received for the automobile industry a higher level of protection.[172] Before the actual factory occupations, however, no agreement had been reached. When the occupations began, De Benedetti, president of the LIT, contacted Corradini, undersecretary for internal affairs, and reported to the Turinese association that "the government has no clear policy direction and wishes to make no pledge, not even distant or formal, of defending the industrialists, a task it had completely abandoned." The only assurance De Benedetti received, with the Mazzonis case obviously in mind, was that "the government would not have proceeded with the requisition of occupied factories."[173]

Perhaps the industrialists' greatest mistake was to have mixed syndical action with political action directed toward the government's fiscal policy. As Sinigaglia pointed out, for years the industrialists had lectured the workers on the need to keep politics outside syndical relations. Now they themselves had violated this dictum and reaped the consequences: a project of worker control was forced upon them as the only means of ending what had been at the outset a narrowly circumscribed syndical issue.[174] Because of their ill-considered gamble, the *bacillus bolshevicus,* which appeared to have been exterminated after the April general strike, spawned anew as factory councils now exercised total control over red-bedecked factories.

Though factories were occupied throughout Italy, in no other city was the action so massive in scale as in Turin. On the first Sunday,

[171] Ibid., p. 1710; Abrate, *Lotta sindacale,* pp. 293–6.
[172] Castronovo, *Agnelli,* p. 248–55; Spriano, *Occupazione,* p. 127; Vallauri, "L'atteggiamento del governo Giolitti, II," *Storia e Politica* 4 (Apr. 1965): 234.
[173] Abrate, *Lotta sindacale,* pp. 294–5.
[174] Sinigaglia, "Nuovi rapporti," p. 109.

Fiat workers decided to continue production. The factory council declared: "Demonstrate that you know how to overcome fatigue, hardship, and danger for the emancipation of humanity from the capitalist clique."[175] In an *Ordine Nuova* article entitled "Red Sunday" Gramsci claimed:

The social hierarchies are broken, the historical values are inverted, the executing classes, the instrumental classes, have become *dirigente* classes. Placing themselves in command, they have found in themselves representatives, men who assume all the functions of producing an organic society, a living creature from an elementary and mechanical aggregate. . . . Today, Red Sunday, the action of the metalworkers will, by the workers themselves, lead to the first historical cell of the proletarian revolution that will spring forth from the general situation with the irresistible force of a natural phenomenon.[176]

Gramsci's revolutionary prediction was characteristically optimistic. Nevertheless, precipitated by the massive occupations, public discussion for the first time began seriously to focus on the need to transcend capitalism. Whereas few people had taken Labriola's twaddle on cooperatives and factory councils seriously in July, by September, both in the press and in Parliament, unprecedented attention was given to worker participation in production. No less than Agnelli, for purely tactical reasons, proposed turning Fiat into a cooperative; Sinigaglia advanced his own scheme for stock-sharing with the aim of eventual worker ownership and control of the major firms.[177]

Bourgeois reaction at home and abroad was confusion and alarm. Albertini believed that the only way out of the situation was to give power to the Socialists. As Spriano comments, "The man of order preferred even a socialist order to the existing disorder."[178] Writing in the *Corriere della Sera*, Albertini fully expressed the exasperation of bourgeois opinion:

By this time, we have nothing further to concede. What else can be desired from this bourgeoisie? The regime is dying not so much because its enemies desire it as because the political formula that its governments obey is mortal. The time for decision has arrived: either the bourgeoisie will give itself a government, if there is still time and if a man can be found, if the man finds a

[175] Spriano, *Occupazione*, p. 72.
[176] Gramsci, *L'Ordine Nuovo*, pp. 163–7.
[177] Sinigaglia, "Nuovi rapporti," pp. 106–26.
[178] Spriano, *Occupazione*, p. 131.

following; or it will give the responsibility of power to the Socialists and to the heads of the CGL.[179]

Giolitti, with measured aloofness, remained on vacation at Bardonecchia during most of the conflict. The foreign press could not make heads or tails out of what was unfolding; a Buenos Aires newspaper went so far as to report that the government abandoned Rome to seek refuge in the hills of Bardonecchia.[180] Although such contemporary observers as Labriola, Salvemini, and Einaudi thought that revolution was possible during the occupations, more recent scholarship suggests that this would have been highly unlikely given the absence of certain objective conditions (the urban–industrial proletariat's lack of national presence and its isolation from other social strata; the lack of effective organizational ties between the industrial cities of the north) and subjective conditions (the lack of a revolutionary party that might have directed the amorphous, locally based, and spontaneous movement, imposing unitary discipline over antagonistic factions within the Socialist Party and CGL). It should be remembered that the occupations initially had been a *defensive action,* as FIOM thought it impossible to conduct another strike after the defeat in April. No preparations had been made to take the step from factory occupations to revolution, nor did the *ordinovisti* wish to risk such action alone, after having already suffered the perils of isolation in April. A national meeting of CGL was called for 9–12 September, where revolutionary action was discussed and voted down, thereafter to be derisively called "the revolution of the votes."

The reformist leadership of the CGL placed the revolutionary burden upon the Socialist Party in general and the *ordinovisti* in particular. Were they ready to assume responsibility for such a move? The answer was no. Togliatti, representing the Turinese section of the party, was asked if the workers of that city, the avant-garde of the Italian proletariat, were prepared for armed struggle? "We will not attack alone," Togliatti responded, "to do so a simultaneous action in the countryside and especially in the nation would be necessary. . . . The revolution, if there is to be one, ought to be Italian, otherwise the two most daring cities, Turin and Milan, would be overpow-

[179] Maier, *Recasting Bourgeois Europe,* p. 188; Spriano, *Occupazione,* pp. 201–6.
[180] Spriano, *Occupazione,* p. 116.

ered."[181] D'Aragona, secretary of the CGL, had thereby sought to shield himself from *ordinovisti* criticism:

We interrogated the Turinese comrades because we believed that Turin was the best prepared city for an action of this type. We asked them: are you prepared to conduct the struggle if we transfer it to the political arena? And they answered us: if it's a question of defending the factories, we can do so; if it's a question of leaving the factories to conduct a struggle in the streets, we would be finished in ten minutes.[182]

The reformist leadership of the CGL decided that the real objective of the struggle was not "revolution" at all but rather "the principle of syndical control of the firms" (note the use of "syndical"). This position became the basis for a possible agreement between the CGL, the government, and the industrialists. The CGL leadership then confronted the Socialist Party: if you want a revolution, we will resign from the direction of the CGL and you lead it. Against the reformist position, a revolutionary one was advanced and a vote taken. The revolution was defeated 591,245 to 409,457, with 93,623 abstentions. Without the CGL's participation, the Socialist Party refused even to consider further action. As Spriano sardonically comments: "The revolution accepted to be democratically postponed *sine die*."[183]

Giolitti, who had communicated to the industrialists that he would not intervene, claimed to have had insufficient military force either to protect the factories or to liberate them. In any event, what was he to do? Bombard them with cannon?[184] Giolitti refused to be backed into a corner by industrialists over his "inaction." When he was attacked in the Senate by Dante Ferraris over his handling of the occupations, Giolitti rather sarcastically reminded Ferraris that he had been minister of industry under Nitti when the government requisitioned the Mazzonis factories.[185] Giolitti was confident that as the occupation progressed, workers would learn the error of their ways. As he stated in his autobiography, the occupations were essentially similar to the

[181] Salvemini, *Origins of Fascism,* pp. 279–80; Spriano, *Occupazione,* pp. 103–4.
[182] Spriano, *Occupazione,* pp. 104–5.
[183] Spriano, *Occupazione,* pp. 112–13; Vallauri, "L'attegiamento del governo Giolitti, II," p. 228.
[184] Vallauri, "L'attegiamento del governo Giolitti,II," p. 294; Spriano, *Occupazione,* pp. 57–8.
[185] *Atti Parlamentari,* Senato, 26 Sept. 1920, pp. 1710–11.

1904 general strike led by, of all people, his current minister of labor.[186]

Against the industrialists, Giolitti employed the carrot and the stick. On the one hand, he held out the promise (partially delivered) of tariff adjustments and the watering down of his fiscal measures; on the other, he "allowed" the factories to stay occupied and used the banks to apply pressure on the industrialists. De Benedetti, at a 15 September meeting of the LIT, spoke of there having been "exercised on the part of the government incredible pressures, not only flattery and personal threats, but warnings of reprisals on the part of banks."[187]

The triumph of the reformists at the CGL conference, however, allowed for a way out of the impasse between Giolitti and Confindustria leadership, both of whom wanted the conflict to come to a rapid conclusion under terms that would favor moderate syndical leadership over the extremists, yet not compromise managerial authority. After the "revolution of the votes" in favor of syndical control, Olivetti began to meet unofficially with D'Aragona and nurture a more conciliatory attitude among industrial leaders. Above all, Olivetti was a realist. Though the term "control" technically signified nothing more than a labor syndicate's right to audit a firm's accounts so as to be assured that industrialists were negotiating salaries in good faith (thus preventing the type of situation that had actually led to the occupations), Olivetti knew that this would represent a point of departure for, not the end of, worker demands for greater influence in the productive process. And yet the recognition of syndical control, however formal and transient, was the only way that the occupations might be ended, especially after Giolitti himself had made this the basis for a political resolution of the dispute. Thus, Olivetti and Conti (then president of Confindustria) resolved to overcome resistance on the part of industrialists by persuasion and, as we shall see, some measure of chicanery, while attempting, at the same time, to predefine the terms of the final settlement. Illustrative of Olivetti's "realistic" cast of mind are the following remarks from a tapped telephone conversation with Silvio Crespi in Milan on 18 September, the day before the settlement between Confindustria and the CGL was signed:

---

[186] Abrate, *Lotta sindacale*, p. 45.
[187] Consiglio Direttivo, LIT, meeting of 15 Sept. 1920, HAUIT.

The advice of Conti and myself is this: the alternatives are to submit to the government's terms or resist to the limit. Both alternatives obviously might have grave consequences, but given that the situation is one where the government will intervene against the weaker party, which is precisely the industrialists, you know our thoughts. . . . In these conditions, we say it is far better to finish with the situation today because the position of the industrialists will be more grave tomorrow.[188]

What Olivetti and Conti kept secret was the fact that the "government's terms," to which industrialists had to "submit," in fact were *their terms*. The decree that Giolitti issued formally on 19 September was actually drafted by them on 14 September and transmitted to the prime minister, who then "made it his own."[189]

When Olivetti and Conti set themselves in motion, Giolitti marshaled the state apparatus behind the conciliatory effort. Before leaving for Aix-les-Bains on 11 September to meet with Millerand, as if nothing exceptional were taking place in Italy, Giolitti instructed Corradini to have the banks pressure the Milanese industrialists: "In Turin there is the sensation that all will accommodate themselves. There is resistance in Milan, where industrialists will yield if they receive instructions from the banks on which their existence depends."[190] On 12 September Corradini cabled Giolitti that the CGL reformists had triumphed over the extremists with a formula of "syndical control" rather than "socialization of industry," under which the factory councils would have substituted themselves for management. Giolitti then instructed him to proceed, making the formula of "syndical control" the basis for a settlement.[191]

The next day a meeting took place at the office of the prefect of Milan, Alfredo Lusignoli. Present were Albertini, Conti, and Agnelli, as well as Toeplitz (Banca Commerciale) and Pogliani (Banca di Sconto). Reporting to Corradini, Lusignoli mentioned that Conti took a conciliatory position and accepted the principle of syndical control, though many industrialists remained intransigent.[192] On 14 September in Milan the delegate council of Confindustria met and two tendencies emerged: one was a refusal to accept any formula of control except as a governmental *atto d'imperio;* the other was an

[188] Spriano, *Occupazione*, p. 210.
[189] Abrate, *Lotta sindacale*, p. 297; Conti, *Taccuino*, pp. 154–5.
[190] Castronovo, *Agnelli*, p. 251.
[191] Spriano, *Occupazione*, pp. 121–3.
[192] Ibid., pp. 125–6, 157.

acceptance of control "so as to influence it in a way which might not be excessively dangerous." According to De Benedetti, the majority were for nonacceptance, while Conti, who had a mandate to continue consultations at the prefecture, was for preemptive acceptance. Later that day, word was received that Giolitti wanted to meet with the leadership of Confindustria and the CGL in Turin on his return trip from France. In anticipation of this meeting, Olivetti and Conti drafted a decree calling for a joint CGL–Confindustria commission to formulate legislation concerning "the eventual participation of workers in the technical–administrative control of firms."[193]

From the outset, this was a purely tactical move on the part of Olivetti and Conti; their sole purpose was to settle the conflict and end the occupations. They never intended to see such control actually proceed, feeling confident that they could obstruct the work of this joint commission. To cite Conti's diary:

> Since it is easy to foresee that a commission of this nature will never succeed in formulating any reasonable legislation, the matter will finish for now without winners or losers. Unfortunately, a real crisis of production is imminent and of the control commission nothing more will be said. . . . Now it is up to the government to name the commission which must prepare the legislation. I am sure that nothing will come of it.[194]

Conti and Olivetti were to have it both ways: they would actually write the terms of the settlement *and* have it appear to irate Confindustria members as if this settlement were an *atto d'imperio,* the sole condition under which they could be dragged, *malgré eux,* toward conciliation.

The meeting between Giolitti and the leaders of Confindustria and the CGL went according to plan. Conti feigned opposition to any form of control. Giolitti, claiming the time had come to give workers responsibility in the productive process, imposed "his" draft decree upon the recalcitrant industrialists. The following day, 16 September, Confindustria's national council met and after eleven hours of heated discussion accepted the principle of control, where "it establishes neither monopoly nor the prevalence of workers' syndicates and signifies collaboration and co-responsibility of the various elements of production."[195] Even in this more innocuous form, the resolution

[193] Abrate, *Lotta sindacale,* pp. 296–7.
[194] Conti, *Taccuino,* pp. 154–5.
[195] Abrate, *Lotta sindacale,* p. 297; Spriano, *Occupazione,* 129–30.

was not unanimous but passed by a vote of twenty-one to fourteen (opposition being led by Rotigliano of Ilva). The joint commission was established, and the original salary dispute settled in the workers' favor. As for payment to workers for goods produced during the occupation, it was left for individual firms to determine the value and make salary payments accordingly.[196]

Reaction in Turin to the settlement was bitter. During the conflict, Turin had been the only industrial center to fall almost completely under the control of factory councils; of 199 firms occupied, 85 had been administered by these bodies.[197] When FIOM held a national referendum to confirm acceptance of the settlement, Turin was the only city where a compact minority was for continuation of the struggle and remained in many of the factories, particularly those of Fiat. De Benedetti resigned his presidency of the LIT in anger on 20 September, after attacking both the government and Confindustria for their laxity in failing to make the emptying out of the factories a precondition for any settlement. The prefect of Turin, Taddei, who had earlier requisitioned the Mazzonis factories, recommended that the Turinese industrialists make salary increases greater than those negotiated in Rome in the hope of breaking the impasse. Specifically, he recommended that workers be paid for all the days of the occupation, regardless of the goods produced. Though Agnelli agreed, both AMMA and the LIT were rigidly opposed to conceding anything beyond the provisions of the Rome settlement. Incidentally, this was also Buozzi's position, since the Rome accord was a syndical pact between the CGL and Confindustria which had to be universally accepted.[198]

It was at this point that Agnelli assumed the role of a major protagonist, convinced that the situation had to be "forced" so that the drama would come to a speedy conclusion. On 27 September, at a meeting of AMMA, he announced his intention to sign a separate agreement based on the prefect's formula. Agnelli then announced his resignation as president of AMMA, saying that Fiat could no longer remain a member because it would soon bear a "proletarian label" and be transformed into a cooperative. According to Castronovo, Agnelli's definitive biographer, four motives were behind this bold

---

[196] Spriano, *Occupazione*, pp. 132–3.
[197] Castronovo, *Agnelli*, p. 255.
[198] Abrate, *Lotta sindacale*, pp. 299–300; Castronovo, *Agnelli*, pp. 255–8.

and unexpected move: (1) to speed the withdrawal of occupying workers from the factories; (2) to pressure the other industrialists toward acceptance of the prefect's formula; (3) to give greater momentary credibility to Giolitti's decree on syndical control; and (4) to pressure Fiat's major stockholders into affording him complete managerial autonomy.[199] On all four counts, Agnelli was completely successful. He had never been very precise as to the form a Fiat cooperative might take; these were details to be settled later. It soon became apparent to Fiat workers that Agnelli's package had been, according to Castronovo, "an able diversion or even less, an empty box." Responding to the workers' rejection of his cooperative proposal, Agnelli played his role of "captain of industry" for all it was worth, claiming that this was further proof that workers were incapable of assuming responsibility for a firm's direction, adding: "The rejection of the cooperative proves once again that the industrial leaders, in the interest of industry and the nation, have more courage than worker leadership in blazing new paths."[200]

Nor was Agnelli finished. On 3 October he exploded another bomb, setting in motion a new set of pressures: both he and Fornaca threatened to resign from Fiat. "I cannot continue to work having for collaborators 24,000 enemies," he declared. With this move Agnelli hoped to alarm public opinion and force Giolitti to ensure that syndical control stopped far short of challenging managerial authority. To all, even Gramsci and Gobetti, Agnelli was the very symbol of a competent industrial organizer. If he could no longer function in this new ambience of worker participation, perhaps it was time to brake all further steps in this direction. Agnelli also used the ploy to secure needed loans. Rather than see him resign from Fiat, the Banca Commerciale and Credito Italiano quickly came forth with 150 million lire. Furthermore, Agnelli used the threat to regain absolute managerial authority in Fiat – to be, as it were, returned by plebiscite.[201] As Gobetti had occasion to say, Agnelli knew the value of forms and gestures. By 30 October, Agnelli had even regained the sympathy of Fiat workers, judging from the following description of his mother's

[199] Castronovo, *Agnelli,* pp. 260–76.
[200] Ibid., p. 267.
[201] Ibid., pp. 264–76.

funeral as reported in *Corriere della Sera:*

At the stately funeral of Signora Agnelli, 3,000 workers took part. By decision of the leaders of the workers' organizations, production was suspended in all of Fiat's fourteen plants during the ceremony as a sign of mourning. As the body was carried from the parish church, a significant episode took place. One of the members of the *commissione interna* of Fiat Centro, a regional Socialist officer, approached Commendatore Agnelli and said in a loud voice, "Return with us." A representative of the clerical workers, in the name of all the others, expressed the same desire. Commendatore Agnelli, overpowered with emotion, was speechless but extended a long handshake to the two spokesmen of the firm's employees.[202]

By the end of October, Agnelli once more was president of AMMA, undisputed autocrat of Fiat, and a popular captain of industry. At a time when other Turinese industrialists had faltered and lost their sense of the moment, he had almost single-handedly brought about a return to normalcy. As Abrate suggests, he alone had been able to transcend "the abstraction of principles and adapt himself to the objective exigencies of reality."[203]

Olivetti, now secretary of Confindustria (based in Rome), returned to Turin on 29 October to address a special meeting of the LIT. Once again, as he did after every setback, Olivetti sought to turn weakness into strength, underscoring the need for greater unity and discipline. Other forces, he argued, had conspired against the industrialists and contributed to their momentary defeat. Yet the industrialists themselves bore major responsibility: they had shown poor judgment in remaining intransigent over salary concessions, and internal disunity had also left them vulnerable:

We must, however, recognize having brought this upon ourselves with our frivolity and dissension. Chateaubriand affirmed that "a regime dies by its own hand." We must all remember that bitter conflict between two powerful groups, headed by the Banca Commerciale and the Perrone brothers, which helped foment and aggravate that campaign of lies which laid the groundwork for the factory occupations and threatened to dry up, with the downfall of industry, each of the country's most productive sources.[204]

---

[202] Ibid., p. 276.
[203] Abrate, *Lotta sindacale*, p. 304.
[204] Ibid., p. 337.

The red wave ends

The workers emerged from the factory occupations with modest salary increases and a vague promise of control, yet demoralization and fratricidal dissension had become prevalent with the movement's failure to attain a revolutionary outcome. Never again would the proletariat launch another major campaign nor even maintain the level of strike activity that characterized the last half of 1919 and the first half of 1920. From October 1920 until the March on Rome two years later, it was continually on the defensive. Three factors are significant in this respect. First, beginning in January 1921, the workers' organizational forces fragmented, with the split producing a separate Communist Party. In October 1922, the Socialist Party split into maximalists and reformists, and the ties between the CGL and all of the separate Marxist parties were severed. Second, the economic crisis of 1921, which led to wide-scale unemployment (102,156 in December 1920; 512,260 in December 1921), was effectively exploited by the industrialists to impose discipline. Third, national politics took a rightward swing, evidenced by the relative success of "constitutionalist" parties in the local election of November 1920, the rise of rural Fascism between November 1920 and June 1921, and the formation of an anti-Socialist Blocco Nazionale during the national election of 1921. After the Livorno Congress in January 1921, when the Socialist Party split to the Left instead of the Right, Giolitti gradually discarded his reformist program aimed at enlisting the support of a collaborationist Socialist Party and looked to the Right for an alternative base of support.

Confindustria lost no time in mending its associational wounds and launching an offensive – this time publicly – against Giolitti's fiscal program, as well as the projected legislation on syndical control. Orders were given from Rome, and executed locally, to combat the project by marshaling the press as a vehicle for proindustrial propaganda, by sponsoring public meetings on the subject (in Turin, Milan, Rome, Florence, Venice, Naples, and Trieste), by enlisting the support of commercial associations, by recruiting respected academicians and professionals to denounce the control concept, and by lobbying in Rome among parliamentary deputies and locally among the various liberal associations.[205]

---

[205] Confindustria Circulars: P.N. 1128, C. 1175, 6 Mar. 1921.

Needless to say, the architect of this initiative was Gino Olivetti. From the outset — as early as 7 October 1920 — he had sought to undermine Giolitti's contention that syndical control would be a step toward class collaboration and increased productivity by identifying the project rather as a Trojan horse, penetrating the fortress of capitalism with revolutionary Socialism. Given Gramsci's writings on factory councils and on the need for prefigurative–transformative structures able to function under capitalism to prepare workers for the new order, and even statements by reformists like Turati that worker control was but a first step toward further Socialist conquests, Olivetti focused attention on the essentially *political,* rather than the illusory technicoadministrative, nature of the project.[206] In Confindustria's academic journal, *Rivista delle Società Commerciali* (later transformed into the *Rivista di Politica Economica*), which he himself edited, Olivetti had professors attack the control project. For example, Manfredi Siotto Pinto claimed that "the industrialists were asked, in substance, to discuss the type and length of rope with which they were to be hung."[207] In this rather erudite organ, Olivetti also contributed an essay ("Riccordi vecchi e cose nuove") on the failure of the *conseil d'encouragement pour les associations ouvrières,* established in France in July 1848 with a subsidy of three million francs, to aid workers' *ateliers* and promote an early form of *autogestion.*[208]

The joint commission appointed by Giolitti to draft control legislation broke down by 22 November. According to Confindustria, "the two delegations agreed that all further discussion was useless and that the work of the commission should be terminated."[209] The immediate cause of the rupture was the CGL's attempt to extend application of control to the hiring and firing of workers, outside the scope of the original decree but necessary, according to the CGL, because of the economic crisis that had already led to substantial layoffs. The industrialists objected on principle, claiming that this would destroy the freedom of contract, hamper the hiring of the most-qualified workers, and burden industry with bureaucratic constraints. Moreover, industrialists refused to concede this power because it had been, and would

[206] *L'Informazione Industriale,* 7 Oct. 1923.
[207] *Rivista delle Società Commerciale,* July 1920, Oct. 1920, Dec. 1920; *Rivista di Politica Economica,* Jan. 1921.
[208] *Rivista di Politica Economica,* Feb. 1921.
[209] *Atti Parlamentari,* Camera, Documenti: Disegni di leggi e relazioni, meeting of 8 Feb. 1921, p. 20.

be again, a weapon in their hands to maintain discipline.[210] Each separate delegation presented its own draft. The minister of industry reviewed both and, in consultation with the Consiglio Superiore dell'Industria (an advisory body of Parliament), presented the government's draft on 8 February 1921.

Though the government's draft was clearly a compromise between the two positions, and Confindustria had been successful in prevailing upon the industrialist members of the advisory council to annex a resolution calling for a delay in adopting the measure because of the delicate economic moment, Confindustria nevertheless attacked the government's draft, and had it attacked, as vigorously as it had attacked the CGL draft earlier. The CGL draft called for two levels of control: one at the firm, where workers would elect representatives to attend board meetings and have access to information regarding costs, profits, productive methods, marketing, and salary scales; the other at the national level of the particular industrial sector, where the data on individual firms would be collected and the situation of that sector ascertained for contractual purposes. Hiring would take place exclusively through employment offices administered by worker and industrialist syndicates. Layoffs were to follow specified conditions, including the reduction of the work week to thirty-six hours before such action could be taken. Compulsory arbitration also was mandated in conflicts between labor and capital.

The government's draft – which, as Confindustria mockingly noted, excluded state industries – had no form of control at the firm level but established control commissions at the national level for each branch of industry. These control commissions, composed exclusively of workers, had the right to appoint delegates in individual plants to collect data but not to attend board meetings. Separate industrialist commissions were also provided, which could send delegates to participate without vote at control commission meetings and prevent publication of material they judged prejudicial to industry. Norms were also included governing the hiring and firing of workers and were substantially similar to those contained in the CGL draft.

---

[210] Catalano, *Potere economico*, pp. 177–8; *CGII Annuario 1927*, pp. 119–26; Confindustria Circulars: P.N. 660, C. 170, 10 Feb. 1921; P.N. 776, C. 172, 14 Feb. 1921.

Confindustria's draft merely provided for joint worker–employer control commissions at the national level by sector. Workers had no elected or delegated status with regard to control in individual firms. Data were to be furnished from the firms directly to the control commissions, and such data were confined to salaries only, not the financial structure of the firm or its technical apparatus. No provisions were made concerning hiring and firing.

Moreover, the report affixed to the Confindustria draft, unlike those of the other two, was patently polemical, attacking the very concept of control. It briefly raised a number of objections that had been previously aired in the association's press campaign (that industrial secrets would be revealed; that workers were too incompetent to understand, and too irresponsible to be entrusted with, vital data; that control commissions should not be composed entirely of workers; and that no norms should be established regarding hiring and firing, an exclusive domain of the employer). But the thrust of Confindustria's argument concerned *the political nature of control,* as well as its effect of undermining necessary factory authority. The CGL, it argued, formally maintained that the objective of control was to know the state of industry. Yet in numerous public statements, and in the joint commission meetings, the CGL indicated that it also expected veto power over managerial decisions that conflicted with its assessment of the data. This not only would make swift decisions impossible but would undermine managerial authority and prevent the industrialist from executing his directive function in the most efficacious manner. Even without a formal veto, Confindustria argued, continual surveillance would immobilize the vital organs of industry. "Vivisection may be an excellent means to study the functions of life, but it usually costs the existence or at least some vital functions of the subject." The time and effort spent in this type of control not only would be unproductive but would be downright counterproductive:

We are convinced that if industry is to live, it is imperative that confusion be avoided concerning who must command and who must obey. It is imperative that he who commands not be a censurable and dismissable agent of the masses, who, to the contrary, must be directed. It is strange that while the necessity of hierarchy in industry has been recognized in Lenin's Russia, our organizers do not wish to take note of this instructive experience but want to give possession and direction of factories to the workers.

The "real motive" behind the CGL's project, Confindustria argued, was political: to prepare for the transition to Socialism.[211]

By the middle of March 1921, Giolitti called for new national elections and began to assemble an anti-Socialist Blocco Nazionale. In exchange for their support, industrialists demanded the dismantling of his "demagogic" fiscal program, as well as an end to any further consideration of control. Giolitti agreed, as his attention was no longer directed toward the reformist Left but to the Right. The control legislation was never formally debated on the floor of Parliament before or after the May elections; in effect, it was buried in committee. By March 1921 it had become a nonissue; not even the CGL lobbied for it any longer, realizing that the divided Left lacked sufficient strength in Parliament or in the nation to push it through without Giolitti's support. Therefore, exception must be taken to interpretations of Fascism which suggest that killing of the control legislation was one of the rewards that industrialists received for having backed Mussolini. According to Spriano:

With the changed relation of forces, the joint commission formed by Giolitti never succeeded in formulating a unitary text; negotiations dragged on wearily. Giolitti presented his own draft in February 1921, but the Chamber discussed it neither in that nor in the successive legislature, and all the various projects (that of the CGL, Confindustria, Giolitti, the CIL [Confederazione Italiana del Lavoro] and PPI [Partito Popolare Italiano]) remained dead letters. No one would speak of it again. All the burning debates of September 1920, all the interrelated debates then on its contents (class control, syndical control, state control, participation, and stock-sharing) were dropped as soon as the workers' forces were no longer capable of realistically imposing any control on production and on the management of the firms.[212]

The 1921 economic crisis, in any case, would have weakened the bargaining position of workers' syndicates. Confindustria decided to take full advantage of rising unemployment to renounce or renegotiate existing labor contracts and impose greater factory discipline; workers were in no position, materially or spiritually, to sustain further strikes. Already before the war had ended, Olivetti suggested that the wartime level of employment could not be maintained and that workers who had been attracted by high salaries to the urban—

[211] *Atti Parlamentari*, Camera, Documenti: Disegni di legge e relazioni, meeting of 8 Feb. 1921, pp. 1–33.
[212] Spriano, *Occupazione*, pp. 166–7.

industrial areas would have to return to the land.[213] Officially, of course, Confindustria denied the CGL's charge that industrialists were deliberately taking advantage of the economic crisis to retract gains made by workers during the 1919–20 period. Olivetti, in a letter to Beneduce, the new minister of labor, claimed that rising unemployment was simply an objective consequence of the crisis. It was also a necessary consequence of the technical restructuring of productive processes; the most efficient industrial capacity, however deleterious its unfortunate short-term effects, was, after all, in the long-term interests of the nation. Once again, a neutral technological veil was summoned forth by the industrial ideologue to mask an essentially class-specific argument.

I maintain that the industrialists ought not to profit from the crisis by diminishing the moral position of the proletariat, and in this sense, instructions have been given for some time which you have seen confirmed by the facts. However, it would be well to reach an understanding on this point: it is certain that our industries cannot support those so-called moral conquests for which they must contribute to workers' organizations or see diminished the possibility of technically and economically ordering work processes in a manner most useful to the ends of production or adhere to obligations of this kind. You yourself will understand that this restoration of the industrialist's position is necessary after the wave of sovietism of the past years and after the industrial crisis, which is far from finished, necessitated a complete rearrangement of the productive order.[214]

Given the political and economic conditions of 1919, industrialists had been willing or forced to exchange high salaries and "moral conquests" for greater rationalization. By 1921 such a trade-off was no longer necessary and, if anything, industrialists would attempt to impose a return to the status quo ante.

The workers' syndicates asked for a reduction of working hours in order to maintain as high a level of employment as possible. Confindustria insisted upon an intensification of production and a reduction of variable costs. In a circular dated 23 March 1921, Olivetti advised industrialists to renounce or modify existing labor contracts in accordance with these objectives. "As a general rule, the reduction of personnel rather than working hours would be most suitable in the interest of industry." With the reduction of working hours, "the firms

---

[213] Abrate, *Lotta sindacale*, p. 183.
[214] Confindustria Circulars: P.N. 1128, C. 1175, 6 Mar. 1921.

are constrained invariably to maintain a sizable proportion of their costs." The policy advocated by Confindustria, furthermore, would stimulate a return to agricultural occupations and be "an effective break upon the phenomenon of urbanism." As for the restoration of factory discipline: "The industrial organizations, finally, consider it to be a supreme necessity of industry to reestablish discipline in the factories and to attain a better technical ordering of labor through a careful selection of the workforce. The crisis offers a propitious circumstance to realize these objectives, which coincide with the fundamental bases of industrial life."[215] Reflecting a growing convergence between the Right-moving Giolitti and the industrialists, the prime minister himself invited workers to "return to the land" and did not promote reformist welfare measures which might have alleviated urban–industrial unemployment.[216] In fact, it was during this very period that Giolitti abolished the political price of bread.

In Turin massive layoffs at first were resisted by the workers' syndicates, but by now the industrialists had the upper hand. In early March 1921, Michelin, after having already laid off 6,500 of its 14,000 workers, announced its intention to cut another 800. On 12 March the suspended workers refused to leave the factory and work was suspended. At this point, the firm requested intervention by the police, who themselves occupied the building. Michelin kept the factory locked until early April, when workers agreed to return on its terms.[217]

Almost simultaneously Fiat announced the layoff of "at least 1,500 workers." Agnelli, to be sure, publicly maintained that such a move was necessary to reduce costs and better weather the economic crisis. Privately, at an AMMA meeting, he maintained that the time had come to "eliminate from the factories all the Communist elements, the factory councils, and all those workers who impeded the control of production."[218] Fiat's *commissione interna* insisted upon a suspension of the announced layoffs, as well as the reduction of working hours. Agnelli responded by declaring a lockout, due to the "systematic opposition of the workers' organizations and the *commissioni interne*" and also the "abusive presence in the factories of numerous

[215] Ibid., P.N. 136, C. 189, 23 Mar. 1921.
[216] Castronovo, *Agnelli*, p. 286.
[217] Abrate, *Lotta sindacale*, p. 346.
[218] Ibid., p. 348.

suspended workers."[219] Once again, public forces were used to clear Fiat's factories, and Agnelli announced that they would not be reopened until each and every worker personally signed a statement that he would execute whatever the management requested. After a month, 8,300 workers had signed, and 1,300 more indicated a willingness to do so. The Fiat factories reopened unhampered thereafter by any further infractions of discipline. Gramsci's moving article "Men of Flesh and Bone" reflected the general sense of resignation which now permeated the once revolutionary city.[220]

By the spring of 1921 it had become fully apparent that revolution was no longer on the horizon. Had the proletariat not suffered from such sharp ideological divisions, organizational inefficiency, and poor leadership, it might have, at best, held its own during the second postwar biennium. Lacking this, the Italian working class was objectively and subjectively incapable of stemming the political involution that would culminate in Fascism. Already on 25 April 1921 the Camera del Lavoro in Turin was burned by the Fascists. Immediately, the Socialist press held the industrialists responsible, though the industrialists themselves were shocked and outraged by the incident. At a meeting of the LIT three days later, concern was voiced that an erroneous identity might be made in the public consciousness between industrialists and Fascism.[221] The new president of the association, Giuseppe Mazzini, who with Gino Olivetti was running as a candidate on Giolitti's Blocco Nazionale, disclaimed in a political speech the day after the fire any connection between industrialists and Fascism:

Even today a Communist journal identifies industrialists and Fascists, and yesterday it suggested that an order for the destruction of the Camera del Lavoro came from Confindustria via a telegram from Rome. It would do well, both for the Fascists and for members of the LIT, to emphasize that Fascism is one thing and industry another, that Fascism serves to defend, not industry, but our institutions and the state.[222]

Industrialists, as we shall see, were proud to the point of arrogance in claiming that they single-handedly beat back the "Communists" without recourse to third parties. They had never called for or con-

---

[219] Castronovo, *Agnelli*, p. 288.
[220] Gramsci, *Socialismo e fascismo*, p. 154.
[221] Abrate, *Lotta sindacale*, p. 348.
[222] Consiglio Direttivo, LIT, meeting of 29 Apr. 1921, HAUIT.

doned *squadristi* violence and were among the first to demand a demobilization of the Fascist militia after the March on Rome. As the astute, anti-Fascist Piero Gogetti recognized, "Fascism has not known how to be the avante-garde of modern industry. . . . In Piemonte and Lombardy the industrialists prefer dealing with Buozzi rather than Mussolini."[223]

If anything, industrial associations had been too successful in confronting the workers' movement as a belligerent force, rather than coopting the reformist syndicates through a policy aimed more toward the regulation and institutionalization of class conflict. Here, associational leaders found themselves in the same paradoxical situation as we noted in the prewar period. On the one hand, there was an expressed desire, as well as a number of concrete actions, to establish conciliatory relations with an "institutional partner" so as to contain "impulsive" behavior that in their eyes interrupted production to the detriment of both classes. On the other, industrial associations so humiliated reformist syndicates in the major postwar conflicts that whatever precarious measure of legitimacy these might have commanded among the rank and file was further eroded, leaving the proletariat fragmented and "undisciplined." Both in public and in private, industrialists expressed genuine respect for such labor leaders as Buozzi (something, incidentally, they would rarely, if ever, do with regard to Fascist labor leaders). Even during their darkest moment, negotiating a final settlement of the factory occupations, Confindustria leaders dealt with their CGL counterparts as objective adversaries, not detested enemies. A notation from Conti's diary is illustrative of this:

The curious thing is that meanwhile, between me and my adversaries, relations were being created which I will call cordial, even if the term may sound excessive. The other evening Buozzi said to me: "But are you not convinced Senator that by now we are the *padroni*, that the revolution is under way and nothing can stop it? Why not prepare yourself to come with us. We have need of men like you." I thanked him, laughing at the offer, observing that while in Russia there was no real bourgeoisie, with good fortune we have one that is cultivated, intelligent, and hardworking; not at all disposed to let ourselves be suppressed. . . . Leaving Buozzi, D'Aragona, and company, I did not fail to note that we had finished with reciprocal sympathy. They had defended their class and I had defended mine; but our relations had always remained cordial.[224]

[223] Castronovo, *Agnelli*, p. 269.
[224] Conti, *Taccuino*, pp. 153–5.

In any case, that syndical relations did not develop into a well-regulated, institutional pattern was hardly the sole fault of industrial leadership. While perhaps they might have been more effective in favoring the reformist syndicates, it is unlikely that this alone would have altered fundamentally the internal fragmentation of the proletariat. The record indicates that, indeed, Confindustria did make significant concessions to FIOM and the CGL, only to see these duly negotiated labor contracts rejected by the rank and file. Generally speaking, industrial leadership treated the workers' syndicates in a heavy-handed manner only *after* the latter had failed to enforce the very contracts that they had in good faith negotiated. Since the syndicates could not check pervasive indiscipline, industrialists felt compelled to impose a solution unilaterally. Buozzi himself admitted in April 1921 that his "one great error" was "to have allowed for two years in Turin, without sufficient intransigence, an experiment to continue which we predicted at the end of the Florence conference of November 1919 had to lead inevitably to dissolution."[225]

The major point, however, is that by the spring of 1921 industrialists had fully triumphed at the level of class conflict, and unlike the agrarians, they had done so on the basis of their own internal strength and organizational resources, not by employing external agents to terrorize workers into submission. As Lyttelton correctly observes, "Terror was at odds with the rationality of modern industry. In a city like Turin, the industrialists were proud of the superior quality of their workforce, and aware that it had one weapon of protest at hand, namely emigration to the factories of France or Switzerland."[226] Not only were Fascist squads not used by industrialists in the major cities, but an essential source of diffidence toward Fascism on the part of industrialists was the fear of stirring up worker agitation anew in reaction to squadrist activity, now that order had finally been restored by *them* in the factories.

Illustrative of a generalized perception among industrialists that the threat of "Bolshevism" had passed was Mazzini's characterization of 1921 as "one of the more tranquil years."[227] Gramsci himself recognized that by August 1921 (fourteen months before the March on Rome), the situation had fundamentally changed: "The bourgeoisie

---

[225] Castronovo, *Agnelli*, p. 291.
[226] Lyttelton, *Seizure of Power*, p. 213.
[227] *L'Informazione Industriale*, 20 Apr. 1923.

takes courage. The bourgeoisie today feels secure after having over-come a grave danger."[228] Mussolini, as we have seen, noted a pro-found change in the "psychology of the masses" and tried to check provincial Fascists from speculating on the threat of Bolshevism any further, as this was beginning to alienate public opinion. The battle at the level of class conflict had already been won, and yet the political crisis of liberalism remained and deepened.

Industrialists and the political crisis

Though we have analyzed in considerable detail the growing alien-ation of the *borghesia produttrice* from the *borghesia politica,* we should not anticipate a single moment of catharsis in which a commit-ment to liberalism was purged and unconditional support given to Fascism. Our research indicates that the standard instrumentalist in-terpretation of the relationship between industrialists and Fascism is not only factually incorrect but analytically crude and mechanistic; that is, at a certain point, industrialists found in Fascism a superior political vehicle, more responsive to their sectoral needs, and conse-quently severed their bonds with the traditional liberal *classe diri-gente*. As Guarneri indicates, most industrialists retained their liberal party membership until 1926, when new syndical legislation – which they opposed – compelled membership in the Partito Nazionale Fas-cista (PNF). Actually, some industrialists, like Pirelli and Mazzini, delayed joining the Fascist Party until 1932.[229]

In fact, what transpired between 1919 and 1922 was less a matter of industrialists forsaking liberalism for Fascism but rather, as we have been suggesting, a growing convergence between liberalism and Fascism. During these critical years, there emerged no significant programmatic or ideological contrast between the two political forces such that they could be viewed as antithetical or fundamentally dis-tinct. As Maier notes: "In sum, there could be no liberal anti-fascist stance, because with rare exceptions liberals wanted fascism to share in power."[230] That said, it must be further recognized that industrial-ists played a relatively minor role in the transformation of Fascism from a rather marginal political movement into a determinant na-

[228] Gramsci, *Socialismo e fascismo*, p. 265.
[229] Guarneri, *Battaglie economiche*, 1:54.
[230] Maier, *Recasting Bourgeois Europe*, p. 338.

tional political force. It was the landowners who found in the hitherto urban middle-class movement an effective weapon to be employed in securing conditions for their own long-term survival, making it the spearhead of agrarian reaction. It was Giolitti who, for his own tactical reasons (and with no prodding by industrialists), included the Fascists in his Blocco Nazionale, bestowing upon them political respectability and a significant presence in Parliament. If, in the unlikely case, Fascism's political success could be traced to any single source, it certainly could not be found in the instrumental machinations of industrialists, who, having "played the card of liberal democracy" and found it wanting, now "played the card of Fascism," foisting it upon an otherwise sound and resilient body politic. Rather, the success of Fascism was due to the breakdown of traditional liberalism in the face of mass politics: its failure ideologically and organizationally to penetrate newly mobilized social strata; its incapacity to mediate within its diffuse institutional framework and transformist modus vivendi a wider spectrum of opposing, formally organized interests; its utter lack of any specific center of gravity or organic base within the fragmented bourgeois bloc which might have served as a positive aggregating pole.

As belated members of the bourgeois bloc and the liberal *classe dirigente,* rather than as industrialists per se, we must now focus our attention on the political activity undertaken by industrial associations during the period at hand. More than any other bourgeois fragment, industrialists were ascendant both ideologically and organizationally. Their failure to reconstitute the disaggregated bourgeois constellation, to become its hegemonic faction, is of far greater relevance in reconstructing the relationship between industrialists and the rise of Fascism than the more narrow instrumentalist hypothesis based on some specific sectoral exigency, a hypothesis that is factually unfounded. Seen from this perspective, what the industrialists *failed to do* may be far more significant than what they did do, as it was their self-stated intention to impose *direzione* upon the *borghesia politica,* as well as the bourgeoisie in general. Thus, the relationship between industrialists and the rise of Fascism was indirect, rather than direct, of hegemonic default rather than hegemonic success. Within the realm of concrete politics, rather than that of mere aspirations, industrialists proved capable only of defending their own particular sectoral interest, not generalizing that interest ideologically and organizationally to encompass the whole of the bourgeoisie and ultimately the whole of civil society.

Lacking *direzione* (authoritative leadership based on unity, organization, and self-consciousness) provided by a hegemonic element, the bourgeoisie's success at the level of class conflict could not be subsequently converted into sufficient political capacity to ensure the permanence of a liberal order, which, by definition, would have required a high level of legitimacy, or the voluntary consent of ruled classes, as well as *dominio,* or coercion. Without such hegemonic leadership exercised by the industrialists, the replete *classe dirigente* thus found itself in an immobilized, disaggregated state, needing some exogenous force to mediate between its own constituent fragments, as well as between the bourgeois bloc as a whole and lower-class strata. That exogenous force, that negative aggregation, was Fascism.

We turn our attention now to a detailed study of the political activity of industrial associations during the postwar period. As previously mentioned, the strict prewar separation between syndical and political activity, which marked the first stage of associational development, already had begun to break down during the mobilization. However, given the "precorporatist," rather than liberal, nature of the wartime regime, such political activity was essentially oriented toward administrative–bureaucratic policy formulated and enforced by the executive. After the armistice, the legislature, awakened from its state of hibernation, once again regained centrality. Thus, for the first time, industrial associations felt compelled to engage in electoral-mobilizational politics, to establish themselves as a hegemonic force within the heterogeneous constellation of liberal parties and associations, trying to give this amorphous aggregate a direction, a coherence, a center of gravity.

Such a "takeover," however, was made difficult by two major factors. First, the liberals had no preexistent national party organization that might have been penetrated and eventually commandeered. Liberal parties and associations were locally based and reflected the interplay of local interests, though at the national level they were mechanically combined into aprincipled and unstable heterocephalous coalitions by predominant personalities on the basis of short-term and limited trade-offs. Second, concentrated in the northern industrial triangle, industrialists were not a true, extensively organized national class. Industrialists (the dominant fragment of the *borghesia produttrice*), agrarians, bankers, and commercial interests only formed national – and *separate* – confederations during 1919–20. They were all late and relatively inexperienced political contestants, entering the structurally altered arena of mass politics after having experienced an associationally debilitating interval of precorporatism. By the time the November 1919 national election was held, the most significant of the postwar elections in terms of creating a situation of legislative stalemate and immobilization, Confindustria had been in existence but a few months and did not even attempt to orchestrate a national electoral strategy, leaving this instead to the initiative of regional associations.

Once again, the LIT was the pacesetter. Under the general guidance of Olivetti and the direct leadership of De Benedetti (who, at the time, was president of both the LIT and the Società Promotrice), industrialists formed a Partito Liberale Economico in conjunction with regional agrarian associations. The new party sent several members to Parliament, including, as its leader, Gino Olivetti. It was conceived as an autonomous "third force," situated between the democratic (Giolitti, Nitti) and conservative (Salandra, Sonnino) poles of the liberal aggregate; *ministeriali* (government supporters) to be sure, but autonomous representatives of the *borghesia produttrice*, no longer dependent political clients. Thus, the new party intended to pressure both liberal wings to its own advantage.[231]

Despite the fact that the Socialists had scored impressive gains, De Benedetti's evaluation of the November 1919 national election was neither unduly apprehensive nor even pessimistic. First, as he argued in a speech to the *Società Promotrice*, the Socialists' strength was more apparent than real, more a reaction against the weak program and leadership that the liberals had offered than confirmation of a positive mass attraction toward the Left. Of forty million Italian inhabitants, the membership of the Socialist Party was, by their own figures, only 88,482. A large number of voters, he maintained, did not participate in the election, and others voted Socialist in mere protest against "the mistaken policies of the Government." A reconstituted liberal party, oriented toward the programmatic interests of the *borghesia produttrice*, would thus have a potentially large electoral base to exploit. Second, under the logic of proportional repre-

---

[231] Castronovo, *Agnelli*, pp. 205–9.

sentation, syndical and professional organizations would gain prominence over more traditional electoral groupings, leading to a more
"organic representation of class interests." De Benedetti expressed
ambivalence toward this tendency leading to the return of "medieval
corporatism," in conflict with the ideals of liberal individualism, yet
he argued that proportional representation might, nevertheless, be
turned to the industrialists' advantage:

> Certainly no one can fail to see what essential importance associative forms
> are destined to assume, associative forms such as ours. . . . When suffrage is
> organized on the basis of groupings and collectives responsive to particular
> economic and social functions, when delegated representatives of organized
> classes and strata will be sent to legislative assemblies, can you not see what
> a useful function our association will be able to perform as we set out in the
> new direction? In an age when it seemed that each of us might have reached
> the ideal of individual liberty and personal sovereignty, we find ourselves
> hurled centuries backward by the force of new events. We find ourselves
> retreating toward a corporatist regime of classes, orders, strata, and trades, a
> throwback to the Middle Ages.[232]

Disenchantment on the part of industrialists toward the Nitti government had been mounting during the first three months of 1920,
due to continuing apprehension over the fiscal crisis of the state
(especially the effects of the political price of bread) and its perceived
weakness in the face of mass unrest and sporadic land and factory
occupations. However, the industrialists' dramatic victory in the April
general strike and their effective formation of volunteer committees
for civil order gave them added impetus to expand their political role.
Whereas in France, as Maier suggests, the government had been
actively involved in the spring 1920 victory over labor, in Italy the
government appeared fainthearted and inept. Industrialists felt that
they had won by virtue of their own resistance.[233] In De Benedetti's
words, they had been "the unique force which acted in defense of
social order, shoring it up in the face of government weakness. . . .
Yes, let us say it, and without false modesty: if today there is still
order, if all the social classes can enjoy some measure of well-being, if
production has not been stopped, and if property is still respected,
this is our work."[234] In a word, as the very symbols of bourgeois
resistance and as the guardians of public order, industrialists had not

[232] *L'Informazione Industriale*, 2 July 1920.
[233] Maier, *Recasting Bourgeois Europe*, pp. 176–7.
[234] *L'Informazione Industriale*, 2 July 1920.

only earned the moral right but felt compelled to assume the burdens of political leadership.

With the November 1920 local election in sight, they gave rise to a new party, the Partito Liberale Democratico in May 1920. While the Partito Liberale Economico had been narrowly sectoral and independent from the local liberal associations, the new party was intended to take over those associations and meld them into a homogeneous force, penetrate the executive council, and eventually take it over.[235] There was discussion in the LIT about the possibility of buying a newspaper to distribute free to workers and about the need to cultivate public opinion. Instead, the LIT gave subsidies to newspapers that assumed a proindustrialist position; Agnelli, independently, bought one-third interest in La Stampa.[236]

As we saw, industrialists were generally relieved when Giolitti first returned to power in June 1920; at last, so they thought, the authority of the state would be restored. Not wishing to attack his fiscal reforms publicly, they stalled on granting salary increases, hoping that in return for salary concessions the prime minister would lighten the load that his fiscal policy had upon industry. This gamble, of course, backfired in the form of massive factory occupations that ended in the politically sanctioned demand for worker control. Though Gino Olivetti recognized the industrialists' mistaken judgment, he could not condone Giolitti's feigned impotence in the face of this wide-scale violation of constitutionally guaranteed property rights. After all, FIOM had threatened to occupy the factories two weeks before such action was actually taken; some preventive action might have been planned. Once again, as he charged in 1913 (when Giolitti threatened not to protect factories against possible worker violence), Olivetti accused the prime minister of the selective use, or non-use, of executive power to impose a solution from above, thereby undermining the very concept of the state as absolute guardian of public order and protector of constitutional rights. "The state is in its essence a juridical construction. If this breaks down, even in a particular instance, the state falls and that which it represents, the social order."[237] Industrialists would thus emerge from the factory occupation crisis with two political imperatives: first, and foremost, to make themselves the

---

[235] Consiglio Direttivo, LIT, meeting of 7 May 1920, HAUIT.
[236] Castronovo, Agnelli, p. 277.
[237] Abrate, Lotta sindacale, p. 305.

major protagonists behind a new "bloc of order" in the coming local election, taking control, wherever possible, of local liberal associations, as well as taking credit, where successful, for Socialist defeats; second, to launch a concerted public attack against Giolitti's fiscal program, because more subtle means had failed.

The November 1920 local election marked a reversal in the trend toward increased Socialist strength; constitutionalist forces captured every major city except Bologna and Milan, both of which remained in Socialist hands. It appeared as if De Benedetti's evaluation had been substantially correct; there was, indeed, a potentially large pool of voters that liberal forces could mobilize who had previously abstained or cast a Socialist protest vote. In cities of over 100,000 population (except Bologna), there was a pronounced increase in voter turnout compared to the 1919 national election (in Turin, from 58 percent of the eligible voters to 65 percent; in Genoa, from 44 to 55; in Milan, from 59 to 74; in Florence, from 52 to 62; in Rome, from 30 to 48). Moreover, the total constitutionalist vote rose from its 1919 total of 47 percent to 56 percent, while the Socialist total dropped from 32 percent to 24 percent. As Maier comments, a "bourgeois revival was underway in Italy as elsewhere."[238]

In preparation for the November 1920 local election, Olivetti came to Turin from Rome to impress upon the LIT the importance of a victory over the Socialists and the necessity, therefore, of overcoming reservations about the political character that industrial syndicates were increasingly assuming. Within the LIT there was a minority "syndicalist" current headed by its former president, Craponne, against political activity on principle. Olivetti argued that since workers' syndicates make direct contributions to the Socialist Party, "no one should then wonder that bourgeois parties are sustained by industrial associations." He prevailed upon the LIT to contribute 800,000 lire to the constitutionalist list, suggesting that they also constitute "a solid political organization the day after the elections, without losing a moment, so as to have in hand a moral and political force that could be substituted for the existing liberal association if necessary." Since industrialists were the principal contributors to the liberal association, Olivetti argued that they should have a determinant voice in its direction. Mazzini, concurring with Olivetti, maintained:

[238] Maier, *Recasting Bourgeois Europe*, p. 189.

The responsibility for the current disastrous disorganization of bourgeois parties lies a bit on all. It is necessary that the industrialists, fortified by the bourgeoisie, come to be better valued and their work given greater account so that if one day it might appear necessary to take control of the Associazione Liberale Monarchica, the non-industrialist members will not resign. It is necessary, therefore, that before taking material direction of the *borghesia politica*, industrialists take moral direction, and this organization of continuous defense ought to be undertaken day by day with the greatest shrewdness and attention.[239]

The electoral victory of the *blocco di difesa sociale* produced a sense of euphoria within the LIT, although the propriety of the new political course continued to be debated.

Meanwhile, local industrial associations were encouraged by Confindustria to attack openly Giolitti's fiscal programs and the project of worker control through the press and in public meetings. Particularly prominent in this campaign was Giuseppe Mazzini, who was conceded two lengthy interviews in *Il Sole* and *La Stampa* during January and February 1921.[240] Indicative of Mazzini's combative tone is the following response, after a detailed refutation of Giolitti's fiscal program, to the question whether such measures were really necessary for political reasons:

I do not admit at all to such heresy. Industry is industry and politics is politics. Do you think one can go on with such programs? War profits tax? Political reasons. Uninhibited occupations of factories? Political reasons. Registration of stocks in the bearer's name? Political reasons. Workers' control? Political reasons. Ah, enough of such politics which is nothing but demagoguery, which is nothing but the ruin of industry and of the nation.

Mazzini realized that Giolitti's fiscal measures were aimed at overcoming Socialist opposition to terminating the political price of bread, but he argued that this is the type of solution that is worse than the problem itself. "When industry is ruined, having bread at its natural price, rather than at the political price, will be poor consolation."[241]

Meanwhile, Giolitti, for economic and political reasons, was beginning to abandon his reformist programs. Economically, the deepening crisis lent weight to the argument made by industrialists and professional economists like Einaudi that the nation was in too delicate a period to support such experiments, which drained the state treasury,

---

[239] Consiglio Direttivo, LIT, meeting of 6 Nov. 1923, HAUIT.
[240] Mazzini's interview was reprinted in *L'Informazione Industriale*, 6 Jan. 1921.
[241] Ibid., 17 Feb. 1921.

discouraged investment, and exacerbated unemployment. The example of England was cited, whose economy was far stronger than that of Italy, but which, nevertheless, terminated a similar war profits tax in the hope of stemming unemployment.[242] Politically, as we have seen, Giolitti began to shift to the Right as a response to the bourgeois revival in the cities, the rise of agrarian Fascism in the country, and the foreclosed possibility of absorbing reform Socialists after the party split to the Left rather than the Right.

Giolitti announced in March 1921 that national elections were to take place in May, and he proceeded to form a Blocco Nazionale of the constitutionalist parties. By then, industrialists had become a significant political force, determined to make their support contingent upon programmatic concessions – in particular, modification of Giolitti's fiscal program, termination of the project on worker control, and inclusion of industrialist candidates on the Blocco Nazionale list.

For the first time Confindustria took the initiative in actually coordinating electoral mobilization, rather than deferring to regional associations as it had done earlier. Its central committee ordered member firms to pay twenty lire per worker into a special electoral fund. However, because some of the deputies who had been previously elected with their financial support had failed to "sustain in the Chamber the defense of industrial property and the principles of sound economy, industrialists now would insist upon programmatic clarity before funds were allocated." Regional industrial committees were established that were to follow strictly directives handed down by Confindustria's central committee and to form alliances with agricultural and commercial associations. Such activity was to be based on four fundamental premises:

1 Protection of the fundamental principles of order, property, and especially savings
2 Free development of individual initiative
3 Adoption of fiscal legislation suited to the present contingencies
4 The inopportunity of social experiments in the present period of crisis and reconstruction[243]

By early May 1921, the legislative project on worker control had been tabled. At the same time, industrialists were assured – in confi-

---

[242] Catalano, *Potere economico*, p. 277.
[243] Confindustria Circulars: P.N. 110, C. 190, 28 Mar. 1921; P.N. 110, C. 193, 15 Apr. 1921.

dence – of modifications in fiscal policy, especially the war profits tax. The skeptical Craponne wanted to make these assurances public but was restrained by Agnelli, who urged greater tact. A week before the election, Confindustria, responding to these private assurances, assumed as its official position that because of the deepening crisis, no tax on excess war profits could possibly be paid. Three weeks after the election, Giolitti proved true to his word; the period in which the tax had to be paid was extended by five years.[244]

Assured that the program of the Blocco Nazionale would exclude any mention of control and "other aspects of Giolitti's policy against the interests of industry," and that candidates unsympathetic to industrialists were to be excluded from the list, while industrialists were to be included, the LIT subsidized one-third of the bloc's expenses in Turin. Because Fascist candidates were included on Giolitti's list, the May 1921 election marked the first time that industrial associations made direct contributions to the Fascists, though the size of these contributions was relatively small, based on what we know of Turin (Fascist candidates received 23,500 lire of the 1,098,419 lire the LIT spent on the election).[245] Some LIT members, like Craponne and Freschi, still doubted the value of the association's new course. Freschi, referring to the performance of Dante Ferraris as Nitti's minister of industry, claimed that some of the worst defenders of industry in Parliament and in the government were "industrialists-turned-politicians." To this, Olivetti and Mazzini, both successful candidates on Giolitti's list, objected. Mazzini offered to resign as president of the LIT while running for elective office, but the association's executive council, at the urging of Olivetti, rejected the resignation and approved his insertion in the Blocco Nazionale as a "mandated" representative of industry. Olivetti felt that the poor performance of industrialists-turned-politicians did not spring from the fact that they were industrialists but rather from the fact that they spoke as private individuals and not as "representatives of a class or of an organization." This weakness could only be remedied if industrial associations became increasingly political and overcame their syndicalist purity. One LIT member, Pola, carried away by the logic of Olivetti's position, went so far as to suggest that industrialists distribute electoral propaganda in the factories. Here, Olivetti coun-

---

[244] Abrate, *Lotta sindacale*, p. 341.
[245] Consiglio Direttivo, LIT, meeting of 9 Apr. 1921, HAUIT.

seled restraint. Politics should be kept out of the factories, otherwise industrialists would have no moral right to prohibit political agitation by workers. After all, it had been the industrialists who maintained that "in the factory one works, one does not discuss."[246]

Olivetti received the largest preference showing on the Blocco Nazionale list, outpolling even the Giolittian deputy and future prime minister Luigi Facta by 112,000 votes. Mazzini also did well and was elected. At a banquet held in their honor, Ferracini, vice-president of the LIT, claimed that "the industrial class is the avante-garde of the bourgeoisie," and Olivetti maintained that "the industrialists were at the point of becoming the class around which all the activity of the nation was oriented."[247] Industrialists, on the whole, were once again elated with their electoral performance, as well as their demonstrated capacity to impose programmatic direction upon the liberals. And yet, in reality, they remained at the "economic–corporate" level, successful only in "defending" their sectoral interests. Contrary to pronouncements like those cited above, they had not substantially altered the structure, composition, or ideological content of liberalism. At best, they merely shifted the balance of liberal forces more in their favor. The political crisis of liberalism, however, continued and deepened; no strong, stable, and legitimate government was in sight. What good was the attainment of greater weight within the unaltered ship of Italian liberalism if that ship had already shown itself unseaworthy in rough water and inclined perilously toward sinking by virtue of its own structural weakness even after the red storm had passed?

Unlike the French Bloc National upon which it was modeled, Giolitti's Blocco Nazionale reaped no substantial electoral victory over the Socialists or the Partito Popolari which might have yielded a viable parliamentary majority. The Socialists lost only 17 seats of their former 156 (123 of the new total were official Socialists; 16 were Communists); the Partito Popolari actually had a net gain of 7 seats. The constitutionalist parties increased their representation from 239 to 275; in the main, this increase was accounted for by the addition of 35 new Fascist deputies. In the major industrial cities, only Turin registered a marked decrease in the Socialist vote (63 percent in 1919; 43 percent in 1921). Elsewhere, as in the rural zones

---

[246] Ibid.; Abrate, *Lotta sindacale*, p. 362.
[247] *L'Informazione Industriale*, 16 June 1921.

of Romagna and Ferrara – where the Socialist vote fell from 67 to 32 percent and from 62 to 38 percent respectively – the decrease was due, not to electoral support for the Blocco Nazionale, but rather to the brutal effects of agrarian Fascism.[248]

As a political instrument, a national bloc is fundamentally an electoral device to unite factions incapable of aggregating themselves into a unified party structure. At best, it is a poor substitute for a ruling party or a ruling coalition, because heterogeneous elements willing to make defensive compromises for the sole purpose of competing against Socialist parties in elections are seldom willing or capable afterward of maintaining a requisite measure of unity to maintain a stable government. Even in France, it should be noted, the victorious Bloc National had broken down by 1924, when it lost a national election to another heterogeneous electoral bloc, the *cartel des gauches*. In Italy, not only had the Blocco Nazionale failed to win a decisive victory, but its constituent elements, markedly more heterogeneous than those in France, began to fly apart the day after the electoral battle. The right wing of the bloc was anything but *giolittiani*; composed of 35 Fascists, 11 Nationalists, and 21 followers of Salandra, it lost no time in attacking the government. So too did Nitti's following, programmatically close to Giolitti but loyal to their own leader, whose personal and political relations with the prime minister had soured. Meanwhile, since the Blocco Nazionale had been specifically directed against Socialists and Popolari, even moderates of the two mass parties now refused their cooperation. Of significance, in this regard, was the cabinet resignation of the Popolare Filippo Meda, Giolitti's minister of the treasury. The new legislature, which was to sit until April 1924, one and a half years after the March on Rome, was even more heterogeneous and unmanageable than its predecessor.

Thus, the Blocco Nazionale, which was to have unified the bourgeois forces and altered the composition of Parliament, and thus resolve the political crisis, reflected instead the disarray of Italian liberalism. The two successive prime ministers, Bonomi and Facta, even had they been as competent as Giolitti – which they clearly were not – were to have no base either in Parliament or in the country, not even the minimal majority necessary to break the legislative stalemate

[248] Maier, *Recasting Bourgeois Europe*, pp. 326–7.

and begin to overcome the stasis in public policy. Giolitti realized that such policy could only be conducted over the head of Parliament and thus had requested full executive power in fiscal and administrative matters, but the legislature refused to yield such prerogatives to the old wizard, whose transformist magic now failed him, prerogatives it would concede to Mussolini little more than a year after he assumed office.

Measured against their hegemonic pretenses, the industrialists' reaction to the deepening political crisis was generally passive and thoroughly inadequate. As a pressure group, capable of defending its sectoral interests, Confindustria was without equal. But as a national directing force, capable of ideologically encompassing the universal interests of the bourgeois aggregate and organizationally reconstituting its fractured political linkages, Confindustria was patently deficient. Having definitively won its major syndical battles during the *biennio rosso*, Confindustria, during the next biennium, would successfully force a substantial revocation of Giolitti's remaining fiscal measures and compel the *borghesia politica* programmatically to adopt its economic demands. Yet, when all is said and done, these were of relatively minor significance as long as the very political bases of bourgeois dominance were fast eroding. At the very moment Confindustria attained economic leadership of its class, political leadership – by default rather than volition – had passed into the hands of Mussolini.

With regard to Giolitti's remaining fiscal reforms, Bonomi in August 1921, two months after becoming premier, would suspend application of the law requiring registration of stocks in the bearer's name and so modify the terms of the war profits tax that *La Finanza Italiana* would characterize the revision as "a noteworthy disavowal of the fiscally absurd and practically unfeasible criteria which presided in the compilation of the preceding regulation." During the months to follow, consumers in general (and especially the poorer classes) would shoulder the fiscal burden of the state, as indirect taxes were increased.[249]

Having neutralized Giolitti's fiscal program, Confindustria, in the months to come, would call for a concerted campaign against "useless government expenses," a campaign similar to those begun earlier in England and France to help solve the economic crisis: a sharp reduction in the size of the state bureaucracy and reprivatization of those na-

[249] Alatri, "La Fiat dal 1921 al 1926," pp. 301–2; Guarneri, *Battaglie economiche*, 1:47–9.

tional industries which were operating at a substantial deficit.[250] In early April 1922, the executive council of Confindustria made preparations for the creation of a Parliamentary Economic Alliance, which was to serve the dual functions of distributing propaganda favoring the reduction of state expenses and pressuring Parliament from within to act on such demands. Although the "alliance" would include agrarian and commercial representatives, as well as a number of moderate Fascist economic "experts" (e.g., De Stefani, Corgini, Gray, Ciano), it was clearly dominated by Confindustria and was presided over, naturally, by Gino Olivetti. On 28 June 1922, the Parliamentary Economic Alliance issued a lengthy manifesto calling for a number of fiscal measures already being discussed in England, France, and the United States, among which were the following:

1 The effective reduction of spending by the state bureaucracy, which should be reduced in size to its prewar stature.
2 The renunciation of each new expense and revision of those already approved
3 Reform of the public services, with the gradual elimination of all deficits
4 Limitation on the emission of treasury bills
5 Abandonment by the state of all functions not strictly necessary[251]

The manifesto was favorably received by the national press, the *Corriere della Sera* of 28 June 1922 calling it an "opportune appeal" and the one program that might save Italy. The manifesto also impressed the Fascists, who, at this time, were well on their way toward revising their economic program in a liberal direction. Corgini, a member of the alliance, was coauthor of the August 1922 Fascist economic program, which, it will be recalled, drew such favorable comment from the liberal economist Luigi Einaudi and stressed reform of the state bureaucracy, privatization of state industries, limitation of public works programs, abolition of unnecessary state organs, revision of social legislation that "fetters production," and an increase in indirect, rather than direct, taxes (which were "already elevated to limits incompatible with the development of a private economy").[252]

Industrial leaders such as Olivetti, Benni, and Mazzini participated

---

[250] Confindustria Circulars: P.N. 235, C. 235, 8 June 1921; P.N. 389, C. 225, 19 Oct. 1921.
[251] Ibid., P.N. 529, C. 296, 11 Apr. 1922; P.N. 300, C. 292, 18 May 1922; P.N. 550, C. 300, 28 June 1922.
[252] De Felice, *Mussolini il fascista*, 1:330–2.

in the founding of the ill-fated Partito Liberale Italiano (PLI) during mid-October 1922, two and a half weeks before the March on Rome. Although the one account of this event, written by Alberto Giovannini, secretary of the new party, yields little insight regarding which groups or interests played a predominant role in the midst of the personalistic and regional rivalries that continued unabated, the mark of Confindustria is readily apparent when one examines the program formally adopted, particularly the preface and five of the document's nine points.[253]

Never before in national politics had production, private property, and fiscal policy aimed toward investment rather than social welfare attained the predominance they reached in 1922, in large measure due to the initiatives of Confindustria. Such economic policy was now

---

[253] Giovannini, *Il rifiuto*, pp. 91–101. Relevant sections of the PLI program are as follows:

"We believe in class collaboration and in international solidarity. The first we must carry out day by day, emphasizing it in the process of production and promoting those particular types of enterprises which best ensure it. Above all, we must achieve it by nurturing production as a superior ideal, that it is the common duty to work not only for personal gain, which passes, but for the Nation, which remains, combating every doctrine which pretends to divide capital from labor. There are, as Giuseppe Mazzini said, two classes truly opposed and divided: the class of those, proletarians and capitalists, who contribute gainful labor and continue for the common good; and the class of those, proletarians and capitalists, who attempt to usurp the fruit of another's labor and live without producing. . . .

"2. Return of the State to its normal political and juridical functions, limiting its action to integrating the energies of citizens where this is lacking or insufficient, besides creating the economic, social, and political foundations for the realization of the agricultural, industrial, and commercial potential of the country, taking into account diverse sectoral and regional conditions. . . .

"4. Civil education of the people inspired by the indomitable concepts of *famiglia, patria, e umanità;* public instruction which would favor collaboration among the various classes, in opposition to the principle of class conflict. Integrative public education so that the schools can better perform their function.

"5. Defend the principle of private property, considered as the hinge and function of the social order, as well as the principle of saving, [which is the] source of property, favoring with opportune measures the acquisition of agricultural, industrial, and commercial properties by the classes who labor with their minds and hands.

"6. Freedom of economic initiative – commercial, agricultural, and industrial – with the suppression of every fetter and privilege. Eventual reduction of tariff protection. Defense of the freedom of organization.

"7. Balancing the budget, which has been the special attention of the liberals. Revision of demagogic fiscal policy, simplification and generalization of the taxes. Lowering of the tax rates, with grave penalties for fraud. Reduction of public expenses through the simplification and diminution of state functions, including the administration of public services: railroads and the postal, telegraph, and telephone system. Where this cannot be accomplished, passage of these services to private management."

championed by both liberals and Fascists; together with the demand for a restoration of order and the authority of the state, this "Manchestrian" economic policy was the programmatic hinge on which the convergence of the two parties was anchored. Confindustria by now was recognized as the most powerful interest group in the country, a potent organizational force with which each and every constitutionalist party had to reckon. As we shall see, organizational unity and the competence of its leaders allowed for a degree of autonomy unmatched by any other employer association before and after the March on Rome. Yet autonomy was not hegemony. Although capable of defending its associational integrity and the interests of industry, Confindustria was unable to make itself a directing political force, capable of playing an active, rather than defensive, role in national politics. During the final stage of Fascism's supersession of liberalism, it was never more than a relevant though indeterminate factor, successful only in making clear to both liberals and Fascists, by now programmatically indistinct, that no party would any longer be able to make political gains at the expense of industry.

As Piero Melograni suggests, industrial leadership shared the conviction, common to all major liberal spokesmen (e.g., Giolitti, Salandra, Albertini, Croce), that "Fascism, opportunely channeled, might positively contribute to the renewal of national life."[254] The qualification "opportunely channeled" is of paramount importance; industrial and liberal leaders both envisioned Fascist participation in a broadened liberal government, not handing the reins of state power to Mussolini. This outcome, although the objective consequence of their incapacity and inaction, was not their subjective intent or the result of their direct, purposive action. Neither industrial nor liberal leaders, as Mussolini well knew, were prepared for any such leap into the dark. Rather than see Mussolini, a suspect and unknown political quantity, as prime minister, industrialists were actually preparing for another Giolittian or Salandran government. To forestall this traditional solution to a traditional parliamentary impasse, Mussolini hastened to create an extraparliamentary crisis by mobilizing a Fascist March on Rome, an action that liberals were unprepared to counter and that industrialists, who in no way were previously informed or consulted by Mussolini, sought unsuccessfully to prevent. To compre-

---

[254] Melograni, *Gli industriali e Mussolini,* p. 9.

hend the industrialists' behavior in the face of the March on Rome, we shift the analysis from an examination of Confindustria's relations with the liberals to an examination of its relations with the Fascists.

Industrialists and Fascists

By now it should be obvious that industrialists did not partake of the narrowly instrumentalist relationship that the agrarians had developed with Fascism. Without recourse to external agents, they had successfully defended their class position. Although not achieving hegemony over the other bourgeois forces, industrialists nevertheless had displayed an unmatched capacity for the autonomous advancement of their sectoral interests. For these reasons, we have argued that the relationship between Fascism and the industrialists was not rooted in any necessary sectoral exigency but rather must be sought at the more general level of the bourgeois bloc's declining political capabilities, the multifaceted crisis of Italian liberalism to which we have devoted so much attention. Industrialists were not directly responsible for Fascism's transition from an insignificant movement into a national political force; responsibility here lies with the agrarians and liberal politicians (particularly Giolitti, who included Fascists in the constitutionalist Blocco Nazionale). Nor were industrialists directly responsible for Fascism's eventual status as the ultimate arbiter, as a negative aggregator, between the heterogeneous and heterocephalous bourgeois constitutionalist parties; responsibility here lies more with the bourgeoisie in toto as a historically inadequate *classe dirigente* rather than with the industrialists, who, as one bourgeois fragment, failed to unify these parties by successfully imposing their hegemony.

With the benefit of hindsight, we know that the industrialists, more than any other class fragment, would benefit from Fascism. But how is this to be explained? Methodologically, it is better to leave open the question as to how much these relative benefits reflected the intrinsic bias of Fascism as a generic regime type, as distinguished from how much these relative benefits reflected the specific organizational capacity and political skill of industrialists in overcoming potentially dangerous, anti-industrial tendencies within Fascism, thereby preserving, if not actually extending, their sectoral autonomy. This, however, is a question to be considered when dealing with Fascism in power. It is analytically separate from the question as to whether before the March on Rome, industrialists might have looked upon Fascism either as a preferred regime type or even as one that they could comfortably, if not unconditionally, support. It is also separate from the question as to whether, indeed, industrialists purposively acted in such a manner that one might attribute to them one of these positions or the other.

As reasonable as such analytic questions might appear from a post factum perspective, they become increasingly abstract, if not totally devoid of real meaning, when one tries to grapple with Fascism as an unfolding historical phenomenon, hardly conscious of itself and its "telos" (if, indeed, it had one) at each developmental step, particularly the first tentative few. As we shift perspectives, meanings, perceptions, and intentions — to say nothing of "necessary" causal relationships — lose their a posteriori clarity. No one, not even Mussolini (as he was later to admit), knew where Fascism was going on the eve of the March on Rome, much less what the nature of a generically Fascist regime would be. Naturally, Fascism was born within a given web of historical contingencies; the March on Rome, after all, did not appear on a tabula rasa. These contingencies, however, like Mussolini's bases of support, were multiple and often contradictory; they conferred upon the new phenomenon no fixed nature or clear sense of orientation. In other words, what Fascism was — its nature, its direction — remained to be constituted, and constituted it was, as we shall see, in often the most improvised manner imaginable. We have already seen that Fascism changed significantly in program and even internal composition between 1919 and 1922. Who could have known, much less reasonably predicted, how it would develop thereafter? For agrarians, who in the main had already definitively broken with liberalism and abandoned themselves to Fascism, such weighing of alternatives was less problematic; objectively speaking, they had little choice. Not so, however, for the industrialists, who to the very last moment worked for the return of another liberal government during October 1922, even one, especially one, headed by Giolitti. With Giolitti, of course, they had fundamental differences; nevertheless, he was a known quantity, the one liberal leader who still might be able to dominate national politics. As for Mussolini being entrusted with the reigns of state power, Mazzini, certainly not the most anti-Fascist of the industrial leaders, put the question well on 11

October: "How can we, men of the Right, say without hesitation that Fascism is a party of the Right and not, perhaps, really a political party of the Left?"[255]

As incredible as it may seem in retrospect, industrial leadership never even considered the possibility of a Mussolini government, much less a Fascist coup. When rumors to this effect began to circulate in late October, they attempted to break the revolutionary movement and convince Mussolini to enter a cabinet headed by Giolitti or Salandra. On 2 November, a few days after the March on Rome, Alessandro Freschi, at a LIT meeting, wryly suggested that it was a bit late to consider what attitude to adopt toward Fascism now that Mussolini was in power. Echoing the consensus of this meeting, Freschi suggested that relations with the existing Socialist labor organizations should remain unchanged, labor contracts in force should be respected, and the industrialists should prevent Fascism from being interpreted as a "reaction against workers at the service of the industrialists."[256]

No less confused than everyone else by the events of October 1922 were the Communists. If the historical significance of Fascism were so obvious at this time, certainly they, along with the Socialists, should have mobilized more than purely symbolic resistance. Yet such actions as mass demonstrations, general strikes, and so on, were never ordered, nor did they spontaneously erupt. Socialists and Communists were too busy fighting each other to act jointly against Fascism, which, according to Pietro Nenni, "no one took seriously."[257] Bordiga, who was head of the Partito Comunista Italiano (PCI) and had his own early version of what later would be called the "social-Fascism line," held that since Fascism was convergent with "democratic Socialism," it had no need to destroy democratic institutions; thus, he foresaw a "liberal and democratic Fascism."[258] Zinoviev, sitting in Moscow – the best spot for Comintern officials to observe Italian Fascism – made the rather curious claim that "from a historical point of view" the Fascist coup was a "comedy."[259] Trotsky, recollecting the Italian situation in 1931, stated – as Gramsci himself

---

[255] *La Stampa*, 11 Oct. 1922; Sarti, *Fascism and Industrial Leadership*, p. 35.

[256] Consiglio Direttivo, LIT, meeting of 2 Nov. 1922, HAUIT.

[257] Paolo Spriano, *Storia del partito comunista italiano*, 4 vols. (Turin: Einaudi, 1969), 1:232.

[258] Ibid., p. 241.

[259] Ibid., p. 239.

admitted – that Communists failed both to comprehend the nature of Fascism and to prepare for the eventuality of a Fascist *pris du pouvoir*.[260]

Trotsky goes on to admit that Fascism was then "a new phenomenon, not yet fully formed." Thus, the Italian Communists' tragic error was regrettably understandable. And yet, one might ask, if Fascism was a novel phenomenon, as yet lacking a discernible nature, why should it be presumed – as it often is – by Marxist scholars that the industrialists, unschooled in the intricacies of dialectical materialism, were sufficiently clairvoyant, in marked contrast with Socialists and Communists, to have foreseen what a fascist regime would "inexorably" become and thus self-consciously "push" it to power? If the Italian situation during the fall of 1922 was sufficiently uncertain to befuddle the most self-conscious representatives of the proletariat, how can one believe that industrial leadership somehow knew from the outset the path that Fascism was destined to travel, that it could be nothing other than their facile instrument? This, indeed, is one of the major paradoxes plaguing standard post factum, instrumentalist treatments of the industrialists' role in the rise of Fascism, for, in fact, their apparent omniscience is never demonstrated with concrete evidence but simply inferred on the basis of events to follow. Thus, the argument is as clear as it is superficial: given the fact that industrialists made disproportionate gains under Fascism, they *must have* known what Fascism was to become and therefore *must have* actively promoted it in clear preference to troublesome liberalism.

Having raised logical doubts regarding such a mode of analysis, we proceed with a descriptive account in an attempt to discover, rather than infer, what the industrialists indeed perceived and what actions in fact they took.

Before the March on Rome, there had been three significant instances of collaboration between industrialists and Fascists: the formation of the Comitato di Organizzazione Civile, participation in the Blocco Nazionale, and creation of the Parliamentary Economic Alliance. In each instance, Fascists were strictly a dependent element, one of many, never the predominant element; never were Fascists the "saviors" or even the "representatives" of the industrialists.

The Parliamentary Economic Alliance, though indicative of a grow-

[260] Ibid., p. 231.

ing convergence between liberal and Fascist economic programs, was the least politically significant of the three collaborations. All this parliamentary group did, in fact, was to issue a manifesto. Yet even here one may discern a movement of Fascists toward the industrialists, not vice versa; there was never any doubt as to who dominated the alliance organizationally and ideologically. Insofar as the alliance had any bearing upon subsequent events, this was to be seen in Fascist programmatic modifications reflecting the alliance's Manchestrian manifesto (e.g., the Rocco–Corgini economic program, Mussolini's Udine speech). The two more significant instances of collaboration – the Comitato di Organizzazione Civile and the Blocco Nazionale – were anything but harmonious and hardly inspired industrialist confidence in Fascism.

As mentioned earlier, the Comitato di Organizzazione Civile was organized by the LIT during the general strike of April 1920 to help maintain civil order and to see that public services functioned. It was strictly committed to legality and was open to all "regardless of political tendency." During the spring and summer of 1921, tensions between the committee and the Fascists began to surface due to the latter's refusal to remain within the bounds of legality. In a speech delivered on 6 July 1921, De Benedetti mentioned that a number of Fascists had to be expelled from the committee for having committed acts of violence; these acts were in violation of the committee's program and "tended to impair that discipline of individual minds and energies which constitutes the first and foremost principle of our Organization." Referring to the reaction of the committee's officers to this expulsion, De Benedetti continued, "This energetic act was approved by the overwhelming majority of officers, who saw a tendency developing which was absolutely noxious to our Organization."[261]

The Blocco Nazionale, it will be recalled, was an initiative of Giolitti, not the industrialists. The latter had little to do with the actual composition of the bloc other than to insist that Giolitti include a number of industrialist candidates and exclude those hostile to the interests of industry. There is no evidence that Fascist participation was called for by industrialists or, for that matter, that they in any way objected. Fascist participation was linked to Giolitti's own politi-

[261] Comitato di Organizzazione Civile, 1921, file at HAUIT.

cal agenda (to divide Mussolini from D'Annunzio, pressure the So-cialists and the Partito Popolari, and "transform" Fascism), not to any sectoral needs of industry. Nevertheless, industrialists were an-gered that Mussolini, who owed his election and that of the thirty-four other Fascist deputies to inclusion in the bloc, immediately bolted, declaring his full independence. A postelection police report concerning the reaction of Milanese industrialists stated that they were displeased, "fearing that Mussolini in the Chamber will now follow his own lead in antagonism with their interests."[262] Their displeasure with Mussolini increased when on 21 May 1921 he an-nounced that Fascism was tendentially republican and indicated his intention to seek an understanding among Popolari, Socialists, and Fascists, rather than work with Giolitti. Concerning industrialist reac-tion to this, another Milan police report reads: "The comments made in various environments are infinite and could be summed up in a single word: *delusion*. Authoritative personalities express their regret; industrialists explicitly affirm that Mussolini has attempted another extortion to obtain more money; ordinary voters declare that in the future they will abstain from voting."[263]

The Blocco Nazionale experience hardly demonstrated to the indus-trialists Mussolini's reliability as a politician, much less his stature as a potential prime minister. If they feared that as a deputy he would follow his own lead in antagonism to their interests, blackmailing them with leftist threats to obtain more money and greater autonomy, is it at all likely that industrialists would enthusiastically welcome Mussolini as head of government and that they would be instrumental in placing him in that position?

To association leaders like Mazzini, Fascism emerged as a sponta-neous reaction to Communism; as such it was but another extremist "ism," beneficial, to be sure, in combating Communism when there was the threat of revolution but hardly an appropriate solution once that threat had ended. Speaking to the Associazione Liberale Demo-cratica on 31 January 1922, Mazzini affirmed that there were essen-tially two political forces in the country, "one of transformation, the other of revolution; the first legal and pacific, the second violent and outside the law." Liberals, according to Mazzini, constituted a transformative force, while both Communists and Fascists constituted

---

[262] De Felice, *Mussolini il fascista*, 1:93.
[263] Ibid., 97.

the revolutionary force. "With gradual transformation there is civil progress and this ought to be the tendency of the liberal–democratic party, while the other is the flag of all the extreme parties, whatever color they might represent." Mazzini concluded the speech advocating, not reaction, but collaboration with the reform Socialists, as together reformists and constitutionalists would have three hundred votes in Parliament, a large enough majority to effectively govern.[264] Confindustria reacted to the two Facta government crises of July and October 1922 by supporting Bonomi in the first and Giolitti in the second.[265] Mussolini was never even considered until the March on Rome was already under way and the king had refused to sign a decree declaring martial law.

This is not to say that Mussolini's support for industrialists during the April 1920 general strike, his productivism, and his growing economic liberalism failed to impress a number of industrialists, among whom was Giovanni Silvestri, president of Confindustria from December 1919 to May 1920.[266] Yet Conti, who succeeded Silvestri as president, took note of Mussolini's inconsistencies (e.g., his initial support for the workers during the September 1920 factory occupations) and exaggerated sense of violence ("roba soreliana," as he put it in his diary).[267] In any event, though there might have been varying degrees of personal sympathy for Mussolini on the part of some industrial leaders, there is no evidence that this in any way signified serious consideration of Mussolini as a potential prime minister.

The fall of the first Facta government and the violent Fascist reaction to the ill-timed Socialist *sciopero legalitario* in July 1922 elicited an unusually firm and unambiguous statement by Confindustria as to its position in the face of the deepening political crisis. On 15 August, Confindustria declared:

Perhaps the day is not too distant in which it is necessary to discuss forcefully the relations between politics and industry. By now we are passing through a series of interminglings, orientations, and inferences. In Italy, even industry is intersected by political manifestations and initiatives. For that reason, it is necessary to consider even this side of the new industrial life, as well as the fact that by now one has the sensation that our class is one of the few bourgeois categories still imperfectly but certainly solidly organized.

[264] *L'Informazione Industriale*, 2 Feb. 1922.
[265] De Felice, *Mussolini il fascista*, 1:327–9.
[266] Conti, *Taccuino*, p. 169.
[267] Ibid., pp. 165, 253.

By now the industrial class is tired of seeing industry considered a *corpus vile* on which every type of social experiment is permitted. For three years, it has been subjected to every ordeal and torment. From the tyranny of Bolshevik agitations to the demagoguery of fiscal legislation, to the systematic weakness of governments that have squandered more security of the juridical order every day, Italian industry has suffered and suffers hard blows, while the world economic crisis beats upon it. And in this succession of conflicts and blows, it was left alone to struggle.

Its relative success in this struggle was accomplished by virtue of its own organizational strength, not recourse to others. In a barb directed against the pseudoheroic posturing of Fascists, the statement continues:

Today political parties claim leadership in the battle against Bolshevism, but in 1919 and 1920 it was industrial organization alone which sustained the battle: the twelve days of the Turinese general strike, the far worse time of April 1920, were sustained and won solely through the industrialists' force. It was this which was eventually successful, even against the will of the authorities, in resisting the daily attempts at subverting the bases of the economic and social order, which is the essential part of the political and civil order.

Fascists had merely "accelerated the evolution" against Bolshevism by succeeding, like previous "isms," in attracting a following among the confused and uneducated masses, who, in this situation, became a "field of conquest." Industrialists regretted being depicted as enemies of working-class organizations, as they had always shown themselves to be "loyal and open adversaries." In any event, Confindustria wished to make clear to all that it would remain committed to its traditional moderate–reformist position, one it was quite capable of defending in the future as it had in the past:

For our part, we repeat that which we have maintained for years: the productive order cannot be a field for political battles; industry cannot continue to be the terrain on which it is permissible to promote demagogic action for whatever motive; and the industrialist who has the responsibility for industry cannot renounce the free directive function which constitutes his raison d'être. . . .

Ready to continue with all their energy the slow, patient, and tenacious work so as not to be submerged by natural or artificial crises, the Italian industrialists – whom a recent document of the League of Nations recognized as the most liberal of Europe – will maintain their efforts as fellow citizens and collaborators. As such they have the duty, and for whom should be reserved the liberty, to organize themselves as they deem best.

It would do well for parties to begin to understand that it will not be possible to make their political fortune on the shoulders and at the expense of industry.

If the past has not given sufficient lesson, we may have to think once again of conducting another operation to rescue industry. Then we shall surely take note of who is on our side.

Commenting on this statement, which appeared in *Organizzazione Industriale* on 15 August 1922, Melograni correctly points out that there is nothing to indicate that industrialists saw Fascism as the unique means of resolving the political crisis. At best, Fascism was treated as just one of the political parties warned to take note of Confindustria's demonstrated capability; at worst, Fascism was just another "ism." Melograni continues:

In substance, the industrial leaders, knowing that they would have to make a choice, did not orient themselves toward a "reactionary" solution. Rather, they understood that to safeguard their sectoral interest they would have to attempt a compromise with other political forces. It was for this reason that in the summer of 1922, and again during the March on Rome, they acted so that power might be entrusted to a liberal exponent.[268]

Directing our analysis now toward industrialists' attitudes and actions during the fatal autumn of 1922, we should recall the three reasons for their wariness toward Fascism, according to Cesare Rossi, Mussolini's closest lieutenant: (1) that the primitive leftist character of Fascism had not been fully superseded, (2) that disruptive reactions in the factories might be provoked anew, and (3) the absolute nonexistence of any nuclei of Fascist workers in the factories on whom industrialists could count. In addition to these, we may note three more: (4) preoccupation with the programmatic radicalism and monopolistic tendencies of the Fascist labor syndicates, (5) concern that a joint industrialist–Socialist effort at opening trade relations with Soviet Russia might be placed in jeopardy, and (6) hostile personal relations between industrialists and some sectors of Fascist leadership.

The development of Fascist labor syndicates will be fully treated in the next chapter. Here we merely indicate two issues preoccupying industrialists and already manifest before the March on Rome. The first was an initial step toward what would later be called *sindacalismo integrale,* or the attempt at situating industrialist and worker syndicates within one corporatist structure headed by the principal

---

[268] Melograni, *Gli industriali e Mussolini,* p. 28.

Fascist labor leader, Edmondo Rossoni. Already in June 1922, Rossoni announced his intention to organize small businessmen, an action that threatened Confindustria's attempt to extend its associational scope to this same category. The second issue concerning the Fascist syndicates was the demand that they be granted a representational monopoly over the workforce. Just as industrialists had traditionally refused on principle to concede such a monopoly to Socialist syndicates, they refused on principle to consider such a monopoly with regard to Fascist syndicates. On 25 September 1922, the executive council of Confindustria passed a resolution to this effect, adding "it is absolutely necessary that industry and the productive order not be a field for political battles and social experiments."[269] This resolution immediately caught the attention of the Fascists, Michele Bianchi noting in the 7 October edition of *Popolo d'Italia* "a certain equivocal attitude of industrial representatives in a recent meeting of Confindustria." At a 6 October meeting of the LIT, Mazzini mentioned informing a representative of the Fascist syndicates that industrialists would negotiate with them when they commanded a majority of the workers but would not, in any case, hire only Fascists.[270]

Ironically, in the months immediately preceding the March on Rome, industrialists, rather frigid in their relations with the unrepresentative Fascist labor syndicates, had been engaged in a new collaborationist initiative with the CGL and reform Socialists regarding trade relations with Russia. Both Confindustria and the CGL had a stake in rapidly overcoming the economic crisis. As Castronovo put it, "It was in the common interest in surmounting the economic depression: the resumption of production and enlargement of exports would have favored expansion of both investments and employment."[271] While the American and west European markets were blocked by high tariff walls and dominated by powerful international cartels, Russia, possessing a wealth of raw materials and an immense market for manufactured goods, provided an opportune opening, especially now that the NEP had been instituted by the new Soviet regime, which seemed intent upon rapid economic development and ending its isolation from foreign markets.

On 17 May 1922, Conti noted in his diary that since the danger of

---

[269] *Organizzazione Industriale* (hereafter cited as *OI*), 1 Oct. 1922.
[270] Consiglio Direttivo, LIT, meeting of 6 Oct. 1922, HAUIT.
[271] Castronovo, *Agnelli*, p. 346.

Communist expansion had passed, trade relations with the West might well alter the very nature of the new Russian regime. "We are not far from hoping that ending the Russian isolation might promote an internal transformation of the country. Until now, Communism has been maintained by isolation; the renewal of relations with the rest of the world will perhaps help initiate in Russia a return to the conditions and methods of the world economy." Actually, at the level of international relations, Italian industrialists were relatively enlightened, in relation to both the prototypical "economic nationalism" allegedly characteristic of *grand capital monopoliste* and the actual conservative French policy (the famous *cordon sanitaire*) of the Poincaré government, which Conti explicitly criticized. Yet this was no simple commitment to abstract principles; the Italian orientation was conditioned by its lack of raw materials, as well as its subordinate status within the Western economic community. As Conti noted, Russia could remedy domestic deficiencies in grain, oil, and mineral resources in return for Italian assistance in economic development.[272] Industrialist interest in penetrating Russia had been expressed by the LIT as early as 1913; preliminary contacts, however, had been suspended with the outbreak of war.[273] Conti's exploratory mission and Confindustria circulars[274] indicate continued interest in the postwar period as well. However, given the new NEP orientation and the reform Socialist Oddino Morgari's willingness to assume the role of Agnelli's Russian "import agent" during the spring of 1922, the time for concerted action now had arrived. Though a reformist, Morgari was on excellent personal terms with Lenin, whom he had met at the Zimmerwald and Kienthal conferences.[275]

As early as March 1920, Morgari had contacted Olivetti, who he knew was interested in sponsoring a Russian trade initiative, but the April general strike and the later factory occupations blocked further collaboration. In February 1922, however, Morgari began to correspond with Agnelli, and by late March, Olivetti had requested Morgari to expand the scope of his efforts "beyond the ambience of Turin and Fiat." On 28 March, a meeting in Rome was held to establish a Comitato per le Iniziative Italo–Russo; in attendance were leaders of

[272] Conti, *Taccuino*, pp. 80–1.
[273] Alatri, "La Fiat dal 1921 al 1926," p. 305.
[274] Confindustria Circulars: P.N. 3583, C. 94, 5 Apr. 1920; P.N. 4174, C. 203, 30 Apr. 1922.
[275] Alatri, "La Fiat dal 1921 al 1926," p. 305.

the respective syndical confederations (Confindustria: Olivetti, Agnelli, Pirelli, Bocca, Guarneri, Targetti, De Benedetti; the CGL: Buozzi, D'Aragona, Morgari, Baldesi, Colombino; as well as Turati of the Socialist Party). An executive council was established, comprised of four industrialists and four Socialists.[276] At the same time, Conti and Olivetti used their parliamentary positions to influence the Facta government, which established a special commission to begin negotiations with a Russian delegation for a new trade agreement. The commission, headed by Conti (and including Olivetti, Pirelli, and Benni), worked quickly, and a trade agreement was signed by the end of May.[277]

These efforts continued until the March on Rome, and when Mussolini indicated, shortly after assuming power, that he had no objection to the project, this industrialist–Socialist initiative persisted well into 1923 with Morgari still the advance man. Industrialists, however, had no way of knowing *prior* to the March on Rome how this important initiative would be affected, both in Russia and in Italy, by Mussolini's ascension to power. It is hard to imagine that fear that this effort might be undercut by Fascism would not have been an additional source of anxiety on the part of industrialists. Not only is it significant that industrialists still valued collaboration with Socialists before and after the March on Rome, but on the particular subject of improving trade relations with Russia, it appeared that Socialist collaboration was virtually indispensible. There was precious little in the Fascist program, or in Mussolini's pronouncements regarding the Socialists, to have inspired much confidence in this regard.

We come now to the sixth source of industrial diffidence toward Fascism: hostile personal relations between some industrial leaders and some sectors of Fascist leadership. Curiously enough, at the time of the March on Rome, many industrialists were considered by Fascist leaders and followers as unsympathetic to the movement, if not outright anti-Fascists. The president of Confindustria, Raimondo Targetti, had a brother who was a Socialist deputy. So extreme was the Turinese Fascists' dislike of industrialists that Raoul Ghezzi, a "Fascist of the first hour," felt constrained to author a tract entitled *Communisti, industriali e fascisti a Torino, 1920–23*, which was explicitly aimed at convincing local Fascists that industrialists were not their adversaries but rather two groups who "did not understand

---

[276] Castronovo, *Agnelli,* pp. 248–52.
[277] Conti, *Taccuino,* pp. 181–2.

one another." In a sense, Turinese Fascists were frustrated by their utter superfluousness; they never "conquered" the city before the March on Rome, nor could they ever launch a punitive expedition "in grand style." Worse still, Turinese industrialists continued to maintain cordial relations with the Socialists and CGL leaders while they actually spurned relations with the local Fascists. Ghezzi tried to argue that the liberal Turinese industrialists, if not "true" Fascists, were "pre-Fascists"; that is, they were the ones who "took command of the city" and had "confronted the Communists" before Fascists were strong enough to do so. Ghezzi actually had to defend Agnelli and Olivetti against charges of anti-Fascism, praising them, moreover, for their intelligence and competence.[278] Instead of improving, however, relations between industrialists and Fascists in Turin actually deteriorated after the March on Rome, as we shall see in the next chapter.

Olivetti, both before and after the March on Rome, was a frequent target of Fascist invective. His disarming intellect, soft-spoken yet caustic wit, aristocratic bearing, and political adroitness would eventually lead, as we shall see later, to a trial by a specially constituted Fascist "court of honor" in 1926. Although cleared of anti-Fascist charges, Olivetti, given "his political origins and entirely typically liberal spiritual formation," was judged a "Fascist by adaptation."[279] According to Antonio Stefano Benni, who would become president of Confindustria in 1923 and remain in that position till 1934: "My life as president was not one of the easiest, given the hostility the Fascist government already had in the period preceding my nomination toward the secretary, Gino Olivetti, and pressures – not to say more – which were applied on me to force his removal."[280]

Of significance in the days immediately preceding the March on Rome was a vicious attack upon Olivetti by the Fascist leader and publicist Giovanni Preziosi, a defrocked priest, inveterate anti-Semite, and so thoroughly malevolent that even Mussolini bore his presence only with difficulty.[281] In 1913, Preziosi had founded a Nationalist

---

[278] Raoul Ghezzi, *Comunisti, industriali e fascisti a Torino, 1920–23* (Turin: Eredi Botta, 1923), pp. xiii, 27, 161, 181–6.

[279] Vertenza Olivetti file, HAUIT.

[280] "Benni," in Istituto della Enciclopedia Italiana, *Dizionario biografico degli italiani* (Rome: Societa Grafica Romana, 1971), 8:558–62.

[281] On Preziosi see Hamilton, *The Appeal of Fascism*, p. 107; Renzo De Felice, "G. Preziosi e le origini del fascismo," *Rivista del Socialismo* 17 (Sept. 1962): 493–526.

journal, *La Vita Italiana,* whose contributors included Pantaleoni, Pareto, and even Hitler (author of a 15 August 1922 article on German Jews, signed "a Bavarian"). Having in separate articles relished the assassination of Walter Rathenau, praised American and Polish anti-Semitism, and warned of the Jewish peril in Italy, Preziosi turned upon "that dear democrat Olivetti," on 15 September 1922, accusing him of secret ties to the Socialists and calling upon Confindustria for his elimination. On 15 October, two weeks before the March on Rome, Preziosi attacked Olivetti once again:

Olivetti represents the true Jewish disintegrator. The politics of internal disintegration and dissolution of live energies, so well described in the *Protocols of the Elders of Zion,* have in him a daily agent of realization. . . . The methods followed by industrial organizations of always seeking to obtain the security of their profits at the price of reformist concessions, and at the price of continuously endowing Socialist organizations – and especially their leaders – with prestige, are his work. The industrialists, who find an agent of their adversaries there where they have need of an animator, yield, criticize, and mutter deep within. Fascism finds in him an instinctive enemy.[282]

Two weeks before the March on Rome, Olivetti was thus accused of being a secret agent of the Socialists, a Zionist parasite, and an "instinctive enemy of Fascism." And yet, two weeks after the March on Rome, Olivetti was accused by the Socialist leader Turati of being the Fascists' principal *marionettista:* "Honorable Mussolini, I see the pointed and Semitic nose of Honorable Olivetti emerging all too visibly from behind your shadow."[283]

That two such opposed and contrasting instrumentalist charges, both tinged with an anti-Semitism uncommon to pre-1938 Italy, could be made against Confindustria's dominant personality would seem to suggest a rather ambiguous perception of the association's role with regard to the March on Rome, if not its fundamental relationship to Fascism before the coup. Such perceived ambiguity, in part, is attributable to the predominantly private nature of Confindustria's politics. Only rarely, as with the 15 August manifesto, did the association issue a political position. To men such as Olivetti, Conti, Agnelli, and Benni, the intimacy of ministerial *antichambre* or the prefect's office was more congenial for discussions relating to public policy and for communicating their position on specific issues

[282] *La Vita Italiani,* 15 July 1922, 15 Aug. 1922, 15 Sept. 1922, 15 Oct. 1922.
[283] Rossi, *Padroni del vapore,* p. 44.

than the press, public meetings, or even party assemblies. If we are to follow Confindustria's actions before and during the March on Rome, we must concentrate on this private ambience.

Luigi Facta's second government was universally recognized as being a transitory expedient, to remain in office only until one of the major liberal leaders could work out a suitable *combinazione*. Negotiations toward this end had been in progress even before the fall of Facta's first government in July 1922. On 12 October, a Confindustria delegation sought a meeting with Alfredo Lusignoli, prefect of Milan. Present were Olivetti, Targetti, Conti, Benni, and Pirelli. The substance of the meeting was communicated the following day by Lusignoli in a letter to Giolitti:

> Yesterday, a most authoritative commission of industrialists asked to see me; among others present were Senator Conti, Deputies Olivetti and Benni, Commendatore Targetti, president of the industrial federation, and Alberto Pirelli. These gentlemen related to me their most grave preoccupations with regard to the financial situation and Fascism, which they maintained had to be channeled. They fear that some delay might provoke a grave crisis whose consequences cannot be calculated. They suggested that by now all Italy awaits another Giolittian ministry and there is no need to hide it. The industrialists declared that they are most favorably disposed toward the return of Your Excellency to power, persuaded that the two predominant questions (the financial situation and public order) will be vigorously met with your exceptional authority. They are disposed to make all sacrifices, asking only that in the formation of the cabinet, the necessities of the moment are taken into account, effected by the actions of strong men, not compromised (their words) by parliamentary maneuvers. They fear, in a word, the return of men who, according to them, have already been disvalued by past actions. I informed them that in my position as prefect, I did not feel authorized to hear such considerations. They replied that their appeal was to my position as senator, rather than prefect, who could transmit upward their public requests. They even suggested that by now everything was in dissolution: public works for which poor provision was made, the administration of justice, which is in maximum disorder. They repeatedly emphasized the financial situation and the need, without hesitation, to form a new ministry presided over by Your Excellency. They repeated many times their desire that I make their intentions known to Your Excellency and to the prime minister.[284]

This letter indicates a definitive position favoring Giolitti on the part of Confindustria. Although industrial leadership had consider-

---

[284] De Felice, *Mussolini il fascista*, 1:328–9; Melograni, *Gli industriali e Mussolini*, pp. 31–2; Nino Valeri, *Da Giolitti a Mussolini* (Milan: Il Saggiatore, 1967), pp. 181–2.

able difficulties with Giolitti's past performance, they felt – as did Mussolini himself – that he was the only liberal leader possessing sufficient skill and authority to arrest the accelerated political decline that had marked the Bonomi and Facta governments. Despite these past difficulties, Giolitti was a known quantity, someone with whom these pragmatic industrialists knew how to deal. The same could not be said of Mussolini. In their private writings, industrialists recognized that Giolitti, as a politician, faced imperatives different from and at times opposed to their own; after all, he had been steward of the general interest, while they defended only the interests of industry. Guarneri, for example, admitted that Giolitti had ably handled the factory occupations, praising his "realistic spirit," as well as his "strong and courageous politics."[285] Writing in his diary on 12 October 1922, the same day as the meeting with Lusignoli, Conti expressed the same admiration for "this man who, with his simplifying spirit, knew how to talk of the most important things with such *bonhomie* and calm serenity."[286] With good reason, De Felice remarks:

Confindustria, for so long as it was possible (that is, until the moment the king called upon Mussolini to form a government), never thought of a Fascist government, but only a coalition cabinet in which Fascists might also have participated. It is extremely significant that its major efforts were directed, on the one hand, toward breaking the revolutionary Fascist movement and, on the other, toward bringing Giolitti to power.[287]

What blocked Giolitti's return to power was not Confindustria but rather the internal blockage of the liberal system. In February and October 1922, Giolitti, despite prolonged negotiations, could not assemble the requisite *combinazione*. Having formed the Blocco Nazionale with Fascist participation against the two mass parties, the Socialists and Popolari, he could not easily entice them now to participate in a new government which, thus constituted, would necessarily have been anti-Fascist. Giolitti asked, "What good could come from a Sturzo–Treves–Turati *connubio*?" He himself admitted to his chief negotiator that such a government "would almost inevitably lead to civil war."[288] Giolitti might have returned to power if the Popolari,

[285] Guarneri, *Battaglie economiche*, 1:45–7.
[286] Conti, *Taccuino*, pp. 185–91.
[287] De Felice, *Mussolini il fascista*, 1:328.
[288] Valeri, *Giolitti*, pp. 335–6.

less intransigently anti-Fascist than the Socialists, had consented; however, their leader, Don Sturzo, once again exercised his famous veto, as he had done twice earlier in February and July. Intense personal dislike had always marked the relationship between Giolitti and Don Sturzo; the former finding it incredible that a party leader could be a priest and not even a member of Parliament, the latter resenting the old politician who personified corruption as well as the anticlerical tradition of the laic liberal *classe dirigente*. The veto, however, was based on Don Sturzo's refusal to support a government including Fascists.[289] Ironically, the Popolari would several weeks later send two ministers to join the new Mussolini government. Don Sturzo, to be sure, objected, but by then the church already had begun to undercut the progressive Sicilian priest's party leadership (he would resign as secretary in nine months) and seek accommodation with Mussolini.[290]

Industrialists, of course, were well aware of the Popolari's opposition. On 12 October, Giolitti sought a meeting with Conti, during which he stated his intention to form a cabinet "with large Fascist participation," tentatively offering Conti the Ministry of Industry. Afterward, in his diary Conti registered a personal doubt that Giolitti's initiative would succeed, "given the sure opposition of the Partito Popolare."[291] Nevertheless, amid speculation that Salandra or Orlando might succeed Facta, Giolitti remained Confindustria's preferred choice. Authoritative sources, such as the *Corriere della Sera* (and other major newspapers), as late as 24 October confidently reported that another Giolitti government would soon be installed.[292]

As rumors began to circulate concerning the March on Rome, Conti met several times with Mussolini, who remained in Milan, the "moral capital of Italy" (and close to the Swiss border, should the operation fail). "The purpose of my visits," recorded Conti in his diary, was "the attempt to break the revolutionary movement."[293]

Basing his judgment largely upon a reconstruction of one of these meetings (26 October) given in a speech by Alberto Pirelli ten years later, Ernesto Rossi suggests that the industrialists wholeheartedly

---

[289] Ibid., pp. 366–8.
[290] Lyttelton, *Seizure of Power*, p. 97; Salvemini, *Origins of Fascism*, pp. 370–1, 391–3.
[291] Conti, *Taccuino*, p. 191.
[292] Melograni, *Gli industriali e Mussolini*, p. 34.
[293] Conti, *Taccuino*, p. 192.

supported the Fascist initiative. Pirelli, indeed, did say (*ten years later*) that the industrialists – after raising questions concerning the nation's credit abroad, government bonds, and currency exchange rates – were "filled with admiration in finding a man who could discuss these problems with reflection, with a vivid sense of their importance and complexity, revealing the will to dominate even this subject."[294]

By 1932, of course, industrialists and others were hard at work rewriting their histories so as to retrospectively – and opportunistically – establish their early Fascist affiliation, especially their affirmative role in the March on Rome. Actually, one is struck by the relatively moderate tone of Pirelli's speech, given that it was delivered at a special celebration commemorating the tenth anniversary of the March on Rome, where ritualistic posturing was more to be expected than dispassionate and disinterested historical reconstruction.

A vastly different account, highlighting the industrialists' shock and apprehension, is offered by Cesare Rossi, who was present at these meetings. In an 18 November 1955 article in *Il Tirreno* critical of Ernesto Rossi's study *I padrone del vapore,* the former Fascist leader states:

Professor Rossi dwells much upon the visit made to the *Popolo d'Italia* by a commission of industrial leaders, among whom I remember Benni, Olivetti, and Alberto Pirelli. It is argued that on the morning of Saturday, 28 October, they demonstrated their solidarity with and encouragement for the "head" of the expedition in progress, that with the Blackshirts they were playing their ultimate card. The visit did not have this character at all. Mussolini several minutes later said to me: "I'm rather tired of persuading them. They fear reactions in their factories. They think even of our eccentricities. It's useless; they are tied to the old liberal and parliamentary world." That step, according to me, was the product of preoccupations and fears over social complications, not a gesture of encouragement and solidarity.

Then, many years later, when the triumphs of the dictator had multiplied and everyone was eager to appear among those present and loyal at the hour of the decisive evening, that some industrialists exclaimed "we were also there!" is understandable, given the contagion of exhibitionism and servility. But the truth is that the industrialists – especially the most prominent ones and their syndical organizations – resisted more than the other classes Mussolini's successful *coup de main.* During those days, I met with Benni and Olivetti two more times, in the late evening of Saturday the 28th at the prefecture of Milan, and the next day on the train while in transit with

---

[294] Rossi, *Pardoni del vapore,* pp. 38–9; Sarti, *Fascism and Industrial Leadership,* p. 27; *OI,* 30 Nov. 1932.

Mussolini to the capital. Even then, the two leaders of Confindustria were not at all tranquil or enthusiastic about what was happening.[295]

In a similar vein, Alfredo Rocco, writing in *Idea Nazionale* one year after the 28 October meeting took place, suggested that the industrialists were still unsuccessfully trying to convince Mussolini to enter a government headed by Salandra or Orlando and were "alarmed" by the turn of events.[296] As Melograni notes, this reconstruction, written in 1923, has special significance, since at the first anniversary of the March on Rome, no one, especially industrial leadership, had any interest in being depicted as alarmed or hesitant.[297] Further examples of diffidence, if not opposition, on the part of industrialists toward the March on Rome could be cited. On 29 October, Mussolini offered the Ministry of Industry to Conti, who refused it, "not wishing to participate in a government born of revolution." Conti wrote in his diary, "Personally, I cannot fail to see the dangers of the new situation and the manner in which it has been achieved. Yet I trust that the good sense of the people and the shrewdness of the new leaders chosen among the various parties will save us from the former and cause the latter to be forgotten."[298] Another industrial leader, Giacinto Motta, expressed the hope that the march would be resisted by force.[299]

Once the king had summoned Mussolini to come to Rome and form a government, the other constitutionalist parties agreed to participate in the new cabinet. No significant disturbances of public order or spilling of blood took place. Then, the initial doubts of the industrialists began to give way to a sense of guarded optimism, characteristic of all liberals, that the revolutionary interlude had ended, that Fascism had been channeled, and that "normalization" could proceed. Now that Fascism was normalized, Conti hoped it would be able to "forget its origins, collaborate with the other parties, and thus be of benefit to the country."[300] As we saw earlier, Albertini felt that once in Rome, Mussolini would come under the liberals' influence. It should be remembered that neither the industrialists nor

---

[295] Melograni, *Gli industriali e Mussolini,* pp. 36–7.
[296] Rocco, *Scritti,* 2:745–6.
[297] Melograni, *Gli industriali e Mussolini,* pp. 36–7.
[298] Conti, *Taccuino,* pp. 192–3; see also a similar reaction on the part of Alberto Pirelli in his *Taccuini, 1922–43,* pp. 22–4, 45–8, 70.
[299] Melograni, *Gli industriali e Mussolini,* pp. 35–6.
[300] Conti, *Taccuino,* p. 191.

the liberals referred to Mussolini's government as *il governo fascista*, but simply as *il governo nuovo*. As Sarti has pointed out, the official Confindustria endorsement of the new government, though enthusiastic in tone, never once mentioned the word "Fascist." In essence, it was a restatement of those convergent economic principles by now programmatically common to both liberals and Fascists: defense of property rights, necessity of discipline, appreciation of individual initiative, recognition of the importance of the *borghesia produttrice*.[301]

Was the March on Rome a point of arrival, Fascism being finally absorbed within the liberal state, as the old *classe dirigente* believed, or was it merely a point of departure, as radical Fascists (syndicalists, intellectuals, *squadristi*), soon to threaten a "second wave," insisted? A liberal–Fascist government had come to power for unknown duration; how would the "experiment" – as it typically was referred to – unfold? The contradictory bases upon which the new regime had been founded would soon come to light both within the Fascist movement itself (e.g., revisionists and normalizers against intransigents and syndicalists) and between Fascists and elements of the old liberal *classe dirigente,* contemptuously regarded by radical Blackshirts as opportunistic *fiancheggiatori* (supporters). Strategically situated between these crosscurrents was Mussolini, who, rather than give unqualified support to any, carefully mediated between all, making everyone ultimately dependent upon him personally.

The March on Rome had not resolved any of the substantive contradictions plaguing the liberal state; instead these merely assumed new and more obscure forms, less subject to public debate and parliamentary initiative, more subject to selective, extralegal violence summoned or sanctioned from above, as well as the private mediations of Mussolini. A radically new regime had not yet been instituted; political pluralism and constitutional liberties were not yet juridically nullified. Still, there had been no return to normalcy. Instead, a new political indeterminacy, rooted in the hybrid basis of the new government, substituted itself for the old – one that was more sinister, to be sure, for Fascism's declared enemies but yet was far less reassuring to its so-called *fiancheggiatori,* as we shall see, than the traditional literature on Fascism would suggest.

[301] *OI,* 1 Nov. 1922.

4. Liberal–Fascism

During the course of the past two chapters, we have traced a growing convergence between Italian liberalism and Fascism in reaction to the postwar crisis. Here we shall treat what may be called a liberal–Fascist regime, Mussolini's government from the March on Rome until 3 January 1925. On that day, Mussolini abruptly sought to resolve from above the legitimation crisis that had been set off by the assassination of the Socialist deputy Giacomo Matteotti, ushering in the transition to an explicitly authoritarian regime, antiliberal in theory and in practice.

Before beginning our analysis, however, it will be suggestive briefly to consider reaction to the Fascist government on the part of non-Italian liberals. Not doing so might lead the reader to believe that the attitudes of Italian liberals were somehow unique, that they had ruled themselves out of the broader liberal universe of discourse. It should never be forgotten that whatever Fascism might have represented when Mussolini came to power in 1922 – or, for that matter, until the 1935 Italian invasion of Ethiopia – Italy certainly had not been relegated to pariah status in the international community. Retrospective impressions of Italy's unholy alliance with Nazi Germany against the Spanish Republic, and then against the western liberal world in 1939, have largely eclipsed the rather favorable image afforded Mussolini and his regime by an assorted collection of governments, statesmen, journalists, intellectuals, and celebrities during the first half of the Fascist epoch. Recalling this earlier period, A. J. P. Taylor has noted:

Mussolini was the most admired public figure in Europe except among the socialists who saw through him from the start. Ramsay MacDonald praised him. Austen Chamberlain spent family holidays with him. Successive French statesmen courted him in dreary procession. . . . I never went to Italy during Mussolini's time. Few followed my example.[1]

---

[1] *New York Review of Books,* 5 Aug. 1976.

In England, respectability was conferred upon the new regime almost immediately with a royal visit by King George in May 1923. That same year, the noted historian G. M. Trevelyan, a man of unquestionable liberal sympathies, wrote: "Let us not be impatient with Italy if she is for a moment swerving from the path of liberty in the course of a very earnest attempt to set her house in order and to cope with the evils which the friends of liberty have allowed to grow up."[2] Recent studies of the British press[3] and Foreign Office[4] indicate that while informed opinion had little sympathy for any English version of Fascism, in Italy – that tumultuous land of "sturdy beggars" (to quote Lord Salisbury)[5] – it was the best that might be expected. As late as January 1927, that is, after the Matteotti assassination and the authoritarian consolidation of power, Winston Churchill, chancellor of the exchequer, told a press conference in Rome that "if I had been Italian, I should have been wholeheartedly with you from start to finish in your triumphant struggle against the bestial appetites and passions of Leninism." Churchill acknowledged that "your movement has rendered a service to the entire world . . . it has given the necessary antidote to the Russian poison." Questioned by Labor opposition, Prime Minister Baldwin said that he found nothing reprehensible in Churchill's comments.[6]

Speaking of Mussolini, Sir Austen Chamberlain (foreign secretary) said, "I am confident that he is a patriot and a sincere man; I trust his word when given and I think we might go far before finding an Italian with whom it would be as easy for the British government to work."[7] Reacting to criticism in November 1926 by Sir Ronald Graham, British ambassador in Rome, and Oliver Harvey of the Central Department of the Foreign Service, that Mussolini was becoming a tyrant, Chamberlain angrily replied:

It is easy to denounce "tyrannies" and I have no love for them, but are these generalities very helpful? Was life safer in Italy before the March on Rome? Was law better observed? Was the average Italian as free even as he is today?

[2] R. J. Bosworth, "The British Press, the Conservatives and Mussolini, 1920–34," *Journal of Contemporary History* 5 (1970): 171.
[3] Ibid., p. 171.
[4] P. G. Edwards, "The Foreign Office and Fascism, 1924–29," *Journal of Contemporary History* 5 (1970): 153–61.
[5] Bosworth, "The British Press," p. 165.
[6] Procacci, *History of the Italian People*, p. 425; *Lavoro d'Italia* (subsequently cited as *LI*), 21 Jan. 1927.
[7] Bosworth, "The British Press," p. 170.

There is no greater mistake than to apply British standards to an un-British condition. Mussolini would not be a fascist if he were an Englishman living in England. Is Mr. Harvey certain that if he had been an *Italian* living in prefascist Italy he would not have joined a fascio?

There is little doubt as to how Chamberlain himself would have acted. "If I ever had to choose in my own country between anarchy and dictatorship, I expect I should be on the side of the dictator."[8]

American reaction to the Mussolini government, in the main, was substantially similar to that of the British. Celebrities, such as Douglas Fairbanks and Mary Pickford, toured Italy and were photographed in poses sympathetic to the regime.[9] The Hearst publications, the *Chicago Tribune,* and the *Saturday Evening Post* all were consistently pro-Fascist, the last offering its readers a serialized edition of Mussolini's autobiography.[10] While the *Nation* was hostile to Fascism from the very start for its violation of civil liberties, the *New Republic,* under the editorial guidance of Herbert Croly, saw in Fascism a new form of "pragmatic progressivism," experimental in nature, nondoctrinaire, and committed to moral regeneration.[11] Progressives like Charles Beard, Samuel McClure, and Lincoln Steffens saw in corporatism a bold institutional means to overcome the divisiveness of unregulated class conflict. Returning from a visit to Italy, McClure declared that the principle of corporatism was "a great forward step and the first new ideal in government since the founding of the American Republic."[12] According to Beard, corporatism had "brought about by force of the State the most compact and unified organization of capitalists and laborers into two camps which the world has ever seen."[13] Although the State Department worried that "the pretty red radical" Ida Tarbell would write "violent anti-Mussolini articles" when she was sent to Italy by *McCall's* in 1926, the former muckraker, to the contrary, held that the Fascist labor laws constituted an admirable social experiment and described Mus-

[8] Edwards, "The Foreign Office," p. 156.
[9] The Fairbanks–Pickford tour of Italy was given extensive coverage in *LI* during April and May of 1926.
[10] John Diggins, *Mussolini: The View from America* (Princeton: Princeton University Press, 1972), pp. 27, 48.
[11] Ibid., p. 13.
[12] Ibid., p. 28.
[13] Ibid., p. 227.

solini, who "kissed my hand in the gallant Italian fashion," as a "despot with a dimple."[14]

The American government's response to the Fascist regime was similarly sympathetic. Richard Washburn Child, himself a former muckraker, and ambassador to Italy at the time of the March on Rome, became a close confidant of Mussolini, whose "autobiography" he helped write and edit (also writing an introduction for the English edition).[15] Within the United States, harassment and the threat of deportation were used by the government to muzzle criticism by Italian anti-Fascists in exile.[16] In 1926, the U.S. Debt Commission announced that Italy was to be afforded a significantly lower interest rate on its war debts (0.4 percent) than England (3.3 percent) and France (1.6 percent). Congress approved the debt terms, despite a stormy debate which centered on the fact that within a week after the Debt Commission released its proposed terms for Italy, the Morgan Company announced a loan to the Italian government of $100 million at a rate of interest thought excessive. Congressional opponents charged that the two events taken together suggested U.S. affirmation of Mussolini's consolidation of power, as well as a bonanza for Wall Street.[17]

This brief and hardly exhaustive digression on foreign reaction to Mussolini's government before 1935 is not intended to establish the existence of a uniformly positive consensus toward Italian Fascism. That, indeed, would be to simplify matters and to overlook liberal opposition to Italy's authoritarian drift from the very start. Our sole intention rather is to suggest a more ambiguous liberal posture toward Fascism than contemporary understanding has chosen to recall. We have seen that some liberals publicly acknowledged positive virtues in Fascism; others went so far as to say that had they been Italian, they too would have joined the Fascists. This summary of foreign reaction is not meant to exonerate the action of Italian liberals or absolve them of their political responsibility for contributing to twenty years of despotism. If anything, perhaps, it raises larger questions pertaining to the very nature of twentieth-century liberalism and

[14] Ibid., pp. 28–9, 63.
[15] Ibid., p. 27.
[16] Ibid., pp. 119–43.
[17] Ibid., pp. 152–6, 270–6.

its complex relationship to non-Communist authoritarian regimes, and, in this case specifically, to its relationship to Fascism.

To return to the Italian domestic situation, it was commonly felt that the king's call to Mussolini to form a government signaled the "constitutionalization" and "normalization" of Fascism. No one at that time, as opposed to later, made reference to the *governo fascista,* for there had been no perceivable break as yet with traditional liberal politics. In Parliament, the Blackshirts had but three dozen deputies, less than 7 percent of the total. Besides Mussolini, who personally held the ministries of foreign affairs and the interior, the cabinet consisted of only four Fascists as against ten non-Fascists.[18] Extremists within the Fascist party (the PNF), who had been pressing for an all-Fascist cabinet, were quick to voice their disappointment at both the composition and general orientation of the new government, threatening a "second wave" unless Mussolini quickly rewarded them the spoils of the "revolution."

Mussolini, fully aware of the limits of his power and the indeterminacy of the political situation, acted with caution and moderation. Given the fractured, nonhegemonic nature of political relations, no postwar governments other than those based upon shaky coalitions had emerged. Mussolini's was no exception, and it was only his uncanny ability to mediate between contradictory tendencies to his own personal advantage that enabled him to survive where others had failed. Yet his coalition was to be of a different nature: it was not simply a mechanical aggregate of different groups and parties which separately retained their organizational integrity and political base; rather, it was oriented toward the gradual undermining of their autonomy by either whole-scale absorption (separating leading personalities from their organizations, separating organizations from their political base) or repressing them to the point that they could no longer effectively function.

The Nationalists were absorbed by the Fascists within six months. Through dealing directly with the Vatican, promising in exchange for its support solution to the "Roman question" (later realized in the Lateran Treaty), Mussolini was first able to isolate the Left and Don Sturzo within the Partito Popolari, and then to prevail upon the church to disown the Catholic party *tout court.* With the liberals

---

[18] Mack Smith, *Italy,* p. 373.

Mussolini was successful in exacerbating divisions between democrats and conservatives, prevailing upon major liberal personalities to run on the Fascist electoral list in 1924 (rather than run separately as liberals) and tap the liberals' major sources of funding, the employer associations. Through intermittent repression, although never juridically prohibiting their legal existence, Socialists and Communists were rendered immobile and ineffective.

These strategies, of course, were not fully apparent at the outset. Though the Mussolini government was not the one liberals would have preferred, his commitment to a liberal–productivist economic policy and the maintenance of civil order, essential elements of the aforementioned liberal–Fascist convergence, gave them confidence that until a new liberal *combinazione* could be amalgamated, the Fascist "experiment" represented a timely stopgap. With varying degrees of enthusiasm, this was the position of liberal–democrats like Giolitti, Amendola, and Nitti, as well as liberal–conservatives like Salandra, Croce, Albertini of the *Corriere della Sera,* and Bergamini of the *Giornale d'Italia.*

Amendola, later to become leader of the Aventine secession and fall victim to Fascist violence, advised a friend that while faith in democratic principles must be reaffirmed, they should nevertheless "proclaim the duty of everyone to support the work of the new Mussolini ministry insofar as it is committed to restore order, discipline finance and economy, giving Mussolini our best wishes for that success which would mark an end to the era of tribulation and the beginning of our country's necessary inevitable ascent."[19]

The *Giornale d'Italia* of Rome was blatantly pro-Fascist. This newspaper, close to Salandra and Croce, advocated closer collaboration between liberals and Fascists. On 24 February 1923, it claimed that "the principles which inspire the two parties are identical, and we liberals can claim the honor, so to speak, of having been pre-Fascists when it was fashionable to be democrats." The liberal party (PLI) announced its "open support for the work of the government," and its secretary, Alberto Giovannini, tried unsuccessfully to form a federation between the liberal and Fascist parties.[20]

The great liberal philosopher Benedetto Croce gave his support in the Senate to Mussolini's government even after the Matteotti

[19] De Felice, *Mussolini il fascista,* 1:393.
[20] Alatri, *Origini,* pp. 105–6; Lyttelton, *Seizure of Power,* pp. 107–10.

assassination and praised Fascism in interviews carried by the *Giornale d'Italia*. On 27 October 1923, Croce said: "Where are the forces which can oppose or succeed the present government? I do not see them. All I can see is a terror returning to the anarchy of 1922. It is because of this that no man of good sense wishes for a change in regime." When asked by his interviewer whether or not there was a contradiction between his faith in liberalism and his acceptance of Fascism, Croce replied: "None whatsoever. If the liberals lacked the force and the ability to save Italy from the anarchy which was rampant, they have only themselves to blame. In the meantime, they must accept and acknowledge the cure, whatever its source, and prepare themselves for the future." In an interview with the *Corriere Italiano* on 1 February 1923, Croce continued in the same vein: "I consider so excellent the cure to which Fascism has submitted Italy that my main worry is that the convalescent may leave her bed too soon and suffer a relapse."[21] During May 1923, Croce's protégé, Giovanni Gentile, resigned from the PLI and joined the Fascists, writing to Mussolini that the liberal tradition was no longer represented by the liberals of today "but in fact by yourself."[22] Though Croce and Gentile would eventually become estranged when the former emerged after 1925 as Fascism's most notable intellectual opponent, their shared acceptance of Fascism *during this period* only reflected the broad liberal consensus vis-à-vis Fascism.

Aware that support for or tolerance of his government was conditional and temporally limited, Mussolini at once set out to broaden his political base. As a negative aggregation, mediating between a variety of groups that neither singly nor collectively could impose direction upon the immobilized government, Fascism had achieved prominence before the March on Rome through Mussolini's political skill – in particular, his capacity to represent, better than any other agent, the negative claims of these aggrieved groups. This capacity to make different and at times contradictory promises to different constituencies, however, became limited once Mussolini assumed power. As prime minister, the Fascist leader was now to be held responsible and accountable.

Though many observers have taken note of Mussolini's characteristic mix of force and consent, our periodization of liberal–Fascism (1922–5), followed by nonintegral corporatism (1925–35), suggests

[21] Hamilton, *The Appeal of Fascism*, pp. 70–1.
[22] Ibid., pp. 68–9.

a shift in the relative portion of these components from an emphasis on the consensual to one on the coercive. Until opposition parties could be either absorbed or neutralized, until some measure of internal discipline could be imposed upon the intransigent Fascists, and until sufficient control could be exercised over the state apparatus, Mussolini never dared – as he did on 3 January 1925 – to resort to force alone. Even then, Mussolini went to great lengths in an attempt to overcome by consensual means the legitimation crisis posed by the Matteotti assassination before all margin for maneuver had been swept from under his feet.

Though indiscriminate Fascist violence, beyond Mussolini's control, continued throughout this period, and though behind Mussolini's gestures of compromise lay the potential threat of selective violence, some observers saw Mussolini's behavior as a new variant of traditional transformist politics, seemingly without any coherent direction or center of gravity. Yet behind this appearance of seemingly aimless compromise, a profound structural transformation was taking place. In reality, each successive step was directed toward progressively undermining the autonomy of existing parties and associations while, at the same time, consolidating the personal political power of Mussolini. This point is of fundamental importance, for if by the end of 1924 Mussolini had exhausted his capacity to mediate between contradictory interests and tendencies, it is nevertheless the case that his strategy had so devitalized real and potential opposition that no force, singly or in aggregate, could fill the political vacuum triggered by the Matteotti crisis and present itself as a viable alternative. In that sense, one might say that if by the end of 1924 Mussolini had exhausted his mediating capacity under conditions of liberal—Fascism, by this time there no longer existed the practical need for such sweeping mediation. Consensual politics – punctuated, to be sure, by sporadic violence – was necessary only so long as there existed autonomous loci of power and the credible threat that Mussolini might be replaced. This is the reason that at the outset, limited as he was, Mussolini conditionally accepted the practice of parliamentary liberalism. By the end of 1924, however, he emptied this form of its vital competitive substance, laying the groundwork for a successive authoritarian form. Hence, when the Matteotti assassination led to a crisis of liberal—Fascism, Mussolini was able to summarily disown that form and begin the transition to an integrally Fascist regime.

Just as Mussolini short-circuited the Popolari's relationship with the Vatican, isolating the Catholic Party from its base, he similarly sought to neutralize the Socialists by pulling the CGL from its orbit. The Socialist trade-union confederation, as we have seen, had already broken its pact with the Socialist Party (PSI) before the March on Rome, when that party split into three separate entities (the Communists, the maximalists, and the reformists). As he had done on several occasions before coming to power, Mussolini now made no secret of his interest in the CGL. On three separate occasions – October 1922, December 1922, and July 1923 – Mussolini entered into negotiations with the CGL with the aim of appointing one of their leaders to a cabinet post, first as minister of labor, later to head the newly created Ministry of the National Economy.[23] Although the CGL, much to the dismay of the Socialists, was ready to accept, in each case these initiatives were effectively blocked by an intra-Fascist alliance of provincial intransigents and syndical leaders. Wanting to penetrate the industrial proletariat, and privately conceding the Fascist syndicate's incapacity to do so, Mussolini continued negotiations with the CGL right up to the Matteotti crisis. According to one source, even as late as 1928, Buozzi, then an exile in Paris, was asked to return and head the Fascist syndical confederation.[24] However, given the relative strength of anti-Socialist sentiment within the Fascist ranks, and the post-1925 rightward trajectory of the regime, such a move, even if personally desired by Mussolini, was virtually impossible.

With the liberals Mussolini was a good deal more cautious. Though they possessed no organized mass base, liberals nevertheless were the traditional *classe dirigente*. What was lacking in sheer numbers and modern organization was compensated for, in part, by the assets one would expect from a traditional elite: political professionalism, ties to dominant economic interests, cultural leadership, and general influence over public opinion through the major newspapers. Though they lost their political dominance, few liberals initially saw this as a permanent, irremediable demise. Rather, as Croce and others imag-

---

[23] On the negotiations between Mussolini and the CGL during October 1922, December 1922, and July 1923, see Cordova, *Sindacati fascisti,* pp. 107–8, 115–18, 164–79; De Felice, *Mussolini il fascista,* 1:377, 594, 602, 607, 912; Lyttelton, *Seizure of Power,* pp. 95, 103–4, 231–6. Before the March on Rome, Mussolini told Massimo Rocca that if he came to power he would need CGL representatives in his cabinet; see Massimo Rocca, *Come il fascismo divenne una dittatura* (Milan: Edizioni Librarie Italiane, 1952), p. 116.

[24] Haider, *Capital and Labor under Fascism,* p. 95.

ined, Mussolini's government would be a brief parenthesis. After reestablishing order, the Fascists were to be either absorbed or summarily dismissed. Beyond their other assets, liberals had far greater representation in Parliament and influence over the state bureaucracy than the Fascists. Without liberal support, Mussolini could not have come to power; without their continued backing, he could not have initially remained in office.

Liberals were primarily interested in the restoration of constitutional order and overcoming the immobility preventing implementation of economic and administrative reforms necessary for Italy's postwar recovery. For reasons already stated, it appeared that Mussolini perhaps was the only man capable of taking such action. Mussolini, on the other hand, was primarily interested in overcoming the political fetters in which he found himself. Among other things, this meant maximizing his position for the next general election, which he hoped might yield him his own, rather than an inherited, majority. A significant parliamentary majority was essential, for it would lessen Mussolini's dependence upon both liberals and Fascists, especially if these two parties were to run not on separate lists but jointly on Mussolini's own national list. Without reassuring the liberals, while at the same time undermining their autonomy, he could not succeed. Yet, as we shall see, mediating between liberal and Fascist constituencies was not an easy task.

Soon after coming to power, Mussolini requested from Parliament, and received with liberal backing, extraordinary powers for administrative and economic reform. Using rather eclectic, nondoctrinaire criteria, Mussolini set out to realize such common liberal and Fascist programmatic demands as the consolidation of overlapping governmental agencies, reduction in the number of state employees, and revision of the tax system. In addition to more minor consolidations, the Ministry of the Treasury was fused with that of Finance, the Ministry of Labor and Social Welfare with that of Industry and Commerce, and finally, the Ministries of Agriculture, Industry, and Commerce were combined into a unitary Ministry of the National Economy. In all, some 65,000 state employees were eliminated.[25]

Responsibility for economic and tax reform was placed in the hands of Alberto De Stefani, minister of finance. Regarded as the

[25] Aquarone, *Stato totalitario*, pp. 8–11.

leading economist of "early" Fascism, De Stefani was a professor of economics whose policies were close to those of the liberals. As Shepard Clough put it, "He sought not only to produce more revenue with greater simplicity and less tax evasion, but also to arrange the tax structure so that people with capital could be encouraged to invest."[26] In effect, this meant a regressive tax structure whose burden fell disproportionally upon low-income groups. He replaced a tax on luxury items with a general sales tax and reduced inheritance and the tax on personal incomes of business managers and corporation executives. De Stefani's major fiscal reform, a new personal income tax, was designed to promote production by taxing only the income of physical persons, not business firms. According to Sarti, "He hoped that exempting business firms from the new tax would stimulate production and that the resulting rise in production would be reflected in higher incomes. The government could then tax these higher incomes without interfering with business operations."[27] In the hope of attracting outside capital, De Stefani exempted foreign investment from taxation. A twenty-five-year exemption from the building tax was conceded for the construction of stores, offices, and hotels, and the tax rate was reduced on new industrial construction. Finally, De Stefani formally abolished Giolitti's fiscal measures, which, as we have seen, had been informally dropped or amended under the governments of Bonomi and Facta.[28]

Besides these tax reforms, which also included abolition of anachronistic tolls levied on goods transported across municipal lines, De Stefani sought to realize liberal and Fascist demands calling for the removal of government from the economy wherever possible. He abolished commissions for fixing fair prices and rent control, withdrew government subsidies from cooperatives, and reprivatized state monopolies in life insurance, telephones, and matches.[29] In all, De Stefani managed to reduce state expenses from 35,461 million lire in 1922 to 21,832 million in 1923. By the end of 1924, not only was the state budget balanced, but receipts exceeded expenditures for the first time since the war.[30] Though some of the credit for this feat must be

[26] Clough, *Economic History*, p. 223.
[27] Sarti, *Fascism and Industrial Leadership*, pp. 51–2.
[28] Clough, *Economic History*, pp. 223–5; Romeo, *Breve storia*, pp. 134–6; Sarti, *Fascism and Industrial Leadership*, pp. 51–2.
[29] Clough, *Economic History*, p. 224; Rossi, *Padroni del vapore*, pp. 42–59.
[30] Clough, *Economic History*, p. 224.

given to the previous administration and to an upswing in the business cycle, it is doubtful that such a recovery from the 1921 fiscal crisis could have taken place through normal parliamentary practice. De Stefani carried out these measures, in the main, through special decrees under the extraordinary administrative and fiscal powers granted Mussolini.

If liberals were reassured by Mussolini's administrative and fiscal policies, they were clearly less satisfied that civil order and the authority of the state were, in fact, being restored. In contrast with conciliatory gestures of Fascism in Rome, the periphery remained a theater of brutal, indiscriminate violence and abuse in authority on the part of the provincial *ras* and their squads. The 1921 rift between Mussolini and the provincial intransigents had never been fully resolved; now, as before, they acted and spoke as if they had nothing to gain and everything to lose from normalization. If Mussolini's mediations were to be successful, these autonomous loci of Fascist power would also have to be neutralized, for they too constrained his freedom of action. A frontal assault on these provincial elements initially was as impossible as it was vis-à-vis the liberals. They, too, had residual strength and Mussolini needed their support as a countervailing force in dealing with the liberals. Just as he did before the March on Rome, Mussolini continued to present himself as the only man capable of controlling the Fascists. This time, however, the price Mussolini would demand was more personal power as the head of government. Certainly there were limits, for with either too much or too little provincial violence Mussolini would lose credibility, yet within these limits he operated with uncommon finesse. As De Felice acutely notes, Mussolini's strategy toward the liberals enabled him to enjoy the threat of a "second wave" without having to assume responsibility for it.[31]

When Mussolini came to power, the PNF still lacked a hierarchical, centralized structure, such that recalcitrant elements could be disciplined from above. Fascism, at this time, was rather a loose collection of feudal fiefdoms *(rassati)*. According to Lyttelton, "a multitude of petty bosses in the villages and small towns imposed their parochial tyranny."[32] It is within the context of Mussolini's struggle against the provincial intransigents and their uncontrollable illegalities that one

[31] De Felice, *Mussolini il fascista*, 1:546.
[32] Lyttelton, *Seizure of Power*, p. 167.

must examine the creation of such new, centralized, and hierarchic party structures as the Fascist Grand Council and the Militia, the 1923–5 "revisionist" polemic, and the 1924 elections. During the period of liberal–Fascism, a process began whereby the PNF would undergo a full-scale structural reconstitution from its original semi-feudal, decentralized status to its bureaucratization and subordination to Mussolini's cabinet, to its ultimate "sacrifice to the state," becoming little more than a devitalized, passive, and fully choreographed organization. The Grand Council, appointed by Mussolini and acting under his tight control, replaced the old *direzione* as the "supreme organ of the party." One of the first acts of the Grand Council was to create the Militia. The various locally based squads were to be placed within a centralized national structure whose leadership, including non-Fascist military officers, was appointed from above according to the criterion of fidelity to Mussolini (to whom loyalty was pledged, rather than to the king). Since this would have deprived the *ras* of their private squads, and the squads of their license for indiscriminate, unsanctioned violence, they resisted, unsuccessfully, the slow but ultimately definitive articulation of this new organ, which, unlike the Grand Council, immediately received legal recognition.[33]

To combat the intransigents ideologically and to reassure liberals who were expecting normalization, Mussolini initially encouraged the Fascist "revisionists" in their bitter polemic against provincial Fascism. While intransigents called for the elimination of all non-Fascists from political life, revisionists, stressing the technological and modernizing potential of Fascism, argued for seeking the collaboration of non-Fascist experts possessing much needed talent, skills, and competence. As early as January 1923, the *direzione* of the party admitted the paucity of such talent within their ranks. "The State is not yet completely in the hands of Fascists because, as there are few men in our party qualified to hold important offices, it is necessary to await the appearance of new technical and administrative talent."[34] Competence groups *(gruppi di competenza)* had been mentioned in the PNF constitution of 1921 but remained only on paper until the March on Rome. Then, Massimo Rocca, a revolutionary syndicalist turned

[33] Aquarone, *Stato totalitario*, pp. 18–24; De Felice, *Mussolini il fascista*, 1:431–8. See also Aquarone, "La Milizia Voluntario nello stato fascista," *La Cultura*, May and June 1964, pp. 259–71, 360–74.
[34] Lyttleton, *Seizure of Power*, p. 165.

monarchic Fascist, was assigned the task of their further development and organization. Addressing the Grand Council in March 1923, he said:

A party such as ours – having such consciousness of the importance of technical problems and intending to both technologize and spiritualize public life, classifying men by virtue of their productive capacity and not the party label they bear – must preoccupy itself with developing cadres of a new *classe dirigente* charged with the technical reorganization of Italian life.[35]

Competence groups, on the one hand, were to serve as a bridge to experts who had hitherto remained aloof from the party and, on the other, were to be the nuclear organ of a future corporatist order, dispassionately mediating between the syndicates of labor and capital, as well as between these and the state.[36]

Those who were attracted to such technological aspirations were primarily students whose educations had been interrupted by the war. In the military, as one of them recalled, they had been socialized to hierarchical norms, which stood in sharp contrast to the bumbling inefficiency of postwar civilian governments. According to this source, Camillo Pellizzi, "the word 'competence' acquired the significance and popularity of a true political slogan" (that being, as it were, "make way for competence!").[37] Their weight, however, within the party was relatively small; they were young intellectuals in a philistine mass movement and made their mark mainly as journalists, writing in such organs as *Critica Fascista* and *Epoca*.

Besides Rocca, the other notable revisionist was Giuseppe Bottai, later to head the Ministry of Corporations. In 1923 he founded *Critica Fascista*, a journal explicitly conceived to promote the development of a new *classe dirigente* and to reveal the limitations of provincial Fascism, which was inadequate to the tasks of governing the nation, managing the state and the economy, developing a new and intellectually credible ideology, and securing consensus for the regime among the population at large.

The revisionist polemic officially began on 15 September 1923,

---

[35] Massimo Rocca, *Relazione al Gran Consiglio Fascista di marzo 1923 sui Gruppi di Competenza* (Milan: Imperia, 1923), p. 17.

[36] On the *gruppi di competenza* see Aquarone, "Aspirazione technocratiche del primo fascismo," *Nord e Sud* 11 (Apr. 1964): 109–28; Cordova, *Sindacati fascisti*, pp. 101–6; Camillo Pellizzi, *Una rivoluzione mancata* (Milan: Longanesi, 1949), pp. 15–27.

[37] Pellizzi, *Rivoluzione mancata*, pp. 15–27.

when Rocca's article "Fascism and the Country" appeared in *Critica Fascista*. He lambasted the "provincial satrapies with their opposition to culture, to technical capacity, and to intelligence." He bemoaned the growing separation between Fascism and the nation, between the party and Mussolini. The provinces were quick to respond: *La Scura* of Piacenza, *L'Assalto* of Bologna, *Camicia Nera* of Treviso, and most important, Roberto Farinacci's *Cremona Nuova*. Farinacci, intransigent of intransigents, called for Rocca's head, and the 27 September meeting of the party's executive committee called for Rocca's expulsion. Mussolini, however, threatened to side publicly with Rocca unless the executive committee resigned. The final decision would be made by the Grand Council, which suspended Rocca from the party for three months.

Mussolini, who did not want to highlight his own struggle with the *ras*, gave initial encouragement to the revisionists, letting them take full responsibility for the attack. Then, to avoid a major crisis within Fascism and, once again, appear as the ultimate arbiter between conflicting tendencies, Mussolini imposed a compromise.[38] A second revisionist polemic would break out again in May 1924, this time without Mussolini's encouragement. Rocca refused Mussolini's order to cease and was formally expelled from the party by the Grand Council on 15 May. Having to choose between Rocca, who had no significant following within the party, and Farinacci, spokesman for the provinces, Mussolini sacrificed Rocca. Farinacci would soon suffer a similar fate, becoming an unwitting instrument in Mussolini's hands. But by now, Rocca was expendable, having partially accomplished Mussolini's aim: the enunciation of an intra-Fascist attack on provincial Fascism's legitimacy. Defending Rocca to the point of provoking a major crisis within Fascism, with the provinces mobilized against Rome, was still too risky. Besides, as De Felice notes, Mussolini was in the process of negotiations with the CGL and did not want these jeopardized by a major factional split. With Rocca gone, there might be a trade-off: an end to revisionism in exchange for the provinces' acceptance of a CGL representative in Mussolini's cabinet. However, the Matteotti assassination, one month later, made this a moot point.[39]

With the expulsion of Rocca, the competence groups, so identified

---

[38] On the revisionist polemic see De Felice, *Mussolini il fascista*, 1:546–53; Lyttelton, *Seizure of Power*, pp. 180–2; Salvatorelli and Mira, *Storia*, 1:301–3.

[39] De Felice, *Mussolini il fascista*, 1:595.

with his person, were devalued and eventually dropped. They had failed to attract the nonparty experts they had sought and, according to Pellizzi, reflected more intrinsic incompetence than competence in any case.[40] Fearful of expulsion, Bottai discreetly retreated from a formal "revisionist" position, though he continued, unsuccessfully, the substantive struggle for a Fascist managerial revolution.

The Grand Council, the Militia, and the revisionist polemic were all aimed at undermining the autonomy of the *ras*. Mussolini would use the 1924 election to neutralize the provincial leaders politically, at the very same time they were being subjected to greater organizational discipline and hierarchy. According to De Felice, the election would serve to "pull the rug from under intransigent Fascism, demonstrating to the various Farinaccis that the success of Fascism was not dependent upon them, that for him they were not necessary; rather, the reverse was closer to the truth: if they did not wish to be isolated, they were the ones who had to support him." Further, by making himself the fulcrum of a large national bloc, consisting of atomized individuals rather than party groups, Mussolini could further marginalize traditional parties while dominating his own.[41]

A necessary step in this strategy was replacing proportional representation with a new electoral law giving any party or bloc that received the largest number of votes two-thirds of the seats in the Chamber, an automatic absolute majority. Though the opposition parties were against this revision, Mussolini, working through the Vatican, managed to get the Popolari to abstain. The liberals, who blamed the postwar parliamentary stalemate on proportional representation, gave the bill their backing both in committee (on which Giolitti, Orlando, and Salandra served) and in final deliberation. The law was enacted on 18 November 1923.

Liberals deluded themselves that the new law would promote the process of normalization. Though from the outset, Mussolini boasted to Parliament that he could have "transformed this drab, silent hall into a bivouac for my squads; I could have barred Parliament and established an exclusively Fascist government,"[42] he continually noted that the Constitution had been respected: no dictatorship had been created, and no special laws or special courts had been estab-

[40] Pellizzi, *Rivoluzione mancata*, p. 38.
[41] De Felice, *Mussolini il fascista*, 1:337.
[42] Mussolini, *Scritti*, 4:8.

lished to deal with opponents. Instead, a coalition government had been formed with respected representatives from the traditional parties.[43] In fact, in his speech to the Chamber on the revised electoral law, judged by Salvatorelli and Mira to be "the most parliamentary discourse he ever delivered,"[44] Mussolini asked for the collaboration of all, making specific reference to the CGL, and recognized the constitutional function of opposition. Not only did Mussolini appear moderate on domestic issues, but he promised an unadventurous foreign policy as well, recognizing treaties entered into by previous governments and hoping to normalize relations with the Soviet Union.[45] Even La Stampa, least sympathetic to Fascism of all the major newspapers, sounded an optimistic note. On 26 May 1923, it observed that Mussolini was at a crossroads, having to choose between violence and a return to the Constitution. If, as it seemed, Mussolini was opting for the latter, he should benefit from liberal cooperation.[46]

Preparations for the April 1924 election were begun in January of that year. Mussolini was successful in having the PNF's national council appoint a five-member committee, known as the pentarchia, to determine the composition of the national list, or listone (the big list) as it was called. The pentarchia were all members of Mussolini's entourage and adopted his criterion for inclusion, not that of the intransigents. Whereas the intransigents demanded that all members of the listone accept the PNF program, Mussolini's only condition was that they accept his government's national program. Although the listone was modeled, in part, on Giolitti's 1921 Blocco Nazionale, it had this important difference: the listone was not a mechanical aggregation of different parties but rather a collection of individuals who in joining had explicitly renounced any contingent party ties or discipline. Mussolini had refused to make any electoral alliances with parties as such.

The PLI, as Lyttelton suggests, "lived down to Mussolini's expectations."[47] Its executive committee took no official position other than a decision not to present its own list. Members were free to choose

---

[43] Ibid., 3:8–17, 29–36, 4:68–82, 149–77.
[44] Salvatorelli and Mira, Storia, 1:293.
[45] Mussolini, Scritti, 3:8–17, 281–5.
[46] Lyttelton, Seizure of Power, p. 126.
[47] Ibid., p. 138.

between running on the *listone* or on a "parallel" (nonopposition) list. Giovannini, secretary of the party, joined the *listone,* as did most other liberals, including Salandra, Orlando, and De Nicola. Giolitti was offered thirty places on the list for his followers, as well as an appointment to the Senate (to which he replied that he would sooner renounce his manhood). Instead, he chose to form his own parallel list with a specific liberal identity. Piero Gobetti, with characteristic insight, saw the whole operation as the triumph of a new *trasformismo;* by denying autonomy to sympathetic parties, Mussolini hoped to absorb their membership into a unified government majority. The "masterpiece of Mussolinism" was Mussolini's success in making himself the major liberal leader, the one to whom liberal members of the *listone* would owe their election.[48]

In characteristic fashion, Mussolini instructed prefects to prevent any preelectoral violence; once again, such instructions were largely ignored. Not only was the election "made" in traditional Italian custom (partisan poll watchers, vote fraud, open voting), but sixty to one hundred Socialist candidates (according to Matteotti) were not allowed to freely circulate in their districts. A maximalist candidate was shot in Reggio Emilia, and numerous opposition candidates, including Popolari, were brutally beaten.[49]

The *listone* and the progovernment bis-list received 65 percent of the votes cast. Nevertheless, a geographical breakdown indicates limits to the national penetration of these lists; they were stronger in the south than in the north and were stronger in the small towns than in the large cities. In the south they received 81.5 percent of the vote, compared to 76 percent in the center and 54.3 percent in the north.[50] In none of the large cities, except Rome, was an absolute majority obtained (Milan, 38.4 percent; Turin, 36.6; Genoa, 47.2; Venice, 36.5; Naples, 49.6; Palermo, 30.4).[51]

The election was a notable victory for Mussolini, giving him a legislature with which it would be far easier to deal than the preceding one, which had but three dozen Fascists. It appeared as if he had successfully transformed Parliament, blurring the liberal and Fascist distinctions in his majority, indeed so much so that different sources

[48] De Felice, *Mussolini il fascista,* 1:586.
[49] On electoral violence see Salvatorelli and Mira, *Storia,* 1:314–19.
[50] De Felice, *Mussolini il fascista,* 1:586.
[51] Lyttelton, *Seizure of Power,* p. 146.

gave different counts on just how many Fascists, as opposed to liberals, figured in the 374 governmental seats. Apparently it was becoming increasingly difficult to tell a Fascist from a liberal: the *Corriere
della Sera* first claimed that there were 275 Fascists, then reduced this
number to 230; *Giornale d'Italia* put the number at 250; Cesare
Rossi provided a list of 150 names which he designated as liberal
rather than Fascist, indicating the Fascist count as somewhere between 200 and 270.[52]

The new legislature opened on 24 May 1924. Six days later Giacomo Matteotti delivered his swan song, challenging the validity of
the election, if not the very legitimacy of the regime itself. As
Salvemini described it:

He recited at length the instances of threats and acts of violence and of
general tampering with ballots and returns. In conclusion, he moved that the
elections should be declared void and without effect, and that new elections
should be held under conditions that would allow the voters freedom to
express their preference. There was highly dramatic tension in the Chamber.
Matteotti's speech was interrupted at almost every sentence by cries, denials,
insulting remarks, and threats of the Fascist majority, but the fearless deputy,
calm and unmoved, continued his indictment of Fascist violence to the end.
Then he turned toward his colleagues and said in the same calm, firm voice,
"And now get ready for my funeral." He knew well that by his act of courage
he had forfeited his life.[53]

Eleven days later, while en route to Parliament, Matteotti was kid-
napped and murdered. On 12 June the opposition formed what was
called the Aventine secession; in a strongly worded manifesto they
declared that they would not return to Parliament until there was a
return to a constitutional regime. Hoping to paralyze the Chamber by
their absence and provoke a moral crisis that would force the king to
ask for Mussolini's resignation, the Aventine took no direct action;
that is, no strikes or public demonstrations were called. Rather naively, they thought that a dignified and essentially passive protest
would topple the regime. Composed of various opposition elements,
the Aventine could agree upon no common strategy or alternative
program beyond the compromise of passive resistance. The Communists pushed for a general strike, but the majority preferred indirect
action, thinking it might have greater effect upon the king and liberal

[52] Maier, *Recasting Bourgeois Europe*, p. 439.
[53] Salvemini, *Origins of Fascism*, pp. 398–9.

members of Mussolini's majority, who might be alienated by mass demonstrations. Yet the king, once again fearful of the designs of his pro-Fascist cousin, the duke of Aosta, would not act. Though liberal spokesmen like Giolitti, Salandra, Orlando, and Albertini would eventually declare their opposition, they would neither support the Aventine nor constitute themselves as an alternative third force.

The liberal–Fascist regime had run its course, yet what could take its place? Opposition there might have been, but an opposition that, however morally superior, was fragmented, and – thanks to Mussolini – organizationally emasculated and devitalized. Where was an alternative force that might not only lead the nation out of the crisis but prevent a feared return to the days of the *biennio rosso?* This was the fundamental question haunting the most enlightened elements of the bourgeoisie, Confindustria included. Once again, the political incapacity of this class stood revealed; once again, it demonstrated its inability to generate its own distinctive program, modernize liberalism so as to penetrate the other social strata, compete with the by now weakened mass parties, and lead the nation.

What then was the liberal–Fascist regime of 1922–5? We have suggested that it was a tentative, contradictory, and unstable outcome of the 1921–2 liberal–Fascist convergence. In contrast with the regime to follow, it represented continuity with the traditional liberal regime in terms of the juridical definition of the state, public policy, and patterns of class dominance. For a limited time, Mussolini's mediations and the threat of violence had delayed the necessity for a definitive rupture with the past and the construction of a generically new antiliberal state, one that juridically proscribed party pluralism, syndical freedom, a free press, and other civil liberties associated with liberalism.

Industrialists and liberal–Fascism

Standard instrumentalist treatments of the relationship between industrialists and Fascism stress the decidedly probusiness bias of economic policy that followed the March on Rome as obvious confirmation of a quid pro quo. In his 1955 study, *I padroni del vapore*, Ernesto Rossi entitled a chapter dealing with this period "Bills Falling Due" *(cambiali in scadenza)*. In 1972, when a good deal of contrary evidence was readily available, the noted economist Sylos-Labini wrote: "Immediately after being thrust to power, the Fascist Party paid its account for the financial and political help obtained in the preceding years from the big bourgeoisie."[54] How else could one explain such phenomena as formal abolition of Giolitti's fiscal reforms, reprivatization of state monopolies, termination of subsidies to cooperatives, Agnelli being appointed a senator, and so on?

As is often the case, the most "obvious" explanation is the least probing and satisfactory. We have already questioned the adequacy of such an instrumentalist interpretation by noting Confindustria's relative strength and lack of dependence upon Fascism, as well as its limited financial and political support for Fascism. Furthermore, we have noted that although Giolitti's fiscal reforms were *formally* abolished by Mussolini's minister of finance, De Stefani, they had been administratively rescinded during the latter part of Giolitti's own government, as well as under the successive governments of Bonomi and Facta. Lyttelton is closer to the mark in observing that by the end of 1921, a year before the March on Rome, industrialists had achieved most of their economic objectives; moreover, they credited this to their own organizational influence, not reliance upon external forces.[55] We have also seen that by the fall of 1922, Confindustria's economic demands had been substantively adopted not only by the liberal and Fascist parties but indeed by a broad segment of informed public opinion, including such leading economists as Einaudi, Pantaleoni, Bachi, and Mortara.[56] Far from being viewed by contemporaries as a narrow, self-interested position, one could well say that Confindustria's liberal–technocratic, productivist program had been recognized as perhaps the only means, given the dynamics of capitalism, to overcome Italy's economic crisis. In an era of pre-Keynesian economics, there seemed no way to end the nation's recession other than a liberal–productivist program oriented toward encouraging industrial investment, increasing national income, reducing state expenses, and balancing the budget.[57]

Appointment to the Senate was conferred upon individuals who had distinguished themselves in their various professions. Given the

---

[54] Rossi, *Padroni del vapore*, pp. 42–59; P. Sylos-Labini, "Sviluppo economico e classi sociali," *Quaderni di Sociologia* 4 (1972): 402. A similar judgment is rendered by Salvatorelli and Mira, *Storia*, 1:246.

[55] Lyttelton, *Seizure of Power*, p. 210.

[56] Abrate, *Lotta sindacale*, p. 400.

[57] De Felice, *Mussolini il fascista*, 1:399–400.

international stature of Agnelli, not only as a "capitalist" but also (as even Gramsci had recognized) as an "innovator and organizer of production," it was to be expected that eventually he would be awarded the rank of senator, whatever the specific nature of the regime in power. In fact, few contemporaries saw Agnelli's appointment as an immediate "reward" for services rendered to Fascism. Baldesi, one of the CGL's dominant personalities, marked the occasion by writing a laudatory article for a special edition of *Informazione Industriale* celebrating Agnelli's appointment. Significantly, the Socialist's remarks received greater prominence than those of Domenico Bagnasco, local head of the Fascist syndicates.[58]

Agnelli is reputed once to have said, "We industrialists are government supporters by definition."[59] By that he meant that industrialists rarely, if ever, frontally opposed any given government; rather, they sought to maintain a supportive relationship with each ministry so as to better influence the specific policies vitally touching upon their interests. The magnitude of such support, however, was never absolute and unconditional but was contingent upon a pragmatic assessment of governmental performance. Mussolini's government was no exception to this long-standing pattern. As with other actors, running the ideological gamut from Nationalists to Communists, Confindustria did not believe that the newly formed coalition government would reconstitute itself as an antiliberal regime, much less remain in power for twenty years. Because the Manchestrian Fascist economic program was convergent with its own, Confindustria was hardly hostile to the new government. After all, in his first speech as prime minister to the Chamber of Deputies, Mussolini stated:

The guidelines of our domestic policy may be summarized in these words: economy, work, discipline. The financial problem is fundamental: the budget must be balanced with the greatest possible speed. A regime of austerity; intelligent utilization of funds; help to all the productive forces of the nation; an end to all the residual *bardature di guerra*.[60]

Given Mussolini's inconsistent past, however, such promises were not taken at face value; nor was worker antipathy toward Fascism overlooked. Fearful that identification with Fascism might provoke

---

[58] *L'Informazione Industriale*, 10 Mar. 1923; Abrate, *Lotta sindacale*, pp. 379, 392; Alatri, "La Fiat dal 1921 al 1926," p. 304; Castronovo, *Agnelli*, pp. 377–81.
[59] Guarneri, *Battaglie economiche*, 1:57.
[60] Mussolini, *Scritti*, 3:14.

reactions in the factories, suspicious of the demagogic rhetoric and stated aims of the Fascist syndicates, and disturbed by the primitive leftism and gangsterism which still typified certain Fascist elements, especially at the local level, Confindustria kept its symbolic and practical distance: it did not intervene or even comment upon the revisionist–intransigent polemic raging within Fascism, its leaders retained their PLI membership, it refused to favor Fascist syndicates in any way or change May Day to 21 April (the Fascist *festa nazionale*), and it did not permit its members to join the Fascist *gruppi di competenza*.[61]

As we shall see, alone among the other employer confederations, Confindustria, despite pressure and actual threats, refused to affiliate itself with Fascism, sacrifice its associational autonomy, or modify its long-standing commitments to syndical pluralism and the public–private distinction.[62] Throughout the duration of liberal–Fascism, Confindustria reaffirmed the liberal–technocratic position that had informed associational development from the very outset: support for a nonbelligerent foreign policy allowing for extensive foreign trade, maintenance of public order and respect for the Constitution, autonomy of the productive realm, defense of absolute managerial authority, and direct labor negotiations between apolitical syndicates representing capital and labor. Confindustria immediately called upon the new government to avoid an adventurous foreign policy and to modify a law calling for the obligatory hiring of war invalids, arguing that such legislation, although well-meaning, violated industrial rationality (i.e., hiring should be based solely on skill and qualification, no other criteria).[63]

Such independence and "agnosticism" with regard to Fascism made Confindustria the target of virulent criticism by Fascist syndicalists and intransigents. The association sought both to neutralize such pressure and to influence public policy by forging a personal relationship with Mussolini himself, rather than deal substantively with Fas-

---

[61] On the May Day controversy see Abrate, *Lotta sindacale*, p. 383. On Confindustria's position regarding the *gruppi di competenza* see the CGII circular C. 351, 10 Sept. 1923, which seems to contradict Massimo Rocca's claim that after some hesitation the major representatives of industry supported the *gruppi di competenza* (Rocca, *Come il fascismo divenne una dittatura*, p. 132).

[62] The Confederation of Commerce announced its official adherence to Fascism on 18 February 1923; the Confederation of Agriculture was forced to merge with the Fascist FISA on 20 Feb. 1924.

[63] *CGII Annuario 1923*, pp. 91, 151.

cism per se, and especially the Fascist syndicates. Reflective of this orientation was Antonio Stefano Benni's elevation to the presidency of Confindustria in February 1923. Though Benni was a member of Salandra's political following, he had established cordial relations with Mussolini and the more moderate Milanese Fascists before the March on Rome. Unlike such other cultivated, upper-class Confindustria leaders as Olivetti, Conti, and Agnelli, Benni was a rather pedestrian, self-made man. Although Lyttelton exaggerates somewhat in his comparison of Olivetti ("a man of wide learning and general knowledge, cynical and astute") with Benni ("an uneducated philistine who appeared obtuse"),[64] it is nevertheless the case that Olivetti, as general secretary, continued to be the effective head of Confindustria, whereas Benni's role was mainly that of a public spokesman and mediator, articulating positions developed and even authored by Olivetti.

As was the case with many Fascist leaders, Benni too had come from humble origins. With the death of his father, he was forced to give up his studies and go to work for Ercoli Marelli at the age of fifteen. There he worked his way up the ranks, eventually to head the electrical firm, a rather uncommon accomplishment in status-conscious Italy. With industrial prominence came political opportunity, and Benni was elected to the Chamber in 1921 as part of Giolitti's Blocco Nazionale. Though given to rhetorical excess and viewed, unlike other Confindustria leaders, as sympathetic to Fascism, Benni never wavered in his commitment to the association's autonomy nor, for that matter, in his personal loyalty – despite relentless Fascist pressure – to Olivetti.[65] Benni was Confindustria's personal link to Mussolini; at the same time, the hard-line Fascists, deeply suspicious of the *éminence grise*, Olivetti, viewed him as a more sympathetic industrial representative.

De Felice and Melograni have noted that Confindustria's attitude toward Fascism was essentially similar to that of the larger liberal community; that is, Fascism, "properly channeled" and "normalized," might positively contribute toward the restoration of order, the

---

[64] Lyttelton, *Seizure of Power*, p. 213; see also Guarneri, *Battaglie economiche*, 1:67–8.

[65] On Benni see *OI*, Mar. 1923. Lyttelton makes the undocumented and highly dubious claim that Benni, unlike most of the other major industrialists, "had made direct use of fascist help" in reestablishing control over his workers (*Seizure of Power*, p. 212).

authority of the state, and economic recovery.[66] Rather than "pro-Fascist," they were *Mussoliniani,* believing that with their support, Mussolini might be capable of directing both his government and the PNF in this direction. Castronovo similarly refers to this as a desire to transform Fascism into a liberal–conservative force through the personal mediation of Mussolini. "In sum, it was a question of guaranteeing the constellation of power around Mussolini at the governmental level, while at the same time encouraging the process of normalization and absorption of the minor Fascist elements, driving away the more intransigent currents, and enlarging the bases of consensus to embrace other political forces."[67] Industrialists and liberals certainly had no interest in seeing Fascism become a dictatorship, which would destroy the traditional political framework. Conti, writing in his diary on 27 November 1922, dismissed the possibility that Italy might be heading in this direction. After all, he noted, Mussolini appeared more "an innovator than a dictator."[68]

Like the liberals, industrialists became progressively frustrated at recurrent Fascist violence and the retarded pace of normalization. Agnelli and Motta were among the first personally to call on Mussolini to halt *squadristi* violence and demobilize the Militia.[69] In contrast with Rome, the periphery was out of control; at the local level, relations between Fascists and industrialists were far from ideal. The *ras* and syndical leaders, often at odds among themselves, tried to impose their will upon industrialists, no matter what consequent problems this caused for Mussolini in Rome. And nowhere was this antipathy between local Fascists and industrialists greater than in Turin, the one major city that Fascist squads never conquered, where industrialists continued to negotiate with Socialist, not Fascist, syndicates, and where the workers repeatedly elected CGL representatives to the various *commissioni interne,* excluding Fascists from these bodies.

On 18 December 1922, the famous *fatti di Torino* took place. Local Fascists went on a violent rampage against Socialists, and eleven workers were murdered and another twenty-seven injured. This provoked a collective protest from the Turinese industrialists,

---

[66] De Felice, *Mussolini il fascista,* 1:319–401; Melograni, *Gli industriali e Mussolini,* pp. 9–10.
[67] Castronovo, *Agnelli,* p. 399.
[68] Conti, *Taccuino,* p. 198.
[69] Castronovo, *Agnelli,* p. 373; Rocca, *Come il fascismo divenne una dittatura,* p. 193.

who sent a delegation to visit Mussolini in Rome.[70] Despite his reassurances, relations between the Turinese *ras*, Cesare Maria De Vecchi,
and the industrialists continued to deteriorate to the point that the
prefect rushed a telegram to Mussolini on 26 June 1923 warning that
De Vecchi was preparing a major attack against the *"plutocrazia
industriale,"* Agnelli in particular.[71] For this and other provocations,
De Vecchi was removed from Turin and given a one-way ticket to
Somalia, where he became a colonial governor. Local Fascist hostility
toward the industrialists in general, and Agnelli in particular, continued. In November 1923, an attempt was made to physically attack
the head of Fiat.[72] This caught the attention of Gramsci, who, unlike
other Communist writers, stressed the underlying tension between
industrialists and Fascists:

The Fascists then accused the Turinese industrialists of cultivating anti-
Fascism in the masses, of preferring to negotiate with the reformist syndicates, of firing Fascist workers, of impeding the development of the national
corporations, etc. They even tried to attack the head of Fiat, Senator Giovanni Agnelli, in a local cafe. The situation became very serious for the
industrialists, as well as for the Government.[73]

In this regard, we have already noted the tract written by Raoul
Ghezzi, a "Fascist of the first hour," who defended industrialists,
particularly Olivetti and Agnelli, against charges of anti-Fascism.[74]

Defeat of the revisionists within the PNF was still another indication that normalization and collaboration with non-Fascists was not
progressing. To the industrialists, who did not comment on the intra-
party polemic, defeat of the revisionists certainly must have indicated
as well resistance to the government's liberal economic policy. Indeed,
the authors of the Manchestrian 1922 Fascist economic program,
Corgini and Rocca, were among the first major personalities to be
expelled from the party: Corgini in May 1923, Rocca a year later.
Throughout 1923–4 the minister of finance, De Stefani, was under

---

[70] On the *fatti di Torino* see Lyttelton, *Seizure of Power*, pp. 152–3, 212–13; also
Renzo De Felice, "I fatti di Torino del dicembre 1922," *Studi Storici* 4 (Jan. 1963):
51–5; *La Stampa*, 22–3 Dec. 1922.
[71] ACS, Ministro dell'Interno, Gabinetto Finzi, Ordine Pubblica (1922–4), busta 9,
fascicolo 89.
[72] Castronovo, *Agnelli*, p. 390.
[73] Antonio Gramsci, *La construzione del partito comunista, 1923–24* (Turin: Einaudi,
1971), p. 521.
[74] Ghezzi, *Comunisti, industriali e fascisti a Torino*.

continual attack in the intransigent press for his "tepid" Fascism and for "consorting with non-Fascist elements."[75]

Of all Confindustria's sources of anxiety during the period of liberal–Fascism, however, the threat to its autonomy posed by the Fascist syndicates was clearly the most ominous. Not only was the association attacked, but, as one Confindustria official put it, so were "the unity of command inside the factory and the position of responsibility of the manager."[76]

Confindustria and the Fascist syndicates

It has often been pointed out that in contrast with German Nazism, Italian Fascism was significantly more "leftist" in terms of its original program, as well as in the composition of its original membership, so many of whom, starting with Mussolini himself, came from the ranks of the Socialists and revolutionary syndicalists. Thus, it should come as no surprise that the Fascist syndicates, led by men like Edmondo Rossoni, who had dedicated their lives to class struggle, were looked upon with wariness by industrialists. Once again, however, a shift in historical perspective is necessary to appreciate the full significance of the threat to industrialists posed by the Fascist syndicates. If, as is often the case, one takes a post factum, cost–benefit view of Fascism (i.e., who *ultimately* gained and lost), then the Fascist syndicates, rendered marginal and ineffective, appear at best as inadequate and at worst as self-conscious "stooges for the capitalist bosses" and, in any case, hardly worthy of concern. On the other hand, if we pursue the methodology which has informed this study, casting aside hindsight and reconstructing the development of the Fascist phenomenon as it actually unfolded, then it will become immediately apparent why industrial leadership never took the radical aspirations of Fascism for granted.

During 1923, when the conflict between Confindustria and the Fascist syndicates reached its most acute stage, many observers anticipated a definitive break with Fascism on the part of industrialists because of the syndical question. Salvemini, agreeing with Amendola, wrote on 6 January 1923: "It is probable that the Nationalists, military officers, Salandra's followers, large industrialists, and agrarians will begin to be suspect of Mussolini and of the worker organizations

---

[75] De Felice, *Mussolini il fascista*, 1:452–3.
[76] Guarneri, *Battaglie economiche*, 1:56.

grouped under the Fascist banner, as well as the Militia and the squads which swear loyalty to Mussolini." In early April, writing once again about the Fascist syndicates, Salvemini continued: "Now the industrialists are no longer very content with Mussolini. They are not as manageable as they wished." At the end of April, referring to information passed along to Donati, editor of the Catholic newspaper *Il Popolo,* Salvemini noted: "An industrialist of Turin told Donati that in his circle people are beginning to ask themselves if it might now be wise to pay the Communists to fight the Fascists!"[77] In early May, the future Communist leader Palmiro Togliatti wrote to Gramsci in Moscow that "the industrial classes are rather wary of the new regime, fearing unpredictable developments in the class struggle with Fascist syndicates."[78]

To comprehend such concern on the part of industrialists, a brief treatment of the Fascist syndicates and their leader, Edmondo Rossoni, is in order. Rossoni's affiliation with the revolutionary syndicalists predates World War I. Along with Massimo Rocca, A. O. Olivetti, and Arturo Labriola, all of whom spent time in the United States between 1910 and 1912, Rossoni helped establish the Camera Italiano del Lavoro in New York City. He also edited the revolutionary syndicalist newspaper *Il Proletario* and worked with Big Bill Hayward as an organizer for the Industrial Workers of the World (IWW) in New York and Hoboken. As was the case with Mussolini in those days, Rossoni was yet to discover patriotism and Nationalism. Just as Mussolini in 1911 would call the Italian tricolor "a rag to be planted on a dung-hill,"[79] Rossoni gained notoriety that same year for publicly spitting on the Italian flag at a New York demonstration.[80] However, as he later would recall, the pretenses of proletarian internationalism could not be squared with the despicable treatment of Italian workers, and so he returned to Italy in 1913 with the aim of fusing Nationalism with class struggle.[81]

[77] Melograni, *Gli industriali del gruppo dirigente,* pp. 53–4.
[78] Togliatti, *La formazione del gruppo dirigente,* pp. 53–4.
[79] Mack Smith, *Italy,* p. 323.
[80] Salvemini, *Origins of Fascism,* pp. 130–71.
[81] On Rossoni's background see Rossoni, *Le idee della ricostruzione* (Florence: Bemporad, 1923), pp. 12–13; Diggens, *Mussolini,* p. 87; Rocca, *Come il fascismo divennne una dittatura,* p. 29; Louis Rosenstock-Franck, *L'economie corporative en doctrine et en fait* (Paris: Librarie Universitaire Gambier, 1934), pp. 12–13. See also John Tinghino, *Edmondo Rossoni, from Revolutionary Syndicalism to Fascism* (New York: Peter Lang, 1990).

Having supported the war, Rossoni attended the Inter-Allied Labor Conference at Leeds (17–22 September 1918), organized by Samuel Gompers to plan postwar strategy. That year, Rossoni helped found the journal *L'Italia Nostra,* an organ of the Unione Sindacale Milanese, whose motto was "The Patria is not to be denied but conquered." In June 1918, he helped form the Unione Italiana del Lavoro (UIL), which, among other demands (recognition of the *commissioni interne,* dissolution of trusts, minimum salaries, an eight-hour day), called for the reorganization of production on a syndical basis, thus realizing the Sorelian idea of a syndical state. As Rossoni put it: "It is therefore necessary to be precise in saying that by dictatorship of the proletariat we mean a government of workers' syndicates."[82] As we shall see, this concept formed the basis of what Rossoni would later call *sindacalismo integrale.* True to the characteristic revolutionary syndicalist disdain for political, rather than syndical, action, Rossoni imposed upon the UIL "absolute autonomy" from all political parties, as well as the rule that all of its leaders must remain strictly apolitical.[83] An example of what he meant by direct syndical action was the UIL-led occupation of the Franchi-Gregorini factory in Dalmine during February 1919, the first such occupation of the postwar period.

Besides fusing Nationalism with revolutionary syndicalism, Rossoni developed another action-oriented concept, which he called the "struggle of capacities" *(lotta delle capacità).* Touched by the war-induced productivism which we have previously treated, Rossoni insisted that the "dynamic law of history" was not, as Marx had thought, class struggle but rather "the struggle of inferior groups who had acquired the capacity to fulfill functions which the superior groups had lost in corresponding measure."[84] Accordingly, industrialists had the right to occupy their positions only till such time as workers, organized into new syndicates, had mastered the requisite competence to take command. In the name of production, during a transition period, there should be cooperation between industrialists and workers, but not within the old, degrading context of *padroni* and servants.[85] The function of capital was active in the early stages

---

[82] Cordova, *Sindacati fascisti,* p. 87.

[83] Ibid., p. 7.

[84] *LI,* 2 Nov. 1922. See also Cordova, *Sindacati fascisti,* pp. 111–15; Rosenstock-Franck, *L'economie corporative,* p. 29; Rossoni, *Le idee della ricostruzione,* p. 5.

[85] Rossoni, *Le idee della ricostruzione,* p. 31.

of industrialization, later becoming passive and ultimately parasitic when "speculation interfered with production." To Rossoni and his followers, the capitalist system "depressed and annulled production rather than stimulating and developing it." Industrialists, in the main, were "apathetic, passive, and ignorant." Therefore, Rossoni called for elimination of "monopolist exploitation, elimination of 'parasitism,' elimination of the *caste passive* in favor of new 'active elements,' and the reordering of production 'exclusively upon technical and scientific values.' "[86]

From a consideration of doctrine, we pass now to the organizational ties between Nationalist syndicates and Fascism. As Mussolini would recall before the Grand Council on 15 March 1923, when the Fascist movement was born at Piazza San Sepolcro in March 1919, no thought was given to the syndical question, much less the creation of new Fascist syndicates.[87] Already by that time, Mussolini had begun his elusive flirtation with the CGL, hoping to sever it from the Socialists and give Fascism a mass base in the industrial proletariat. Finding no immediate opening there, he attempted an alliance with the UIL. In fact, his *Popolo d'Italia* was the only newspaper to cover the UIL's formation and to support the Dalmine occupation as a "productivist strike." Yet here Mussolini, as would happen again in the future, came up against Rossoni's autonomist position. Though there was a faction sympathetic to collaboration with the Fascists at the UIL congress in October 1919, Rossoni's position remained dominant. Actually, not only did Rossoni once again condemn political affiliations in general, but he went on to accuse the Fascists in particular of being reactionary. "Our syndical purity" must not be prejudiced, he said, by appearing "in the eyes of the great public, not as an independent syndical organism, but as an appendage to parties hostile to Bolshevism. . . . the Fascists, despite their revolutionary coloration, work in reaction to Bolshevism."[88]

Because the UIL had earlier adhered to the July 1919 international general strike and then supported the public-services strike of January 1920, both of which Mussolini condemned, the Fascists denounced the UIL in favor of the new so-called *sindacati economici* (or white-

---

[86] *LI*, 22 Dec. 1922, 28 Dec. 1922.
[87] *Il Gran Consiglio nei primi dieci anni dell'era fascista* (Rome: Nuova Europa, 1933), p. 44.
[88] Cordova, *Sindacati fascisti*, p. 23.

collar unions), which emerged in reaction to these strikes. In November 1920, the Confederazione Italiana dei Sindacati Economici (CISE) was formed. Fascists joined the new organization, which participated in the 1921 election as part of Giolitti's Blocco Nazionale; some, like Farinacci and Arpini, ran as CISE candidates. By October 1921, the Fascists had gained sufficient strength within the CISE to form their own breakaway organization, the Confederazione Italiana dei Sindacati Fascisti. However, within the new organization, a split emerged between a Milanese faction, close to Mussolini, who wanted party control over the syndicate, and an autonomist faction, led by Rossoni, who had left the UIL to head the Camera del Lavoro of Ferrara. Although the new confederation was born "under the impulse of Fascism," Rossoni denied that any party, even the Fascists, could propel workers toward emancipation. "Political parties cannot help the organized masses, but only obstruct their path."[89]

A meeting was held in January 1922 to reconcile these opposing factions. For the last time – one should note, ten months before the March on Rome – Rossoni argued for autonomy from the party. The meeting ended with a compromise: a new organization would be formed, the Confederazione Nazionale delle Corporazione Sindacale, which was to be autonomous in name but in fact under the control of the PNF. Two weeks later, Rossoni was elected general secretary of the organization, and a journal was launched, Il Lavoro d'Italia. As Michele Bianchi put it, "the cadaver of apoliticismo assoluto was unanimously buried."[90] Rossoni realized that without the agrarian assault upon the red and white leagues and upon Socialist town administrations, the Fascist syndicates could not have glided through Emilia – Romagna like a black vacuum cleaner, coercively collecting dispersed agricultural workers. As he himself admitted, "without the action of Fascism, which has broken the hegemony of the reds and the whites, our union movement would not exist."[91]

Rossoni made Lavoro d'Italia his personal forum, articulating the concepts previously discussed. During the spring and summer of 1922, when the PNF adopted a Manchestrian position, Lavoro d'Italia also spoke of "emptying the state of its economic functions,"[92]

[89]   Ibid., p. 51.
[90]   Ibid., pp. 52–5.
[91]   Lyttelton, Seizure of Power, p. 218.
[92]   LI, 18 May 1922.

though Rossoni meant that these should be assumed by syndicates rather than revert back to private interests. Accordingly, he also argued in June 1922 that employers too should be organized within the national Corporazione.[93] When the program of the Corporazioni was approved in November 1922, it bore Rossoni's stamp: *lotta delle capacità*, productivism, organizing employers.[94] By the beginning of 1923, Rossoni's tone was becoming increasingly demagogic. Employer associations, like Confindustria, were "completely controlled by anti-Nationalist forces."[95] New employer associations, organized by his Corporazioni, were set up to realize Rossoni's program of *sindacalismo integrale*. By this Rossoni meant that autonomous worker and employer syndicates should no longer exist; instead, they both should be part of one unified "integral" structure whose leadership would make all productive and distributive decisions. Practically, this meant forcing existing employer associations to join the Corporazioni or be replaced by new ones created by Rossoni.

It is highly unlikely that Mussolini agreed with Rossoni's initiatives; after coming to power, he paid relatively little attention to the Corporazioni. As we have noted, Mussolini then was more intent upon bringing a CGL representative into his cabinet, if not absorbing the entire Socialist confederation within the Fascist orbit. After all, Rossoni himself had openly admitted that the urban–industrial proletariat was still in Socialist hands and had yet to be penetrated by his Corporazioni.[96] However, Mussolini's failed November 1922 initiative with the CGL led to two immediate consequences: first, it galvanized an alliance between the Fascist syndicates and the intransigents (led, respectively, by Rossoni and Farinacci); second, it forced the Corporazioni to give up formal autonomy, becoming in December 1922 the Confederazione delle Corporazioni Sindacale Fasciste.

If the Corporazioni had the support of the intransigents, those elements of the PNF interested in normalization were openly critical. Lumbroso, a dissident Fascist, was disgusted with their counterproductive demagoguery:

In their meetings and in their journals the leadership gave vent to bombastic demagoguery based on the "rights of the proletariat" and the "exploitative

[93] Ibid.
[94] *LI*, 2 Nov. 1922.
[95] *LI*, 25 Jan. 1923.
[96] *LI*, 17 Aug. 1922.

bourgeoisie," threatening, on each occasion, the agrarians and industrialists with the use of the *manganello* and caster oil. Such demagoguery was all the more stupid because they did not support any concrete program of economic demands and succeeded only in disgusting those proprietors who sincerely desired to promote class collaboration, without at all intimidating those other greedy and odious proprietors who wished to make use of Fascism as an arm to take back from workers and peasants benefits conceded in the preceding years.[97]

Revisionists were openly critical of the Fascist syndicates. Rossoni could not accept the fact that the *gruppi di competenza* were given the status of nuclear organs of a future corporatist order rather than his own Corporazioni. He thus attempted to constitute his own separate competence groups, provoking a sharp rebuke from Massimo Rocca on *pseudo gruppi di competenza* formed without official authorization.[98] Bottai, destined to become undersecretary of corporations, and a bitter personal enemy of Rossoni, continually fought to prevent the party and government from affording Rossoni's syndicates monopoly status. Until these could demonstrate that they were "real organizations and not phantasms," giving them monopoly status would only further alienate the working class, still loyal to Socialist syndicates, from the regime.[99] Later, in 1925, Bottai would take Rossoni before a special Fascist disciplinary court for having accused him of serving interests "anything but Fascist."[100] Even the intransigent Curzio Malaparte would come into conflict with Rossoni, challenging him to a duel, which apparently both survived.[101] Finally, the Nationalists opposed Rossoni's program of *sindacalismo integrale*. They certainly had no qualms against forcing workers to join one compulsory syndicate but demanded that the state control the syndicate rather than vice versa. As the Nationalist leader and future minister of justice Alfredo Rocco put it: "The State, especially the Fascist State, cannot allow the constitution of states within the State. Organization ought to be a means to discipline the syndicates, not a means to create potent and uncontrollable organisms which might threaten the State."[102]

---

[97] De Felice, *Mussolini il fascista,* 1:404.
[98] Cordova, *Sindacati fascisti,* p. 165.
[99] Ibid., p. 171.
[100] ACS, Segretaria particolare del Duce, 64/R, Bottai, sottofascicolo 2, vicende politiche. See also Cordova, *Sindacati fascisti,* p. 454.
[101] Cordova, *Sindacati fascisti,* p. 453.
[102] Rocco, *Scritti,* 3:991.

What was Confindustria's attitude toward the Fascist syndicates? Previously, we noted that in early October 1922, shortly before the March on Rome, Mazzini reported to the LIT's executive council that he had told the local Fascist syndical leader that when his organization represented a majority of the city's work force, the LIT would deal with it, but would never, in any case, hire personnel exclusively through it.[103] A month after the March on Rome, Confindustria, both in a private circular to its membership and in its official public organ *Organizzazione Industriale,* announced that all existing labor contracts were to be rigorously honored until their natural expiration and that any violation of this order by member firms should immediately be called to the association's attention.[104]

Following Melograni, one might briefly enumerate the reasons behind this attitude: (1) there had been no break, either called for by the government or understood in the public consciousness, with traditional liberal–pluralistic syndical practice; (2) according to such practice and long-standing association policy, so long as the majority of workers adhered to Socialist syndicates, these would continue to represent the proper syndical counterpart and bargaining unit; (3) dealing with phantom syndicates, having no real following in the factories, might lead to violent reactions on the part of Socialist workers, as well as – from the other side – coercion on the part of the Fascist *ras,* squads, prefects, and national government, should conflict develop between industrial associations and Fascist syndicates; and (4) the existing contracts, negotiated with Socialist syndicates during the 1921 recession, kept salaries low at a time when the economy began to show signs of recovery.[105]

To this list, one might add still another reason readily apparent from a reading of private industrialist documents as well as public statements: an obvious antipathy, on the part of Confindustria, for the program of the Fascist syndicates, so clearly at odds with its own liberal–technocratic conception of industrial order, as well as the association's continued autonomous existence. Moreover, there were deep-seated reservations about the background and professional competence of Fascist syndical leaders. It is significant that in their public

103 Consiglio Direttivo, LIT, meeting of 6 Oct. 1922, HAUIT.
104 Confindustria Circular, Confindustria Library, Rome: P.N. 611, C. 313, 27 Nov. 1922, OI, 1 Dec. 1922.
105 Melograni, *Gli industriali e Mussolini,* pp. 55–6.

and private communications, no respect for or admiration of Fascist syndical leaders can be found; this is in sharp contrast to the frequent expressions of such sentiments regarding Socialist syndical leaders, such as Buozzi. If anything, Fascist syndical officials at both the national and the local levels were viewed with thinly veiled contempt as being crude, demagogic, and unworthy of any confidence.

The year 1923 became one of major apprehension for Confindustria because of Rossoni's aggressiveness in pursuing a maximalist program of *sindacalismo integrale* and a minimalist program calling for monopoly status for the Corporazioni. Rossoni's demands were met with an ambiguous response – not one of frank disapproval – from Mussolini, who did not want to paint himself into a corner and restrict his room for maneuver. No doubt, Mussolini might have given private assurances to Benni, but how sincere were such assurances in light of Mussolini's past record, as well as the fact that he was continually talking out of both sides of his mouth, uttering different, and contradictory, pronouncements to different audiences? It should be remembered, for example, that at the very height of his "Manchestrian period" – that is, in September 1922, one month before the March on Rome – Mussolini wrote in *Popolo d'Italia* that "fascist syndicalism does not exclude the possibility that in a far-off tomorrow producer syndicates may be the cells of a new type of economy."[106]

During 1923, Rossoni pushed the Corporazioni in three concomitant directions: (1) absorption of the major employer associations; (2) destruction of the remaining Socialist and Catholic syndicates, while attaining monopoly status for the Fascist syndicates; and (3) obstructing any attempted fusion between Fascist and non-Fascist syndicates.[107] The last refers to Mussolini's repeated attempts, sometimes through the mediation of D'Annunzio, at promoting a unitary syndical body in which the CGL would be an equal or perhaps senior partner. Since this had less impact upon relations with Confindustria, except in forcing an alliance between Rossoni and Farinacci oriented, in part, against the industrialists, our attention will be focused on the first two directions: absorption of employer confederations and the quest for monopoly status.

Absorption of employer confederations was an essential prerequisite for Rossoni's program of *sindacalismo integrale,* launched in

[106] Haider, *Capital and Labor under Fascism,* p. 97.
[107] Cordova, *Sindacati fascisti,* p. 131.

January 1923. As *Lavoro d'Italia* put it, "After the defeat of red leaguism, it is impossible not to condemn the autonomous leaguism of the employers. This constitutes a permanent danger and would justify a rekindling of autonomous leaguism on the part of other classes." Further:

That there exist worker syndicates operating under Fascist discipline is apparently okay, but the demand that employers also be placed under the same rule seems to them an offense beyond their dignity! They begin to grumble against Fascism, which only yesterday they understood to be a club used against workers. They secretly curse Fascist syndicalism as a deviation and a betrayal of their magnanimous ideals.[108]

Rossoni's strategy for realizing *sindacalismo integrale* was twofold: first, he established parallel employer associations in agriculture (Federazione Italiana Sindacati Agricoltori; FISA) and commerce and industry (Corporazione dell'Industria e del Commercio); second, he sought to pressure the Fascist Grand Council into officially supporting *sindacalismo integrale* and monopoly status for the Fascist syndicates.

The Grand Council, it will be recalled, was under Mussolini's control and reflected his position as mediator between antagonistic tendencies within the party, as well as between Fascism and its non-Fascist *fiancheggiatori* (supporters). Given opposition to Rossoni's program both within the PNF and on the part of liberal supporters, Mussolini was not about to jeopardize his "impartiality" or lessen his broad, if contradictory, base of support so early in the game. What followed, then, was a series of ambiguous pronouncements by the Grand Council on the syndical question.

In January 1923, the Grand Council gave token support to the concept of *sindacalismo integrale* by forbidding members of the PNF from belonging to non-Fascist syndical organizations and recognizing the value of organizing all productive categories, workers and employers, in Fascist syndicates. At the same time, it also recognized that few employers were PNF members; thus most were not obligated to join Fascist syndicates. Employers, then, were not compelled as a category to adhere to the Corporazioni; existing non-Fascist employer associations were merely expected to assume a more benevolent attitude toward the Fascist syndicates.[109]

Rossoni was undeterred and continued his attacks on the employer

[108] *LI,* 18 Jan. 1923.
[109] Cordova, *Sindacati fascisti,* p. 134.

associations, Confindustria in particular. He repeatedly charged that this body should change its name, since it was not, in fact, a confederation of industry but of industrialists. To represent industry, one would have to develop a new organism embracing *all* productive categories; then one could "speak of industry in terms of the organic and inseparable wholeness of the productive process." Only the Corporazioni could be an "instrument of discipline and of harmony in production." The syndical problem should be thus confronted and solved in a true Fascist fashion: "if there is one precise task today for the Corporazioni, it is to ask Fascism to resume its march, ridding itself of rubbish like the so-called *fiancheggiatori*."[110] *Lavoro d'Italia* threatened that the Militia was not created for use against the Communists only, but also against industrialists and agrarians who could not define themselves as Fascist and who were not prepared to accept any sacrifice. Unlike the newly constituted Corporazione dell'Industria e del Commercio, Confindustria was "completely controlled by antinational forces," had "unjustly profited" from discipline that Fascism had imposed upon the workers, and was incapable of giving the industrial class new and innovative leadership informed by Fascist idealism.[111]

Just before the next meeting of the Grand Council, which was to deal again with the syndical question, *Lavoro d'Italia* reaffirmed the right of the Corporazioni to organize employers, since the Corporazioni represented "the totality of Italian national and syndical life." Just as no political action was to be taken outside Fascism, there was no place for economic and syndical action outside the Corporazioni.[112]

There were two tendencies at the 15 March 1923 meeting of the Grand Council: a minority position, advanced by Rossoni and Farinacci, in favor of *sindacalismo integrale* and monopoly status for the Fascist syndicates; and a majority position, articulated by Corgini, favoring the autonomy of employer associations and against monopoly status. The outcome, once again, was ambiguous, reflecting Mussolini's own position: the Corporazioni were recognized as "one aspect of the Fascist revolution" whose discipline all Fascists should unconditionally obey; yet the Grand Council also declared itself

[110] Ibid., pp. 140–1.
[111] *LI*, 25 Jan. 1923, 1 Mar. 1923.
[112] *LI*, 15 Mar. 1923; Cordova, *Sindacati fascisti*, p. 148.

against any syndical monopoly. Fascism should seek harmony among workers, managers, and employers; but this was to be developed through propaganda and education.[113]

Rossoni interpreted this resolution to mean that "now collaboration takes place exclusively within the Corporazioni."[114] Olivetti gave Confindustria's interpretation: "for us this means freedom of organization." As for that part of the resolution calling for a regrouping of workers, managers, and employers under Fascism – a rather boiled-down and compromised version of *sindacalismo integrale* – Olivetti haughtily retorted: "a respectable opinion, like all those frankly professed, but still questionable."[115] On 20 March, Benni met with Mussolini, whose reassurances Confindustria immediately made public; Confindustria was "not to be touched or diminished."[116] In return, Mussolini asked that the leaders of Confindustria and the Corporazioni meet on 30 March to establish a basis for more cordial relations. Since such a basis was obviously lacking, nothing of substance came out of the meeting, which was strictly formal and ceremonial in nature. Interviewed the following day, Benni said: "The Fascist Corporazioni proposing class collaboration find in Confindustria a most secure ally. One may only hope that from a unity of intent and common effort, conducted independently and separately, agreement might be more easily reached on one goal: the industrial and economic development of Italy and its ascent in the world."[117] Stripped of symbolic references to class collaboration, unity of intent, common effort, and industrial development, the substance of Benni's remark is to be found in the parenthetical phrase "independently and separately." The issue at hand, after all, was either *sindacalismo integrale* or autonomy.

If, as Abrate suggests, Mussolini acted with moderation so as not to find himself against a "united employer front" led by Confindustria,[118] reaction from both Fascist syndicalists and intransigents was bitter. Because of Confindustria's stand, the confederations of commerce and agriculture took courage and asserted their autonomy

---

[113] *Gran Consiglio primi dieci anni*, pp. 39–45; Cordova, *Sindacati fascisti*, pp. 149–50.
[114] *LI*, 15 Mar. 1923.
[115] *Giornale d'Italia*, 20 Mar. 1923; Abrate, *Lotta sindacale*, p. 380.
[116] *OI*, 1 Apr. 1923.
[117] Cordova, *Sindacati fascisti*, pp. 152–7.
[118] Abrate, *Lotta sindacale*, p. 381.

from the Corporazioni as well. The intransigent press was outraged. *L'Impero* gave its full support for *sindacalismo integrale* and called the industrialists traitors against whom force might be necessary.[119] *Il Caffaro* attacked the industrialists' equivocation,[120] while *L'Assalto* wrote:

> If Fascist law, which subordinates the interests of categories and classes to the superior national interest, has been imposed upon the workers, then the same law – pleasing or not to the various Olivettis and Doninis of Italy – ought to be imposed on the agrarians and industrialists more or less organized in the Confederations of Industry and Agriculture. Otherwise, class struggle, thrown out the window, reenters through the front door. Fascism does not want to become, as the Socialists affirm, a bourgeois reaction against labor and the workers. It is said and repeated to the seven winds that Fascism is above the bourgeoisie and above the proletariat. Well then, this superior law must be applied everywhere and to all. Otherwise Fascism would be partial and would signify with such partiality the beginning of its fatal ruination.[121]

Despite Mussolini's assurances, Confindustria was preoccupied with the growing intensity of this attack. During April 1923, Olivetti wrote three detailed analyses of the syndical situation, which were sent to regional associations.[122] From the information contained in Olivetti's communications – a detailed account of factions within the Fascist syndicates, who said what at past meetings, and what was to be discussed at future meetings – it is clear that the industrial association had an impressive intelligence capability. Olivetti noted that most of the Fascist labor organizers were profoundly discontent, "speaking openly of the failure of syndical action as it had been delineated and theorized by Fascism." Some were contemplating sending an explicit warning to Mussolini, telling him that it was impossible to proceed unless they could back up their demands with strikes or unless employers too were made subject to Fascist authority. One of two paths had to be chosen: either "passing on to a syndical struggle against the industrialists with strikes and agitations or imposing Fascist discipline

---

[119] *L'Impero*, 1 Apr. 1923, 8 Apr. 1928.
[120] *Il Caffaro*, 15 Mar. 1923.
[121] *L'Assalto*, 15 Mar. 1923.
[122] All three of Olivetti's analyses may be found in the historical files at Confindustria headquarters in Rome; copies may also be found at the HAUIT. They are reproduced in full in Abrate, *Lotta sindacale*, pp. 393–7. Besides Olivetti's analyses, two other analyses were written by Confindustria officials, probably not Olivetti himself, although they reflect his thinking. These are dated 21 Apr. 1923 and 23 June 1923.

upon the industrialists, forcing them to accept solutions to labor conflicts made by an external force. In the present situation, the extreme means of syndical struggle are prohibited, yet there is no class collaboration since unitary discipline is not applied to workers and employers alike."

Fascist syndicates, Olivetti continued, could not compete with Socialist syndicates. They were "clearly inferior to the Socialist organizations insofar as they were obliged to follow the discipline of the Government, even support and defend it when it is unpopular with the masses." And it was precisely this weakness that compelled the Fascist syndicates to continue with the program of *sindacalismo integrale:*

This inferiority is however compensated by the fact that *sindacalismo integrale fascista* can move into the employers' camp, gaining from one side what it loses from the other. Corresponding to such a situation of fact, the theoretical construction of Fascist syndicalism is based on organizing all the factors of production as a necessary condition to ensure class collaboration. The employers' syndicates thus become a condition sine qua non for Fascist syndical activity. If they remain autonomous, then the whole system becomes unbalanced and in danger of collapse. Suspended between the political exigencies of the Government and the resistance of autonomously organized industrialists, Fascist syndicates would have no possibility of life, let alone development, once the exceptional political situation of today has passed.

From this perspective, according to Olivetti, *all* employer confederations would have to be organized by the Fascist syndicates. Organizing the agrarians, yet leaving industrial associations independent, would be "unjustifiable in theory and dangerous in practice. Unjustifiable in that no serious rationale could be given for necessarily absorbing agrarians within Fascist employer syndicates and not the industrialists; dangerous in that the independence which industrialists maintain against Fascist organizations, without doubt, would incite the other employer categories."

Such were the imperatives of the situation for the Fascist syndicates. However, given Mussolini's tentative support for an autonomous Confindustria, how might the Fascist syndicates proceed with their plans? To Olivetti, it was clear that there was but one path. Confindustria's weak flank lay with the unorganized small and medium-sized industrialists. Were the Fascist syndicates successfully to organize these, the ground would then be prepared for a frontal assault on Confindustria:

By now it is an accomplished fact that within Fascist syndicates are small-scale industrialists who, for the most part, do not belong to Confindustria. This affords the Fascist syndicates a precious freedom of action, if the action is ably executed, since the boundaries between small, medium, and large industry are neither defined nor definable. It is a matter, therefore, of cleverly, patiently, and unobtrusively absorbing single industrial elements within the Corporazione of industry. And then, when this has undergone considerable development – development which Mussolini cannot oppose, for this would mean refusing the enrollment of industrialists who are Fascist or are said to be Fascist – the mask could be thrown off and accounts settled with Confindustria, confronting it either with whole-scale passage into the Corporazione or a struggle to the bitter end.

Organizing small and medium-scale industrialists thus became a major priority for Olivetti. In fact, this was not the first time he had shown interest in organizing the relatively atomized elements of these categories. Two weeks before the March on Rome, Confindustria sponsored the "First National Convention of Small and Medium Industry," which was held in Turin.[123] Now, however, it was absolutely imperative that the association aggressively pursue these categories. A circular was distributed to regional offices, announcing such a campaign; at the same time, a special Central Committee on Small Industry was established in Rome. The circular specifically stated that small industrialists were not to form an independent organization; they might become a separate section but must be tied directly to Confindustria.[124]

The Grand Council met again to discuss the syndical question on 1 May 1923. Rossoni attempted to force a dramatic choice upon Fascism's central organ: either support the concept of *sindacalismo integrale* or declare its failure. "Compel the employers to enter by force the Fascist Corporazioni to carry out, under the advice and guidance of the Government, the collaborationist experiment, or renounce the experiment, restoring to the workers full liberty of action."[125] Apparently, Olivetti's analysis had been right on the mark: the Fascist syndicates would have to extricate themselves from the present situation, and the alternatives were clear. However, the choice was not theirs to make. So long as the syndical question was overdetermined

---

[123] A pamphlet entitled *Il primo congresso nazionale delle piccola e media industria, Torino, 14–16 ottobre 1922* may be found at the HAUIT.

[124] Confindustria Circular C. 343, no date, though it is filed between 7 and 27 Aug. 1923.

[125] Cordova, *Sindacati fascisti,* p. 159.

by more global political considerations, Mussolini and the Grand Council would continue equivocating. Hence, still another pronouncement, even more ambiguous than the preceding two, was forthcoming: Fascist syndicates represented a "qualitative minority" which aspired to no monopoly, just as the old worker and employer organizations had no recognized monopoly. To coordinate relations between the PNF and the Corporazioni and to encourage "full appreciation of the syndical and technical forces of Fascism," a commission was named.[126] No specific position on *sindacalismo integrale* or autonomy was expressed. The net result of the meeting was the creation of a commission whose tasks were neither well specified nor immediately apparent.

Benni felt reassured. Addressing Confindustria's delegate assembly on 27 June, he said: "Every attempt to divide our ranks has been in vain and will continue to be so in the future; of this I am certain. . . . The attacks that have been made against us and, through us, against the industrial class, do not scare us. Only the strong become objects of discussion and opposition."[127]

During the summer of 1923, there was a subtle shift in the position of the Fascist syndicates. The immediate realization of *sindacalismo integrale* was improbable, as was the PNF's support for open syndical struggle. The only way out of the impasse was to call for a juridical redefinition of the state's relation to syndicates, reasserting, in this context, their claim to monopoly status. These views were first aired at a meeting of the Corporazioni's national council on 1 July. Armando Cassalini called upon the government to supersede the agnosticism of the liberal state, which left labor conflict to bargaining between parties, and to impose instead "juridical validity on contracts stipulated between those syndicates that did not partake of 'antinational' activity." If Confindustria's autonomy, for the moment, could not be touched, its freedom of action would at least be narrowed by legally defining the "red syndicates" out of existence. Once again, such strategy reflected the Corporazioni's objective weakness before both Confindustria and the Socialist organizations. Bramante Cucini argued that it was inadmissible for the industrialists to stipulate contracts with those organizations which still represented a majority of the workers, since these were anti-Fascist and antinational. If

---

[126] *Grand Consiglio primi dieci anni*, p. 61.
[127] *OI*, 1 July 1923.

Confindustria wished to continue as an autonomous body, outside the framework of the Corporazioni, it would have to deal, nevertheless, exclusively with Fascist syndicates. All syndicates would be juridically recognized, meaning – in this context – that they would become organs of the state. As such, the whole framework of labor relations would be fundamentally altered. No longer would syndical activity be free and competitive, but, in effect, it would be regulated by the state through newly created labor courts. These concerns of the Fascist syndicates were especially pressing because during the summer of 1923, Mussolini was in the midst of another set of negotiations with the CGL.[128]

Without, at this time, addressing the question of juridical recognition, Confindustria issued a public communiqué opposing monopoly status in general, reminding Rossoni's followers that this was a basic associational principle that had never been sacrificed, "even in more difficult times." Furthermore, the statement continued, the Grand Council had specifically declared itself against syndical monopolies.[129]

During early October 1923, industrialists were denounced for allegedly violating labor contracts, leading an offensive against the Fascist syndicates, and isolating Mussolini from Fascism. Such charges were made at a number of regional meetings of the Fascist syndicates where local leaders vented their frustration against the government as well. CGL leaders, such as D'Aragona, Buozzi, and Colombino, "too frequently had access to ministerial antechambers," while the Grand Council was favoring Confindustria. In fact, on 27 July, Benni and Olivetti were invited to participate at a Grand Council meeting, the first time that non-Fascists had ever been solicited by the Fascist body to express their views. Domenico Bagnasco, at one of these regional meetings, vehemently denounced the industrialists of Turin, the city where he headed the Fascist syndicates. It was necessary, he said, "no longer to act with sentiment but with force, the only way to subject all adversaries to Fascist discipline. Fascist syndicalism must be defended against the industrialists' offensive, but above all it is necessary to defend Fascism and Mussolini, who the industrialists are attempting to isolate from Fascism."[130] Following Bagnasco's remarks, greeted with "prolonged applause," this 17 October meeting passed a resolution

---

[128] Cordova, *Sindacati fascisti*, pp. 162–3.
[129] *Corriere della Sera*, 24 Aug. 1923.
[130] Cordova, *Sindacati fascisti*, pp. 182–3.

calling for "a most severe, intransigent battle against the industrialists, who are even now turning to the residues of red syndicalism to combat the Fascist syndicates."[131]

As if this were not enough, Bagnasco went on to accuse the Turinese industrialists of actually subsidizing Socialist organizations and newspapers, as well as paying the foreign press to denigrate Mussolini's occupation of Corfu.[132] Bagnasco's timing belied his real intention, that of upsetting Confindustria's cordial relations with Mussolini, who was scheduled to visit the Fiat factories in Turin the following week. The attempt backfired. Mussolini met with Olivetti, Benni, and Agnelli in Rome, once again reassuring them; he then reprimanded Rossoni. A telegram from Mussolini to the prefect of Turin speaks for itself:

Syndical question raised exactly on the eve of my departure for Turin seems inopportune to say the least. Stop. . . . There is no need to create dissension right at the time of my arrival in Turin. Stop. It is necessary to at least avoid bitter polemics.[133]

For his part, Olivetti quickly set out from Rome to Turin and prevented the LIT from adding to the tension by making public hostile sentiments aired in private meetings.[134]

Earlier, it was suggested that for Mussolini the syndical question was overdetermined by larger political concerns. By the fall of 1923, this had become fully apparent. Already he had indicated his intention of calling national elections to strengthen his position against both liberals and Fascist intransigents, to have "his own" majority in Parliament.[135] Here, the confidence of Confindustria was critical were he to have the support of the larger economic community. This meant tilting the syndical balance in its favor. Thus, on 16 November 1923, the Grand Council issued the following resolution:

The Grand Council recognizes that the majority of Italian industrial forces are grouped within Confindustria; declares that it does not intend to cause schisms or diminutions in the moral and technical efficiency of this organization; and insists that this Confederation take account of that in its relations with the Fascist workers' syndicates.[136]

[131] Abrate, *Lotta sindacale*, p. 384.
[132] Consiglio Direttivo, LIT, meeting of 18 Oct. 1923, HAUIT.
[133] Cordova, *Sindacati fascisti*, pp. 184–5.
[134] Consiglio Direttivo, LIT, meeting of 18 Oct. 1923, HAUIT.
[135] De Felice, *Mussolini il fascista*, 1:554–8.
[136] *Gran Consiglio primi dieci anni*, pp. 116–17.

To counterbalance, in the eyes of the Fascist syndicates, this strong preference for Confindustria, the Grand Council went on to declare: "In the agricultural camp, the employer association recognized by Fascism is the Federazione Italiana Sindacati Agricoltori Fascisti," an employer association organized by the Corporazioni, rather than Confagricoltura, Confindustria's autonomous counterpart. Although the Grand Council explicitly denied that this conferred monopoly status upon FISA, Confagricoltura's days were numbered, and in February 1924, an imposed FISA–Confagricoltura fusion took place, against the expressed will of the latter, resentful of Confindustria's preferential treatment.[137]

Mussolini's next step in reassuring Confindustria was the so-called Pact of Palazzo Chigi, 21 December 1923, signed by the industrial association and Rossoni's Corporazioni. In exchange for a vague promise that the two bodies would intensify their efforts at mutual collaboration, Confindustria obtained official repudiation of *sindacalismo integrale* so far as industry was concerned. Mussolini publicly affirmed that the autonomy and integrity of Confindustria would be respected, announcing that now Rossoni fully understood the difference between industry and agriculture.[138] As Felice Guarneri of Confindustria put it, the Pact of Palazzo Chigi planted a "tombstone on Rossoni's *sindacalismo integrale.*"[139] Olivetti, asked in an interview to comment on the consequences of the pact, answered:

It established the fact that the industrialists will be organized within Confindustria. Equivocations and misunderstandings are thus condemned to disappear. One should note that the Prime Minister proclaimed the necessity for a united industrial front and that the General Secretary of the Fascist Corporazioni declared that industrialists less inspired by the national interest were those who remained outside our confederation, those, that is, undisciplined by the organs of Confindustria.

When asked if this meant the end of *sindacalismo integrale,* Olivetti replied: "That certainly. All that remains is the spirit."[140] As if any doubts remained regarding Confindustria's status, Mussolini issued the following press release on 24 January 1924:

[137] On Confagricoltura's resentment see their letter to Mussolini of 12 Nov. 1923, ACS, Segretaria particolare del Duce, 25/242R, Inserto H, 11–12, 1923.
[138] *OI,* 1 Jan. 1924.
[139] Guarneri, *Battaglie economiche,* 1:66.
[140] *OI,* 1 Jan. 1924.

Inasmuch as there exists no syndical monopoly, it is still opportune to recall that in the deliberations of the Fascist Grand Council, in the expressed thoughts of His Excellency, Mussolini, and in the Pact of Palazzo Chigi, the unique industrial organization recognized as living and operating in the orbit and under the direction of the National Government is Confindustria, with headquarters in Rome, presided over by Honorable Benni, which represents, without distinction of region and branch of industry, the overwhelming majority of small, medium, and large industrialists. Any attempt to form other industrial organizations, a useless dispersion of energy, should be considered as unauthorized by the Head of Government and by the responsible organs of the Fascist Party.[141]

A month later, on 26 February 1924, Mussolini addressed the executive council of Confindustria, saying that all industrialists, large and small, should work toward bringing Confindustria to peak efficiency, "not dispersing energy, not creating duplicates, not seeking out sly or artificial divisions that might paralyze the continuity of economic life and that, in any case, would not have the Government's moral recognition."[142] Industrialists formerly organized by Rossoni's Corporazioni were absorbed by Confindustria.[143]

The Matteotti crisis and the collapse of liberal–Fascism

By the time national elections were announced, many of the industrialists' earlier apprehensions had been relieved: the Fascist syndicates had been tamed, and there had been a marked decrease in strikes, as well as a decrease in the level of unemployment. The number of workdays lost in industry due to strikes in 1923 had fallen to 295,929, compared with 6,600,000 in 1922 and 16,400,000 in 1921.[144] Unemployment decreased from 381,969 in December 1922 to 258,580 in December 1923 and would sink to 150,449 by December 1924. To some degree, these statistics reflect a post-1922 upturn in the world economy; however, the new regime was given major credit for leading the nation toward recovery, not simply because it happened to be the incumbent government, but because of its liberal–

---

[141] Confindustria Circular: 23 Jan. 1924; Cordova, *Sindacati fascisti*, p. 239.
[142] *OI*, 1 Mar. 1924.
[143] ACS, Segretario particolare del Duce, 87/WR, Rossoni, sottofascicolo 1, anonimi.
[144] Melograni, *Gli il industriali e Mussolini*, p. 52.

productivist economic policy and latent threats to meet labor agitation with force.[145]

Confindustria thus supported Mussolini's *listone* with money and men. They did so, however, as liberals, not as Fascists, although, as we have argued, the line of demarcation between these had become rather muddy. Such support did not prevent tensions from emerging between the government and industrialists. In Turin, as the prefect Palmieri reported to Mussolini: "The prominent men of the LIT are masters and financiers of the famous liberal association of Via Genova, where Professor Giovannini often visits to recite his melancholy dissertations on liberty and where, despite every declaration to the contrary by Olivetti and company, some supporters deride the Government." In the words of the prefect, this Associazione Liberale Democratica contained "hostile and insecure elements," to the point that those industrialists who wanted to give full adhesion to the government and to be independent of the PLI formed a new association, the Unione Liberale Monarchica.[146] Thus, despite the fact that both liberal associations supported the *listone*, as did Confindustria, there were significant differences of position as to the nature and degree of such backing. Some leaders of the LIT suggested that support should also be given to Giolitti's parallel list, though no determination can be made, given available evidence, as to how much support, if any, was actually afforded.[147]

In all, some twenty representatives of Confindustria were elected on the *listone*, including Benni, Olivetti, Motta, Mazzini, and Ponti. Satisfaction at such a relatively large industrial presence in the Chamber of Deputies was accompanied by continued apprehension caused by the unprecedented level of electoral violence and intimidation. Conti, for example, sent a sharply worded telegram of protest to Mussolini and later he met with him to convey "the citizens' disgust for the acts of vandalism committed, insisting on the damage done to the government and the Nation by these acts."[148]

The assassination of Matteotti and the Aventine secession in June 1924 threw the regime, if not the very premises of liberal–Fascism,

---

[145] De Felice, *Mussolini il fascista*, 1:397.
[146] ACS, Ministero dell'Interno, Gabinetto Finzi, busta 9, fascicolo 89, telegrams dates 8 Nov. 1923 and 9 Jan. 1924.
[147] Abrate, *Lotta sindacale*, pp. 403–7; Castronovo, *Agnelli*, pp. 401–4.
[148] Conti, *Taccuino*, pp. 205–6.

into disarray. For the next six months, Mussolini attempted to reassure both liberals and the extremists within his party. Yet the divide opened by the Matteotti crisis was so profound that promises made to one side only provoked the wrath of the other, to the point that neither had confidence in Mussolini's credibility or in the future of his government. However, as we have argued, neither side was capable of autonomously generating a viable alternative. Eventually, Fascist intransigents forced Mussolini's hand at the end of December 1924; ironically, this had the effect of leading directly to the creation of an authoritarian state, which then allowed Mussolini to definitively settle accounts with them shortly thereafter.

In mid-June 1924, some members of the cabinet (De Stefani, Oviglio, Federzoni, and Gentile) threatened to resign unless Mussolini purged the government of all morally suspect subordinates and handed over the minister of the interior to Federzoni. After some hesitation, Mussolini agreed. Finzi was removed as undersecretary of the interior, and De Bono as head of public security. Cesare Rossi was fired as Mussolini's press secretary, later to be arrested for complicity in Matteotti's murder. On 1 July, Mussolini added two liberals to his cabinet, Casati and Sarrochi, as well as one moderate Catholic, Cesare Nava. Such moves gave tentative satisfaction to the liberals, judging by the Senate vote of confidence (the Chamber was in summer recess): 225 votes to 21, with 6 abstentions. One liberal senator who voted for the government was none other than Benedetto Croce, who explained his position in an interview carried by *Giornale d'Italia* on 10 July:

You know that I have always maintained that the Fascist movement was sterile of new institutions, incapable of giving form, as its publicists boast, to a new type of state. For that reason, it cannot and ought not be anything other than a bridge to a new, more severe liberal regime within the framework of a new, stronger state. . . . Since Fascism is not up to creating a new constitutional and juridical framework which might be substituted for that of liberalism, it must maintain itself with the same violent methods of its beginning, perpetuating a state of affairs which ought to be opportune and transitory. . . . One must not expect or desire that Fascism fall suddenly. . . . It is necessary for Fascism to complete its process of transformation. This is the significance of the prudent and patriotic vote of the Senate.

As might be expected, the provincial intransigents responded to these concessions by Mussolini with violence and harsh polemics. The threat of a "second wave" was rekindled in such intransigent journals as *Conquista dello Stato, Il Selveggio, Battaglie Fasciste,* and especially *Cremona Nuova,* edited by Farinacci, who offered to defend Dumini, one of those charged with Matteotti's murder. Mussolini then took three steps to placate the intransigents. First, he declared to the Grand Council that he was "antinormalist" (normalization, he claimed, was anti-Fascism pure and simple, a return to the discredited liberal regime).[149] Second, he announced the formation of a "Committee of Fifteen," later ridiculed by anti-Fascists as the "Committee of Solons." This body was charged with developing constitutional revisions of a corporatist nature which would overcome the "agnosticism" of the liberal state in labor relations (e.g., juridical recognition of syndicates, labor courts, compulsory arbitration). Third, Mussolini tilted the syndical balance in favor of the Corporazioni. On 19 July, he received the Turinese syndicalist leader Bagnasco, telling him: "If the industrialists refuse class collaboration, we must find other means."[150] This was the beginning of the so-called *svolta a sinistra* (turn to the left). The Grand Council, which had given Fascist syndicates little previous support, now pledged its "ardent sympathy to the workers presently engaged in syndical struggles under the leadership of the Corporazioni" and invited all Fascists "actively and vigilantly" to participate in labor controversies so that they would be resolved in favor of the workers.[151] Once the green light was given, Rossoni's syndicates called a number of strikes, the most important being that of the miners in Valdarno. The PNF, "recognizing the justice of the workers' cause," contributed 50,000 lire to the strike fund.[152]

Confindustria naturally was alarmed, both because one of its initial fears, that industrialists might find themselves pitted against syndicates that had the backing of the party and the government, had been realized, and also because Rossoni's new program of *corporativismo integrale,* first announced in April 1924, seemed to be gaining official support.[153] Unlike *sindacalismo integrale,* which sought to absorb employer associations within the Corporazioni, *corporativismo integrale* was decidedly etatist: syndicates representing different classes

---

[149] Maier, *Recasting Bourgeois Europe,* p. 551.
[150] Cordova, *Sindacati fascisti,* p. 273.
[151] Ibid., p. 274.
[152] Ibid., p. 281.
[153] *LI,* 19 Apr. 1924; see also 1 Mar. 1924.

would remain autonomous as such but be jointly subject to a higher state corporative body, which would mediate labor disputes and make productive decisions. The new program called for juridical recognition of one compulsory syndicate per worker or employer category, obligatory collective contracts, compulsory arbitration, and special labor courts. Such a program, of course, was no more acceptable to Confindustria than *sindacalismo integrale*. What did it matter if the industrial association were formally autonomous but substantively subject to higher state authority, one that would impose exogenous political criteria on productive decisions, thereby limiting the managerial autonomy of individual industrialists?

Confindustria responded by sending two circulars on the syndical question to its membership, one marked *riservatissima* and the other *riservata*. These advised industrialists to make salary concessions where possible, but in no case should there be departures from standard "juridico-moral" contractual norms (e.g., conceding a monopoly to one syndicate or agreeing to hire exclusively through a syndicate). These instructions were to be "followed scrupulously" so that on "important and grave matters of principle" industrialists would not "find themselves deprived of a common direction."[154] Publicly, Olivetti gave an interview to *La Tribuna* on 24 July 1924 critical of the Fascist syndicates' "useless and demagogic verbal violence." When asked if Confindustria would sacrifice the principle of absolute and unfettered managerial authority, which he had earlier addressed in the interview, Olivetti responded:

No. Confindustria has always defended and maintained this principle intact. Just as we never yielded to Socialist impositions, we neither can nor will yield before those who put forth demands previously rejected, even when these may be colored with collaborationist assertions.

After categorically rejecting the recognition of any syndical monopoly, Olivetti was asked about Confindustria's position on state intervention in the productive process. His response:

State intervention in this area is very dangerous. Let us be clear on this. The state certainly has the duty to promote and guide pacification, even in the economic realm. But it has neither the ability nor the means to pass itself off as an arbitrator or judge in economic situations, or to take upon itself the

---

[154] Confindustria Circulars: C. 969, 10 Aug. 1924; also nonnumbered circular of 23 July 1924.

responsibility of gauging what can influence the financial situation of a firm subjected to all the fluctuations of international competition. . . . In a general sense, peace in the economic realm will be better maintained the less this realm becomes once again a field of passions and of political speculations.

Olivetti's position, while officially representing Confindustria, was shared by the larger liberal community, alienated by the summer "turn to the left" and talk of corporatist legislative projects. On 21 July, the most consistently pro-Fascist liberal paper, *Giornale d'Italia,* after enumerating all the forms of support liberals had given the government, asked, "After all this, what do you still want from the liberal bourgeoisie, Honorable Mussolini?" Five days later, the newspaper ran an article suggestively entitled "A Little Prudence Wouldn't Hurt," highly critical of the government's prejudicial intervention in labor conflicts.

Critical though it was of recent government policy, Confindustria had not commented on the larger question of the regime as such in the wake of the Matteotti murder. True, it joined with the CGL in calling for a ten-minute work cessation to honor the fallen Socialist martyr,[155] but it did not comment on the assassination and its political implications. This "silence" provoked a polemic against the association on the part of some liberals, illustrious but few, who clearly wanted a break between liberalism and Fascism, which, in their eyes, required the support of Confindustria. On 30 July, Luigi Albertini, editor of *Corriere della Sera,* sent the following letter to Einaudi, the paper's influential economist:

Here in Milan, Amendola and I have done what we could do to get Confindustria to vote in its meeting today a resolution condemning the second wave, the nights of St. Bartholomew, bullets for the opposition, and all the rest the *squadristi* have done. We have not been successful. Everything was put off; in reality, they don't want to do anything. In these conditions, after having talked with Alberto [Albertini], it seems to me that you might write a signed article taking note of this silence and asking the industrialists what they think of the second wave. On the Stock Exchange one notes a profound unease and a state of uncertainty which did not exist before the assassination of Matteotti. Are relations between industrialists and the government so intimate and firm to prevent them from expressing a sincere opinion without incurring the wrath they fear? . . . Many industrialists say that they must sustain the given state of affairs for fear of still worse, not seeing that if the given state of affairs is not energetically remedied, still worse is inevitable.

[155] *L'Informazione Industriale,* 22 June 1924.

The longer illegality lasts, the more there is to fear for the future. . . . These are my ideas that you might further elaborate, complementing them with your own in an article which corresponds with our purpose and which might induce cynical types like Olivetti and obtuse types like Benni to reflect upon what they are doing. The article, of course, is a very delicate matter and its wording should be carefully weighed.[156]

On 6 August 1924, the *Corriere della Sera* published Einaudi's famous article "The Silence of the Industrialists," which stated:

The industrialists do not approve of threats, but pretending to consider the agitated loudmouths innocuous maniacs, they insist on the preeminent necessity of strong government. They maintain that social tranquility, the absence of strikes, the intense productive upturn, the balanced budget, are goods which are tangible, effective, and of greater long-term importance than harm done due to the loss of political liberty, which, after all, interests a tiny minority of Italians. First, there is the need to work, produce, and create the material conditions for a comfortable life; to think, to struggle politically, are purely ideal goods that one can do without. The more cynical, the more adherent to an unconscionably materialist conception of life, add that it's well worth the tribute in money and liberty to be saved from the danger of Bolshevism, anarchy, and the destruction of wealth. Either the present regime, with all its restrictions on liberty, or Bolshevism. Between the two the choice is obvious. Fatally, the restoration of ordinary parliamentary practice, of freedom of the press, would mean a return to the methods of Giolitti and Nitti, of cajolery and weakness toward the red parties. As Kerensky was fatally followed by Lenin, would we want to fall into the horrors of Bolshevism? So ask the men of finance. . . . The industrialists' politics of silence in such a dramatic moment assumes the appearance of servility in the eyes of the public. Is it not more dangerous to have the workers think that their own humiliation is the price paid by their employers' complicity?

Einaudi, who personally knew many of the Confindustria leaders and was well aware that they never viewed Mussolini as their savior from Bolshevism, deliberately exaggerated in the hope of provoking a public response. On 12 August, Giovanni Silvestri, on his own behalf and without consulting Confindustria, replied in *Il Secolo*. Silvestri, who had been president of the association from December 1919 to December 1920, insisted that industrialists thought only of work and not politics:

The tried and true industrialist has, if not a horror, certainly an aversion for politics. He gives it a half hour in the morning and a half hour in the evening,

---

[156] Melograni, *Gli industriali e Mussolini*, p. 75. Melograni presents an excellent and detailed analysis of the Einaudi polemic with the industrialists on pp. 74–96.

flipping through the newspapers. But then, during the day, his thoughts are completely dedicated to his work, to his business.[157]

Einaudi lost no time in tossing back a caustic reply, entitled "The Lesser Evil." This appeared on 14 August in *Corriere della Sera:*

> ... if everything finished there, if the politics of the industrialists were limited to reading the papers in the morning with their coffee and in the evening before retiring, with consequent protests against journalists incapable of going forth for the good of the country, then, everyone would agree, things would simply be lamentable. But that's not the way it is, or at least not for the industrialists who write, who formulate resolutions, who lead professional associations. Above all, that's not the way it is with industrialists who intervene in politics to the sound of millions, founding and subsidizing newspapers. They profess a theory of politics, just as they profess a theory of economics. ... Reading what Silvestri says, it seems as if castor oil, the bludgeon, and the loss of freedom of the press ought to appear to Italians as small things compared to the horrors of Russian Bolshevism.

Throughout the month of August, the Einaudi polemic generated numerous articles in the press, though no response came from Confindustria, whose silence now assumed growing political significance. The association's leadership was embarrassed by Silvestri's simplistic reply to Einaudi, yet it carefully had to weigh the consequences of a public statement hostile to the government. What effect would this have on the conflict with the Fascist syndicates, now that they apparently had the support of the party and the government? What possible alternative was there to the present regime, something Einaudi himself never considered while deriding industrialists for allegedly maintaining "either Fascism or Bolshevism"? Finally, what would the economic consequences be? This was hardly a facile question, given the fact that during the years 1922–5, Italy had registered the greatest boom yet recorded, one not equaled until the so-called economic miracle after World War II. According to Melograni, the index of industrial production (1938 = 100) passed from 54 in 1921 to 83 in 1925; that is, an increment of 54 percent in four years. "In the world, during those years, only Japan experienced a more rapid industrial development; the other nations, including the United States, developed either at rates lower than that of Italy or saw a regress in their economies (as in the cases of Austria, Germany, England, and

[157] Ibid., p. 79.

Russia)."[158] In this light, the sentiments expressed by Camillo Olivetti in *La Voce Repubblicana* of 6 September 1924 are of great significance. Founder of the famous office-machine firm, a social visionary, and one-time member of the Socialist Party, outside the Confindustria orbit and as anti-Fascist by conviction as an industrialist could possibly be, Camillo Olivetti nevertheless acknowledged the productivist policies of the government. It had succeeded where the old *classe dirigente*, with its "anti-industrial mentality," had failed: "the Fascist government has been the only Italian government to concern itself with the conditions of industry and to not consider industrialists as people *convenable et conspuable à merci*, as have all the other governments, excepting none, that have succeeded one another in Italy for fifty years."[159]

Yet who could say with confidence that the order, discipline, and productivity which Mussolini had brought to Italy in the past was not over? Since the Matteotti assassination, these attributes were hardly characteristic of economic and social life. Such sentiments were voiced by *Industrie Italiane Illustrate*, a publication not affiliated with Confindustria but usually close in outlook:

So long as Fascism represents the element of order, quiet, and the possibility for serene and profitable work, industry will be with the Government. But if Fascism represents – even indirectly – an element of disorder and gives way to derangements, to tumultuous manifestations, and to ill-advised strikes, then it might no longer find us agreeable. All that which impairs and paralyzes work, provoked by any side, cannot have our approval. . . . In the present moment, we can no longer take a position, because we are at a change in circumstances. . . . For now ours can only be an attitude of cautious waiting.[160]

All these crosscurrents raised by Einaudi's polemic began to surface within Confindustria during the fall. At a 4 September meeting, originally called to discuss syndical matters, Olivetti asked that the leadership address the problem of Confindustria's relationship with the government and the PNF. After Benni rather emphatically stated that he agreed with Silvestri's response to Einaudi, Olivetti took the floor and stated that as an officer of Confindustria and as an elected deputy, he requested the association to take a responsible position:

[158] Ibid., p. 50.
[159] Ibid., p. 82.
[160] Ibid., p. 108.

It is not possible that at so grave a moment all that the Italian industrialists have to say is that they are not interested in politics because they work from morning to evening in their factories. If that were the case, I could not rule out the possibility that one fine day we may awake and find the black flag of the Corporazioni flying over our factories. Such a day I would not want to see; there is no cause to believe that the black flag is any better than the red. We must therefore do something, go to the head of the government and tell him that things cannot go on this way. Mussolini will understand that we want nothing but the establishment once again of legality. Without peace inspired by profound sentiments, not imposed by bludgeons, not even industry can survive and prosper.[161]

Everyone present, except Jarach, voted in favor of Olivetti composing a memorandum to be transmitted to Mussolini. After at least three drafts, which Conti helped revise, a delegation consisting of Benni, Olivetti, Conti, and Pirelli presented it to Mussolini on 9 September.[162]

The memorandum began with the problem of syndical relations. After reaffirming that industrialists "do not request and do not deem suitable or possible any politics of repression with regard to the working class," there followed Olivetti's characteristic criticism of state intervention, as well as a call for syndical freedom. This was not only a statement of principle but an obvious criticism of the summer "turn to the left."

The industrial class has always held that the principle of collaboration in production, substituted for the principle of class struggle, ought to govern relations between employers and workers. It has acted and it acts according to this directive. It believes that the intervention of the state ought to be limited to promoting this principle in the national interest, abstaining from other specific action in a field in which the difficult equilibrium can only be attained through the absolute respect for the laws protecting the liberty of industry, the liberty of labor, and the liberty of organization; eliminating, so far as possible, all political influence from the economic realm and guaranteeing that the state will not yield or use its power and authority in favor of one class or the other, especially for contingent and opportunistic reasons of the moment.

---

[161] Letter from Olivetti to Mazzini, dated 8 Sept. 1924, which accompanied the text of the Confindustria memo to Mussolini, HAUIT.; see also Abrate, *Lotta sindacale*, pp. 422–3.

[162] Three separate drafts of the memo to Mussolini may be found in the historical files at Confindustria headquarters in Rome. Apparently Olivetti distributed it to some of the regional associations, as a copy was sent to Mazzini, president of the LIT. It may be found at the HAUIT.

The memorandum then went on to ask for greater impartiality and equal treatment for all, an end to corporatist legislative projects, which were both misinformed and discouraged initiative, nonpartisan administration, and the guarantee of individual rights:

The state has not yet entirely reestablished its prestige and power, but this will surely happen:

1. If the state will exercise the means and powers it has at its disposal for the defense of its existence and of civil order with the guarantee of equal treatment for all, truly assuming the position of an entity superior to all parties and just toward all citizens.

2. If the state will not submit to continual changes, or the possibility of continual changes, in its legislation, which destroys the sense of stability and continuity in civil life, impedes the formation of a popular conscience that conforms to the laws, instills the idea that it is necessary or sufficient to change legislation rather than customs, impedes the application of rules, which are presumed transitory, flounders upon the exigency of reality, destroys interest, and discourages energy and initiative.

3. If the state will ensure that the law is applied to all and will make certain that its functionaries act with a major sense of objectivity, without distinction to party or political influence.

4. If, within limits established by laws pertaining to the actions that single citizens may take without harm to the rights of others and the interests of the state, the government will guarantee that the sphere of individual action will not be touched.

5. If the state will allow for a selection of individuals and agencies according to their real value, ensuring that in public life personal interest is not placed before the general interest.

The mere enunciation of these principles called into question the very framework and practice of Fascist administration. The memorandum went on to say that "a new *classe dirigente* may be in formation but is not yet formed. In the meantime, the state should not only accept but solicit and value the active collaboration of all those in the national parties who are ready to give, with unity of intent and tranquility of spirit, their labor and their solidarity to implement a concrete program directed toward reaffirming the greatness of the Nation." Stripped of its rhetorical excess, this was nothing less than a call for a broad coalition government based on explicitly liberal, not Fascist, principles.

In a letter to Mazzini accompanying a copy of the memorandum, Olivetti was somewhat less than sanguine as to its ultimate effect.

"Either he will listen to us, making it possible for liberal ministers to remain in his government and silence those among his followers who yell the loudest and wish to kill off half of Italy, or he will not listen to us, in which case it is absolutely unforeseeable what might happen." It would be the king, not the liberals and industrialists, who would ultimately force Mussolini to choose between these alternatives, according to Olivetti. "I must sincerely tell you that in my opinion his decision will depend very little upon what we do. Others who are above us will be, with their conduct, the real determinants of his decision." If it appeared that Mussolini would remain in power by force, Olivetti advised Mazzini to tell the Turinese industrialists to prepare for an attack by Rossoni:

In any case, we will remain at our posts and defend ourselves as best we can. But I want to tell you this, and you pass it on to the others in Turin. If there are clear signs that he intends to remain by force, make yourselves small, let fall any question of unity, scatter, and don't expose your flank to a frontal assault by R., who hasn't forgotten the humiliation of 1923 and is waiting for his chance.

The Confindustria memorandum was never made public, although its substantive content was leaked to *La Stampa* of Turin, which ran an exposé on 17 September. This was followed by favorable comments in the opposition press, including the Socialist *Avanti! La Voce Repubblicana* wrote, "The simply enormous value of this document of the industrialists has no need of comment." *Giornale d'Italia* recognized the commonality between the industrialists' position and that of the other alienated national forces: "this step by Confindustria is analogous to the attitude of liberals, veterans, and war invalids, in short, all the national forces collaborating with the Government who want to make known to Honorable Mussolini that he must resolutely choose the path of legality."[163]

Among the government's supporters, the next to act were the liberals. The PLI met on 4–7 October at Livorno. After rejecting a resolution that would have given approval to the government's policy, another resolution was passed by a large majority that called for autonomy among the liberal deputies, even though they had been elected on the *listone*. The resolution also listed a number of demands

[163] Melograni, *Gli industriali e Mussolini,* pp. 91–5.

similar to those specified earlier in the Confindustria memorandum.[164]

Yet if the liberals and the industrialists began to loosen their ties to the government, they were nevertheless incapable themselves of generating an alternative. There was talk of a return of Giolitti to power and later talk of negotiations regarding a possible Giolitti–Salandra–Orlando government, but these never materialized. Even the liberals' attempt to get the king to intervene came to naught. After the Confindustria memorandum in September, the association took no further action. By default it encouraged its members either to act individually or not at all. Of the Confindustria leadership, Conti went the furthest, first by encouraging a group of prominent liberals to seek royal intervention, then actively working for Giolitti's return. On 3 December 1924, he delivered an impassioned speech in the Senate, reaffirming points raised in the memorandum and calling for Mussolini's resignation.[165] As for the vote of confidence in the Chamber on 15 November, Motta was absent, Ponti abstained, and the other major industrial leaders (including Benni, Olivetti, and Donegani) voted in support of the government. When it was the Senate's turn, Conti abstained, and the other industrialists voted in support of the government. Since no alternatives to Mussolini were present, and since there was no doubt whatsoever that the government would win handily in both houses of Parliament, what could be gained for the interests of industry by antagonizing Mussolini, especially now that the "turn to the left" seemed to target Confindustria for militant action?

In the meantime, both Fascist syndicates and provincial intransigents began to distance themselves from Mussolini as well. Mussolini had encouraged the summer "turn to the left" in part to prevent an anticipated rise in CGL membership and to secure mass loyalty when it was most needed by projecting a prolabor Fascist image. In September, Mussolini intended to undercut Rossoni by encouraging a secessionist faction within the Corporazioni. Two events, however, forced him to end the initiative: the Confindustria memorandum and the

---

[164] *L'Informazione Industriale*, 10 Nov. 1924; De Felice, *Mussolini il fascista*, 1:678–80. On 22 Nov. 1924, Olivetti presented a resolution to the Chamber calling for "a secure, complete, and impartial application of the law rather than the continual tendency to change legislative regulations and norms" (Giovannini, *Il rifiuto*, pp. 424–5).

[165] *Atti Parlamentari*, Senato, 3 Dec. 1924, pp. 344–8.

assassination of one of the Corporazioni leaders, Casalini.[166] The political climate resulting from these events was such that a countervailing force was needed to maintain pressure on the industrialists, now drifting away from the government and toward the opposition, while the intransigents would not have tolerated a move against Rossoni's leadership, especially now that one of his high command had been murdered. Yet soon after the summer "turn to the left," Mussolini began moving toward a more moderate position and gave the syndicates little support.

In November, the directorate of the Corporazioni sent a letter to Mussolini which, after pointing out that they remained loyal while "false friends every day are dropping their masks," asked:

1 Does Fascism intend to recognize the doctrine of the Corporazioni as its own syndical program?
2 Does Fascism intend to furnish the Corporazioni those means (syndical legislation, collaboration between Party and Corporazioni) necessary to actuate in every field its program of *sindacalismo integrale?*[167]

Receiving no answer, one faction of the Corporazioni leadership, led by Fioretti, advocated the removal of the Fascist label from the syndicate's name. In an interview on 3 December, Fioretti said: "Think of how we have been hurt by the attitude of the Government and the Party toward Confindustria, which then paid back Fascism in a way that we all know and, behind the sly and intelligent diplomacy of Signor Olivetti, has kept in reserve the most insidious weapon to destroy, or at least paralyze, Fascism."[168] During the closing days of December, when the intransigents were threatening to break with Mussolini, Fioretti led the argument in the executive council of the Corporazioni for finally removing the Fascist label.

The intransigents, long fed up with Mussolini's equivocations, were outraged at the prime minister's circular to the party of 30 November, calling for conciliation with the government's allies and the end of *squadrismo:* "It is necessary to liberate the party from all elements who are unfit for the new settlement, from those who make a profession of violence."[169] Provincial Fascists thought that Mussolini might

---

[166] Cordova, *Sindacati fascisti,* pp. 283–94.
[167] Ibid., p. 311.
[168] De Felice, *Mussolini il fascista,* 1:668.
[169] Lyttelton, *Seizure of Power,* p. 258.

be trying to save himself at their expense. The Nationalist Federzoni took over the Ministry of the Interior and began making arrests. To this, the provincial intransigents responded "either everyone in jail or no one." On 31 December, a delegation of thirty-three Militia consuls met with Mussolini, demanding that he move against the opposition and release all Fascists from behind bars. Renewed acts of violence broke out in Florence, Pisa, Bologna, and elsewhere.[170] Articles were running in the intransigent press similar to the one by Malaparte entitled "Fascism against Mussolini."

On 3 January 1925, Mussolini addressed the Chamber of Deputies. After challenging anyone to bring impeachment charges against him, he accepted the "full political, moral, and historical responsibility for all that has happened." Finally, the *coup:* "You may be assured that within the next forty-eight hours after my speech, the situation will be clarified in every field."[171]

[170] Ibid., p. 264.
[171] Mussolini, *Scritti,* 5:7–16.

5. Industrialists and nonintegral corporatism

During the period of liberal–Fascism, Confindustria had never been forced to define itself as Fascist. It had retained an autonomous liberal identity, giving conditional and contingent support – as did liberals in general – to Mussolini as prime minister of duly constituted government, not to Mussolini as Duce, much less to Fascism per se. By the beginning of 1925, in the aftermath of the Matteotti crisis, the four-year liberal–Fascist convergence had broken down. No longer was there manifest concern shown by Mussolini for continuity with the traditional liberal state, nor was there further talk of normalization. By the end of 1925, foundations for a new, distinctively antiliberal state had already been laid, the final edifice to be fully erected in subsequent years.

Forced at the end of 1924 to choose between liberal *fiancheggiatori* and intransigent Fascists, whose respective demands could no longer be reconciled within the faltering framework of liberal–Fascism, Mussolini tentatively sided with the intransigents. Within two years, however, they too would be neutralized, as the party was reduced to little more than a disciplined and pitifully dependent extension of the state. Quite apart from the need to substitute a new juridical order for the negated liberal state, more pressing problems (civil unrest, continuing Fascist violence, and four separate attempts on Mussolini's life) led to a whole series of party directives and repressive laws: the squads were demobilized, the party was "purified" of recalcitrant elements, and local leadership was made subservient to the prefect. Aventine deputies were stripped of their parliamentary immunity; freedom of the press was abolished, and leading liberal journalists like Albertini, Frassati, and Salvatorelli were forced from *Corriere della Sera* and *La Stampa;* non-Fascist parties and associations were prohibited; and the so-called head of government was rendered independent from Parliament and given discretionary power to disapprove proposals before they were actually presented to the Chamber, and to rule by decree.

344

Celebrating the third anniversary of the March on Rome, Mussolini renounced his earlier Manchestrian understanding of the state and enunciated a new political formula: "everything in the state, nothing outside the state, nothing against the state."[1] Six months later, he declared:

We live in a Fascist state. We have buried the old liberal–democratic state, and thus we are in a state that controls all the forces that vitally affect the Nation. We control the political forces, we control the moral forces, we control the economic forces. We are then in a full Fascist–corporatist state.[2]

The political arena was now exclusively Fascist. This is not to say that Fascism had indeed gained full control over all of civil society, as Mussolini would boast with characteristic overstatement, or that contradictions within the Fascist movement and between the movement and its supporters had been fully resolved. Rather, the political arena was exclusively Fascist in that the atomized and fragmented non-Fascist forces, which had been unable to constitute an alternative to Fascism before 1925, were subsequently prevented from pursuing any overt political action whatsoever. The bourgeois public sphere, which by the turn of the century had already been lacerated by Socialists and Catholics, was now imperatively restructured. It was stripped of its autonomy, as the state itself directly mobilized consensus from above, imposing official and incontrovertible definitions of reality.

During 1925, Confindustria had to adjust to the new reality if, as Abrate suggests, it were to "save what was savable of the industrialists' syndical and economic organization, preserving a limited sphere of autonomy."[3] Until October 1925, Confindustria stubbornly refused to end its "agnosticism" toward Fascism or to retreat from its principled stand against limiting syndical freedom, recognizing monopoly status on the part of Fascist syndicates, and yielding to compulsory state arbitration in labor conflict. However, when it became all too apparent that maintaining such a position ran the far greater risk that the association might find itself locked outside a narrowed political arena in which vital decisions affecting production were being made, Confindustria yielded on these points and eventually changed its official name to the Confederazione Generale Fascista dell'Industria Italiana.

[1] Mussolini, *Scritti*, 5:162.
[2] Ibid., p. 310.
[3] Abrate, *Lotta sindacale*, p. 447.

Besides gaining a permanent seat on the Fascist Grand Council, Confindustria – now formally "Fascist" – was able to exploit the internal contradictions and doctrinal ambiguities of Fascism to its own relative advantage. Within the Fascist orbit, Confindustria was literally the only group possessing independent resources, a clear sense of purpose, technical competence, effective organization, and exceptional leadership. If, as Mussolini claimed, everything was to be within the Fascist state, nothing outside it, Confindustria was to become, as one of its leaders would later put it, a "state within the state, a rugged rock inaccessible even to the superpower of the party." Thus:

All of us remained at our posts; for Confindustria nothing changed whether with regard to its internal organization or its spirit, even when, in 1926, it obtained juridical recognition in accordance with the laws and added to its old name the attribute "Fascist." The party that, since its rise to power, had been able to alter at its pleasure with the force of a veritable earthquake syndical leadership in all the other categories of employers and workers was stopped before the doorstep of the Confederation of Industry and never succeeded in imposing its own men. . . . That Confindustria in those years was a powerful body cannot be seriously contested. But the secret – if not of its power, then certainly of the incontestable prestige that it succeeded in establishing – was to be found in the fact that the Confederation had at the center of its national and territorial organizations executive councils composed of the best and most respected representatives of the various industrial sectors, and leaders endowed with great experience, in full harmony among themselves, who had been well formed much before Fascism had appeared on the horizon.[4]

And yet if *lo stato corporativo* stopped at the factory gate, one should not overhastily concur with orthodox Marxist interpretations of Fascism as "the regime of monopoly capital," for that would be to impose a necessary and immanent telos upon a regime that had, as we have seen, no fixed trajectory. Such a view cannot adequately account for the tension and abrupt discontinuities in the relationship between Fascism and the industrialists that we have observed in the pre-Fascist and liberal–Fascist periods, or for the essentially defensive and rear-guard actions of Confindustria during the later period of nonintegral corporatism. That Confindustria was able to not only survive but actually extend its authority was due more to the consummate political skill of its leadership and to the internal weakness of

---

[4] Guarneri, *Battaglie economiche*, 1:55–6.

Fascism than to the actual intentions of Fascist leaders or to some suprahistorical "cunning of reason." There is reason to suppose that in the absence of such a relatively effective Confindustria strategy, Italian Fascism might have developed in ways far more threatening to capitalism. Both Sarti and Romeo have observed that under Fascism the state had more latitude for control over the economy than in any other nation at the time except for the Soviet Union.[5] Confindustria never saw their own surrender of control as inevitable. As we noted earlier, and as we shall see again, other employer confederations were sufficiently intimidated by Fascist leadership to momentarily sacrifice their autonomy until Confindustria, acting as a type of intransigent associational pacesetter, came to the rescue and checked such assaults upon *iniziativa privata*.

Finally, it should be observed that Confindustria's victory was, at best, partial. Although absolute managerial authority was preserved at the factory level, and Confindustria came to assume significant authority in administering economic policy, it is nevertheless the case that the *context* of economic policy became increasingly political and irrational from a strictly economic point of view (e.g., setting the lira for reasons of prestige at the noncompetitive level of ninety to the pound sterling, ruralism, encouraging population growth, autarky, the invasion of Ethiopia, the alliance with Germany against England and France). At the level of public policy, both foreign and domestic, Confindustria exercised little or no initiative. Here the association, at best, could negotiate subsequent trade-offs to the relative advantage of industry *once fundamental decisions had already been made;* it reacted rather than acted.

From liberal–Fascism to nonintegral corporatism

In the last chapter, we concentrated on the legitimation crisis set off by the Matteotti assassination and Mussolini's growing inability to reconcile opposing interests within the constraining framework of liberal–Fascism. Before beginning our treatment of the transition to nonintegral corporatism, two essentially economic problems must be further specified that had significant political bearing. These, together with the political problems treated earlier, jointly contributed to the drift to-

[5] Romeo, *Breve storia*, pp. 173–4; Sarti, *Fascism and Industrial Leadership*, p. 124.

ward a more authoritarian regime: (1) a severe balance of payments problem, leading to inflation and devaluation of the lira; and (2) Italy's need to borrow foreign capital and resolve its war debts.

Although Italy's index of industrial production (1922 = 100) continued to increase until 1925 (1923 = 116; 1924 = 138; 1925 = 157), importation of foreign grain to compensate for a bad harvest in 1924 and the continuing need to import lacking raw materials pushed the commercial deficit to 8,177 million lire in 1925, compared to 5,258 in 1922. In reaction, Italian currency began to fall precipitously on international money markets; the lira, which against the pound sterling had been 91.5 in December 1922 and 109.9 in December 1924, slipped to 117.5 in January 1925, 138.5 in June, and 144.9 in July. Despite the government's attempt to support the lira in international markets, it continued to decline, reaching a low of 153.7 in July 1926.[6] At this point, the devaluation of the lira was no longer an economic problem but a political one of major significance. Inflation and speculation on stocks, which grew more intense, threatened to undercut Fascism's middle-class base, particularly those strata living on savings, pensions, fixed incomes, and rents.[7] Moreover, the consequent rise in prices and decrease in real wages threatened to provoke another round of labor agitation unless the situation was stabilized. Furthermore, runaway inflation and potential social unrest threatened to jeopardize Italy's attempt to borrow foreign capital and secure favorable terms for the repayment of its war debts.

These domestic and international economic constraints also contributed to the supersession of liberalism in favor of state intervention and a directed economy. The free play of market forces, upon which economic liberalism was based, could no longer be risked. Only a more authoritarian government would afford necessary coercive power simultaneously to launch a "battle of grain" (increasing the national quota and limiting imports) and a "battle of the lira" (controlling credit, salaries, costs, and prices). Economic stabilization, in other words, required new forms of political control, and these, in turn, when compounded by the legitimation crisis of liberal–Fascism, called for a juridical restructuring of the state.

---

[6] Renzo De Felice, "I lineamenti politici della 'quota novanta' attraverso i documenti di Mussolini e Volpi," *Il Nuovo Osservatore* 7 (May 1960): 374–7.

[7] Vittorio Foa's introduction to Pietro Grifone, *Il capitale finanziario in Italia* (Turin: Einaudi, 1971), p. xxxv.

Thus, the liberal nightwatchman state was to be rejected in favor of one no longer constrained by the public–private distinction or limited by constitutional guarantees of associational pluralism and inviolable individual rights. At the ideological level, this imperative gave rise to a host of ready-made literati who railed against the unconscionable hedonism of liberal political economy and the degenerative effects of the French Revolution, both of which, it was argued, broke down a natural communitarian moral order, placed the atomized, self-seeking individual above the state, and upended natural hierarchies of quality in the name of social leveling. Invoking such authorities as Plato, Aristotle, and St. Thomas against such targets as Rousseau, Locke, and Marx, sages like Gino Arias heralded a new state in which *homo corporativus* would arise from the transmuted soul of *homo oeconomicus*. Competition between amoral and materialistic individuals and classes would give way to a harmoniously ordered social totality based on functionalism and natural inequality. Associations would not be voluntary and oriented toward the defense of private interest but would be compulsory and oriented toward the realization of collective interest. Within this new organic order, there would be no empty space or unaffiliated individuals; everyone was to be *inquadrato* (or framed) within functionally specific, corporative associations linked directly to the state.

So much for the general corporatist weltanschauung. For our purposes, there are three corporatist spokesmen who merit attention both because of threats they posed to Confindustria and because of the role they played in the development of the Fascist state: Edmondo Rossoni, Alfredo Rocco, and Giuseppe Bottai.[8] On Rossoni, little more need be added to what has already been said. Coming from the tradition of revolutionary syndicalism, his objective was the realization of a syndical state with no external political mediation. As we have suggested, his program of *corporativismo integrale* was but a cosmetically altered version of *sindacalismo integrale* – a tentative concession that the Fascist syndicates were not as yet prepared to assert their dominance over the party and the state, though this remained Rossoni's ultimate objective.

Rocco, appointed minister of justice in 1925 and author of the most significant pieces of corporatist legislation, had as "integral" an

---

[8] Franklin Hugh Adler, "Italian Industrialists and Radical Fascism," *Telos* 30 (winter 1976–7): 193–201.

understanding of social organization as Rossoni, though his version was essentially conservative and authoritarian. Rather than a state subordinate to syndicates, Rocco viewed syndicates, those of workers *and* employers, as subordinate to the state – passive and dependent vehicles for carrying out directives issued from above, while at the same time imposing discipline upon their members.[9]

Bottai, who headed the Ministry of Corporations from 1926 to 1932, had the most dynamic and technocratic corporatist conception of the three. Having been an ardent supporter of the ill-fated *gruppi di competenza,* the *consigli technici,* and the recommendations of the Committee of Solons, Bottai advocated a bottom–up, decentralized, regionally based order whose propelling force would be a new middle-class managerial elite. Around him he attracted the brightest of the young Fascist theorists, who collectively argued in such journals as *Critica Fascista, Primato,* and *Archivio di Studi Corporativi* for the creation of this new *classe dirigente.* Against the demagogic, class-bound conception of Rossoni and the static, etatist conception of Rocco, Bottai wanted corporations and their component syndicates to be directed by specially trained professionals, and toward that end he created a school for syndical officials in Genoa in 1928.[10]

Rossoni's aspirations were blocked by the failure of the Fascist syndicates ever to gain a foothold in the urban–industrial proletariat, as well as by resistance on the part of Confindustria, Bottai, Rocco, and Mussolini himself, all of whom, for different reasons, feared the disruptive potential of a powerful syndical force headed by a firebrand like Rossoni. Bottai's aspirations were blocked by the failure to create a new managerial elite, a project resisted by vested economic interests, the traditional state bureaucracy, and the PNF. Only Rocco's authoritarian conception would attain partial realization, for this most closely conformed to Mussolini's desire to use the state as his personal political instrument, yet not without resistance on the part of Confindustria.

---

[9] On Rocco, see Gaeta, *Nazionalismo italiano;* Paolo Ungari, *Alfredo Rocco e l'ideologia giuridica del fascismo* (Brescia: Morecellini, 1963).

[10] On Bottai, see his diary, *Vent'anni e un giorno* (Milan: Garzanti, 1977; also Sabino Cassese, "Un programmatore degli anni trenta: Giuseppe Bottai," *Politica del Diritto* 1 (1970): 404–47; Alexander De Grand, "Giuseppe Bottai e il fallimento del revisionismo fascista," *Storia Contemporanea* 4 (1975): 711–30; Giordano Guerri, *Giuseppe Bottai: un fascista critico* (Milan: Feltrinelli, 1976); Bruno Uva, *La nascita dello stato corporativo e sindacale fascista* (Rome: Carucci, n.d.), pp. 3–79.

Within the emergent corporatist order, parties had no essential function to perform. First non-Fascist parties were prohibited, then the PNF itself was sacrificed to the state. The intransigents who had forced Mussolini's hand at the end of 1924, and who continued to indulge in counterproductive acts of violence, had to be neutralized. By the time the dullard Achille Starace was appointed party secretary at the end of 1931, the PNF had been thoroughly devitalized and depoliticized, reduced to a "predominantly choreographed role."[11] More than 180,000 refractory elements had been expelled, primarily *squadristi* from the provinces who refused orders to demobilize and enroll in the Militia.[12]

The end of party pluralism and reduction of the PNF to a subservient state organ were mirrored in the syndical sphere. The so-called Rocco labor law (3 April 1926) made the existence of non-Fascist syndicates virtually impossible; by the end of 1927 the Socialist CGL and the Catholic Confederazione Italiana dei Lavoratori (CIL) disbanded themselves. Under the new Fascist labor law, the previously autonomous syndical sphere was placed firmly within the state orbit. All syndical entities had to be jurdically recognized by the government, their statutes had to be officially registered, and their leadership approved. Whereas employer syndicates generally elected their own leaders, who then had to be formally approved, leadership was appointed from above in workers' associations. These appointments were typically based on political criteria; frequently the individuals involved had neither productive nor syndical experience.

During the period of liberal–Fascism, Mussolini repeatedly attempted to co-opt the urban–industrial proletariat; after 3 January 1925, he abandoned any hope of winning the confidence of this refractory force. Speaking to the Chamber on 26 May 1927, he concluded that Fascism would have to wait for a new generation of workers, indoctrinated by Fascist youth organizations, to replace the present generation of *irriducibili*.[13] A decade later, the situation was unchanged, according to intelligence reports.[14] Discipline was to be exacted where consensus had failed. Not only were workers legally compelled to join the Fascist syndicates, but to ensure that these never

---

[11] Aquarone, *Stato totalitario*, pp. 182–3.
[12] De Felice, *Mussolini il fascista*, 2:184; Aquarone, *Stato totalitario*, p. 181.
[13] Mussolini, *Scritti*, 6:45.
[14] Aquarone, *Stato totalitario*, p. 228.

became a potent organizational force counterposed to the government, Rossoni's unitary confederation, the Corporazioni, was "busted" (the so-called *sbloccamento*) into separate federations.

We shall deal in detail soon with Confindustria's position on the Rocco labor law and future corporatist restructuring. Here, we shall note only that although the industrial association was eventually forced to yield in its opposition to such provisions as compulsory syndical monopolies and compulsory arbitration by newly created labor courts, it was successful in blocking creation of the mixed employer–employee syndicates favored by both Rossoni and Rocco. This was a highly significant victory and set a pattern for future corporatist development; though only one employer and one worker syndicate was recognized per category, they were to retain separate and distinct organizational structures and were not fused into one integral form.

It was suggested earlier that one motive force behind Mussolini's drift toward a more authoritarian state was the need to dominate domestic economic forces in an international market situation wherein the lira was falling uncontrollably in value and Italy was in need of foreign capital. This is not to say, however, that Mussolini's actual economic policy was either rational or in any way pleasing to Confindustria.

When a wave of speculation caused by a rise in prices and a fall in the purchasing power of the lira first became manifest in the spring of 1925, De Stefani enacted a number of stringent measures to control terms of investment (such as raising the discount rate and limiting the purchase of stocks on margin) and to limit the rush to buy foreign currency. The medicine proved inordinately strong and a sharp market decline followed. On 10 July 1925, De Stefani was replaced as minister of finance by Giuseppe Volpi, who had figured prominently in the industrial community (he had been president of the Società Italiane per Azioni and would be a future president of Confindustria).

In many accounts of Fascism it has been suggested that this substitution had been "forced" by Confindustria, and that Volpi's appointment was simple confirmation of the association's influence on economic policy. Although it would be absurd to argue that industry did not benefit, in the main, from Volpi's policies, a number of qualifying points must be made. First, Confindustria was certainly not alone in its criticism of De Stefani's policy; the file compiled on this matter in the Archivio Centrale dello Stato is replete with criticism by the entire business community (e.g., various municipal chambers of commerce, stock exchanges, and currency account agents).[15] Second, unlike De Stefani, a former economics professor who had no diplomatic experience, Volpi possessed extensive diplomatic and international commercial expertise, a quality – it should be stressed – to be highly valued in negotiating Italy's war debts and foreign loans.[16] Third, on the single most important economic issue of his ministerial tenure, the revaluation of the lira, Volpi was totally unsuccessful in preventing Mussolini from imposing his famous "quota 90" (Volpi consistently argued for an exchange rate of 125 lire to the pound sterling). In some measure, just as Mussolini had appointed Farinacci party secretary to exert his will over the Fascist intransigents, the appointment of Volpi and the quota 90 may be seen, as De Felice has suggested, as a similar "proof of force" against the industrialists.[17]

Ten days before his famous speech at Pesaro (18 August 1926), when Mussolini pledged to defend the lira "to the last breath, to the last drop of blood," he wrote to Volpi claiming that "the fate of the regime is tied to the fate of the lira."[18] Regardless of the consequences, the lira was to be set at 90 to the pound sterling, the exchange rate in effect shortly before the March on Rome. Despite warnings from industrialists on the effects this would have on exports, prices, salaries, and employment, Mussolini was unmovable. Each time industrial representatives approached him to reconsider, Mussolini threatened an even lower rate than 90. In response to Volpi, he suggested a rate of 80–85; in response to Conti, a rate of 50![19] Olivetti, understandably preoccupied with the matter, commented, "that man . . . is really capable of killing all of us by bringing the exchange rate to five lire to the dollar."[20]

In his diary on 22 May 1927, Conti caustically attacked the notion

---

[15] ACS, Presidenza del Consiglio dei Ministri, 1925, 9/9, n. 872.
[16] Volpi, beyond numerous international dealings on behalf of the Banca Commerciale, had negotiated a peace treaty with Turkey in 1912 and was governor of Tripoli from 1921 to 1925.
[17] De Felice, *Mussolini il fascista*, 2:223, 239–43, 282. On the quota 90 policy see De Felice, "I lineamenti politici della 'quota novanta' "; Clough, *Economic History*, pp. 229–72; Salvatore La Francesca, *La politica economica del fascismo* (Bari: Laterza, 1972), pp. 14–20.
[18] De Felice, "I lineamenti politici della 'quota novanta,' " p. 379.
[19] Ibid., p. 384; Conti, *Taccuino*, p. 241.
[20] Sarti, *Fascism and Industrial Leadership*, p. 115.

that currencies could be altered by simple force of will, regardless of objective economic and technical constraints:

> Plight of dictatorships: to give rise to flatterers who, to ingratiate themselves with the master from whom they await favors, interpret his ideas, pushing them to a limit beyond reality and common sense. The discourse of Pesaro has created the popular illusion that one can go on to infinity with the revaluation, arriving even to the point where the lira is worth its weight in gold. In the world of journalism and politics, because of excessive significance given to the discourse, there has been a servile and obsequious attempt to attribute to Mussolini magical powers capable of changing the realities of life.[21]

Failing to alter Mussolini's position on revaluation, Conti – acting against the advice of Volpi – openly attacked the policy on the floor of the Senate in the presence of Mussolini, who was angered at the prolonged applause that followed Conti's oration. *La Stampa*, controlled by Agnelli, attempted to publish a full text of Conti's speech, but it was sequestered.[22] Subsequent entries in Conti's diary are replete with criticism of the regime's economic irrationalism; in one instance, Mussolini responded to Conti's criticism by baldly asserting that economic matters "never stopped the March of History."[23]

Conti was not alone in his criticism. Through Volpi and his own intelligence reports, Mussolini was fully aware of the industrialists' dissatisfaction. Some, like Riccardo Gualino, were particularly upset with how the consequences of revaluation would conflict with the industrial expansion which had been promoted during the earlier productivist period of liberal–Fascism. In a terse letter to Mussolini, Gualino minced no words:

> Think that the Italians were pushed to construct, construct, construct, construct; recall that the industrialists were advised to augment their plants to increase exports and were praised for this. And then consider how today those who followed these governmental directives are being punished. They find themselves with factories devalued because of revalued debts, with grandiose plants built and paid for while the pound sterling equaled 125 lire. They must devalue their capital and reduce production without hope of later being able to retake lost ground since, in the meantime, foreign firms are occupying markets which Italians had conquered with so much effort.[24]

---

[21] Conti, *Taccuino*, p. 241.
[22] Ibid., pp. 242–4.
[23] Ibid., p. 350.
[24] De Felice, "I lineamenti politici della 'quota novanta,'" p. 390.

The consequences of the revaluation policy were as the industrialists had feared. In only six months, from September 1926 to February 1927, domestic prices rose 18 percent, while in England and the United States they declined by 8 percent. Exports dropped from 18.2 billion lire in 1926 to 15.2 billion lire in 1927, damaging key sectors, like automobiles, which exported 61 percent of its product (compared to American auto firms, which exported 14.3 percent of their product, and German auto firms, which exported 7.7 percent).[25] The general index of industrial production (1922 = 100) dropped from 165.8 in 1926 to 163.7 in 1927, while unemployment rose from 181,439 to 414,283.[26] Even during the Depression, the lira was kept at an artificially high rate, despite the fact that the dollar and the pound sterling were devalued; the number of lire a pound sterling would buy went from 90 to 58.07 in December 1934, while the rate of lire to the dollar also fell from 18.60 to 11.73. As Clough observed, this made Italian goods and services noncompetitive in foreign markets, hurting the tourist trade as well.[27]

Confindustria, while unsuccessful in opposing the revaluation policy, nevertheless succeeded in negotiating a number of extremely important compensatory trade-offs. Production costs clearly had to be lowered; and in the absence of an equally strong countervailing syndical force, this burden was placed on the workers. A 10–20 percent salary reduction was put into effect in October 1927, but exploitation of labor was intensified through greater use of labor-saving machinery and Taylorism, that is, an accelerated rhythm of production at lower pay.[28] This amounted to Americanism without Fordism: in the United States, at least initially, the rationalization of work was accompanied by salary increases. More than ever before, Italian factories became rigidly hierarchical, and managerial authority was absolute. To some degree, this was but an extension of earlier development; however, because of new constraints imposed by the revaluation policy, this form of industrial discipline became objectively necessary rather than simply desirable. As we shall see, the government's labor policy gave full recognition to this imperative,

[25] Romeo, *Breve storia*, p. 156.
[26] Ibid., pp. 155–7; Clough, *Economic History*, pp. 229–30.
[27] Clough, *Economic History*, p. 251.
[28] Paola Fiorentini, "Ristrutturazione capitalistica e sfruttamento operaio in Italian negli anni '20," *Rivista Storica del Socialismo* 10 (Jan. 1967): 144–5.

blocking any attempt by Fascist syndicates to interfere with the "technical ordering of production," thus guaranteeing a military-like, chain of command in the factory.

Still another irrational aspect of Fascist economic policy which preoccupied the industrialists was the so-called ruralist campaign that began in 1927 and its concurrent demographic battle. To some degree, ruralism was a product of Mussolini's inability to resolve a number of the economic and political contradictions previously mentioned. The great industrial expansion that had occurred during the productivist period of liberal–Fascism had the consequence of increasing the population of urban–industrial workers. This group, as we have seen, was the least politically secure of all; the relationship between Fascism's failure to penetrate the urban–industrial proletariat and ruralism was made clear by Mussolini in his previously mentioned speech of 26 May 1927. While on the one hand admitting that Fascism would have to wait for the present generation of "the so-called proletariat" to die off, on the other Mussolini attacked urbanism as destructive, a "sterilizing force" when compared with the attributes of *piccola proprietà rurale*. Not only was the urban population politically insecure, it also had a greater propensity to consume than the rural population; thus, in Mussolini's eyes, it disproportionately contributed to Italy's inflation. Speaking to the Senate in June 1926, Mussolini praised the rural population "rooted in the soil, those who are still sufficiently barbaric not to overvalue the so-called advantages of modern comforts."[29] For political, economic, and demographic reasons it was thus necessary, as Mussolini said, to "ruralize Italy, even if this takes thousands of millions and half a century."[30] From such premises there ensued an expensive, though marginally successful, effort at land reclamation and preventing migration from the countryside to the city.

Confindustria could not publicly criticize this absurd effort at increasing the population of an already overpopulated nation or condemn ruralism as such. Benni and Olivetti argued instead that agriculture alone was incapable of sustaining Italy's growing population, that industrial investment resulted in proportionately higher employment opportunities than rural investment, and that all of the great

---

[29] Mussolini, *Scritti*, 5:294.
[30] Melograni, *Gli industriali e Mussolini*, p. 198.

modern nations had a solid industrial base.[31] In the end, ruralism turned out to be an empty threat, articulated for essentially ideological reasons. Mussolini was still too much of a realist to place industry in jeopardy and thereby exacerbate Italy's already formidable economic problems. Nevertheless, ruralism was still another indeterminate and irrational factor which Confindustria had to endure, not of its making and certainly not to its liking.

Nonintegral corporatism

Before beginning our treatment of nonintegral corporatism, it will be instructive conceptually to explore what its opposite, integral corporatism, might have signified; the practical shortcomings of the Italian case might thereby be more clearly delineated. For an ideal type of *corporatisme intégral et pur,* we turn to perhaps the most lucid, analytically rigorous treatise on corporatism written during the interwar years, Mihail Manoilesco's *Le siècle du corporatisme.* Trained as an engineer and later becoming a professor of political economy in Bucharest, Manoilesco also held a number of ministerial posts in Romania (minister of communications and public works, minister of industry and commerce, governor of the National Bank).[32] An authority on the various schools of corporatism developing in Europe during the 1930s, he was naturally a keen observer of Italian theory and practice. Together with Werner Sombart, he was one of the honored foreign guests invited to attend the international corporatist conference held at Ferrara in May 1932.

For Manoilesco, corporative entities would have to be "integral" and "pure": integral, because they would include all the associations of civil society; pure, because they would themselves constitute the base – *la seule base légitime* – of legislative power. In contrast with Rocco's conception, corporations were not to be subordinated to

---

[31] Benni's speech of 20 March 1926 to the Grand Council may be found in ACS, Segretario particolare del Duce, fascicolo Gran Consiglio del Fascismo, sottofascicolo A, 1926; *OI,* 1 Jan. 1929; also Olivetti's long introduction to a volume entitled *L'industria Italiana,* published by Confindustria in 1929 to commemorate its tenth anniversary.

[32] On Manoilesco see Philippe Schmitter, "Reflections on Mihail Manoilesco and the Theory of the Political Consequences of Delayed Development on the Periphery of Europe," in Kenneth Jowette, ed., *Social Change in Romania, 1860–1940* (Berkeley: Institute of International Studies, 1978), pp. 117–39.

external state power; rather, they were to be the unique source of such power.[33] The state would have no external power of *surveillance* over the corporations, for that would contradict *le principe de l'autonomie corporative*. A corporative parliament would control executive power, not be subordinated to it; "this is a major point which distinguishes *corporatisme pur* from *corporatisme subordonné*."[34] In *Le siècle du corporatisme*, Manoilesco presents a model of corporatism predicated on a decentralized, rather than centralized, state, recognizing, at the same time, a division of power.[35]

Measured against the conception of *corporatisme intégral et pur*, Italian Fascism was found wanting. Classes in the old sense – that is, hierarchy based primarily on property – had not been abolished but actually legalized in the juridical recognition of separate and distinct syndicates representing capital and labor. To Manoilesco this was little more than *"une concession à la tradition du dix-neuvième siècle et au monde ancien."*[36] Instead of being *intégral et pur*, Italian corporatism was *partiel et subordonné*. The corporations were neither unitary nor did they embrace all of civil society; moreover, they were subordinated to the external authority of the state.[37] Instead of promoting the decentralization and division of political power, the Fascists had concentrated such power in the hands of the state executive, which showed little confidence in the corporations: "The Fascist system strikes us as much too rigid. It doesn't seem to give the corporations the confidence they merit. It might be said that these daughters of the regime are suspected by the regime itself."[38]

Manoilesco's skepticism toward Italian corporatism was shared by Bottai, Spirito, and Pellizzi, all of whom envisioned a thoroughgoing technocratic transformation of society. Instead, the Italian corporative edifice lacked substance; it merely occupied formal political space, while all significant decisions were made elsewhere. With characteristic wit, Salvemini entitled a chapter on corporatism in *Under the Axe of Fascism* "Looking in a Dark Room for a Black Cat Which Is Not There." The Ministry of Corporations was created in 1926,

---

[33] Manoilesco, *Le siècle du corporatisme* (Paris: Librairie Félix Alcan, 1934), p. 17.
[34] Ibid., p. 274.
[35] Ibid., pp. 150–1, 348.
[36] Ibid., pp. 108–9.
[37] Ibid., pp. 94, 150, 345.
[38] Ibid., p. 276.

but the corporations themselves were not constituted until 1934. As Alberto Aquarone observes:

> But the creation of the ministry without the corporations – the outer cover, so to speak, without the substance – was characteristic of Fascism in relation to the corporative system: an attitude of giving preference always to the administrative, and therefore traditional, aspect rather than to the political and economic aspects, which should have provided its really creative and original features.[39]

If, in 1926, there was corporatism without corporations, Bottai bitterly noted that by 1934 there were "corporations without corporatism."[40] The context in which corporative bodies were finally born was fully compromised and bureaucratized. According to Pellizzi, they were "dead before birth" in the "intentions and effective possibilities of the regime."[41] The National Council of Corporations (Consiglio Nazionale delle Corporazioni), which had been hailed with such fanfare at its founding in 1929 as a bold new organ of coordination and planning, was a rubber-stamp body with no effective autonomy or power. According to Louis Rosenstock-Franck, the major French student of Italian corporatism, *"Le Conseil ne crée pas, il enregistre."*[42] Aquarone, author of the major monograph on the juridico-institutional development of the Fascist state, aptly characterized the council as *"più fumo che arrosto."*[43] Elsewhere, Aquarone has written that the council's

> duties were mainly consultative, but it was also given legislative powers to regulate collective economic relations between the various categories of production; this provision was described by Mussolini as revolutionary, "the keystone of the whole law." In point of fact, the National Council of Corporations made very little use of these powers, whether by fixing prices, establishing quotas, or imposing particular methods on producers. For the most part, agreements in this field continued to be concluded directly between the categories concerned and were negotiated at the ministries under the watchful eyes of the higher authorities. Even the Council's consultative role was of no great importance; indeed many of the major decisions of economic policy in those years – for example, the creation of IRI – were taken without even asking the opinion of that organization which the Duce had defined as the

[39] Alberto Aquarone, "Italy: The Crisis and Corporative Economy," *Journal of Contemporary History* 4 (Oct. 1969): 44.
[40] Cassese, "Programmatore anni trenta," p. 427.
[41] Pellizzi, *Rivoluzione mancata*, p. 65.
[42] Rosenstock-Franck, *L'économie corporative*, p. 298.
[43] Aquarone, *Stato totalitario*, p. 193.

General Staff of Italy's Economy, "the thinking brain that prepares and coordinates."[44]

Aquarone's reference to the Istituto per la Ricostruzione Industriale (IRI) is highly significant, for that parastate organ, created in 1933 to counter the effects of the Great Depression by assuming devalued stocks and securities held by the major banks, had no effective links whatsoever to the corporative system. IRI, the major example of state intervention in the Italian economy, was placed in the hands of a neutral, non-Fascist technocrat, Alberto Beneduce, a former Socialist who had actively opposed Fascism before withdrawing from political life in 1925.[45] Not only was economic policy formulated and administered outside the corporative framework, but the actual relationship between labor and capital within the factory was substantively unaltered by the new order. As Felice Guarneri, a high-level Confindustria functionary, observed: caught between the industrialists, who feared that the corporations would interfere with the productive process, and the Fascist syndicates, which sought to use the corporations to "penetrate the citadel from which they had been hitherto denied," the corporative state "remained in the misty confines of a vague doctrinal conception and in the verbal experiments of tiresome academicians."[46]

Here, however, it is necessary to insist upon a rather important point. It would be incorrect to presume that the growing superficiality of corporatism was an "immanent" or "necessary" development, so obvious as to be taken for granted by those to whom it might have otherwise constituted a substantial threat. We should prudently refrain from invoking some form of suprahistorical logic and approach the failure of corporatism in concrete political terms; that is, by identifying the interests and accounting for the actions of those most likely to have been adversely affected by integral corporatist development. Corporatist proponents, as we have seen, were divided among themselves in terms of both theoretical conception and practical intent; fragmented into antagonistic groups, they represented no autonomous and unified force that could be mobilized in the name of

---

[44] Aquarone, "Italy: The Crisis," pp. 44, 49; Sabino Cassese, "Corporazioni e intervento pubblico nell'economia," Il Foro Amministrativo 7 (July 1969): 481.

[45] Sarti, Fascism and Industrial Leadership, pp. 116–25; see also Grifone, Il capitale finanzario, pp. 78–110; Romeo, Breve storia, pp. 158–95.

[46] Guarneri, Battaglie economiche, 1:144–9.

corporatism. Against corporative development were three separate, though convergent, sources of opposition: the PNF, the state bureaucracy, and, of course, employer associations, most significantly Confindustria.

Elements within the PNF resented the fact that corporatist institutions were displacing the original preeminence of the squads and local *fasci*. The corporatist tide appeared to carry with it a whole host of parasites and *arrivisti*: theoreticians, philologists, and experts who had little to do with the movement's "heroic struggles" and "intransigent spirit." In a letter to Mussolini, dated 1 January 1930, Augusto Turati, secretary of the PNF, openly polemicized against the emergent corporative framework: "a much too cumbersome complex of organisms which legitimate their existence by, above all, complicating things. Technocrats, annotators, experts, judges, and professionals have ascended." Turati argued that the essential problem of corporatism was regulating labor contracts, and this would best be done through direct negotiations between syndicates that authentically represented employers and workers. Two years later, an intelligence report on the PNF stated that corporatism had been the object of malicious comments "by Fascist elements who neither see, comprehend, nor approve of its function."[47]

The traditional state bureaucracy feared that a competitive corporative bureaucracy might undermine its authority and prerogatives. As early as September 1927, Belluzzo, minister of the national economy, put Bottai on notice that his ministry had no intention of becoming a subsection of the Ministry of Corporations.[48] Traditional state bureaucrats adjusted to the new order by becoming nominal Fascists while continuing, more or less, to operate as they had earlier. Even within the new Ministry of Corporations, executive positions remained a monopoly of the traditional bureaucracy. Aquarone observes that ten years after its constitution, all incumbents of upper- and middle-level posts had entered the state administration before the March on Rome.[49] De Felice also has called attention to the "subterranean action" – ranging from passive resistance to outright

[47] ACS, Segretario particolare del Duce, Carteggio Riservato, 1922–43, fascicolo 242/R: Gran Consiglio, sottofascicolo 8, inserto A; Aquarone, *Stato totalitario*, pp. 196–7, 530–2.

[48] Aquarone, *Stato totalitario*, p. 137.

[49] Ibid., p. 75.

obstructionism — of the pre-Fascist bureaucrats against the corporative order.[50] Lacking a firm basis within the bureaucracy itself, or the possibility of creating an entirely new one, all Bottai and his followers could do was write occasional and rather futile polemics in *Critica Fascista* against the "very little comprehension that certain zones of the bureaucracy have demonstrated toward the corporative order."[51]

We come now to the third source of resistance to the development of an integrally corporative order: Confindustria, intent upon "saving the savable" and conserving some measure of autonomy. It sought to do so by simultaneously pursuing three concomitant strategies: (1) entering into a symbiotic relationship with the state bureaucracy to jointly preserve traditional structures and processes of interest mediation; (2) preempting and conserving as many categories as possible within its organizational sphere during the process of corporative ordering (*inquadramento*); and (3) contributing to the ideological and juridical development of corporatism, *malgré eux*, in such a manner as to render corporatism as innocuous as possible.

Collusion between Confindustria and the traditional state bureaucracy, noted by Aquarone and De Felice,[52] was hardly a phenomenon that escaped the attention of Bottai. On 30 August 1927, the young undersecretary of corporations wrote a memo to Mussolini "on the conduct adopted by the Confederation of Industry against every legislative initiative directed toward developing, concretizing, and delineating the tasks, organization, and powers of the Ministry of Corporations and of corporative organs." While other employer associations had "positively contributed" in an effort to develop legislative norms which would regulate terms of employment, "the Confederation of Industry profited by having had prior knowledge of the proposal, applying pressure on various Ministries in the hope of provoking difficulties with the presentation of the project. The Confederation has declared itself absolutely opposed to the very concept of such a law." In like tone, Bottai continued his attack on Confindustria:

Now it does not seem, above all, in line with discipline that such behavior be permissible for an association which is subject to the vigilance and tutelage of the Ministry of Corporations. If the unitary principle of the state is to become

---

[50] De Felice, *Mussolini il fascista*, 2:345–6.
[51] *Critica Fascista*, 1 Oct. 1927; De Felice, *Mussolini il fascista*, 2:345–6.
[52] Aquarone, *Stato totalitario*, p. 193; Renzo De Felice, *Mussolini il Duce* (Turin: Einaudi, 1974), pp. 157–78.

a reality, it must have contact with the Government exclusively through this Ministry, never acting in contrast with acts of censure and criticism as if it were a state in the state or a power superior to the state. The mentality of those who direct the Confederation of Industry has remained unchanged. Openly, and without even feigning to conceal it, they pursue a line which aims at the annulment of the corporative order of the state, and thus the Fascist regime. . . . I beg Your Excellency to have this report discussed in the Council of Ministers, where the Confederation of Industry boasts – upon what basis I do not know – of possessing the patronage of several Ministers.[53]

In fact, Bottai's accusations and suspicions are partially confirmed by the testimony of Confindustria's Felice Guarneri:

For their part, industrialists, represented by Confindustria, were decisively opposed to such a corporative orientation, having as allies – strange to say – a major part of the state administration that dealt with production, exchange, and credit. These people feared that intervention by the corporations might limit their scope of initiative or render their tasks more difficult and burdensome. . . . With that the corporations, structurally heavy, choked by complicated procedures, surrounded by the distrust of producers and the state administration, began their life as institutions operating in a void, without influence either upon the organization of the state of which they were part or upon the organization of production over which they were to have become coordinating and disciplinary instruments.[54]

Still another source, Giuseppe Belluzzo, minister of the national economy, alludes to Confindustria's colonization of the state apparatus in pursuit of its private interests. "Men of great ability and experience, the best elements of the Italian bureaucracy, have long since passed into the framework of the confederations of employers. *It is the confederations and not the state who control the national economic system,* and who have created a state within a state to serve private interests which are not always in harmony with the general interests of the nation."[55]

One might call Confindustria's second strategy "preemptive *inquadramento.*" *Inquadramento,* it will be recalled, refers to the "framing" of particular categories within more inclusive corporative structures. In a corporative order, the relative strength of any given sectoral confederation is partially dependent upon the scope of its

---

[53] ACS, Presidenza del Consiglio dei Ministri, Gabinetto Atti, 1919–36, busta 297.
[54] Guarneri, *Battaglie economiche,* 1:282–5.
[55] Gaetano Salvemini, *Under the Axe of Fascism* (New York: Citadel, 1971), pp. 384–5.

inclusiveness in relation to real or potential adversaries. Here, Confindustria was particularly effective in absorbing as many categories under its jurisdiction as possible, thereby preventing them from gravitating toward other organizational orbits. Though it lost its transportation sector, which eventually became autonomous, Confindustria gained landlords, artisans, and industrial cooperatives.[56] Most important, it absorbed industrial managers and experts, categories that might have posed a substantial threat if autonomously organized or placed within the Fascist labor syndicates. Initially, Rossoni's syndicates argued that industrial managers and experts were employees and therefore should be part of their organization. When this effort failed, and industrial managers and experts were absorbed by Confindustria, the Fascist syndicates then unsuccessfully launched a protracted campaign demanding their autonomous status (congruent, they argued, with the so-called three factors of production: *capitale, lavoro, e tecnica*).[57] From another perspective, were managers and experts granted autonomous status, Bottai's group might have had greater success in realizing its aspiration of constituting a new managerial elite which would displace the old industrial class and directly control production. So long as industrial managers and experts were subsumed by Confindustria, such a project was virtually impossible.

We come now to Confindustria's third strategy, subverting corporative development from within through subtle ideological and juridical posturing. Paradoxically, corporatism's growing organizational marginality was met — judging by the number of tracts written and orations delivered — with increased ideological salience. One elderly liberal, Ettore Ciccotti, complained to the Senate that a "new Tower of Babel" was being erected; so many corporatist publications were being produced that it appeared as if this were the major means whereby the government intended to solve Italy's unemployment problem. Rather than actually read a massive new volume recently printed by the government, Ciccotti chose to weigh it instead: "*4 chili e 900 grami,*" he reported to the Senate with mordant precision.[58]

Confindustria self-consciously contributed to this growing corpo-

---

[56] Sarti, *Fascism and Industrial Leadership,* pp. 83–4.
[57] *LI,* 21 Dec. 1922, 28 Dec. 1922, Jan. 1923, 28 Apr. 1926; *Lavoro Fascista* (subsequently cited as *LF*), 10 Dec. 1929, 17 Jan. 1930, 1 Mar. 1931, 7, 21, Aug. 1932, 1, 2, 14 Nov. 1932.
[58] *Atti Parlamentari,* Senato, 14 Mar. 1930, p. 1967.

ratist mystification and pseudohistorical humbug that inundated Italy, hoping that potentially conflictual issues relating to production might thus be dissipated within the dense obfuscatory mist. A reader who chronologically wades through Confindustria's publications from 1919 through the Fascist epoch will observe an abrupt break in 1926, as liberal–Fascism gave way to nonintegral corporatism. Before 1926, Confindustria showed nothing but outright contempt for "theoretical abstractions" concerning productive relations; it had been openly critical of corporatism as such, as well as other notions of an *economia associata* which arose from the war mobilization. After 1926, such criticism suddenly ceased, and Confindustria publications gave conspicuous coverage to corporatism, but corporatism of the most innocuous stripe: Gino Arias's Thomistic abstractions, accounts of ancient Rome and the Middle Ages, and critiques of the French Revolution and the hedonism of liberal political economy.[59] In fact, criticism was vented only against particular corporatist theoreticians whose formulations posed a potential threat, and this occurred but twice: when Massimo Fovel attempted to demonstrate that a "true" corporatist salary could only be reached when profit was set at zero,[60] and when Ugo Spirito argued at the Ferrara conference on corporatism that property should be transferred from private hands to the corporations.[61] Nor did the intellectually dexterous Gino Olivetti fail to rise to the occasion; the liberal Confindustria theoretician, who had made innumerable anticorporatist statements prior to 1926, became an overnight expert on the subject. By 1933, Olivetti had given a course on corporative law at the University of Turin and had authored two hefty volumes on the subject which were cited in official government bibliographies.[62] Nothing was taken for granted; at the 1932 Ferrara conference, Confindustria sent the largest single delegation and Olivetti personally led the broadly based attack against Ugo Spirito's "Communist thesis" on proprietary corporations.

While ideologically promoting an innocuous interpretation of corporatism, Confindustria sought to develop within Fascism a new technocratic legitimacy for the industrialist, one that might counter

[59] *OI*, 15 Dec. 1927, 15 Jan. 1928, 1 Feb. 1928, 1 Mar. 1928; *Rivista di Politica Economica*, March 1929, July 1929, Oct. 1932, Mar. 1934, July 1934.

[60] *OI*, 15 Jan. 1932.

[61] *OI*, 15 May 1932.

[62] *OI*, 1 Mar. 1929; *10 anni della carta del lavoro* (Rome: n.p., 1937), bibliografia essenziale, p. 591.

Bottai's group, carve out an autonomous niche for industrial production within the emergent corporative order, and help justify the intensification of labor (rationalization, Taylorism, mechanization) triggered, as we have seen, by Mussolini's monetary policy. Finally and unambiguously, Confindustria now had to define itself in terms of Fascism. The problem was to select an appropriate ideological formula, and here the only one appropriate was that of Fascism's early technocratic aspirations. Olivetti lost no time in building upon Confindustria's pre-Fascist productivism, such that the "captains of industry" alone were projected as the indispensable, technically competent harbingers of a new Fascist productive order.

Conspicuous, in this regard, was Confindustria's founding of Ente Nazionale Italiano per l'Organizzazione Scientifica del Lavoro (ENIOS) in October 1925, the very same month, significantly, in which the association formally renounced its agnosticism before Fascism, signed the Pact of Palazzo Vidoni, and began to chart its new course. The executive council of ENIOS was nominated by Confindustria, and its general secretary, not surprisingly, was Gino Olivetti. Besides publishing a journal, the mission of ENIOS was to disseminate propaganda stressing scientific management and the efficacy of private initiative. Additionally, ENIOS occupied space that otherwise might have been filled by technocrats unsympathetic or even hostile to private industry; it was, after all, the only officially recognized Italian association concerned with industrial rationalization. Obviously pleased by the foreign respectability brought to his regime by ENIOS's sponsorship of an international conference on scientific management held in Rome during early September 1927, Mussolini personally greeted delegates from all the major industrialized nations, as well as from Russia, Cuba, Argentina, India, and Siam. Among the honored guests – Confindustria left no stone unturned – was the widow of Frederick Winslow Taylor, founder of the very concept of scientific management.[63] Besides his course on corporative law in Turin, Olivetti also gave a course on scientific management in Rome, where he later helped create, through ENIOS, an institute of industrial psychology.[64]

[63] OI, 15 Feb. 1926, 15 Apr. 1926, 1 June 1926, 1 Apr. 1927, 1, 15 Sept. 1927; on ENIOS see also Giogio Pedrocco, Fascismo e nuove tecnologie (Bologna: CLUEB, 1980); and Giulio Sapelli, Organizzazione lavoro e innovazione industriale nell'Italia tra le due guerre (Turin: Rosenberg & Sellier, 1978).
[64] OI, 1 May 1930, 15 Nov. 1932.

Confindustria's new Fascist–productivist posture was based, as we have suggested, on its earlier precepts: an autonomous realm of production that followed its own objective logic and therefore was subject to its own separate exigencies; the indispensability of private initiative; and the technical necessity of absolute managerial authority. Dropped, at least formally, were explicitly liberal assumptions concerning an inviolate public–private distinction, syndical and political pluralism, and a doctrinal bias against state intervention. For these was substituted the compulsory, hierarchical "leadership principle" of Fascism. Interestingly, the word "capitalist" was never uttered; instead, the industrialist was an "organizer of production," the "chief of the enterprise," or, as Mussolini himself put it, an "officer" of production (as distinguished from "soldier–workers"):

The capitalist, as depicted in pre-Socialist literature, no longer exists. There has been a separation between capital and management, between industrialist and capitalist. Capital, with the emergence of joint-stock companies, has been dispersed to the point of pulverization. . . . While capital and the capitalist have become anonymous, the manager of the enterprise has become primary, the captain of industry, the creator of wealth. As in military terminology, the industrialists may be considered "officers" of production over the great army of workers.[65]

Mussolini's formulation, opportunely repeated by Confindustria whenever the occasion called for it, was but a more accentuated version of statement that Benni had made two years earlier, on 30 March 1926, before the Grand Council. Instead of likening production to an army, Benni compared the factory to a small technical state.

In substance, even the factory is a small technical state in which one must apply the same principles of authority which govern a state. Permit me to say that just as the parliamentary state failed to meet its objectives, so with the constitutional factory. Interference with authority is not possible; in the factory there can be only a technical hierarchy required by the productive order itself. To insist upon this principle, and upon its complete application, corresponds perfectly to the necessity of industry, to the interest of the Nation, to the Fascist concept.[66]

Such ideological posturing, interesting perhaps in itself, would be of limited political significance had not Confindustria been able to have it translated into public policy, and especially to have it incorporated within the new juridical norms and positive law of the Fascist

[65] Mussolini, *Scritti*, 6:231.
[66] ACS, Segretaria particolare del Duce, 27/242/R5, sottofascicolo 4, inserto C, 30 Mar. 1926.

state. Although this will be treated in detail later, we might note here Confindustria's success in having the following three principles explicitly specified in the Carta del Lavoro: (1) it was management's responsibility to order production; (2) it was the responsibility of employer associations to promote the perfection of production and the reduction of costs; and (3) state intervention was appropriate only when private initiative was lacking or inefficient or when the vital interests of the state were at play. Although the Carta del Lavoro, the so-called Magna Carta of corporatism, was only a statement of principles and lacked de jure status, it nevertheless served as the normative basis for future positive law and set the parameters for further corporatist debate. The industrialist, or more generally, the employer, was thus afforded privileged status from the very outset of Italian corporatism. This need not have been the case. As we shall see, the other employer associations were prepared to accept a far more restrictive draft of the Carta del Lavoro until Confindustria, alone, succeeded in inducing the government to make necessary revisions, including the abovementioned principles.

Whereas both Bottai's group and the Fascist syndicates separately tended to interpret Mussolini's pronouncements, the Carta del Lavoro, and successive pieces of corporatist legislation as *points of departure,* Confindustria insisted that these were to be *points of arrival,* basic and immutable principles. Having gained acceptance from Mussolini and from the Carta del Lavoro for its productivist rationale, Confindustria could then oppose all proposals that compromised the autonomy of industry on "technical grounds," rather than naked class interest, stemming from the "exigencies of production," which, of course, only it fully understood. Indeed, "exigencies of production" became a Catch-22-like phrase, formally recognized in law and fully respected in administrative practice. Thus, for every compulsory norm promulgated to "discipline" or to "regulate" production, industrialists were always afforded discretionary latitude. For example, a law was issued stating that workers were to be hired exclusively through employment offices run by the Ministry of Corporations, giving preference to Fascists and veterans.[67] Industrialists,

---

[67] Compulsory hiring through employment offices of the corporations was already anticipated in the Carta del Lavoro, Article 22 and was put into effect with the law of R.D. 29 Mar. 1928, n. 1003 – Disciplina nazionale delle domande e dell'offerto di laboro. See *Codice Corporativo 1926–35* (Rome: Cremonese Editore, 1935), pp. 81–3.

however, as "organizers of production" knowing the technical requirements for each post, were free to choose among all workers – Fascist and non-Fascist – registered at these employment offices. As we shall see, there were numerous complaints that industrialists used this latitude to discriminate against Fascist workers, to which Confindustria replied that, as "good Fascists," they could not denigrate the principles of hierarchy and competence by hiring unqualified workers simply because they wore black shirts! Such discretionary latitude in hiring became all the more significant during the Great Depression, when the Ministry of Corporations and the Fascist syndicates both attempted, with little success, to impose strict employment guidelines on industry, guidelines that Confindustria maintained were neither technically feasible nor economically justified. Even under conditions of massive unemployment, industry had to follow its own logic and not be subject to unwarranted interference.

From a general treatment of the transition to nonintegral corporatism, we turn our attention now to the specific development of Confindustria during this period. We shall concentrate on its analysis of the changed political arena and its new strategy vis-à-vis Fascism: working from within to make sure that the prerogatives of industry would be protected; seeing to it that corporative institutions and practice were kept spinning within a relatively harmless circle beyond whose periphery all substantive economic decisions were made. The major contours of this strategy, as well as the general constellation of sympathetic and hostile forces, have already been delineated. The task now is one of narrowing the focus to the confederation itself, filling in with greater detail its relation to the nonintegrally corporatist state. What follows, then, is an account of Confindustria's actions with regard to a series of consecutive corporatist measures from 1925 to 1934, measures that laid the foundations for a new institutional order.

1925: the year of transition

As we saw earlier, the Matteotti crisis was brought to an abrupt termination with Mussolini's speech of 3 January 1925. Neither the Aventine secessionists nor the liberals who remained in Parliament, singly or in aggregate, had been able to constitute an alternative. After its September 1924 communiqué to Mussolini, Confindustria took no official position on the Matteotti crisis; individual industrialists tended to reflect the larger division among progovernment and opposition liberals. On 13 January, a final meeting of the opposition liberal deputies was called by the three former prime ministers: Giolitti, Salandra, and Orlando. Participating were a number of industrialists, including Motta and Ponti. Several days later in Milan, progovernment liberals held a rally whose participants included Benni and a number of other prominent industrialists. Conspicuously absent were Pirelli and Conti.[68] Writing in his diary on 7 January, Conti expressed shame at the turn toward dictatorship, finding consolation only in the fact that he himself had not voted confidence in the government. In his analysis, the Aventine secession had been a tragic mistake, as the Fascists were thus left masters of the Chamber. Unlike Giolitti, who remained at his post, the secessionists bore some measure of responsibility for what had happened by having renounced, with no alternative strategy, any possibility of effective legal opposition in Parliament.[69]

Meanwhile, the *svolta a sinistra* within Fascism was still in effect. Intransigents and syndicalists, who had forced Mussolini's hand during the closing days of December 1924, continued their attacks against the bourgeois *fiancheggiatori*. Thus, *Lavoro d'Italia*, Rossoni's journal, threatened on 3 January that "1925 must be the year of clarification." As De Felice suggests, Mussolini was not yet strong enough to stifle the leftist current but opportunely chose to exploit the "syndical arm" against industrialists, hoping thereby to pressure them toward a position of direct and unqualified collaboration.[70] On 23 January, the Grand Council passed a resolution encouraging Fascist syndicates to strike if necessary, while at the same time criticizing "resistance and obstacles on the part of some groups of employers."[71]

During February and March, a number of strikes were called by the Fascist syndicates, most notably involving metalworkers in Brescia and Milan, demanding salary concessions and exclusive representation. Despite unprecedented demagoguery by syndical leaders like Rossoni and Razza (e.g., threatening to use the squads and the *manganello* against industrialists) and support for the Fascist syndicates by the PNF, the industrialists held firm. After remaining somewhat

[68] Melograni, *Gli industriali e Mussolini*, pp. 117–18.
[69] Conti, *Taccuino*, pp. 213, 201.
[70] De Felice, *Mussolini il fascista*, 2:91.
[71] *Gran Consiglio primi dieci anni*, p. 180.

aloof so as to appear "above the parties," but nevertheless concerned that the strikes might adversely affect Italy's delicate situation in international money markets, Mussolini stepped in and mediated a compromise on salaries only. FIOM, however, called for a two-day continuation of the strike in Milan, which, according to police estimates, was respected by 75 percent of the workers, thereby underscoring, once again, the Socialist confederation's status as labor's true representative.[72]

The strikes, which ended with minimal salary concessions and no recognition of monopoly status for the Fascist syndicates, had proven embarrassing for Fascism; once again, the facts belied verbal commitments to class collaboration. On 25 April, the Grand Council passed another resolution on the syndical question, threatening the freedom of action of both the Fascist syndicates and Confindustria. The use of the strike was now to be considered an "act of war," and accordingly, the Fascist syndicates would have to obtain "preventive authorization" from the PNF before they could initiate such action. On the other hand, "some employer organizations" would have to respect the provisions of the Pact of Palazzo Chigi, "otherwise Fascism would take necessary measures, breaking the monopoly of those organizations which placed their individual interests against the general interests of production and the Nation."[73]

Rossoni, aware that this new restriction on strikes would further inhibit the ability of his syndicates to compete effectively for the loyalty of industrial workers, sought once again to act directly on Confindustria, hoping to force some agreement from above. He publicly charged industrialists with trying to divide the working class to maximize their own interest: "At the moment when Fascist syndicalism is on the verge of becoming an absolute force in the field of labor, the industrialists, playing a most dangerous game, have tried to resuscitate the old red organizations. . . . With the famous *divide et impera* the industrialists think they are playing a clever game, but they are grossly mistaken." With that, Rossoni renewed his campaign for *corporativismo integrale:* monopoly representation, a unitary employer–employee structure, compulsory arbitration.[74]

Confindustria's reaction to the 25 April Grand Council resolution

---

[72] Cordova, *Sindacati fascisti*, pp. 356–78; Uva, *Stato corporativo*, pp. 92–172.
[73] *Gran Consiglio primi dieci anni*, pp. 193–5.
[74] *LI*, 3 May 1925.

was swift and unambiguous. Benni, addressing an assembly on 28 April, reaffirmed the association's traditional commitment to syndical pluralism, calling "unprofitable" any attempt to impose "an obligatory and monopolistic regime on this matter which was still in continuous formation and evolution." Although Confindustria was always prepared to "promote effective economic development in harmony with the interests of the country," it rejected the very idea of *corporativismo integrale*. The assembly then passed a resolution denying that it had forgotten the "spirit of the Pact of Palazzo Chigi" and affirming the full right of industry tranquilly to continue its autonomous task, not becoming "an experimental field for every social and political initiative." Here, the association repeated the same fundamental objection to external political interference in the realm of production that it had made earlier against Giolitti's reforms and Gramsci's factory council program. As Benni reiterated, "the field of industry must not become an experimental field for all the tendencies, all the passions, all the political parties."[75]

Actually, from the very beginning of 1925 Confindustria had been attacking the concepts of syndical monopoly and compulsory arbitration in its academic journal, *Rivista di Politica Economica* and in its *Annuario 1925*. Regarding the concept of a juridically recognized syndical monopoly:

One must not forget that syndicates exist and live for the protection of those whom they represent in the competitions between labor and capital, more or less pacific, more or less collaborationist. In the determination of a point of equilibrium in these competitions, a number of economic and social factors and coefficients are at play that operate effectively only when they are left free to run their course. The state, in absolute terms, can have no function other than impeding these competitions from departing from the bounds of legality. . . . But it cannot intervene and substitute its judgment for the action of economic and social factors and coefficients without rendering more difficult, if not impossible, the attainment of a point of equilibrium, without establishing a fictitious, artificial, and therefore mistaken equilibrium destined to cause unjustified damage to one of the parties and often to the economy of the country.[76]

[75] *OI*, 1 May 1925.
[76] Giovanni Balella, "Sul riconoscimento giuridici dei sindacati," *Rivista di Politica Economica*, Jan. 1925; Umberto Ricci, "Il sindacalismo giudicato da un economista," *Rivista di Political Economica*, Feb. 1925.

This, of course, is none other than the position that had been put forth by Olivetti during the formative prewar period of associational development. As had been argued earlier, the Confindustria *Annuario 1925* went on to attack state intervention in labor conflict, especially compulsory arbitration, as "antijuridical and antieconomic; by now definitively condemned in theory and in experience." By state intervention, Confindustria meant not only final resolution of conflicts but any interference in "the internal and external life of the syndicates." By "compelling determinate categories of citizens to associate," the state would necessarily abuse and distort the purpose of syndicates.

Compulsory arbitration was impossible, Confindustria argued, because one could neither rationally calculate and balance all the economic, psychological, political, and social factors at play in labor conflicts nor establish a neutral organism truly above the parties involved, capable of adjudicating purely on the basis of set juridical formulas. This was especially true for Italian jurists: "let us say it frankly: in Italy, unfortunately, even among bourgeois classes, an anticapitalist mentality prevails which detests, despises, or envies the industrialist much more than the *rentier* and which does not comprehend the function that the industrialist performs in the national interest." Furthermore, in those cases where compulsory arbitration had been tried (e.g., Australia, Norway, Kansas) the results were counterproductive; there occurred even more strikes than before.[77]

Besides these reasons of long-standing principle, industrialists resisted the monopolist aspirations of Rossoni's syndicates on two further grounds. First, the Fascist syndicates were nonrepresentative and had no substantial footing in the factories; they were an extraneous element whose only source of potential support was political, the PNF and the government. Second, as Rossoni himself observed, it was to the industrialists' advantage to keep workers divided, not only between Fascists and Socialists but also between Socialists and Communists. As we noted, industrialists refused to concede monopoly status to the Fascist syndicates during the strikes of February and March. During the late spring and summer, they refused another of Rossoni's demands: abolishing the worker-elected *commissioni in-*

[77] *CGII Annuario 1925*, pp. 417–32.

terne and replacing them with *fiduciari di fabbrica* appointed by the Fascist syndicates.

The issue of the *commissioni interne* became particularly explosive in Turin, where industrialists adopted a policy of dealing directly with these bodies rather than with the syndicates. On the one hand, this enabled them to keep the city's militant workforce fragmented; on the other, it enabled them to avoid having to choose publicly between Socialist and Fascist syndicates. As Agnelli declared in *La Stampa*, Turinese industrialists dealt directly with their workers' elected representatives; "that outside the factory the *commissioni* belong to this or that organization is something which does not preoccupy us at all because it is not our concern."[78] In a similar fashion Mazzini dealt with the prefect of Turin, who expressed concern that "only in Piemonte contracts are not stipulated with the Fascist syndicates." Mazzini, president of the LIT, responded that "the industrialists, even those closest to Fascism, maintain that the *commissioni interne,* regularly elected by the entire workforce, constitute the most adept organ for normal relations with management."[79]

Since the *commissioni interne* were freely elected, Fascist representatives never were able to compete with those nominated by FIOM or the Communists (who ran separately). In the April and June elections at Fiat, FIOM and the Communists won a clean sweep.[80] On 18 August, knowing that a representative of the Fascist syndicates was en route from Rome to negotiate a new contract with Fiat, Agnelli hastily assembled some members of the *commissioni interne,* all Communists, and negotiated a preemptive pact. When the Fascist representative arrived, Agnelli informed him that it would be impossible to negotiate a new contract, since another pact was already in force.[81]

Meanwhile, Mussolini had not committed himself to one side or the other. During the early summer of 1925, he gave signs of trying to placate the industrialists, after first having encouraged the Fascist syndicates. On 22 June, he told a Fascist congress in Rome that "we must have syndicalism without demagoguery."[82] On 8 July, he sent the following telegram to all prefects:

[78] *La Stampa*, 17 Mar. 1925.
[79] Abrate, *Lotta sindacale*, p. 438.
[80] For a breakdown of the Fiat elections see Uva, *Stato corporativo*, p. 209.
[81] Abrate, *Lotta sindacale*, pp. 439–40.
[82] Mussolini, *Scritti*, 5:109–18.

Secretary of industrial confederation alerts me to a rekindling of syndical conflicts promoted by the Fascist Corporazioni. You must energetically make it understood that in this most delicate moment for Italian finance such agitations are crimes harmful to the Nation. Avoid them vigorously and when they break out conclude them as rapidly as possible.[83]

It was also in July that Mussolini substituted Volpi for De Stefani as minister of finance. As Volpi almost immediately set out to negotiate Italy's war debt and foreign loans, it appears that Mussolini's major concern at the time was maintaining labor peace so that Volpi's mission might meet with success. Accordingly, he called for Confindustria and the Fascist syndicates to meet in Rome during September and reconcile their outstanding differences.

At the same time, a polemic was raging within Fascism over the deliberations of the Committee of Solons, whose corporatist recommendations were close to Bottai's position. The Solons, disregarding Rossoni's strident objections, voted against unitary and obligatory syndicates. This polemic, carried out mainly between Rossoni and Bottai, was pushed off dead-center at the end of August with Mussolini's approval and support for a position laid out by Alfredo Rocco, soon to be minister of justice. Rocco advanced a conception of corporatism more suitable to Mussolini's immediate interests, one asserting the dominance of the state over syndicates and individuals.[84] As early as 1920, Rocco had advanced the basic outlines of this conception: mixed obligatory syndicates, compulsory arbitration, creation of labor courts, and an end to "class self-defense" (strikes and lockouts).[85] Bottai attacked the conservative, top–down nature of Rocco's conception, which saw corporatism only as a disciplinary – not as a creative – phenomenon, but he was publicly reprimanded by Mussolini and judiciously relented.[86]

Given what has been said, the fall 1925 meetings between Confindustria and Rossoni's Corporazioni must be viewed in terms of imminent corporatist restructuring, not mere rapprochement. Judging from private and public communications, Confindustria resisted as long as possible Rossoni's demands for monopoly status and the substitution of Fascist *fiduciari* for the freely elected *commissioni interne*. The

---

[83] Cordova, *Sindacati fascisti*, p. 416.
[84] Ibid., pp. 424–6.
[85] Rocco, *Scritti*, 1:641–2.
[86] Cordova, *Sindacati fascisti*, p. 427.

industrial association clearly recognized that some preference would have to be conceded to the Fascist syndicates, but not at the expense of cutting all ties with non-Fascist organizations.

In Turin, the LIT met on 15 September to discuss the situation. Acutis, head of the Itala automotive firm, complained that the Fascist syndicalists were men "of the worst quality, without even that minimum of courtesy which is necessary in negotiations where there is a contrast of interest." Grottanelli argued that it would be dangerous to abolish the *commissioni interne,* especially if they were to be replaced by *fiduciari.* Fano agreed, adding that the limited penetration of the Fascist syndicates was hardly the fault of the industrialists. Tedeschi held that "opposition to nonelected *fiduciari,* appointed from the outside, ought to be uncompromising." Freschi argued that although "in the past the government could intervene in labor disputes as a third party with a moderating function, with the *fiduciari* the industrialists would be dealing with an emanation of the government whose intervention would now be permanent, direct, and partisan."[87]

On 25 September, Olivetti briefed the LIT on the status of syndical negotiations in Rome. Confindustria had been forced to yield on the question of monopoly status and abolition of the *commissioni interne.* In the face of "complete inaction" on the part of non-Fascist workers' syndicates, Confindustria "could not put itself against both the party and the government, which today attribute to the decisions of the Confederation a character of support or opposition on the question of exclusive representation by the Corporazioni." As for the *fiduciari,* Olivetti reaffirmed Confindustria's absolute refusal to compromise; "no governmental or corporative authority within the factory would be acceptable."[88]

Another source on the Rome meetings is the following interview (*La Giustizia,* 25 September 1925) with "a noted industrialist from northern Italy" who had been a participant:

I have no reason to hide the fact that the prevalent thought in the industrialists' camp is decisively antimonopolist; thus, the decision of Confindustria should have been contrary to the request of the Fascist syndicates. I don't believe, however, that the conclusions of our meetings will be completely negative for obvious reasons.

[87] Abrate, *Lotta sindacale,* pp. 441–2.
[88] Ibid.

— Would you tell us the reasons why you and the majority of your colleagues are against monopoly?

They are double in nature: theoretical and practical. Is not the principle on which property rights are based economic freedom? Why then should we industrialists renounce it? Aside from disturbances to production which might follow recognizing a monopoly that would offend the syndical rights of a conspicuous part of the workers, we have no interest in assuming binding obligations with any organization. We want and need to have our hands free.

— But then how can one explain the fact that at the meeting at Palazzo Vidoni the representatives of Confindustria adhered to Rossoni's position, at least insofar as one can gather from the communiqué released by the Corporazioni?

That is not exact. In the Rome meeting of 10 September, the representatives of the Corporazioni posed two questions: abolition of the *commissioni interne* and syndical monopoly. The industrialists resisted one as much as the other. Then, in transition, they declared that they might yield on suppressing the *commissioni interne* but reaffirmed their formal reserve on the question of monopoly. This attitude was fully confirmed in successive industrialist conferences.

— We cannot hide our amazement in learning that the representatives of Confindustria battled the representatives of the Corporazioni over the defense of the *commissioni interne*.

That's not the point. They saw in the substitution of *fiduciari* for *commissioni interne* a remedy worse than the affliction. Speaking for myself, I have no difficulty in declaring that the recognition of *commissioni interne* – of course, when their competence is clearly defined – never bothered me. . . . If one overlooks a period of aberration, during which some tried to make them organs of workers' power in the factory, no one can deny that *commissioni interne* have acted, generally, as an element of moderation and conciliation. . . .

— Do you believe that the Corporazioni will adopt an attitude of intransigence if the industrialists decide against their request for monopoly?

Everything depends upon the wishes of those in control. It seems that the Prime Minister, in a recent meeting which took place here in Milan, took account of the positions put to him by the industrialists. But everything, at this time, might already have changed.[89]

Mussolini, who had been wavering between syndical pluralism and monopoly status during the final days of September, finally opted for the latter. The Pact of Palazzo Vidoni between Confindustria and the Corporazioni was signed on 2 October. Each organization assumed

---

[89] Melograni, *Gli industriali e Mussolini*, pp. 133–5.

exclusive representation for their respective categories, the *commissioni interne* were abolished but *not* replaced by *fiduciari*. If there was disappointment in the industrialist camp that Confindustria had conceded on the questions of monopoly status and abolition of the *commissioni interne,* there was manifest relief that no compromise was struck on the question of *fiduciari*. One anonymous Turinese industrialist related to *Il Mondo* on 3 October that

we knew that the *commissioni interne effectively and exclusively* represented the workers. These Fascist *fiduciari* which appeared on the horizon instead represented too much and too little. Too little, if one takes account of their scarce following among the masses; too much if behind them stood the Fascist Party and – as we are repeatedly told – the government. I had often endured bitter struggles with the *commissioni interne,* and some of these have left bitter memories, but I never questioned that behind these men who came to talk with me, sometimes discourteously, stood most of my workers. Instead, if and when I were to talk with Fascist *fiduciari,* who would I really find before me? The workers? Certainly not, because – at least here in Turin – workers who belong to the Corporazioni must number about zero, and even if the reform had passed, the *fiduciari* certainly could not delude themselves or make others believe that they really were the interpreters of the workers' thoughts and sentiments. Then perhaps they represent the Fascist Party? I do not believe that the party has the right to interfere in internal syndical questions. The government? In this case, being a man of order, I would yield. But if that's the way it is, I would prefer it if the Prefect would send for me and say: "I order you to sign the agreement on the following terms." I could then appeal to higher authorities if the decision seemed unjust to me; but in the meantime, I would comply, knowing clearly how I ought to behave. But it wouldn't be easy to do this much with the *fiduciari* of today, who would simply present themselves as the exponents of the workers and then later could transform themselves into spokesmen for the party or, worse, *missi dominici* of the government.[90]

Although, with the Pact of Palazzo Vidoni, Rossoni finally obtained his major demand, monopoly representation for the Fascist syndicates in all labor pacts, it proved a Pyrrhic victory indeed. With the abolition of the *commissioni interne* and the failure to have *fiduciari* substituted in their place, workers' syndicates were stripped of any presence whatsoever within single factories. As Aquarone observes: "The Pact of Palazzo Vidoni, while ensuring a single syndicate normative power in matters relating to collective labor contracts, at the same time sanctioned an authoritarian factory structure, stripping

[90] Cordova, *Sindacati fascisti,* pp. 428–9.

from the workers of individual firms any possibility of directly monitoring the application of contractual norms in their favor."[91] At the signing ceremony, Mussolini declared that in the factory there must be "one hierarchy, a technical one," adding that "there should be no talk of *fiduciari*."[92] With these words, to be tactically repeated by Confindustria later on, absolute managerial authority was officially sanctioned. Furthermore, as Olivetti publicly affirmed, "if monopoly represented a gain for the workers, it also represented an advantage for the industrialists."[93] Confindustria now became the exclusive, legally sanctioned representative of all industry, extending its control over firms that had formerly remained outside the associational fold. It was no longer possible for a rival industrial confederation to form, or for determinate industrial interests to arrive at separate agreements with the Fascist syndicates, thereby breaching the associational front.

Before proceeding, one final observation must be made regarding the Pact of Palazzo Vidoni of 2 October 1925. If this marked a definitive rupture with Confindustria's prior theory and practice, representing a fatal step from liberalism toward corporatism, it should be fairly obvious that the association's hand had been forced. Doctrine and attitude had to make way for survival within a fundamentally changed political context in which Confindustria, alone, could no longer risk pitting itself against the regime. Outside the Fascist orbit remained only the wasted residue of liberalism, Socialism, and the *popolari,* none of which had been willing or able to pose as a viable alternative or even act to contain further Fascist development. That Confindustria was left with no alternative was recognized by other notables at the time. On the very day that the pact was announced, Guglielmo Emanuel wrote to Luigi Albertini:

The industrialists say that faced with a lack of energy on the part of the liberals, they did not want to expose themselves to a split. A month ago the government demanded the recognition of a syndical monopoly, announcing – at the same time – that otherwise this would be decreed. The industrialists limited themselves to fighting against the *fiduciari*, although they had no hostility toward the *commissioni interne,* which the Corporazioni wanted to suppress. They added that for the moment (as had already happened in

---

[91] Aquarone, *Stato totalitario,* p. 122.
[92] *OI,* 15 Oct. 1925. *Impero,* 7 Oct. 1925, reported Benni stating that discipline in the factories was to be "rigorously respected" and that there was no place for "extraneous elements" such as *finduciari.*
[93] *Giornale d'Italia,* 6 Oct. 1925.

various provinces like Liguria, Toscana, and Emilia) the workers have submitted to contracts negotiated by the Corporazioni. If in the future the CGL
regains strength, it will be up to them to overcome the Fascist monopoly. For
now, they are not moving and one cannot ask the industrialists to fight if they
will not themselves fight.[94]

The CGL and the Socialists were busy exchanging mutual recriminations with the Communists. At no time either before or after the
Vidoni pact did they singly or jointly demonstrate in any significant
way. With justification Abrate notes:

Paradoxically, the strongest defenders of the liberty of the trade unions,
which themselves were more than ever afflicted by incurable internal disputes,
were the representatives of industry. In trying to protect their own autonomy,
they had to defend the principles of free trade-union representation. In the
face of the almost complete passivity or the negative results from the spas-
modic activity of the large workers' federations, Industry, in October 1925,
was obliged to enter the Pact of Palazzo Vidoni. Through the exclusive and
mutual recognition of Confindustria and the Corporazioni, this pact signaled
the decline of Italian trade unionism for the next twenty years.[95]

October 1925 was to be the key month in the transition from
liberal–Fascism to nonintegral corporatism; it began with the Vidoni
pact and ended with Mussolini's new formula "everything in the
state, nothing outside the state, nothing against the state."[96] Four
days after the Vidoni pact, the Grand Council passed a resolution
explicitly rejecting the pluralistic corporatist recommendations of the
Committee of Solons, affirming instead the authoritarian, etatist, corporatist conception of the new minister of justice, Alfredo Rocco:
"The Grand Council of Fascism recognizes that the syndical phenomenon, a necessary and irrepressible aspect of modern life, must be
controlled and *inquadrato* by the state." One obligatory worker and
employer syndicate was to be recognized per category, a Labor Court
was to be established for the purpose of compulsory arbitration,
and the so-called *autodifesa di classe* (class self-defense) was to be
prohibited.[97] This resolution of the Grand Council was then developed into a comprehensive new syndical law, bearing the name of its
author, Alfredo Rocco. On 25 October, the initial draft of this "law
on the juridical discipline of labor relations" was presented to Parlia-

[94] Melograni, *Gli industriali e Mussolini*, p. 140.
[95] Abrate, *Lotta sindacale*, p. 11.
[96] Mussolini, *Scritti*, 5: 140.
[97] *Gran Consiglio primi diece anni*, pp. 204–6.

ment. With characteristic hyperbole, Mussolini called it "the most courageous, the most audacious, the most innovative, therefore the most revolutionary" of the laws yet passed by the Fascist government.[98]

Frontal opposition to the syndical law – whose passage, in any case, was a certainty – would have been strategically disastrous for Confindustria. Now that it was patently obvious to all concerned that no liberal, Socialist, or Catholic alternative to Fascism was any longer possible, the industrial association could not afford to be isolated from a regime intent upon making policy decisions affecting its vital interests. It was better to adopt a more subtle strategy, working from within to minimize the potential threat to industrial autonomy by raising "technical," rather than principled, objections to specific details, especially those that were more substantive than formal in nature. Thus, during November, when the syndical legislation was still in committee, Benni and Olivetti dropped the doctrinal opposition they had always maintained regarding the legitimacy of any juridical incursions into syndical relations, raising instead specific objections against mixed syndicates and compulsory arbitration. In this more limited endeavor they were successful. By the time Rocco's legislation reached the floor of Parliament, mixed syndicates were reduced to a vague provision whereby employer and worker associations might occasionally meet in some common form, but the associations themselves were to represent employers and workers *separately;* that is, no integral organism was created, the word *corporazione* was not even mentioned.[99] Arbitration before a newly constructed Labor Court (Magistratura del Lavoro) was made compulsory for agriculture but *not* industry.

When, in early December, the syndical legislation was debated in Parliament, Rossoni and Barbiellini-Amidei (an agrarian representative) challenged the exclusion of industry from compulsory arbitration. As Sarti suggests, Benni and Olivetti found themselves in a difficult political corner: having to oppose compulsory arbitration and yet not explicitly state their lack of faith either in Fascist syndicates or in the regime.[100] Not surprisingly, they attempted to extricate themselves from this dilemma by emphasizing the fundamentally tech-

---

[98] Aquarone, *Stato totalitario,* p. 126.
[99] See Article 3 of the Rocco labor law; Aquarone, *Stato totalitario,* p. 44.
[100] Sarti, *Fascism and Industrial Leadership,* pp. 69–78.

nical nature of industrial relations (and thereby the specific function and competence of the industrialist, as opposed to a juridically trained labor magistrate), invoking Mussolini's explicit recognition of the principles of hierarchy and discipline. Benni argued that the figure of the modern industrialist was progressively distinguishing itself from the figure of the capitalist; the former was an organizer of production who directed his firm, not in his private interest, but in the superior interest of the nation.

> This directing function we have always defended and always will; it is the unique reason for being of the industrialist. It is his competence, his experience, his intuition and will that constitute the real and solid bases of every factory. . . . It is not possible to admit interference with industrial authority when the fundamental elements of his function are in question: the possibility to select collaborators as he sees fit, to allocate tasks in such a way as he deems best, to imprint on his firm that organization of labor and force of unitary impulse without which industry cannot survive or prosper. . . . A factory is a miniature state, which, as the example of Italy demonstrates, prospers and multiplies when the will of he who knows best has the possibility of making itself valued and obeyed.

Benni reminded the Chamber that Italy was still in a delicate financial situation and thus caution should be exercised. If the syndical reform were to have any chance of success, it should not compromise those principles of hierarchy, discipline, and order that Mussolini himself had articulated. For this reason, Benni added, "in the present situation we are against the reconstitution of medieval-like organisms" which might confuse or appropriate functions (a thinly veiled gibe at corporatism). Informed by the principles of hierarchy, discipline, and order, industrialists would support syndical reform with – as Benni clumsily if suggestively put it – "audacious prudence" (*con ogni audace prudenza*).[101]

When challenged by Rossoni and Barbiellini-Amidei on the fairness of establishing compulsory arbitration for agriculture and not for industry, Benni replied that when the legislation was still in committee he had opposed compulsory arbitration for both. A judge, he argued, lacked the technical competence to make such decisions: "I believe that intervention by a judge in establishing labor contracts would lead to the end of Italian industry." Rossoni cut Benni off: "Not for a song. With Bolshevik syndicates, yes; but Fascist syndicates, no. It is

---

[101] Ibid., p. 74.

an erroneous presupposition."[102] Barbiellini-Amidei accused Benni of indifference to the Fascist revolution, adding that industry never demonstrated the same unquestioning devotion to Fascism as did agriculture. "We are prepared to apply Fascist legislation; you are not." Wandering even further from the issues at hand, Barbiellini-Amidei then accused the industrialists of subsidizing the anti-Fascist press, while swearing that agrarians had never given a penny for such purpose.[103]

In response to repeated doubts as to the Fascist faith of Confindustria, as well as to Rossoni's pointed question on why the industrial association had not added the denomination "Fascist" to its name, Olivetti rose to speak. He and Benni, as representatives of Confindustria, were being treated like "Daniels in a lion's den." Barbiellini-Amidei responded that they might be Daniels but asked, who were the lions? Olivetti, of course, named Barbiellini-Amidei, haughtily adding, "though only one from the country." To the question why Confindustria had not added the denomination "Fascist," Olivetti responded somewhat elliptically: "When one accepts a law such as this, in which the intervention of governmental authority on men and things has reached such a point, one accepts not only the government but the regime." Yet, "for an intuitive question of dignity," Confindustria would not add the denomination "Fascist" upon the simple invitation of Rossoni.[104]

The difference in commitment to Fascism between industry and agriculture was alluded to also by Rocco in explaining why he, as minister of justice, had agreed to the exclusion of industry from compulsory arbitration. While agrarians had shown themselves to be "mature" enough for such a social experiment, "industrialists had held themselves apart from the Fascist renewal and were in a position of minor spiritual preparation." Their objection to compulsory arbitration, furthermore, might be due to "theoretical preconceptions derived from the doctrine of economic liberalism."[105]

On the question of compulsory arbitration, Mussolini finally intervened, stating that the syndical law would "remain mutilated" were industry to be afforded special treatment. In contrast with his position

---

[102] *Atti Parlamentari*, Camera, 9 Dec. 1925, pp. 4887–9.
[103] Ibid., p. 4888; ibid., 10 Dec. 1925, pp. 4914–19.
[104] Ibid., 11 Dec. 1925, pp. 4934–5; *L'Informazione Industriale*, 17 Dec. 1925.
[105] Rocco, *Scritti*, 3:973–4, 991–3.

at the signing of the Pact of Palazzo Chigi in December 1923, when he publicly lectured Rossoni on the essential differences between industry and agriculture, Mussolini now affirmed that there should be no "neat separation between the two economies." The Duce concluded that "as things stand, I believe that the Confederation of Industry can and will take this step because the advantages will well outweigh any inconveniences."[106]

After such a statement, Confindustria was left with no choice other than to accept the principle of compulsory arbitration, although Olivetti was quick to propose an amendment, which was passed, whereby individual labor contracts would be reviewed by the highest syndical associations before being subject to the authority of the Labor Court.[107] This right of preliminary review made the procedure of arbitration more time-consuming and cumbersome, encouraging the settlement of labor controversies outside court. For this and other reasons, the Labor Court played a rather marginal role; by 1927, only forty-one collective labor controversies had reached the court, and of these only sixteen were actually settled by court decision.[108] As Sarti points out, the enactment of the Rocco labor law signified an indefinite postponement of realizing the corporative state: "Organized industry was in the state but not of the state. The aspirations of revolutionary syndicalists, fascist revisionists, and integral nationalists were frustrated once again."[109]

Still, if Confindustria had been able to limit the more threatening aspects of the Fascist syndical reform, it did so at the eventual cost of its formal independence vis-à-vis Fascism. The December 1925 debates on the Rocco labor law indicated the degree to which Confindustria's fidelity to the regime was called into question. With further legislative reconstruction clearly on the agenda, Confindustria and its representatives could no longer afford to be isolated from fascism per se or absent from such key policy organs as the Grand Council. Already Olivetti's defense in Parliament of the association's political loyalty signaled a turning point in Confindustria's formal relations with Fascism. On 15 December, at Palazzo Venezia in Rome, Con-

---

[106] *Atti Parlamentari,* Camera, 11 Dec. 1925, pp. 4956–60.
[107] Ibid., pp. 4964–5.
[108] Aquarone, *Stato totalitario,* pp. 133–6.
[109] Sarti, *Fascism and Industrial Leadership,* p. 76; *Atti Parlamentari,* Camera, 12 Dec. 1925, pp. 4964–5.

findustria announced its official adherence to Fascism and its new denomination: the Confederazione Generale Fascista dell'Industria Italiana. In Turin, the president and vice-president of the LIT, Mazzini and Tedeschi, resigned in protest, though neither they nor any of the other association leaders were able to pose an alternative strategy to Olivetti's pragmatism. Indeed, Mazzini would later be elected as a deputy on the Fascist list in the 1929 plebiscite, join the executive committee of Confindustria, and in 1943 become a member of the Camera dei Fasci e Delle Corporazioni (which replaced the traditional Chamber of Deputies in 1939).[110] Fascist intransigents, on the other hand, resented the belated and opportunistic PNF membership of liberal Confindustria leaders like Olivetti and Agnelli. In this regard, perhaps the most revealing incident was Olivetti's being taken before a specially constituted Fascist "court of honor" by the "consul" of Mantova, Giuseppe Moschini.

The Olivetti–Moschini conflict began several days after Confindustria took on the Fascist denomination. Moschini, writing in *La Voce di Mantova* (19 December 1925), accused Olivetti of anti-Fascism and claimed that none other than Benni told him, "he's a Jew, what do you expect?" Drawing no public response from Olivetti, Moschini came to Rome and demanded the resignations of Olivetti and Benni, both "unworthy to head a Fascist organization." Moschini even went to the point of searching the city for Olivetti and, eventually finding him at a restaurant without a Fascist Party badge, proceeded to insult the Confindustria leader. As the urbane Olivetti did nothing but ignore Moschini's histrionics, the frustrated Fascist intransigent left in a huff and sent an insulting note – addressed to a "Fascist for personal advantage" – challenging Olivetti to a duel. A preliminary meeting of their respective seconds stopped a shade short of degenerating into a farcical brawl, and then the affair was referred to the secretary of the PNF, who appointed a court of honor headed by Enrico Corradini. Besides charging Olivetti with refusing to respond to his public attacks or to confess to being an "agent" of the Masons, Moschini asserted:

> 2 On 17 September 1924, after the Matteotti assassination, Olivetti presented the Prime Minister with a communiqué fixing the terms

[110] *OI*, 1 Jan. 1926; *Impero*, 17 Dec. 1925; Abrate, *Lotta sindacale*, pp. 446–7; Melograni, *Gli industriali e Mussolini*, p. 157.

for Confindustria's adhesion to the regime and asking for the suppression of the Militia.

3 Confindustria, of which Olivetti is Secretary, of having sent telegrams of condolence and reprimand concerning the death of
Matteotti, with the manifest intent of laying direct and indirect
responsibility upon the Fascist regime.

4 Olivetti of having signed a resolution of the Chamber which counseled the regime and the government not to alter the Constitution.

5 Olivetti of having given an anti-Fascist speech in Turin, following
the Matteotti assassination, though he had entered the Chamber as
a deputy on the ministerial list.

6 Olivetti of never demonstrating, either personally or through Confindustria, disinterested adhesion to the regime and to the party.

The court of honor affirmed Moschini's good faith and praised him
as a "Fascist of the most lively, energetic, and combative tempera-
ment." Nevertheless, it cleared Olivetti of being an anti-Fascist. Given
his political origins and "typically liberal spiritual formation," Olivetti was judged a "Fascist by adaptation."[111] Speculation concerning Olivetti's anti-Fascism continued, even among anti-Fascist exiles
based in Paris. Their organ *Corriere degli Italiani* attributed the following private remarks to the secretary of Confindustria on 6 April
1926: "Mussolini is a criminal idiot who understands nothing and is
capable of nothing. Fascist syndicalism is putrid, ignorant, and dis-
honest. I prefer a hundred times over dealing with the red *commissioni*. With them there was honesty and intelligence."[112]

Though it is doubtful that the prudent secretary of Confindustria
would have made such a statement, or have made it within earshot of
anyone remotely likely to have passed it on to the anti-Fascist press,
the fact that it appeared at all is indicative of the perceived skepticism
which marked Confindustria's "conversion" to Fascism. Just as Olivetti was judged a "Fascist by adaptation," the same might be said
of Confindustria itself. In the fundamentally altered political context
of 1925, the association adapted its principles, strategy, ideology –
even its name – in order to protect itself and industry from far more
radical Fascist measures which, no doubt, would have been instituted
as a vindictive *diktat* against the industrialists had Confindustria's
"agnosticism" continued. By now the choice was brutally simple:
either Confindustria would risk its survival and rule itself out of a

[111] See file labeled "Vertenza Olivetti" at HAUIT.
[112] Melograni, *Gli industriali e Mussolini*, p. 158.

political arena that had become exclusively Fascist, or it would formally adapt itself to the new regime in the hope of working from within to substantively preserve as much of industry's autonomy as possible. By now, for better or worse, there were no other alternatives; Fascism, so to speak was the only game in town.

Working from within

By the end of 1925, a new political framework was in the process of being erected, yet it still lacked substance and definition. Such ambiguity within the emerging regime led to a good deal of posturing and jockeying for position. Almost immediately, Confindustria and Rossoni's Corporazioni were vying to impose their respective syndical programs under the general terms of the new labor law.

Rossoni made it clear that for his organization the Rocco labor law was nothing more than a *punto di partenza* to be quickly superseded by the full institutionalization of *corporativismo integrale*.[113] This, he repeatedly asserted, was the "true Fascist syndical idea." To reject it, as did the industrialists, was therefore tantamount to rejecting Fascism itself.[114] Fascism called for a "totalitarian solution" to production in which each sector would be "rationally organized by a specific national corporation."[115] And if workers had given up their absolute liberty, equal sacrifice was to be exacted from the industrialists (whom Rossoni now referred to as "vampires" and "profiteers"). His tone becoming ever more threatening, Rossoni asserted, "We should not delude ourselves that words alone may disarm these profiteers; jail and the *manganello* are needed to discipline such rabble in any context, in any period."[116] At a minimum, the present leadership of employer organizations should be purged and replaced by sincere Fascists.

It is inadmissible to affirm absolute liberty for capital without giving it to labor to battle for its conquests. Fascism has denied worker classism, so it cannot therefore allow capitalist classism. If it is allowed for one, it will arise in the other. . . . If we wish to follow the intransigent method of Fascism, we must proceed in this way: select the ten percent of the employers who are

[113] *LI*, 20 Feb. 1926.
[114] *LI*, 23 Apr. 1926, 5 May 1926, 21 Apr. 1926.
[115] *LI*, 5 May 1926.
[116] *LI*, 9 Jan. 1926.

Fascists by sincere faith and place them at the head of the employer organizations, forcing the others to obey rather than remain as *condottieri* of these bodies.[117]

Furthermore, ad hoc and intermittent labor–capital organisms, like the mixed commission that negotiated the pacts of Palazzo Chigi and Palazzo Vidoni, were no longer adequate. After the Rocco labor law, they had to be replaced by permanent structures with authority to coordinate and discipline the various elements of production.[118]

Confindustria, for its part, wanted to preserve as much of the status quo ante as possible. In no case was it prepared to go beyond the general provisions of the Rocco labor law toward a more integrally corporative order. However, rather than chance a public polemic, the industrial association chose to utilize its influence within the traditional ministries and on the Grand Council, where Rossoni, by this point, had little support, especially after his erstwhile ally, the intransigent Farinacci, had been undercut by Mussolini. Benni, taking full advantage of his new permanent seat on the Grand Council, attacked Rossoni for his irresponsible demagoguery toward employers in general and Confindustria in particular. During the Grand Council meeting of 30 March 1926, when Benni likened the factory to a "small technical state," he countered Rossoni's concept of *corporativismo integrale* and charges of "classism" by invoking the Fascist principle of hierarchy and reaffirming the directive function of the industrialist:

It is said that Confindustria is classist, just as the Socialists used to say that it was reactionary. If "classism" means that it egotistically promotes the interests of only one part of the citizenry, I deny it. But if "classist" means that Confindustria defends the function and mission of the industrialist, well then I believe it is only doing its duty. The industrialist is the one who gives life to new initiatives, who gives impulse to the factories, who directs, who has responsibility for it not only before the stockholders but before the Nation. The industrialist is the one who confronts risks, who must resolve problems and overcome new and old obstacles, who gives confidence to the factory, who seeks out markets, who coordinates the efforts of all his collaborators, who searches for new methods to perfect production, who fights large and small battles every day, not only for himself but for his workers. This is the great function of the industrialist, that which gives him the right to exist, that which gives him the right to demand – in the fundamental interest of the Nation – to be left to perform his rightful duty with that tranquility and serenity welcomed by the Duce of

[117] *LI,* 21 Apr. 1926.
[118] Ibid.

Fascism for the future of the Patria. Never have the masses provided the energetic impulse for action: it has always been the leaders.

Corporativismo integrale, Benni argued, would conflict with the essential logic of productive hierarchy. Mussolini himself had declared that in the factories there could only be a technical hierarchy and no interference with managerial authority. Syndical relations, therefore, had to recognize the reciprocal rights and functions of industrialists and workers, not confuse them to the detriment of national production.[119]

Confindustria tried to further isolate Rossoni after the announcement, during the spring of 1926, that a new Ministry of Corporations was to be established. In a letter to Mussolini, Olivetti claimed that the industrialists were alarmed over "rumors" that Rossoni was to head the new ministry, placing "in Rossoni's hands not only the workers' organizations but also those of industry, agriculture, and commerce." While "not believing these rumors," Olivetti rhetorically asked: "Is it possible that supervision over these organizations might be entrusted to him, giving him the possibility of legally dominating them all?" Olivetti went on to suggest that the demagogic Rossoni might then use this position to further his own interests, not those of Mussolini. Better to appoint a "neutral person," Olivetti counseled, especially in so formative a period.[120]

Now it is highly improbable that the astute secretary of Confindustria seriously thought that Mussolini, disdainful of any autonomous concentrations of power within Fascism, would have appointed Rossoni – whom he personally disliked and distrusted – minister of corporations. Most likely, Olivetti used news of the new ministry as the pretext for a private, gratuitous attack on Rossoni, who, as luck would have it, was under attack from other quarters as well. Alfredo Rocco and A. O. Olivetti (a revolutionary syndicalist, longtime associate of Mussolini, and no relation to Gino Olivetti) both had earlier advised the breakup of Rossoni's intersectoral Corporazioni into separate syndicates; otherwise, they warned Mussolini, Rossoni might become too powerful to control effectively.[121] Rossoni himself

---

[119] ACS, Segreteria particolare del Duce, Carteggio Riservato, 1922–43, fascicolo 342/R, Gran Consiglio del Fascismo, sottofascicolo A, inserto C, Mar. 1926.

[120] A copy of Olivetti's letter to Mussolini, 1 May 1926, may be found in the historical files at Confindustria headquarters in Rome. It is partially reproduced in Abrate, *Lotta sindacale,* p. 459, and in De Felice, *Mussolini il fascista,* 2:273.

[121] De Felice, *Mussolini il fascista,* 2:270–1.

showed reserve toward the idea of a Ministry of Corporations as such, separate from and superior to his organization, and attacked those who publicly suggested dividing the Corporazioni into separate associations to match those of the employers. Rather, he argued, the employers should follow his example and form their own inter-sectoral body. "We must not renounce the unitary Fascist system; it is the employers who should imitate us."[122]

Meanwhile, Confindustria used its influence to modify some of the provisions contained in the original draft of the "norms for actua-tion." Rocco had made this available to Confindustria for review, and Olivetti immediately drafted a letter to Mussolini criticizing a number of provisions that would have shifted the balance of syndical power from central to regional associations, forced employer associations to contribute half the sum for the expense of assistance programs run by workers' associations, allowed prefects and ministers to suspend associational deliberations, and made such documents as company books available for public scrutiny. All the provisions were subse-quently dropped from the final draft, although Olivetti was unsuc-cessful in his attempt to retain Confindustria's transportation sector, which now became autonomous.[123]

After the Ministry of Corporations was constituted (without the simultaneous formation of actual corporations), the next step in non-integral corporatist development was promulgation of the Carta del Lavoro on the Fascist Labor Day (21 April 1927). Hailed by sympa-thetic literati as the Magna Carta of corporatism, derisively dubbed *fille de la Summa Theologica* by Rosenstock-Franck,[124] the Carta attained immediate international attention. Werner Sombart claimed it was the most audacious reform of recent times,[125] and subsequent authoritarian regimes in Iberia and Latin America would use it as a model for similar labor charters. Perhaps its historical status would have been less spectacular had it been known that the Carta was hardly the bold, organically conceived document announced by the Fascist press but rather the simple product of opportunism and com-promise.

---

[122] *LI*, 17 May 1926.
[123] The letter is dated 1 May 1926. Olivetti's handwritten draft may be found in the historical files at Confindustria headquarters in Rome. The final draft may be found at ACS, Presidenza del Consiglio dei Ministri, 1927, 3/5, n. 761.
[124] Rosenstock-Franck, *L'économie corporative*, p. 403.
[125] *OI*, 15 Nov. 1928.

As De Felice suggests, Mussolini's primary motive in proposing a labor charter was to offer the workers symbolic compensation for the unemployment and salary reductions they had suffered as a result of the quota 90 monetary policy. Here it was symbolically necessary to link the revaluation of the lira with a further corporative step that would formalize certain moral and social-welfare guarantees while at the same time place something in the otherwise empty hands of the Fascist syndicates that they could bring before their disgruntled proletarian constituency.[126] Indeed, throughout 1927 there was a rising tide of resentment within the PNF and the Fascist syndicates against employers who were "profiteering" from the austere fiscal measures, much as they had presumably done during the war. Suardo, head of the Ministry of Corporations, claimed that "the battle today is directed against the old economic *classe dirigente.*" After having broken the backs of the reds, Fascism must now move against the "*plutocrazia,* degenerates of capitalism, who will pay their share even if they cloak themselves under the sign of the Littoria."[127]

Rossoni's demagoguery, of course, went on unabated. The state should intervene against the "inertia of the *borghesia produttrice,*" who were nothing more than "inepts, if not deserters and enemies." Further: "now the inepts have no right to direct the economic life of the Nation; the state, which represents the interests of all, must correct the deficiencies of their activity when this shows itself harmful and dangerous for the country."[128] Once again, Rossoni called for formation of *fiduciari di fabbrica,* as well as equal division of corporate profits and compulsory hiring through employment offices run by his Fascist syndicates.[129]

At the very end of 1926, it was announced that the Grand Council would soon discuss fundamental principles to be incorporated in a Fascist labor charter. The various confederations of capital and labor were sent a preliminary draft and asked to transmit their comments to Turati, PNF secretary. Though this preliminary draft has apparently been lost, it seems to have reflected Rossoni's demands for concrete provisions on labor contracts, minimum salaries, working hours, and terms of employment to an extent that the em-

---

[126] De Felice, *Mussolini il fascista,* 2: 284.
[127] Ibid., pp. 283–4.
[128] *LI,* 29 Aug. 1927.
[129] *LI,* 12 Jan. 1927, 9, 24, February 1927.

ployers, eager to protect their freedom of movement, were unwilling to accept.

In an unusual display of unity and common frustration with having to deal with syndicates that presumed always to have the backing of the government and that were ready to denounce as "anti-Fascism" any sign of resistance, the five employer confederations sent a collective letter to Turati on 27 December 1926 affirming "the necessity to give the Carta del Lavoro a physiognomy completely different from that which would result from the draft given to us for comment." Though it is impossible, given the present state of documentation, to discern authorship of this letter, Confindustria's influence is readily apparent in the employers' effort to both discredit Rossoni and limit the scope of the prospective labor charter. The letter began with a scathing attack against "some heads of the workers' syndicates who continue to follow an orientation in complete contrast with the directives of the Regime."

Apart from the arrogant and sometimes uncouth manner which is used in certain cases, aside from the fact that even the most recently appointed secretaries of the smallest workers' syndicates assume the right to speak in the name of the Duce and the secretary of the PNF, it is deplorable that every time employer associations cannot agree to the demands presented, judging these contrary to the necessities and interests of production, their leaders are accused of anti-Fascism, of incomprehension, of a backward classist mentality and are threatened with disciplinary political action. For such militants, collaboration often means blind agreement to the most absurd demands they can think of advancing, while each resistance to their overbearing attitude comes to be defined as anticollaboration, anti-Fascism, and antinational conduct. . . . The trips that the head of the abovementioned Confederation makes in the various regions of Italy leave a path of morbid excitation in the spirit of the workers, who are not and cannot yet be completely transformed in their attitudes, excitation which leads to indiscipline, malcontent, and the rise of new pretexts that can be traced with mathematical precision to wherever the leader of the workers' syndicate has passed. One can well understand the reasons. The Honorable Rossoni, received and accompanied with sovereign honors by the highest authorities in the provinces with choreographed pomp – that is, to have the masses believe that he alone is the authorized interpreter of the thought and will of the regime – the Honorable Rossoni, we say, despite the collaborationist veneer of his words, never ceases, especially recently, to make accusations and ferocious insinuations in his speeches against the employers, their associations, and the leaders of these, resorting to images and expressions which too easily sway the minds and naive spirit of the workers.

The employers' letter, echoing Confindustria's long-standing contempt for developing legislative norms to regulate productive relations, claimed "it is not, in any case, possible to establish one unitary norm adaptable to the various branches of production, or within one branch, to all the various kinds of activity." Should the Carta attempt to specify and standardize labor contracts, this would lead to the "formation within the firms of a bureaucratic organization of production unresponsive – rather, prejudicial – to the exigencies of productive life." Once again, production was depicted as an autonomous realm, having its own inner logic and exigencies which defied both public regulation and public interference. This point was made rather sharply in the employers' criticism of norms relating to the hiring of personnel, specifically, giving preference to Fascist workers. Here the employers could invoke Mussolini's statements on productivism, technical hierarchies, and the elitist nature of Fascist syndicalism. As "good Fascists," the employers argued that hiring and the allocation of productive tasks must be based exclusively on competence, not merely the possession of a party card, and that the employer, as the organizer of production, was the only authority capable of making such judgments.

Determination of the technical, moral, and disciplinary requisites can only be left to the authoritative judgment of the employer because he is the leader of and responsible for production. He therefore has the right to choose his employees, the personnel he retains the most qualified – from a technical, moral, and disciplinary point of view – for the task to which he intends to assign them. Hence, it follows that any formula which might tend to establish obligatory preference can have neither judicial force nor practical effectiveness.[130]

As for the obligation to hire Fascists or give them preference, one should note that six months earlier, in June 1926, Benni had communicated Confindustria's view to Mussolini that a segment of the working class neither was nor wished to be Fascist. "As it is indispensable to also make use of such personnel, it is clear that the abovementioned obligation cannot be admitted." Even were employers constrained by law to give preference to Fascist workers, rather than be obliged to exclusively hire these, Benni warned Mussolini that "it would not impede – as practice has demonstrated – the

---

[130] ACS, Segreteria particolare del Duce, Carteggio Riservata, 1922–43, fascicolo 242/ R, sottofascicolo 5, inserto A.

manifestation of charges on the part of professional and political organizations against the judgment of industrialists, who in many places would certainly be accused of anti-Fascism whenever they might assume non-Fascist personnel."[131]

On 7 January 1927, the Grand Council passed a general resolution "reaffirming the right of the state to establish norms regulating production and national labor according to the principles of the new order whose premises are contained in the legislation on the discipline of collective relations."[132] Bottai, who in November 1926 succeeded Suardo as head of the Ministry of Corporations, was given the task of convening meetings between the interested parties and drawing up a mutually acceptable draft of the Carta. Bottai was successful in getting the other four employer confederations to agree to Rossoni's demands for concrete provisions regarding labor contracts and enlarged scope for state intervention through corporations yet to be formed. Confindustria, however, refused to retreat from the position articulated earlier in the collective employers' letter.[133] As Bottai informed Mussolini, "The two most intransigent positions are: on the one side, that of the Confederazione Nazionale dei Sindacati Fascisti, which intends to realize in the Carta *concrete* guarantees for the workers tied to a system a bit too rigid, one that might render more difficult the natural development of collective contracts conceived as the fundamental characteristic of the syndical order. On the other side is the position of the Confederazione Nazionale dell'Industria, which tends to assume till now an antagonistic stance with respect to the Corporation, something of fundamental importance in the Fascist conception."[134]

Bottai thus composed two separate drafts of the Carta: one reflecting the position of Rossoni and the four employer confederations; the other that of Confindustria. The former, besides enumerating specific guarantees on such conditions of work as night labor, promotions, vacations, sickness, and hygiene, recognized the state as "the supreme regulator and moderator of relations between productive

[131] Ibid.
[132] *Gran Consiglio primi dieci anni*, pp. 262–3.
[133] De Felice, *Mussolini il fascista*, 2: 291–2; Melograni, *Gli industriali e Mussolini*, pp. 191–3.
[134] De Felice, *Mussolini il fascista*, 2:292.

classes"; attributed to the Corporazioni an organizing, directive role in production; stipulated that during economic crises, profits would be reduced the equivalent degree as salaries; and severely limited the employers' ability to hire non-Fascists. The latter, far shorter in length and far more general in tone, stated that "private initiative is the fecund source of production"; attributed to the Corporazioni only a consultative role; assigned to employers' associations the tasks of pursuing technical perfection and disciplining production; and gave the employer full liberty to hire without obligation or preference regarding Fascist workers.[135]

After receiving Bottai's two drafts, Mussolini at first attempted to modify the one reflecting Confindustria's position but then assigned Rocco the task of striking a compromise. Despite Rocco's characteristic affinity for state intervention, his draft one-sidedly favored Confindustria's position: private initiative in the field of production was "the most useful and perfect instrument" in furthering the social interest; state intervention was justified only when private initiative was lacking or when the interests of the state were at stake; employer associations were charged with the technical perfection and coordination of production; and the provision on hiring was virtually identical with that of the pro-Confindustria draft. Perhaps because it was too conservative and supportive of Confindustria to accomplish its intended propagandistic objective, Mussolini and the Grand Council revised Rocco's draft by making a few concessions to Rossoni: from "the most useful and perfect instrument" in the field of production, private initiative was minimally downgraded to "the most effective and useful instrument"; while the employer was responsible for production, the worker was an "active collaborator"; while state intervention was still exceptional (when private initiative was lacking or the interests of the state were at stake), such intervention could now assume the form of control, encouragement, or direct management; employers had to hire workers through employment agencies run by the Ministry of Corporations but were allowed to choose among all the workers registered, giving preference to those belonging to the PNF and to Fascist syndicates.[136]

[135] Both drafts are reproduced in ibid., pp. 525–37.
[136] Ibid., pp. 537–47.

Despite the opportunism and compromise marking its origin, the Carta del Lavoro from April 1927 onward was to be the fundamental document of Italian Fascism, the seminal source of all subsequent ideological, juridical, and institutional development. Most important, positions advanced by the various conflicting currents within Fascism had to be based on particular constructions and selective readings of the Carta's thirty immortal, if eclectic, articles.[137]

In countering pronouncements made by Fascist syndical leaders and technocratic corporatists like Bottai and Spirito, who despite their own differences argued that the Carta superseded the free play of interests characteristic of liberalism, affording the state an active, directing role in the economy, Confindustria emphasized the primacy of individual initiative and absolute managerial authority. The state was not to substitute itself for individual initiative or play a directive role as such but instead was to represent – in some general sense – the national interest and function as a passive moderator between competing particularistic interests, not unlike the view of the state as umpire in more modern pluralist formulations:

It is intuitive, moreover, that the function of the state in the new order is not meant to be a substitute for or diminish individual initiative, which remains complete and is encouraged to attain the maximum efficiency possible. The function of the state is exclusively understood to harmonize the various interests, which remain distinct and unsuppressed. One could certainly not conceive of collaboration if there did not exist diverse interests, each having autonomous representation, while all contribute toward a common end, which is the general interest of the state.

In this light, Fascism was not to be understood as the restoration of medieval corporatism ("exhausted forms and systems of the past"), as "some superficial observers have believed." Instead, it has "realized, in a certain sense perfected, the 'productivism' of Saint Simon."[138] Fascism aspired to maximize the productive potential of the nation; this, however, was understood by Confindustria to be synonymous with maximizing private initiative. In contrast with the conception of integral corporatism, we may note Confindustria's deliberate emphasis on the continued existence of "diverse interests, each having autonomous representation." Here, too, it should be pointed out that the industrial association held up the United States

---

[137] Rosenstock-Franck, *L'économie corporative*, p. 168.
[138] *OI*, 1 Dec. 1927.

as a model to be emulated, a case – interestingly enough – where the scope of state intervention was more restricted than in any other capitalist system.

Olivetti, Confindustria's instant expert on corporatism, was to base the association's position on this rather liberal, nonintegral reading of the Carta. Thus, at the Ferrara conference on corporatism in 1932, Olivetti attacked Spirito's concept of proprietary corporations and Spirito's claim that there was too great a residue of liberal ideas in the Italian corporative system by simply quoting the text of Article 7:

The Corporative State considers private initiative in the field of production as the most efficient and useful instrument for furthering the interests of the Nation. The private organization of production being a function of the national interest, the organizer of the enterprise is responsible for productive policy before the state. From the collaboration of productive forces is derived among them reciprocal rights and duties. The employee – manager, clerk, or worker – is an active collaborator in the economic enterprise, direction over which belongs to the employer, who is responsible for it.

Olivetti concluded that the Carta, far from negating private initiative, regarded it as a "positive fact" and defined corporatism as a system specifically constructed to maximize its potential and value.[139] In his 756-page volume on corporative law, Olivetti returned to Article 7 of the Carta and, in contradistinction to Spirito's "Communist thesis," situated corporatism exclusively within the framework of capitalism (this, one might add, despite the fact that the actual term "capitalism" is not to be found anywhere in the text of Article 7).

This means that the Fascist State recognizes capitalism as its economic system; one, that is, which is based upon private property and, aside from traditional juridical concepts derived from Roman law, best conforms to the interest of the Nation. It is important to emphasize this point because some wish to affirm that in the Fascist State the property owner has no rightful title but is simply a manager of his property in the collective interest. Such affirmation has no basis in our legislation, which explicitly recognizes the right of private property.[140]

Olivetti then went on to explicate the second part of Article 7, concerning the hierarchy of functions in the field of production:

[139] *Atti del secondo convegno di studi sindacali e corporativi, Ferrara, 5–8 maggio 1932*, 3: 147–8.
[140] Gino Olivetti, *Corso di Diritto Corporativo* (Turin: University of Turin, 1933), pp. 83–4.

As for this economic system, the Carta del Lavoro is noteworthy for having specified another point: that of the distinction in reciprocal functions between the organizer of the enterprise, that is, the employer, and the employee (manager, clerk, or worker). *The Carta del Lavoro attributes to the former the direction of the enterprise for which he shoulders the responsibility, and refers to the latter as an active collaborator in it.* At first glance, such determination might appear superfluous inasmuch as it corresponds to the nature of things that he who has responsibility for the enterprise ought to also have the powers necessary to order that enterprise in the manner he believes most useful for the end of production. But, in reality, the affirmation of the reciprocal relation of the two elements contributing to production has not been superfluous for two reasons: first, *because it underscores one more time that corporative discipline does not replace the directive function and the responsibility of the organizer of the enterprise* – it does not, that is, impair the authority of the employer in the factory; second, to react against tendencies that were determinate in other places and that, before the Fascist regime, appeared even among us, tendencies subversive of the disciplinary ladder and productive hierarchy, which subjected the direction of the enterprise to the influence and intervention of the employees.[141]

Until Italy was to feel the full effects of the international depression, when – in Mussolini's words – the "crisis in the system" became a "crisis of the system," Confindustria's interpretation of the Carta was generally accepted by the regime and the Duce himself. If, at times, Mussolini was critical of "indifferent liberalism," he made it clear that Fascism did not represent "state Socialism." Rather, "the regime respected and would have respected private property, it respected and would have respected private initiative."[142]

However, once again we should point out that there was nothing inherent in Fascism itself to explain Mussolini's concurrence with Confindustria's position, especially when one recalls the somewhat strained relationship between the dictator and the industrial association throughout 1926–7 over the quota 90 fiscal policy and the ruralism campaign. Though Confindustria formally became Fascist at the end of 1925, it had not yet declared its absolute loyalty to Mussolini nor had it yet adopted a public posture of unqualified collaboration with the regime. As we noted, industrialists were repeatedly attacked in the Fascist press, and as late as May 1927, Conti attacked Mussolini's fiscal policy in the Senate.

Both Conti's speech and Agnelli's attempt to have it published in

---

[141] Ibid., pp. 93–4.
[142] Mussolini, *Scritti*, 8: 121, 6: 16.

La Stampa sparked another series of articles in none other than *Popolo d'Italia* during the summer of 1927. These attacked the self-interested behavior of the *capitani d'industria* in general and their stand on the quota 90 policy in particular.[143] With some measure of overstatement, the *Corriere degli Italiani* in Paris declared that the industrialists were now ready to abandon Fascism,[144] and Suardo, a member of Mussolini's cabinet, delivered a scathing speech (cleared by the Duce) against the industrialists at a meeting of Fascist leaders in Bologna on 4 July 1927.[145] The next day, Arnaldo Mussolini proclaimed on the front page of *Popolo d'Italia,* the necessity for the PNF, after the conquest of political power, to move toward the conquest of the command posts of the economic forces of interest to the general life of the nation.[146]

Were Confindustria to be successful both in negotiating compensations to offset the harmful effects upon industry of the quota 90 policy (e.g., reduction of costs through salary reduction, further rationalization) and in having its minimalist interpretation of the Carta del Lavoro upheld, a new understanding would have to be struck with Mussolini. In return for such trade-offs, Confindustria would have to end its criticism of the quota 90 policy, as well as demonstrate unqualified acceptance of the policies and person of Mussolini, by now fully in command of both the PNF and the state apparatus. Confindustria, at least formally, would subsequently fall into line; all public criticism of the regime was terminated, and a conspicuously servile, pseudoheroic adulation of the Duce characterized all its oral and written statements, in marked contrast with its previous independence. Concurrently, to carve out a niche for itself within Fascism, as well as legitimate further rationalization, Confindustria, as suggested earlier, developed a distinctively technocratic role for itself. The association, that is, cast itself as the primary agent of Fascist modernization, building upon the productivism and technocratic themes previously treated. American industrial organization, scientific management, and rationalization became dominant motifs, presented almost as national imperatives, were Italy, in the short run, to cut costs, thus making Italian goods competitive again in international markets,

[143] *Popolo d'Italia,* 10, 24 June 1927, 5 July 1927.
[144] Melograni, *Gli industriali e Mussolini,* p. 214.
[145] Ibid., p. 216.
[146] Ibid.

and, in the long run, to increase the industrial potential of the nation, thus relieving the traditional and now intensified demographic pressure by generating employment opportunities, which the agricultural sector could not provide.

Benni lost no time in closing the breach caused by the quota 90 policy. Already in April 1927, a month before Conti's speech, he had declared to *Popolo d'Italia* that rumors concerning the industrialists' disapproval of Mussolini's monetary policy were nothing but "stupid nonsense"; nevertheless, every effort to reduce costs and rationalize production would have to be made so that Italian goods might still be competitive.[147] In September 1927, Benni published a curt reply to the *Times* of London, which on 16 August had claimed, as had the anti-Fascist *Corriere degli Italiani,* that Italian industrialists were thoroughly disillusioned with Fascism and longed for a return to the liberal state. "The Italians are profoundly grateful to the Fascist Government for having reestablished order, discipline, and hierarchy in the factories."[148] Also, in September 1927, Confindustria (through ENIOS) sponsored an international conference on scientific management in Rome. Speaking consecutively in Italian, French, English, and German, Mussolini modestly pronounced himself a "pioneer in their area," having stressed the application of scientific management, or, as he put it, "unity of command and direction, prohibiting the dispersion of effort and energy."[149]

Still another sign that Confindustria was trying to close the breach between itself and Mussolini and publicly fall into line was a declaration in celebration of the fifth anniversary of the March on Rome. Written in characteristic Fascist style, heretofore totally foreign to the pages of *Organizzazione Industriale,* the statement begins: "It has been five years since Italian youth, inspired and led by a great Chief, began the great movement to restore national discipline, renew political thought, and lay the unshakable basis for a reorganization aimed at restoring the destiny, prosperity, and power of Italy." In like style, the statement ends:

Thus, in Year V of the Regime, the forces of production have held their trenches; thus today the industrialists serenely confront the new year with the firm will to fulfill, in the daily effort of a profoundly quiet and laborious life, their duty toward the enterprise, toward the Regime, and toward the Nation.

[147] *OI,* 1 Apr. 1927.
[148] *OI,* 1 Sept. 1927.
[149] Mussolini, *Scritti,* 6: 86; *OI,* 15 Aug. 1927.

As for the actual substance of this statement, stress was placed upon the productivist aspects of the newly approved Carta del Lavoro, which would contribute toward a "major increase in the wealth of the country." Significantly, no mention was made of the distributive or social-welfare aspects of the labor charter. Far more important, however, was Confindustria's public and unambiguous affirmation of the quota 90 policy, formally ending the one immediate and remaining bone of contention between Mussolini and the industrialists. Year V, or 1927, was one in which;

> through the far-seeing will of the Chief of Government, Italy, proudly assuming full control over its own currency, has given the world proof of the discipline and will with which the Nation follows the Duce in this severe but necessary task, for its complete economic recovery and for the maximum security of its future as a great Nation.[150]

The culmination of this reconciliation between Confindustria and Mussolini would occur in June 1928, when the association organized the first national congress of Italian industrialists. It took place in Rome a month after Rossoni's syndicates held their national congress, where industrialists had been denounced and threatened with a new wave of labor agitation. Confindustria brought more than six thousand of its constituents to the capital. Speaking to this assembly, with Mussolini in attendance, Benni reaffirmed the association's support for the quota 90 policy. "The Confederation can only salute with great satisfaction the decision of the Chief of Government, clearly enunciated and rigidly applied, to leave the situation of uncertainty which might have led to disastrous consequences." However, for industry both to operate effectively under constraints imposed by the monetary policy and to offset the effects of Italy's demographic imbalance, absolute managerial authority and rationalization were essential to "coordinate, concentrate, unify, and standardize: in short, to organize production in the most economic manner." Technocratic themes were stressed as never before, judging from the topics of the major address: the problem of rationalization; science and industry; America, Europe, and Italy.[151]

It is highly significant that at this transitional point in corporative restructuring, the United States – a rationalized capitalist system par excellence – would be a model for Italy to follow, one that, in

[150] *OI*, 31 Oct. 1927.
[151] *OI*, 1 July 1928.

Confindustria's eyes, stressed private initiative, optimal efficiency, hierarchy, and discipline, yet at the same time was characterized by minimal state intervention and institutional rigidity. A fortnight before the national congress, the *Organizzazione Industriale* anticipated this new theme with an article by Olivetti, "The Spirit of Industrial Initiative and American Prosperity." Olivetti argued that American prosperity was due less to its natural resources than to "its methods employed, directives applied, and systems realized to achieve the maximum effect with the minimum force."[152]

This theme was further developed at the Confindustria congress by Alberto Pirelli, who argued that both Italy and the United States disconfirmed Karl Marx's prognostication as to the imminent and inevitable self-destruction of capitalism. Pirelli stressed the themes of elitism and engineering, quoting no less an authority than Herbert Hoover. He took pleasure in comparing the words of the American president with the text of Article 7 of the Carta del Lavoro: "The Corporative State considers private initiative in the field of production as the most efficient and useful instrument for furthering the interests of the Nation." Pirelli also suggested that the ambience within the American factory was something to be emulated:

Visiting American factories one notices a sense of great discipline, together with a sense of friendship. I was impressed at seeing the national flag displayed on the walls. In more than one factory I saw signs saying "smile and obey," a motto that I believe would bring pleasure to our Chief of Government (lively applause).

In contrast to integralist and collectivist conceptions of corporatism, as distinct from liberal capitalism embellished here and there with feigned corporatist sentiments, Pirelli's analogy between the United States and Italy concluded:

There is in all of this a truly interesting parallel with the principles that represent in Italy too a reaction against collectivism. The specific conditions and methods are different, but the principles at the base of the two experiments, American and Italian, are the same: the exaltation of individual effort, the necessity that individuals be educated to realize that their efforts must be directed toward a common good, the cooperation between individuals and classes for the attainment of such a common good.

Mussolini, obviously pleased with Confindustria's choreography, observed that "the world has never seen the spectacle of an assembly

[152] *OI,* 1 June 1928.

such as this," noting that "thousands upon thousands of industrialists from all regions of Italy had come to give their full support to the Regime." Industrialists, he said, were no longer "capitalists," as depicted in the old literature, but "productive officers leading the great army of workers." In return for giving their "full support to the Regime," Mussolini promised the industrialists that fiscal pressure would be alleviated through tax reductions and lower salaries, adding, "In Italy, for obvious reasons, a Fordist policy of high salaries is not possible."[153] Americanism without Fordism, whereby rationalization signified the intensified exploitation of labor without commensurate wage increases, thus characterized economic policy during the late 1920s. *Popolo d'Italia,* previously critical of the industrialists, now affirmed the intellectual, scientific, and moral stature of Confindustria, approving also the association's emulation of America. At the same time, Benni – in the pages of Mussolini's monthly *Gerarchia* – asserted that the national congress had served as a final "clarification" regarding ill-founded rumors of discord between Confindustria and the Duce. "The pervasive applause, repeated and vibrant, signified to Benito Mussolini a protest against the skeptical affirmations which some had attributed to the industrialists, showing instead their complete solidarity with the difficult and complicated work of reconstruction."[154]

As relations between Confindustria and Mussolini gradually improved during the course of 1928, it should come as no surprise that Rossoni and the Fascist syndicates found themselves progressively marginalized. In fact, during November the Corporazioni would be "busted" (the *sbloccamento*) into six separate sectoral federations, paralleling those of the employer associations. Thereafter, Confindustria would find itself confronted with a Fascist federation of industrial workers numbering 1,200,000, rather than the earlier "superconfederation" of 2,800,000 members headed by Rossoni. Though it is often claimed (without documentation) that Confindustria demanded the *sblocco,* closer investigation indicates that the breakup of Rossoni's organization was due primarily to causes internal to Fascism itself.

First, it will be recalled that already at the time of the Rocco labor law and its "norms of actuation" (1925–6), there had been talk of breaking up the Fascist labor confederation, which represented a

[153] *OI,* 1 July 1928.
[154] *Popolo d'Italia,* 21 July 1928; *Gerarchia,* 1 July 1928.

potentially threatening concentration of power under the headstrong Rossoni. After all, the Corporazioni constituted the largest mass organization existing in Italy at the time, having more than double the membership of the PNF (2,800,000 as against 1,131,981).[155] Furthermore, Rossoni was never actually appointed by Mussolini to head the organization but had been elected and reelected by acclamation at the annual congresses.[156]

Second, the *sbloccamento* must be viewed from the perspective of institutional reordering associated with the transition from the so-called syndical phase to the corporative phase of Fascism. Bottai, minister of corporations and Rossoni's bitter political enemy, argued throughout 1928 that the power of both employer and worker syndicates would have to be limited, as these were subordinated to the state. Syndicalism was not, he argued, an end in itself, either in doctrine or in fact, for this would place in doubt the directing, integrating, and coordinating role of the state. Bottai explicitly denied that "this so-called revolutionary syndicalism" was, as Rossoni argued, "the historical premise on which corporatist development was based."[157] Furthermore, under the terms of the new law on electoral representation (presented to the Chamber in March 1928), Rossoni's organization, if left intact, might have had disproportionate political influence. This law provided for professional, rather than territorial, representation; that is, professional associations, according to their size, were to nominate a proportionate number of candidates to the Grand Council, which then was to formulate a single government list subsequently presented to the voters in a plebiscitary fashion. Had it not been for the *sbloccamento*, Rossoni's organization might have played a major role in constituting the new Chamber, nominating 440 of the 1,000 candidates (compared with 320 nominated by employer associations).[158]

Finally, Rossoni had made numerous personal and political enemies within Fascism. As De Felice has pointed out, both Bottai, minister of corporations, and Turati, secretary of the PNF, entered into an alliance to undermine him.[159] Whereas Bottai wanted the

[155] Melograni, *Gli industriali e Mussolini*, p. 241.
[156] Haider, *Capital and Labor under Fascism*, p. 214.
[157] *Critica Fascista*, 11 May 1928.
[158] De Felice, *Mussolini il fascista*, 2: 334.
[159] Ibid., pp. 330–7.

Fascist syndicates made directly subordinate to his own ministry, Turati feared that the Fascist syndicates might overshadow the party if left unchecked. Other Fascists were disgusted by Rossoni's pretentiousness and demagoguery. In January 1928, Rossoni actually wrote a poem, which he entitled "Il Canto del Lavoro," and had the operatic composer Mascagni set it to music. Through Rossoni's influence, the work was performed with huge orchestras and choruses in many of Italy's giant piazzas. *Lavoro d'Italia,* of course, gave the "composition" exceptional coverage, including an article describing precisely how the normally audacious Rossoni, *fier comme un pou sur son fumier,* was smitten by the Muse. The whole affair was ruthlessly ridiculed by the intransigent journal *L'Impero,* which, among other hostile pieces, ran a vicious satire on Rossoni, whose face was appended to a ridiculous-looking bird which bore the classification *rossoniolus corporativus.*[160] Lastly, it should be noted that relations between Rossoni and Mussolini had always been strained. Before the March on Rome, Rossoni stubbornly resisted the party's domination over his syndical organization, defending the "autonomist" position typical of revolutionary syndicalism. After the March on Rome, Mussolini repeatedly ordered Rossoni to tone down his rhetoric, which sounded like that of the old "reds." When the prefect of Milan complained to Mussolini in September 1927 that Rossoni was making inflammatory speeches, claiming that the government was losing the "battle of prices" because of unrestrained avarice on the part of capitalists, Mussolini promptly ordered Rossoni to "convoke no more meetings and deliver no more speeches. There is no need to casually offer polemical opportunities to all the anti-Fascists of the world." These "intensely demagogic affirmations," Mussolini claimed, not only undercut the prefect of Milan's attempt to control the cost of living but called into question the monetary policy of the regime as well.[161]

On 21 November 1928, Mussolini ordered the *sbloccamento,* arguing that this was necessary to create symmetrical balance between employer and worker confederations as a precondition for future corporative development.[162] By way of precaution, the prefects and

[160] *LI,* 5 Jan. 1928; *Impero,* 7, 20 Jan. 1928, 26 Feb. 1928.
[161] ACS, Segreteria particolare del Duce, 87/WR, Rossoni, Edmondo, sottofascicolo varia, 20, 22, 23 Sept. 1927.
[162] *LI,* 2 Dec. 1928.

police were instructed to intercept all communications between the Corporazioni's central headquarters and provincial offices. Rossoni, according to police reports, was "infuriated" but realized that resistance was impossible. These reports indicate broadly based solidarity within the syndical organization with Rossoni, as well as bitter criticism of the government ("it is said that by acting this way the government has delivered the working masses into the hands of the industrialists"). Rossoni, while maintaining his seat on the Grand Council, was subjected to a well-coordinated smear campaign. Among the charges directed against him were improprieties with union funds, being the "greatest enemy of the Duce," and – most incredible – having fled to Russia.[163]

With the *sbloccamento,* Rossoni's project was fully discredited, and the Fascist syndicates were stripped of any residual autonomy and influence. No longer was any pretense made of their "representing" the legitimate interests of labor against capital or being anything other than a disciplinary agency of the state. This was signaled by Arnaldo Mussolini, writing in *Popolo d'Italia* on 24 January 1929: "Syndicalism, in order to be a vital and live force in the state, must depart from demagogic pretensions, from belligerent attitudes toward capital. It should not fall into the 1923 conception of *sindacalismo integrale,* which was a mixture, however noble, of ingenuousness and political paternalism."

The relative weakness of the Fascist syndicates in the political sphere was paralleled by their relative ineffectiveness in the productive sphere. The new, so-called Corporative Chamber that resulted from the plebiscite of 24 March 1929 was neither new nor essentially corporative. Of the 400 deputies, half had been members of the preceding legislature; 47 percent of the Chamber were not "corporative" representatives of the productive forces (i.e., worker and employer confederations) but rather PNF members casually assigned to such categories as professionals, public servants, veteran associations, and cultural societies. Yet in the 53 percent of the Chamber that was "corporative," employers were overrepresented in aggregate (33 percent as against the workers' 22 percent) as well as in each of the various productive sectors. Thus, for example, Confindustria, which

<hr>

[163] ACS, Segreteria particolare del Duce, 87/R, Rossoni, Edmondo, sottofascicolo anonimi, Pubblica Sicurezza, Rome, Nov. 1928 and 12 Aug. 1928; Ministro dell'Interno, 18, 19 June 1929.

had 70,000 members, had 31 deputies, while the Confederation of Industrial Workers, with a membership of 1,200,000, had 26 deputies. Furthermore, a number of prominent leaders of the Fascist syndicates had been excluded from the government list, but no such exclusions were made among names designated by the employer associations. In the new Chamber, Confindustria was represented by such leading personalities as Olivetti, Benni, Motta, and Ponti, and Mussolini appointed eight additional industrialists to the Senate.[164]

We turn now to the relative weakness of the Fascist syndicates in the productive sphere. Their final dramatic initiative, launched against the industrialists during the last half of 1929, was occasioned by two factors: (1) the further rationalization of work and salary reductions caused, as we have seen, by the government's monetary policy; and (2) the lack of any syndical presence within the factories, allowing the industrialists, in effect, to adopt such measures onesidedly, without any participation of or consultation with the Fascist syndicates. Accordingly, the syndicates attacked "scientific management in general and the "Bedeaux system" in particular while at the same time again demanding recognition of *fiduciari di fabbrica*.

The Bedeaux system had been developed by Charles Bedeaux, a native Frenchman who emigrated to the United States, where, in 1918, he designed a system for the Imperial Furniture Company of Grand Rapids which "scientifically" calculated workers' salaries. Based on Taylor's time–motion studies, Bedeaux established "laws" and "coefficients" whereby each worker's earnings were a function of the optimal efficiency computed for his specific task.[165] *Lavoro Fascista* argued that under the Bedeaux system and other forms of scientific management, employees were working harder and earning less.[166]

To remedy this and other grievances, *fiduciari di fabbrica* were necessary. Though *fiduciari* had attained de facto status in a limited number of factories, Confindustria steadfastly refused to grant them formal recognition. The industrial association simply recalled Mussolini's words at the signing of the Pact of Palazzo Vidoni in October

---

[164] Aquarone, *Stato totalitario,* pp. 154–9; De Felice, *Mussolini il fascista,* 2:473–8; Melograni, *Gli industriali e Mussolini,* pp. 253–5; Rosenstock-Franck, *L'économie corporative,* pp. 248–55.
[165] Fiorentini, "Ristrutturazione capitalistica," pp. 148–9.
[166] *LF,* 10 June 1929 through 3 July 1929.

1925, when the issue of *fiduciari* had first been raised: that in the factory there should be "one hierarchy only, a technical one," and that "there should be no talk of *fiduciari*." Confindustria further noted, as if it were equally significant, that "in America no one would dream of asking for anything resembling *fiduciari di fabbrica*."[167]

Lavoro Fascista, all too aware of Mussolini's words, as well as Confindustria's continual assertion that the Carta del Lavoro guaranteed absolute managerial authority and the industrialists' responsibility to increase production and cut costs (Articles 7 and 8), argued that the *fiduciari* would not constitute another hierarchy but instead would serve as a necessary link between the syndical association and the individual worker in the factory. The Carta, they held, also established equal juridical status between employer and worker associations and stated that the worker was an "active collaborator" in the economic enterprise (Articles 6 and 7). Furthermore, locked outside the factory gates, syndical representatives could neither ensure that labor contracts were rigorously followed nor have the relevant information with which to negotiate new contracts.[168] Without *fiduciari,* that is, the Fascist syndicates could not fulfill their essential responsibilities; they would always be in an inferior position when dealing with industrial associations.

> On the one side sits the representative of the employers' association armed with technical arguments, charts, and statistics, supported by the willing testimony of the managers, who belong to their association. On the other sits the representative of the workers' syndicate, who, forbidden entry into the sacred interior of the factory, can only argue on the basis of assertions (necessarily incomplete) made by the interested party. The contrast is obvious.[169]

For their refusal to recognize *fiduciari,* industrialists again were accused of "classism" and of masking their true liberal convictions behind verbal commitments to corporatism. This charge was made by *Lavoro Fascista* against Olivetti when he argued that private initiative should not be "disoriented by sinister threats or by groundless anticipations" but left instead to its "natural functioning."[170] Several days later, *Lavoro Fascista* argued that industrialists were in bad faith

---

[167] *OI,* 1 Sept. 1929.
[168] *LF,* 28 Apr. 1929, 7, 9 May 1929, 2, 10, 11, 14 July 1929, 9 Aug. 1929.
[169] *LF,* 9 May 1929.
[170] *LF,* 5 May 1929.

harking back to the Vidoni pact, because that had been superseded by further corporative development. In hiding behind "literal or arbitrary interpretations" of earlier Fascist legislation, industrialists revealed "an entirely liberal tendency."[171]

The attack on the industrialists reached a peak at a meeting of the Fascist Federation of Industrial Workers in Milan on 2 July 1929. They were accused of having financed Fascism for reasons of narrow self-interest, of blatantly violating labor contracts, and of deliberately provoking discontent among the workers to drive them from Fascism. Against integral forms of corporative collaboration, industrialists always raised abstract questions of principle. "Not Fascist principles, because Fascist collaboration has no need of such obstacles. All this formalism is intended to leave the door open to a return to the liberal economy. They fear a corporative economy and dream of a return to economic liberalism." These sentiments, expressed by Arnaldo Fioretti, president of the Federation of Industrial Workers, only served to confirm Confindustria's suspicions of the *fiduciari,* as well as the intentions of the Fascist syndicates. Whereas earlier Fioretti had argued that *fiduciari* would not represent another hierarchy in the factory and would not interfere with the technical ordering of production, he now called for "an integral revision of the productive process." Fascism now would have to "penetrate the factories" in order to establish the necessary preconditions for corporatism and block the path leading to a covert return to liberalism.[172]

Confindustria reacted to the campaign for *fiduciari* with self-confident prudence. Though by no means certain of the outcome, the association's prior strategy (vis-à-vis the Vidoni pact, the Rocco labor law, and the Carta del Lavoro) had been successful in both enlisting the support of Mussolini and having codified into Fascist legislation the very principles now called into question by the Fascist syndicates: private initiative, an absolute and unitary hierarchy in the factories, and the industrialist's supreme and undivided responsibility to perfect production and reduce costs. Thus, Confindustria, perhaps fearing that it could only jeopardize an otherwise favorable situation, chose not to engage in a public polemic with the Fascist syndicates until the regime gave clear indication that formal rejection of *fiduciari* was imminent. Until such time, the association worked quietly through

[171] *LF,* 9 May 1929.
[172] *LF,* 2 July 1929.

existing channels where they could raise formalistic objections against *fiduciari* and gratuitously attack the Fascist syndicates for not conducting themselves in a similarly responsible manner (but, instead, engaging in public demagoguery more akin in form and in substance to the "old reds" than what one might expect of disciplined Fascists). Accordingly, at the outset of the *fiduciari* campaign, Confindustria sent a memorandum to Mussolini reminding the Duce of his earlier statements and arguing that *fiduciari* would both undercut the newly established syndical relationship between national employer and worker associations and undermine factory discipline:

Your Excellency, the Head of Government, receiving the representatives of the organizations which had signed the Pact of Palazzo Vidoni, declared that one should not even talk of *fiduciari di fabbrica*. . . .

Recently, however, some important syndicates have issued instructions calling for the formation of *fiduciari di fabbrica*. Furthermore, they have even conducted polemics in the press against employers' associations, which, adhering purely and simply to the orders of the head of Government and to collective contracts, have instructed all firms not to recognize such *fiduciari*.

Aside from considerations as to this manner of proceeding, without doubt shameful, the Confederazione Generale Fascista dell'Industria, in expressing its own views on the question of *fiduciari* before the Central Intersyndical Committee, respectfully submits the reasons why the institution of *fiduciari*, having functions to perform within single firms, is absolutely inadmissible.

In fact, one of the fundamental principles of the corporative order, found in the spirit and content of all syndical order, is that association always finds itself matched against association.

This is a necessary and sufficient condition because in relations of work the syndicate can and must represent the interest of its category. It is evident that if the interest of the category of the workers is at stake, the counterposed interest of the category of employers is consequently also at stake; that the association of the latter has the right and the duty to tutor this interest directly, just as is the case with the opposed association of workers.

The institution of *fiduciari di fabbrica*, in practice, would *shatter the workers' syndicates into a series of sindacati di fabbrica and would also thus annul the employers' association.*

From the standpoint of factory discipline and hierarchy, the institution of *fiduciari* could only have the gravest of effects. *The existence in the factory of a person who duplicated the powers of an organism of public law, the syndicate, that is, of a worker who in the factory defends his colleagues against the employer, can only lead to deleterious consequences from both a psychological and a material point of view. . . .*

It would thus annul the principle, *put forth by the Duce, that "in the factory there ought to be only one hierarchy, a technical one."*

Accordingly, the reasons which argue against the institution of *fiduciari* are of a double nature – of principle and of practice, which reciprocally act upon one another: on the one hand, the juridical and social essence of the very corporative order of the state and the application of its syndical laws; on the other, the foundation of discipline and hierarchy in the factories. *The institution of fiduciari di fabbrica would carry us backward; with one step it would set back progress made by the Regime during the past four years.*[173]

Although not as yet directly commenting on *fiduciari* in its public organ, *Organizzazione Industriale,* Confindustria nevertheless took note of industrial trends in Russia to make the point still again, as it had done earlier in the pre-Fascist factory council polemic, that even under a Communist system, hierarchy and discipline were recognized as being absolutely essential to maintain production. In 1929, Stalin removed Mikhail Tomski as head of the Russian syndicates in a new effort to impose greater discipline upon the workers while at the same time issuing a directive conferring increased authority upon management. Thus, it is no accident that *Organizzazione Industriale,* on 1 June 1929, gave maximum coverage to statements made by Tolstopiatov, commissar of labor, concerning the chaotic state of industry in Russia and the need to reestablish discipline and hierarchy:

Tolstopiatov summed up in a few words the unique remedy possible: reestablish hierarchy; give back to each individual charged with directive and technical functions the authority necessary to fulfill them; place order, discipline, coordination, and distribution of work among those attributes indispensable for fulfilling such functions; specify relations of authority and define tasks and responsibilities. For a system of collective command – which in an individual enterprise is nonsense – a system of individual initiative and command is being substituted. . . . The point of departure is precisely this: production is not a theory, nor a tart that anyone can cook at will. It follows from the precise, methodical, and well-ordered deployment of determinate factors, each one of which has a function, in itself important, but subordinated to a rigidly unitary direction, framework, and program. As all the elements which contribute to the same end are essential, coordination must be harmonious and compulsory. An industrial firm, from this perspective, is synonymous with hierarchy.

The syndical question was addressed by the Central Intersyndical Committee on 6 and 10 July. Although no definitive resolution concerning *fiduciari* emerged from these meetings, Mussolini, in no un-

---

[173] ACS, Presidenza del Consiglio dei Ministri, Gabinetto Atti, 1919–36, busta 521, fascicolo 18/2, n. 6970.

certain terms, vented his displeasure at the comportment of the Fascist syndicates, in particular at what took place at the previously mentioned congress of the Federation of Industrial Workers in Milan. According to the official minutes of these Central Intersyndical Committee sessions, Mussolini accused the federation of having suggested the preeminence of syndicates over the corporative order and of having "used a demagogic nomenclature (*classi padronali, ceti padronali, padroni*) which predates the epoch of Karl Marx." There was "no need whatsoever" of holding any further syndical meetings which, like that of Milan, "had a completely demagogic tone."

Fioretti, clearly on the defensive, denied that the Milan meeting had been called for demagogic ends and denied that his organization intended to launch a new "syndical phase" to the detriment of the "corporative phase." Fioretti claimed that although it was true that many syndical representatives had been depressed in the aftermath of the *sbloccamento,* the Milan meeting had been "deformed by the press." Mussolini immediately shot back, "By your press?" Fioretti, fully aware of *Lavoro Fascista*'s reportage, sheepishly replied, "Yes, even by ours."

Benni, following Mussolini's lead, seized the moment to counterattack with an overdose of self-righteous indignation. The minutes read:

Benni: Declared that the Milan meeting had greatly impressed the industrial camp for its form as well as its substance. Many preoccupations were expressed. It was claimed that the industrialist was not a Fascist by conviction but only for personal gain. He rose against this point of view, affirming that Italian industry had always done its duty toward the Nation. They should remember that beside the 500,000 casualties of the war lay numerous dead from the industrial camp who sacrificed capital and family for the economic affirmation of the Nation and who fell in the breach. One should recall that the industrialists were the only ones to oppose the Bolshevik tide during the occupation of the factories. Defending their factories, they defended not only their own interests but those of the Nation's economy. He argued, moreover, that in attacking one category of industrialists, the whole class was attacked. Industrialists bore the mark of original sin. This characterization, he confessed, discouraged and disheartened the entire category.

Mussolini concluded the session by praising the industrialists' "spirit of initiative" and "utilization of scientific discoveries." However, reacting to Benni's overstated profession of the industrialists' "Fascist faith," Mussolini expressed clear doubt:

Mussolini: As for the Fascist spirit of the industrialists, there is no need to exaggerate one way or the other. The Duce affirmed his ample reserve about many industrialists as Fascists. As a representative example, he mentioned Gualino.
Benni: Said that Gaulino is a speculator, not an industrialist.
Mussolini: Then cited Senator Agnelli, a good Giolittian liberal who attentively oversees his industry and, as such, is respected. But the first one who would say he is not a Fascist is Agnelli himself. To be a Fascist, many moral, intellectual, and physical qualities are necessary. Furthermore, one must be so born. Senator Agnelli apparently was born too early.

Mussolini then cited Pirelli, a first-rate manager "who should not be considered a Fascist, because he simply isn't." Further, "all these may be forceful, active, and genial industrialists, but as for Fascism they had to be pulled along." Nevertheless, Mussolini concluded – with evidently more concern for practical politics than logical consistency – that Confindustria, as an organization, "ought to be considered Fascist."

Although no specific position was taken on the issue of *fiduciari* during these meetings of the Central Intersyndical Committee, two significant points should be made. The first is Mussolini's criticism of the Milan meeting of the Fascist syndicate, where, after all, the major issue had been recognition of *fiduciari*. Second is Mussolini's concurrence with Benni's analysis of the nation's delicate economic situation and consequent policy recommendations: favoring all forms of rationalization and giving the most ample liberty to industrial managers in this regard; reducing public expenses to ease tax pressure; readjusting the distribution of the tax load in such a manner to favor investment; allowing private capital to flow spontaneously toward the most remunerative investments without being diverted toward public works; and – most significant, given the transition from the syndical to the corporatist phase – "impeding the progressive bureaucratization of the Nation, the increase of minimally productive personnel resulting from the constitution of public and semipublic organisms lacking any productive function."[174] Without as yet formally declaring himself on the issue of *fiduciari*, Mussolini was clearly favoring the Confindustria position: absolute managerial authority was to be spared "demagogic" incursions and there was to be no "integral revision of the productive process," as Fioretti had demanded in Milan. In fact, the

[174] ACS, Carta Cianetti, busta 4, fascicolo Comitato Centrale Intersindacale.

very logic of capitalist accumulation and reproduction was to be left intact.

Shortly after these meetings of the Central Intersyndical Committee, both Bottai and Arnaldo Mussolini publicly supported Confindustria's position on the *fiduciari*. Bottai, of course, had always been skeptical of the intentions and actual competence of the Fascist syndicates. Though at times he questioned Confindustria's commitment to corporatism, he never denied for a moment the technical competence of Italian industrialists or the necessity for absolute managerial authority. Speaking at a Confindustria gathering in early July, Bottai declared that no one could question, "and certainly not the workers' syndicates, the right of the employer to give his enterprise that organization of work which is most conducive to maximize production. Not only does the employer have this right, considering his position of responsibility for the enterprise, but this right becomes his duty, considering the position of the employer vis-à-vis the national interest. This is both a right and a duty because of the responsibility he must bear every day regarding the supreme necessity of national production." *Organizzazione Industriale,* in its preface to a full transcript of Bottai's speech, underscored the fact that the minister of corporations had defended the substance and spirit of Fascist legislation against "dangerous deviations" which had been put forth by "some organizations" in the press.[175]

During August 1929, Arnaldo Mussolini attacked the concept of *fiduciari* in the authoritative *Popolo d'Italia.* Concurring with the position that Confindustria had advanced, Mussolini's brother charged that *fiduciari* would undermine the newly constructed syndical framework and might, if instituted, eventually become new loci of power beyond the control of syndical hierarchies, making a mockery of Fascist discipline. He, too, made the connection between *fiduciari* and the errors of Bolshevism, arguing that "economic imperialism derives from a perfect capitalist system. Thus, it is North America which moves toward the conquest of new markets."[176] Although the Wall Street crash was but two months away, American capitalism, as contrasted with Russian Bolshevism, was for both Confindustria and the regime a model and standard of economic rationality.

In the wake of Mussolini's statements and of attacks by Bottai and

[175] *OI,* 15 July 1929.
[176] *Popolo d'Italia,* 23 Aug. 1929.

Mussolini's brother, the Fascist syndicates began to moderate their tone and retreat. *Lavoro Fascista* now described the issue of *fiduciari* as *"una questione non drammatica,"* while advancing a blatantly weakened conception of the intended functions of these new bodies.[177] It was only at this point that Confindustria chose to go public with a polemic. Invoking the same Trojan horse argument it had made against factory councils and Giolitti's project on worker control, the industrial association argued that the real design behind such seemingly harmless bodies was one of gradually enlarging and transforming their original functions to the point of eventually subverting factory discipline and constituting the basis for a new, and necessarily irrational, economic order. Thus, Confindustria mocked the recent minimalist conception of *fiduciari*, which *Organizzazione Industriale* now referred to somewhat caustically as *"fiduciari* 2nd edition." This was little more, in Confindustria's eyes, than rhetorical artifice to mask revolutionary intent. The real issue concerned "an apparently innocuous organ which tomorrow will assume its true aspect." This secret intent was betrayed by the "classism" and demagoguery which typified the original *fiduciari* conception, where industrialists had been depicted as exploiters and anti-Fascists in need of constant surveillance by "true Fascists" intent on promoting an "integral revision of the productive process." Citing the Carta del Lavoro, as well as statements made by Mussolini, Confindustria argued that industrialists were "fully obedient to the concepts and directives of Fascism" and were dutifully defending their leadership function, as well as the "Fascist" principles of private initiative, hierarchy, and discipline:

In substance, the principle on which the entirety of the workers' demand is based, that from which it develops, is clear: the boss, if his authority is unchecked, commits injustices, violates labor contracts, exploits (the word is not used, but the concept is clearly there) the workers, who find themselves in a state of subjugation and moral inferiority, notwithstanding – one reads – the laws and directives of the regime. It is therefore necessary that close by him, in front of him, there be another power representing the workers: one who watches over him, who perpetually controls him, who supervises him, who is ready to intervene in the defense of the oppressed workers, who, furthermore, becomes the exponent and custodian of Fascism and Fascist principles before the concealed anti-Fascism or afascism of the heads and

---

[177] *LF*, 9 Aug. 1929.

managers of the firm, who are thusly judged simply because they might not act as the *fiduciario* says they must act. . . . Now the industrialists clearly declare that they cannot entertain any form of *fiduciario* more or less attenuated, because this would introduce into the factory a new element of power, of command, of control, and thus an obstacle to production. Defending their function and their powers as leaders of industry, industrialists intend to do their duty as Italians and as Fascists, fully obedient to the concepts and directives of Fascism. . . . The industrialists do not dramatize the question of *fiduciari*. They are far too filled with the desire to build, too habituated toward action, to assume theatrical gestures.[178]

The attacks by the Fascist syndicates in public speeches and newspaper articles were more or less doomed to failure for essentially two reasons. First, given the relation of forces within Fascism, the syndicates had already been internally fragmented, as well as isolated from any other Fascist current with which they might have formed a strategic alliance to promote or impose their interests. Second, a necessary precondition for the success of such attacks would have been the existence of a relatively autonomous public sphere, which might have allowed not only the free expression of demands aimed at a mass audience but also the capacity to mobilize such a mass constituency outside – or, if need be, against – official channels, by now intentionally narrowed and unidirectional, hierarchical, and unresponsive to demands emanating from below.

We have seen that the corporative organization of the state was self-consciously aimed at eliminating such a public sphere characteristic of liberalism, substituting in its place a centrally controlled, imperatively ordered command state which sought to frame and discipline all of civil society. In a sense, one might say that the Fascist syndicates were checkmated even before the *fiduciari* campaign, whereas Confindustria, already relatively secure in terms of the relationship between the official understanding of corporatism and its own position, as well as in terms of its relationship with Fascist leadership, quietly acted through the official channels that it itself helped form, never having to seriously defend itself in some nonexistent public sphere. In fact, the Fascist syndicates' only real chance of success would have been Confindustria's committing some strategic blunder, such that Mussolini might have used the threat of *fiduciari* as a vehicle to force the industrialists back into line. Confindustria, by now *formally*

[178] *OI*, 1 Sept. 1929.

Fascist and *formally* loyal to Mussolini, committed no such blunder; prudently it abided by the unstated, though mutually understood, ground rules governing its actions vis-à-vis the regime.

On 9 September 1929, the Central Intersyndical Committee unanimously rejected *fiduciari,* both in principle and in practice.[179] In the fundamentally changed political situation of 1938–9, the question of *fiduciari* would be posed by the Fascist syndicates once again, this time with limited success. Mussolini, angered by the lack of support he had received from the industrialists for his increasingly adventurous and belligerent foreign policy, launched a protracted "antibourgeois" polemic. Only then, virtually on the eve of the Second World War, were *fiduciari* instituted, *not,* however, as originally conceived but rather in the "attenuated" version, what Confindustria had called "*fiduciari* 2nd edition." Official guidelines specifically stated that *fiduciari* must absolutely not interfere with the hierarchical and productive order of the firm or have direct contact with the directors regarding labor relations. "The *fiduciari,* in sum, ought to be communication organs of the party and of the syndicates."[180]

The *sbloccamento* of 1928 and the failed campaign for *fiduciari* in 1929 marked the definitive demise of the Fascist syndicates either as a residually autonomous force within Fascism or as an effective countervailing force to Confindustria. As Aquarone concludes in his study of Fascist labor policy, no sooner did the Fascist syndicates henceforth demonstrate "an excessive vigor in sustaining worker demands or in trying to boost the morale of the workers with modest propagandistic activity than they were immediately accused of 'Communist' or 'subversive' tendencies, of incomprehension of the social conception of Fascism, of inciting class struggle."[181] Or, as Salvemini quipped in his classic study of Fascism, "labor has in the Fascist corporative state no more active part than have the animals in a society for the protection of animals."[182]

The old guard, which still represented the revolutionary syndicalist aspirations of the postwar period, were progressively replaced by younger "professionals" of bourgeois origin trained at Fascist labor

---

[179] *OI,* 15 Sept. 1929.
[180] Alberto Aquarone, "La politica sindacale del fascismo," *Il Nuovo Osservatore,* Nov.–Dec. 1965, pp. 887–8.
[181] Ibid., p. 882.
[182] Salvemini, *Origins of Fascism,* p. 419.

schools, men primarily interested in advancing their political careers rather than representing labor as such. These, according to Aquarone, were "true and proper public functionaries, responsible directly not to their respective bases but to superior political hierarchies which could in practice transfer them at will from one locality to another without the slightest concern for consulting the interested workers."[183] Older intransigents who resisted this full-scale regimentation of labor were forced out of leadership posts, as was the case with Fioretti, who was pressured to resign as head of the Federation of Industrial Workers for having opposed a general salary reduction in November 1930.[184]

Confindustria and the Great Depression

With the coming of the Great Depression, Confindustria found itself in a precarious position; all the international and domestic constants upon which it had based its actions were now dramatically altered. The 1920s trend toward a free flow of capital, goods, and labor came to an abrupt halt in the 1930s, as Italy's major trading partners, even England, initiated protective measures. Foreign trade, upon which the export-oriented Confindustria firms were dependent, declined by two-thirds from 1929 to 1933.[185] Domestically, the value of stocks and securities fell an average of 39 percent (many falling in excess of 50 percent), the index of industrial production fell from 100 to 66.8, and unemployment jumped from 300,000 to 1,010,000.[186]

The deepening economic crisis called into question some of Confindustria's most basic maxims: the essential vitality of liberal political economy (with its presumed self-corrective market mechanism), the autonomy of industry, and even productivism itself. Prior to the Depression, Confindustria had been successful in identifying corporatism with capitalism while at the same time invoking the United States, significant for its robust economy and lack of state intervention, as a model for Italy to emulate. Now Mussolini, who began his parliamentary career by claiming that "the true history of capitalism

---

[183] Aquarone, *Stato totalitario*, pp. 224–5.
[184] De Felice, *Mussolini il Duce*, p. 195. See also Leonardo Rapone, "Il sindacalismo fascista: temi e problemi della ricerca storica," *Storia Contemporanea* 13 (Oct. 1982): 4–5.
[185] Clough, *Economic History*, p. 247; Romeo, *Breve storia*, pp. 160, 444.
[186] Aquarone, "Italy: The Crisis," p. 38; Romeo, *Breve storia*, pp. 160–2.

is just beginning,"[187] argued that the "crisis in the system" had become a "crisis of the system."[188] Furthermore, if there were anything
to emulate about the United States, it was hardly "degenerate"
laissez-faire capitalism but rather the bold interventionist steps that
the new Roosevelt administration had recently undertaken, suggesting
in the minds of some – on both sides of the Atlantic – a strong affinity
between the New Deal and Fascist corporatism.[189]

As the Depression deepened, Mussolini's criticism of capitalism and
the bourgeoisie grew progressively more demagogic. On 17 October
1932, he asked whether the crisis was merely another cyclical phenomenon or "the transit from one epoch of civilization to another."
A year later, on 14 November 1933, he found the answer: "the crisis
has penetrated so profoundly within the system that it has become a
crisis of the system. No longer a trauma, it is a constitutional mal-
ady." Mussolini then went on to specify three periods of capitalist
development: 1830–70 was dynamic; 1870–1914 was static; 1914 to
the present was decadent, the stage of "supercapitalism."[190] In March
1934, Mussolini began his antibourgeois polemic, which would grow
particularly intense during the late 1930s. "But one danger can still
threaten the Regime: this danger can be represented by what is commonly referred to as 'bourgeois spirit,' spirit, that is, of satisfaction
and adaptation, tendency toward skepticism, toward compromise,
toward the comfortable life, toward careerism."[191] Taking their cue
from the Duce, official propagandists immediately invoked such new
terms as *plutocrazia, supercapitalismo,* and *superfinanza,* terms that
found their origin in Marxism and that had formerly been banned
from the official Fascist lexicon.

Industrialists, as Sarti suggests, now found themselves in a dangerous dilemma: "They could not afford to refuse public assistance, nor
did they want to risk public regulation by accepting public assistance."[192] What Confindustria feared most were two interrelated
threats: (1) the enactment of obligatory norms for industry through
which the state might impose "counterproductive" and "bureaucratic" policies regarding prices, cartel formation, plant construction,

[187] Mussolini, *Scritti,* 2:182.
[188] Ibid., 8:257–73.
[189] Ibid., 9:10, 10:105, 8:121, 257–73.
[190] Ibid., 8:257–73.
[191] Ibid., 9:43.
[192] Sarti, *Fascism and Industrial Leadership,* p. 98.

and employment quotas; and (2) a more integral development of corporatism, as a vehicle both to administer such obligatory norms and to fulfill the symbolic and propagandistic needs of a regime which aspired not only to mediate new social tensions engendered by the Depression but also to demonstrate corporatism's superior capacity to institutionally overcome the crisis-prone, atomistic tendencies of liberal capitalism.

Faced with these threats, Confindustria once again tried to salvage as much of the status quo ante as possible in a defensive effort to preserve some measure of autonomy against the state. This meant resisting all attempts at regulation and further corporatist development. Not uncompromising resistance, to be sure, for within the Fascist political arena this would have only rendered industry an even more vulnerable target and would have certainly led to strategic defeat. Rather, Confindustria would continue its more pragmatic tactic of raising particularistic objections to specific policies and, where these were nevertheless adopted, neutralizing them by either having itself made the actual administrative agency (as in the case of compulsory cartels) or quietly not cooperating with external regulatory organs. Here, for example, Confindustria would frustrate the Ministry of Corporations with the selective use of its information-gathering capacity, superior to that of all other private associations and the state bureaucracy itself. It simply withheld vital information while at the same time flooding the understaffed ministry with trivial data.[193]

Confindustria's resistance to state regulation entailed an ideological dimension as well. Mussolini and his Fascist literati, as we have seen, now began to polemicize against *supercapitalismo,* arguing that "decadent" large-scale enterprises could no longer be considered private entities beyond public control. Speaking to the Senate on 15 January 1931, Mussolini asserted:

When a private enterprise exceeds certain limits, it is no longer a private but a public enterprise. An artisanal enterprise would be private, but when an industry, a credit institution, a business, or a bank controls several thousand million lire and employs several thousand persons, how is it possible to think that its misfortune is a personal affair of the director of the enterprise or the stockholders of an industry? By now it is of interest to the entire Nation and the State.[194]

[193] Ibid., p. 103.
[194] *OI,* 15 Jan. 1931.

By 1934, when many of the large banks and corporations had been rescued with assistance from IRI, Mussolini declared that "when a firm makes appeal to the capital of all, its private character ceases; it becomes a public matter or, if you prefer, a social matter." When, as he claimed, three-fourths of the Italian economy is within the hands of the state, those who still talk of a liberal economy "make me laugh – laugh and cry at the same time." Had he wanted to introduce state capitalism or state Socialism, he "would today have the necessary, sufficient, and objective conditions to do it."[195]

Taking his cue from this, Olivetti set out to recast the image of Italian industry. Unlike the supercapitalism of the plutocratic nations, where the economy was dominated by highly vulnerable large-scale concerns, Italian industry was based on small- and middle-scale units. Furthermore, unlike foreign large-scale concerns, "artificial" in nature and dominated by bankers and speculators, these smaller Italian firms preserved an organic relationship between worker and owner such that the latter, in contrast to owners of foreign large-scale firms, was still the effective manager.

This "smallness" argument was invoked by Olivetti during the course of a December 1932 parliamentary debate concerning a law that would compel all industrialists to obtain government approval before enlarging or altering their plants. Rather than attack the measure itself, which would have gotten nowhere, Olivetti sought to limit the provision to only those firms whose past performance merited regulation, excluding from such control the vast majority of relatively healthy small firms. As Olivetti argued:

This character of our industrial activity, whose central group is represented by 40,000 firms employing more than two million workers, half the workforce, whose total employees range from 10 to 500 each, this characteristic of small and medium industry explains why our industries run at a capacity vastly superior to that of other countries. These smaller organizations are more easily adaptable to changes imposed by circumstances.[196]

Though unsuccessful in limiting the provision itself, Olivetti at least made sure that Confindustria was the administrative vehicle responsible for recommending building permits.

Olivetti also employed the smallness argument against Ugo Spirito

[195] Mussolini, *Scritti*, 9:18, 94.
[196] *OI*, 15 Dec. 1932.

at the Ferrara conference on corporatism in 1932. Spirito argued that during the course of capitalist development, from family firms to joint-stock companies, there had been a progressive separation between ownership and management, the former becoming more and more parasitic while the latter became ever more indispensable. The point now had been reached when the two elements entered a terminal phase of contradiction. Joint-stock companies had so extended themselves that the public–private distinction, a vestige of early capitalism, had been historically superseded. Fascism could now transcend this dualism, and with it end class-divided society, but only by taking the next obvious step: abolishing large-scale property ownership and vesting it in the corporations – in other words, establishing proprietary corporations.[197]

Olivetti lost no time in attacking Spirito, first at the conference, then shortly after in *La Stampa*. The secretary of Confindustria, no doubt, saw a dangerous convergence between Spirito's "Communist thesis" and the formulation advanced by Mussolini (who, incidentally, had read and cleared Spirito's address prior to the Ferrara conference); that is, beyond a certain size, private enterprises became public in nature. Assuming his preferred pose of a realistic empiricist doing battle against abstract and dogmatic theorists, Olivetti denied any such unilinear development of capitalism. Giant trusts had enjoyed their "quarter of an hour in the sun," but the Depression clearly demonstrated that they lacked the vitality of smaller firms, which would, more likely than not, typify the economy of the future. Furthermore, the vitality of smaller firms was directly attributable to the personal risks and the greater competence demonstrated by their owner–managers:

In these firms, even in the past, administration had been much more austere and farsighted than in those firms where the directing functions have been assumed by a delegated administrator or an employee. These men might be very capable; but in substance they manage the money of others, they are not permanently bound to the future of the firm nor do they risk their patrimony. Often they are appointed, not by the stockholders, but by banking institutions, whose interests they represent even when these do not coincide with the interests of production.[198]

Did Olivetti really believe in this smallness argument, or was it merely another instance of his astute ideological adaptation, similar

---

[197] Spirito's address and his response to Olivetti are reproduced in Ugo Spirito, *Il corporativismo* (Florence: Sansoni, 1970), pp. 351–65.

[198] *La Stampa*, 20 May 1932.

to that marking his 1925–7 "conversion" to corporatism? The evidence is unclear. On the one hand, he never employed the smallness argument until *after* Mussolini's 1931 statement on unit size. Moreover, as we have seen, from 1906 until the Depression, Olivetti had consistently emphasized Taylorism, rationalization, productivism, and Americanism, all certainly more typical of large, rather than small- or middle-sized, firms. Not only that, but Confindustria, like earlier industrial associations, had been a product of the larger Italian firms, whose interests it reflected to a far greater degree than those of small- and middle-sized firms, which had never manifested any eagerness to associate and had become members of Confindustria largely through compulsory *inquadramento*. On the other hand, many of Italy's more successful large-scale firms (e.g., Fiat, Pirelli, Olivetti) had retained the characteristics that Olivetti subsumed in his smallness argument, particularly the pivotal role of the self-interested, owner–manager. What clearly preoccupied Olivetti the most was the possibility, with increased state intervention, that industrialists might become little more than dependent managers taking orders from bureaucratic and incompetent regulatory bodies. This preoccupation was obviously present in a November 1933 speech he delivered to the Turinese industrialists, warning them to refrain, as much as possible, from requesting state assistance:

I know very well that in this period of difficulties and obstacles many industrialists would gladly exchange their position as head of their firms for that of mere state functionaries placed in charge of given factories, so that they would not be exposed to the risk of failure because they would always be assured of external assistance. But the day this mentality triumphs, becoming that of the great majority rather than that of a base minority, private industry will be finished and the industrialists will have nothing more to do. . . . The day on which you cut from the cycle of economic activity its mainspring, the principle that the greatest remuneration for economic action should go to the most able and capable, when all are reduced to the common denominator of employees, secure that someone else will subsidize all losses, you will no longer derive profits from your own efforts – when profits there may be – and your function must necessarily disappear because you no longer have a distinctive raison d'être, other than being a manager. Those among you who have technical proficiency may become good administrators, but industrialists you no longer will be![199]

As the economic crisis intensified, Confindustria was less successful than it had been earlier in affecting the formal articulation of public

---

[199] *OI,* 30 Nov. 1933.

policy. Unable to block or modify significantly legislation it judged inimical to industry's interest, Confindustria nevertheless was still capable of ensuring that in the actual execution of such policy either the "exigencies of production" (as it defined them) would be respected or passive, noncooperation would be tolerated. This may be seen in three areas where obligatory norms were established for industry despite Confindustria's opposition: compulsory cartels (*consorzi obligatori*), authorization for enlarging or modifying plants, and employment policy.

In two of these areas, compulsory cartels and authorization for enlarging or modifying plants, Confindustria had itself established as the administrative agency; it was not the ultimate authority, which juridically was the Ministry of Corporations, yet given the technical competence and information-gathering superiority of the former, as contrasted with the small, poorly trained staff of the latter, Confindustria's recommendations were largely rubber-stamped. With regard to authorization for enlarging or modifying plants, all applications were reviewed and evaluated by Confindustria, which then passed them on to the Ministry of Corporations for final approval. Few of its recommended applications seem to have been subsequently rejected; in any event, violation of the law carried a 10,000 lire fine, a mere pittance in relation to benefits which might accrue from such capital investment.[200]

The issue of compulsory cartels was first raised in 1930. As suggested earlier, one consequence of Mussolini's quota 90 policy was increased rationalization and consolidation. Cartels were being formed in many of the key industrial sectors over which the state had no control. Bottai and other prominent Fascist leaders proposed making membership in the cartels obligatory for a given sector, with regulation vested in the Ministry of Corporations. When Arnaldo Mussolini, writing in *Popolo d'Italia* during April 1930, gave his support to the proposal, Benni immediately responded with a published critique. Rejecting the concept of obligatory cartels out of hand, Benni argued that "faith and collaboration" could never be imposed but would have to emerge naturally from the voluntary cooperation of interested parties.[201] Four months later, the executive council of Confindustria formally expressed itself as "completely op-

---

[200] Sarti, *Fascism and Industrial Leadership*, pp. 107–10.
[201] *OI*, 1 May 1930.

posed to any form of obligatory cartels."[202] It was not until 1932, when the economic crisis had deepened, that the proposal was reconsidered and enacted into law, despite the reservations of Confindustria, which argued for the continuation of voluntary cartels.[203] Posing the question as to why industrialists had such a "phobie des consortiums obligatoires," Rosenstock-Franck concluded, "Parce que tout consortium obligatoire est formé avec l'intervention de l'Etat et peut être soumis ultérieurement à la surveillance du Gouvernement."[204] Once again, however, the Ministry of Corporations lacked the staff and competence to administer so complex a policy, and Confindustria was delegated first-line regulation. Still very much a "state within the state," the industrial association saw to it that these compulsory cartels were essentially consensual: they would have to represent at least four-fifths of any given sector, and their deliberative assemblies could take action only if two-thirds of the members were present.[205]

We turn now to the question of employment policy, which, naturally, became more pressing as unemployment became a mass phenomenon. Here, Confindustria invoked its "exigencies of production" argument, fearing that public policy oriented toward the maintenance of artificially high levels of employment, while politically expedient, would cripple industry's efforts at rationally adapting itself to the crisis. Reacting to employment demands put forth by the Fascist syndicates, the industrial association claimed:

The defense and development of production within the framework of the national interest in fact represent the only means capable of truly ensuring in a lasting and efficacious way the greatest possibility of employment in each firm and industry in general. . . . It is indispensable that direct action taken to meet the crisis not prejudice any more gravely the efficiency of the productive organism, because in such case the effect would be diametrically opposed to that desired.

Not at all persuaded by Confindustria's position, the Fascist syndicates responded:

The development of production undoubtedly represents the *normal* remedy for unemployment. But it is also a remedy of an essentially automatic character whose process would require a relatively long time. To say *at this moment*

[202] *OI*, 15 Sept. 1930.
[203] *OI*, 15 Feb. 1932.
[204] Rosenstock-Franck, *L'économie corporative*, pp. 374–6.
[205] Guarneri, *Battaglie economiche*, 1:274–8.

that the unique remedy for unemployment resides in the development of production is to say, in a certain sense, that the remedy is to be found in the gradual disappearance of the problem insofar as it presupposes that production must necessarily reach that level where it could reabsorb all or a major part of the unemployed.

On the one hand, the Fascist syndicates were advocating a number of specific employment measures which would be obligatory for all industrialists (e.g., preference for PNF members in hiring and job retention, limiting the right of the employer to choose among all workers registered at the labor exchanges, ending overtime and shortening the workday so that additional workers could be hired). On the other hand, Confindustria rejected the general idea that obligatory norms could be universally applied to diverse sectors with distinctive productive exigencies and raised technical objections to each of the requested measures (e.g., in some sectors shifts could not be shortened, and even where they could, the presumption that in each locality there was a sufficient number of qualified workers was not only unwarranted but would, in any case, necessarily raise productive costs, since additional social security contributions would have to be made for each new worker).[206]

Pragmatically realizing that some accommodation would have to be made, Confindustria aimed at reaching agreements with Fascist syndicates sector by sector, thereby hoping to contain the issue of employment policy within the syndical sphere (where its competitive advantages had been clearly demonstrated) rather than allow the issue to become politicized to the point that the government might intervene and set obligatory norms from above. Here, it would make a number of concessions (e.g., eliminating overtime, shortening shifts so that a significant number of workers already employed might be retained), though none fundamentally undercut managerial autonomy or altered the previously established, juridically sanctioned prerogatives of the employer within the enterprise. Citing Fascist doctrine and the Carta del Lavoro, Confindustria successfully argued that the fundamental consideration in either hiring or firing a worker had to be technical competence, not possession of a party card. Bottai, as

---

[206] The letter from Pirelli to the Fascist Federation of Industrial Workers, dated 3 Aug. 1934, and the letter of Cianetti to Confindustria in response, dated 13 Aug. 1934, are in Confindustria Circulars, Confindustria Library, Rome: C. 1919, 3 Aug. 1934; C. 1934, 1 Sept. 1934.

head of the Ministry of Corporations and a technocratic reformer in his own right, assured the industrial association that "membership in the Party or Syndicates cannot constitute in itself a title of preference regarding the assumption or maintenance of employment if the employee does not have professional merit, the fundamental criterion of selection."[207] On similar grounds, Confindustria argued against limiting the employer's right to choose in hiring from among all workers registered at the labor exchanges. Here, at least at the formal level of legislation, it was less successful. In February 1935, the Grand Council voted to limit this choice to skilled workers only. In practice, however, it appears as if this restriction was never put into effect, given the difficulties – continually alluded to by Confindustria – concerning precisely who should make the skilled–unskilled determination and according to which specific criteria.[208]

From a treatment of Confindustria's resistance to public regulation and obligatory norms, we now turn to the association's actions regarding further corporative development during the Depression. The two issues were, of course, intrinsically related, since corporative bodies, at least in theory, were supposed to plan, regulate, and administer all productive activity. It will be recalled that Olivetti had deliberately articulated a version of corporatism which conformed – so far as it was substantively possible – to the logic of liberal capitalism. The function of corporatism, he argued, was to realize fully the potential of private initiative. Furthermore, we have seen that until the Great Depression, Mussolini tended to share this view in his public pronouncements. However, with the coming of the Depression and the growing emphasis on state intervention, Olivetti's minimalist position was subjected to new challenges.

Whereas Olivetti had hoped that the Carta del Lavoro would represent the final step of corporatist development, other important forces – Bottai's group, the Fascist syndicates, Mussolini – were committed to further corporatist institutionalization. Bottai was intent upon making the Ministry of Corporations not only the predominant ministry of the state apparatus but the incubator for a new *classe dirigente* which would undercut traditional elites and lead Italy into a new and qualitatively superior historical epoch. The Fascist syndi-

---

[207] Ibid., C. 14340/05193, 11 Oct. 1930.
[208] *10 anni della Carta del Lavoro*, p. 347; *OI*, 17 Mar. 1935; *CGII Annuario 1933*, p. 601.

cates saw in further corporatist development an opportunity to re-
dress the syndical imbalance with employers and to play a major role
in decisions regarding production. Mussolini's interest in corporatism
was largely ideological and propagandistic; that is, corporative innovations would help confer legitimacy upon his regime both at home
and abroad. Abroad, corporatism would be seen as a bold solution to
the crisis of liberal capitalism and confirmation that his was not a
static dictatorship; at home, corporatism would confer at least symbolic rewards upon those whose material aspirations had yet to be
met.

These forces – Bottai's group, the Fascist syndicates, and Mussolini – thus had different, if not thoroughly irreconcilable, interests.
Bottai, while truly committed to real, rather than symbolic, innovation, retained his cynicism toward the bureaucratic, self-interested
syndicates. The Fascist syndicates, in turn, remained suspicious of
Bottai and the Ministry of Corporations, which, in fact, did little to
help them cultivate their constituency other than by replacing proletarian with petit-bourgeois leaders. Mussolini, meanwhile, became
increasingly predisposed toward personal rule. Incapable of effectively delegating authority, compulsively concerning himself with all
areas of decision making (even the most trivial), continually shuffling
cabinet and party appointments, the Duce – rhetoric aside – remained
an authoritarian mediator, not an innovator, one who would not
permit any autonomous concentration of authority that might short-
circuit his pyramidal political network or limit his prerogatives. Thus,
while these three elements were jointly committed to further corporatist development, singly they were often acting at cross-purposes.
Small wonder then that little was substantively accomplished, especially when one takes into account the forces opposed to corporatism:
the traditional bureaucracy, the party, and employer confederations
led by Confindustria.

Following the Carta del Lavoro, the next important step was formation of the National Council of Corporations. Originally created
in 1926, along with the Ministry of Corporations, the National Council had not as yet functioned. Bottai, who wanted to transform this
paper phantom into a dynamic organ which would coordinate all
economic policy, presented draft legislation to the Grand Council in
April 1929, giving the National Council of Corporations not only
advisory functions but the authority to pronounce obligatory norms.

During November and December 1929, the measure was brought to the Chamber, hotly debated, and finally approved. Controversy, not surprisingly, had centered on the third paragraph of Article 12, which gave the National Council authority to set "norms for the regulation of economic relations among the various categories of production represented by the legally recognized syndical associations."[209] Broadly interpreted, this would cover such areas as prices, credit, marketing, wages, and output. Benni, speaking for Confindustria, claimed that such a measure would violate Article 7 of the Carta del Lavoro, which recognized private initiative and the employer's responsibility to order production, while Bottai invoked Article 6 of the Carta, which gave the corporations the power to "set obligatory norms regarding the discipline of labor relations and also the coordination of production."

Commenting on the tone and substance of statements made by some during the parliamentary discussion of the law, Benni remarked: "One has the sensation that private initiative is an evil which should be placed under the vigilance of the state." The primary task of the National Council, Benni continued, should be to "place every producer in a condition to continually increase and improve his capacity and his means, orienting and directing them to the advantage of the Nation." This entailed, not the confusion of functions, but recognizing – as the Duce himself had said – that some must command and others obey. Those charged with the responsibility of directing production, he argued, must be given unimpeded powers to do so, unburdened by directives from some external source.

The more an external force – even that of syndical organizations – intervenes, not to persuade but to compel the individual producer to operate in a determined way, the more his responsibility is diminished, as well as the possibility of demonstrating his value, his capacity, his technical competence. If, as some have said, there is the possibility that a superior organ – even composed of syndical representatives – might come to establish what and how he should produce, as well as the price at which it should be sold, it is easy to see that private initiative would not be stimulated but restrained and impeded.

Bottai was quick to respond to Benni's self-interested defense of private initiative, rhetorically asking why the industrialists had not been similarly alarmed when the state impinged upon the private

---

[209] *Codice Corporativo*, p. 113.

initiative of Italian workers, ordering a 20 percent salary reduction. The minister of corporations argued that private initiative was not being negated but placed in a new reciprocal relationship with syndical initiative and corporative initiative, affirming that private initiative alone, or giving it primacy, would represent a simple return to liberalism.[210]

Confindustria eventually yielded on the question of principle because the law afforded the National Council of Corporations no autonomy whatsoever.[211] The National Council could meet only when convoked by Mussolini, who set the agenda and whose assent was necessary before it could use its normative authority.[212] This was hinted at by Benni, who during the parliamentary debate suggested that important economic issues should continue to be dealt with by Mussolini's cabinet, not the National Council of Corporations. Citing a recent example where coordination was needed between the silk industry and credit institutions, Benni commended the simple manner with which Mussolini called in the interested representatives, heard their views, and rendered a speedy decision:

The Duce posed the problem, heard the views, and recognized that it was urgent, useful, and necessary that something be done. He brought his decisions to the Cabinet and in three days the question was resolved, concrete collaboration in action. The same thing can happen, for the good of Italy, even after the National Council of Corporations is instituted. When the house is burning, the Chief of Fascism and the Fascist Government do not wait for byzantine discussions, even if corporative; they seek immediate remedies to extinguish the fire.[213]

As Rosenstock-Franck wryly noted, "If an accord between industrialists and bankers could be reached in Mussolini's cabinet at the Palazzo Venezia, one might ask what function the National Council of Corporations might serve."[214]

By this point, Confindustria was relatively satisfied with the relations it had cultivated with the traditional ministries and Mussolini. Were the industrial organization to have opposed the legislation, such informal relations might have been jeopardized. Thus, somewhat

[210] OI, 1 Jan. 1930.
[211] Guarneri, Battaglie economiche, 1:284–5; Rosenstock-Franck, L'économie corporative, pp. 268–9.
[212] Codice Corporativo, pp. 107–34.
[213] OI, 1 Jan. 1930.
[214] Rosenstock-Franck, L'économie corporative, pp. 268–9.

cynically it gave its support for this corporatist milestone. After all, Mussolini's interest had been served; all producers had rallied behind this "revolutionary" step. Speaking at the inaugural session of the National Council, Mussolini ironically trumpeted the one controversial provision of the law (Article 12, Paragraph 3, cited above), which he had no intention of putting into effect. This paragraph, which gave the National Council power to set obligatory norms, was the "keystone of the entire law, for these three lines alone the law merits the appellative revolutionary. . . . In Article Twelve there is all of the corporation as intended and desired by the Fascist State."[215]

With that this revolutionary institution, this "thinking brain which prepares and coordinates," began its lackluster life, crippled at birth. As suggested earlier, it made little use of its advisory or normative powers; economic decisions continued to be made in traditional ways, outside the corporative framework, even the creation and administration of new organs of state intervention like IRI. The National Council, which met infrequently, merely rubber-stamped decisions that had already been made elsewhere. While conducting research, during 1933, for his classic study of Italian corporatism, Rosenstock-Franck asked a high official at the Ministry of Corporations why the National Council had never used its normative power to fix prices, impose productive methods, or set quotas. He was simply told: *"Nous sommes jeunes, attendez!"*[216]

From the formation of the National Council of Corporations in 1930 to the actual constitution of the corporations themselves in 1934, no further institutional steps were taken. The period, however, was marked by a high level of attention, scholarly and propagandistic, devoted to the subject of corporatism. As Salvemini quipped in the preface to his *Under the Axe of Fascism:* "Italy has become the Mecca of political scientists, economists and sociologists, who flock there to see with their own eyes the organization and working of the Fascist Corporative State."[217]

Confindustria, for its part, contributed to this pervasive mystification, filling its publications with corporatist fluff and participating in events like the Ferrara conference, where corporatism could be equated with capitalism and the promotion of private initiative.

[215] Mussolini, *Scritti*, 7: 192–3.
[216] Rosenstock-Franck, *L'économie corporative*, p. 297.
[217] Salvemini, *Under the Axe of Fascism*, p. viii.

Speaking against Ugo Spirito's Communist thesis, Olivetti reminded the so-called *enfant terrible de la doctrine corporative*[218] that corporatism was not only a natural product of the "Greco-Roman tradition" but "the best barrier of Western civilization against the invasion of oriental and Asiatic Bolshevism."[219] Beyond Spirito himself, Olivetti was concerned with a tendency among some of Bottai's followers at the School for Corporative Studies at Pisa to see a convergence between Fascism and Communism, not the antithesis Confindustria desired to exploit for its own ends. That school, in fact, not only published a new anthology of Marx's writings but translated essays by Stalin, Molotov, and Ginko.[220] Furthermore, none other than Werner Sombart, one of the celebrated foreign participants at the Ferrara conference, also advanced the convergence thesis, arguing that while the nineteenth century was dominated by economics, the twentieth century would be dominated by politics. Fascism and Communism were but two reflections of the same universal tendency.[221]

Spirito's thesis was poorly received by all the Italian delegates present, except for Fovel and Bottai. Trying to respond to criticism, Spirito was rudely interrupted. He had clearly gone too far, presenting an opportune pretext for the quick-minded Olivetti to lead – in the name of the majority – opposition against him, thereby undercutting as well the befuddled representatives of the Fascist syndicates, caught between the Scylla of Spirito's academic extremism and the Charybdis of Olivetti's pious orthodoxy. Only afterward would they bitterly comment in *Lavoro Fascista:*

> However, if the Spirito thesis was unacceptable, and it was, no less acceptable was the false indignation of those who profited from the error to express, in a type of shamefaced corporatist orthodoxy, that which they did not understand and that which they understood too well. In fact, after the Ferrara conference, the most convinced defenders of Fascist integrity walked arm-in-arm with those who still consider the corporative order as an evil by now inevitable, acceptable only because of the discipline it ensures.[222]

In his concluding remarks at the end of the conference, Bottai, somewhat embarrassed by Spirito, yet pointedly disdainful of Olivetti,

[218] Rosenstock-Franck, *L'économie corporative*, p. 240.
[219] *Atti del secondo convegno di studi sindacali e corporativi*, 3: 147–8.
[220] Ugo Spirito, "Interpretazione del corporativismo," *Il Diritto del Lavoro* 34 (1965): 281; Cassese, "Un programmatore degli anni trenta," pp. 422–3.
[221] *Atti del secondo convegno di studi sindacali e corporativi*, 3: 9–10.
[222] *LF,* 3 June 1932.

identified two tendencies that had revealed themselves: one "static," the other "dynamic." Although Spirito might have taken a "step outside corporatism," he nevertheless represented dynamism, the tendency with which Bottai too identified himself, as opposed to the one that

would like to place the corporative order, like a dead butterfly, in the album of science; that which would stop it, bind it to existing positions and structures, considering it definitive and perfect, maybe even exalting its perfection beyond what is really called for. The representatives of this tendency, fellow delegates, wear an extraordinary corporatist mask, but a mask of cardboard. Under the mask is still the pale face of liberal Hamlets who, between being and not being, prefer having been.[223]

The Ferrara conference marked the high point of corporatist debate in Italy. Thereafter Mussolini, wanting to institute the corporations in as nonpolemical a climate as possible, ordered a halt to rhetoric that might stir up waters he wanted tranquil before launching the crowning edifice, which was certainly light enough to float in any case.[224] At the end of June 1932, less than three weeks after the Ferrara conference, Bottai was removed as minister of corporations, a position which Mussolini now assumed himself. Bottai had been too critical of the "acorporative" drift in public policy and too hostile toward Confindustria to promote the broad, if vacuous, consensus at which Mussolini was now aiming. Even before his remarks at Ferrara, Bottai, speaking before the Chamber on 24 February 1932, had claimed that the major obstacles to corporatism were "those who either conserved an individualistic and monopolistic mentality or those who enjoyed the tranquility of acquired positions."[225]

The elimination of Bottai, however, was in itself part of Mussolini's larger political strategy of removing prominent Fascists from high positions and replacing them with short-tenured, neutral bureaucrats who would simply administer policy set by the Duce himself. With the growing institutionalization and bureaucratization taking place during the 1930s, Italy, paradoxically, was becoming less and less of a distinctively "Fascist" state and more of an essentially personal dictatorship. In his memoirs, Bottai clearly noted the intent and consequences of Mussolini's "investiture by rotation" tactics: "He

[223] Giuseppe Bottai, *Esperienza corporativa* (Florence: Vallecchi, 1934), pp. 533–47.
[224] De Felice, *Mussolini il Duce*, p. 11.
[225] Ibid., pp. 290–1, 175; Cassese, "Un programmatore degli anni trenta," pp. 422–3.

wished to obtain, and obtained, around him a government squad which claimed authority only through him; not a harmoniously united *classe dirigente,* but men in series, interchangeable. His dream . . . was a government of functionaries."[226] Bottai was not alone; the July 1932 changing of the guard included Rocco (minister of justice), Grandi (foreign minister), and Mosconi (minister of finance). To this list can be added the 1930 elimination of Turati (secretary of the PNF) and Bianchi (minister of public works), plus the 1933 elimination of Balbo (minister of aeronautics) and Arpini (undersecretary of internal affairs).

Nor was the changing of the guard from above limited to positions in the government and in the PNF. Before the corporations were finally instituted in February 1934, Mussolini forced the resignation of all those who headed the employer and worker confederations, including the leadership of Confindustria. The president, Benni, was replaced by Pirelli and later Volpi; Olivetti's position as general secretary was divided into three separate offices (general services, labor services, and economic services). That three men had to fill Olivetti's shoes was itself an indication of his extraordinary energy and competence. It was rumored, according to Guarneri, that the actual decree forcing the resignation of all confederation leaders had been specifically issued with the primary intent of eliminating Olivetti from the political scene. Abroad when the decree was announced, Olivetti was met upon his return to Italy by a colleague from Confindustria who told him: "to subdue one Jew they have slain ten Christians."[227] However, due to the autonomy that industrialists had managed to preserve for themselves, as well as Olivetti's considerable international stature, he remained Italy's employer representative to the International Labor Organization, while maintaining executive positions in the following associations: ENIOS, Comitato per il Prodotto Italiano, Ente Nazionale di Propaganda per la Prevenzione Infortuni, Istituto Cotoniero Italiano, Associazione Nazionale Fascista degli Industrial Cotonieri, and Confindustria's academic journal *Rivista di Politica Economica.*

When the Nazi-inspired racial laws were put into effect, during 1938, Olivetti expatriated to Switzerland and then to Argentina. He

[226] Giuseppe Bottai, *Venti'anni e un giorno* (Milan: Garzanti, 1949), p. 96.
[227] Guarneri, *Battaglie economiche,* 1: 70.

died in 1942, while undertaking a study, not surprisingly, of Japanese industrial expansion.[228]

Little need be said concerning the corporations established in 1934; they had no more autonomy or authority than that afforded in the 1929 legislation creating the National Council of Corporations. As Pellizzi, who saw Fascism as a technocratic *rivoluzione mancata*, suggested, the corporations created in 1934 were "dead before birth."[229] If corporatism ever really had a chance of taking root, this only could have happened during the relatively open period from 1926 to 1929, before Confindustria had consolidated its position and before the trend toward bureaucratization had assumed the proportions reached during the 1930s. With Bottai removed from the Ministry of Corporations, and his talented group confined to teaching and writing, "official corporatism" lacked men of competence and vision. Then again, even had Bottai remained at his post, it is unlikely that corporatist development would have been significantly different. If before 1932 Bottai lacked the capacity and autonomy to carry out his project, what could he have accomplished after 1934? As he himself confessed in a 1952 retrospective, the 1934 law had created "corporations without corporatism, without, that is, a political atmosphere in which they could act and react." All too evident, he noted, were "concessions made to the state bureaucracy, on one side, and the party bureaucracy on the other."[230]

Despite the changing of the guard in the government, the party, and the confederations, Confindustria carried on much as before. As Federico Maria Pacces wrote in Bottai's *Critica Fascista* on 1 January 1937:

Still cast aside by the administrative apparatus of the state, the corporations meet, discuss, and approve "declarations," while the firms produce as before and the ministers proceed as before, acting directly – not through corporative channels – in approving or rejecting requests, issuing administrative directives, and drafting decree-laws. The doctrine, if it remains, is mortified, extended – ethereal and irresponsible – between the clouds of a utopia.[231]

Yet, what does carrying on as before, in fact, mean? Certainly not dictating policy or pulling the strings of Fascist marionettes, as

---

[228] Abrate, *Lotta sindacale*, p. 460.

[229] Pellizzi, *Rivoluzione mancata*, p. 65.

[230] Giuseppe Bottai, "Verso il corporativo democratico o verso una democrazia corporativa?" *Il Diritto del Lavoro* 26 (1952): 132–8.

[231] *Critica Fascista*, 1 Jan. 1937.

proponents of the instrumentalist interpretation of Fascism suggest. We have seen in considerable detail how Confindustria was compelled to adapt itself to Fascist policy, not vice versa, preserving, as best it could, some measure of autonomy. This is not to say that Confindustria was without influence and that Fascist leadership did not take the association's position into account when formulating public policy. Nevertheless, we have encountered a number of important instances when public policy clearly ran counter to Confindustria's expressed wishes, when the association, as it were, was forced into line. Such influence as Confindustria had was mainly limited to effective reaction, negotiating favorable trade-offs once public policy had already been set. And its influence was due, as we have argued, less to some objectively necessary relationship between Fascism and *grand capital,* than to the association's superlative leadership and effective strategy when constrained to "operate from within", in particular its capacity to maintain unity among Italian industrialists, foreclosing the possibility of a *divide et impera* strategy, used so successfully in another context (by Hitler in fragmenting German industrialists), and its single-minded pursuit of the interests of industry by exploiting the contradictions and inconsistencies of Fascism to its own advantage.

This was a limited victory at best. As the 1930s progressed, Mussolini's personalistic–bureaucratic regime embarked upon an ever more economically irrational, belligerent, and proto-Nazi path: autarky, the alliance with Germany, racial legislation, and finally war against England and France, Italy's traditional allies. Confindustria played no formative role in any of these measures. Though the association could not assume a position of formal opposition, privately leaders like Ettore Conti expressed nothing but bitter disdain for such policy and resentment that the Fascist experiment had led the once proud liberal nation into the confines of a disgraceful dictatorship.[232] Private property remained, to be sure, but the entire framework of economic action became increasingly political and, as such, became ever more constraining, inflexible, irrational, and beyond the influence of Confindustria.

[232] Conti, *Taccuino,* pp. 322–4, 342, 349–51, 389–90, 392–3, 399–400, 406–11, 426–9, 433.

Conclusion

Our study questions the adequacy of interpretations that either (1) reduce Fascism to the status of a class-specific project of the industrialists; (2) suggest a programmatic, psychological, or habitual affinity between industrialists and Fascism; or (3) presume determinate influence on the part of industrialists regarding the genesis and subsequent consolidation of Fascism.

To sustain the instrumentalist interpretation, one would have to specify a class-specific, distinctively authoritarian political alternative to the liberal state that industrialists self-consciously entertained, an end toward which Fascism was to be the requisite means. One would also have to demonstrate that the industrialists' action-oriented principles, programmatic demands, and actual political practices were so informed and directed. This interpretation is clearly disconfirmed by the evidence.

So, too, are interpretations that suggest a programmatic, psychological, or habitual affinity between industrialists and Fascism. In contrast with the frequent, though undocumented, claim that Italian industrialists acted like *padroni* whose habits and attitudes toward production and workers were semifeudal and despotic, we have seen that industrial associations were grounded in a distinctively modern understanding of productive and syndical relations, based upon the most-advanced concepts regarding such relations at the time, including a clear recognition of the essential function workers' syndicates were to play in modern labor relations and of the need to develop an institutionalized modus vivendi with them.

Our study questions the adequacy of interpretations that either reduce Fascism to the status of a class-specific project of the industrialists or presume their determinate influence in the rise and consolidation of Fascism. Not only are such interpretations fundamentally flawed, they draw attention away from the overarching political context within which this relationship must be situated: the crisis tendencies and progressive self-negation of Italian liberalism. Accordingly, we have attempted to reconstruct the political development of industrialists within this systemic failure of the liberal state to adapt itself to an age of mass politics and organized capitalism. In the post–World War I conjuncture, Italian liberalism and Fascism were essentially convergent; there was no distinctive liberal alternative to Fascism at the time of the March on Rome, nor was there a viable non-Fascist alternative at the time of the Matteotti crisis. Fascism was less a product of the industrialists' class-specific action than a product of the structural and conjunctural crises of the liberal political system. Industrialists, as we have seen, were far less implicated in Fascism's ascendancy than the large landowners and liberal politicians; they had fought their class-specific battles without recourse to a white guard and without ever having entered into a direct political alliance with Fascists. To the contrary, we have indicated that their class-specific demands had been met before the March on Rome, an action which they actually tried to prevent. If anything, they were apprehensive at the prospect of a government led by Fascists and worked to the very last moment for the formation of yet another liberal government headed by Giolitti.

These apprehensions continued well into the period of liberal–Fascism. Toward Fascism they were agnostic at best, though supportive of Mussolini's feigned commitment to normalization. Thus, they were critical of Fascist acts of violence, the establishment of a Fascist militia, and integrally corporatist initiatives. Important industrialists like Conti and Pirelli declined ministerial portfolios in Mussolini's new government, despite repeated solicitations. Confindustria responded to the Matteotti crisis by calling for a broadly based coalition government and by stubbornly defending syndical pluralism, recognizing that their own autonomy vis-à-vis Fascism might well be tied to the continued autonomy of free workers' syndicates. After the Matteotti crisis, when it was clear that a non-Fascist alternative was no longer possible, they formally embraced Fascism in order to have some influence upon public policy affecting industry and to attempt a transformation of Fascism from within, exploiting its internal contradictions, entering into subterranean alliances with forces that also sought to conserve subsystem autonomy, and advancing a characteristically minimalist concept of corporatism. Throughout it all, industrialists remained substantively committed to the liberal–technocratic position which had informed associational development from the very beginning of the century. They *reacted* to changes in Italian political life, including the transition from liberalism to Fascism, without ever initiating such changes or fundamentally determining outcomes along the way. Through adroit political practice, they managed to conserve a relatively ample degree of autonomy for industry but could only negotiate subsequent trade-offs to the relative advantage of industry once policy had already been formulated.

Hence, it would be erroneous to define Fascism as their instrument. The relative advantages that industrialists negotiated were due largely to their own political skill and to what other groups, such as workers, were prevented from doing. Thus, although class conflict under the Fascist regime was asymmetrically skewed in their favor, repression of workers per se was rooted more in the internal dynamics and narrow political exigencies of Fascism. The need to reduce salaries was necessitated by Mussolini's irrational quota 90 fiscal policy; without cutting labor costs, artificially overvalued Italian goods could not compete in world markets. Confindustria opposed Mussolini's fiscal policy resolutely and publicly; having lost this battle, it negotiated compensatory trade-offs, including the generalized salary cuts. Confindustria resolutely and publicly opposed the authoritarian, monopolist drift of Fascist labor policy, refusing to compromise its classically liberal position on syndical freedom until such opposition was foreclosed both by the juridical restructuring of the Fascist state and by the total failure of non-Fascist unions to mobilize in their own defense and against the regime.

For the Fascist regime, workers represented the principal antagonistic force; it was this relation, rather than the intentions and practices of industrialists, that accounted for their relative disadvantage under Fascism. This is not to say that industrialists refrained from taking full advantage of the situation, but after the Matteotti crisis, how could they have acted otherwise? Until that crisis was resolved in the creation of a characteristically antiliberal, anti-Socialist, nonpluralist regime, industrialists had refused to give preference to Fascist syndicates and continued dealing with Socialist syndicates, which they openly recognized as the elected and authentic representatives of their employees. Monopoly status for the Fascist syndicates and the corporative restructuring of syndical relations were literally forced upon the industrialists by the Fascist regime; such policies were demonstrably not their preference nor to their liking. It was not so

much that the regime was proindustrialist as that it was antilabor.
The industrial proletariat thus suffered under a double burden: as the
class opponents of a relatively well organized and well led industrial
class; and as the political opponents of Fascism, which, after 1925,
made it clear that no opposition to the regime was to be permitted.

At no time could it be said that industrialists somehow opted for
Fascism, having found liberalism an unacceptable alternative. Not
only was there no viable liberal alternative to Fascism, given the
structural and conjunctural contradictions we have specified, but liberals did not subjectively recognize themselves to be non-Fascist or
anti-Fascist during the transformative period of liberal–Fascism. The
political success of Fascism was both external to the actual political
actions of industrialists and antithetical to their perceived interests. It
might be said rather that Italian liberalism negated itself and was
subsumed by Fascism. Situated within this externally induced transformation, certainly not its propelling agent, industrialists in fact
remained remarkably consistent in defending their earlier liberal–
technocratic position against the integralist and statist aspirations of
Fascism and in trying to preserve as much of the liberal status quo
ante as possible. The industrialists' residual liberalism, even under
conditions of full Fascism, was never lost on such diverse Fascist
leaders as Rossoni, Bottai, Rocco, and even Mussolini himself.

That liberal–technocratic position, however, was at times myopic,
naive, and clouded by ambiguities. Did traditional liberalism, even in
the most favorable of cases, provide an adequate political framework
within which industrial–capitalist development could effectively proceed? Given the particular problems associated with belated development, as well as the distinctive material and cultural constraints which
typified Italian development, did traditional liberalism represent an
appropriate political framework for rapid capital accumulation and
industrial expansion, one that would respect and value the so-called
exigencies of production? In other words, might not the liberal–
technocratic position that the industrialists so vigorously promoted
and defended have been itself fundamentally flawed from the very
outset?

Although doctrinally committed to the classic liberal public–private, state–civil society distinctions, such that the productive and
political spheres were understood to be both autonomous from one
another and based on essentially distinct underlying principles, indus-

trialists never fully grasped the relationships underlying this formal dualism. Falling between the cracks of their technocratic fetishism, on the one hand, and their nonreflective, characteristically vacuous Italian liberalism, on the other, was an awareness of both the political assumptions implicit in their view of productive relations and a recognition of the fact that these presumed objective, universal, and nonpolitical relations in reality were bounded and perhaps overdetermined by political contingencies. Industrialists thus failed to recognize, much less reconcile, the contradictory undercurrents flowing beneath their rather formalistic liberal–technocratic position, primarily between (1) a liberal, pluralistic order where competitive parliamentary practice prevailed over ascriptive authority relations, such that no category of citizens could legitimately advance private hierarchical claims and be backed by public coercive power; and (2) an imperatively ordered, internally illiberal productive order whose inner logic required absolute authority, rigid hierarchy, and unquestioning discipline.

What then was the status of these twin commitments to a liberal polity and a hierarchic productive order? If not mutually exclusive, were they so skewed toward the latter as to justify the claim that the industrialists' productivism in fact prefigured or necessitated an illiberal, authoritarian political regime such as Fascism? Such a hypothesis has been advanced in a highly suggestive, if overly dogmatic, essay by Vittorio Foa. Foa argues that the industrialists' conception of factory hierarchy provided the model upon which the Fascist sociopolitical order was based, that "the discipline in the factory had to be guaranteed by an extension of discipline to the outside, embracing the entire arc of social relations." While recognizing that Fascism was not a deliberate project of the industrialists, Foa argues that "the relations between Fascism and *grande capitale* must be gauged at the level of the system, not on a subjective plane." Thus:

Fascist violence was a direct expression of the agrarians, even though in industry there were episodes where Fascists acted as a white guard; the Fascist formula of worker repression and stabilization was accepted and not promoted at a political level by the industrialists. However, they had, at the factory level, furnished the model. Destroying syndical liberty, they liquidated the unique counterbalance of Giolittian reformism and opened the way to an institutionalization of class violence.[1]

---

[1] Foa, introduction to Grifone, *Il capitale finanziario,* p. xxxii.

We shall return momentarily to the question of whether or not industrialists indeed destroyed syndical liberty at the factory level, proceeding directly to the more important point raised by Foa, that of mass consent, for if the industrialists' hierarchical concept of productive relations were to be realized within a liberal political order, it would have to be accepted by workers as legitimate rather than be simply imposed:

The industrialists were sincere when they disclaimed any affection for black squads and Fascist destruction; they would have certainly preferred consensual discipline, a subaltern though voluntary collaboration on the part of workers. But in those conditions, with as yet insufficient margin for a mass organization of consensus (that is, a new reformism), Fascism emerged as an available solution, one which based itself on the authoritarian model furnished by modern production and thus could respond, despite subjective opinions, to the exigencies of productive capitalism and especially grand industry.[2]

Despite his reductionist logic, Foa's point is nevertheless instructive in that it attempts to situate the relationship between industrialists and Fascism within a broader context, rather than simply presume an immediate identity between the interests of industry and those of Fascism. In post–World War I Italy, he argues, the conditions were as yet insufficient for a mass organization of consensus, which industrialists clearly would have preferred to Fascism. With this conclusion we are in substantial agreement, though our argument is based less on the overriding significance of the modern factory as a prefigurative Fascist model than on a contextual analysis of the long-term and conjunctural insufficiencies of Italian political development. Modern factories, to state the obvious, existed throughout the capitalist world, but the success of Fascism was limited to those cases where consensus, the self-proclaimed basis for liberal-bourgeois rule, either had broken down or had never been organically developed. Our treatment of Italian political development, focusing upon the bourgeoisie's incapacity to constitute itself as a hegemonic class capable of constructing an institutional framework and articulating a mobilizing ideology with which to secure and conserve mass consensus, was an attempt to specify precisely that context distinguishing Italy from those states which underwent the transition from market capitalism to organized capitalism without a Fascist interlude.

[2] Ibid., p. xxiv.

Within the context of such development, material constraints were by no means inconsequential. Italy's economic marginality and belated industrialization limited the degree to which reformist policies, effected elsewhere for the express purpose of preempting mass demands and securing consensus, could be undertaken. Moreover, the materially induced form of consensus characteristic of so-called post-industrial consumer societies, which might have better mystified class relations or at least have taken the sharp edge off anticapitalist radicalism, had not yet presented itself in Italy or anywhere else in Europe. Thus, the alluring prospect of *la dolce vita,* manufactured and universalized by what Adorno called the "culture industry," was as yet unavailable to rescue or substitute itself for the distinctive bourgeois public sphere which in Italy had been so congenitally weak and precociously lacerated by autonomously generated and unmediated mass claims for participation and redistribution.

Industrialists were late and not altogether welcome entrants into the Italian bourgeois bloc. They could not fundamentally reconstitute this bloc in their own image or significantly compensate for the social disaggregation and institutional fragility which had been the consequence of prior bourgeois development. In all essential characteristics, their attitudes and action-oriented principles were no different from those of industrialists in the more-advanced liberal nations. This is perfectly understandable, since the latter served both as a model and as a source of orientation, whether or not the experience of such foreign industrialists was at all relevant or responsive to the Italian reality. In any event, we have discovered no distinctively authoritarian orientations that set Italian industrialists apart from their counterparts in the liberal–democratic nations, nothing that would suggest a distinctive predilection toward antiliberal, authoritarian politics.

Industrialists advanced a liberal–technocratic form of productivism, distinct from the etatist–corporative productivism of the nationalists and Fascists, though they failed to effect the political transformations and secure the mass consensus that would have made this possible. Contrary to Foa's claim that they destroyed syndical liberty at the factory level, thus liquidating an essential basis for liberal reformism and opening the way for an institutionalization of class violence, industrialists actively sought just that institutional partnership with workers' syndicates in the hope of regulating class conflict so that production might be less subject to impulsive disruptions. The

industrial associations we have studied recognized workers' syndicates from the very outset, as well as the mediating role they were to
play in modern industrial relations. Indeed, these associations – contrary to Foa's claim – championed the cause of syndical liberty well
into the Fascist period, until the regime, against their will, ended such
liberty for political reasons of its own having little to do with the
industrialists per se. Not only was there an unquestionable gap between this co-optive and regulative conception of syndical practice
and the perhaps overly combative posture industrialists assumed
when mediation had broken down and strikes ensued, but the latter
was less the product of an intentional desire to destroy the opposition,
and thus the very basis for future mediation, than frustration caused
by the failure of workers' syndical leadership to discipline their members and have them abide by duly negotiated contractual provisions.
Here, too, developmental factors are highly significant, because the
historical incapacity of labor's syndical leaders to legitimate a bureaucratic, collaborationist modus vivendi with industrialists, the very
basis of modern reformism, was at least partially attributable to
long-term worker alienation from the liberal bourgeois order. This
alienation was rooted specifically in the repressive policy of pre-
Giolittian governments, a policy that only encouraged within the
proletarian subculture a proclivity toward extremism, especially anar-
chism and revolutionary syndicalism, rather than moderation.
Worker moderation might have been generated had the Italian bourgeoisie developed an affirmative, universalizing ideology and an inclusive, rather than exclusive, response to real or potential grievances.
Giolitti's well-meaning attempts at reform did not fundamentally alter
the situation, since they did not address the fundamental problems or
alter the traditional institutional framework.

   With the collapse of Fascism and the birth of a new Italian republic,
liberalism reappeared as a residual political phenomenon, quickly and
permanently marginalized by Marxism and Christian Democracy,
which, unlike liberalism, were mass political movements, organizationally extensive and firmly grounded in Italy's two subcultures.
Interestingly enough, the newly constituted Confindustria immediately embarked upon a post-Fascist program of liberal–technocratic
productivism based on the very principles that had informed associational development from the outset, as if the experience of Fascism
had taught them nothing or as if the antiliberal tendencies of the new

dominant mass parties were generally irrelevant to the association's future development. Liberalism was the only tune they knew and, after all, was the norm in other Western nations, particularly the United States, which continued to serve as their model and point of orientation. How appropriate this liberal–technocratic productivism was to Italy, and, normative commitments aside, its chances for success in the Italian political arena, were questions never realistically addressed.

Private industry as the motor of development, the optimality formula, managerial authority, the exigencies of production, the public–private distinction, and the dangers of state intervention are themes that have characterized Confindustria's stance throughout the history of the Italian Republic. Little of substance has been added since Gino Olivetti elaborated them from 1907 to 1921, just as little of substance had been added during Fascism.[3] For better or worse, Confindustria has shown remarkable continuity, despite major changes of regime and less dramatic shifts in the general equation of Italian political life (e.g., the "opening to the Left" and the "Centro-Sinistra" of the 1960s). Generally speaking, this long-term continuity has not been noted by scholars who have studied Confindustria during the post-Fascist years, whether an understandable consequence of period specialization or the fact that the association rarely, if ever, refers to its activities during Fascism and literally never to those who actually led the association during those years, most significantly Gino Olivetti. Insofar as Fascism and corporatism were discussed in the early days of the Republic, they were cited as dangerous, illiberal aberrations of unchecked statism whose only cure could be a rapid return to liberal economics and politics. For example, Angelo Costa, first president of the reconstituted Confindustria, called for a rapid dismantling of the corporatist superstructure, eliminating IRI as quickly as possible, and limiting the role of the public sector in terms strikingly similar to Olivetti's attack on Italy's World War I industrial mobilization (the

[3] On Confindustria in the post-Fascist period see La Palombara, *Interest Groups in Italian Politics;* Gloria Pirzio Ammassari, *La politica della Confindustria* (Naples: Liguouri Editore, 1976); Lorenzo Caselli, *Spett.Le Confindustria* (Rome: Edizioni Lavoro, 1980); *Gli imprenditori e la political industriale* (Bologna: Il Mulino, 1982); Alberto Martinelli, "Organized Business in Italian Politics," *West European Politics* 2 (Oct. 1979): 67–87; Marco Maraffi, *Politica ed economia in Italia* (Bologna: Il Mulino, 1990); Liborio Mattina, *Gli industriali e la democratazia* (Bologna: Il Mulino, 1991).

so-called *bardatura di guerra*). Costa and later Confindustria leaders would attack labor's attempts at establishing a presence in the factory which might interfere with managerial authority (e.g., *consigli di gestione* in 1944–5; *delegati di reparto* and *consigli di fabbrica* in 1968–9) in terms strikingly similar to Olivetti's attack on factory councils in 1920–1 and, for that matter, his critique of internal commissions even before World War I. Guido Carli, who became president of Confindustria in 1976, would bemoan the loss of real industrial entrepreneurship which attended those firms that had passed to the public sector or that sought greater state support in terms strikingly similar to Olivetti's November 1933 speech to the Turinese industrialists warning them that despite the Depression's debilitating impact, reliance upon state assistance would undercut their very function and raison d'être.[4]

Nevertheless, Confindustria was remarkably successful during the early years of the Republic, particularly during the so-called golden period, 1947–53: it maintained its representational monopoly over all segments of industry; it cultivated effective clientelistic relations with relevant sectors of the state administration, particularly the Ministry of Industry and Commerce; and it differentially benefited from a conservative economic policy (the so-called Einaudi line) which stimulated growth by keeping salaries low while encouraging rapid capital accumulation and industrial rationalization. Without doubt, Confindustria was the most powerful interest group in the country during this period: *interlocutore primario* vis-à-vis the government and the ruling Christian Democratic Party (Democrazia Cristiana; the DC).

Yet the association's early success was due primarily to the favorable, yet quite transitory, political context of the time, one characterized more by the relative weakness of other players than Confindustria's own inherent strength. The cold war led to a marginalization of leftist parties and a division of the labor movement along ideological lines, with the American government and the Roman Catholic Church playing major roles, leaving the DC under Alcide De Gasperi as the politically hegemonic force after the key election of 1948. Confindustria entered into a symbiotic relationship with the DC: the association benefited from the party's conservative policies, and the party bene-

[4] See p. 423

fited from the association's material support. Central to the relationship was a close personal friendship between their respective leaders, De Gasperi and Costa, as well as the suppression of the DC's integralist and communal–populist factions, which had political programs of their own and looked with suspicion on Confindustria.

By the mid-1950s, however, this relationship began to unravel. After De Gasperi left the political scene in 1954, the DC moved further to the Left, trying to enlarge its mass base and area of consensus, eventually culminating, under Amintore Fanfani's leadership, with the Centro-Sinistra. The longer the DC remained in power, the less it needed Confindustria's backing; its control of the state opened up other sources of funding, especially as the public sector grew in size and influence under its partisan sponsorship. Confindustria's ideological commitments were liberal and secular; its relationship with the DC had been instrumental, not principled, and contingent upon the continued dominance of conservatives within the party. By 1956, Confindustria had become sufficiently alienated from the DC's dominant faction to organize its own autonomous political initiative, promoting an employers' "superconfederation" (the so-called Confintesa), which gave support to the DC's marginalized right wing and sought to "revitalize" the liberal party (PLI), with which it was ideologically most closely associated. By all accounts, even those of Confindustria in later years, this effort was a colossal failure and had no impact, except negatively, on the political landscape. DC leadership, meanwhile, had adopted a populist program of social reforms that included expansion of the public sector and nationalizing electricity. By the end of the decade, a separate ministry had been created to promote firms in the public sector, which were, moreover, legislatively severed from Confindustria (the so-called *sgancimento*) and organized within a new, separate association, Intersind. This situation not only opened up a significant division in the industrialists' camp but created a major breach in labor negotiations, since the Intersind firms – not directly subject to market mechanisms – tended to make concessions that the private firms of Confindustria felt excessive and unwarranted. Meanwhile, another new association of small industrialists, Confapi, was organized in response to the presumed hegemony within Confindustria of the giant firms. Thus, Confindustria emerged from the 1950s in a weakened position, never again to attain the dominance it initially enjoyed. Politically isolated and no longer the sole voice for Italian industry, Confindustria even saw its larger member firms circumvent the organization, pursuing separate, self-interested strategies with labor, various factions of the DC, and other parties of the ruling coalition, as well as local party notables and sections of the state bureaucracy.

The public sector continued to grow at the perceived expense of private firms, such that the state now controls roughly 50 percent of Italian industry. Already in 1969, Confindustria claimed that of the twenty largest Italian firms, only four or five could be considered effectively private and autonomous from public power.[5] The state-controlled sector, despite early commitments made by its leaders to broad social goals, degenerated into a swamp of DC clientelism, inefficiency, unproductive labor, and scandal. By the late 1970s, studies by Giorgio Galli, Alessandra Nannei, Luigi Gasperini, Antonio Mutti, and Paolo Segatti were published in Italy dealing specifically with this phenomenon and bearing such suggestive titles as *Italia occidente mancato, Il capitalismo assistenziale, La borghesia di stato, La nuovissima classe,* and *Stato e capitalismo assistenziale.*[6] A central target of these and similar studies has been the politician–managers of the public sector, the so-called *borghesia di stato.* Neither private owners nor a class of competent technocrats who elsewhere in Europe have promoted neocapitalist rationalization, this Italian state bourgeoisie has been portrayed as a parasitic, self-regarding alliance of public-enterprise managers and political brokers who form the "real," though hidden, government (*sottogoverno, criptogoverno*), which, unlike the formal one, has never, until recently, been in a state of crisis but, as Norberto Bobbio has suggested, indeed has grown stronger and seemingly more indispensable as the latter has grown weaker.[7] Some economists, like Nannei, have even likened this "new class" to Djilas's celebrated analysis of Eastern-bloc systems: one-

[5] "Una politica per l'industria," in *Confindustria e società: una rilettura di "una politica per l'industria" a del "rapporto Pirelli"* (Rome: Quaderni dei *quale impresa:* 1, 1979), p. 141.
[6] Giorgio Galli and Alessandra Nannei, *Il capitalismo assistenziale* (Milan: SugarCo., 1976); Giorgio Galli and Alessandra Nannei, *Italia occidente mancato* (Milan Mandadori, 1980); Alessandra Nannei, *La nuovissima classe* (Milan: SugarCo., 1978); Antonio Mutti and Paolo Segatti, *La borghesia di stato* (Milan: Mazzotta, 1977); Luigi Gasperini, *Stato e capitalismo assistenziale: il caso italiano* (Florence: G. D'Anna, 1978).
[7] Norberto Bobbio, "Democracy and Invisible Government in Italy," *Telos* 52 (summer 1982): 41–55.

party dominance, parasitism, unproductive labor, black and underground markets, self-reproducing elite privileges, and so on.

Confindustria, of course, attacked this distorted development of the state sector, complaining that the private firms had to operate efficiently, according to the exigencies of the market, whereas firms operating in the public sector were subsidized, protected from market controls, and managed according to no formalized rational criteria against which they could be judged and held accountable. From the association's perspective, there was no reason to expect a higher level of performance from the state-controlled firms than that amply demonstrated in the provision of basic public services, so far inferior to those provided in other Western "statist" systems such as France or the social democracies of northern Europe despite the fact – or possibly because of it – that Italy had by far the highest percentage of workers in the service sector actually employed by the state (Italy, 30 percent; West Germany, 18.9 percent; France, 12.9 percent; Belgium, 14.1 percent).[8] And those who paid the freight, as it were, for this ever-expanding load were the private firms, which created the wealth to support both social welfare and state parasitism, private firms – as Confindustria repeated – whose market constraints, national and international, were recognized by neither labor syndicates nor the government, and whose very capacity to produce was being undercut by an emergent social and political system which failed to acknowledge that productivity was the fundamental factor making all social goods and benefits possible.[9] For these reasons, "relaunching the firm" (understood as the private firm) and its "centrality" became dominant ideological themes for Confindustria in the late 1970s and 1980s. During his presidency, Guido Carli raised the polemic to unprecedented heights in numerous speeches, public statements, and especially in a best-selling, 128-page paperback interview on Italian capitalism with one of Italy's leading journalists, Eugenio Scalfari. Carli, who is credited with actually having invented the term *borghesia di stato*, argued that Italy somehow had managed to combine the worst elements, rather than the best, of Western and Eastern systems: it lacked the relative efficiency and productivity of capitalism; it

[8] Rapporto annuale sul situazione del paese, Censis, Rome 1973, cited in Ammassari, *La politica della Confindustria*, p. 156.
[9] For Confindustria's views on the state sector, see its publication *Gli imprenditori e la political industriale*.

lacked the relatively extensive and generous social benefits of Socialism. "We are in such a condition because we have the worst of both
systems: we have undercut the industrialist without eliminating him;
we have opened the door to state intervention without programming
it. We have corrupted, at the same time, capitalism and Socialism. We
couldn't have done worse."[10]

And yet, polemics aside, all Confindustria has done by way of
posing an alternative is recycle old formulas, even when existing
leadership or disgruntled groups of "young industrialists" within the
association's ranks issue major statements at critical moments bearing
imposing titles like "Una politica per l'industria." Such reports are
invariably sophisticated, informative, and well written, yet at the
same time rather abstract, politically irrelevant, and soon forgotten
by everyone but their authors and scholars. The best example of
this occurred in May 1969, when the "central committee of young
industrialist groups" issued an eleven-part, 300-page report with the
assistance of the Centro Luigi Einaudi in Turin. Responding to the
dramatic social unrest of 1968–9 and to the perceived inadequacies
of the "old guard," represented by Costa, the report essentially was a
repackaging of old themes and a renewed call for liberalism, bolstered
by an impressive compendium of concepts and theorists current in
American political science (in fact, the citations could well have been
a required reading list for any graduate-level comparative politics
class offered in the United States at the time: Almond and Verba,
Banfield, La Palombara, Eckstein, Lijphart, Pye, Russet, Finer, Sart-
ori, Tocqueville – even Marcuse).

The report was an excellent critique of the state, the political
class, the party, and interest-group systems, as well as Italian political
culture. Yet, as the report asserted, critique was not enough; it was
now time for industrialists "to participate and anticipate," to develop
a new strategy that might "arrest the deterioration and create in the
country conditions for a Western democratic form of modernization."[11] And this was none other than the idealized conception of a
"modern" society that characterized American political science when
"modernization theory" was in vogue: one (understood to be the
actual American political system) where the "civic culture" was secu-

---

[10] Guido Carli, *Intervista sul capitalismo italiano, a cura di Eugenio Scalfari* (Bari:
Laterza, 1977), p. 68.
[11] *Confindustria e società*, pp. 31, 136.

lar, pragmatic, and accommodating; where there was a robust network of autonomous, voluntary associations that articulated interests; and where competitive, nonideological political parties
aggregated those interests into responsive programs. Quite aside from
the fact that this in itself was a highly questionable perception of the
American political system, it had nothing whatsoever to do with
Italian politics past, present, or future. Yet, based on this model,
the report called for "liberating" civil society from the "ideological
deformations" of Italian party politics, "secularizing" the political
culture, and "informing" it with new values. This would be done
largely by the promotion of "new demands," as autonomous associations, pragmatically pursuing their largely self-interested, nonideological agendas, forced a change in the party system, making it more
responsive: a revisionism in the Communists (PCI); a secularization
of the DC ("eternally oscillating between conservative immobility and
demagogic populism"); a reformism in the Socialists (PSI); while
liberals (PLI) and Republicans (PRI) would be "courageously projected toward the democratic resurrection of those liberal ideals
whose weariness is among the decisive causes of the current decay in
the democratic forces."[12]

Little of this came to pass. The political changes that did occur
happened for reasons quite separate from the report's scenario, not
because of significant alterations in the interest-group structure and
its relationship to the party system, or an altered political culture.
The report did lead to some internal changes within Confindustria,
proposed by the so-called Pirelli report, and helped clear the way for
a "new guard" (Leopoldo Pirelli, Giovanni Agnelli, Guido Carli) to
assume leadership, but the association has managed neither to effect
significant change in the Italian political system nor to recoup its
earlier influence. If not political outsiders, Italian industrialists, as
Guido Carli put it, "have never been considered full-fledged members
of the establishment, members of the governing class." The very
estrangement between the *borghesia politica* and the *borghesia produttrice* that we observed early in the formation of the industrial class
remains. Carli adds:

In some cases, it is true, the governing class has rendered great service to the
men and to the classes which retained economic power, but always firmly

[12] Ibid., p. 298.

maintaining the substantial division of tasks and roles. The industrialists were above all concerned that the State might help them in their affairs, but an identification was lacking. An industrialist felt and feels it his duty to serve the firm, not the State with the same intensity. In fact, industrialists have never furnished political personnel, as commonly happens in England, the United States, France, and Germany. Let us remember that Pompidou was a banker from the Rothschilds; that many American public officials, whether Democrats or Republicans, come from business and return to business after leaving office. Meanwhile here in Italy this crossing over has never happened; it might create a scandal, but above all industrialists, with few exceptions, would not feel it a natural thing.[13]

And yet it could be argued that this estrangement from politics has deprived Italian liberalism of precisely that force which might have helped transform Italy into the type of society anticipated in "Una politica per l'industria" and, in fact, presupposed by Confindustria every time it complains about the way things ought to be. The problem might not be with its long-term identification with liberalism but the fact that its commitment has been largely ritualistic and rhetorical, though certainly not insincere. As the young industrialists who produced "Una politica per l'industria" themselves recognized, Italy never managed to develop "an intelligent reformism of the Right" comparable to those produced in different periods by English Conservatives and American Republicans. And since an intelligent reformism of the Right was lacking, "the initiative for each reform in Italy remains solidly in the possession of the Left. And since the Left is immature and doctrinaire, sinning alternatively between excessive timidity and maximalism, the reforms they produce are produced badly and contest the interests of the productive class."[14]

It has been observed by Giorgio Galli and others that Italy lacks a "mature bourgeois political culture" that could confront Marxism and Christian Democracy, and this is due largely to the political abdication of the industrialists.[15] No doubt such accusations are partial and overstated, since the insufficiencies of Italian liberalism are more attributable to the peculiarly weak form of development which over the long term has marked the Italian bourgeoisie as a whole than they are to the inaction of one of its fragments, which, in fact, never exercised hegemony over the entire bloc. And yet it is clear that only

[13] Carli, *Intervista*, pp. 72–3.
[14] *Confindustria e società*, p. 163.
[15] Cited in *Confindustria e società*, pp. 72–3.

this fragment, the most dynamic and powerful, could assume the kind of leadership critics such as Galli presuppose. When all is said and done, it might be argued that industrialists are the only group in Italy that ever elaborated a coherent developmental strategy which, for all of its presumed limitations, can nevertheless claim greater practical success than those strategies articulated and put into practice by Marxists and Christian Democrats. If this is so, then the absence of industrialists from more direct and open engagement in Italian political life is all the more lamentable. By remaining on the sidelines and quietly adapting themselves to a progressively more corrupt modus operandi with the ruling political parties, they lost the moral and practical authority for national leadership or at least the possibility of standing for something other than the pervasive systemic corruption which surfaced recently as Tangentopoli, an indictment not only of the *classe politica* but of the entire Italian *classe dirigente*.

Index